"Profoundly affecting . . . flows with the amazing clarity and delicacy of a fine novel."

—*DAILY MAIL*

"A nuanced and compelling picture of life in the diaspora."

—*NEW STATESMAN*

"Filled with vibrant characters, rich in historical detail, this excavation also bears the traces of its author's passion at the injustices of a terrible history, which now again can seem too close for comfort."

—*OBSERVER* (UK)

"With high drama, heart-breaking tragedy, thwarted love and walk-on parts for Pablo Picasso, Marc Chagall and Christian Dior, Freeman's memoir House of Glass would feel too neat if it were a novel. It certainly reads like one, and if I were a film director I'd be snapping up the rights."

—*JEWISH CHRONICLE*

"Researched with diligence and written with love, it triggers the same shock of recognition that comes from colorised film; black-and-white history flooded with bright detail, human warmth."

—*SUNDAY TIMES* (UK)

"Breathtakingly compelling."

—*EVENING STANDARD*

"*House of Glass* addresses themes of assimilation, identity and home."

—*HAARETZ*

"With a historian's unflinching loyalty to accuracy, often relying upon unredacted records chronicling official cruelty, Freeman masterfully recreates the very dark atmosphere of the times. Freeman's skill as a writer . . . provides dimension, character and emotion to the individuals whom we meet and come to know throughout the book. Freeman is also to be commended for the delicate literary touch and neat turns of phrase that she employs to depict situations of high or low drama."

—*CANADIAN JEWISH NEWS*

"Freeman's book is the sort every grandchild of Holocaust survivors longs to write. . . . It's a deep dive, an illumination of lives previously unknown—a looking glass through which kaleidoscopes of homes destroyed; parents, cousins, and lovers dragged to their deaths; and bodies furtively huddled in dark shadows suddenly appear before our eyes."

—ELECTRIC LITERATURE

"A magnificently vivid re-creation of her Jewish family's experience of twentieth-century Europe, from a Polish shtetl reminiscent of Isaac Bashevis Singer's stories and Marc Chagall's art, via Parisian haute couture to the Résistance and Auschwitz, Hadley Freeman's book is also an acute examination of the roots, tropes, and persistence of anti-Semitism, which makes it an urgently necessary book for us to read right now."

—SALMAN RUSHDIE

"This is a startlingly original book, remarkable and gripping."

—EDMUND DE WAAL, author of *The Hare with the Amber Eyes*

"This is an utterly engrossing book: one that manages to be an intimate family history and a meticulously researched account of a shocking period of world history at the same time. It may be an overused term of approbation, but it truly is unputdownable."

—NIGELLA LAWSON

"*House of Glass* is extraordinary. It reads like a mystery and a memoir and a gripping history of the last century. Armed with a shoebox filled with her grandmother's keepsakes, Hadley Freeman reconstructs the story of a family that the Holocaust tried to erase. Freeman doesn't hide from the gray spaces people inhabit during wartime, or shy away from drawing the terrifying parallels to today's iterations of those ancient hatreds. It's a brave and wonderful book."

—NATHAN ENGLANDER, author of *What We Talk About When We Talk About Anne Frank*

"If you have a heart, this book will break it. Hadley Freeman forces us to understand the myriad responses of her family members to the anti-Semitism that sent many to their deaths while sparing others. She, like Dostoevksy, has produced a work that must stand as a classic of love and redemption."

—CHARLES GLASS, author of *Americans in Paris: Life and Death Under Nazi Occupation*

ALSO BY HADLEY FREEMAN

The Meaning of Sunglasses

Be Awesome

Life Moves Pretty Fast

HOUSE
of
GLASS

*The Story and Secrets
of a Twentieth-Century
Jewish Family*

HADLEY FREEMAN

Simon & Schuster Paperbacks

NEW YORK   LONDON   TORONTO
SYDNEY   NEW DELHI

Simon & Schuster Paperbacks
1230 Avenue of the Americas
New York, NY 10020

First Simon & Schuster trade paperback edition March 2021

SIMON & SCHUSTER PAPERBACKS and colophon are registered trademarks
of Simon & Schuster, Inc.

For information about special discounts for bulk purchases, please contact
Simon & Schuster Special Sales at 1-866-506-1949
or business@simonandschuster.com.

The Simon & Schuster Speakers Bureau can bring authors to your
live event. For more information or to book an event, contact the
Simon & Schuster Speakers Bureau at 1-866-248-3049 or
visit our website at www.simonspeakers.com.

Interior design by Paul Dippolito

Manufactured in the United States of America

1   3   5   7   9   10   8   6   4   2

Library of Congress Cataloging-in-Publication Data

Names: Freeman, Hadley, author.
Title: House of Glass : the story and secrets of a
twentieth-century Jewish family / Hadley Freeman.
Description: New York ; London ; Toronto : Simon & Schuster,
[2020] | Includes bibliographical references.
Identifiers: LCCN 2019049707 (print) | LCCN 2019049708 (ebook) |
ISBN 9781501199158 (hardcover) | ISBN 9781501199206 (ebook)
Subjects: LCSH: Glass family. | Holocaust, Jewish (1939–1945)—France—Biography. |
Jewish refugees—United States—Biography. | Freeman, Hadley—Travel.
Classification: LCC DS135.F9 G534 2020 (print) | LCC DS135.F9 (ebook) |
DDC 940.53/18092 [B]—dc23
LC record available at https://lccn.loc.gov/2019049707
LC ebook record available at https://lccn.loc.gov/2019049708

ISBN 978-1-5011-9915-8
ISBN 978-1-5011-9920-2 (pbk)
ISBN 978-1-5011-9922-6 (ebook)

All photos are from the Hadley Family Archive except for page 301, from Billy Farrell/BFA.com.

For my father, Ron Freeman, and my Grandma Sala

Contents

"Getting this hysterical about [anti-Semitism] on the other side of the world is sane?"

"When she talks about it, it's not on the other side of the world, it's on the next block."

"And that's sane?"

"I don't know what it is! I just get the feeling sometimes that she KNOWS something, something that . . . It's like she's connected to some . . . some wire that goes half around the world, some truth that other people are blind to."

—*Broken Glass*, Arthur Miller, 1994

FAMILY TREE

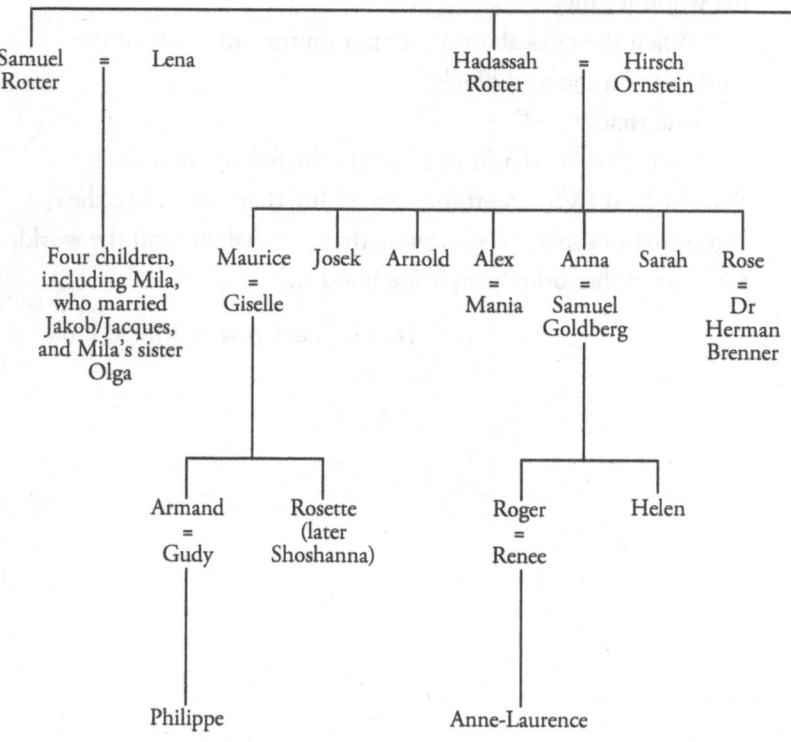

Samuel Rotter = Lena

Hadassah Rotter = Hirsch Ornstein

Four children, including Mila, who married Jakob/Jacques, and Mila's sister Olga

Maurice = Giselle

Josek

Arnold

Alex = Mania

Anna = Samuel Goldberg

Sarah

Rose = Dr Herman Brenner

Armand = Gudy

Rosette (later Shoshanna)

Roger = Renee

Helen

Philippe

Anne-Laurence

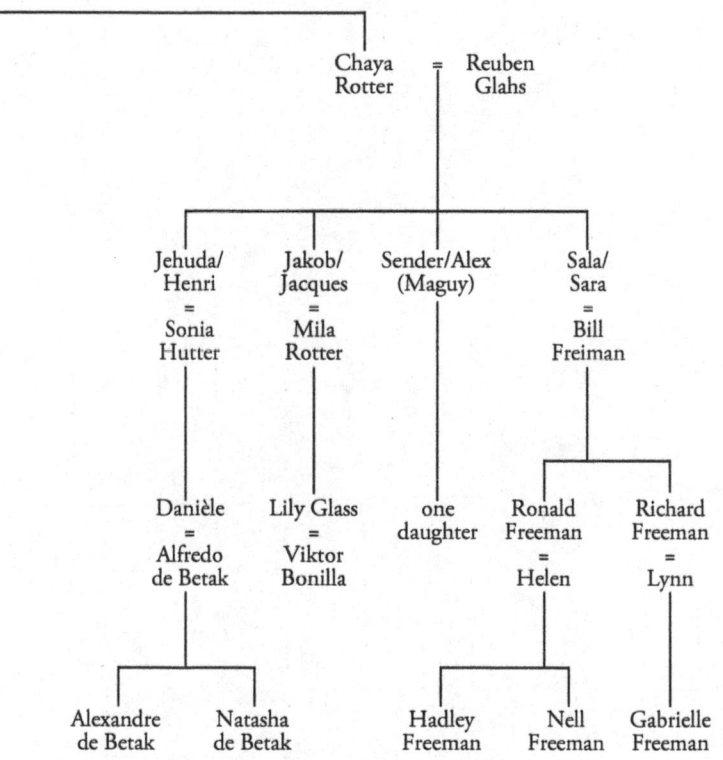

Introduction

I stood up to shut the closet door and that's when I spotted the shoebox, right at the back, behind a pile of leather handbags. It was burnished red, although it looked almost gray, covered in over a decade's worth of dust. Surely, I thought, it would just contain another pair of slightly battered kitten-heeled sandals. But still, I'd come all this way, I might as well look inside. So I sat back on the floor, pulled it out, and opened it. I did not find shoes. Instead, it was filled with the secrets my grandmother had managed to keep all her life and some years beyond.

The road that led me to rifling through my grandmother's closet a dozen years after she died began, for me, twenty-three years earlier, in 1983 when I was five years old. That was the year my parents took me to Europe for the first time to meet my French family: my grandmother's oldest brother and his wife, Henri and Sonia Glass; another brother, Alex Maguy; and their last surviving cousins, Alex and Mania Ornstein. My grandmother, Sala, also joined us there, flying over from her home in Florida, where she lived with her American husband, my grandfather Bill.

My dad was keen for us to meet them all, perhaps to balance out our family tree: where my mother's side was fruitful, with its abundance of American aunts, uncles, and cousins scattered generously around the United States, from Washington, DC, to Cincinnati to Seattle, my father's side was comparatively barren. Until this trip it had consisted in my mind solely of my grandparents and my uncle, my father's younger brother, Rich, all clustered together in Miami. I knew my grandmother had had to leave her relatives behind in France when she escaped what was vaguely described to me as "the war," and this, my father said, was why I didn't have much family on his side. He didn't explain where the family was on his very American father's side, and I was too young then to think to ask why.

My mother's family was warm, rambunctious, and close, and I always looked forward to seeing my cousins, whom I thought of as quasi-siblings. But when we visited my paternal grandparents, they snapped at one another continuously, which scared me because I never saw my parents fight. Also, for reasons I was in no way capable of articulating then, I found my grandmother difficult. If pressed, I would have said she was "weird," but what I meant was that she seemed sad, and sad adults are confusing to children, especially ones as sheltered as I was. When we'd visit them in Miami, my grandfather, in his white trousers and golf shirts, would sit with us by the hotel pool on the candy-colored sun loungers, enjoying the sunshine, letting my sister and me twirl his enormous mustache. My grandmother would sit under an umbrella, separate from us. She was further protected from the sun by a wide-brimmed hat, various Hermès—or Hermès-esque—silk scarves wound in complicated knots around her neck, a mini Dior handbag in her lap. She looked as distinctly French as my grandfather looked American, with the naturally soft, elegant looks of a Renoir painting, but now overlaid with the melancholy of a Hopper one.

Often by the pool she would read the French fashion magazines her brothers sent her from Paris, and despite having lived in America for forty years by the time I was born, she clung tightly to her French accent. So it made sense to me that she would come with us to France. After all, she was, emphatically, French.

I flew with my parents from New York to Paris, and then took a train to Deauville, a seaside resort in Normandy. Deauville looked then and still looks now frozen in the mid-twentieth century, with its grand hotels and long beach dotted with large colorful beach umbrellas, to which liveried waiters brought three-course meals on silver trays. We went there to meet the French relatives because that is where they liked to go on holiday from their homes in Paris, albeit rarely with one another.

Sala eating lunch in Deauville, under Alex Ornstein's umbrella

Even though I was only five at the time, my memories of this holiday are clearer than of ones I took in my teens and twenties. Partly this was from the novelty of being outside America for the first time, and the experience was as jarringly formative as the first day of school, or my first job. But it's also because my family takes so many photos, and more photos were taken of this holiday than of most people's weddings, mainly by the family photographers, Henri and my father. We are also a family of anecdotalists, and it is impossible for me to separate now what I actually remember about this trip, and what I remember from the photos and stories told afterward. Am I remembering actual memories or are they memories of memories? In my family, the line between the two is not always clear. But everything I have written here about this trip has been corroborated by those wise enough to make this distinction better than me (my parents, in other words).

On our first night in Deauville we arranged to meet everyone at the front of the hotel dining room before dinner. I assumed that my French family would turn out to be like my American one, and I'd be running up and down the beach with my new relatives the way I ran around

Cincinnati with my cousins, because in my five years of experience that's what extended families were like. But when we arrived in the dining room, a group of impossibly old people was waiting for us, none of whom looked predisposed to run anywhere. Only two of them could speak English, Alex Maguy and Sonia. The rest just smiled and nodded at me, and I, gripping my mother's hand, shyly did the same back. Deauville, it turned out, was nothing like Cincinnati. So it was with some relief that I saw my grandmother arriving, the last of the group—at least I knew her and she spoke English. But instead of joining us, she hung back, watching her siblings and cousins. Just as I was about to go over to her, I noticed something I'd never seen before: she was crying. And then she turned around and rushed out of the room.

"What's wrong with Grandma?" I asked my mother, but she shook her head at me and held her finger to her lips. I looked up at my father for an answer but he was looking toward where his mother had disappeared and went after her.

Alex Maguy—whose real surname was Glass, like Henri and Sonia's, as well as my grandmother's originally, and it didn't occur to me to ask why he'd apparently changed it—had a cabana on the beach, and my parents said I could use it to change in and out of my swimsuit. Having one's own cabana seemed to me the absolute pinnacle of cool, but that was before I saw what Alex Ornstein had on the beach: his own giant umbrella, red with a blue flag on top, and every day we would all meet under it for lunch, attended to by smartly dressed waiters. Even though it was Alex Ornstein's umbrella, Alex Maguy dominated those lunches. He was small, bald, and tough like a bullet, but he loved talking with my father, as well as with his cousin Alex Ornstein, whom he occasionally embraced fondly. He didn't give hugs to my sister or me, but he seemed to enjoy talking with us, telling us about the famous artists he knew, none of whom we'd ever heard of, because we were, respectively, three and five years old. When I got lost on the beach one day, it was Alex Maguy and his cabana I looked for, because I knew he'd know how to get me home.

Like my grandmother, Sonia was short and had red hair, but where Sala was thin, quiet, and melancholic, Sonia was a solid ball of vibrating energy. With her bright hair, pink lipstick, and blue eye shadow, she looked like a firecracker. She taught my sister and me how to play bridge and introduced us to pain au chocolat, which was even more exciting than bridge. In the mornings she would meet us in the hotel lobby and walk us onto the beach, where she seemed to know every person on the boardwalk.

"Who was that?" I asked once, after she'd had a long, involved conversation with an older American lady about their respective dogs.

"I have no idea," she replied, marching onward.

Sonia's husband, Henri, was, at six feet, about a foot taller than his wife and siblings, but gentler than them, and at eighty-three still strikingly handsome. He would catch my eye across the table and make apologetic smiles for not being able to speak English, and he would often hold my grandmother, stroking her hair like she was still his baby sister. When Sonia and Alex Maguy argued viciously over lunch, Henri would just sit back, letting it blow over. We all knew you shouldn't get between a firecracker and a bullet.

Alex and Mania Ornstein were the frailest and in many ways the easiest-going members of the groups, often acting as peace brokers between Sonia and Alex Maguy. Being an Ornstein seemed to be less complicated than being a Glass.

Despite Deauville's differences from Cincinnati, I had a wonderful holiday. I was introduced to French culture essentials, such as triple-scoop ice cream cones and baguettes. But the grown-ups occasionally seemed to be grumpy, especially Sonia and Alex Maguy, who were barely able to sit at the same table by the end of the holiday. This was the first time in decades that all of them had spent any time together. It was also to be the last.

At the end of the week, I went back to the United States with my parents and sister, and soon after, slowly, inexorably, everyone I met in Deauville died. My grandmother died in 1994, when I was sixteen. She had made a life for herself in America but she never stopped seeming sad to me, and her sadness never stopped unnerving me. As a result I never let her get close to me. By the time she died, I was closed off in my own sadness, hospitalized for anorexia, which kept me from her funeral. For years afterward, thinking about all this made me feel things I still couldn't articulate so, again, I probably would have said it made me feel "weird," but what I really meant was that it made me feel terrible. So I deliberately didn't think about her, or any of my French family, at all.

But when I became an adult, I suddenly couldn't stop thinking of them. Moments I had barely noticed at the time, yet they made enough of an impact to leave a footprint in my memory, began to surface: my grandmother reaching out for Henri's hand in Deauville, as if he—or she—were about to drift away; Alex all alone in his grand apartment in Paris in the 1990s, surrouned by Piccasso and Matisse paintings; Sonia and Alex not even speaking to one another at my bat mitzvah, despite living almost their whole lives as neighbors in Paris.

I was ashamed of how I'd pushed my grandmother away, and that I'd never asked my French relatives about their pasts when they were all alive. But then, no one else did either: my father, my uncle Rich, and Henri and Sonia's daughter, Danièle, hardly ever talked to their parents about their pasts.

We all knew lightly penciled outlines of stories, but nothing concrete, and certainly nothing that seemed provable. I knew that my grandmother, along with her mother and brothers, lived in Paris in the 1930s. At some point, through Alex Maguy, she met my American grandfather and went with him to the States. I knew that Alex had fought in the war, and was then captured and sent to a concentration camp, but somehow escaped, and I knew he had worked as a fashion designer and then an art dealer after the war. I knew there was also another brother who had not survived the war. About Henri and Sonia's past, I knew almost nothing.

It felt increasingly apt that the one time I had met them all was in Deauville, because Deauville is a picture-perfect image of an idealized French past. My grandmother—with her chic French fashion, her home full of French art and magazines—was herself an image of idealized Frenchness and, in her obvious homesickness, embodied a longing for the France of her past. I knew there was a story, but even thinking about it felt like touching a bruise, and I started alternately tapping this sore spot and then running away in horror at what I was doing. Just an afternoon trip to an archive to look for the Glasses' birth certificates, for example, would exhaust me so much emotionally I'd have to take a two-hour nap afterward. I hid my early files and notebooks in the backs of various cupboards around my apartment, kidding myself that I wasn't doing what I was, in fact, starting to do.

When I was in my midtwenties, I came up with an idea of how to write about my grandmother in what seemed like a painless way: I would write about her relationship with fashion. By now I was working as a journalist in London, and my grandmother had used her wardrobe to make a defiant statement about her identity. While other Jewish grandmothers in Miami wore shapeless muumuus or badly fitting clothes in garish prints, my grandmother always looked like she was going to a fashion show, even if she was just going to the supermarket. Her hair and makeup were always impeccable, her accessories exquisite. She wore distinctly French styles—Yves Saint Laurent–like peasant tops, Chanel-esque jackets— proudly emphasizing her non-Americanness through her clothes.

At this point, my uncle Rich was living in my grandparents' former apartment and, fortunately for me, he hadn't thrown away any of her old things. So I flew there, simply intending to go through my grandmother's closet and describe her wardrobe, using it as a sort of meta way to write about her, because writing simply about her without any proxy still felt like staring straight into the sun. And so, after arriving at what was now my uncle's apartment, I opened her closet door and began.

Her dresses were still carefully preserved in the dry cleaners' plastic wrap, and still smelled of her mix of Chanel perfume and Guerlain face powder (even her cosmetics were strictly French). I sat on the floor, making sketches of her shoes, her bags, her scarves, until I'd filled up my notebook. And then I saw the shoebox at the back. This is what I found inside:

A small photo album with a carved wooden cover, filled with pictures of Henri and Alex looking younger than I'd ever seen them. There were also several photos of my grandmother as a child. Later in the album there were photos of her as a young woman embracing a man whose face had been scraped out by someone's—presumably my grandmother's—fingernail

A professional photo of my grandmother in her late twenties that someone had ripped into quarters, and taped back together but missing one quarter

A couple of xeroxed pages from a book titled *The Dressmakers of France.*

Three letters from someone called "Kiki," all dated during the 1940s and sent from Los Angeles, but in French

Photos of a balding man in round spectacles I'd never seen before, including one in which he was in army uniform, and two in which he was with a group of men. On several of the photos my grandmother had written in her distinctive cursive "Jacques"

A pencil drawing of Jacques, mounted on cardboard, on which the artist had written "Camp de Pithiviers, 22.VI.1941"

A rectangular metal plate on which the words "Glass Prisonnier Cambrai 1940" were written

A photocopied note on which someone had written, in French, that "la famille Glass" was hiding in Paris under an assumed name

A telegram from the International Committee of the Red Cross, apologizing for the "distressing news contained within"

Photos of Henri, Sonia, and Danièle when she was a baby

Newspaper clippings about Alex Maguy

Several photos of Alex with Pablo Picasso

A scrappy piece of paper folded into quarters on which someone had drawn a man, pointing a gun at his own head, and the tip of a cigarette had burned through the paper where the gun was pointing at the man's head. It was signed "Avec amitié, Picasso."

*　　*　　*

I put everything back in the shoebox, the shoebox in my bag, and flew home the next day. I knew I had a story now, and it wasn't about fashion.

Over the next decade, I followed these clues to trace the lives of my grandmother and her brothers. Sometimes they confirmed and filled in stories I'd already vaguely known, sometimes they told me things I'd have never imagined about my family. In some cases I uncovered truths that I know were meant to be hidden forever, and I then seriously questioned the morality of what I was doing, rummaging around in my relatives' closets that they'd long ago closed for the last time. After all, that I had found my grandmother's shoebox of tokens from the past was not, I knew, a sign that she had wanted it to be discovered: It was a testament to how quickly she was incapacitated by her stroke so that she was unable to destroy it before she died.

Yet I also knew that the stories I found could not be allowed to fade away, like a black-and-white photo in the back of a closet. The more I researched, the more the story went beyond the personal past to the political present, and it is probably no coincidence that I finally committed to writing this book in the shadow of the Brexit referendum and Donald Trump's 2016 election. Neither of those political shifts was about keeping the Jews out, but they were about keeping out vaguely defined "outsiders."

Alongside that, open anti-Semitism was on the rise throughout Europe in a way I never thought I'd see in my lifetime, from the far right and the far left. A 2018 survey found that one in four Europeans believe Jews have "too much influence in conflict and wars across the world" and one in five think they have "too much influence in media and politics."[1] In France, which is where most of my family's story is set, anti-Semitic acts rose by 74 percent between 2017 and 2018;[2] meanwhile, in America the Anti-Defamation League reported that in that same period anti-Semitic attacks doubled.[3] Of course, it's easier to ignore the lessons of the past when the past itself has faded to nothing: according to two recent surveys, 41 percent of Americans do not know what Auschwitz is[4] and one in three Europeans know "little or nothing" about the Holocaust.[5] Reading these news stories quashed any concerns I had that writing about the past, or my family, was self-indulgent.

But ultimately, the reason this story had kept such a hold on me was the people involved, each one such an extraordinary force of personality that I couldn't shake them off decades after they died. My grandmother and her brothers, once so close, took very different paths during the war, and each of their stories represents a separate strand of the Jewish experience through the twentieth century. Learning about them provided me with not just a map for what was behind me, but one that explained where we all are today. "If you don't know the past, you can't understand the present and plan properly for the future," Chaim Potok writes in *Davita's Harp*. What I found about the past and present is in this book.

Hadley in Deauville

HOUSE
of
GLASS

Chapter I

THE GLAHS FAMILY—
THE SHTETL

Austria-Hungary, 1900s

Sender, Sala, and an Ornstein cousin in Chrzanow in about 1916

enri, Jacques, Alex, and Sara Glass loved being French, and the reason was that they weren't French and their names weren't Henri, Jacques, Alex, and Sara Glass. They were born Jehuda, Jakob, Sender, and Sala Glahs in what is now Poland but was then still Austria-Hungary. This caused further confusion about the nationality of the Glasses in life and death: Alex was often described in newspaper articles in his lifetime as "Austrian," and Sala's death certificate states her place of birth simply as "Austria." This was echoed by several of her friends from later in life who told me that she spent her early years "in Vienna, I think." In fact, Sala grew up more than 250 miles from Vienna, and the Glahs family probably never visited what is now Austria at all. They were from Chrzanow, once a busy market town whose name derives, with a memorable lack of romanticism, from the Polish word for horseradish (*chrzan*), a local specialty. Its region was more elegantly named Galicia, in what is now Poland's southwest corner.

Chrzanow was a typical early-twentieth-century eastern European shtetl, or Jewish village, the kind that's so familiar from popular culture that even those who lived there describe it through the prism of art, flattening reality to something close to cliché. The very few times my grandmother referred to her childhood she talked about it in reference to *Fiddler on the Roof,* and the memoir of a townsperson who lived there at the same time as the Glahs siblings described its picturesque side streets as looking "like those in Chagall's paintings, poor and crooked." [1] When I visited Chrzanow in 2018 my guide compared it to the towns in stories by Isaac Bashevis Singer. But Chrzanow has its own unique qualities that lift it beyond the generic. Back when the Glahses lived there, it was known for its surrounding dark forests of densely packed silver birch trees where the children would hide to avoid their parents and schoolteachers. It also had an exceptionally pretty central square, fringed with colorful houses and shops, where people from miles away would come to do their shopping. Today it is better known for the more dubious accolade of being only 12.5 miles from Auschwitz, so close the two towns considered themselves to be sisters.

None of the Glahs siblings ever spoke about their childhoods, and if they mentioned Poland at all they'd spit with disgust and move on, no elaboration necessary. So, without personal anecdotes to act as my starting point, I turned to historical documents. If my family had been one of the famous Jewish dynasties—the Rothschilds, say, or the Freuds, or even the Halberstams, a wealthy family who lived in the region at the time—this would have sufficed. But they were not, and it did not. There aren't many records of the individual billions of poorer lives from Europe's past, people who leave only footprints in the sand that blow away as soon as they are buried; people who leave, at most, unidentifiable black-and-white photos behind them—their faces blankly solemn for the photographer's studio, the flash bleaching them of personality—or perhaps a brief mention in a census locked away in an obscure government vault that proves they once existed and nothing more. These people are merely referred to by history as "the poor," "the peasants," "the illiterate," even though their lives are far more revealing of the times in which they lived than those of the grander families whose lives are faithfully recorded ever after by historians.

My father mentioned that back in the 1970s my great-uncle Alex claimed to have written a memoir, which was never published, but my father couldn't remember if he'd ever even seen it, let alone read it. If it existed at all, it had surely long been thrown away, but it seemed more likely that this was another one of Alex's many implausible boasts, that he once wrote a memoir that somehow no one had ever seen. The idea that Alex could have ever had the patience to sit down and write an entire book seemed about as likely as my hanging out with Picasso. But one day in 2014, my father's younger brother, Rich, emailed from Florida: he had found Alex's memoir among my grandmother's possessions. A week later it arrived, a bulky FedEx package, the pages untouched for at least twenty years, since my grandmother died. It was typed in French on loose-leaf paper and Alex had almost certainly dictated it to an assistant who then typed it up, because it read just as Alex talked, in his gruff, colloquial, rat-a-tat stream of consciousness: "I still have my Yiddish accent. I've never tried to correct it. I love Yiddish. It is my mother tongue. The language I spoke when I knew hunger. When I fought those degenerate Poles who wished me dead," he wrote on the first page. It was like he was standing in front of me in his flat in Paris, shaking his finger wildly, as if jabbing it at invisible opponents. (The first time I saw Joe Pesci in a movie I nearly fell off my seat in shock because, if you swap the Italian heritage for a Jewish one, Pesci looks—and talks, and swaggers, and gesticulates—a lot like my great-uncle Alex did.) My father, with characteristic heroism, translated all 250 pages of Alex's memoir for me from French to English. (My French is fine, but in no way is it strong enough to handle Alex's punchy slang with occasional swoops into Yiddish.) But before he sent the translation back to me, he warned me to read it with at the very least a skeptical eye: Alex's tendency toward self-mythology was infamous, and not even those closest to him ever really believed the things he said about himself. So, while this memoir was an astonishing find, I opened it expecting to read a somewhat deadening litany of Alex's triumphs. Instead, I was amazed to discover that the first thirty pages or so was a detailed and humble account of his childhood in Chrzanow, a period of his life he certainly never discussed with any of us. Instead of focusing on himself and his glories, he wrote heartfelt descriptions of his family and their struggles, and lives that had been hidden in darkness for over a century burst into the light.

Jews had lived in Chrzanow since 1590, when the town's first Jew, a man called Yaakov, settled there.[2] Yaakov clearly had quite an impact, because by the beginning of the twentieth century more than 60 percent of the town's inhabitants were Jewish,[3] and one of its main industries was manufacturing Judaica, such as Torah scrolls and mezuzahs.[4] The town square was bordered by 120 specifically Jewish shops, their signs written in both Hebrew and Yiddish, while the open market within was where women shopped for kosher food and headscarves. When the Glahs children were born, Chrzanow even had a Jewish mayor, Dr. Zygmunt Keppler, a lawyer. From its top office to its lowest social order, Chrzanow was a Jewish town.

This was the tail end of what was a brief and relatively golden age for Jews in the Austro-Hungarian Empire. Anti-Semitism certainly existed there, most infamously in the Hilsner Affair, a series of trials that took place in 1899–1900, in which a Jew, Leopold Hilsner, was accused of blood libel and spent nineteen years in prison before finally being pardoned. But Emperor Franz Joseph I had a fondness for the Jewish religion, and under his rule, Austro-Hungarian Jews emerged from the ghettos and became part of society as the emperor gave Jews equal rights, and financed Jewish institutions. This is why there seems to have been such a flourishing of Jewish productivity in the Austro-Hungarian Empire between 1848 and 1916, from such people as Theodore Herzl, Stefan Zweig, and Sigmund Freud: it's not that this generation of Jews was uniquely talented compared with previous ones, it's that they were granted a then-unique amount of freedom.

The Chrzanovian Jews were mostly poor, but their lives were better than they ever had been or would be again. They had a friendly relationship with the Catholic Poles in the neighboring countryside who came into town to go to church, do their shopping, and take their children to school, where they were taught alongside the Jewish children.[5] Chrzanow also had a great financial advantage in its proximity to the Three Emperors' Corner, the border dividing Russia, Germany, and Austria, and the city lay on the main highway that connected eastern and western Europe, meaning traders from all over came through it. So, although it was a very Jewish town, it was also a very international one, and the townspeople regularly mixed with many other ethnicities and nationalities. Back then, this was a wonderful financial advantage for the town's Jews; very soon, it would become one of their greatest misfortunes.

One person who never trusted her neighbors was Chaya Rotter. Born in 1873 and the youngest of three children, she grew up in Chrzanow. Despite her lifelong closeness to multiple other countries, she spoke only Yiddish and Polish. She had little interest in mixing with anyone but her own kind.

On March 13, 1898, when she was twenty-five, she married someone who was ostensibly her kind in a wedding arranged by her parents. Reuben Glahs was a Jewish scholar five years younger than she and also from Chrzanow. But in truth, they were a deeply unlikely couple, in looks as much as temperament. In the very few photos that remain of her it is clear she was a large woman, solid rather than fat, with much-remarked-upon large feet and a face not even a poet could describe as beautiful.

But her most extraordinary feature was her eyes. On her medical notes later in life they were described simply as "blue/gray," a description that suggests either enormous self-restraint or irony on the doctor's part. In fact, they went in two different directions at the same time, which made her look both wild and watchful.

Reuben, by contrast, was dark haired, delicate, shorter than Chaya, and strikingly handsome, like a young Adrien Brody. Unlike Chaya, he was fluent in multiple languages—German, Polish, Russian, Yiddish— and the only person in Chrzanow other than a rabbi who could read and write Hebrew. Where Chaya was tough, practical, and energetic, Reuben was gentle, scholarly, and slow. In his memoir, Sender—Alex, as I knew him—draws frequent comparisons between his parents, invariably to his mother's disadvantage, no matter how neutral the differences were he was describing: she liked to debate furiously in the market square, washing the family's dishes around the central well where the townswomen gathered, while he preferred to sit with his friends in the cafés, listening and nodding and drinking coffee. She was ambitious for more, whereas Reuben thought you should be happy with what you have. Between them they represented the different attitudes peasant Jews had about their place in the world at that time: Should you fight for a better life than the one you were born into, or should you meekly sit back and be grateful for what you were given? Chaya and Reuben never really resolved this difference between them, and their marriage was less than blissful.

"She believed herself, quite falsely, to be from a higher social class than his. So she treated my father with indifference. I saw her coolness to him. It pained me, for my father was a man of deep goodness, of noble heart and intelligence," Sender wrote in his memoir, in one of many passages laying out at length his mother's flaws and his father's perfection.

As the daughter of a poor tailor, it's unlikely Chaya really thought of herself as being in a higher social class than anyone else, and Sender's allegation almost certainly says more about his feelings for his mother than it does about Chaya's feelings for Reuben. (And these feelings were also somewhat ironic, given that, in temperament and ambition, Sender was much more like his mother than his father.) But it is also likely that Reuben was a disappointment to her. When they met, he was a handsome man celebrated in the town for his intellect, but Chaya soon learned you can't eat intellect. He worked diligently from the day of his wedding, but life only got harder for them because of his unfailing inability to earn any money. He tried his hand at being a tailor, a glassblower, a potato picker, a translator, and, finally, a Singer sewing machine traveling salesman. Each career was less successful than the last. They were desperately poor, and became more so with each child born. After an initial stillbirth in 1900, Jehuda, Chaya's favorite, was born in 1901, followed shortly by Jakob in 1902, then Sender in 1906, one more stillbirth, then a little girl, Mindel, in 1908, who died from illness as a child, and finally Sala in 1910. For a decade, Chaya was almost continually pregnant and hungry.

The children's early years were both difficult and blissful. They were in a constant state of near starvation, dreaming of food that wasn't even available to buy, not that they could have afforded it anyway. One day, a piece of cheese appeared in the window of one of the shops in the town square, beneath a glass bell. The town's children, including Jakob and Sender, stared at it in wonder: cheese! With holes! Several inches thick! No one had ever seen such a marvel, and they watched longingly as one of the wealthy Chrzanovians from the town's poshest street, Aleja Henryka (Boulevard Henry), went into the shop, bought it, bagged it, and walked home with it, without giving any of them even a crumb. But Sender got his own back on his rich neighbors: Whenever he smelled good cooking in one of their houses, he would sneak around the back, look through the kitchen window, wait for the cook to step away, then climb in, pocket a meatball, and run into the forest to eat his prize. His mother, secretly pleased at her youngest son's pragmatic approach to life, pretended not to notice the grease stains on his trousers.

They lived on a street called Kostalista in a ruin of a building, in a two-room apartment on the second floor, so dark you could barely see more than three feet in front of you in the daytime. (Chrzanow didn't get electricity until 1912.) The windows looked out onto a barren courtyard filled with firewood for the long, bitter winters. The apartment was cold, dirty, and dangerous, and the children, particularly Sender, occasionally fell out the unprotected windows, crashing down headfirst onto the paving stones outside.

Despite all the hunger and near-death tumbles, life for the children was happy. Little Sala, sickly from birth with weak lungs, would stay at home with her mother during the day, contentedly cooking and sewing. Occasionally when she was allowed out, she would play with her pretty cousin, Rose Ornstein, who was about the same age as her. The two would make dolls out of clothespins. The boys nominally went to the local grammar school with non-Jews in the morning and then Hebrew school in the afternoon, but only Jehuda actually attended classes. He especially liked his Catholic Polish teacher, who taught him in the morning, and the teacher liked him, even coming over to the Glahses' home for the occasional kosher dinner. But Jakob and especially Sender preferred to run through the streets and play football with their seven Ornstein cousins, Rose's brothers, who were roughly the same ages as they were: Maurice, the eldest and therefore the leader; Josek, who was two years younger than Sender but so brave when it came to stealing food that Sender graciously considered him an equal; quiet and shy Arnold; and Alex Ornstein, the baby of the boys. (As well as Rose, there were two other Ornstein girls, Anna and Sarah.) The Ornsteins were the children of Chaya's older sister, Hadassah, who managed to produce eight children in a decade, all sweet-natured and easygoing despite having to fight for a spot around the dining table at every meal. They lived around the corner from the Glahs family, on Aleja Henryka, named after a converted Jew,[6] because their father, Hirsch, was comparatively wealthy. But Sender never mentions feeling socially inferior to, or jealous of, his cousins in his memoir. Instead, he describes the thrill of dashing up Aleja Henryka with his brother and cousins, Sender and Josek pocketing some meatballs on the way and heading into the birch tree woods, where there was a large sandpit, a stone quarry, and a lake. They would eat Sender and Josek's takings and hide from their parents for hours, playing make-believe and kicking a "football" that was a rolled-up bunch of rags.

The Glahs family kept kosher, and Reuben, like all the Jewish men in Chrzanow, went to prayers every Shabbat and on the holy days, walking to the Great Synagogue off the market square around the corner from their house. They were Orthodox, but not ultra-Orthodox, like many of their fellow townspeople who dominated the town's local politics, in their heavy black clothes, long beards, and side curls. In the very few surviving photos of the Glahs children from this period, which I found in Sala's and Henri's albums, the boys often wear yarmulkes, but they don't have side curls or wear traditional clothes, and Sala is generally wearing pretty, frilly dresses, while Chaya never covered her hair, as ultra-Orthodox women do. Their lives were informed by Judaism, but not controlled by it, and compared with many of their neighbors they were almost scandalously modern.

Throughout Galicia at this time there was a growing schism among the Jews regarding tradition versus progress, with the heavy-coated conservatives on one side and the less tradition-bound Jews on the other. The latter argued for a modern approach to Judaism, influenced by the Haskalah, the Jewish enlightenment, which emerged in the late eighteenth century and argued that Jews should maintain their secular distinctiveness but should also take more part in the modern world, such as adopting modern dress and broader education. It looked at Judaism as an evolving cultural identity rather than a restrictive religious one. Ironically, this ideology that pushed for integration would later contribute to the rise of Zionism, partly because many Jews later realized that, no matter how much they assimilated, they were still persecuted, and therefore Jews needed a Jewish homeland.

But in Austria-Hungary in the early twentieth century, the idea of a Jewish state was so far away it might have been on the moon. Given that traditional Jews far outnumbered progressive ones in Galicia in general and Chrzanow in particular, the whole debate was ostensibly moot for Chrzanovian Jews. But Jehuda, a talented scholar from an early age who would likely have read about the Haskalah, argued for his family to adopt a more progressive approach to Judaism. In his memoir, Sender describes, with palpable retrospective awe of his big brother, how at the young age of twelve Jehuda urged his parents to be less obviously Jewish and to assimilate more with the Germans or Poles—to try to speak their language more instead of always relying on Yiddish, for example. Chaya waved her son away and continued to speak Yiddish loudly in the town square. Reuben similarly couldn't countenance giving up what he saw as his primary identity. But as a compromise, he allowed himself to be persuaded by Jehuda to change the spelling of their surname from Glahs to the more westernized Glass—something simultaneously strong and fragile, able to withstand pressure but prone to breaking. Jews' names as a whole in this period were unfixed, mutable—a sign it seemed to them at the time of their adaptability. But it was also an indication of the instability of their lives, and was seen as part of the "rootlessness" that would soon be used against them.

All four of the children idolized their gentle, loving father, who raised his hand only once: to Sender (of course), when he announced at age four, on the way to synagogue, that he didn't believe in God, and the strike was so half-hearted it felt more like a pat. Although Chaya was undoubtedly the more assertive parent, it was Reuben's looks that were dominant. Jehuda, Jakob, and Sala all inherited Reuben's delicate, pretty appearance—Jakob in particular, whom Reuben named after his beloved late father,* looked so similar to him the neighbors used to joke they probably had the same fingerprints. He was also the most like his father: gentle, passive, and easily pushed around—Jakob skipped school only because Sender told him to do so. Jehuda, quiet and self-contained, inherited his father's intellectual curiosity, but he was more reliable and

---

* Reuben is the son of Jacob in the Old Testament, so the name is traditionally translated as "son of Jacob."

practical. As for baby Sala, her father loved to buy pretty dresses for his little daughter, while Chaya, judging from photos, would not have recognized a pretty dress from an ugly one if it hit her in the face in the marketplace. But Reuben always took care over his appearance, even when he was reduced to wearing almost literal rags. The Glass children all inherited his appreciation of aesthetics, and for the rest of their lives they dressed carefully and stylishly, a lifelong show of love for their father.

The only child who resembled and acted like Chaya was Sender. According to family lore, Sender was "born fighting," because when he came out of his mother he was silent, so the midwife slapped him. It was the last time in his life Sender lost a fight. From the age of six he was getting into scrapes at school daily. He wasn't bothered by the blood and bruises as long as he won the battle, and he always fought until he won. Sender was born on December 25 and his mother referred to him as "little Jesus," a teasing reference to his dominating personality, which was in inverse proportion to his physical size. Unlike his brothers, Sender was short, something he later put down to "deprivation," although he never explained why his brothers both grew to over six feet, about a foot taller than him. But Sender wasn't just a stubby little fighter—he was also a dreamer, and what he dreamed of was escape. He loved to hear his father describe places he'd read about like Paris, London, Venice, cities of such beauty they made the Chrzanow synagogues look like nothing, Reuben said. Sender loved his father, but he would never be like him, slaving away for no recognition. What was the point of working hard without reward? At the age of eight, Paris was far beyond his reach, so he came up with a plan to go to the closer and yet almost equally exotic Trzebina, a town a little more than four miles away where people from Chrzanow went when they needed a dentist. Sender told his mother he had a terrible toothache and Chaya let him take the train on his own with his favorite cousin, Josek Ornstein. The town itself was something of a disappointment, but the freedom of travel thrilled Sender so much he was, for once, almost speechless. Even though it meant the boys had to suffer a hideously painful tooth extraction by the dentist, the journey was worth it. So much so, they did it again, costing them another tooth. Still worth it.

"It was a world of superstitions, of quarrelling rabbis, quarrelling Hasidim, where thousands of Jews lived, twenty synagogues, where the air was so fresh. I sometimes felt, in lieu of food, I was nourished by the Carpathian air," Sender later wrote. But then World War I started and everything that had been good about the children's lives instantly turned very, very bad.

When Chaya waved her husband off to war she must have had few hopes of ever seeing him again. Reuben couldn't even walk up Aleja Henryka without losing his breath, and that one time he gave Sender a smack he, rather than Sender, had cried—how on earth was such a man going to survive life in the Austro-Hungarian army? But like many Jewish men, Reuben felt intense loyalty to Emperor Franz Joseph I because of his kindness to the Jews. An educated man like Reuben would have been all too aware that it was very much in his best interest, as a Jew, to defend the emperor. So he signed up to fight pretty much as soon as his country declared war on Serbia. But there were, surely, few more unlikely soldiers than Reuben Glass.

Chaya was now, essentially, a single mother at the age of forty-one, with four children aged thirteen, twelve, eight, and four. There was no way she could look after them on her own. Her older sister, Hadassah, was busy enough with her own seven children and her brother, Samuel, was busy with his four. No, she needed a man to take charge of the household, one who would look after the family and look after her. She didn't have to search too far to find just the one she needed.

Jehuda was only thirteen, but when his father went off to war he became the head of the household. Chaya relied on him, not even like a wife on a husband but a daughter on a father, and this was to be their dynamic for the rest of their lives. It was an obligation Jehuda quietly shouldered with enormous patience. "Jehuda," Chaya would say proudly to her children and, later, her grandchildren, "iz die beste." (Sender, on the other hand, she would describe as alternately a *pshakrev*—dog's blood, a Polish curse—or a mitzvah, a blessing, depending on his notoriously changeable mood.) Despite still being at school, Jehuda, as he later recounted in his own notes, supported the family, working for the library in the evenings and on the weekends, and he tried, with minimal success, to get his brothers to go to school. He, too, started missing school: his 1916/17 school report says he missed 145 hours that year, but he still got straight A's. But as Chaya became more demanding, and life in Chrzanow became more difficult, what he really wanted was to get out. Whereas Sender looked to schemes and tooth extractions as his means of escape, Jehuda realized academia might be his ticket.

Food became increasingly scarce in Chrzanow as the war went on, and the Jews were used as the scapegoats for everyone's suffering; Polish authorities started confiscating their goods, claiming, falsely, that they were trading on the black market. The local halls in town, where the Jews had often held cultural committee meetings, were suddenly off-limits to them.[7] Both Sender and Jehuda watched all this, and started talking more openly about leaving the town. Jakob laughed at their concerns, and insisted the Jews would be safe in Chrzanow, as they always had been. Little Sala, who had Jehuda's quietude and Jakob's gentleness, revered her three older brothers, and agreed with whichever one seemed to be taking charge, which in this case was generally Jehuda. But any talk of leaving Chrzanow could only be talk for now: they weren't going anywhere until the war ended and their father returned.

But it was becoming almost impossible for them to stay. In late October 1918 there were rumors that a pogrom was being planned, organized by the Polish authorities. On November 5, 1918, six days before the end of the war, the first town in the newly liberated Poland to suffer such an attack was Chrzanow.[8]

They came at night. The townspeople heard them before they saw them, "a savage screaming crowd that seemed like a monster. They were attacking animals, wild beasts from the guts of hell. From their distorted snouts came cries of a horrible hatred which I found impossible to understand," Sender wrote. Polish men and women tore through the town, ransacking the synagogues, smashing the Jewish shop windows. The Jews ran to their homes, frantically locking the doors behind them. The Glass family hid under a bed, both Sala, who was eight, and Chaya, forty-five, clinging to seventeen-year-old Jehuda in terror. After an hour or so of listening to the terrifying noises outside, twelve-year-old Sender scrambled out from under the bed and, ignoring the cries of his family, ran out to join the few Jewish men who were attempting to fight back. In the dark, he tried to make out the faces, but they were so obscured by hate and fury they looked more like wild boars than humans to him— except one. As he watched the group charge up his street, he looked at the leader and realized he recognized him: it was Jehuda's former tutor, the Christian Pole who came over for dinner occasionally. As he looked closer, he recognized some more: people who came in every Sunday to go to church, the man who occasionally gave him a bit of cheese in the market, women who had bought sewing machines from his father. He saw a well-respected judge, Court President Wierszbyicki, he saw scholars, and he saw peasants and thugs—all sectors of Polish society—and here they all were, beating up his friends, trying to burn down his house and kill his family.

"Something in me died in the face of this inhuman explosion of savagery," he later wrote. "From that day, my childhood was over."

The pogrom lasted twenty-four hours, and Sender did as much as a young boy could to fight back, tripping the men as they charged in to ransack the empty stores, kicking their horses. At one point he was slashed across the forehead with a knife and, decades later, Sala could still remember her terror when her brother stumbled through their door in the morning, blinded by blood pouring down into his eyes from his deep head wound, half-crazed with adrenaline; for the rest of her life she associated Poland with that vision of violence. In one night, almost all the town's Jews were left destitute, their money and livelihoods taken from them by their own countrymen. When the war ended six days later, few celebrated.

From then on, attacks on Jews became common in Chrzanow and in the surrounding area, especially from the so-called Polish liberation army, which emerged after Poland's liberation at the end of the war. Its members were known as "the Hallerchiks" in honor of their leader, General Haller, and they would roam through Chrzanow, ripping the beards off any Jews they encountered, tearing the skin and laughing at the bloodied faces, and if they came across a clean-shaven Jew, they would beat him for his lack of religiosity. They justified these attacks by citing the increasingly popular theory that Jews were not loyal to Poland, but were instead Bolsheviks, plotting to overturn the government. Neither the Hallerchiks nor the Chrzanovians could have known it at the time, and certainly the Glass family didn't, but they were at the emerging forefront of a relatively new kind of anti-Semitism, one which would shape the twentieth century and their lives. And it would linger, like a strange stray black cloud, over the lives of their children and grandchildren.

The theory that Jews are political destabilizers, working against whatever country they live in, is a more modern and politically inflected form of anti-Semitism than the traditional and religiously based one, which held Jews responsible for Jesus's crucifixion. It emerged in the eighteenth and nineteenth centuries as a reaction against the social and economic changes in Europe stemming from the French Revolution, when the old monarchical hierarchies were toppled, followed by the spread of industrialization and urbanization across the continent. These two enormous shifts combined to create a new liberal, capitalist social order, one in which citizenship was based on civic participation and equality, as opposed to bloodline and history—forward-looking rationalism over backward-looking nationalism.[9] Thus, Jews could be seen as citizens as opposed to outsiders. Opponents of the Enlightenment, however, argued for national purity, celebrating a country's heritage as opposed to its modern future, and during the nineteenth century there was a rise in anti-Semitic sentiment as those who failed to benefit from the new economy blamed the Jews. In 1845 the French writer Alphonse Toussenel claimed, "Protestants and Jews . . . have controlled public opinion in order to favour trafficking and rigging the market, blocked every defence of royalty and of the people, put the producer and the consumer at their mercy so that in France the Jew reigns and governs."[10]

These beliefs found validation in the infamous 1903 document *The Protocols of the Elders of Zion,* which emerged just as the Glass children were being born. It claimed that a mysterious Jewish cabal was controlling governments and the media, and even though *The Protocols* was quickly exposed as a hoax, it shaped the dominating anti-Semitic narrative of the twentieth century. This really began to take hold after World War I, when nationalism escalated in response to the economic devastation across the continent, although specific takes on it slightly differed. In one version of this theory, Jews are greedy money-hoarders who control a country's government through their connections and wealth, puppet masters pulling the strings. In the other version, the one promoted by the Hallerchiks, Jews were communist revolutionaries looking to overthrow a country's government. But the message of both versions is the same: Jews are political disruptors working against the people and for themselves, which is just a new take on the old idea that Jews are not really citizens of the country in which they were born, so cannot be trusted. In other words, anti-Semitism becomes another form of xenophobia.

This theory has retained a tenacious hold on the popular imagination despite everything Jews endured in the twentieth century. In the twenty-first century it can be seen in the right wing's demonization of George Soros, the Hungarian American philanthropist and Holocaust survivor who has been vilified by the American,[11] Hungarian,* and

---

* During his 2017 campaign for reelection, Hungarian prime minister Viktor Orban claimed that Soros was planning to resettle a million refugees in the European Union and give them thousands of euros each, and claimed "[Soros] wants to transform Hungary into an immigrant country." "Hungary Says EU's 'Irresponsible' Migrant Policy Poses Threat to Jews," *Reuters,* April 16, 2018.

British far right* as a suspicious manipulator plotting to control the global order and bring chaos into the lives of peaceful citizens.†‡

The campaign for Brexit—which went on near simultaneously with the vilification of Soros, and crossed left and right party lines—would have appealed to the Hallerchiks with its dreamy-eyed talk about hard borders, heritage, and national purity. Nigel Farage, Brexit's most influential architect, has long talked darkly about "the new world order" and argued that "globalists have wanted to have some form of conflict with Russia as an argument for us all to surrender our national sovereignty and give it up to a higher global level."[12] It is hard not to hear the echoes of the Hallerchiks' insistence that Jews, those citizens of nowhere, were working against Poland for some kind of greater global domination, but Farage determinedly stuck his fingers in his ears and insisted any sug-

---

* Nigel Farage has made many claims about Soros, including that he "wants to break down the fundamental values of our society and, in the case of Europe, he doesn't want Europe to be based on Christianity." "Farage Criticised for Using Antisemitic Themes to Criticise Soros," *The Guardian*, May 12, 2019.

† President Trump repeatedly implied in October and November 2018 that Soros was funding the so-called migrant caravan, a group of thousands of desperate Central American migrants seeking asylum in America. Various other Republicans and far-right commentators also pushed that allegation, and many people believed it. One believer was US citizen Robert Bowers, who reposted a comment that said, "Jews are waging a propaganda war against Western civilization and it is so effective we are heading towards certain extinction." On October 27, 2018, Bowers shot and killed eleven Jews in a synagogue. This did not stop President Trump from continuing to endorse the entirely unfounded theory that Soros was funding the caravan. ("Trump says he 'wouldn't be surprised' if unfounded conspiracy theory about George Soros funding [migrant] caravan is true," John Wagner, *Washington Post*, November 1, 2018.)

‡ And this mentality is not limited to the right. The former leader of Britain's Labour Party, Jeremy Corbyn, has been repeatedly criticized for what many see as flirtations with anti-Semitism. One especially egregious example hit the news just as I was starting to write this book in 2018, when it emerged that in 2012 he appeared to express support on Facebook for a mural that depicted stereotypically Jewish-looking bankers playing Monopoly on the backs of slaves. (Corbyn insisted that he "did not look more closely at the image.") "Jeremy Corbyn Regrets Comments about 'Anti-Semitic' Mural," BBC, March 23, 2018.

gestion of anti-Semitism was "wide of the mark."* From "bolsheviks" in the 1920s to "globalists" in the 2010s, the euphemisms for anti-Semitic and nationalist beliefs might shift over time, but the underlying stories remain remarkably constant.

Contrary to everyone's expectations, his wife's presumably most of all, Reuben did return from the war, but only barely. He had fought in the Second Battle of the Piave River in June 1918, in which the Italian army crushed the Austro-Hungarian army. This battle was the beginning of the end of the Austro-Hungarian Empire. Nearly 230,000 men were killed, but Reuben was not one of them. He was, however, gassed badly, and his lungs were damaged irrevocably. Somehow he limped through the rest of the war, further depleting whatever strength his lungs had left, and got home, where he walked in the door and collapsed in the front room.

But when Reuben realized how poor his family had become in his absence, with Sender stealing food for the family table and Sala wearing rags, he forced himself to return to work. Reuben didn't have a pension from the army, and the family desperately needed the money, so he went back to hawking Singer sewing machines around the countryside. But there aren't many worse careers for a man with broken lungs than that of traveling salesman, schlepping through sooty towns on dirty trains in cold nights. "My father was very, very ill, and there was no medicine for him. As if we could afford medicine. He had to return to work, to continue his endless travels as a sewing machine salesman for a miserable little salary. Great sadness infected our home," Sender wrote.

---

* Similarly, in her first Conservative conference speech after becoming prime minister soon after the referendum, Theresa May attacked "global elites" and claimed, "If you believe you are a citizen of the world, you are a citizen of nowhere." Vince Cable, the then leader of the Liberal Democrat party, said at the time, "It could have been taken out of *Mein Kampf.* I think that's where it came from, wasn't it? 'Rootless cosmopolitans'?" "Vince Cable: Theresa May's Tory Conference Speech 'Could Have Been Taken Out of *Mein Kampf,*'" Anoosh Chakelian, *New Statesman*, July 5, 2017.

Reuben did not last long at his job, but the sadness did. One night Reuben came back to the apartment after another trip, went to bed, and never got up again. For the next few years he lay there, sick, in horrendous pain, racked with a violent cough that seemed to rip his lungs apart with every hack.

After the war, the Glass family was still in their old home but in an utterly unfamiliar land. The deeply anti-Semitic National-Democratic (ND) Party was on the rise in Poland. At the Versailles Conference in January 1919, the Polish delegation, co-led by Roman Dmowski, cofounder of the ND Party, fought unsuccessfully against signing the minorities protections section of the Treaty of Versailles. Dmowski and the Polish politicians complained that it suggested Poland and the Polish people were oppressors as opposed to victims, which was how they saw themselves, and not without some merit. Poland was decimated after the war, after German, Austrian, and Russian troops had marched back and forth across it, destroying railways and agriculture, and the ensuing poverty led people to look for targets to blame. Dmowski insisted, in familiar rhetoric, that "international Jewry" was plotting Poland's destruction, and the Catholic Polish media repeatedly and openly associated Jews with evil.[13] This didn't do much to stem the attacks against Jews in Poland.

The Ornstein cousins had already left Chrzanow to go to Paris, and after the first pogrom the Glass family knew they had to go, too. Like a strikingly high number of Jews in the early 1920s, Jehuda went to Prague for university,[14] which the family somehow managed to pay for. So Jakob was the first of the family to go to Paris, in 1920 when he was eighteen years old, followed shortly thereafter by fourteen-year-old Sender. But Chaya and Sala stayed behind with Reuben, as he could not survive the journey, and the three of them alone endured the terror of multiple pogroms and increasing anti-Semitism. Finally, in 1925, after years of pain, Reuben died.

For the rest of their lives, the Glass children referred to Reuben's death as one of their most formative and traumatic experiences, despite all they later endured. Jakob and Sender were both living in Paris at this point, and the former wept for the only adult he knew who never berated him for his deficiencies, while Sender, who idolized his father, both despite and because he was so different from him, raged with fury against his death. Fifty years later, he dedicated his memoir to his father, "the man I loved most in my life." Sala, still only fourteen at this point, cried for her father, who had made her feel pretty and loved and safe. Chaya leaned on Jehuda more heavily than ever, demanding he come home from university to help her.

Jehuda didn't cry when his father died. It was perhaps at that point that he learned not to cry because he pretty much never did so. And yet, he was utterly bereft by the loss of his father, who was the only member of his family who saw him for who he was and not what he was, the oldest, most dependable son. But he tucked his grief behind his implacable exterior, like the creased photo of his father that he hid inside his stiff wallet for the rest of his life. Almost thirty years after Jehuda died, I found that wallet in a storage box in the basement of his daughter Danièle's building. It had slipped into the lining of an old suitcase and I happened to discover it by accident. I pulled it out and looked through it, hoping to find something that would reveal a little of Jehuda's later life: receipts, perhaps, or scrawled notes. But the only thing in it was the photo of Reuben, a century old by that point, the only memory Jehuda kept on him at all times, until he, too, was a memory.

Almost as soon as Reuben died, Chaya and Sala went to Paris. The world in which the Glass children had grown up, the eastern European Jewish shtetl, based on community but also dependent on peaceful interactions with outsiders, was dying. Like Reuben, it had no place in this harshly emerging modern era. So both he and it were buried in Chrzanow's Jewish cemetery, filled with other Jews whose families, if they were lucky, were forging new lives across Europe, leaving behind neglected gravestones and much more.

None of the Glasses ever returned to Chrzanow, except one, once. In the 1970s, Sender—now known as Alex—visited Poland on a trip organized by some of his fellow veterans of the Foreign Legion. He went, very reluctantly, back to a country he associated only with death, pogroms, and hunger. But he went because he was interested to see how many Jews were left where he grew up, and how they were living. What he saw devastated him. The town that he remembered as surrounded by forests and countryside was, he wrote, now "an open, heavily polluted field." The only things he recognized were "the brutish mugs" of the Polish people he saw in the marketplace—otherwise, everything from his childhood was gone: his home, the synagogues, the Jews.

Chrzanow fell into German hands almost the day World War II was declared, September 1, 1939. This was not a surprise to the Chrzanovians: the month before, they'd watched the long caravans of desperate people marching down the long highway between Katowice and Krakow that ran through Chrzanow, as civilians who lived near the German and Polish borders fled into the countryside for safety. Adolf Hitler had been pushing the myth that communism was a Jewish plot for almost a decade, borrowing the story from anti-Semitic nationalist movements in various countries, including Poland. Meanwhile, the theory that Polish Jews were working for the Soviets, and had even been responsible for the Great Purge of 1936–1938, in which up to 1.2 million people were killed in Russia, had become so widespread it was generally assumed to be fact, and Polish nationalists referred to Jews collectively as traitors.[15] Chrzanow was infused with panic, and the wealthier and cannier sent their female relatives, children, and valuables out of the city to safety.[16] But many did not. Because so many of the town's Jews knew and did business with the Germans, they refused to believe that the Germans would actually hurt them, their longtime neighbors, friends, and colleagues.[17] For neither the first nor the last time, the Jews were overoptimistic about the benevolence of outsiders. On September 4, 1939, the Nazis entered the city and immediately began to terrorize the Jews. But as much as the actions of their neighbors and former colleagues shocked them, an even bigger surprise to the Chzarnovian Jews was how keen their countrymen, the Poles, were to betray them.

"They were the ones who pointed out the Jews to the German soldiers, who couldn't tell the difference between Jews and Poles. They didn't know any German but with sign language they pointed out 'Jude!'" one resident of the town later recalled.[18] More than 15,000 Jews—almost the entirety of Chrzanow's Jewish population[19]—died in the Holocaust, rounded up and sent just down the road to their sister town, which many of them would have visited before, where they were murdered.[20] Ironically, the pogroms that had so terrified my grandmother and her family actually saved their lives, because they propelled the family out of Poland before the 1930s. Had they stayed, they all almost certainly would have been killed.

I went to Chrzanow in the spring of 2018, forty years after Alex visited, almost exactly one hundred years after the Glass family started to leave. My father traveled there with me, as did my father's cousin Anne-Laurence Goldberg, Anna Ornstein's granddaughter. Chrzanow itself wasn't quite as grim as when Alex had visited, when it was still under communist rule: there were typical Eastern European tower blocks around the outside, but also pretty streets in the center, bordered with houses freshly painted in dusky pinks, yellows, and greens as they had been back when the Glasses lived there. Yet it still feels like a town from which something's been sucked out, and what's been sucked out are the Jews. In 1920, Jews represented 55.5 percent of the town's population. Today, they officially represent less than 1 percent, although our guide admitted that number was more likely to be closer to zero.

My father, Anne-Laurence, and I walked around the town, retracing the stories Alex told in his memoir. The square where Chaya used to wash the dishes and do the shopping is still there, but none of the Jewish shops that bordered the square remain. Of the town's twenty synagogues, not a single one remains. The Great Synagogue, where the Glasses prayed, was destroyed in the 1970s to make room for a parking lot. All that remains of it is a broken concrete wall, heavily graffitied. In fact, the Jewish cemetery where Reuben is buried, which somehow survived the war, is pretty much the only sign that Jews ever lived there at all. He lies in a quiet corner, shaded by the former Galician forest where his children once ran. He is near his daughter Mindel, who died as a child; his father Jakob's gravestone lies on the other side of the cemetery, next to the great family tomb for the wealthy Halberstam family, like a humble sentryman keeping guard. Reuben was not one for making public statements in life, but in death the deeply carved Hebrew letters on his tombstone act as an uncharacteristically defiant show of Chrzanow's Jewish legacy.

The week before my father and I booked our tickets to go to Chrzanow in 2018, the Polish president, Andrzej Duda, signed into law an anti-defamation bill making it illegal to attribute responsibility or complicity for the Holocaust to the Polish state.* This law, President Duda said in a national broadcast, "protects Polish interests . . . our dignity, the historical truth . . . so that we are not slandered as a state and as a nation." In a century-spanning echo of Dmowski's complaint in 1919, Duda objected to the idea that Poland was ever an oppressor. Instead, he said, stories about Poland during World War II should focus on Poland's suffering and glory.

This bill was not a surprise to anyone who had followed the Law and Justice Party since they came to power. In 2016, President Duda threatened to take away a national honor from Jan Tomasz Gross, an American citizen born in Poland and one of the world's experts on the Holocaust.[21] Gross wrote in an essay that the Poles killed more Jews than the Germans did, a claim other historians have backed up as correct. Yet Duda insisted this was "an attempt to destroy Poland's good name," and while in Poland, Gross was hauled in for five hours of questioning.[22]

No doubt, Poland endured one of the most brutal occupations of any country invaded by the Germans, and the Poles, whom the Nazis considered to be *untermenschen* (inferiors), suffered horrifically. Yet it is also true that part of the reason 90 percent of Poland's Jews were killed dur-

---

* Five months after this bill was passed, after international outcry about this law, Duda downgraded it from a criminal offense to a civil one. So it's still wrong to suggest Poland was complicit with the Nazis, but you probably won't go to jail for saying so.

ing the war, one of the highest percentages in Europe, is that they were
denounced, hunted, and killed by the Poles themselves, before, during,
and even after the war. Just one year after the end of World War II, on
July 4, 1946, soldiers and civilians led an attack on the Jews in the Polish
town of Kielce, killing more than forty. They had survived the Holocaust
and returned to what was in many cases their homeland, only to then
be killed by their fellow citizens. After what became known as the Kielce
pogrom, many of the surviving Polish Jews left the country and few have
ever returned. Before World War II, more than three million Jews lived
in Poland, the biggest Jewish population in Europe; today it is estimated
to be about ten thousand. By comparison, more than fifteen thousand
Jews live in Miami Beach. More than fifty thousand Jews live in the
north London borough of Barnet.

Poland had been a deeply anti-Semitic country long before the Nazis
turned up, as the Glass family knew well. So while there certainly were
brave Polish individuals who tried to help the Jews during the war, they
were very much the exceptions.[23] Even after the war, many in Eastern
Europe, including Poland, continued to refer to Jews as Bolsheviks, suggesting that what happened to them was in some way their fault, and
certainly not Poland's. That mentality still exists today: by outlawing
suggestions of Polish complicity, President Duda and his Law and Justice
Party are trying to create "a narrative of heroic Polish victimhood," the
New York Times said,[24] one that absolved them of any wrongdoing in
World War II. An official to the president said any Jews who criticized
the law, who claimed that Polish anti-Semitism helped to enable the
Holocaust happening on Polish land, were merely "ashamed [that] many
Jews engaged in collaboration during the war."[25]

Just down the road from Chrzanow is the Auschwitz-Birkenau Museum and Memorial. While my father, Anne-Laurence, and I were in
Chrzanow, the nationalist and pro-government Polish media was accusing the museum of downplaying the deaths of Poles in the camp and
focusing instead on what was described as "foreign narratives"—in other
words, the Jewish stories.

"Foreign, and not Polish narratives reign at Auschwitz. Time for it to stop," wrote Barbara Nowack, a former local councillor for the Law and Justice Party. The home of at least one guide at the site was vandalized in March 2018, with someone spray-painting "Poland for the Poles" across the outside alongside a Star of David equated with a swastika.[26]

None of this would have surprised the Glasses. It did, however, surprise me. Because I went to Auschwitz-Birkenau before visiting Chrzanow with my father and Anne-Laurence (whose grandparents had been killed there), what struck me was how much emphasis was placed on the Polish victims. Seventy-five thousand non-Jewish Poles were killed in Auschwitz, which is shocking, but so were the 1.1 million Jews, and looking around at the exhibitions, signs, and tours I felt like the memorial was suggesting some kind of equivalence between the Polish and Jewish suffering in the camp. There is even a gift shop in the car park outside, run by the local municipality, which sells Polish tourist tat. Because nothing makes one more desirous of buying an "I Heart Poland" coffee mug than a trip to Auschwitz. "An Auschwitz gift shop" is surely the ultimate Jewish joke, and its intention is clear: Auschwitz, it is saying, is about Polish victimhood and triumph. The Jews were a side issue.

"In all Holocaust sites there is a tendency to emphasize the nation's suffering and German culpability," Martin Winstone from the Holocaust Educational Trust told me in 2018:

> Auschwitz was one of the very few concentration camps where non-Jewish Poles were killed, so it's not surprising Polish suffering is emphasized there—although, of course, far more Jews were killed there. But so much depends on political and social climates. Even just five years ago people would have said Poland was being really honest about its history. But with this government in power they are trying to limit discussions of Polish culpability, and these efforts aren't actually aimed at the international community, but at the people in Poland—teachers, academics—who are trying to tell the true story. A huge amount of Polish identity is based on the idea that Poles were

victims of the German occupation, but that doesn't mean some of them didn't also perpetrate it. Every country wants to have heroic narratives of the war, and what this all shows is how vulnerable historical truth is.

Back in Chrzanow, we found the building where Anne-Laurence's grandmother, Anna Ornstein, and the rest of the Ornstein cousins lived on Aleja Henryka. It was large and imposing, with fretted ironwork around the balconies, preventing any children from rolling off. It was painfully different from the crumbling semi–death trap where the Glasses lived, as described in Alex's memoir. We eventually found the Glass family's street, after figuring out it had been renamed from Kostalista to Lipstada. Their house had long since been torn down, which wasn't a surprise—I hardly expected a condemned building from a century ago to still be standing. But what I saw around the corner made me stop and stare. There, on the side of a building just behind where the Glasses once lived, was fresh graffiti: "Anty Jude." This was a tag from a fan of the Wisla football team, whose supporters refer to themselves as the "Anty Jude gang," in opposition to the Widzew team, which is associated with the Jewish community in the way Tottenham Hotspur Football Club is in England. The Anty Jude label is defended by supporters as mere larky banter—only the most po-faced seeker of victim status could confuse it with *real* anti-Semitism, they say. At a Polish league game in 2013 between Wisla and Widzew, there were chants of "Move on, Jews! Your home is at Auschwitz! Send you to the gas chamber!" A Polish municipal prosecutor decided these were not criminal offenses.[27]

Not even being less than four miles from Auschwitz made this graffiti artist rethink leaving this tag. If anything, it may have encouraged him. My father winced when he saw it and looked away, but I think the Glasses would have appreciated the aptness of seeing this on their neighbor's building in 2018. Almost a century after they left everything they had and knew to go to France, their old town—their old country—was still very much vindicating their decision.

Chapter 2

THE GLASS SIBLINGS—
IMMIGRATION

Paris, 1920s to early 1930s

Sala in France, 1929

Of course, to the Glasses, their decision to move from Poland to Paris in 1920 felt utterly personal: their hometown was suddenly under threat from violent pogroms; the Ornstein cousins were already in Paris, so they could help them once they were there; Paris wasn't unreachably far from where they were. This random set of circumstances, it seemed to them, happened to blow them toward the French capital.

But as is often the case with events that feel specific to us in the moment, the Glasses' move was wholly typical of both their time and their demographic. Between 1880 and 1925, 3.5 million Jews left central and eastern Europe, and 100,000 of them went to France,[1] most for exactly the same reasons as the Glasses: they were fleeing the pogroms, and they knew people in Paris. Between 1900 and 1935, the number of Jews in France tripled,[2] and by the end of that decade Paris had the third-largest Jewish community in the world, surpassed only by New York and Warsaw.[3] So not only were Jews likely to feel at home there, they were also likely to have relatives there who would help them settle in, as the Glasses did. New York was too far away for many eastern European immigrants, and Warsaw too close to the danger from which they were fleeing, so Paris was the logical third option. Even more appealing for immigrants in the 1920s was that, at this point, France—unlike the United States or the United Kingdom[4]—had never imposed an anti-immigration statute that capped the number of (primarily Jewish) immigrants allowed in. Instead, the country was known as *une terre d'asile* (a nation of asylum), and as a result, by the late 1930s, Paris had a Jewish population of 150,000, of whom 90,000 were immigrants from eastern Europe, including 50,000 Poles.[5] France, these Jews imagined, would be their salvation, away from pogroms and rampaging peasants. There was even a popular Yiddish phrase suggesting as much: *lebn vi Got in Frankrykk*[6] (live like a king in France). Although seeing as there was a similar phrase about Poland, describing it as a *Pardisus Judeorum* (a Jewish paradise),[7] the Polish Jews at least ought to have known better than to put too much faith in old Yiddish sayings.

France's appeal to fleeing Jewish immigrants went deeper than mere pragmatic considerations. In 1791 it became the first country in western Europe to liberate Jews* and so was associated in many Jews' minds with liberalism and tolerance. Immigrant Jews weren't especially bothered by the Dreyfus affair,[8] the notorious case in which Alfred Dreyfus, a Jewish artillery officer, was accused of passing confidential French military

---

* The first country in the world to liberate Jews was, ironically enough, Poland, five hundred years earlier.

documents to the Germans and was unanimously found guilty by seven judges of treason 1894. He was finally exonerated in 1906 after another (non-Jewish) Frenchman, Ferdinand Walsin Esterhazy, was proven to be the culprit. The French army had mounted a massive cover-up to obscure Dreyfus's innocence and more than a century on, the case remains one of the most notorious examples of anti-Semitism. Many eastern European Jews at the time, however, saw it differently. At least, they reasoned, in France, these arguments happen in the public sphere, an improvement from what they saw in their countries, where their relatives and friends were lynched and dumped.

"We saw the Dreyfus affair as part of history, and touching only on a part of the populace, the military. It seemed to us a sort of literary anti-Semitism, the product of old, reactionary fanatics. What had really touched us was the Beilis affair. For us poor Jews, the Beilis affair had a terrifying resonance when the pogroms began, because it seemed like it could happen anywhere," Sender wrote, referring to the vehemently anti-Semitic 1911 case in Russia, in which Menahem Mendel Beilis, a Hasidic Jew, was falsely accused of killing a thirteen-year-old Ukrainian boy, and the murder was associated with the blood libel. West, in other words, was infinitely preferable to east.

And in the main, France was happy to have the Jews. After the Dreyfus affair, which exposed systemic French anti-Semitism under the shaming bright lights of publicity, anti-Jewish feelings subsided.[9] The anti-Semitic newspaper *La Libre Parole*, which once had a circulation of more than 300,000 copies, folded, and even Maurice Barrès, one of the leaders of the anti-Semitic right at the end of the nineteenth century and during the Dreyfus affair, wrote in his 1917 essay "Les diverses familles spirituelles de la France" that Jews should be considered one of France's "spiritual families" because of their courage during the war.

But there was a practical element to France's embrace of Jews as well as a moral one: 1.4 million Frenchmen died in World War I, and the country desperately needed workers. So much so that in 1927 the Naturalization Act was introduced, reducing the requirement for naturalization from ten years to three, making it even easier, and quicker, to get immigrants into jobs.[10] The eastern European immigrants were shunted into industries that were seen as Jewish, such as the textile and garment trades, furniture making, and watch and jewelry repair. Most of these were based in or near the Marais, the Parisian quarter that was once chic but now something of a ghetto. Just a few years before the Glass family arrived, New York's Yiddish newspaper *Der Forverts* ran an article about the Marais: "The alleys are frightfully dirty, the houses mostly old ruins . . . Without exaggeration one can find from twelve to fifteen persons living in two small rooms . . . The largest and best room serves as the atelier; one eats where one can and sleeps in a dark hole without a window."[11] This was where many immigrants settled, and it was so popular with Jewish immigrants it became known as the *Pletzl*—Yiddish for "little place."

Jakob was the first to arrive in Paris, when he was just eighteen years old, and he adhered so faithfully to the trends of his demographic that the outlines of his story at times veer toward textbook. He rented a small flat near the Pletzl, on rue de Cléry, because it was close to his Ornstein cousins, and he got work as a furrier in the Pletzl, not because he knew anything about fur but because his cousin Josek, the second-oldest Ornstein, worked in the fur trade and helped him find a job. Jakob spent his days in the Pletzl, tending to animal skins in a darkened room, and he loved the simplicity of his work and life. In the Pletzl he could live as he had always done, surrounded by Poles and Yiddish speakers. If he never left his neighborhood, and there was rarely any need to do so, he barely had to remember he had left Chrzanow at all.

Sender, however, felt very differently. The fourteen-year-old arrived not long after Jakob, on a train full of other eastern European immigrants. His clothes and speech immediately marked him as a foreigner, so he was shunned by the French commuters around him as he walked through the train station. It was there that he saw and learned his first French word: *sortie* (exit). Following Jakob's instructions, he caught a bus from the station and stared out the window in astonishment at the beauty of Paris. His occasional trips to the dentist in Trzebina hadn't prepared him for anything like this. He stared out the bus's window at the elegant architecture and even more elegant people in amazement. When he arrived at his new neighborhood, next to the Pletzl, his heart sank into his shoes. It looked to him like Jakob had found the one ugly part of Paris and was making him live there. He walked through the dirty and noisy streets looking for rue de Cléry, and when he saw Jakob's poky flat, he understood how little Jakob had changed his life to live here, whereas Sender had come here to change everything. He also grasped that he was expected to become a traditional immigrant Jewish tailor like his brother and beloved Ornstein cousins, and he knew that he would never, ever do that. He loved few people more than Jakob, and no one more than his father, but he looked at their lives of drudgery, and although there was a part of him that admired their humility in enduring this, he knew life had more to offer and he would grab it. Jakob and Reuben expected nothing from life; Sender demanded everything. He had not come all this way to continue living like a Polish peasant. Despite having had such a circumscribed childhood, Sender's ambitions were boundless, and from what his father had always told him, and what he had seen on his bus ride to the Pletzl, he knew Paris could provide what he sought.

"In Paris there was such gaiety. It dazzled the eyes. In Paris, on the terraces of the great restaurants, people drank wine and were happy. It was the image of happiness on earth. 'This life is impossible. It must be better, elsewhere': these words turned in my head during the long Chrzanow nights. So, it was true. Life could be marvellous. Paris is where I was reborn," he wrote in his memoir.

After rejecting the life of a tailor, spending his days sitting on a bench in the Pletzl, Sender decided to be a couturier. He wanted his name above the door of his own salon, like those he saw on his daily walks around the city, when he eagerly escaped the Pletzl to explore the ritzier neighborhoods around rue du Faubourg Saint-Honoré and Place Vendôme. Lanvin, Schiaparelli, Vionnet, Patou: that's who he wanted to be like, not just another Jewish tailor. There was, however, a small problem: he didn't even know how to sew on a button.

Not for a second did Sender see this as a possible impediment to becoming a world-famous fashion designer. If anything, that it was such an unlikely path for him to choose only made him more determined to succeed. So, undaunted, he found a job as an apprentice at a garment workshop, where he learned how to cut, sew, and drape while working twenty-four-hour shifts. And when he finished a shift, he came back to his and Jakob's flat and practiced sewing for another twenty-four hours. It infuriated him that he was so bad at it, and his anger drove him to work harder: he wouldn't, he explained to his bemused brother, stop until he became good. His cousin Josek was one of the few who understood his ambitions, because, like Sender, Josek was smart, but he considered himself too smart to take such an absurd risk as trying to be a couturier, whereas Sender felt he was too smart not to.

"Life," he wrote, "was not going to pass me by anymore."

Over the next few years, while Sala and Chaya stayed in Chrzanow with Reuben, and Jehuda continued his studies in Prague, Jakob worked quietly as a furrier in the Pletzl, and Sender, then in his mid-teens, threw himself into couture and Paris life. He slogged his way through the workshops and got apprenticeships with small couturiers around the Saint-Martin neighborhood, making a name for himself as an exceptionally hard worker and a perfectionist. "Couture is a strange business, and the apprenticeship is very difficult, a permanent war between head and hand. My imagination ran faster than my fingers," he later wrote. "But my teachers taught me the secrets of the couturier's magic hands. I learned how to create clothes in which women are made younger and more beautiful."

Couture might seem like an odd career path for one who used to relax by getting into brawls in the streets of Chrzanow. But what fashion meant to Sender was beauty, and beauty represented the opposite of Poland. It was a bulwark against the suffering he saw his father endure. "In my little Chrzanow world, there were no paintings at all, no beauty.

But I always felt a growing hunger inside me for it, and I arrived in Paris famished for this beauty. Different from other immigrants who came to France mainly to earn money, I wished to educate myself constantly, to continue the Jewish traditions but also to open myself to French culture. I participated in the life of the country. Everywhere I went something new was happening, and I hurried to make up for lost time. I wanted to know everything, to devour life like a man eating a big chunk of meat," Sender wrote.

While he spent his weekdays learning how to make beautiful clothes, he spent his weekends and nights learning how to make a beautiful world. Jakob liked to hang out at the cafés in the Pletzl with his cousins and other Jewish tailors. Sender was not averse to cafés, but he wanted to find a new life, not cling to his old one. Not long after he arrived in Paris, he met Marc Chagall, who was already an established artist, at Café Koretz, a small hangout for Yiddish speakers in the Pletzl with only five or six tables. Over dishes of stuffed carp, cake, and tea, the two would talk about politics and share memories of their hometowns that still haunted them both. It was through Chagall that Sender became aware of modern art and artists, and he was soon spending his weekends at the Musée du Luxembourg, then Paris's only museum of modern art. When Sender would invite his brother to come with him on weekends to look at the Cézannes and Monets, or to look in the windows of the French couturiers on the Grands Boulevards, Jakob would wave him away.

"We don't know anything about painting, why would we spend our weekends doing that? Let's have fun instead," he'd say. And when Sender would storm off toward the Louvre on his own, Jakob would head to his local café to see his friends, all of whom were also Jewish immigrants, to read the Yiddish newspapers, to drink, to joke, to do nothing.

So Sender looked elsewhere for like-minded companionship. Through Chagall, he became increasingly close to artists who, like Chagall and himself, were Jewish refugees, such as Jules Pascin and Moïse Kisling, known to his friends as Kiki. These three artists—Chagall, Pascin, and Kisling—were all part of the École de Paris, a term coined by a critic to refer to the sudden influx of immigrant artists who had all, for reasons very similar to Sender, washed up in Paris in the interwar period. ("École de France," on the other hand, referred to French-born artists, who tended to be more traditional stylistically, and they somewhat resented the attention these new avant-garde foreigners got from the art critics.) All of them were several decades older than Sender, and it's likely that Sender, the fatherless teenager in a new strange land, saw them as paternal figures. Chagall would refer to Sender fondly as "our youngest friend," and if he was ever away too long from the cafés, because he was working so hard, one of the artists would come looking for him, bringing a cup of soup in case he was ill. For the first time in Sender's life, he had friends.

By 1925, Sender had earned enough through his apprenticeships so that he was able to send money for Chaya and Sala to come join them in Paris after Reuben died. They initially lived with him and Jakob on rue de Cléry, four people crowded into a studio flat barely big enough for one. Like Jakob, Chaya loved the Pletzl for its reassuring familiarity. The local bakeries sold challah, not croissants. The Polish synagogue was only a few yards away. Chaya had managed to move halfway across Europe without changing her daily life a jot, and in all the years she lived in Paris she never learned a single French word. Chaya had never trusted outsiders anyway, and after her experiences in Chrzanow, she believed if the French didn't see her they wouldn't hurt her.

But while Chaya and Jakob felt similarly about the Pletzl, Sala shared Sender's feelings about Paris. After living for so long in fear in pogrom-torn Chrzanow, Paris's beauty amazed her, and although as a sickly teenage girl she was largely stuck inside, she longed to explore the city like her older brother. Sender had never paid much attention to his sister before, but when she arrived in Paris she was a fifteen-year-old beauty who looked, Sender realized, not unlike the models in the fashion magazines he had taken to buying whenever he had spare change. She had wavy dark hair, high cheekbones, and large round eyes, which seemed to get bigger in Paris as she tried to take in everything around her. Of equal interest to Sender was the fact that she idolized him, making her his only sibling who took his dreams seriously. When Sender had a day off and if Sala was feeling well enough, he would take her with him around the city, and the two Polish teenagers walked together down the Grands Boulevards, staring through the big windows of the fashion salons, looking at the elegant French ladies choosing fabrics while the couturiers bowed and flattered them. Decades later Sala would describe those walks to her family, still audibly thrilling at the memory of seeing such elegance and being with her brother.

Sender also brought her to the museums and introduced her to art, which she had never seen before in her life. Sometimes he would also bring some of his Ornstein cousins, in particular his favorites Josek and Alex, one tough like him and the other sweet-tempered and easygoing. (All his life, Sender was drawn to two types of men: either tough, competitive men like himself and Josek, or calm and gentle ones like Jehuda, Jakob, and Alex Ornstein.) He showed them his favorite designers and artworks, because the parts of Sender's character that he felt he had to suppress to get ahead in the world he expressed through art and fashion. He told his sister that he loved the Impressionists because "of their femininity." When they went to the Musée du Luxembourg together, Sender would stand for hours in front of a Monet painting.

"This fills my soul with delight," he told her.

Sala's soul was also delighted by Paris, with all its beauty, art, and fashion. Her weak lungs, however, suffered wretchedly in the dirty Pletzl. Jehuda arrived in Paris later that year, after he finished his studies in Prague followed by a brief period in Danzig where he worked as an engineer to make some money, and when he heard his sister's chronic cough, he took charge, like the father figure he was to her. For the next half decade, Sala was in and out of sanatoriums her biggest brother found for her up in the mountains, physically recovering but mentally rotting in lonely solitude, time and life drifting away. They were lonely, isolating, and disorienting, these giant white buildings up in the sky, so far from her new home and even farther from her old home, too far for any of her family to come visit her. They did, however, make her better, and the doctors finally put a name to her suffering: she had pleurisy, an inflammation of the tissue layers in the lungs, and although they couldn't cure it yet, the rest and clean air began to soothe the pains in her chest she'd had so long she assumed it was simply part of the human condition. Until one day they lifted, and it was like clearing dirt from her eyes. Life didn't have to be obscured by pain after all.

Jehuda's feelings about Paris were much closer to Sala's and Sender's than Chaya's and Jakob's: as soon as he arrived he knew this city was home, because it didn't feel like his old home. The sophistication of the people and architecture, the delicious food, even the waiters with their short vests and white aprons looked thrillingly chic to him as they carried out long, thin-stemmed glasses of wine to their patrons: it was all so different from the unrelenting drabness of Chrzanow, and he loved it all.

Jehuda was known in his family as the intellectual one, but he was also deeply aesthetic. He'd always loved Western culture, especially the art, and as a student in Krakow he proudly if somewhat eccentrically wore a chimney sweep's hat, as tall as a stovepipe, much to his brother Jakob's bemusement and his brother Sender's admiration. Fashion allowed this shy young man to carve out some self-expression, and it wasn't until he got to France that this expression found its shape and flow.

Initially he stayed in a tiny one-room flat near the rest of his family, on a loud and busy main road. Almost as soon as he arrived, he told his siblings they should all change their Polish names to the French equivalents, just as he once urged his father to change their surname. Jehuda understood, as he had known in Chrzanow, that shucking off their heavy Yiddish and Polish labels would only ease his and his sibling's paths in life, and this was when the young people born Jehuda, Jakob, Sender, and Sala Glahs were reborn as Jules, Jacques, Alex, and Sara Glass. Unfortunately, Jehuda hated the westernized version of his name, "Jules," as he thought it pretentious, a quality he abhorred above all. So he found what felt like a legitimate way around this rule of his own making by adopting the French version of his middle name, Henoch. He could be who he wanted, but within certain self-imposed parameters, and so he become Henri. It sounded respectable and French to him, and he liked it so much he instantly made the change official: in 1926 he received a certificate from l'Administration Supérieure Confessionnelle Israelite de la Paroisse stating "Jehuda Henoch Glass shall hereon be known as Jules Henri Glass."

And yet, despite the Glass siblings' eager embrace of their French names, they did not apply for naturalization, even after the Naturalization Act the following year in 1927. In retrospect, this seems like a baffling decision, and yet it was one many foreign Jews took. Like a lot of immigrants, the Glass family arrived in Paris with a wariness of local officials and a suspicion of registering one's presence with the state. After all, being known as Jewish hadn't helped them much back in Poland. Of more immediate concern, applying for naturalization involved a large amount of time-consuming paperwork and the assistance of a lawyer. To the cash-strapped Glass family, whose ability to read French was, at this point, patchy at best, this made it an impossibility. And so they opted to remain unnaturalized, relying on work permits and the goodwill of France to immigrants. There was no reason to doubt the latter would change, they believed. The French had let them in, after all.

But being unnaturalized meant the Glasses couldn't vote, which probably didn't bother Henri much, and they had to carry identity cards, which very much did. As well as restricting immigrants to certain geographical areas, identity cards determined what professions they could work in. Despite his degrees, Henri didn't have many career choices when he arrived in Paris, as the Ornstein cousins had warned him ahead of time: Josek Ornstein was celebrated for his intellect back in Poland, but in Paris he worked as a furrier. Henri, the trained engineer, similarly learned to shrink his ambition and shelve his dreams, going into business with his brother Jacques. Neither of the two oldest Glass brothers were natural businessmen, let alone tailors, as was soon to become all too clear, but Henri managed to save up just enough to get his own apartment over the river, far from his family and among the native Parisians in the 7th arrondissement.

Eventually, all the Glasses found their own apartments. Alex was driven out of the apartment by his mother. Alex and Chaya, as alike in temperament as they were in looks, were utterly impossible flatmates and they fought viciously, usually about what Chaya deemed to be Alex's "dissolute" lifestyle of staying out late and drinking alcohol.

"Get your own place if you want to live like this," she said.

"This *is* my place!" he snapped back, which was true, as Chaya and Sara were still living in his and Jacques' apartment. But Alex had had enough of living with his family, so he simply walked out of the Marais, bought a newspaper, looked in the property section, and went to the first available apartment that he could afford, around the corner from Gare de l'Est. He gave the landlord forged identity papers, so he wouldn't know how young he was, and because Alex didn't have enough money for a bank account, he got his more well-known employers and customers to provide references, hoping their names would dazzle the landlord. He was right. Alex was still only a teenager, and he looked at least four years younger because he was so small, but he already knew how to game the system.

Chaya moved out soon, too, to a little apartment on rue des Rosiers, the central spine of the Pletzl, and Sara lived with her in between stays in the sanatoriums. Back then, rue des Rosiers was filthy and almost intolerably noisy (a terrible place for someone to stay while recovering from pleurisy). Today, it is a very chic street, partially pedestrianized so visitors can shop that little bit more easily at boutiques like Lululemon and Annick Goutal. Few signs of the street's earlier Jewish life still exist—there is a Jewish bakery at one end, although alone on this street of high-end shops it feels more like a heritage tourist site than something connected to the life of the area, fancy dress among the fancy dresses. A more revealing remnant of the past can be found next door at 16 rue des Rosiers: a plaque commemorating the memory of five former inhabitants, including a twelve-year-old (Rosette Lewkowicz), a two-year-old (Viktor Wajncwaig), and a one-month-old (Paulette Wajncwaig), who were killed in the Holocaust "par les Nazis, par ce que nés juifs. Avec la complicité

Sara and Chaya in their apartment on rue des Rosiers

active du gouvernement de Vichy" (by the Nazis, because they were born Jewish. With the active complicity of the Vichy government).

The Glass brothers could now focus on building their lives in Paris. For Alex, this meant becoming a couturier. He lived on his own but managed to save up enough money so that after finishing his apprenticeships, instead of working for a designer, as most other young aspiring couturiers did, he decided instead to achieve his dream: at the age of only twenty, he opened his first couture salon. He called it Alex Maguy instead of Alex Glass, and he gave varying reasons for this over the years. In his memoir, he says Maguy "sounded more Parisian"; he once told my father, Ronald, it was to make him sound like a typical Frenchman. He also claimed it was in honor of a friend's wife who was called Maguerite. And maybe those reasons are true. But perhaps Alex was also making a further break between his new life as a Parisian couturier and his old life as a Polish peasant, and by taking an entirely new surname he was putting a definitive division between his new, independent life and the emotionally enmeshed one he had with his family. Henri was not the only sibling who understand that changing one's name was an effective way to break from the past.

Alex's salon was small and basic, a two-room former office space, a far cry from the plush silk-strewn luxury he and Sara had seen through the windows of Lanvin and Patou. But the details were irrelevant because he had done it: he had his own couture company, at 29 rue d'Argenteuil, near the Palais Royal and just around the corner from the great couturiers. He had never even been allowed in any of their showrooms, having been relegated only to the backrooms with the other trainees and workers, but now he had one of his own. It was, by any measure, an incredible achievement, especially for a designer who was hardly more than a teenager. Few rushed faster to achieve their dreams than Alex: "I had never been in a salon de couture and had no idea what they were like, but that was of no importance. I wanted to be Number One. The best," he writes. In the encyclopedic catalogue *Paris Couture Années Trente*, the entry about Alex (who appears just before Mainbocher) begins, "This house of

A friend, Sala, and Alex

couture was run by an extremely young man." But the catalogue under-
estimates Alex in saying that his first show was in 1937. In fact, it was
eleven years earlier as Alex sent out invites as soon as he moved into his
salon, summoning potential clients and the press to see the first collection of "the Napoleon of couture." Of all the things Alex lacked at various points in his life—food, stability, support—self-belief was never one
of them.

The only person who was more proud of Alex than Alex himself
was his sister. Almost eighty years after Alex opened his couture house,
I found among my grandmother's belongings several photocopies of the
pages about Alex in the 1956 book *The Dressmakers of France,* by Mary
Brooks Picken and Dora Loues Miller. Alex sent the photocopies to my
grandmother, even signing them on the back, and she kept them for the
rest of her life. It's easy to see why the entry about Alex appealed to them
both, because it gives a real, and merited, sense of just how extraordinary
Alex's achievement was:

> He started his house in 1926. And it was *his* house—he had no part-
> ners, no financial backers. *He* was his house. And that was rare, for
> the combination of designer and businessman is a difficult role to
> maintain successfully over a period of years. His passion had always
> been painting—and in his studio the walls were covered with truly
> unusual paintings. An intimate of the great Kisling, he was also a
> friend of most of the living artists of his day who were considered
> significant. Perhaps that association explains his continued inspira-
> tion for creation. Where he obtained or inherited his business ability
> is unexplained. Perhaps that came from his sympathy and under-
> standing of many types of people—businessmen as well as artists.

Alex had grown up in a world as disconnected from couture as it was
from space exploration, and given how bad his father—and brothers—
were at business, Picken and Miller's comment about his business ability
being "unexplained" is quite an understatement. But Alex taught himself

to be good at business, because he knew he needed to be so to succeed. Beauty was an ideal, but Alex had learned from his father's struggles that one cannot eat ideals. Fashion, it seemed to him, was a way of living in a world of beauty but also making money from it—an aesthetic practice but also a commercial one.

As well as being inspired by the paintings in his studio that were mostly by his new friends, he got inspiration from the city he lived in, taking in all the Parisian elegance he saw around him, digesting it, and re-creating it through clothes. He took the long dresses worn by the high-society women he saw in Renoir's paintings and subtly modernized them, getting rid of the corsets and raising the hems and cropping the sleeves. For his first show he riffed on the outfits worn by the jockeys at Longchamps, that most Parisian scene of high society—everything, for him, was about paying homage to the beauty of Paris and trying to add to it. The critics loved it: the journalist from *L'Officiel,* the upmarket French fashion magazine that is still popular today, described him as "so talented" but worried that he would become disheartened with how hard the business was.

They were right to worry: not a single one of his outfits from his first collection sold. Although Alex had chosen the more ostensibly glamorous profession when he opted for being a couturier near the Place Vendôme over working as a tailor in the Pletzl, he had actually opted for the much harder job. As a tailor, he would likely have been working for a contractor, who would have been in charge of selling the clothes to department stores or smaller shops around Paris.[12] This was how Jacques worked, and it saved him from having to deal with retail issues, which he could never have done. As a couturier, and a young and unestablished one, Alex had to deal with everything: the designs, the sewing, the marketing, the customers, and the production. As one historian later put it, "Running a fashion salon [in Paris in the 1930s] took the skill of a military general; securing the assurance of a faithful following demanded the diplomacy of a minister of state."[13]

But Alex had one thing in his favor: he never, ever admitted defeat.

After he failed to sell any outfits from his first collection, he shed "one tear of frustration" and then promptly gathered up his designs, walked around the corner, and sold them to the more established houses around the corner. Each of the houses asked if they were exclusive—in other words, no other house would have these patterns—and Alex unhesitatingly said yes, even while he had the money for selling the same designs to different design houses in his back pocket. According to Alex's memoir, the ruse was quickly discovered by Nina Ricci, then working at the design house Raffin, and she summoned in the young designer to explain himself. Anyone else would have run away in fear, or at least crawled into the meeting cringing with contrition, but Alex was defiant.

"Alex, it was not nice of you to sell this design to other houses," the fearsome white-haired designer said to him.

"Please forgive me, but I am just starting out, what did you expect?" he snapped back.

Fortunately, Madame Ricci already liked Alex, having met him when he did an apprenticeship at Raffin, and she asked him why he wanted to be a designer, when it was such a hard career.

"Because I burn with new ideas—young ideas, which you don't see in couture," he replied. "I want to give woman the most natural beauty possible, rid her of the straitjacket of corsets, to make her supple. I want to invent a new elegance in harmony with the modern world, dressing woman as lightly as possible. I dream of Paris, and the legendary elegance of its women. I would be proud to make a contribution to couture!"

When he finally paused for breath, Madame Ricci offered him a job at Raffin, but Alex refused. He was betting, against every possible odd, that he could make it on his own.

Henri and Jacques thought they were playing it safer than their younger brother by staying in the Pletzl, slogging it out in the garment trade. In the early 1930s, they were also running a wood-carving shop, although "running" was something of an overstatement. By the spring of 1931, both of their businesses were bankrupt and people were coming after them for debts. But while Jacques merely shrugged at this development, seeing it as yet another hurdle in a life from which he expected nothing but hurdles, Henri was completely mortified. He'd loved his father but he had not studied so hard to live on the edge of bankruptcy as Reuben had done, and, unlike Jacques, he could not bear the humiliation of being dragged through the legal system. His ambitions might not have been as high as Alex's, but he had a greater sense of pride than Jacques, and he hoped for more from life than his brother. Otherwise, what had been the point in coming to Paris at all? There was, he was sure, a better life out there for him.

By the early 1930s, all of the Glasses were living in Paris. Sara had come home from the sanatoriums for good, healthy at last, living with her mother on rue des Rosiers and starting to think about what she wanted from life. Henri was also figuring out what he wanted to do and, like Sara, was in a city so beautiful he hardly believed he could call it home. Alex was working as a couturier, just as he'd dreamed he would, and Jacques was—occasional court appearance aside—working

Sara Glass

steadily as a furrier in the Pletzl, just down the road from his mother, which was as much as he'd ever asked for of life. They were all, in their different ways, content, planning for what they imagined would be an uninterrupted future in France, working, living, and maybe one day loving as they wished, and always within comfortable walking distance from one another. They had escaped what they thought were the worst of times and created lives for themselves in the most beautiful city in the world. Their story of immigration was, they would all have agreed at that time, successful. And in just a handful of years, everything that they had worked so hard to achieve would be taken away from them again by the very thing they had tried so desperately to escape.

Chapter 3

HENRI—ASSIMILATION

Paris, 1930s

Young Jehuda

Just as life was becoming good for the Glass family personally, it was getting extremely bad for Jews in Europe generally. By the early 1930s, the Great Depression crisis bit into France, traveling eastward from the United States, while at the same time eastern European Jewish refugees were running westward toward France for safety. This confluence of international disasters resulted in a resurgence of the French anti-Semitism that had been dammed back after World War I, and the immigrants who were once so welcomed for filling the gaps in the workplace were now attacked for stealing French jobs. The Metz Chamber of Commerce declared, "These foreign competitors, highly undesirable, have become a veritable plague for honest French merchants." In 1931, the president of the French Medical Association complained about "this legion of Jews" coming into the medical profession.[1]

Politicians and commentators pushed three lines of attack against the immigrant Jews in France: that they were taking jobs from the French, that they were Bolshevik revolutionaries determined to destroy France, and that they were diseased criminals. François Coty, the perfume magnate who owned two newspapers, *L'Ami du Peuple* and *Le Figaro*, was so horrified by the growing numbers of German Jewish refugees arriving in the city after Hitler's election that he suggested they were a German plot to destroy France from within, and his papers relentlessly pushed this theory.[2] In 1934, Gaetan Sanvoisin wrote in *Le Figaro*, "Hitler has sent us some 50,000 German Jews who are, for the most part, extremely dangerous revolutionaries."

Any immigrant Jew who arrived in Paris expecting to find some kind of kinship with the French Jews was disappointed. The two groups were miles apart from one another, mentally and physically. Unlike the immigrants, who were largely workers, the native Jews were more bourgeois and they certainly didn't live in the Pletzl. They lived in the posher parts of the city and worked in liberal professions, such as banking, medicine, and law.[3] They spoke French, not Yiddish; many did not bother celebrating the Sabbath; and they looked at these immigrants as potential threats to their hard-fought efforts to be part of the French bourgeoisie.[4] In other words, they were assimilated, and to the eastern European immigrant arrivals, the French Jews seemed to them to be even more foreign than the French Catholics; differences with those you expect to be on your side are always more shocking than those you know to be your opposite. To the French Jews, the immigrants were embarrassingly backward, and their reluctance to relinquish their old traditions was baffling. Hadn't they learned from the past that they needed to blend in? They knew these new arrivals would only exacerbate the anti-Jewish feelings in the city and make life worse for them.[5] To differentiate themselves from these coarse newcomers, who were rapidly making up more than half of the city's Jewish population and thus becoming a highly visible representation of Judaism to the French, many native Jews pointedly defined themselves in opposition to them. They described themselves as French first, and they complained that the new arrivals were too dirty, too noisy, too loud with their Yiddish—too obviously Jewish, in short.[6]

How much of one's ancestral identity must one give up to live in the modern world? How much do the actions of one part of a group reflect on the whole? Is a refusal to blend in a show of strength or self-defeating rigidity? And must the choice always be between assimilation and self-ghettoization? Could there not be an option of inclusion, which allows for a minority group to retain its distinctive identity without this being seen as a threat to the majority? Natives and immigrants, Jewish and otherwise, have argued these questions for centuries, with each other and with themselves, and they will do so for centuries more. In the case of the native and immigrant Parisian Jews, the debate was irresolvable, not least because the two groups largely stayed away from one another. The French Jews didn't want to be associated with the immigrants, and the immigrants reacted to that rejection in what would soon turn out to be the worst way possible: they remained separate from French life.[7] During the 1920s and 1930s, immigrant Jews formed their own little communities in Paris, creating pockets of mini-Polands, -Russias, and -Lithuanias, in the Pletzl and around the Bastille and Belleville. Although this gave them a sense of community in their new country, its advantages were to prove brutally short term. Because the ghettos kept them separate from the rest of the city, the immigrants remained unknown, strange, not French, and thus, later, easy to sacrifice.[8] But in a similar vein to what the Chrzanow Jews thought of the Poles and later the Germans, so the immigrant Jews in Paris believed of France: surely their neighbors would protect them. And again, like the Chrzanow Jews, they were to be proven wrong.

Chaya especially and Jacques largely typified the behavior of immigrant Jews: they remained unassimilated and stayed among Polish Jewish immigrants. Henri, Alex, and Sara, by contrast, were more on the side of the French Jews. To them, Poland was a backward pit of hate and ignorance. Next to cultured, beautiful Paris, where people weren't beating them up in the street, there was no question in their minds with which country they wanted to identify.

Alex and Sara had been happy to slough off their Polish identities as soon as they arrived in Paris. They were born in 1906 and 1910, respectively, and so largely associated Chrzanow with the war and pogroms. But Jacques and Henri had lived there longer, and for that reason Jacques struggled more to shrug off his past entirely: he considered himself French but he remained rooted in the world of other immigrants, rarely mixing with native French people.

Henri, however, made a seamless chameleonic break. Strikingly tall—at least six foot two—and handsome, with a broad forehead and dark deep-set eyes, Henri set out to become a proper Frenchman. He learned the language quickly, and while Alex proudly kept his Yiddish accent all his life, Henri soon sounded entirely French. His reasons were more personal than political: Poland to him represented his father's death, and his years away studying had taken him farther, geographically and mentally, from the shtetl world. For Henri, Poland was the past; France was the future.

Jewish assimilation had a complicated history long before Jehuda Glahs became Jules Henri Glass. Chanukah, now one of the best-known Jewish holidays, is a celebration of Jews who refused to assimilate, as it's a festival in memory of a small group of Jews who in 167 BC disobeyed their Greek-Syrian oppressors by not worshipping their gods. And yet the only reason Chanukah—always a minor holiday on the Jewish calendar—is so well known now is because of its proximity to Christmas. As a result, Chanukah has turned into a quasi-Jewish Christmas, and so, with an apt kind of Jewish irony, Chanukah itself has become assimilated.

And yet, especially after the Haskalah, the Jewish enlightenment in the late eighteenth and early nineteenth centuries, many Jews saw assimilation as a positive, progressive step; being part of the modern world instead of hiding from it behind shtetl walls, disguised within thick, heavy black clothes. Assimilation meant, as it did to Henri, having more options than one's parents did. But others felt the cost of assimilation both too high and impossible. Jews would always be seen as the vilified outsiders.

Some of the most influential thinking about Jewish assimilation was inspired by events in Paris shortly before the Glass family moved there. After witnessing the Dreyfus scandal, Theodor Herzl, the Jewish journalist and political activist, rejected his earlier writings urging Jewish assimilation. Instead, he became the father of modern Zionism, telling Jews they would never be safe no matter how much they assimilated, so they should stay true to their identity and establish a Jewish homeland. Assimilated Jews loathed this theory, as they saw it as undermining all their efforts to become a part of their country's civic life. And yet these efforts were, in the eyes of others, pointless: many non-Jews then believed that Jews could never be truly assimilated into a Western country, and the question of how much they could be, or whether they could be at all, was known as the Jewish Question. So Herzl's turnaround was, in the context of his time, pretty understandable.

Assimilated Jews could argue that Zionism was ultimately analogous to what German writers such as Theodor Fritsch, author of *The Handbook of the Jewish Question*, suggested when he argued that Jews should be kept separate, even banished, so as not to contaminate the Aryan race. This partly explains why some of the earliest and most enthusiastic supporters of Zionism were not Jews, but rather evangelical Christians and anti-Semites, and there was and is some, but by no means a complete, overlap between the two groups. Evangelicals believe that Jews returning to their homeland will hasten the return of the Messiah. Alongside this, Zionism still has enormous popularity among anti-Semites, who are a lot less concerned with providing the Jews with a homeland than they are with simply segregating them.* Herzl saw where matters were heading for Jews in Europe long before others did.

France might have been known as *une terre d'asile*, but the French most definitely did not see themselves as a nation of immigrants. Immigrants were expected to assimilate, and those who kept themselves separate and retained their original identity were seen as suspicious. Antipathy to what critics would call the self-ghettoization of immigrants and what defenders would call immigrants' distinctive identity was prevalent on both the left and the right in France,[9] and this attitude was hardly unique to France or the early twentieth century. In pretty much every Western country today there is a belief that people who come to a new country should assimilate, almost as a show of gratitude, or at the very least politeness. Today this is mainly—but not solely—voiced by the right and is aimed largely at black and Muslim immigrants instead of Jewish ones.

France had a particular interest in cultural assimilation because of the country's principle of laïcité, roughly translated as secularism. Laïcité was instituted in 1905 with the separation of church and state, meaning that state funding was withdrawn from religions in order to place all faiths on an equal footing and protect schools in particular from the Catholic church. Whereas in America today the separation of church and state means the state cannot interfere in religion, in France it means all signs of religion are banned in the public sphere, because

---

* One of the weirder background noises going on as I wrote this book was the seemingly never-ending obsession of former British politician and now somewhat dimmed left-wing firebrand Ken Livingstone, and his certainty that Hitler "supported Zionism" when he came to power in 1933. According to Livingstone, because Hitler supported getting the Jews out of Europe, this meant he supported Zionism, as if Jews going to Israel of their own accord is analogous to Jews being persecuted and expelled, with all their worldly goods confiscated. Livingstone's obvious mistake was to conflate self-determination and freedom of movement with ethnic cleansing. Livingstone finally quit the Labour Party in May 2018, two years after he developed what I would call "Hitler Tourette's" and became incapable of talking about anything but Hitler's alleged Zionism. https://www.theguardian .com/politics/2017/mar/30/ken-livingstone-repeats-claim-nazi-zionist-collaboration.

Republic takes precedence over religion, or as the 1905 law puts it, "the Rpeublic neither recognizes nor employs nor subsidizes cults," but it guarantees the freedom of these "cults," as long as they do not upset the public order. Laïcité remains a cherished principle in France today, even if it does cause occasional controversy, such as whether it encourages assimilation or further self-ghettoization from those who do not wish to give up, say, their religiously ordained headscarves and clothes. For Chaya, it provoked the latter: aware that she was not part of or welcome in French bourgeois society as she was, she stayed firmly in the Pletzl. Henri, Alex and Sara, who had the active desire to assimilate, did otherwise.

Despite what right-wing politicians today suggest, assimilation is neither simple nor the answer. There exists, allegedly, a magical sweet spot where immigrants are assimilated enough so as not to offend natives with their jarringly exotic customs, but not so assimilated that they are stealing natives' jobs and diluting the culture of the country. Immigrants are blamed by the media and politicians for not locating this spot themselves, but no one else has ever been able to define its whereabouts either, primarily because its location shifts depending on a country's economic situation.

By the 1930s, growing numbers of French people came to see dangers in the idea of Jews assimilating, mixing among them unrecognized. After the relaxation of naturalization laws in 1927, right-wing newspapers and politicians spoke doomfully about immigrants taking jobs as well as Jews corrupting French society with their Bolshevik ideas and infecting the people with their strange foreign germs. When it came to assimilation, Jews couldn't win—mix into the culture and they were condemned, stay separate and they were damned. The Jewish Question was becoming a seemingly irresolvable puzzle, and it would not be long before someone offered up the Final Solution.

Today, Jewish assimilation remains controversial, and while you still hear anti-Semites warning against it, some of the most striking critics are observant Jews, who use the same arguments as those advanced by the rabbinical traditionalists of the nineteenth century. (And their fidelity to those arguments is, in their eyes, the point.) According to a study carried out by the Rabbinical Centre of Europe in 2014, as many as 85 percent of Jews in Europe are assimilated, leading one member of the Israeli Chief Rabbinate Council to lament, "The assimilation in the shocking numbers that we see is worse than the Holocaust we saw."[10]

You don't need to be assimilated, or Jewish, to find this statement repulsive. But it is true that recognizably observant Jewish people and communities are far less commonly seen in Europe today than they were at the beginning of the twentieth century. That's not just because the Holocaust killed off so many of them[11] and many of the survivors went elsewhere (Israel, mainly), although both of those factors are certainly part of it—it's because the successive generations have assimilated. Contrary to what Herzl and many others thought, Jewish assimilation has proven to be more than possible—it has become inevitable. As society has become increasingly secular, and Jews have made secure lives for themselves in Western countries, often intermarrying with other faiths, the story of Jewish identity in the late twentieth century became a story of assimilation. Whether Jews are truly accepted depends on which Jew you ask, and how many times they've been accused on social media that day of being part of a Zionist conspiracy. But in terms of Jews living, working, and socializing with non-Jews, this has become such a non-issue it's almost hard to believe there was a time when it was otherwise, although that time is still very much in living memory: my grandparents would have been horrified if my father had married a non-Jewish woman, but my parents could not have cared less about the religion of my sister's and my chosen partners. Jews have become more assimilated with each successive generation, and this is certainly borne out by my family. And for us, the path that led us here began with Henri.

All the Glass siblings were style-conscious, thanks to Reuben's influence, but Henri approached fashion the most methodically, because it was part of his process of becoming French. He studied how his neighbors looked and he copied them, buying three-piece suits when he could find them secondhand; double-breasted wool coats with velvet collars; starchy white shirts and silk ties; and always a hat. Henri's style was yet another thing Alex admired about his brother, and whenever he could find the material, he made pocket handkerchiefs for him, which Henri would carefully iron and then fold neatly to stick out of his breast pocket. In everything, from his studies to his appearance, he was utterly meticulous.

He was also a very private person, so when I started to research him I originally worried he might be the lacuna in the book, as he never talked about himself.

"Did your father leave anything that might tell me about the past—an address book, perhaps, or even old calendars?" I asked his daughter, Danièle, the first time I interviewed her for this book in her flat in Paris.

"Oh yes, a couple of things. Come down to the basement, I'll show you," she said mildly.

I walked down the stairs behind her, expecting, at most, some old birthday cards, perhaps a business card or two. She unlocked the door to her building's storage unit, and there were four suitcases, each containing every receipt Henri ever got, every business transaction he conducted, every letter he received, and every photo he ever took, all perfectly filed in perfect French. Henri's careful bookkeeping was a reflection of his naturally precise nature but also of his lifelong fear that the authorities would one day call him to account because he wasn't truly French. As a result of it, I probably now know more about the minutiae of his business affairs than I do about my own.

For Henri there was one big hurdle to his assimilation into French society: his failing businesses with Jacques. By 1931 the letters from lawyers were threatening the brothers with jail, each one another kick at his dreams. You can't be a respectable Frenchman if the bailiffs are after you, Henri thought sadly. At last, one spring day, the worst letter arrived, telling him to meet the lawyer's assistant in Gare Saint-Lazare, in la Salle des Pas Perdus—the Room of Lost Steps, the poetic French name for the hallway or waiting area in railway stations or courthouses—and she would serve him with bankruptcy papers. He dressed wearily that morning, putting on his three-piece suit, fully expecting this to be the end of his brief Parisian life. Instead, it marked the true beginning of it.

Sophie Huttner, also known as Sonia, was born in 1905 in Kopyczynce, a small city about 310 miles to the east of Chrzanow, in what is now Ukraine. Born into a middle-class Jewish family and exceptionally bright from a young age, she moved to Paris in 1928 to study at the Sorbonne,[12] but she really came to experience life, and she certainly succeeded in that. At the time she arranged to serve this tall, quiet man with bankruptcy papers, she'd had at least two boyfriends, a Prussian prince and a man from Barcelona, and she later hinted there had been more; Sonia had always been popular with boys, and it was not hard to see why. Although not beautiful the way Sara was—Sonia's features were earthier and less delicate—she was sexy, smart, funny, and flirtatious, and she knew how to tip her head down and then look up at a man through her lashes with an irresistible little smile. And as soon as Henri saw her, waiting for him in the Room of Lost Steps, he fell hopelessly in love.

Although both were Jewish and raised in Austria-Hungary, their backgrounds were utterly different. Henri's father had been a traveling salesman, whereas Sonia's father was a government official. Henri had to learn French when he arrived in Paris, but Sonia had grown up speaking it, because her nanny had been a dispossessed French aristocrat. Sonia didn't even really have to work, and she lived comfortably on her family's money for her first few years in France. But she was too smart to sit around, and she had enough drive to power the whole of Paris. She was fluent in a half dozen languages: French, Polish, German, Spanish, English, and Portuguese, and she could easily switch between them in conversation. So she worked as an interpreter at several companies and as a secretary at others, and it just so happened that she was working as a secretary at a lawyer's office when she was sent to serve papers at Gare Saint-Lazare.

Henri was thirty-one when he met Sonia, but I could find no record of any other girlfriends in his past—no names mentioned among his letters, no teasing references by Sonia during their long lifetime together. It is entirely possible she was his first girlfriend, and he was certainly besotted by her. Henri was a keen photographer, and while he took, at most, a few dozen photos of his family, he took hundreds of photos of Sonia during their courtship: here's Sonia looking up coquettishly on a bridge; here's Sonia in a beret, tight pencil skirt, and sexy halter-neck top, plucking a leaf from a bush. Henri loved to photograph her, and Sonia loved to be photographed, posing with the ease of one who never lacked confidence about her looks. In one photo, taken in someone's room, Sonia poses by a bed in a pair of high-waisted trousers and jacket. In the second picture, she has taken the jacket off to reveal a skimpy vest top, and she is now sitting on the bed. In the last, she has rolled the straps of her vest off her shoulder and she is lying on the bed and spreading her legs, looking into the camera with a sexuality so frank it is unnerving. I found

Henri and Sonia shortly after they met in Paris, 1930s

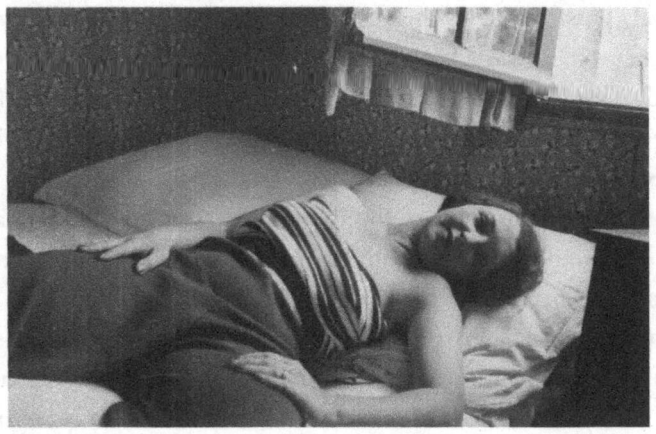

Sonia

these photos among Sonia's possessions, twenty years after she died, and I let out a yelp when I got to the last one; you don't expect to find eighty-year-old evidence of your great-uncle and great-aunt's love life on an average Tuesday afternoon.

And apparently it was a very happy love life: Henri and Sonia got married on Christmas Day, 1932, in Lwow, not far from where Sonia grew up, so her family could attend. Adolf Hitler would become chancellor of Germany just a few weeks later, but among the dozens of cards and letters the couple received from Sonia's relatives and friends back home, many of whom would be killed in the Holocaust within a decade, there was only joy and hope for the future: "May you have a long and happy wedded life! Love, The Liebermans"; "Wishing joy and long life, The Zygfryd Reizs"; "God bless the newlyweds and their families on this happy day, The Koenigow Mlyniecs." And in one of Sonia's scrapbooks, I found a telegram from her new sister-in-law in France, dated 25/12/1932: "Bonheur bonheur bonheur de tout coeur—Sara."

Henri didn't have as much money as the Prussian prince, and maybe wasn't as exciting as the man from Barcelona. But Sonia chose him because, as she explained to their daughter decades later, "I saw he was a good son and brother."

Which was not to say that she was wild about his family. Chaya she quickly got the measure of when Henri took her to his mother's flat on rue des Rosiers and she saw how much Henri longed to get some kind of independence from his mother. So she fashioned herself between them, stepping in whenever Chaya asked Henri to accompany her to synagogue or to do her shopping at the local kosher markets. Jacques, Sonia thought, was sweet, the sweetest of them all, only lacking in backbone. Sara bemused her with her love of fashion. But Sara told her how happy she was to have a *real* sister—she'd had Mindel, but Mindel had died so long ago, and she had Rose Ornstein, but Rose was really her cousin. Sonia was her sister! She'd desperately wanted a sister, and Sonia, touched, told her she felt the same.

Alex was a different story—Sonia and Alex loathed one another from the moment they met. Alex couldn't believe that his idolized older brother—so tall and so handsome!—who, in his mind, could have had his pick of any Frenchwoman in Paris, would choose this short, dumpy Polack. Henri had been a father figure to Alex for pretty much all of his

Sonia and Sara

life, ever since Reuben went off to war, and he reacted to Sonia's arrival like that of a petulant child to a new stepmother. He thought she was ugly, fat, and unworthy of his brother. And Sonia, who sized up Alex about as quickly as she did Chaya, saw in Alex an arrogant bully. Neither of them ever found cause to alter their first impression.

But family aside, Henri and Sonia were blissfully content newlyweds. Sonia had a much easier relationship with her past than Henri, because her childhood had been much happier. There were no tortured issues about identity, assimilation, or nonassimilation for Sonia: she had grown up multilingual, so flitting between nationalities felt utterly natural to her, and her language skills were so good she was often mistaken for a native of multiple countries. And yet, even though Sonia spoke Polish and Yiddish, they almost always spoke to one another in French.

Soon after they were settled in their new apartment, on rue Victor Cousin, just next to the Sorbonne, they held a housewarming supper for the Glasses, to compensate for the fact that none of them could travel to Lwow for the wedding. Henri took a photo of the evening to commemo-

Henri, Sonia, Sara, Chaya, and Jacques in Henri and Sonia's
apartment shortly after their marriage

rate it, and I found the picture, eighty years later, in a small envelope on which he had written "famille." Henri is the first one you notice in the photo, because he is the only one standing. In fact, he appears to be in mid-leap, as he has presumably dashed into the photo frame after having set up the camera. But even in his haste, his three-piece suit sits perfectly on him and every hair is perfectly in place. The only difference about him in this photo compared to previous ones is how happy he clearly is: he is making an unabashed open-mouthed smile and both hands are resting gently on the collarbones of Sonia, who is sitting in front of him. Sonia looks a little more solemn, and with her drooping shoulders and somewhat raised eyebrows she looks like she's asking the camera on the exhale, "Can you believe I'm stuck with this lot now?" By contrast, Sara next to her looks absolutely delighted. She is twenty-two and a striking beauty; her confident pose, with her chin resting coquettishly on the backs of her fingers, makes her, for once, overshadow her usually more dominating sister-in-law. Chaya is seated next to her, a little in the shadows, and, as usual, her eyes are going in two different directions, one looking suspiciously at the viewer, the other at Sonia. And finally there is Jacques, not quite as smartly dressed as Henri, but still stylish and very handsome, with the same finely drawn features as Sara. He is holding a French newspaper, on the front page of which is a picture of Marshal Pétain, who had just been made minister of war, and would in six years time become the chief of state of Vichy France. He would have more to do with the direction of Jacques' life than Jacques could have ever imagined as he dangled the newspaper between his long, thin fingers. Whereas everyone else in the photo is looking at the camera, Jacques is gazing off to the side, as if he were about to head in a different direction from them. Alex is not in the photo. Presumably he declined Henri's invitation.

"My father was brilliant, but he never had any success before he met my mother," Henri and Sonia's daughter Danièle told me. And she was right. One of the first things Sonia did when she and Henri got together was to help him get off the bankruptcy charge, and the second was to extricate him out of business with Jacques. Henri felt enormous guilt about leaving his brother, but as Sonia rightly perceived, Jacques didn't actually care that much about the business, and certainly didn't hold it against his brother for leaving it. At last Henri was free of the work that had caused him so much anxiety and brought him so little satisfaction. He could simply enjoy his happy marriage with Sonia. But he now had another concern: it was 1935, he was thirty-four, and worried.

"My time is running out," Sonia later recalled him saying.

But she already had a plan for him, one more befitting to his education than running a fur and carpentry shop. She had recently met a man who worked at the Sorbonne Science Faculty. He told Sonia that he needed a machine that could reproduce documents quickly and cheaply, and yet no such machine existed in the whole of France. Did she know a man who might be able to help, perhaps one with engineering and photography experience?

Henri had finished his engineering studies a decade earlier, but he hadn't forgotten a thing. Sonia obtained a false identity card for him on the black market so, at long last, he could get a job that utilized his education, and he went to work in the Sorbonne, like the proper Frenchman he longed to be. He could finally leave the Pletzl behind and use the skills he'd studied so hard to acquire at university, just as he wanted to. And Henri wasn't just a good engineer, he was a truly original one. According to his American patent application, which was accepted on February 12, 1940, he made a machine "whereby reproductions may be made on the same scale as the original or on different scales. . . . The prints may be made on glass, negatives, films, or sensitized papers." In other words, he made a machine that reproduced not just documents but blueprints on microfilm and paper, and these reproductions could be to scale or—crucially—shrunk to a much smaller size, making them both easy to store and illegible to anyone until Henri's machine then reproduced them again at full size. This was to become the machine's most important feature, and Henri was using technology that was then at the absolute cutting edge. No other machine in France could do this. Henri named his machine the Omniphot.

Henri working at Photasia

In less than a year, he sold versions of it to the Paris Observatory, the Army Geographic Service (now known as the Institut Géographique National), and the Paris Municipal School of Physics and Chemistry. Henri was so successful that in 1937—just two years after despairing of the direction of his life to Sonia—he showed his Omniphot machine at the Paris fair, where it was spotted by a businessman called Marc Haenel. Monsieur Haenel instantly saw the potential of Henri's invention and convinced him to go into business with him to create their own company, Photosia, where they would do specialist microfilming. Henri agreed. This would prove to be an extremely fortuitous meeting, and just in time, too: Henri's machine would soon be desperately needed by the resistance movement, and his adopted country turned out to need him at least as much as he needed it.

Chapter 4

JACQUES—PASSIVITY

Paris, 1930s

Jacques Glass was born under a bad star. That's what his siblings always said about him, and they would say it fondly, because they really did love him, but, my God, he did have a way of falling into bad luck. When he skipped school in Chrzanow, he alone, among his brother and cousins, was the one who was caught by the schoolmaster. Out of all the immigrants in the Marais who worked in somewhat gray areas of legality, it was Jacques who was repeatedly summoned to the courts to pay various fines. A year after Sonia got him and Henri off the bankruptcy charge, he was summoned to court again for, according to his court record, "employing a woman worker outside the legal hours," for which he was fined 62 francs and 70 centimes in costs (roughly 60 euros today), plus another 5 franc fine, a sizable punishment for a poor immigrant. And yet no one was surprised this happened to Jacques. If there was a hole, Jacques' friends said, he would fall into it.

And he had many friends. Of all the Glass siblings, Jacques was the easiest to get along with. Henri was too shy, Alex so combative, and Sara often away due to poor health. But Jacques was easygoing, always with a ready smile, so everyone liked him. Like his father, he was happiest sitting in cafés with his friends. By the mid-1930s he had—just about—his fur shop, and that was enough for him. Sonia occasionally bustled across the river to see Chaya, or maybe just to check on Jacques, and when she passed his shop it was, invariably, shut. She would then find him around the corner, wasting away the afternoon in a café with friends, and she would upbraid him, astonished at this unabashed show of laziness. If Sonia had ever spoken like that to Alex he would have punched her, but Jacques just smiled and nodded at her, and then moved not an inch. Things did not bother him, and he was perfectly fine where he was. And as much as he frustrated Sonia, she also liked him enormously—it was impossible not to, really. When she would talk about him, even when she was well into her eighties, she would describe him to her daughter as "the best of all the family." "Jacques," Sonia would also later recall, "was wonderful. But too passive."

The idea of Jewish passivity is controversial, and for good reason. The stereotype of the meek Jew in the 1940s who went like a lamb to slaughter has, for a long time, been used by the culpable to excuse their part in the Holocaust. When Israel objected to the 2018 Polish law criminalizing any suggestion that Poland should be blamed for crimes committed during the Holocaust, Andrzej Zybertowicz, adviser to the Polish president, replied that Israel merely felt "shame at the passivity of the Jews during the Holocaust."[1] It has also been used in a more sympathetic manner, by those who mean to show compassion to the Jews but actually end up fetishizing their suffering. Julie Burchill certainly does this in her very weird philo-Semitic book *The Unchosen,* and Steven Spielberg has been accused of doing similarly in *Schindler's List*—unfairly, I think.* And for some Jews, too, the

---

* For example, in "Is Schindler's List Fatally Flawed?" (*Jewish Chronicle,* March 27, 2013), Nathan Abrams argues that the film "serves to embed a narrative of Jewish weakness and passivity, in which Jews were nearly always portrayed as undeserving victims. From this

stereotype of Jewish passivity has fed into their feelings of self-loathing or, at the very least, self-ambivalence: my father's friend and one of the heroes of Operation Entebbe in 1976,[2] the late Michel Cojot-Goldberg, wrote in his autobiography, *Namesake*, about how he felt "ashamed" of his father, who was arrested in Lyon and killed in Auschwitz, and how relieved he later was when he learned his father had briefly escaped from the train to the camps. This, it seemed to Michel, proved his father was not passive after all, but had shown some gumption and not obediently walked toward his own slaughter—as if any Jews, Michel's father included, had much choice, when caught between Vichy laws and German military muscle.[3]

For all of these reasons, Israel has long promoted the self-empowering narrative of Jewish defiance over passivity. But not every Jew in the war was a courageous rebel, any more than every Frenchman was a member of the resistance, no matter how much Israel and France might have claimed otherwise over the years. If for too long the stories of Jewish strength were overlooked, it would be equally untrue to overcorrect that mistake by denying the stories of passivity. There was no single narrative for Jews in the run-up to and during the Holocaust. Jacques, like his father, had been a passive soul since he was a child, always happy with the easiest option. And it was this passivity that led to his greatest misfortunes.

Jacques' first major misfortune looked to him like his greatest good

---

point of view, then, *Schindler's List* is not about the Holocaust or the Jews at all, but a biopic of Schindler and his conversion from ambivalent antihero to righteous gentile." Arguing that a film that is called *Schindler's List* is too much about Oskar Schindler feels like a criticism in search of a point. The Jews *were* undeserving victims and given that they were trapped in Poland in the 1930s and 1940s, powerless and facing unimaginable brutality, arguing that they looked too "weak" or "passive" for the critic's liking flirts weirdly close to victim blaming. As anyone who has read any books about the Krakow Ghetto knows (and the first half of Roman Polanski's autobiography, *Roman by Polanski*, is not a bad place to start), the Jews were weak, because they were weakened by starvation and unarmed but up against the Nazi's military power. The truth is, Schindler did save their lives—they would have been killed without him, and not only is there nothing shameful about that but it is ahistorical to argue otherwise.

fortune. Even more misleadingly, it came from his mother, the person to whom he was most devoted. In 1936, Jacques was thirty-four and still single, and as much as Chaya enjoyed being able to call on Jacques whenever she needed him, she also wanted him to get married, and that was because she wanted him to marry a certain woman in particular.

Mindel Rotter, known as Mila, was the oldest daughter of Samuel Rotter, Chaya's older brother, and she lived in Zakopane, a Polish town about 250 miles to the south of Chzranow. Chaya saw no reason why a cross-continental move should change anything about her children's lives, and she decreed that Jacques should marry Mila, just as she had planned for him when they all lived in Poland.

Henri had sighed. That Jacques should marry his cousin from home was bad enough, given how many possibilities for new futures there were in Paris, but that it should be Mila was the real kicker. Why not Mila's sister Olga? Henri asked his mother. Olga was so pretty and smart and dynamic—quite similar to Sonia, in fact, which might explain Henri's fondness for her. Whereas Mila was, well . . .

Alex was more vocal in his feelings about Mila, and for the rest of his life described her in the most derogatory terms he could come up with, usually combining references to her Polishness with farm animals. He undoubtedly shared those observations with Jacques, but Jacques paid as little attention to them as he did to Alex's commands that he go to museums with him. Jacques might have let Alex push him into skipping school when they were children, but they were adults now, and things had changed. Alex had his path, and Jacques had his, and his path was not to kowtow to his younger brother anymore. Now the person he unthinkingly obeyed was his mother, and so Mila was sent for. She arrived in Paris in 1936, and before he even talked with her Jacques knew he would marry her. Because that was what his mother told him to do.

Jacques and his new wife left the Pletzl and moved just across the river from the ultimate symbol of Parisian pride, the Eiffel Tower, on rue de la Tour. He had found a cramped and dark apartment that had little to recommend it other than that it could just about double as a place for

Mila and Jacques

them to live and work, with the shop where he would restore and store furs at the front and the living quarters at the back, thus saving him some rent. But if he thought moving across the city, or marriage, would get him away from his mother, he was quickly disabused of that notion. Chaya soon moved in with Jacques and Mila at rue de la Tour.

It also turned out to be a pretty poor choice of apartment. According to notes on Jacques later compiled by the Commissariat General aux Questions Juives (CGQJ), the agency established in 1941 to carry out the Vichy government's anti-Semitic policies, the apartment was "extremely small" and "badly located with no passing trade." As a result, the business had "no customers and its assets are immaterial." Jacques had inherited not just his father's looks and passivity but also his utter inability to earn any money.

But he was happier than he'd ever been in his life. Alex was always baffled by his brothers, both so handsome (and, he repeatedly stressed, so tall, a key point for Alex, who was about five foot two), and yet they chose to marry these plain eastern European women. But the very few photos of Jacques from this era show a man who was undoubtedly content. In a photo in the album I found in my grandmother's closet, he is walking down a boardwalk, his hairline starting to recede but his familiar round glasses still in place. Like all the Glass siblings, Jacques loved beautiful things, and in this photo he is dressed precisely in a three-piece suit, but his face is relaxed, and he is making a proud, happy smile as he walks arm in arm with Mila, who smiles uncertainly at the camera. In another photo, taken around the same time, he is posing at what looks like a wedding with almost all of the Ornstein cousins. None of the other Glasses are there, and neither is Mila, but Jacques in his round glasses stands at the back, smiling with his cousins. Within six years of that photo being taken, almost everyone in it would be dead.

Not even Jacques could stay oblivious to how bad things were getting when he would read his newspaper in the local café every day. In July 1934, a law was passed imposing a ten-year delay on naturalized foreigners taking public office or becoming lawyers. In 1935, foreigners had to wait four years to practice medicine, unless they had completed military service.

In 1936, France became the first European state to choose a Jew, the socialist Léon Blum, to be its prime minister. But any optimism Jews in France might have gleaned from this was tempered by the ominous fact that shortly before he assumed office, Blum was nearly beaten to death by anti-Semites associated with the viciously right-wing Action Française league. Four years later he would be arrested and sent to Buchenwald, followed by Dachau and Tyrol, where he nearly escaped execution.

When Édouard Daladier became France's prime minister for the third time in April 1938, just a month before the Anschluss, he used his inaugural address to reassure French voters of his ongoing pacifism (and passivity) in the face of German aggression, promising to take harsh measures against illegal immigrants in France.[4] Fines for visa and employment infractions became more severe and it was suddenly much more difficult for foreigners to get temporary extensions on their residence permits or renew their identity cards. Laws were passed to fine and imprison illegal immigrants, send illegal German immigrants back to Germany, limit the voting rights of naturalized French citizens, and monitor both foreign and naturalized individuals. Anti-Semitic newspapers in France had a huge resurgence at this point: the daily paper *Action Française* was read by 70,000 people per issue; the weekly newspaper *Gringoire*, which regularly cited Jews as the source of all France's problems, was read by 650,000 readers a week. The *Naie Press,* a Yiddish-language daily communist paper published in France, compared the life of an immigrant in 1930s France to that of a man "bicycling in butter."[5]

Long after World War II ended, and even up to the end of the twentieth century, French politicians insisted France was not to blame for its country's actions under Nazi occupation, as Vichy was an illegitimate regime that did not represent the country's values. As late as 1994, President François Mitterrand said, "I will not apologise in the name of France. The Republic had nothing to do with this. I do not believe France is responsible."[6] And yet, as in Poland, the anti-Semitic actions in France during the war were possible only because they reflected something deep within the country's psyche. Anti-Semitism doesn't just emerge like a passing fad; it grows from roots that were already there.

French politicians in the mid-1930s insisted all these new laws were merely for the sake of the country and the economy. Unlike most other Western countries in the late 1930s, France was still suffering from the effects of the Great Depression, and so politicians such as former Prime Minister Albert Sarraut[7] could pretend that the anti-immigrant crackdown was merely a means "to assume control over a foreign population that is becoming excessive and among whom certain elements weigh upon our general economy." The suggestion that this was all simply about jobs and money was somewhat undermined by Sarraut's additional comment that it was necessary to go after "immigrants of all nationalities who, by escaping all verification, successfully infiltrate and eventually constitute an unassimilable mass of often defective individuals, who possess uncertain resources and equivocal morality."[8,9]

After Kristallnacht in November 1938, German and Austrian refugees fled west, even as right-wing French politicians scoffed that reports of the night had been exaggerated. "There were no deaths," declared Charles Maurras, organizer of the deeply anti-Semitic political movement Action Française. (In fact, official records show ninety-one Jews were killed and modern historians suggest the number was almost certainly much higher.) "The prestige of France is not threatened when one burns down a synagogue. One can burn them all. It's not our business and it has no impact on us whatsoever. No diplomatic intervention, no war for the Jews," he added.[10]

Even native Parisian Jews were shocked by the French government's coldness toward the refugees, but many held their tongues to avoid risking accusations of being "unpatriotic."[11] Immigrants like the Glasses who had lived in France for years were in even more of a bind. They had thought of themselves as French, but their adopted country was becoming increasingly hostile toward them, and yet they had nowhere else to go. They had outrun the demons in their home country, but those demons had caught up with them. Not even the most blinkered immigrant who had lived through the Polish pogroms could fail to see the increasingly ominous signs in France as they crept ever closer to his front door. And Jacques, reading his newspaper in his café, would have been forcibly confronted with this reality every day.

So on May 26, 1940, two weeks after Hitler launched his offense on France, Jacques joined the Foreign Legion. Almost a year earlier Alex had joined the Foreign Legion—which was the only French military service open to foreigners at this point—and, just as he did when they were children back in Chrzanow and skipping school, he nagged his older brother to join him. But Jacques probably would have done so anyway without Alex's cajoling. The Glass children still held Reuben up as their moral ideal and, given that he joined the army in World War I to fight for the Austro-Hungarian Empire, it isn't that surprising that the son who was always the most like him would do so, too.

And just as Reuben had realized almost twenty-five years earlier, immigrant Jews in France knew that no matter how bad their country was now, if it lost to these enemies, their lives would become worse. Jacques signed up for the 23rd Régiment de Marche de Volontaires Étrangers, one of various regiments created by the French Foreign Legion to accommodate all the immigrants who wanted to fight for France, some out of loyalty toward the country, others because they saw it as a path toward naturalization. While immigrant Jews generally accounted for 30 percent of the soldiers in these regiments,[12] Jacques' own small unit had double that,[13] and the names are a testament to the loyalty of foreign Jews to their new country, no matter how much it legislated against them: Pinkus Rak, Moise Graf, Icek Zajdenverg. And from this unit of twenty-five men, at least five of the survivors would later be killed in concentration camps.

The 23rd Régiment de Marche de Volontaires Étrangers was a poorly equipped ragtag troop of multiple nationalities and languages, and its life was short, brutal, and eventful. After training in Le Barcarès in the Pyrenees, they were sent on June 3, 1940, to defend Soissons in the north of France, and then went to the south of Paris to try to contain the advance of German armored divisions at Pont sur Yonne. From there, they were then sent back to the north to the Canal de l'Ourcq, where they managed to not just slow down the German advance but kill General Hermann Ritter von Speck, the only enemy general killed during the Battle of France. All of this happened in the space of only two weeks, and yet many had been killed in that short space of time. The 23rd RMVE was dissolved in July 1940.

Jacques did manage to survive, but only because he was taken prisoner. When I was going through the shoebox at the back of my grandmother's closet, it was the small, rectangular metal plate reading "GLASS, Prisonnier Cambrai, 1940" that caused me the most puzzlement: I knew Alex had fought for France, but I was pretty sure he hadn't been taken prisoner. I hadn't considered the possibility that Jacques—the mysterious great-uncle I never met—had also fought.

Cambrai, up in the north of France, was bombed by the Luftwaffe on May 17, 1940, and captured the following day. The Nazis then used

Jacques (kneeling in front) in the Foreign Legion

it as a place to keep some of their prisoners, including Jacques. He was captured during the fighting either around Soissons or Canal de l'Ourcq. The real mystery is how he then got out, which he obviously did because he was soon back in Paris, but there is no record of prisoners being released from Cambrai. There are, however, records of them running away. A British sergeant-major, Frederick Read, was taken prisoner around this time, and he describes in his memoir being held at the barracks in Cambrai in August 1940,[14] where life was monotonous and dispiriting, with the Germans bullying the prisoners with rubber truncheons and shouting orders at them. But every day they were sent out to work in the town at local flour mills, sugar factories, and garages, and these excursions were remarkably unsupervised. Read recounts his own failed escape attempt, which was hampered by his poor language skills. Jacques could at least speak French, albeit heavily accented with Yiddish, so he would have found it relatively easy to hide in the countryside. At least one other man from his regiment was also captured and, according to military records, escaped, so the two might have run off together. It's hard to imagine Jacques running away from the Germans on his own, but with a friend there to encourage him and tell him what to do, the scenario becomes much more plausible. As to the metal plate—"GLASS, Prisonnier Cambrai, 1940"—a fellow prisoner probably made it for him as a souvenir, and perhaps Jacques then sent it to my grandmother as he saw it almost like a trophy commemorating his escape. Or maybe he just wanted his sister to know where he had been and that he was OK. Whichever it was, this would not be the last time he would send Sara mementos from prison.

Jacques was officially demobilized on September 3, 1940, and, even though Paris was now under Nazi occupation, he returned to Mila on rue de la Tour, apparently never even considering that maybe they ought to go somewhere else. But why would he? Jacques was the least assimilated culturally of the Glasses, but of all of them he took his social assimilation for granted the most: he believed that because the French took him in they would therefore never hurt him.

Just three weeks after he returned home, Jacques' assumptions were looking like less of a sure thing. Once France had agreed to stop fighting with Germany on June 22, 1940, it became effectively a collaborator, and Marshal Pétain, an old war hero from World War I, was the new head of state. Under him, the French government fled to the town of Vichy in central France, and the country was chopped in half between German-occupied France and the new Vichy government: northern and western France, including Paris, was occupied by Germany (the Occupied Zone, *zone occupée*), while the south and what little else was left was controlled by Vichy (the Unoccupied Zone, *zone libre*). And Vichy did not wait long to go after the Jews.

On September 27, 1940, the first specifically anti-Jewish legislations came into effect: Jews who had fled to the Unoccupied Zone were prohibited from returning; Jewish shopkeepers had to post a yellow sign in their windows reading "enterprise Juive—Jüdisches Geschäft." A census of Jews in the Occupied Zone was ordered, in which more than 150,000 Jews presented themselves for registration at local police stations, and their names and addresses were then handed over to Section IV J of the Gestapo. Jacques did. In October 1940, all Jews had to have "Juif" stamped on their identity cards. The following year, Jewish businesses in the Occupied Zone were Aryanized—in other words, they were taken away from the Jews—and Jacques was forced to sign over his fur business to Jacques Revillon, the scion of a large fur company. When he joined the Legion to risk his life for France, he had little; now, after fighting for his country, he had even less.

Pétain had been celebrated for his bravery against the Germans during World War I, so much so that he was known as the Lion of Verdun in recognition of his courage at the Battle of Verdun. But as France's chief of state during World War II, he dealt with the Germans by capitulation and active collaboration. Having seen the damage war exacted on France and the French people in World War I, he was willing to do anything to prevent it from happening again, even if that meant submitting to his former enemies. But he went farther than mere obedience.

Vichy France was the only western European country under Nazi occupation that enacted its own measures against the Jews. Despite the claims by French politicians over the years that Vichy was compelled to do this by the Nazis, they in fact came up with anti-Semitic regulations Berlin hadn't even asked for. As Pétain's chief of staff later said, "Germany was not at the origin of the anti-Jewish legislation of Vichy. That legislation was spontaneous and autonomous."[15] When Vichy introduced the "Statut des Juifs" in October 1940 and discriminatory legislation aimed solely at the Jews in June 1941, Jewish people—in the Unoccupied Zone as well as the Occupied one—were excluded from the army, press, commerce and industry, and the civil service, but there was no evidence anywhere that the Germans demanded this of France. As historian Jean Edward Smith later put it, "anti-Semitism was not new to France, but it became one of the hallmarks of the Vichy regime. The Statute on Jews illustrated the Vichy government's willingness to act on its own authority without German pressure and was an ominous sign for the future."[16] The Vichy government even ordered the French police to participate in anti-Jewish thuggery, and the Germans later said they could never have accomplished as much as they did without the help of the French police.[17]

Vichy didn't want to exterminate all Jews like the Nazis did. Not exactly: it wanted to get rid of the foreign Jews, marginalize French Jews, and eliminate Jewish culture from French life[18] to protect the sanctity and unity of French culture. The high number of anti-Semitic fanatics in Vichy—such as Xavier Vallat, the first Vichy Commissioner General for Jewish Affairs, who would soon take a special interest in Alex Maguy—certainly didn't do anything to stop France's anti-Jewish mood. As a result, France quickly proved to be very keen to make anti-Semitic legislation, and in some cases was even more efficient at enacting it than the Germans.

After the war, senior Vichy officials argued that the government felt it had to outpace the Germans in order to save the French Jews and—more pressingly for Vichy—to prevent the fascists from staging a coup in the government. In other words, the way to help the French Jews was by throwing the foreign Jews under a bus, and that by giving the enemy what they wanted they would, in some backhanded way, retain authority. And it is true that the majority of French Jews survived the war. But no government has ever achieved a political, or moral, victory by trying to outpace the far right, let alone actual fascists. The Germans quickly saw through Vichy's strategy and would soon exploit it in their pursuit of foreign Jews, and Vichy—especially from 1942 onward—eagerly helped them, rushing to meet the deportation quotas set by the Germans by sending them Jews—babies, children, the sick—the Nazis hadn't even demanded.[19]

This has caused France some unpleasant reckonings ever since. Serge Klarsfeld, the French activist and Nazi hunter (and, later, a friend of

Alex's), has done more than pretty much anyone in making France con-
front its culpability during the war, and just one instance of this occurred
in 1991. While doing some research at the French Ministry of War Veterans, he happened upon a file of frayed and faded index cards. These were
the remnants of the 1940 census of the French and foreign Jews, which
was used to deport seventy-five thousand people to the concentration
camps.[20] For more than fifty years, historians had thought the cards had
been destroyed, and yet all the while some researchers within the ministry had known the cards existed and kept them hidden. Many in France
were horrified by the discovery—especially, it turned out, those whose
names were on it. So while historians insisted that the list be preserved
for history, those who were on it were terrified by such a prospect.

"How could French historians presume to serenely make use of a
tool that in other times served a racist and criminal system?" one person
wrote to Klarsfeld.

"It's clearly worrying that a listing of categories of citizens exists," said
Jean Kahn, the then head of the French Jewish community.

It didn't matter that most of the people on the census were long dead.
Nor that France was no longer under Vichy and Nazi control. To the
people whose family's names were on it, or who just saw names similar
to their own, the past was ever present and always at risk of returning.
(Eventually, President Jacques Chirac gave the Fichier Juif—Jewish registration file—to the Shoah Memorial in Paris.)

That was how Alex and Henri felt in 1940, and unsurprisingly so,
given what they'd already lived through. So it didn't even occur to Alex
to put his name on the census, and Henri, after careful deliberation with
Sonia, decided against it, too. But Jacques was always different from his
brothers. Despite having been politically aware enough to join the Foreign Legion, he was remarkably resistant to learning the lessons of the
past. So even though he had had to flee his hometown because of anti-
Semitism, and he had just escaped from a Nazi war prison, he still had
a submissive soul. Henri pleaded with him not to register, but Jacques,
urged on by his frightened wife, who believed obedience was a form of

self-protection, dutifully registered himself and Mila as Jewish, giving their home address—which Vichy had anyway, because they were still living in their shop, which had been officially Aryanized. Henri and Alex were horrified when they found out, but he waved their concerns away. He had just saved his life by taking action and disobeying authorities when he ran away from Cambrai, but the only lesson he seemed to have learned from that incident was that he shouldn't try to fight again. No, Jacques felt, it was always better to obey authorities. After all, if you did what they said, why would they hurt you?

Chapter 5

ALEX—DEFIANCE

Paris, 1930s

Alex Maguy, couturier

O n a warm night in the summer of 1936, Alex was in a night-club in Montmartre with his friends. These friends included the artists Moïse Kisling and Jules Pascin, a jazz band leader called Ray Ventura, and several other musicians and artists, many of whom he'd met through his first friend in the art world, Marc Chagall. This was his regular social circle, and tonight was a pretty typical night for him. He met his friends at the glamorous Opéra Comique theater, where they attended the opening night of a new show. They then went to Montparnasse for the cafés there—La Coupole, Le Dôme, Le Café de la Rotonde—that were open late and attracted artistic sorts. There, they met up with Ventura's friend, a young singer called Edith Piaf, and the group then went on to a small club nearby where Charles Trenet was singing. They then headed off to the Montmartre nightclubs, and after that, dancing at the Boeuf sur le Toit, a cabaret where the avant-garde artists hung out until the purple morning hours. It would be another night with no sleep for Alex—there was just too much to do and to see and to drink and to eat. Who has time in Paris to sleep more than one night a week?

In the decade and a half since Alex arrived in Paris, he had lifted himself out of poverty and put himself at the absolute center of the city's artistic and bohemian demimonde. Everything around him was glittering and fabulous, and for the first time in his life, Alex felt like he belonged. The Galician savage, he liked to say, had become the darling of Paris. Forty years later, when writing about this brief period, he described it as "the happiest time of my life." But on that particular night, as he sat in that cabaret, he felt a terrible tug of sadness. Because as he looked around at all that he had, which was everything he had ever wanted, he knew he would have to give it all up.

By 1936, Alex was running a thriving couture house, built up purely by word of mouth, that employed more than sixty people and put out four collections a year. When he had turned down Nina Ricci's offer a decade earlier to work with her at Raffin, he had bet everything he had that he could make it on his own. Against the most extraordinary odds, his bet had paid off.

"[Alex Maguy] was responsible for the livelihood of all of his workers. He was personally concerned with each, from the smallest of the petites mains [the seamstresses] to his salespeople," reads Alex's entry in the book *The Dressmakers of France.* Alex became known for his tailoring and his coats, and long after he switched from fashion design to art dealing, the coats he designed for my grandmother that I saw in her closet were always beautifully made, always with a clever detail like a fluted sleeve or an exaggerated collar, and always still looking new even though my grandmother had been wearing them for decades.

"His own studio, his preoccupation with art, made one suspect he would prefer [to make] evening clothes. But here, too, the fine balance of what was wanted showed him to be an excellent businessman," according to *The Dressmakers of France*.

Alex was so busy he had to hire an assistant to help him with his sketches, as drawing was never Alex's talent. "A distinguished young man, though quite timid, came to show me his sketches," Alex later wrote. "I was quite impressed. He was an extraordinary draftsman, with strong personality revealed by his drawings. His name was Christian Dior." And Alex and Dior, two seemingly very different men, would go on to have strikingly parallel lives over the next few decades.

Like Alex, Dior had found the bohemian Parisian life a thrilling release from the cloistered, closeted world in which he'd grown up, but whereas Alex's life had been circumscribed by poverty, Dior's had been hemmed in by privilege, raised by starchy governesses and a dominating father who disapproved of his son's artistic ambitions.[1]

"I suggested to my family that I should study Fine Arts. There was an outcry! I was not allowed join the Bohemians. To gain time and to enjoy the greatest possible liberty, I was enrolled as a student in the École des Sciences Politiques, which entailed no commitments. Such was the hypocritical way in which I contrived to carry on the life I liked," Dior later recalled.[2]

And the life he liked was a lot like the one Alex did, too: in his autobiography, Dior describes hanging out at the bar Boeuf sur le Toit, going to the Ballets Russes, watching Jean Cocteau films, seeing Josephine Baker on the stage. "What a hectic life! My parents were in despair at having a son who was so incapable of concerning himself with anything serious," Dior writes, and Alex would have sympathized, having had similar arguments with Chaya.

After the Dior family fortune collapsed in the stock market crash, and the art gallery Dior had opened with a friend shut down, Dior started working as a fashion illustrator. Soon he was making sketches for designers such as Schiaparelli, Alex's old friend Nina Ricci—and Alex himself. It was inevitable the two of them would eventually meet as they mixed in the same circles, and it was through Dior that Alex befriended the aspiring designer Imre Partos, a Hungarian Jew, who would become a very important figure in Alex's life in a few years time.

The other illustrator who provided sketches for Alex's label was René Gruau, who became one of Alex's most loyal and enduring friends. He would also, in the next decade, become the most famous fashion illustrator in the world, thanks to his future alliance with Dior. Gruau's fluid, languorous illustrations of Dior's famous New Look collection in 1947 helped to translate what became the most influential fashion breakthrough of the twentieth century to the masses, and he would continue to be the label's artist for more than half a century, coining modern fashion illustration as much as Dior coined modern fashion. John Galliano, head of design at Dior from 1996 to 2011, later said Gruau "captured Dior better than any other" because of their "enduring friendship."[3] And both of them started with Alex in the mid-1930s.[4] Alex might have struggled at times as a designer, but his skill at talent-spotting was pretty much unsurpassable, and this is a testament to his natural and extraordinary sense of aesthethics.

Yet even with Dior's and Gruau's help, the work was punishing. On one day alone, Alex did a fitting with a successful cabaret owner who insisted on drinking from her whiskey bottle as he was draping the fabric around her, and walked through his studio completely naked between fittings, unbothered by the sixty employees working there; another with the French singer Lucienne Boyers, described later in her *New York Times* obituary as "the queen of Paris nightlife in the 1930s"; and a third one with Suzy Solidor, a bisexual cabaret singer who was so popular with artists, including Tamara Lempicka, Jean Cocteau, and Francis Bacon, that she became known as "the most painted woman in the world." After the war she was known as something else when she was convicted of being a collaborator.

He was not a big name, like Chanel or Balenciaga, but he was doing well enough for his company to be valued in the early 1940s by the CGQJ at 2,233,823.30 francs, or almost 90,000 euros today—an unarguably respectable sum. (By contrast, Jacques' business was valued at less than 200,000 francs, or 8,000 euros today.) In his salon, which he moved out of its original office space and into a far more glamorous setting on Avenue Matignon, he had twenty-nine armchairs, proof of the number of clients and journalists he regularly had to seat, and the salon itself was fronted, between a pair of heavy silk curtains, with a large window looking onto the street, through which children could peer into his workplace, just as he and Sara had once looked into Lanvin's.

The two youngest Glasses were always charmed by Parisian style, and as adults they re-created it enthusiastically in their own wardrobes: Alex wore formal three-piece suits and buckets of cologne, with shoes that had two-inch heels for some much-longed-for extra height, and Sara wore berets, wide belts, and peasant-style blouses with tapered trousers. When you move to a new country and don't want to be seen by the natives as a foreigner, you can change your accent, or you can change your clothes, and the latter tends to be easier. It is a way of leaving who you were behind and sending a pleadingly optimistic message to those around you that says, "I know I may not sound like you, but I am one of you." Or maybe it's like being a besotted lover in a new relationship, copying your partner's style. Whichever, it's an expression of love.

And Alex expressed his love for France through his clothes. He built up a successful export business selling a fondly exaggerated image of French chic to, in particular, British and American customers. It was a style that felt a little kitsch for Parisians, but for foreigners this heavily outlined version of French style was a canny formula. It was also one that reflected Alex's status as an immigrant. Like a man who moves to Britain and immediately adopts the mannerisms of Bertie Wooster, or one who moves to the United States and becomes a hardcore baseball fan, or like Henri, for that matter, in his three-piece suits in the 7th arrondissement, it was not enough for Alex to simply be in France. He had to embody that country. As much as he thought of himself as an outsider, there was always a part of him that wanted to prove to the French bourgeoisie that he understood them, and was better than them. So there had to be an exaggeration, an overcompensation, and he made clothes that were Frencher than French.

Alex also turned out to be excellent at selling things. He had watched those obsequious couturiers carefully through the window as a kid, and he was happy to copy them if it sold some dresses. That he did it with his rough Yiddish accent made it seem even more authentic to clients bored of the polished patter they got in other salons. Also, Alex really loved to sell—unlike other couturiers, he did not see it as beneath him to push his goods, to tell women that if they were buying the blue dress they really also ought to buy the red, and maybe to make up a little lie from time to time and say that the English princesses had been in the other day and ordered these skirts, so perhaps the client should, too, as they would soon be the latest fashion. As a salesman, Alex combined the schmooze of French designers with the pushiness of the market traders in the Pletzl and back in Chrzanow, and it was an extremely effective combination.

One of the ironies of fashion design is that a profession ostensibly built to celebrate female beauty has, for more than a century, been dominated by gay men. The question of whether Alex was gay or bisexual was one that was raised in his lifetime by his friends and colleagues, but always behind his back. When I was starting to research Alex's life in Paris I met the now-late designer Ilie Wacs, who worked as a sketcher for Alex in the 1950s. After some preliminary small talk he brought up Alex's sexuality: "He was such a dandy, you know? Always in heels, always heavily perfumed, but he talked about his girlfriends, so we in the studio could never figure it out. Did anyone in your family know?"

No one in the family did. Alex never spoke about his romantic life, and no one dared to ask. It may be that Alex was neither gay nor straight but both and neither: Paris in the 1920s and 1930s was a center for not just the sexual freedom of Josephine Baker but also the sexual fluidity of Jean Cocteau. In the artistic and fashion worlds in which Alex worked, such sexual liberation would have been, if not the openly acknowledged norm, then at least a quietly accepted practice, and the idea of putting a name to such experimentation, to define yourself by who you happened to take to bed on Tuesday, would have seemed as absurd as naming yourself after the color of the jacket you happened to wear on Wednesday. Such things were mutable, and nailing down the sexual preferences of the individuals in Alex's milieu is like trying to fix a wave to the shore.

But while Alex's friends would have been comfortable with homosexuality, his family—and more specifically, his mother—would very much not. Same-sex relationships were not accepted in the world in which she grew up, which was also the world in which Alex grew up, and Alex desperately cared about the good opinion of his siblings and his Ornstein cousins. Certainly in his memoir he takes enormous pains to stress his heterosexuality. He writes about how one of his neighbors initially refused to speak to him "because he believed that all couturiers were homosexuals. But he quickly discovered that I was an exception, a rare exception, to that rule. He soon saw many very pretty ladies coming up the stairs to my place." There are multiple if vague references to various "conquests"—all emphatically female—and dimly described remembrances of young women who desperately wanted to marry him.

These little asides are infuriating in their opacity and almost laughable in their clumsiness. My father had warned me not to take Alex's memoir too seriously, and while I'd been prepared to treat his descriptions of his achievements with some skepticism, it soon became clear to me that the more questionable elements of his story were the references to his personal life. Alex always found it easy to talk about what he did, but how he felt was a very different story. Unlike the shoebox in my grandmother's closet, he fully intended his memoir to be seen by others, so there was a limit to how honest he could, and would, be. If he wasn't willing to discuss the complexities of his sexuality with his family, he certainly wasn't going to do so in a book that he hoped would immortalize his reputation with the public.

Alex's sexuality, like my grandmother's sadness, was something none of us in the family talked about while he was alive or even after he died. It can be hard to see someone you know so well clearly, to fit together the puzzle pieces when your mind can't even grasp how the image should look. But I wondered if the truth was more obvious to those who worked with him. So I asked one of Alex's assistants, who was employed by him in the 1980s, if she ever got any sense of her former boss's sexuality.

"When I knew him he was almost rampantly heterosexual—he was like an octopus around me sometimes," she said. "But I always got the impression that he was largely homosexual for the first half of his life and largely heterosexual for the latter, just from who he was hanging out with at those times. But honestly, I don't think Alex would have ever even thought about it in those terms. It was just who he was at those times."

In the early 1930s, Alex bought a home that was as luxurious as his salon had become: a duplex on the Ile de la Cité, it had large bay windows that looked out over Paris. To help him decorate his apartment he pulled in his friends Christian Dior and René Gruau to advise him. On the walls Alex hung paintings by his friends, such as Pascin and Kisling, and when he threw cocktail parties all of his guests would stand on his terrace and watch the flashing lights of the *bateaux mouches*—tourist cruises—as they sailed up and down the Seine. Even though his working days were exhausting, his nights were relentless: if he wasn't throwing parties in his glamorous apartment, or seeing his siblings, or going out for drinks with his beloved cousins, he was running around Montmartre or Montparnasse with his friends, doing everything. After all, to stay at home and do nothing—like his father did, like his brother Jacques did—was to feel nothing. To do everything was to live. And just as Alex was living exactly as he wanted, he realized he'd have to lose it all.

While Jacques' career was more typical of a Jewish immigrant and Alex's was the more exceptional, when it came to their feelings about the approach of Nazism, it was Jacques who was the unusual one and Alex more archetypal. Jacques' blind belief in France's loyalty toward foreign Jews put him in the minority, while Alex's nervousness was far more common among their demographic. For obvious reasons, eastern European Jews recognized the dangers of Nazism far quicker than French ones, and many realized it was worse than what they had run away from before.[5] Alex was even more pessimistic—or realistic—than most of his peers. His experience in the pogrom as a child had left him with a lifelong cynicism about anyone's loyalty toward Jews and, as much as he loved Paris and became a part of Parisian life, he never kidded himself that he was anything but a foreigner, and his lifelong retention of his Yiddish accent was a statement of that, to himself and to others. He refused to assimilate his tongue, instead defiantly remaining, as he put it, "authentic."

Unlike Jacques, he didn't take his safety in France for granted. So no matter how dazzled he was by his newfound popularity on nights out in Montparnasse, he never forgot the dark forces that had so blighted his childhood and now approached France. He demonstrated against Action Française and Croix-de-Feu, two nationalistic political parties that Alex rightly recognized as riddled with anti-Semitism, and he watched closely their rise and the accompanying national mood for appeasement. Being involved in the art world gave Alex particular clarity of the situation, as Jewish artists were increasingly seen in the 1930s as symbols of destruction of France's heritage. *Le Figaro*'s Camille Mauclair raged against "The Monparno crowd," in which he claimed "the proportion of Semites is around 80%," and he insisted that Alex's friends were conspiring to destroy French art:

"One must admit that if Jews have produced marvellous poets, they have never excelled in plastic arts. How then to explain that the current art market is in the hands of Jewish merchants and critics, and that they therefore push Jewish painters to the forefront of 'living art,' all agreeing to attack the Latin tradition and to obey the spirit of negating criticism, of dissociation, of overturning of values, which is the old Bolshevik base of their race."[6]

By 1935, the major art magazines refused to include even the names of these immigrant Jewish artists in their emphatically French pages. The national mood was becoming all too obvious to Alex.

"In the horror of the pogroms, I had seen the damned beast take form, seen its hideous face. It grew and grew, ever more monstrous. And now it appeared everywhere, here in France, among so-called patriots, but in reality degenerate reactionaries, all wearing the same grinning mask," he wrote.

His first step was to deal with the one member of his family whom he considered to be the easiest to manipulate and the simplest to get out of France: his sister, Sara. In 1937, Alex managed to find a way for her to go to New York and, in doing so, very possibly saved her life. And yet, he doesn't mention this event once in his memoir, or even that his sister left France. This initially astonished me: after all, not only was this a major event in the family, but given how much Alex liked to trumpet his successes, to ignore the fact that he, with great prescience and skill, ostensibly saved his baby sister from the camps seems inexplicable. The most sympathetic explanation would be that by the time he was writing his memoir Alex knew all too well how homesick Sara was in New York, so he couldn't bear to revisit this saga because of the guilt. And there is some evidence in the letters between them over the next few decades that he was aware to some extent of how unhappy she was. But a more likely reason, I think, is that Alex simply didn't think it was that big a deal, not compared with what was happening to him at the time, and so he just didn't bother to write it down. He was writing his story and therefore he focused on himself—he did not want to write about what happened to his sister. And this sums up what it was like to be related to Alex: if he liked you, his generosity was immense, his heart enormous. But these qualities were too often obscured by his infuriating self-centeredness, which sometimes came across as a lack of interest in other people. Alex loved his siblings very deeply, to the point that they were the only people in the world who had the ability to hurt him. They were the bruise on his arm that was too tender to touch. And so while his mother and siblings hardly make an appearance in his memoir during the 1930s, the truth is he tried to save them repeatedly.

When Alex realized he could only get Sara out of France, he set about trying to get French citizenship for himself and his family. He was too late: on September 21, 1937, his application for naturalization was rejected, despite his having lived in France for almost two decades and his growing celebrity. Alex refused to be beaten and so, in defiance of the unarguable odds, he tried again, and once again he was rejected. Devastated, he wrote a furious and heartfelt letter to the government in protest:

> *I was painfully surprised when I learned that my naturalization application had been rejected. The very serious circumstances we are now going through make this refusal even more painful. I am young, brave, fit and eager to have the opportunity to defend this French soil that was welcoming to me and my family. I work with many French people and we fight heart and soul together for our work; it is my dearest desire to now continue the struggle with them—in French— in the most serious of conditions. I hope to have contributed to the renown of French taste and couture abroad. It is for me a moral obligation and an expression of gratitude for your country that make me ask you, sir, to reconsider my application . . .*

he wrote on September 20, 1938. But it was no good; for once, Alex couldn't make a sale. The noose around foreign Jews in France was already too tight. German and Austrian refugees were being rounded up and put into French internment camps; there was no chance France was going to give citizenship to a family of Polish Jews and, Alex realized, even less chance the country would protect them.

He came up with another idea of how to save his family: he would sign up to fight, protecting the home he loved from becoming like the former home he hated. So once France reluctantly joined the war in September 1939, he decided to follow in the footsteps of his friend Kiki Kisling, who had fought in the French Foreign Legion in World War I, and join up. "I'm ready to sacrifice a limb of my body to win this fight against the Germans, my enemies," he told his friends. "If the Krauts win the war, I'll go before a firing squad. So I'm ready to sacrifice a limb of my body to win this fight against the Germans, my enemies."

But it turned out that France wasn't so keen for his limbs. The Legion was already becoming oversubscribed, largely with Spanish Republicans[7] but also because the German and Austrian Jews who had been interned by France were told they would be released if they joined the Legion. So Alex required some help convincing the Foreign Legion that they needed a five foot two Polish-born fashion designer, and he turned to someone who would become a very important part of his life, a man called Colonel Jean Perré.

Alex happened to be the colonel's daughter's couturier, and when she introduced him to her father in the mid-1930s, his eyes must have lit with the same kind of excitement as when he met Chagall or Piaf: here was someone whom he respected, certainly, but who could also be useful to him in his ongoing project to establish himself in France. A large, barrel-chested man, Colonel Perré was an old-fashioned French military man, the kind who believed in France's sovereignty above all. He was anti-Semitic in the way a lot of his demographic was: it wasn't that he specifically hated the Jews, but he didn't want France's innate French character to be altered by a load of suspicious outsiders. But a Jew like Alex, who wrote letters to the government begging to be allowed to defend "French soil"? Well, that was the kind of Jew a military patriot like Colonel Perré could support.

Back in World War I, the colonel was widely seen as the equal and rival of Charles de Gaulle, and the two competed for command of the same regiment. De Gaulle won that contest, but Perré made a name for himself as a skillful tactician with tanks, and in 1919 he went to Poland to command a tank battalion of the first Polish armored units against the Russians. He had a further connection with the Poles: he was in the command staff of the First Armored Polish Brigade and was one of the French advisers introduced in the Polish high command. He was a tough man who respected other tough men, and when he met Alex, an almost aggressively masculine Polish fashion designer, the two formed an immediate bond. Colonel Perré, who was by this point in the high command of the French army, wrote a letter endorsing this young Jew's bid to join the Legion. Doors were swiftly opened and, at last, one of Alex's applications was successful. Just as Alex had always suspected, what mattered in life wasn't what you knew but who.

On October 2, 1939, Alex assigned a manager to look after his salon and said good-bye to his workers, his mother, his brothers, his cousins, and his friends. "Courage," he said to his cousin Josek. "I will see you after the war." Then he took his favorite pieces of art by two of his oldest Parisian friends off the wall in his living room—a small drawing by Pascin of a young woman and a painting by Kisling of a little boy—and he packaged them up and sent them to the Tel Aviv Museum in what was then still Palestine.

"I felt I was doing my duty as an Israeli soldier, as a member of the resistance, as a pioneer, donating to Tel Aviv. I added my brick to the building. I was certain that we would emerge victorious from this struggle. And I was confident that Israel would be born. No one—other than Helena Rubenstein—had ever before made a gift of two paintings to the Tel Aviv Museum," he wrote in his memoir.

This story certainly fit in with Alex's character, but when I read it in his memoir I wondered how much self-mythology was going on here. Could he really have owned museum-worthy art as early as 1939? I called up the museum to ask if Alex and Helena Rubenstein were the first people to donate paintings to the museum, and the museum's archivist firmly denied it. I sighed, and was about to cross the paragraph out in his memoir. Typical Alex, I thought, trying to make himself sound like a big shot and celebrity by proxy. But the archivist then casually added, "But Monsieur Maguy did send those paintings to us in 1939."

"Those particular paintings? In 1939?"

"Oh yes, absolutely. 1939. Other people donated several paintings before him, but those two he sent are still in our permanent collection."

This was to be the first of many instances when I was taught not to underestimate Alex and his claims. Because the story was correct, and he had indeed left his stamp behind him before going off to war. He had just given the tale a brush of showman's pizzazz.

Unsurprisingly, a short, heavily perfumed couturier with a taste for the finer things in life found the Foreign Legion a bit of an adjustment. The French Foreign Legion was and is notoriously tough, even by military standards, and because it, uniquely in the French military, allowed in foreigners, it was filled with the dispossessed from around the world— refugees, vagabonds, and flat-out criminals. German intelligence glee- fully exploited the Legion's rackety admissions practice by stuffing it full of Nazi spies during the 1930s, hoping to destroy the Legion by infiltrat- ing it. Once their ruse was discovered, the German legionnaires were shipped out, but the French authorities retained long-held suspicions about the Legion, and therefore wouldn't let it fight in Europe when France finally entered the war.

Alex (on the left) in the Foreign Legion, 1941

Alex had always prided himself on being a tough foreigner, but even he was taken aback by how tough and foreign his fellow soldiers in the Legion were. Largely made up of Spanish Republicans who fled Franco and Jewish refugees from central and eastern Europe, the Legion was regarded by officers as an unpromising mix of communists and intellectuals.[8] Alex described them as "a mob of rough and tough guys" and, in a rare moment of vulnerability in his memoir, admits he was bullied relentlessly.

"I found it hard to break with Parisian life," Alex wrote. And initially, he barely broke with it at all. Stationed in Barcarès in the southeastern corner of France, Alex would train during the day and then sneak out to the local nightclubs when the rest of the men were in bed, enjoying a social life that wasn't all that different from his life back home. Alex took lifelong pride in getting the better of authority figures around him, but he was remarkably bad at doing so. Just as Nina Ricci had caught him reselling designs, and his mother had caught him stealing meatballs in Chrzanow, Alex's nighttime excursions were quickly exposed when he failed to make it back to the camp in time for reveille and he turned up reeking of booze at the start of inspection. He was promptly put in the stockade, and in his memoir he describes his humiliation at length. "The Legion getting too much for you, Glass? Sorry you enlisted?" his fellow soldiers jeered at him, walking past.

Others would have been cowed into obedience. But Alex felt only defiance and a determination to be tougher than ever. He never felt any embarrassment about describing his falls to others, because they were a chance to show how he rose up and fought back.

From then on, he trained more intensely than anyone else. And he still went out most nights, too—but as a concession, he started wearing a watch so he always got back in time.

Eventually, even Alex had to give up the nightclubs. The training got harder and he was put on night maneuvers as the so-called Phoney War, which lasted from September 1939 to May 1940, neared its end.

"We are being toughened up for war," he later recalled writing to Kisling, who was too old to join the French army this time, so was whiling away the war by painting in his studio in Marseille.

"I hope you'll get leave to come eat a good bouillabaisse here with me in the south," Kisling wrote back. "But for now, forget about Paris. After the victory, knowing you as I do, you'll restart [your business] in no time. For the moment, make war."

On April 17, 1940, Alex had no choice: he and his fellow soldiers were sent to Cherbourg, where they were armed with equipment and packed onto ships. None of them knew where they were going, but they knew it wouldn't be Europe, because French authorities still weren't allowing the Legion to fight on the Continent. The dropping temperature was a hint that they weren't heading southward either: they were going toward the Arctic Circle.

Alex was part of the 13th Demi-Brigade of the Foreign Legion, a unit that had been set up only the month before and would soon gain legendary status. It still has a reputation as "one of [the French army's] most honoured units,"[9] and it was later described by de Gaulle as being "at the heart from the very beginning of the forces of Free France for the liberation of our homeland honourably and victoriously."[10] Formed initially to help the Allies in Finland and Norway, it was put under the command of Lt. Col. Raoul Magrin-Vernerey, a tough military eccentric who personified the Foreign Legion itself: battle-scarred from World War I and saddled with disabilities that should have disqualified him from military service. Various head wounds, and crude attempts to operate on them, had left him with a notorious temper, and either because of or despite that, he was a formidable fighter. Alex worshipped him.

According to Alex's memoir, one night in early May he was keeping watch on the bridge of the ship, the *Ville d'Alger,* when he saw Magrin-Vernerey walking toward him. Above them they could hear enemy planes circling, and Magrin-Vernerey thought he saw fear in the inexperienced soldier's face.

"Don't worry. The planes can't see you. And even if they could, what would they do? Make a big hole in you and you would be dead. Your friends and family would mourn you but for you it would be over," he said with a smile.

But Alex was not one to be teased, even by a lieutenant colonel.

"I don't agree. I came here to fight for my country!" he replied.

Magrin-Vernerey grew serious then, his moods always changing as swiftly as the Nordic sky.

"Don't worry. You'll fight. We'll win."

When his troops asked him why they were there anyway, Magrin-Vernerey treated the question with the same nonchalance with which he first spoke to Alex: "Why? Because my orders are to take Narvik. Why Narvik? For the anchovies, for the Norwegians—I haven't the faintest idea."

In fact, it was for the iron ore. The Germans and Allies were both determined to seize Norway, because both sides realized it was the way to gain control of the iron ore, which was transported out of Sweden and through the Norwegian port, and was so important to the German war machinery. Hitler also saw Norway as a potential naval base, while British forces saw it as a way to open up the Baltic for the Allies. The French saw it as a possible second fighting front a safe distance from France, thus allowing the Legion to battle the Germans without risking harm to France itself or its civilians. The Narvik campaign would turn out to be one of the biggest battles since the invasion of Poland.

On May 13, the 13th Demi-Brigade landed on the Bjerkvik beaches, close to Narvik. As the British battleships and destroyers started firing on the German defenders, and the Luftwaffe fought back, bombing and strafing the beaches, the French Foreign Legion soldiers were ordered to jump overboard, in the middle of the battle, and swim through the freezing North Sea to shore. Weighted down by his artillery, Alex swam in water so cold it felt like it was burning him, and he watched many of his fellow soldiers drown around him, either shot by the Germans or sunk by their own equipment, their terrified faces illuminated by the fires fringing the coast as civilians' homes were bombed. It was like dying at the edge of the world.

"*A moi, la Legion!*" Magrin-Vernerey cried, the Legion's version of "Follow me!" and the soldiers who survived the terrifying landing pressed onward up the beach.

The Norwegian army was an Allied troop but Magrin-Vernerey never really trusted them: "The Norwegian Army is nothing more than a bunch of dull farmers. They are useless. Half of them are paid German spies anyway," he was reported to have said.[11] The Norwegians weren't entirely sure about the legionnaires either. In one book my father bought in Narvik, when retracing Alex's steps, the historian describes them as "not like other soldiers. Many of them were pure bandits, feared and hated by the inhabitants of Bjerkvik and Narvik."[12] Their terror was understandable: thirteen adult civilians and a five-year-old boy were killed during the fighting on the beach, and afterward the legionnaires tore through the few houses still standing near the beach to see if they could find any German soldiers hiding inside, shooting down doors and breaking windows to gain entry, heaping fear on top of trauma for the inhabitants. The French Foreign Legion was not known for its manners.

Fighting alongside them for Narvik was a scrappy patchwork of other international Allied troops, and together they became known as the First Light Infantry Division, which was put under the command of the extremely formidable general Émile Béthouart. This included the 5th Demi-Brigade of Chasseurs Alpins, the 27th Demi-Brigade of Chasseurs Alpins, a mountain troop made up of Polish refugees called the Polish First Carpathian Demi-Brigade, and various Norwegian units. Also fighting with them was the now legendary Captain Marie-Pierre Koenig, a man who had acted with enormous bravery in World War I and would become an essential part of the Allied resistance in this war, too. Between them all, they managed to take Bjerkvik, overcoming the Germans and their firepower. But the 13th Demi-Brigade's battle against the Nazis, and the elements, had only just begun.

Alex and his men were ordered to pursue the retreating Germans up into the barren hills north of Bjerkvik. Even though it was spring, the temperatures were freezing and the mountains covered in snow, making it even harder to spot the Germans, who were wearing white uniforms. Alex was still determined to prove himself and show that he was not the precious couturier the legionnaires initially thought. And so, one night when the men were all resting around a frozen lake in the half-light of the midnight moon, Alex got up, stripped in front of his commanding officers, got a sharp rock, broke through the thick ice on the lake, and dove in, determined to show these old legionnaire war dogs he was as tough as them. It worked: several of these legionnaire officers would become Alex's lifelong friends.

Lake dives aside, the fighting continued. The battles in the hills against the Austrian mountain infantrymen were hard and savage. After enormous loss of life, the legionnaires eventually triumphed and, when they stood victorious on top of their mountain, they were able to wave to the Chasseurs Alpins on top of the neighboring mountain that the Chasseurs Alpins themselves had just seized.[13]

Fighting continued over the Narvik port, and the Germans were retreating. But just as the Legion was nearing Sweden, pushing the Germans over the border and into Swedish internment, they were summoned back home: Germany had broken through French lines, and all troops and equipment were needed for defense. Magrin-Vernerey refused: "My legionnaires and I won't leave until we've taken Narvik," he declared. After a few more days of fighting, in which Alex fought in hand-to hand combat, they accomplished their mission. But any joy they felt was tempered by their frustration at not being able to stay and secure the port, and the German forces would ultimately recapture Narvik. As the 13th Demi-Brigade sailed away from Norway, Alex looked back at the port he and his fellow legionnaires had won, at the cost of ninety-three Legion soldiers and so much suffering in the cold. Dozens of German ships were burning in the harbor, like a giant Viking funeral pyre.

It had been a brutal battle, and Alex had been exceptionally brave. His lake diving turned out to have been unnecessary because his fighting had convinced his superiors that he was a true soldier. Along with the rest of the brigade, he was awarded the Croix de Guerre 1939–1940, but

Alex alone was awarded a Bronze Star, specifically for him, and he was later cited for his courage in the military dispatches of General Béthouart. Alex at last had proven himself.

The port of Narvik is still there, compact and picturesque, fringed with houses in shades of mustard, pink, and red, built on top of ashes of ones that had been destroyed in the battle. At one end is a large bright-red brick building, the iron export terminal, the object of all the fighting eighty years earlier. All day, trains run along the coast toward it, carrying the iron ore. Life continued and continues. Outside the new Narvik War Museum, which opened in 2018 to preserve and tell the stories of the 1940 battle for the port, is a children's playground where sweet blonde Norwegian children play happily on a climbing frame while their parents learn what their grandparents endured. A few miles away from the port are the cemeteries for the fallen French and German soldiers, with the lists of names of the dead, and there you can also see a simple stone memorial thanking the French soldiers, surrounded by a rainbow of small flowers: "La France, à ses fils et à leurs frères d'armes tombés glorieusement en Norvège. Narvik 1940." ["To the sons and brothers of France who fell gloriously in Norway. Narvik, 1940."] Whatever anxieties the locals felt about the legionnaires are long gone, buried with the dead in the ground and in the sea.

The 13th Demi-Brigade sailed back to France, docking at Brest on June 13, 1940, the day before the Nazis marched into Paris. Magrin-Vernerey joined the fight, but it was too late, and Paris fell. So Magrin-Vernerey decided to take his men to Britain and fight from there, alongside Charles de Gaulle and the Free French. Alex and his fellow soldiers went to Trentham Park to be part of the resistance. Alex would lie awake at night, listening to the BBC radio for news from home, learning English from the newscasters' clipped diction. For the rest of his life, when Alex would talk about the BBC he would get a dreamy look in his eyes and say it was his "one source of hope" during that bewildering time. But it also caused him enormous anxiety to hear how Paris was now like a garrison, with the Jews at the mercy of the Vichy laws and

German soldiers. So when Magrin-Vernerey asked Alex to stay in the Demi-Brigade, which became the main unit of the First Free French Division in de Gaulle's Free French forces, Alex refused. He had to return to Paris, he said, where he was responsible for his mother, brothers, and cousins. He couldn't stay in England, he added, because he wanted "to defend French soil and fight my hereditary enemies, the Nazis."

"I know you will do good work," Magrin-Vernerey replied. "We will win this war and meet again, Glass."

Alex was not the only member of his troop to feel that he had to return to France, despite his loyalty to de Gaulle—General Béthouart also said he had to go. De Gaulle took Béthouart to the Rubens Hotel in Victoria for lunch in an attempt to convince him otherwise. Just a week earlier, de Gaulle had made his famous radio appeal from London, in which he told the French people the war was not over for them, despite the fall of France, and he asked for anyone who could to join the French resistance. He asked Béthouart what he thought of the appeal.

"I think that you are right. Someone has to stay and fight with the Allies, but personally I have 7000 men to repatriate and can't in good conscience abandon them before they are safely home," Béthouart replied.[14]

So General Béthouart, Alex, and the rest of the demobilizing soldiers sailed first to Casablanca, where they stayed for a few weeks, and then to Marseille. Among the other returning soldiers was a young man called Jean Seytour. It was a sad return as the soldiers looked at their homeland, a now-humiliated France. But Alex was full of defiance, because he and Seytour had a plan.

"In Grenoble, under the patronage of Béthouart, my friends, including Seytour, swore to form a 'sizaine' [six-pack], a resistance group of men acting under the rule of secrecy," Alex wrote. "Because the Armistice had been signed and defeat accepted. But for us, the resistance had just begun."

Chapter 6

SARA—EMIGRATION

Paris and New York, late 1930s

The day Sara's life changed forever did not seem portentous to her until it was too late. As usual, she woke up in the apartment she shared with her mother on rue des Rosiers, early because she had to get to work, but not so early that her mother hadn't already cooked her breakfast. Sara had never been a good eater, and she never would be, so she picked at the food Chaya had made. And then after kissing her mother good-bye, she walked out of their two-room apartment, down the hall with the communal telephone that had recently been installed for all the residents, out the door, and onto the streets of the Pletzl. It was February 1937 and she was twenty-six years old.

When I started working on this book, I'd planned to focus on my grandmother, but it quickly became clear that was impossible—partly because her and her siblings' lives were so entwined but also because she turned out to be the hardest to research. Whereas her brothers led lives of masculine adventure, which were then recorded in official archives, my grandmother represented the quiet feminine: domestic, private—what George Eliot describes in *Middlemarch* as "a hidden life," and she made sure to hide as much of it as possible. And so, as Eliot says, my grandmother's was a life of "unrecorded acts," which is not an easy proposition for a memoirist. I'd always preferred domestic stories to action ones, but when I started my research I felt myself doing to her what I'd done to her in life: I avoided her. Investigating Alex Maguy's adventures was both practically and emotionally easier than prying into my grandmother's melancholia.

When I at last turned my attention to her, I initially did a kind of displacement activity, searching through archival records for her life, those bureaucratic background cameras ticking off the key moments: here's a marriage, here's a house move, here's a death. But I eventually realized that the reason I wanted to tell my grandmother's story was not because of things that happened to her, as was the case with her brothers, but because of the inner emotional drama that she thought she hid away but never could, not really. We all picked it up from her, but no one ever talked about it, or explained it. My father and uncle didn't ask her about it because they feared exacerbating it, and I didn't ask them about it because I could see how much it pained them. But if I'd pushed her away because of it in life, I could at least try to understand her after she died. And that was a story I was not going to find in archives.

So I had to talk to those who knew her best, and that meant her sons, Ronald and Richard, my father and uncle. I dreaded hurting them by asking difficult questions, but it turned out that what had hurt them most was feeling like they had to keep these stories to themselves. At first they, like me, found it easier to talk about actions than emotions, and my father sent me near-daily emails with attached photos he had of his mother doing things: dancing with her husband in Long Island, visiting him in Paris when he was an adult, sitting with me in New York when I was a child. After several dozen of these, I went to see him and said that I had enough photos—what I needed was details of her life, and by that I meant her emotional life. He went silent and looked down, withdrawing inside his own thoughts. When I went home later that evening, I expected little to come of that conversation. But the next day, he sent a long email detailing exactly what I'd asked for, and then several more over the next few weeks. Slowly, Sara's life, which she'd always kept in the shadows, came into focus.

In the winter of 1937, all of the Glass siblings were happy—happier than they'd ever been, happier than they'd ever imagined they could be. Henri and Jacques were married to women who loved them, Alex was successful in his job. But of all of them, Sara was the most surprised by her happiness because, during her long years in the sanatoriums, she'd had the best cause to assume it would always elude her.

When she finally returned to Paris for good in the early 1930s, Alex frequently took her to the galleries, and while he loved the Monets, the Cézannes, and, most of all, the Picassos, she preferred the Renoirs. At home she painted pictures of Renoir-esque young women, with their soft eyes, chestnut-colored pompadours, and gentle smiles. When at last she was well enough to start working, she decided to do something that let her do the only thing that she had confidence in, and that was draw and paint. She didn't have Alex's manic drive to achieve the impossible, but neither did she have Jacques' quiet acceptance of the least life had to offer, so she enrolled as a nonmatriculated student at the École des Beaux-Arts to study fine art. Every day she would leave the Pletzl and cross the Pont Neuf, walk through the school's grand gates and study in the elegant nineteenth-century building, the chic Boulevard Saint-Germain on one side and the Louvre on the other, Parisian style to her left and classical art to her right. After she finished her course, Sara decided to follow Alex and Jacques into the garment trade, not in couture or as a tailor in the Pletzl, but rather something in between. She got a job at a wholesale clothing supplier making patterns for fabrics sold to the mass market. Decades later, she would show her sons some of the designs she had made: patterns full of color and swirling lines, often with paisley shapes—a psychedelic rejection of the brown drabness of her childhood and the antiseptic, linear whiteness of the sanatoriums. Like Alex, she knew life had more than what she had known, and she was seizing it through her designs. Like Henri, she set out to be as Parisian as possible, not because she thought about assimilation, but because Paris fit her as naturally as a silk dress fits a doe-eyed woman in a Renoir painting.

Some people will move to a foreign country and it will still feel foreign after thirty years, their home country always being their baseline for normality. Others will feel naturally at home after a matter of weeks. The relationship one has with a place is as deeply felt as one's relationship with a person. Sometimes the place that fits you best is what was once unimaginably far afield, and other times it will be the street where you grew up; you might find true love with a holiday romance or you might find it with the boy next door. But no matter how much you love your adopted country, it's harder than people think to bury your origins, especially if you move after puberty, as Sara did. The cadences of our thoughts, never mind our speech, tend to be set by then. Most of us still dream of our childhood home, and when we read scenes in novels set in a home, a school, a park, it's the ones we knew from our youth that we picture, no matter how long ago we left them behind. The mind's eye has a way of snapping us back to the past. So do our parents. I moved from New York to London when I was three years younger than Sara, and like her, I quickly felt at ease in my new home. Yet I still have my American accent, thirty years after moving to London, and this is largely because my parents still have theirs. To speak differently from my parents would require a strength of will and lack of self-consciousness I apparently do not have, and as a result, English people still see me as American.

Sara, however, had no such difficulties. Maybe she did dream of Chrzanow, and maybe she thought of her home on Kostalista when she read books, but she never mentioned it. None of the Glass siblings did. They never pointed to a building and said, "Oh, that reminds me of our school back in Chrzanow," never compared a street in Paris to Aleja Henryka. Chaya never spoke French, and with her heavily accented Polish and Yiddish, she reminded her children with every syllable of their origins. Perhaps because Sara lived with her until she was twenty-six, her crisp French was occasionally sprinkled with the odd Polish or Yiddish expression—when she was tired she would say, "Je suis *feshluffen*," and when she had to carry something she *schlepped* it. But in the main, her identity was wholly rooted in France. I was amazed to discover Sara was as Polish as I am American, because while I come across like a nationality mongrel, she never seemed anything other than French to me.

But while I will always have happy associations with the city of my childhood, Sara did not have that luxury. Her memories of her hometown were terrible: the poverty, the pogroms, her father's protracted death. She left it physically and she also left it mentally. There was no home behind her that she even had the option of returning to; it had disappeared behind her like the ground crumbling away beneath the feet of a cartoon character frantically running for safety. So when she made herself over as French, it was partly because she wanted to, but also because she had to.

And France was good to her in return. By her early twenties she was working in a job she loved and living near the brothers she adored, in a city that made her heart expand just by looking at it. Her beloved cousin whom she played with in childhood, Rose Ornstein, had married a doctor named Herman Brenner, a close friend of Rose's brother Alex Ornstein. Dr. Brenner was very kind to Sara, helping her manage her pleurisy when she was back in Paris, and Sara often went to visit him and Rose in their apartment nearby. She would look around at their happy home and dream of a time she, too, might have her own apartment, away from her mother. And just then, she met a man.

His name has long since vanished in history, because Sara never spoke about him later in life, and her brothers avoided the subject. But he was, Sonia later told Sara's sons, a dental student, Jewish, a socialist, and she loved him. Soon after they met, they were engaged. There are glimpses of him in the photo album I found in my grandmother's closet, or at least of a man who looks like he probably was him: dark haired and young, and in the one photo that survives of them together, handsome and smartly dressed, on a picnic with a group of friends, her arm looped casually through his. As Sara walked to work on that cold morning in February 1937, hours away from when her life would change, she thought about their imminent wedding, and perhaps especially about her life after the wedding. She would move out of her mother's apartment at last, and her life would truly begin. Henri and Jacques were happy in 1937 because they were happily married; Alex was happy because he loved his work. Sara was about to have both professional and marital contentment. She was at that wonderful point in a young person's life when it feels like everything is about to begin and the world seems fringed with joy. And then that evening, when she came home from work, her mother told her that Alex was coming over for supper and he was bringing some colleagues.

The week before in Berlin, Adolf Hitler had given a two-hour-long speech to mark the fourth anniversary of the Nazis' seizure of power in Germany. In a typically rambling and demented speech he promised that "the National Socialist Movement will prevent the Jewish people from intruding themselves among all the other nations as elements of internal disruption, under the mask of honest world-citizens, and thus gaining power over these nations."[1] In France, the ostensibly liberal Popular Front government was adopting a hard-line stance to refugees, as they knew Hitler's rise would mean more Jews would come to France looking for asylum, and this, they concluded, would be problematic. "The problem of German refugees has far more serious demographic ramifications than any other refugee problem has ever had, and it must therefore incline us toward prudence," read one internal foreign ministry memorandum from a few months earlier.[2] The French art world, as Alex knew, had already shut out the Jewish artists in the country.

Sara would not have been thinking about any of that. Alex, however, very much was, as he walked up the stairs to his mother and sister's apartment on that February evening in 1937. And walking behind him was a couple and a thirty-five-year-old man.

When Sara later described this meeting to her children and grand-children, she would tell it quietly, shyly, self-deprecatingly, focusing on the practicalities of how she ended up in the United States. Alex and the second man told it with more enthusiasm and bluster, proud of their active roles in this tale. Sonia had a more wry take on the proceedings. But this is the only story in the history of my family about which there was never any disagreement. Everyone agreed about who was there, what they said, what they thought, and what happened next. But at the time, only one person in the room understood what was actually going on and how this story would likely play out. And that person was definitely not Sara.

The three guests were American: Oscar and Rosa Kellerman,* and Bill Freiman; and he was tall—taller even than Henri. None of the Americans spoke French, and none of the Glasses spoke English, but Bill spoke Yiddish so he acted as translator. They all sat around Chaya's kitchen table—Alex, Sara, the Kellermans, Bill. The Kellermans, Bill explained, were in Paris to do business with Alex, and Bill was going to travel around the Alps once the Kellermans didn't need him any-more—had Sara ever visited the Alps? Sara had no wish to talk about the sanatoriums, so she shook her head. Anyway, there wasn't much room to talk because Alex, as usual, filled the room with his words, saying he'd brought his guests here because he promised them the best kosher food in the whole of Paris, and he talked about which famous person had worn his coat this week and what magazine he'd been in last week. Sara couldn't figure out the relationship between the Kellermans and Mr. Freiman: the Kellermans were obviously married, but, as she would tell her children years later, Mrs. Kellerman seemed to be flirting with Mr. Freiman, plucking at his sleeve, batting her lashes at him, trying to get something from him—attention, acknowledgment—which he clearly had no wish to give. Instead, confusingly, he stared only at her as he told jokes about the things he'd seen in Paris. He said how happy he was to be getting some good Jewish food at last because the French food was

* Because I couldn't track down their descendants, I have not used their real names.

intolerable, and he made jokes about that, too. But Sara never really liked jokes, at least not the kind he was making. He was handsome, but his Yiddish was coarse, rough, working class, and he made no attempt to hide that. Anyway, she'd always preferred men who looked more like her father and Jacques, dark and delicate. With those bright blue eyes and a big handlebar mustache, he was like a cowboy in a Hollywood movie. Sara had never liked cowboy movies: she liked French actors like Maurice Chevalier and Charles Boyer, so chic and elegant. This American, with his jokes and his broad chest, was more like John Wayne.

"Dinner is ready," said Chaya, bringing out the food and taking her seat.

Mr. Kellerman ate hungrily, apparently unaware of or unbothered by his wife's increasingly obvious flirtations with Bill. Sara, as usual, picked at her food, and when Bill asked if she worked, Alex answered for her:

"She's an artist, I told you—really nice paintings, and such a beauty herself all the famous artists want to paint her," he said, to Sara's confusion. Not only was that not true but Alex never spoke that way about her. Sara mostly kept her head down. but every time she looked up, she noticed Bill was staring at her and it unnerved her, so she quickly looked down again. Then, just as Alex was about to launch into another story about his great fashion successes, Bill interrupted him.

"You are the most beautiful woman I have ever seen and I am completely in love with you," he said, looking straight at Sara.

The room went silent.

"Come to America with me next month. I'll get you a return ticket so you can go back if you want. But come with me, I'm an honest, hardworking man and I'll take care of you," he continued, reaching his arm across the table.

Sara did not reach back to take his hand. Instead she made a forced laugh.

"Is this the famous American sense of humor?" she asked.

But he shook his head, shaking off her hint.

"I am not joking, miss. I fell in love with you the minute I saw you. Come with me. I will look after you. I promise," he said.

Sara looked to Alex for help, but for once he said nothing. Her mother also sat there silently. Mrs. Kellerman couldn't understand what was happening but she had a good idea, and she looked like she was about to burst with fury. Only Mr. Kellerman kept eating, utterly unfazed by the scene in front of him. Sara realized no one was going to help her here, so she told Bill that he was clearly drunk and if he didn't stop it she would have to ask him to leave.

Dinner continued awkwardly, with Bill pointedly staring at her and Sara pointedly staring down at her plate. At least, she thought, after this dinner she wouldn't have to see him again. It would be over.

It was not over. Alex brought the American over two more times that week for dinner—without the Kellermans, at least—and both times the scene replayed itself, with him telling Sara that he loved her. If she thought she would be free of him once he finally sailed back to America on March 2, she had once again underestimated him. As soon as he was back home a week later, the phone calls began. Every few days he called her on her building's shared phone, begging her to come join him, telling her he loved her, promising to treat her well. Just one transatlantic phone call in those days would have been a big deal; a dozen was akin to him sending her diamonds. And he continued to beg her to come to America.

Initially she scoffed at his proposals, but Alex started to push her to accept them. (It had been Alex, of course, who gave Bill Sara's building's phone number.) He told her the Nazis were coming and were going to kill them all. This invitation to America was a gift from God and if she turned it down she was as stupid as Mila. If she went to America she would be able to get the rest of them out of Europe—and if she didn't, she was condemning them to death.

"You're going to kill us, is that what you want? You marrying this guy is our last chance," Alex would tell her, while she cried in a chair.

Other times, he would try a different tactic, one covered more in sugar than vinegar:

"He's a millionaire on Park Avenue, he works in the fashion business— what more could you want? He's a handsome guy, and so tall! Taller even than Henri! I've known him for years, he's a great guy," he would say, smilling at her, stroking her pale hand. One man was pulling her to America and the other pushing her, and between them she started to break.

Eventually she went to Henri for help. What should she do? She didn't want to leave her home, her fiancé, her family. But if she didn't, would they all be killed by the Germans? Henri sighed. While he didn't follow the news quite as closely as Alex, he certainly knew about what was happening in Europe, mainly because of Sonia. She read newspapers every day, in multiple languages, and she had been warning Henri about Hitler for years. Henri also had kept some friends from his time in Danzig, and so he knew very well about how that city had been taken over by the Nazis in 1933, and how the Jews had had to flee. Meanwhile, Sonia heard frequently from her family scattered around Poland about the rise of fascist groups there. So when Henri had mentioned Alex's plan to Sonia the week before, after having heard about it from his mother, Sonia said unhesitatingly, "She should go." They'd all lived through pogroms and terror before. The prospect of any of these things returning was not an abstract concept to them.

"You should go," Henri told Sara.

"And that's when your grandmother knew she was going," Sonia later told me.

Sara went to Rose and Herman Brenner's apartment and cried, and they told her she should listen to Henri—maybe Rose and Herman would come live in America, too, one day. Who knew what might happen with the world's politics going the way they were? In what must have been a state close to shock, Sara began to accept that she was going to America to marry a man she didn't know and liked less. She would never have done it just to save herself. But for her whole family? Of course she went.

Alex and Jacques had tried to save their family by going to war. Henri would do his part through his work. The only option open to Sara was the one that countless women had been forced to do before her: marry someone she did not love. It is the traditional form of female sacrifice, so common that it was considered at the time expected and unremarkable.

What would have been extraordinary, in the eyes of those around her then, is if she'd refused to do it.

But how did she explain any of this to her fiancé? Did she say good-bye at all, or just disappear for good? How do you tell the love of your life, with whom you're planning a life, that you're leaving him to marry someone you barely met? Her photo album of her life in France in the 1930s is a wordless yet eloquent testimony of not what she said, but how she felt about leaving behind her love and her life. At some point, she diligently went through it and either tore out whole photos and ripped them up or, with her thumbnail, scored out the faces of the people in the pictures so she wouldn't have to remember them. (She carefully left photos of Henri, Sonia, Jacques, and Alex alone—she didn't have to forget them.) Someone picked up some of the pieces, glued them back together, and stuck them in the album. Initially I assumed it was Sara, having remorsefully mended her photos after destroying them in a fit of high emotion. But my father said it was most likely his father, "walking behind her and picking up the pieces of the photos and tap-ing them together as quickly as she could destroy them." Her husband always thought she was so beautiful, it pained him to see any photos of her destroyed. And then, after her rage had passed and she saw her photos restored, she saved them in her shoebox, where they were safe but she didn't have to look at them. But whoever did the repairing, they couldn't—or didn't—replace the faces she had gouged out, so in several photos my grandmother is standing in Paris, smiling happily, holding the arm of a man with no face—a ghost, a vanished past.

On June 3, 1937, she sailed on the SS *Manhattan* from Le Havre to New York on a ticket Bill sent over for her. "Sara Ryltfa Glass, drafts-man" was how she was described on the passenger list, and in the box for nationality someone wrote "Polish" only to cross that out and write "Heb"—"Hebrew." As in Poland, her Jewishness was now seen as more relevant than her born nationality. As she sailed off, she watched France fade away, the only place she'd ever been happy. She had nothing to think about over the weeklong journey but what she had left behind.

Bill met Sara at the dock. He had a big smile on his face—she did not, but she was relieved that at least the Kellermans weren't with him. They got in his car and as they drove she focused on the sights around her, trying to familiarize herself with this new land she was expected to call home: the cars, the clothes, the advertisements on billboards in a language she did not understand. Next to her, Bill chattered away in Yiddish over the noise of the engine, and when she finally focused on what he was saying, she realized a couple things pretty quickly: he was not a millionaire, he did not live on Park Avenue, and he did not work in the fashion industry. It turned out he barely knew Alex at all. He lived in Farmingdale, Long Island, where he ran a Texaco gas station. Alex had completely lied to her, and the few sketchy images she'd had of her life in the States—living in the city, sharing a life with someone as interested in fashion as her—dissolved into nothing. Instead, she would be living in the middle of what was essentially nowhere, with a man whose life had no connection to her interests and passions at all. But it was too late to go back, because as soon as she accepted Bill's ticket and got on the ship her fate was fixed. Two weeks to the day that her ship docked in New York, she became Mrs. William Freiman.

In Paris, Sara had found a city that encouraged her aspirations and inspired her every day with its beauty. Farmingdale, Long Island, was not Paris. Back in 1937 most of the town's businesses were located on Main Street: the pharmacy, the hardware store, the bank. Kids rode their bicycles up and down it all day in the summer, swerving around cars parked diagonally in front of glass-fronted stores. People lived on side streets and dead ends in identical two-story houses, most of which had an American flag either affixed to the roof or on a pole in the front lawn. There was a cinema in the town, but that was mainly for the kids. When the adults wanted entertainment, they would go to one another's houses for supper and gossip about their neighbors. It was called Farmingdale, Long Island, but it was really Small Town, America.

Sara Glass shortly before she traveled to America

Farmingdale was formed by a series of early-twentieth-century American phenomena. New York, uniquely in the United States back then, had excellent train lines and, as a result, the city was one of the earliest examples of urban flight, with people increasingly moving out of the city and commuting in to work. The American suburbs started to emerge, as immigrants who had arrived in New York in the late nineteenth century realized in the early twentieth century that, instead of living in dirty and diseased tenements on the Lower East Side of Manhattan, they could instead move to comparatively bright and spacious houses outside the city. Suburbia is often depicted as quintessential Americana, but in many cases it was at least partly molded by immigrants, and Farmingdale was, by the time Sara arrived, largely populated by second-generation working-class German and Italian immigrants, who might not have spoken English at home but firmly considered themselves to be American. Just as the suburbs were starting to boom in eastern Long Island, the American aviation industry arrived. Long Island was a natural airfield: situated on the west of the Atlantic, close but not too close to one of America's biggest cities, with large flat plains for takeoffs and landings. When Charles

Lindbergh made his famous transatlantic flight in 1927, he took off from Roosevelt Field, thirteen miles from Farmingdale. This was the golden age of the American aviation industry, and thriving aircraft companies, such as Liberty, Grumman, Republic, Ranger, and Fairchild, needed a huge number of workers. This coaxed yet more people out of the city and into the Long Island suburbs. By the mid-1930s, Farmingdale's population had doubled in twenty years to 3,500.

So Farmingdale looked very American and was shaped by American social shifts. But Sara would also have found it in some ways grimly reminiscent of Chrzanow.

Whereas Chrzanow's name came from the Polish word for horseradish, Farmingdale's original name was the similarly prosaic Hardscrabble. By the 1930s, it was populated by working-class Catholics and Jews, and when Sara arrived, it was, despite the nearby aircraft manufacturers, still a largely rural community; many of her neighbors were potato farmers. And while there obviously weren't pogroms in Farmingdale, there were other problems.

"There was also a lot of racism in the town," William Rappaport, who ran Farmingdale's pharmacy back then, told me. "The John Birch Society had a big presence in Farmingdale, especially during the war. There were marches, meetings, and open anti-Semitism. And that made the Jewish community especially tight-knit."

Alongside the racism, there was, Rappaport said, a suspicion of "difference": "Aspirations, cultural interests, all these were seen as weird, and anything that made you different was weird. So even though the city was just a train ride away, no one would think of going there to see a museum or play. You might go to Brooklyn to see relatives, but that was it. Even reading the *New York Times* was a sign of overintellectualism," he said with a smile. Instead, people were expected to read the local paper, the *Farmingdale Post*.

As in Chrzanow, another small town, there was a feeling that what Farmingdale had to offer should suffice, and anyone who wanted more was getting above themselves—and nothing was worse than that. There were few places less suited to a young Francophile with a love of culture and beauty and with ambitions for a glamorous, fulfilled life than Farmingdale, 1937.

When I visited Farmingdale on a hot spring day, I was struck by how similar it felt to Chrzanow still. Both are pleasant and clean, with pretty streets and friendly people. But it has not been easy for small towns to adjust to the twenty-first century, and on the day I was there Farmingdale felt as silent as an abandoned ranch in an old Western, even on a weekday afternoon. There were vacant storefronts, and the family-run stores had been crushed by the big chains and out-of-town shopping centers. While there are still some aviation companies in Long Island, many such as Grumman have long since closed down and left. With big cities just down the road (Krakow for Chrzanow, Manhattan for Farmingdale), how do you stop the young people leaving as soon as possible, desperate for something to do other than hang out on the same streets they've been hanging out on since they were kids? When I left and returned to the nearby cities where I was staying, it was like slipping from a faded sepia photo into a three-dimensional film. And that's exactly how it felt, in reverse, for Sara, arriving in Farmingdale from Paris eighty years earlier.

Farmingdale was waiting for her when she arrived, and not especially warmly.

"Everyone knew about Bill's French bride long before she turned up," said William Rappaport.

Given how little Bill himself knew about her, their knowledge of Sara was presumably limited to the fact that she was French and she was to be his bride. This was more than enough for them.

"What's wrong with American girls? They not enough for you, Bill?" people asked him.

"If you didn't find anything you wanted in Farmingdale, couldn't you have just gone to New York?" others asked.

Some were simply so stumped as to why handsome Bill would marry a Frenchwoman, they assumed he must have gotten her pregnant while he was in Paris. She was probably one of those kinds of Frenchwomen.

And these questions did not stop once Sara arrived. People asked them of Bill in front of Sara, taking it for granted she wouldn't understand, and not really caring if she did. And soon enough she did understand, because she was good at languages. She heard them muttering about how her husband had had many lady friends, and maybe he still did, maybe that's why he went into the city so much, and she heard them talking about how unfriendly she seemed, how snooty, how superior.

And she probably was snooty or, more accurately, aloof. She realized that none of these people was interested in art, or fashion, or culture—all the things that represented to her high-mindedness, sophistication. These people, it seemed to her, were little different from the Polish peasants. And like her brothers Henri and Alex, she felt that a lack of aspiration was an admission of a lack of soul. Only those who are dead inside fail to want more than the little half-inch of life they've been given.

But Sara was also shy and sad, and these are often mistaken for snobbishness. Talking about her snobbishness was a convenient smoke screen for the simple fact that none of her neighbors wanted to be friends with Sara because she was a foreigner, even though most of them had immigrant parents themselves. But then, they wanted to be American and she did not. She would never be one of them, because she didn't want to be.

"She was a French lady in a rough Long Island town," my father's cousin Ann Horowitz, who grew up in Farmingdale, told me. "She wasn't ever really going to be accepted."

She tried to make a life there: she decorated her and Bill's home in Farmingdale as beautifully as she could, and breakfast and dinner were always on the table on time for him. She would go for walks and get to know the town. But days would go by when she wouldn't speak to anyone but her husband. And on days when he didn't come home, she spoke to no one.

Bill's family were the only people who talked to Sara, as they could talk to her in Yiddish. They all lived close by: his mother, Rose, who lived with them part of the time; his older brothers, Jack and Mike; and his younger sisters, Rita and Sadie. The few surviving children of Bill's siblings, all of whom are in at least their seventies now, stressed to me how much their parents liked Sara: how pretty they all thought she was, how kind they thought she was, and how protective they were of her when they felt Bill wasn't treating her right.

This may all be true, but it wasn't how it seemed to Sara. When my parents got engaged in 1974, Sara arranged to meet up with my mother, her daughter-in-law-to-be, for the first time. As soon as they were sitting down she spoke, in a terrible emotional rush, of how Bill's family had bullied her when she arrived in the States: they made fun of her accent, she said, of her love of art, and of her interest in clothes. "Why are you interested in *that*?!" she recalled them sneering at her. For almost forty years she'd been waiting for a female relative in whom she could confide the pain she'd felt on her arrival in America, and it had festered inside her for decades.

Maybe Bill's siblings did like her, but just didn't know how to reach out to her, or were bewildered by how different she was from them. And maybe she was just too homesick to understand them. But if she felt alienated from her in-laws, that was nothing compared with how she felt about her husband.

Bill was kind—Alex hadn't lied about that, at least—and he really did love her. That turned out to be true, too. He loved to show off his French bride—so beautiful, so classy—but as far as he was concerned, he'd brought her over, provided her with a little house on Cornelia Street, and she could figure out the rest. He'd done her this incredible favor, rescuing her from Europe—what on earth did she have to complain about? But she did complain. She wasn't nearly as grateful to him as he thought she would be.

In another world their marriage could have worked because, in many ways, they were well matched: they both had religious parents but weren't religious themselves, and they both had dreams of a better life than the ones they were born into. But theirs was a match that was forged in lies and impulse and forced into being by politics and circumstance. It would have been a miracle if it had worked, and neither of their families dealt in miracles.

Sara looked at this American, with his coarse jokes and coarser Yiddish, the way assimilated Jews in Paris looked at people like Chaya and the rest of the Pletzl: Didn't he understand he was supposed to hide those parts of himself? Didn't he want to improve his social standing, and not be seen as just another working-class Jew? And didn't he understand that his behavior reflected negatively on her by association? For Sara, Paris had been her step forward, and this American had pulled her back to a life she thought she'd left behind. Bill was smart, so he sensed how she felt, and it hurt him.

And, most of all, she wanted to be with someone else.

"Your mother left her heart in Paris with that dental student," Sonia later told Sara's sons. The fights started not long after they got married. They got worse when Bill revealed that he wasn't going to help bring the rest of her family over from Paris, because it would cost too much. Sara was devastated: the only reason she had married Bill was because she thought it would get her family out of France, and they would be with her in America. But from Bill's perspective, he was the wronged party here. He had certainly not been told that paying for all of his in-laws to come over was part of the deal—in fact, according to Sonia, Alex had promised to support Bill for the rest of his life if he married Sara. But Bill understood sooner than Sara that the promises Alex made during this whole episode didn't amount to much. Bill was able to shrug off such things; Sara, however, was crushed. She was stuck, and now she really was alone. She had given up everything for something that was worse than nothing.

Sara was desperately unhappy; just how unhappy is apparent from looking at the passenger lists of ships between New York and France between 1937 and 1938. In November 1937, five months after she first arrived in the United States, she went back to Paris, presumably using the return ticket Bill had promised her. She returned to New York one month later, but six months later she made another return trip. Six months after that, in November 1938, she went back again. She returned to New York a month later. On none of those trips was she accompanied by Bill.

She didn't, however, forget him. More than twenty years after Bill died, and more than eighty years after it was originally sent, my uncle Rich found a photo among my grandfather's belongings. It was a studio portrait of my grandmother, and she had sent it to him from Paris on one of her trips. It is dated December 8, 1937, and at the bottom, in my grandmother's handwriting, is the inscription, "Pour mon mari cheri, Paris." Whether distance had made Sara's heart truly grow fonder of Bill is a question only she can answer. It seems more likely to me that she felt a wifely loyalty toward him, knew that he was a good man, and felt some gratitude toward him for that. Few relationships are all black or all white. But what is most apparent is that, just six months after marriage, a schism was growing in Sara that would exist for the rest of her life: wherever she was, she felt she should be somewhere else. When she was in France with her family, she felt she should be in America with her husband, and vice-versa. More than half a century later I would see that divide in her myself.

Who was paying for all those tickets? At approximately $130 for a round-trip in tourist class, there is no way Bill would have been able to afford all these trips to Paris, and while Alex would certainly have paid for Sara to go back to New York once she arrived in Paris, he would not have bought her a return ticket so she could then come back again a year later. Perhaps Herman Brenner, Rose Ornstein's husband, helped, but there is no record of that, and it's unlikely he could have afforded it either.

The truth is, no one knows how Sara made three round-trips between New York and France in eighteen months during 1937 and 1938, because neither she nor Bill ever spoke about it, certainly not to anyone alive now. No one even knew about these trips until I happened to spot her name recurring on the old passenger lists, and it was definitely her: Sara Freiman from Farmingdale, Long Island. But where she once had been described as a draftsman, she was now "h'wife"—a housewife. All dreams gone. It's easy to imagine her running back to Paris, frantic to escape her marriage, and even easier to imagine Alex all but pushing her back up the gangplank to go back to New York. And that cycle might have continued forever had

Sara not realized something by the time she docked back in New York on December 1, 1938: she was two months pregnant.

Ronald Michael Freiman, my father, was born July 23, 1939. The doctor who performed the birth botched the job so badly that, eighty years later, my dad still has long, deep scars on his temples from where he was dragged out and nearly crushed by the forceps. The first time Sara saw her son, he was, terrifyingly, covered in blood.

"If my head looks like this, imagine what that butcher did to the insides of my mother," my dad would say when asked about the marks.

Sara couldn't run to her family for comfort anymore, not even after her son's traumatic birth. Once the war had started, most civilian ships were used as troop carriers or freighters. She couldn't even write to her family: from 1939, transatlantic mail was being intercepted by British Imperial Censorship in Bermuda, and some was confiscated. From 1941, it was suspended entirely between America and France, but Sara could not have reached her relatives anyway, because by this point they were all in hiding. For the next three years Sara had no idea if her family was alive or dead.

The only contact she had with anyone vaguely connected to her old life was her occasional correspondence with Alex's friend Kisling, who was at this point living in California, but he was just as ignorant about her family's well-being as she was.

He wrote to her from Beverly Hills on December 6, 1942:

My dear Mrs. Freiman,

I think of you often, I think of poor Alex from whom you are cut off, I think of the worries that is causing you. Really, we have no luck, my poor friend. Each of us who is born over there we are bearing a cross but what can we do? The only weapon we have is hope for this will soon be over and that we will find them all soon again. If you have a moment send me your news, I don't dare ask you the news of Alex of which you probably have more information than me.

I hope your husband is well, as well as your charming child,

Maurice Kisling (Kiki)

Bill took hundreds of photos of her from this era: despite all their fighting, and her disappointing lack of affection, he was always so proud of his beautiful French bride, who made their home so much more stylish than those of his siblings. But few have looked more like a stranger in a strange land than my grandmother in these photos: always in her distinctly French clothing and always standing next to various forms of Americana—a flag, a diner, a supersize car—she is like an exotic explorer among the natives. In one of my favorite photos of my grandmother, taken in 1941, she is wearing a jaunty little three-cornered hat with a peaked top and a beautiful belted coat with exaggerated lapels that was made by Alex. As ever, she is in heels and her makeup and hair are perfect, and she is bending over a little boy—my father—in a snowsuit. She could be a young mother in the Tuileries or on the Champs-Élysées—except she is standing next to a gas pump because she is at my grandfather's gas station in Farmingdale. A friend of mine used to refer to this photo as "granny at the gas station," but I think of it more as Dorothy back in black-and-white Kansas, but in this version she had never wanted to leave Technicolor Oz.

In December 1943, Sara gave birth to her second child—another boy. As she lay in bed recovering from the birth, she listened to the news reports about the Battle of Berlin, in which, on December 17, the Royal Air Force nearly destroyed Berlin's railway system. The Royal Air Force—RAF. The initials kept being repeated in the report: these were the people who were trying to save Europe from the people killing her family, Sara thought. RAF. She named her baby Richard Allen Freiman, known as Rich.

Sara had longed for a girl, whom she could dress in pretty clothes and whose long hair she could style. A girl who could be her confidante, her friend. But she adored her sons, and she poured the love she couldn't give to her husband into her boys. She was a demonstratively affectionate mother, naturally gentle and loving but also desperate to justify to herself the choice she had made that resulted in them being born. If she loved them enough, if they loved her enough, maybe it would have been worth it.

The story of my grandmother confused people—particularly, I noticed, Jewish Americans who generally, and understandably, assume that any story about escaping the war by coming to America is a happy one.

Sara with Ronald and Richard in Farmingdale, mid-1940s

That narrative is a cornerstone of the Jewish American story, yet Sara's story complicated it. When I was ten, I gave a presentation about the Glasses to my Hebrew school class in New York, and although I didn't really have the words to describe my grandmother's unhappiness, I knew enough to say that she'd never wanted to leave Paris.

"But of course she was happy once she got to America, whereas her brothers were very unfortunate to be in France," my teacher, Ms. Meyers, concluded for me, thinking she was being helpful.

I thought of my grandmother, stuck in Miami at that point, still homesick after half a century. And I thought of my great-uncles, Alex and Henri, who were by then happy and wealthy in Paris. Individual lives are always more complicated than sweeps of history, but how could I explain this to Ms. Meyers in my Hebrew school classroom that, by way of interior décor, had a picture of the gates of Auschwitz on one wall? I didn't want to give the wrong answer. So I nodded and sat down at my desk.

Sara had done what she'd had to in order to survive the war. But in saving herself she lost everything that had made her life worth living. Other things took their place—her children, eventually her grandchildren—so I can't say she made the wrong choice, and she would never have said that either. But no, she wasn't happy when she got to America. She was grateful to it for the safety it provided her and the material comforts it brought her. But looking at the photos of her in Farmingdale—her makeup so perfect, her face so sad—it's clear the price she paid for survival was painfully high. "She moved to America but, emotionally, she never really unpacked her bags there," my father said. Sara endured a specifically female tragedy: she gave up not just her true love but her dreams and professional fulfillment in exchange for protection by marriage. Alex got a medal for going to war, and Jacques could send Sara his metal prison plate. But no one was going to give her any plaudits for what she did. While her brothers performed the traditionally masculine roles of carrying out acts of extraordinary bravery, Sara endured the more feminine role of private self-erasure.

Yet as unhappy as she was, divorce was never an option for her. Americans certainly got divorced in the 1940s—in fact, the divorce rate spiked after World War II, when couples who had rushed to marry before the war quickly regretted that decision when the men returned from fighting. But the stigma was still terrible, and like many women of her generation and afterward, Sara could in no way survive as the single mother of two without any kind of familial support. Anyway, that was not what Jewish women like her did. She knew what her role was now: it was to make Bill's meals and look after her boys. When she moved to America, Sara's internal life split: outwardly she existed in the present, but inside she was thinking always of what had been and what could have been, if the war hadn't happened, if she'd stayed and somehow survived, if she moved back there now, if if if. She'd only had a few years of happiness in Paris, and even fewer healthy and happy ones, a mere blink. But the ghosts of those years haunted her. After the war, she promised herself, she would go back to Paris. And thus began Sara's long wait, one that would be much longer than she realized at the time, for her life to begin again.

Chapter 7

BILL—AMERICA

America, 1900s—1930s

Bill had never expected or even especially wanted to go to France, or, as he called it, "Europe." But when his neighbors Oscar and Rosa Kellerman invited him to come with them on a business trip, he thought, *Hey, you only live once.* So he tagged along just for the hell of it.

Except it was possibly for more than the hell of it. Bill was an extremely handsome man, and a good-looking single guy of thirty-five in a small town will attract the eyes of the ladies—one of the ladies whose eyes he caught being Rosa Kellerman. Whether Bill and Rosa actually had an affair no one will ever know, but Sara never forgot how much Rosa flirted with him when she met them in Paris. When I asked my father about it, he said that, thinking about the way Rosa would still moon around his dad, years after the trip to Paris, reminded him of *The Bridges of Madison County*, "not that I would confuse Rosa Kellerman with Meryl Streep." Certainly the ships' passenger lists suggest something was up between them. Even though the Kellermans traveled to Europe frequently for their work in the clothing trade—three times in 1937 alone—they never traveled together. Instead, when Rosa sailed to France from New York in December 1936, her husband had sailed a month earlier. But a certain William Freiman sailed two days after her from the same dock. And when she sailed back in February 1937, she left from Cherbourg. William's ship also left from Cherbourg, a few days later, but her husband, Oscar, didn't return to Farmingdale until April, and he sailed from Southampton. Were William and Rosa staying together in New York and Cherbourg? Sara would have said yes.

If Bill went to France in 1936 to enjoy a flirtation with a married woman under her husband's nose, it wouldn't have been wildly out of character. Bill was many things—funny, handsome, ambitious—but perhaps his most notable quality back then was mischievousness. He was the baby boy in his family, the fourth of five, and he always had a reputation as the cheeky one and a flirt. Among my grandmother's belongings I found a photo of him judging what is clearly a beauty competition. He is standing on stage in a suit holding a microphone, his dark hair slicked back, and on either side of him is a woman in a bathing suit, each wearing a sash that reads *1936*, the year before he sailed to Paris. His pencil moustache is stretching out with his wide smile. He looks pretty pleased with himself.

He and Oscar Kellerman were not close friends—in fact, they hardly socialized at all. But Oscar had learned from his last trip to Paris that he would need to bring someone who spoke either Yiddish or French in order to talk to the fashion merchants there, and it was a lot easier to find a Yiddish speaker than a French one in Farmingdale. It was not explained to Bill that he would be acting as an unpaid translator on this trip; instead, he planned to ditch the Kellermans as soon as they docked in France so he could tour the country by motorcycle and ski in the Alps. But, they told him, if he wanted his return ticket, that would have to wait until after their meeting with this Maguy fellow.

The Kellermans owned a wholesale clothing business, and the reason they traveled to Paris so often was to buy patterns and fabrics on the cheap. Alex had become one of their pattern suppliers, because it was by doing jobs like this that he was able to keep his couture business afloat. He schmoozed the people who ran these companies, but he loathed selling his beautiful designs to what he described as "those *schmatte* merchants," tacky Americans who would tell him to design a sleeve differently so that it wouldn't drag in their macaroni and cheese.

But one American Alex liked right away was Bill. "Your grandfather was a smart man," he would tell me, even though they hardly ever saw one another due to Bill's longstanding belief that he'd been to Europe once and there was no need for him to go again. Bill couldn't have given Alex any money, and he certainly didn't have any power when Alex met him, so I often wondered at Alex's fondness for my grandfather. After all, the number of people Alex truly liked could be counted on one hand, and Bill was very much one of them. He was smart, no question, and tall, which was always an important factor for Alex. But Alex's feelings for Bill seemed to go beyond mere facts and I suspect they lay in how they met, which was through the Kellermans.

Bill disliked Oscar Kellerman about as much as Alex, and neither of them was any good at disguising their feelings. Alex used to recall how he liked Bill so much when he met him with the Kellermans that he invited him over for dinner, and it's easy for me to imagine how that original meeting went, with Bill translating for the Kellermans and him and Alex quickly understanding their mutual loathing of these cheap clothing merchants.

"Tell that piece of dirt that he can go to hell if he thinks he's getting this pattern for less than forty francs," I could picture Alex saying.

"How about thirty francs if he promises his wife won't wear it?" Bill would have responded.

"Deal!"

"Mr. Maguy says you can have the pattern for seventy francs."

"Seventy! That's ridiculous!"

"He says Eleanor Roosevelt bought this pattern when she was last in Paris."

"Wow, really? We'll take it!"

And so on.

I never saw Alex and Bill in the same room together, but I'd have liked to. In some ways they were very similar.

"And you must meet my sister," Alex said to Bill at the end of the meeting with the Kellermans. "She's an absolute beauty, a model. Healthy, fun, and very keen on American men. She always said she wanted to marry one. You're just her type!"

A pretty French girl? Sure, why not. Just for the hell of it.

To Sara and Alex, Bill Freiman looked like the epitome of America, with his broad shoulders, blue eyes, and fondness for cowboy hats. But like them, he was the product of immigration. And also like them, his name was not what he said it was.

Moses Freiman was born in 1902, in a tenement on the Lower East Side of New York. Although he was American by birth, he, along with his brothers and sisters, spoke only Yiddish until he was seven years old. Like Chaya, his mother never learned the language of the country she lived in, and his father spoke only enough English to work. In their neighborhood back then, that was utterly typical. Like the Glasses, his parents, Sam and Rosy Freiman, came from the Austro-Hungarian Empire. They immigrated to the United States in, respectively, 1893 and 1889. Sam probably came for the reason most Jewish men immigrated to America, which was he was looking for a better life. Rosy's story was a little more complicated: she was running away from her family. According to what she told friends later in life, her parents had arranged a marriage for her when she was a teenager, but after the wedding she realized her husband was gay—or, as she experienced it, had no interest in women. As an uneducated, sheltered, Orthodox teenager in eastern Europe, she had no way of explaining the situation to either herself or her family. So instead, she left the marriage and ran away to America to escape her parents' wrath for disgracing the family, somehow scraping the money together to come to New York. A few years later, she met Sam, the same year he arrived, and the two married. If she had run away from her husband back home, this means that when she married Sam she committed bigamy. But it is unlikely she ever thought about it that way, and it certainly didn't break her marital stride: within a decade, they had five children: Michael, Yakov, Sarah, Moses, and Rivka.

Between 1880 and 1924, two and a half million eastern European Jews emigrated to the United States. Close to 85 percent of them came to New York City, and 75 percent of them settled initially in the Lower East Side.[1] This was America's Pletzl. And as in France, the Americanized Jews—who were largely Reform, or not very observant—were less than thrilled by this influx of foreign, Orthodox Jews into their country: "From a religious point of view, the Russian Jew is further from the American Jew than the American Jew is from a Christian or infidel," one New York Jew told the *New York Times* then.[2] But American Jews felt more secure about their position in their country than their French counterparts did, so they worried less about how these immigrant Jews would reflect on them. Although they occasionally lectured them directly, urging them to leave behind what one of the American Jews at the time described as their "impractical, outlandish and medieval beliefs and customs,"[3] they expected this would happen naturally down the generations. And in the main they were right.

By the time Bill was born in 1902, the Lower East Side was the largest Jewish neighborhood in the world and was known as New York's—and, by extension, America's—Jewish ghetto. But that generalizing term does a disservice to the varieties of immigrants and how they created tiny worlds within the crowded and noisy New York neighborhood. Hungarian Jews lived above Houston Street, Galician Jews between Houston and Grand Streets, Romanian and Levantine Jews between Allen Street and the Bowery, and Russian Jews below Grand Street. The Freiman family—occasionally renamed Fryman by census takers—lived at 102 Allen Street, suggesting Sam and Rosy were actually Romanian, even though the US censuses from the time repeatedly described them, as they later would Sara, as Austrian. The building wasn't especially big, but according to the 1900 census, twenty-two other families lived in it, and that is because it was a tenement building.

By 1900, 90 percent of Jews on the Lower East Side lived in tenements,[4] which were five- or six-story homes that had been subdivided by landlords into apartments for families, most just twenty-five feet wide and one hundred feet long, with barely any light, ventilation, or fresh air, for $12 a week in rent. There was no indoor plumbing, just a lone spigot outside that would supply all the water for the building's tenants to clean, cook, and wash, and only one outhouse per every twenty tenants, although rather than walk all the way downstairs and out in the freezing cold to use it, many would use a chamber pot and simply dump the waste out the window, only occasionally checking to see if anyone was walking below. They didn't even have gaslight until the early 1900s, and residents tended to cook with coal, meaning they were living in what were essential pitch-black caves, and they would have to grope their way through the dark hallways to find the stairway and their apartment, feeling their away along the walls with the flat of their palms. Tenements first emerged on the Lower East Side in the 1860s as a solution to over-crowding, but as immigrants continued to move to New York, and the immigrants who were there continued to have children, the tenements themselves became emblems of overcrowding. A tenement apartment that housed four people in 1870 would, by 1900, be home to ten or twelve. They were dirty, dark, and disease-ridden, but for most immigrant Jews in New York they were home, and the Freimans lived in theirs for twenty years.

When Sam Freiman moved his family into a Lower East Side tenement, he was, like most Jewish immigrants in that neighborhood, illiterate. He worked as a peddler, meaning he sold secondhand clothes and rags from the street, and every day he would have to dodge "loafers"—generally Irish-Americans—who hung around on street corners and outside bars and shouted anti-Semitic abuse at him[5] as he worked in the snow and the rain to earn, at best, pennies. A letter written in 1855, when one-third of Jewish wage earners were peddlers, describes the life of a Jewish peddler in the city:

> When the newly arrived Israelite asks what he shall do to make
> a living, he is most commonly advised to go and peddle. Accord-
> ingly a basket is hastily fixed up and he is hurried into the country.
> The country merchants receive [him] coolly and oppose him step by
> step. An acrimonious feeling takes hold of the pedlar's heart—he is
> disappointed and discouraged, and yet he goes on from day to day,
> changes the basket for the bundle, the bundle for the horse and wagon
> peddling, and finally emerges a sleek, thrifty merchant. Have the
> history of one of these men and you have the history of them all.[6]

Sam never became a sleek and thrifty merchant; instead he did something else that was all too common of his demographic: he abandoned his family. Absconding fathers and husbands were so common among the Lower East Side immigrants that one of the several Yiddish daily newspapers in New York at the time had a regular column devoted to missing men. Sometimes they died in a drunken brawl. Sometimes they died of pneumonia after getting drunk and either falling in the river or falling asleep outside in the bitter New York winter. Most commonly they simply ran off, worn down by trying to provide for the multiple children by selling rags. Bill later told his sons that his father was a drunk who died in the gutter, but none of Sam's children ever knew for certain what happened to their father, other than that he disappeared in 1911 and they never saw him again. Like Chaya when Reuben went off to war, Rosy was suddenly a single mother in a country whose language she never learned, with five children to support on her own, aged between seven and sixteen. But unlike Chaya, she did not have Henri to support her. Instead she had Moses.

Moses was nine when his father vanished and the last of the boys to still be at school. Like almost all Jewish immigrant children in the Lower East Side, Moses's older brothers, Michael and Yakov, dropped out of school at eighth grade, because fourteen was the age when children could get work permits and families in the Lower East Side needed money a lot more than they needed educated kids. Many of these kids worked in sweatshops, sewing garments or rolling cigars from 6 a.m. until 11 p.m. for 50 cents a day, in horrifically perilous conditions. In one single fire in a New York sweatshop in 1911, the year Sam left, 146 workers were killed, half of whom were Jewish teenage girls.[7] Because Moses was the last boy at school, this also meant he was the boy who was most at home and became the man of the house, even though he was still in the single digits. Perhaps for that reason, or maybe it was just always in his nature, Moses started getting into brawls in the neighborhood.

"Your grandfather was the wild child in the family. Always a character," my father's cousin Herb Freiman, the son of my grandfather's oldest brother, Michael, told me.

I'd never met Herb until I started researching this book, and I then spent a day with him in Long Island where he lives, not far from Farmingdale. In fact, despite my grandfather having so many siblings, and all of them living pretty much next door to one another for most of their lives, I knew almost no members of his family. But when I walked into Herb's house and saw him waiting for me on the sofa in his living room, my breath caught in my throat: he was the spitting image of my grandfather, who by that point had been dead for twenty-five years. That same cheeky smile, those same bright blue eyes ("the Freiman eyes," Herb said, knowing what I was thinking), and even though he was hooked up to an oxygen tank, the same inexhaustible jokey demeanor. His cousin Ann, Rivka's daughter, also joined us. She was the only one of my father's cousins that I knew as a child before I started working on this book, and I remembered she'd always been extremely thin and careful about what she ate. That was still the case when we met at Herb's, almost thirty years since we'd last seen one another. When she casually mentioned what she weighed that morning, a low number by anyone's standards, Herb shot back, "Well, Ann, the good news is the circus is going to hire you to be the Fat Lady!" When we then went out to lunch at Herb's club and Ann picked halfheartedly at her salad, he teased her again, saying, "Slow down there, Ann. Eat one more grape and you won't be able to fit in the car!" This was exactly how my grandfather used to talk, and while Sara couldn't stand it and thought it tacky, my sister and I thought he was the funniest guy we'd ever known. Herb was similarly delightful. I wished I'd gotten to know him sooner.

"Bill was born with a stutter, so he probably got into fights about that. But he taught himself to speak elegantly, more elegantly than anyone else in the family. But he fought because he wanted to protect his family," Herb said.

My grandfather did talk elegantly—I'd forgotten that. Eloquent and fast, with an enormous vocabulary, without a hint of a Yiddish accent. He also took care to lose what he called his "Jewish accent," by which he meant the rising inflection and nasal tone that is still a vocal signifier of Jewishness in modern pop culture, in everything from Woody Allen movies to *Curb Your Enthusiasm*. As far as Bill was concerned, it was how his family talked, and he was determined to sound different from them. But if he talked well he wrote even better, always in cursive, so florid it verged on calligraphy, and wonderful long letters full of gossip and advice and philosophical thoughts. He was actually left-handed but, through characteristic force of will, he'd taught himself to write with his right hand so as to be able to use a fountain pen without smearing the ink. You'd have never guessed that he didn't speak English until he was seven and was illiterate until he was ten. And that, of course, was entirely the point. Like Alex, Bill dreamed of a better life than the one he was born into, and the ways he spoke and wrote were an expression of that.

There was a reason I knew almost none of his family: he didn't want me to. They were part of a world he wanted to leave behind.

Life in the tenements was brutal. Newspaper headlines from the time give a sense of the chaos and cost: "Three Perish in Midnight Fire! Flames Sweep Through a Big Five-Storey Tenement! Other Tenants Missing!"[8] "Eight Dead By Fire! Awful Tragedy in Hester Street! Woman Burned to Death in Sight of Crowd! Faces of Tortured People Seen at the Windows!"[9] Being a child in the tenements was especially perilous. All the buildings had yards, but these were hemmed in by other buildings and often were where the outhouse was, so were dark and disgusting. Instead, children preferred to play in the street, but because of the lack of decent lighting, cars and bicycles didn't see them. In 1911, when Moses was nine, 183 children in New York were killed by moving vehicles and a further 381 were hit but survived.[10] There were parks and playgrounds, but these were often far away, meaning a three-year-old would have to walk ten or even twenty blocks, dodging cars, just to play on swings. Some mothers in the tenements— especially those who had been abandoned by their husbands—found life so hard that they would put their children on so-called orphan trains that took poor inner-city children out of the metropolis to live with rural families and essentially work as farmhands. Rosy, fortunately, did not do that, but life would have been extremely hard for all of them. Her income was supplemented by Michael and Yakov working, probably in factories, where they would have earned a couple of dollars a week, and it's possible that Sam occasionally sent the family money from wherever he'd disappeared to, but there was no evidence of this. Ultimately, they would have largely had to depend on Rosy's paltry earnings as a seamstress while each of the children looked after one another, each one hurrying after the other in school until they, too, could leave and earn money.

Moses picked up English quickly when he went to school. But he also desperately wanted to earn money to improve his family's situation generally, and as a child he sold ribbons on the street after school. As a teenager he gave driving lessons. He was always looking for a crack in the wall through which he could crawl and find some money. By 1920, just as the Glasses were leaving Chrzanow, Rosy decided it was time to move her family. This might have been partly because of her youngest son, who got in so many fights that, for his own safety, she needed to get him out of the Lower East Side. But also, this was the trajectory of all Jews who wanted to lift their family into the middle classes—they had to get out of the Lower East Side. Many Jews went uptown, or to Brooklyn or Harlem. A friend told Rosy she should go to "the center of the universe" and so, according to family legend, she closed her eyes and pointed to a place on a map of New York. She landed on Long Island.

By the time the Freimans left the city, the Lower East Side was changing irrevocably. Within a decade, it wouldn't even be largely Jewish anymore but instead became an Italian neighborhood. Cities shift and flux, and today when you walk through the Lower East Side there are pickle stores next to Italian delis next to encroaching designer boutiques. During the 1920s, the Jewish population of the Lower East Side plummeted dramatically, from 260,000 to 100,000,[11] and this was partly because of a situation the Glass family in Paris would have found familiar.

Since the late nineteenth century, Congress had been quietly passing laws banning various groups of people from entering the United States. By the time World War I began, these barred groups included such alleged threats to the American way of life as polygamists, lunatics, and Chinese laborers. In 1916, the American lawyer and eugenicist Madison Grant published his still-influential book *The Passing of the Great Race*, in which he stressed the danger of the changing "stock" of American immigration, with more and more people coming to America from southern and eastern Europe instead of what he deemed to be the more superior countries, in the north and west of the continent. The Nordic race, he wrote, was "being literally driven off the streets of New York City by swarms of Polish Jews" and he urged tighter immigration laws "if the higher races are to be maintained."[12] Almost exactly one hundred years later, the president of the United States, Donald Trump, would echo Grant when he told members of Congress in January 2018 that America needed more immigrants from Norway and fewer from "shithole countries," by which he meant El Salvador, Haiti, and certain African nations. Trump was widely condemned for it at the time, but his poll numbers did not suffer. Like Grant's in 1916, it felt like his words were prying open a box of ghouls that America seems to reopen every century. In the first two years of Trump's presidency, the FBI reported a rise in hate crimes motivated by race in America,[13] and attacks against Muslim, South Asian, and Middle Eastern communities rose by 45 percent.[14]

After World War I, national feelings of patriotism made their familiar transition into expressions of racism and anti-Semitism. Just like in France, Jews were associated with radicals, Bolsheviks, and European revolution, and anti-Semitism became not just acceptable but, in many circles in the United States, respectable. The *Dearborn Independent,* a weekly newspaper established by the notoriously anti-Semitic Henry Ford, had, in 1925, a circulation of 900,000, making it the second most popular newspaper in the United States at the time, because it was distributed in all of Ford's car dealerships. At that time, it launched a vicious campaign against so-called Jewish influence in the United States, spurred on by Ford's certainty that Jews started wars in order to profit from them. "I know who started the First World War: German-Jewish bankers," he was widely quoted as saying. Throughout the 1920s, the *Dearborn Independent* ran articles with headlines such as "The International Jew: The World's Foremost Problem" and "Jewish Power and America's Money Famine." In case readers hadn't grasped Ford's point, the *Dearborn Independent* reprinted and distributed *The Protocols of the Elders of Zion,* the already discredited forgery that claimed to show Jewish plans for world domination. Ford eventually closed down the paper and issued an apology, written for him by the then chairman of the American Jewish Committee, Louis Marshall. But even though his views had been criticized at the time, by Jews and non-Jews alike, he was capturing elements of the national mood. F. Scott Fitzgerald acknowledged as much in *The Great Gatsby* when the oafish character Tom Buchanan talks airily about how "if we don't look out the white race will be—will be utterly submerged." Through Tom, Fitzgerald captured—as journalist Pankaj Mishra put it—"a deepening panic among America's Anglophile ruling class."[15]

Grant's book was hugely popular and had enormous political influence. He was close friends with Presidents Theodore Roosevelt and Herbert Hoover, and the former publicly praised his book. He also knew the American politician Albert Johnson, who sponsored the Immigration Restriction Act of 1921, which set a limit of 350,000 immigrants allowed in each year. This, Johnson wrote, would help prevent America from being polluted by hordes of "abnormally twisted," "unassimilable" Jews, "filthy, un-American and often dangerous in their habits."[16] The bill passed easily, but it did not go as far as its supporters had hoped. So in 1924, Johnson, along with Senator David A. Reed of Pennsylvania, turned to Grant as a self-appointed expert on world racial data for statistics that would support tightening quotas on immigrants from southern and eastern European countries. The Immigration Act of 1924, or the Johnson-Reed Act, as well as targeting Jewish immigrants, effectively banned all Arabs, East Indians, and Asians from entering the country. Jewish politicians from across the country, alongside many Catholic ones, tried to fight the bill, defending immigrants' contributions to the country. But it wasn't enough, and the bill passed overwhelmingly in both the House and the Senate.

Grant's influence wasn't limited to 1920s America. It is not a surprise that a book that advocated segregating races with "undesirable" and "inferior" traits, described Jews as "social discards," and endorsed the "one-drop rule"* to prevent mixing between the races would be welcomed in 1930s Germany. Grant's book was the first non-German book the Nazis ordered to be reprinted when they came to power, and Adolf Hitler told Grant, "This book is my Bible." The same book President Theodore Roosevelt described in 1917 as "a capital book; in purpose, in vision, in grasp of the facts our people most need to realize"[17] would, less than

---

* A term from the Jim Crow laws, which classified anyone with black ancestry as black.

twenty years later, become inspiration for the Nazis. Hitler also praised America's restrictions on naturalization as proof that America endorsed the Nazi project, and ultimately the Immigration Act helped to facilitate the Holocaust because it prevented thousands of European Jews from escaping to America, including Anne Frank and her family.[18] Sometimes America isn't quite as far away from fascism as it thinks.

Grant set out to change New York's racial mix and, in that regard, he partially succeeded. Reed's immigration laws had an enormous effect on immigration in general, Jewish immigration in particular, and on the Lower East Side specifically. In 1920, the year before the first of Johnson's laws was passed, there were 800,000 new arrivals into the country, among them 120,000 Jews. By 1925, the numbers had fallen to 295,000 and 10,000, respectively.

When President Trump arrived in office in 2017, he issued an executive order that he himself referred to on Twitter as a "Muslim ban," barring the citizens of seven Muslim countries from entering the United States for a period of ninety days. (Prior to this in 2015, during the presidential campaign, he had called for "a complete and total shutdown" of the country's borders to Muslims, and suggested establishing a government database of all American Muslims, not unlike the 1940 French census of Jews.) Many people—politicians, journalists, Nobel laureates, leaders of Jewish organizations—described the so-called ban as "un-American." But sadly, it was only un-American inasmuch as what America should be; in regard to what America actually is, it was all too American, and Trump comes from a long line of white men who have set out to make America racist again. President Trump was not the first or even the most successful American politician to set out to ban Muslims from the country, and this is a shameful truth about a country that was founded by immigrants for immigrants. But one of the wonderful things about America is there are always people who resist, and people in the 1920s made many of the same points about Johnson that people in 2017 made about President Trump. Dr. I. Mortimer Bloom, rabbi of the Hebrew Tabernacle of West 116th Street, said this at the time:

The immigration restriction bills are a denial and a reversal of long-cherished American ideals and traditions, an affront to the memory of the founders of the Republic, a dagger thrust into the hearts of thousands of human beings who yearn for an opportunity to lead the normal decent life which their own lands deny them and a staggering blow to humanitarians everywhere . . . Not as a Jew, not as one whose co-religionists happen to be seriously affected by the proposed legislation, but as an American steeped in the best traditions of his land, an American who craves for his country to be true to the high and holy mission for which she was called into being, do I cry against these discriminatory, heartless, un-American bills.

With hardly any alterations, Rabbi Bloom's words could have run as an editorial in the *New York Times* or *Washington Post* almost one hundred years later and would have looked completely in tune with the times.

Throughout the 1920s, families like the Freimans were moving out of the Lower East Side, and fewer and fewer Jewish immigrants were coming in to replace them. Although the neighborhood would remain the center of Yiddish-speaking life in America, the Jews themselves were being absorbed across the city. Grant might have succeeded in restricting Jews coming into the United States, but he resoundingly failed to make New York any less racially mixed, let alone less Jewish. Any politician who thinks he can ethnically cleanse America would do himself a favor by learning his history.

As Annie Pollard and Daniel Soyer wrote in their book about New York's immigrant Jews, *Emerging Metropolis*:

New York had already become in some senses a "Jewish city." At nearly a third of the population, Jews were New York's largest single ethnic group, and they profoundly influenced the city's culture, politics and economy. Of course, the city shaped them as well. This was especially true of the second generation, those born and raised in New York, who in the 1920s came into their own as the dominant segment of the community. Jewish immigrants laid the foundation for the Jewish metropolis. Their American-born children and grandchildren built on that groundwork for the remainder of the 20th century.[19]

But this assimilation wasn't entirely straightforward. Ritzier neighborhoods across America barred Jews, and in the 1920s, prestigious universities, such as Harvard and Yale, introduced stiflingly restrictive quotas on the number of Jewish students.* As in France, in the United States the Great Depression then led to a rise in open anti-Semitism; in the 1930s it was the norm in the country's private school systems to have a quota on the number of Jewish students admitted, and the same went for medical and law schools. Meanwhile, Christian applicants were specified in advertisements for white-collar jobs.[20] It was a blatant attempt by America's elite to stop the assimilation of Jews of Bill's generation, the children of immigrants who arrived at the beginning of the twentieth century, and further proof of how close America and France were in their attitudes toward Jewish immigrants between the two world wars, and how differently things could have gone in both countries had they simply had different leaders.[21]

By the time the Freimans had moved out to Farmingdale, most of the children had, like the Glasses, tweaked their names: Michael, Yakov, Sarah, Moses, and Rivka became Mike, Jack, Sadie, Bill, and Rita. Bill, more than the rest of his siblings, was ambitious to make his mark and rise, not just stay for the rest of his life in the Jewish community within Farmingdale.

"Bill always liked to show off, to impress, whereas the others didn't want to draw attention to themselves so much," Herb, Mike's son, told me. "And in the end, he would be the only one to make a relative success of himself, and to get out."

Throughout the day I spent with Herb, who was in his eighties by

---

* Even as late as 1957, my father's university, Lehigh in Pennsylvania, had a strict 10 percent Jewish student quota.

then, and Ann, who was in her seventies, both of them were checking their phones constantly, watching the stock market. Ann had once been a trader on Wall Street, which is where my father worked, too, and that's probably why he remained in touch with her; of his other many cousins, including Herb, I never heard anything.

"How much did you make, Ann? You selling?" Herb would occasionally shout out. He loved it; over his lifetime, he had made an impressive amount of money on the stock market, as proven by his large and stylish house. Ann, too, had done well.

But their parents did not have Bill's drive to get out and get away. Of that generation, only Bill aimed for the golden ring. In 1937 when he went to Paris, he owned a Texaco petrol station in what was then a plum location in Farmingdale, opposite the Republic Aviation manufacturing plant. But he was always cooking up more plans, and his various careers would eventually include making glassware, working as a subcontractor for the military, selling industrial fabrics, working as a stockbroker, and being a real estate agent. He was indefatigable, because he knew he didn't want to just sit on the porch every night, gossiping about the Farmingdale neighbors, and that was why he was still single at thirty-five: he didn't want another Long Island girl. He wanted something different, someone who would show him another kind of life.

When Bill saw Sara in her apartment on that winter's night in 1937, he thought he'd found what he was looking for. She was unlike all the girls he knew at home—she talked about art, and clothes, and style. With her by his side, he wouldn't live the kind of life his siblings did. She would lift him up. Even better, she was a woman who needed rescuing, and ever since he was a child he had been rescuing women, most obviously his mother. So this was a dynamic that felt very familiar to him. But to his shock, it turned out she didn't want to be rescued. Worse, she saw him as a coarse American who dragged her down. Deeply hurt, he would occasionally be cruel to her, telling her he'd been tricked into marrying "damaged goods" because of her weak lungs. Sara withdrew from him even farther. In many ways they were similar, in terms of their backgrounds and their aspirations. But Sara didn't want someone who was like her—she wanted someone different. For the rest of Bill's life, he would only want her. In his eyes, she would always be the beautiful French girl he saw in that dark apartment. But there wasn't anything he could do to make her love him like he loved her.

Whereas Sara was changed irrevocably by her unhappy marriage, Bill was made of tougher stuff. Even when he was ninety, he would joke around with people and call up my father to talk about the stock exchange, always looking for good business opportunities. He never stopped fighting for a better life. Whatever sadness he felt about Sara not reciprocating his love, he proudly hid it from those around him with good humor and inexhaustible energy.

Sara and Bill Glass in Long Island

Herb was the same. As the day I spent with him wore on, I realized certain things in his life were more complicated than they looked—a divorce here, serious health problems there—but he never let any of it dampen his mood. As it got later in the afternoon, one of his daughters quietly told me that her brother, Herb's youngest son, had died in 9/11. As it happened, a friend of mine had also died in 9/11, and I was staying with her parents on the trip to the United States, so I went over and told Herb how very sorry I was for the loss of his son and about my friend. His face collapsed, like a tarpaulin that had its pole removed, and those bright blue eyes looked dull for a second. I felt like I'd reached into his chest, put my finger on the softest part of his heart, and stopped it.

"Yeah, well . . ." he began, his repartee stilled. "Yeah. Thank you."

As well as having the Freiman eyes, Herb had inherited the Freiman way of dealing with tragedy, which was to plow ever onward, distracting himself instead of dwelling. The Glass tendency, by contrast, was to obsess privately about the past forever.

Bill and Sara would eventually leave Farmingdale. His siblings always thought it was Sara who pushed them away, but in truth it was Bill. He wanted to move forward. In Sara, he thought he saw someone who wanted to move forward with him, and he was half right about that: she did want to move forward, she just hadn't wanted it to be with him. And as much as he was able to hide it, that was his tragedy.

Chapter 8

HENRI AND SONIA —
DENOUNCED

Paris, 1940–1943

One of the denunciation letters that was taped to Henri and Sonia's door

When the Nazis marched into Paris on June 14, 1940, a beautiful, bright sunny day, Henri and Sonia were in their apartment on rue Victor Cousin with the shutters tightly closed. Their neighborhood was so quiet Sonia was sure she could hear the marching all the way over on the Champs-Élysées. The few Parisians who were still in town had, like Henri and Sonia, closed their shutters, too, so they wouldn't have to see the German uniforms swarming through their beautiful streets. But for Henri and Sonia, it was also because they didn't want to be seen.

The Nazis' arrival was not a surprise. The French had been waiting for the Germans to attack Paris for weeks, and the reason Henri and Sonia's neighborhood was so quiet was that most of their neighbors had fled the city. Henri and Sonia refused to leave, partly because they couldn't abandon Chaya and Mila, neither of whom was willing to go anywhere, and partly because they didn't believe there was anywhere else for them to go. The road to the south was already clogged with people trying to get out, and there was no way Chaya could make that journey on foot. So they decided to stay where they were, in their beloved apartment. But as Sonia heard the jackboots, she knew they'd have to go into hiding.

Up until that point, they had been cheerful about their life in Paris— or at least they pretended to be so for their relatives.

One of Sonia's cousins in Poland wrote to her in 1939:

Hello dear Zosia,

Do not hold a grudge against me that I do not write so often, although I think of you all the time. You must know the times we live in are not peaceful. Nothing happens here and if something bad happens nobody intervenes. I am sad when I realize that everything we believed in does not matter anymore. It is only a symbol now ... You are full of optimism, that should make me forget about my problems that stop me from sleeping. But all the news we hear suggests everything is worse than it was during the Great War.

On May 25, 1940, Henri wrote what was probably his last letter to his sister before Paris fell, and he spent most of it telling her that everything was fine.

My dear little sister,

Just a word to reassure you that all is well with us. Don't be frightened by what you read in the newspapers. Life in Paris proceeds calmly with full awareness of the gravity of the situation. We are calm and confident. I am showing my machines at a fair in Paris. There are not many visitors, of course, but the ones who are there are potential buyers.

Mother is very well. I am not evacuating her. She will simply

move to Mila's house. This way she won't be alone, Mila neither.
And at Mila's, being on the ground floor, she won't be in any danger.
Jacques and Alex are in the army and fine, the Ornsteins are all
well too. Write to us and don't worry, I kiss you often as well as your
Ronny. Hello Bill!
  Henri

By the time Sara received the letter, Nazis were on the Champs-Élysées and a swastika flag was hanging from the Arc de Triomphe.

How does a Polish Jewish couple live in Paris for the whole of the war and survive? And how could a woman as naturally attention-grabbing as Sonia live under the radar for four years, running away from her natural place in the sun to live in the shadows? Henri never spoke about their years in hiding. Sonia did, but she only ever told half the story. The other part of their story she kept to herself.

Of the 200,000 Jews who lived in Paris when war started, more than half of whom were foreigners, it is estimated that at most only 10 percent refused to register.[1] It is, for obvious reasons, impossible to know how many of those hidden Jews survived. But given they were Polish Jews, who stayed in Paris for the whole of the war and survived, there is no question that Henri and Sonia were exceptional.

Once the Nazis arrived, Henri and Sonia's relatively calm life ended. Most of the anti-Jewish legislation was passed during the first year of occupation, and Jews were banned from being in public places; traveling in certain cars on the metro; owning a bicycle, telephone, or radio; and working in certain professions. They had to be home at certain hours and were allowed to shop only between three and four in the afternoon. Anti-Semitic posters appeared all around the city: *"Il faut aussi balayer les JUIFS pour que notre maison soit propre,"* read a popular one. (We must sweep away the Jews in order to keep our home clean.) From June 1942, Jews had to wear a yellow star at all times so as to make it easier for the authorities to identify them and imminently deport them. Between October 1940, when the anti-Jewish legislation kicked in, and December

1941, the number of known Jews in Paris fell by 18,000: 8,000 had been arrested and were interned as enemy aliens in French camps and 10,000 had vanished.[2]

But Henri and Sonia never registered as Jews. Both of them foresaw the dangers ahead and Sonia, as usual, took charge. She figured out how to buy false identity cards on the black market that claimed they were a Christian German couple called Classe. She also spoke German so fluently she could pass as a native, even to German officers, and Henri could get by. They then rented a tiny apartment on the Avenue des Minimes, under the name of Classe, and left almost everything back in their home on Victor Cousin, so it would look to the police who came looking for the Jewish Glasses like they'd simply abandoned it.

Henri and Sonia's lives were saved by their identity cards, but life in Paris under Nazi occupation was still crushingly difficult. The French had an easier time under occupation than the Polish, because the Nazis didn't consider the French to be *untermenschen*. But their beloved capital city soon became almost unrecognizable. Familiar buildings were now covered with Nazi flags; cinemas—which the French had always loved—were handed over to the Germans and, for example, the Rex Cinema on one of the Grands Boulevards was renamed *Deutschen Soldatenkino* (cinema for German soldiers). Swastikas decked all the great Parisian monuments and propaganda posters were everywhere, warning Parisians to fight against *"le cancer du terrorisme communiste"* (the cancer of communist terrorism). With gas almost impossible to come by, the only vehicles in the streets were German military ones, while the French made do with bicycles, the metro, and their feet. French brasseries were renamed into German and the street signs were similarly redubbed. France's humiliation was total. On the newsstands, only papers approved by Joseph Goebbels, Hitler's minister of propaganda, were on sale, such as the established far-right paper *Le Matin,* which had eagerly become pro Nazi; *La Gerbe* (the Sheaf), a pro-Nazi weekly rooted in racism; and *Aujourd'hui,* a once-independent daily that became pro Vichy and pro Nazi.[3] After the war the editors of some of these papers would be charged with treason, but during the occupation they were almost all that Parisians had to bring them news. While Parisians could see the Germans dining and living it up in the brasseries and the Ritz hotel in the Place Vendôme, they endured near-crippling rationing. The city, one inhabitant wrote at the time, was defined by "silence and misery," and the rations were "barely sufficient to keep people alive provided they remain lying down and don't work."[4]

Henri and Sonia fared better than many of their fellow Parisians. As well as feeding herself and Henri, Sonia looked after Mila and Chaya, and also managed to get enough food on the black market to send to her relatives back home, who then sent her thanks in return:

5th April 1942

My dearest Zosia,

Yesterday I received parcel No5 containing 1 box of melted butter—nothing missing. Today I received 3 parcels together No1, No2 and No3—there was between 80 and 100 grams missing in each of them.

Sweet fruit cakes were all in bits and there were only 9 pieces of butter in a box.

As the post office is not working . . . I am sending this postcard by First Class. Last week they took lots of people from here. My cousin Azyasza H. (76 years old) was one of them. In November they took mum, grandmother, and aunt. We are terrified every single day and nobody knows what happens in a couple of days. It is still a little bit cold here so we burn the fire every other day and we make wholemeal bread as there is lack of it.

I am looking forward to hearing from you. I hope you are healthy.

Lots of love,

Lille Lemberg

Some of her relatives spent as much time in their letters griping to Sonia about family spats as they did thanking her for her bravery and generosity. Not even living in fear of their lives can alter the nature of families.

July 4 1942

My dear Zosia,

I received the olive oil and marmalade, thank you. I think some fruitcakes got damaged in the parcel and 200g of chocolate was missing.

I am worried about mum and on top of that my son and his wife do not respect me. Zenek shouts a lot since he got married. He does not care about his parents any more. I do not speak to him any more and I speak with his wife only when I need something when she goes shopping etc. This is how thankful he is for the fact I have been supporting him financially all his life.

If you have any socks size 8 you do not need, please send me 3 or 4 pairs but no underwear please. Also 20 laxative tablets as I cannot take any liquids and the herbs you sent before are not helpful for constipation. Also shaving cream and lime tea, please. Thank you for looking after me.

Lots of love,

David Lemberg

But Henri and Sonia couldn't look after everyone. One by one, the Ornstein cousins were killed off. And as they were murdered, in scenarios that were both horrific but then unexceptional, the Glass siblings started to fall apart emotionally.

Soon after the war started, Josek Ornstein joined the resistance network Alliance, run by Marie-Madeleine Fourcade, an extremely impressive young woman who wasn't even thirty when she created a web of spies across France. Josek was one of those spies. In Fourcade's book *Noah's Ark: The Secret Undergound,* she refers to him as "little 'Gigot,'" Gigot being his spy name, and the "little" confirming that he had the same build as Alex. Josek was arrested by the French police in 1942 when he was caught trying to cross the demarcation line to get to Paris, and the documents inside his pocket confirmed that he was not only Jewish but a member of the resistance. The police handed him directly over to the Abwehr, or German military intelligence service, who put him in the notoriously brutal Fresnes prison, just south of Paris, where prisoners were starved, threatened, and in some cases tortured.[5] Josek somehow—almost certainly through the Alliance network—managed to get word to Alex, who was now down in Cannes, that he had been arrested and asked for his help.

"I loved Josek," Alex wrote. "As kids we played together and were very close. Knowing him as I did, I was sure he would confess to nothing. When I learned of his arrest I promised myself to do everything I could to save him. Immediately, I went to Vichy to see Perré. Could Perré intercede to free Josek?"

The answer, unsurprisingly, was no. Colonel Perré—who had helped Alex get into the Foreign Legion—was by this point a high-ranking official in Vichy. Since 1940 he had been head of the military tribunal in Clermont-Ferrand in the Auvergne in central France, which not only specifically cracked down on resisters but already had targeted and imprisoned several members of Josek's own resistance network,[6] meaning Perré had personally overseen the incarceration of various Alliance spies like Josek. Moreover, while Perré himself was more interested in the sovereignty of France than Nazism, he was close friends with some of the most deranged anti-Semites in Vichy. One of these friends was René Bousquet, who was then working as secretary-general to the Vichy regime police, and decades later would be indicted for the deportation of 194 Jewish children from France to the death camps.[7]

So as fond as Perré was of Alex, and as much as he considered him to be *le bon Juif*—an exceptional Jew who deserved saving, unlike the others—there was no way he was going to save his Jewish, resistance-fighting cousin. That Alex thought he might says a lot about their friendship.

"I tried all my contacts. Nothing could be done," Alex wrote. On November 30, 1942, at 14:36, Josek was executed at Mont-Valérien,[8] a fortress to the west of Paris, alongside eight other men in his resistance network.[9] One of those fellow Alliance resisters, a handsome young man called Lucien Vallat, left behind a letter he wrote while in prison with Josek. It said, "I think I have done my duty to my country and my comrades, you will never need to blush on my account. That is a great comfort to me. Be courageous. Be courageous, all of you. Farewell, everybody. Farewell, mother."[10] The Germans killed more than a thousand Frenchmen at Mont-Valérien during the war, almost all because they were resistance fighters.

Alex was devastated by the loss of his favorite cousin, the person who he considered as close as a brother and with whom he enjoyed a much less complicated relationship than he had with Henri and Jacques. "To say I was sad would be a huge understatement. I was completely crushed, eaten by remorse to not have been able to save Josek," he wrote.

Alex had always thought that if he befriended as many famous and high-ranking French people as possible, he would be safe and he could save his family. But for perhaps the first time, Alex realized the truth of the current situation. It didn't matter how many French people he knew, and on what side, because the majority of French people didn't care, and if Alex couldn't keep his cousin safe then he couldn't keep himself safe either.

Around the same time as Josek's arrest, Maurice Ornstein, Josek's older brother, and his wife, Giselle, paid a boatman to take them across the river in the town of Chalon-sur-Saône, which would take them into the Unoccupied Zone. They had two children, an especially cherubic little boy called Armand, who was three and a half, and a one-year-old daughter, Rosette. Before they made the crossing they left the children with a family friend in the countryside, arranging to send for them when they got across. They never made it. During the crossing they were shot, possibly by the boatman who had pocketed the money and decided they weren't worth the risk, possibly by a soldier who had spotted them from the shore. Their children, Armand and Rosette, lived with a woman whom Armand today remembers only as "a woman in a white dress"—a nun? A nurse?—who miraculously didn't turn them in but instead cared for them for almost a year. However, little Armand told some of the neighbors that he was Jewish, and the children had to be moved again, fast, this time to another family whose name has long since been lost in history. Armand was even put in an orphanage for a period of time, to try to keep him safe. (Armand, now eighty and still living in Paris, remembers only fragments about this time; the memories have been buried so deeply inside him for so long it's like they never existed at all.) Eventually Giselle's sister Monique walked all the way from Paris out to the countryside where the children were—possibly dozens of miles away, possibly hundreds—took them into her custody, and hid them for the rest of the war.

Rose Ornstein and Herman Brenner

Not long after Maurice's murder, his sister Rose, Sara's beloved almost sister, was on a bus, also trying to cross the demarcation line. Her husband, Herman Brenner, had managed to get to the United States in June 1941, and the plan was that Rose would join him once he had sorted out a place for them to live. Dr. Brenner found a lovely home for them in Queens, not too far from Sara and Bill, much to Sara's ecstatic delight. But by the time Rose set out from Paris it was too late. America had entered the war and it was no longer possible to get visas. As she couldn't get to America from France, she decided to take a bus to Switzerland and somehow get to the United States from there. She hoped that the border police would be too busy to check everyone's passports, because all she had left to cling to were impossible odds. The bus stopped at the border, and when the Vichy police got on and walked down the aisle toward her Rose quickly scribbled on a postcard, gave it to the person sitting next to her, and asked them to send it. No one knew what happened to Rose until Sara finally received the postcard years later, after it had been held up during the war. It was addressed to her in America and it read simply, "They are coming for me. I love you. Good-bye." She was killed in Auschwitz. When Sara finally received that postcard after the war, years after Rose sent it, she screamed and collapsed in her hallway, watched by her toddler son, Ronald, my father.

Also killed in Auschwitz was Rose's sister, Anna, and Anna's husband, Samuel Goldberg, my relative Anne-Laurence Goldberg's grandparents. By the end of the war, of the seven Ornstein siblings, only three survived: Alex Ornstein, who eventually raised his nephew Armand and niece Rosette after getting them from Monique; Arnold Ornstein, who died shortly after the war ended from health problems; and Sarah Ornstein, who went to Israel.

The Ornsteins had come to Paris for safety, and France decimated the family. The only reason the Glasses had come to Paris was because of the Ornsteins—the gentle, sweet, funny, and fun Ornstein cousins, some of them as close as siblings to the Glasses—and the Glasses never really recovered from the devastating loss. They were the roots back to the past,

Anna Goldberg, an Ornstein cousin who was killed in Auschwitz,
with her husband (who was also killed) and their children.
Their son, Roger Goldberg, is on the right.

part of the Glasses' childhood, and when they were killed, the ties that
held the family together began to loosen. Alex never forgave himself for,
as he put it, "failing my brother Josek." But as Alex wept in Cannes over
Josek, he didn't know what danger the rest of his family was in.

They tried to stay alive as best they could, the ones who somehow were living in the shadows. Roger Goldberg was the son of Anna
Ornstein who, along with her husband Samuel Goldberg, was killed
in Auschwitz. Roger and his wife, Renée, were both younger than the
Glasses, but they became extremely close to their older relatives during
the war. Roger and Renée were often separated during the war as they,
incredibly, both managed to travel around France while evading capture.
Their letters to one another are some of the best sources I found for
learning what life was like for the Glasses during the war. But they are
written in an extremely stilted, halting tone, nothing like how Roger and
Renée talked, and occasionally make no sense. This is because Roger and
Renée had to make up a code in order to evade the censors, and despite

Roger and Renée Goldberg during the war

some of the code remaining uncrackable, as the only people who could break it have long since died, it is clear that Roger and Renée were part of a resistance network.

"At Sonia's I learned that the doctor was in the north and that he called one evening. Which surprised me because we would have known but everyone confirms it," Renée writes in 1943. It's possible "the doctor" was simply a doctor, but Renée never wrote in this tone—vague, banal, pointed—in letters before or after the war. So it seems much more likely that "the doctor" and "everyone" referred to particular people in their resistance network.

"Alex is on the coast where he eats a lot of oranges, but he is going to go elsewhere without a doubt," she writes in 1943. In fact, Alex Maguy was nowhere near the coast at this point—he was hiding in the center of the country in the Auvergne. So while he may well have been eating oranges, this sentence was also almost certainly code.

And this, also from 1944:

"Henri had a serious illness, so the apartment is not very healthy. Odette and I would very much like to leave until it is disinfected," Renée writes to Roger. Nowhere does Henri mention being ill during the war, so it is far more likely that Renée was telling Roger that Henri had been nearly captured and they now needed to stay away from the apartment for a while.

Whether Henri and Sonia were also part of a resistance network or not, Henri was certainly part of the resistance effort and they were both nearly caught multiple times. After the Nazis arrived, Henri continued to work covertly at his microfilming company, Photosia, with Marc Haenel. The German army moved into Haenel's building, where Henri frequently came to meet him. "We worked under very dangerous conditions. Nevertheless, we built our machines right by the enemy," Henri later wrote in his records.

Henri's machine, the Omniphot-Microfilm, was so good at photocopying and shrinking blueprints that when the Banque de France contacted Kodak before the Nazis arrived in Paris to ask them to copy their most important documents, Kodak recommended they go instead to Omniphot-Microfilm. Haenel, who was not Jewish, quickly grasped the value of this machine in wartime: industrial plans and public archives could be copied, miniaturized, and stored, protecting them from the Nazis. So he and Henri decided to make this the focus of their business.

"For racial reasons, I was not allowed to be the owner, and Paris being occupied, I was forbidden any activities. But day and night we microfilmed public and private archives. I threw myself into the fight," Henri wrote in a letter shortly after the war ended. "Everything was forbidden to me, of course; yet I built more machines."

French politicians and companies quietly contacted Photosia to ask for help, and Henri microfilmed the archives of businesses, museums, and small towns, saving countless records—of architecture, people's life savings, their homes—from decimation. He could shrink thousands of records down to the size of a thumbnail, which made them both easy to store and unrecognizable to any potential enemies wishing to destroy them. The port authority at Le Havre became one of his clients, so that after the war, when the port was destroyed, Henri was able to return to them the microfilms he'd made of their designs. "Thanks to our help— though modesty should prevent me from saying it—the port of Le Havre was rebuilt in record time," Henri later wrote.

Because Henri was the only person who knew how to work the machine, he had to transport it around the country and do all the microfilming himself whenever the machine was hired for a job. In 1941, he went to the town of Valenciennes in the north of France, which French troops had looted and was now occupied by the Germans. He spent nine months living in the basement of the museum, microfilming the local archives that the mayor had managed to save, plus another two years of repeated visits, according to Henri's meticulous records. Directly across from the museum was the local Gestapo office, in the Valenciennes park. Only once did a policeman come to the museum to see what was happening there. He looked at Henri's identity card—"a total counterfeit," Henri later recalled—and walked away. Henri went right back to microfilming. "It was a very close call. It really could have been the end for me," Henri wrote in a letter.

While Henri was traveling around the country, Sonia was all on her own in Paris, tasked with looking after both Mila and Chaya, the latter of whom insisted on only eating kosher and did not give a damn how hard that was to find in Nazi-controlled, strictly rationed Paris. Every so often Sonia would go back to their apartment on rue Victor Cousin to look through their post and pick up the letters from her family, who still used her old address. One day as she approached the building, she just happened to look up at their apartment window. She saw a hand sticking out, waving frantically. Sonia recognized it as belonging to the concierge of the building, with whom she'd always been friendly, and she knew what her friend was telling her: "The police are searching the apartment for you. Stay away and run away." Sonia ran. Another time, a French policeman did catch her and arrested her for having false papers. Sonia refused to cry, but she pleaded with him, as a Frenchman, to have mercy. He refused. On the steps of the police station, as he was just about to turn her over, Sonia desperately offered him all the jewelry she was wearing—all costume, of course, but it looked real enough for the policeman. He could have pocketed the jewels and still turned her over, but he was kind enough—or dumb enough—to let her go. Another time, she was seized by a German officer and, gathering all her self-control so as to not show the slightest hint of fear, she imperiously told him she was the wife of a high-ranking German politician and if he mistreated her in any way her husband would hear about it. Terrified, the officer let her go. Henri had always known Sonia was an extraordinary woman, but it wasn't until the war that she herself realized how extraordinary she could be.

But the biggest danger for Sonia turned out to be her neighbors. Several times, when she came to rue Victor Cousin to look through the post, she would find letters of denunciation from her former neighbors taped to the front door, telling the Vichy police that Henri and Sonia were still in Paris. Even though it was always extremely dangerous for her to return to rue Victor Cousin, Sonia started coming back more often just to tear the denunciation letters off the door.

Sonia had told me about these letters, and it was a story I assumed I'd have to take on good faith. How do you prove someone tore a denunciation note off a door eighty years ago? On a sunny afternoon a decade after Sonia died, looking through the shoebox in my grandmother's closet, I found out how. Because there, among the photos, was a photocopy of one of the denunciation letters.

The Jewish family, Glass, who lives in Rue Victor Cousin, and who the police are looking for, are currently living at 60 avenue des Minimes on the 5th floor. Their fake identity cards are issued in the name of Classe. This Jewish household continues to live in the city,

It was written in the distinctive curlicue cursive all French children are taught. Every French exchange student I'd had at school wrote like that, as do all my French relatives, for that matter. As much as I know about France's culpability and collaboration during the war, it felt genuinely devastating to see such cruelty written in the familiar French handwriting, like hearing your father shout racist obscenities. Writing about a country behaving badly can feel abstract, clinical even; undeniable evidence of the wickedness of the individuals within is piercingly personal. Later, Henri microfilmed the denunciation letters for Sonia, and they sent some copies to Sara. Even if they rarely talked about this, they wanted to remember it forever and for others to know.

It is estimated that up to a million French people denounced others to the authorities during the occupation, sending between three and five million letters to local and national politicians and law enforcement bureaus,[11] although it is an impossible number to confirm, given that few saved the letters and many denunciations were done by whispers.[12]

"[Denunciation] was a fundamental characteristic of Vichy France. In a sense it was the only way people could express themselves in a country where there were no demonstrations, no rights, no vote: it was the voice of the people, although a mean and petty voice, a way of swearing allegiance to the powers that be," historian Laurent Joly said in 2008 at the world's first international conference on French denunciation in the Second World War.[13] The Vichy government didn't officially encourage denunciations, unlike Italy and Germany, but it certainly didn't discourage them either. The problem for the government was that French people got a little too enthusiastic about them, once they realized that denouncing people was an easy way to get rid of someone who was in their way, whether he was Jewish or not: if you wanted someone's job, or apartment, or wife, denouncing them was a good way to get closer to your goal. And given how tight rations were, there was an extra impetus to denounce one's long-hated neighbor. After all, you might not get their house, but you might at least get their food. False denunciations became such a problem that the Germans started punishing people who made them—in one reported case, sending a woman and her lover to Germany after they falsely denounced her husband[14]—and on January 1, 1942, in his New Year's message to the country, Marshal Pétain announced that anyone who made false denunciations was an "adversary to French unity" and an "enemy of the National Revolution." Real denunciations, however, were a different story. Anyone who denounced Jews living illegally was helping the Vichy regime, and writers in the pro-Nazi French newspapers regularly urged their readers to denounce any foreign Jews they knew, saying it was part of their national duty. But in fact, far from "strengthening national unity," as pro-Vichy propaganda suggested, the culture of denunciations harmed it, with neighbors informing on one another to enrich themselves personally.

In French, there are two words for denunciation: *dénonciation* refers to uncovering something, like discovering a fact, and is a neutral term. *Délation* suggests something more malevolent, something more based in self-interest with a negative impact on others. "Vichy attempted to uphold the distinction between the two words, but to little avail," historian Shannon Fogg writes in her 2003 essay "Denunciations, Community Outsiders, and Material Shortages in Vichy France."

But of course, not all denunciations were false or stemming from petty feuds. Plenty of French people considered turning in Jews to be their patriotic and civic duty, even if they had once been their friends. According to Holocaust historian Serge Klarsfeld, 75,721 Jews from France were deported to the death camps.[15] Not all of those were caught because of denunciations, but these mass arrests and murders would have been a lot more difficult for Vichy to pull off without the complicity of people whom the Jews had once thought were their friends. Henri and Sonia survived the war despite the best efforts of their neighbors and unlike so many Polish Jews in Paris. They were blessed with an enormous amount of ingenuity and even more luck, but not everyone in their family had both or even either of those things. For Jacques there was no need for any French people to denounce him, because he denounced himself.

Chapter 9

JACQUES—CAPTURED

France and Poland, 1940s

Arthur Weisz's portrait of Jacques at Pithiviers

In May 1941, Jacques was at home with Mila on rue de la Tour when he received a green postcard, slipped under his door. It was not from a friend:

> *Prefecture de Police, Paris,*
> *le 10 Mai, 1941*
> *Mr. Glass is requested to present himself, in person, accompanied*
> *by a member of his family or a friend, on May 14 at 7 am at the*
> *Caserne Napoleon to discuss his situation. Please bring ID. Anyone*

*who does not come at the specified day and time risks the most severe
punishment.*

The police commissioner.

Mila was in the early stages of pregnancy and not feeling well, so
Jacques asked his older brother to go with him. Henri not only refused
but begged Jacques not to go either.

"You're going to end up like one of those poor Jews in prison camps!"
Sonia later recalled Henri telling him, referring to the thousands of foreign Jews from "enemy territories" whom France had already incarcerated in internment camps.

Jacques laughed off his brother's concerns. "It is only an administrative matter," he insisted. "I'll be home for dinner."

Early on Wednesday, May 14, 1941, Mila and Jacques left their home
on rue de la Tour. It was already a sunny day, and as they walked together
along the Seine, past the Tuileries and toward the Marais, they looked
to casual onlookers like the image of a happy couple taking a romantic
stroll through some of Paris's prettiest places. Just before 7 a.m. they
reached the Caserne Napoleon, an old barracks, just a few streets away
from where Jacques' mother used to live with Sara. Photos of that day
from contemporary newspapers show a small crowd of Jewish men, waiting for what they thought was a meeting with the police, milling about
in the road, looking serious but relaxed, clutching pitifully small bags,
containing, at most, lunch. When they arrived, the police immediately
told their wives, sisters, mothers, and children who accompanied them
to go back home and pack suitcases for their male relatives and then
return to the Caserne as quickly as possible. This was why the men had
been told to bring someone with them: so they could be sent back to
fetch their belongings. This was not specified on the *billet vert* because it
would have raised suspicions, and fewer men would have come.

After the women and children handed over the suitcases, they were
each given a card telling them when and where they could visit the men,
and then their names and addresses were taken down by the French policemen, who would use them in later roundups. (As well as being right

about what would happen to Jacques, Henri was proven correct in his refusal to accompany his brother.*) Meanwhile, the men were herded onto Parisian buses—the same buses that once took them to work—and driven to the Austerlitz train station. They were then put on specially requisitioned trains and sent to either Pithiviers or Beaune-la-Rolande, what the French newspapers openly described as "concentration camps."

This was the *Rafle du billet vert* (green card roundup), the first official roundup of Jews in France under the Vichy regime. Jacques' bad star was certainly blighting him now, because not only did he get summoned in the very first roundup, he fell victim to it: of the 6,694 foreign Jewish men who had received a summons on a green card, 40 percent refused to obey, either ignoring the instructions or running away. Jacques, obedient to the end, was among the more than 3,700 Jewish and primarily Polish men who believed France could never harm them, and so he did as he was told.[1]

The Glass family took no photos, but I know exactly what Jacques was wearing and carrying and how he was looking that day. One day I was in a library in Paris, looking through a book about the *Rafle du billet vert,* and there, in a photo of men walking along the Austerlitz train station platform, was the unmistakable figure of my great-uncle Jacques. It was the spectacles that caught my eye first: those round wire spectacles that he wore in every single photograph I have of him. But it was his clothes that proved this was Jacques. While most of the other Jews around him are, like him, poor immigrants, and so wearing workmen's clothes, Jacques is so smart he looks fresh from the tailor. He's wearing a neat white button-down shirt, its collar so starched it's almost pointing ahead, dark trousers and shoes, and a trench coat with only its middle button done up, the way fashion followers today still wear it. The only thing that gives away his social class is his luggage, and that's because it was gathered together by Mila, who did not share the Glass siblings' fastidious aesthetics: he is

---

* The Nazis never asked the French to arrest Jewish children along with their parents. That was done entirely at Vichy's volition, partly to fill the deportation quotas imposed by the Germans and partly to spare France what I guess could be described as the administrative burden of thousands of Jewish orphans. Michael R. Marrus and Robert O. Paxton, *Vichy France and The Jews* (New York: Basic Books, Inc., 1981).

carrying a battered suitcase, a dirty cloth bag, and some rolled-up sheets, clearly gathered up in a frantic hurry. He is walking alongside the parked train, already filled with men peering through the windows; he looks focused, not even glancing at the photographer, and he looks scared.

The process that led to Jacques' arrest began eight months earlier, on October 4, 1940, when Vichy passed a law ordering the internment of all foreign Jews in what they called "special camps." More than forty thousand Jews were interned, and the French papers covered the arrests, including the *Rafle du billet vert*, enthusiastically. "These arrests have been carried out in the most correct way," *La Dépêche du Monde* reported the day after the *Rafle du billet vert*. *L'Écho de Pithiviers*, the only local newspaper in its area, was less restrained in its joy. In a front-page editorial headlined "Israel dans le Loiret!," columnist Jean de Nibelle crowed that Jews would now be "behind barbed wire, rather than at the head of our city halls and our great places, as they were previously under the regime of Blume, of Zay, of the Levys and the flea-ridden Semites they brought with them . . . . Today the rule of the Jews is over. France, finally, is protecting herself from them. Thus, the wheel turns! And the Jews, yesterday, all powerful, are today merely miserable animals of concentration camps! After having betrayed and ruined us, here they are reduced themselves, impotent and almost deserving of pity!"[2]

Few people had lived lives with less power than the Jews who were arrested in the *Rafle du billet vert*. Along with the 3,430 Polish Jews and 157 Czech Jews, there were 123 Jewish men officially classified as "stateless." These were poor immigrants who had come to France for a better life than the terrible ones they'd had at home, and whom the Vichy government had gone after because they were easy targets. Jacques was typical of the men who were caught: foreign, ostensibly unemployed, and basically broke thanks to Vichy's increasingly impossible regulations regarding foreign Jewish employment. Jean de Nibelle, in his *Écho de Pithiviers* column, makes the still-popular anti-Semitic reference to Rothschild, as though the men coming to the camps were fat bankers as opposed to

men who lived in basements and often went without breakfast and lunch in order to give their children supper.*

A police report made soon after the *Rafle du billet vert* read that "among certain French Aryan circles, it does not seem that the new rules receive full approval."[3] But these particular French circles were less concerned about anti-Semitism than about the drain on French resources: "It is estimated that these measures all too often reach married men and fathers with families who will be left destitute, and consequently, the children and women will be left in the care of the French government," the report continued.

This reaction to the mass deportation of thousands of men was heartless, but prescient. Without their husbands and sons working, the women struggled. Jacques Biélinky was a Jewish journalist who had come to France in 1909 as a political refugee after surviving the pogroms in Russia. Between 1940 and 1942 he kept a diary, but it wasn't until the *Rafle du billet vert* that Biélinky really started to notice—or at least write about—Jewish persecution in France. Two days after the roundup he writes about the plight of the women left behind: "Huge emotion among the Jewish community because of the mass arrests. Thousands of women with children left without support are worried about starvation. Many women have gone to the police commissioners to beg for food."

Terrified, Jews in Paris went into hiding. Many left the homes in which they were registered, and synagogues, especially those that had been the center of Polish Jewish life, were now almost empty out of fear the police would arrest anyone they saw in there. Jewish aid organizations relied on donations to feed the families of the prisoners.[4]

Despite all he had been through and everything he saw in front of him, Biélinky remained optimistic. On May 20, he writes, "Among Jewish

---

* Incidentally, as I was writing that paragraph about Nibelle I did what no writer should do, which is check Twitter mid-writing. As it happened, someone had sent me an anti-Semitic tweet that included a reference to the Rothschilds. (A Soros reference was chucked in, too, ensuring this version of anti-Semitism was fully up to date.) Anti-Semites maintain traditions at least as faithfully as Orthodox Jews.

circles, it is thought there will be no more arrests and mass internments in camps. A social worker has gone to visit the camps and plead for the sick."

Whatever the social worker did, it wasn't enough for the Jews in France, including Biélinky: in 1943, he was arrested, deported, and killed in Sobibor.

Mila was luckier. She was able to stay in her apartment for another year and a half, largely thanks to Jacques Revillon. Revillon was Jacques' *administrateur provisoire,* who had been put in charge of Jacques' business affairs when it became illegal for Jews to run a business, and he was extraordinarily kind to Mila. He wrote numerous letters to the Comissariat General aux Questions Juives (CGQJ), urging them to let her stay in the apartment, describing the situation as *plus critique.* Given the atmosphere in Occupied Paris at the time, Revillon's kindness to Mila, a very Polish, very Jewish woman, and not an especially easygoing one at that, seems remarkable. And Revillon, it quickly turned out, was an admirable man, in that even though he earned money from looking after Jacques' business, either his conscience or his business sense could not allow him to continue. Eight months after Jacques' arrest, in January 1942—still relatively early in the war—Revillon wrote to the CGQJ, saying he could no longer look after *les affaires Israelites* (Jewish businesses) because doing this work risked "discrediting my company and causing problems with our American customers. . . . This is a very serious imminent threat." Revillon made it sound like the problem was working with Jews, so he was officially relieved of his duties. But the truth was he didn't want to be associated with Vichy. He continued to help Mila throughout the war, writing letters on her behalf to the government about Jacques and allowing her to stay in the apartment for as long as it was safe.

The other person who helped Mila was Sonia. She looked after her throughout her pregnancy and made sure she had plenty of food, holding her hand when she was crying with fear. She also helped Mila make sense of the card she'd been given telling her when she could visit Jacques, and how to get there. Sonia's role was to protect Mila, and between her and Revillon, they did an amazingly good job.

Once Jacques rejected Henri's advice and was on the train at Auster-litz, no one could look after him. The journey to the Loiret in north-central France from Paris is a pretty easy one, taking only a few hours, and Pithiviers is less than 62 miles from Paris. But it was not a pleasant trip for Jacques. Thousands of men all crammed together on the train, confused and fidgety because no one was giving them any answers, all they could do was try to squeeze into a place by a window and watch the countryside roll by.

Eventually they were told that half of them would go to the camp at Beaune-la-Rolonde and half to Pithiviers. Jacques was assigned to the latter, and when they finally reached the train station he got off among 1,700 ragtag men,[5] and marched through the little town with the police. The men all carried their rolled-up bags for what they thought would be a mere few nights' stay, while the townspeople watched them silently, uncertain if they were watching a funny parade or a mournful spectacle.

When the men reached the camp, they walked in through the gates and, as ordered, quietly queued up. They registered their names with the black-booted French guards who were sitting at a small wooden table, recording everyone's information in notebooks. Each prisoner was given a number—Jacques was 470—and assigned to one of eleven barracks. After that, they walked toward what was now their new house.

I went to Pithiviers on a hot July day in 2012 with a group of about thirty other people, on a trip marking the 70th anniversary of when our ancestors had been deported from the camp. We met in the Marais, near the Shoah museum, and boarded a bus, in a pale and presumably unin-tentional echo of the *Rafle du billet vert*. It was a lovely drive from Paris to Pithiviers, past fields of wildflowers and sunflowers, homemade roadside advertisements for foie gras, and colorful houses with red slate roofs. The views became lovelier the closer we got to the camp. There was almost a sense of excitement among the group, as if we were making an important pilgrimage. But it turned out we were making a pilgrimage to nowhere: in Pithiviers itself, nothing remains of the camp today. If it weren't for a stone memorial, its former location would look like just another French suburban street. All signs of the French concentration camp itself have vanished, hastily erased after the war, when France tried to pretend that what had happened had not. We milled around pointlessly on the side of the road and then, with much less excitement, reboarded the bus. I shouldn't have been surprised that Pithiviers had vanished off the earth, but I was, and I felt a vague sense of pointless anger on the drive back to Paris, like I'd been duped by France's postwar subterfuge here, setting aside a day to pay my respects to something that no longer existed. (Five years after I visited, in 2017, it was announced that the long-abandoned Pithiviers train station, where the Jews arrived before being taken to the camp, would be turned into a museum about the French deportations. France's attitude toward its past is at last starting to evolve.)[6]

But even if Pithiviers itself no longer exists, the records, carefully compiled by the black-booted guards, remain. So while it might not be possible to walk among the original barracks with tour groups taking photos, as you can at Auschwitz, it's very easy to get a clear picture of what Jacques' daily life there was like.

Pithiviers had originally been built for German prisoners of war, but when France became occupied, there wasn't any demand for German prisons anymore, only Jewish ones—foreign Jews, that is; no French Jews ever stayed in Pithiviers. The entrance was on a normal pedestrian road—no need to hide the fact that France was interning Jewish immigrants simply for being Jewish immigrants—and conveniently near the railway station so that more prisoners could be brought in with efficient speed. After signing in on that first day in May, Jacques and the other men were directed to the right, toward a row of narrow, regularly spaced barracks—Jacques was originally assigned to barrack 7, then, after more barracks were later built to accommodate the growing numbers of incarcerated men, 11 and then 18. He slept in his barrack, washed there, watched the time go by there. Three times a day he'd walk a short distance to the dining hall, which was next to the infirmary. Management offices were also close by, as was a large vegetable garden. Menus were posted weekly telling the men what they would eat every day. "Monday," read the menu of December 22–29, 1941, "Breakfast—coffee; Lunch—vegetable soup, glazed carrots, and cheese; Supper—vegetable soup, mashed potatoes, and cheese." Never any meat or fish, just vegetables from the garden mashed, pureed, or sugared.

But as prisons went, Pithiviers was not so bad. Family members came to visit twice a month, and there was even a place where the Jews could worship on Shabbos and the High Holy Days. Many of the men there already knew one another from home or through the Foreign Legion—Jacques knew several men in the camp from his regiment. Most important, the French guards didn't beat the inhabitants, and while that was a pretty low bar for describing a place as not bad, it was a crucial one. That the guards were not cruel to them, sometimes even friendly, confirmed to Jacques and the other inhabitants of the camp that they didn't need to be scared. Nothing bad would happen to them in Pithiviers—they were only there because they didn't have the right identity papers, and they needed to be kept there during the war for the sake of the economy. They were safe. It was all OK. Everything was fine.

Most of the men spent their days working on local farms, but Pithiviers itself was not a labor camp. No one had to work, and they did so for free, purely to relieve their boredom. There was also cultural life in the camp: many of the men played chess and there was even a Yiddish theater troupe. Guards encouraged all this because they considered it important to maintaining morale. Decades later, I found a remnant of this cultural life inside the shoebox in my grandmother's closet: on a yellowed piece of paper, mounted on a slab of cardboard, someone by the name of Arthur Weisz had made a pencil portrait of Jacques, round glasses on his face. It is dated the 22nd of June, 1941, and above the date Weisz wrote "Camp de Pithiviers."

Weisz was another prisoner in Pithiviers, and he made many portraits of the inhabitants, who would then send them back to their families as keepsakes. When I made the trip to Pithiviers with other descendants, two of the other people on the bus said they had their own Weisz drawings. For one of them, Weisz's portrait was the only likeness they'd ever seen of their father. Jacques, on the other hand, was well photographed, so I know for certain how accurate Weisz's portrait is, and it is amazingly close. He gave Jacques an air of gravitas that he often lacked in photos, due to his shyness and occasional nervous giggle in front of a camera's lens. Weisz captures his calmness, which Alex and Henri saw as passivity, and his gentleness, which too often came across as weakness. Jacques' arms are thin, a sign of wartime deprivation, but his face is handsome. It is, in truth, the kindest likeness that exists of Jacques and a testament both to Jacques' likability and to Weisz's generosity. (Weisz was later killed by the Nazis in an unlisted concentration camp, but probably Auschwitz.)

This is not the only image I have of Jacques in Pithiviers. Also in my grandmother's shoebox were two black-and-white photos, both stamped on the back, "12 Avril 1942, Camp d'Hébergement de Pithivier LE GES-TIONNAIRE." One photo shows eight men and the other shows nine, and many of the same men, including Jacques, appear in both photos. Both pictures are rather oddly posed: In one, a man is sitting in a bucket and his friends are either holding him in it or pretending to pour water on his head from watering cans. In the other, they are all arranged awkwardly on a ladder in one of the barracks. Photos like these, showing the men larking around and having a merry old time, were often staged by the camp guards and sent home to the prisoners' families for propaganda purposes: *See, everything's fine here! It's basically a holiday camp!* But the forced larking was unnecessary because the men are their own propaganda. They look strikingly healthy after almost a year of living at Pithiviers, and they look happy, making smiles too genuine to be forced. The former is proof of how relatively well they were treated in the camp, and the latter a sign of their complete lack of anxiety about the very near future.

These men all worked in the management (*gestionnaire*) office, a more suitable place for weedy, unathletic Jacques than the fields. Arthur Weisz also stressed in his portrait of him that that's where Jacques worked in Pithiviers, taking particular care over his armband in the portrait, on which he drew a little circle and wrote "Pithiviers Camp d'Internement LE GESTION." Jacques was probably quite good at

Jacques, toward the back

Jacques, far left

helping in administrative affairs, keeping track of which prisoner was in which barrack, punching holes in paper as his time drifted away, drawing up the records I would later use to write his story. But it might have also cost him his life.

When he was in Cambrai in 1940, Jacques went out every day to work on nearby farms, and this is almost certainly how he escaped from that POW camp. Dozens of people from Pithiviers took advantage of the camp's similar lack of security, running away in their early months of incarceration when they went out to work as farmhands. The local police soon put a stop to that and tightened security, but it's entirely possible that, had Jacques been going out to work instead of staying in the camp, he would have run away, too. Maybe his success in escaping from Cambrai would have emboldened him to try again. Maybe he would have sneaked back to Paris, met up with Mila, and gone into hiding with her, with Sonia and Henri's assistance. Or maybe this could never have happened, even if he'd spent all day hoeing potatoes instead of filing papers. Maybe he always would have gone back to the camp instead of grabbing his chance. After all, he chose to stay in the camp, sitting at a desk and following orders, instead of working outside and then running toward the sunset. Stay where you are, don't question things, put your life in the hands of others, just trust—those were Jacques' natural tendencies, and they were how he always felt, whereas his brothers never felt like that. One brother in particular.

According to Alex's memoir, one day in 1941 he went to Pithiviers, determined to get his older brother out. Alex describes a dramatic encounter with a guard who, on realizing he was Jacques' brother, threatened to put Alex in Pithiviers, too.

"I put my hand in my jacket pocket. It was a bluff. I was completely unarmed, not even a pocketknife. But I had my hands and I could strangle him. I was ready to take action and that was obvious," Alex writes.

Having scared off the guard, Alex finds Jacques and tells him he's come to save him.

But Jacques won't leave. He's French, he says. He has nothing to fear.

He's here under the protection of French policemen. He has confidence in them.

"'I'm a French soldier.' These were his only thoughts. French, blind patriot. 'I'm a French corporal in the French army. I've been ordered here so I'm staying.'

"One could weep with rage to see him thus, submissive, obedient, confident," Alex writes.

Whether this scene ever actually happened is impossible to prove. Certainly there's no record of Alex going to Pithiviers, although if he broke in and scared off a guard, there wouldn't be. It's possible that Alex was giving a little showman's pizzazz to a slightly different story that instead Henri and Sonia told their daughter, their nephews, and me, and that Alex also corroborated.

When Jacques was arrested, Mila was two months pregnant. In late December 1941 she gave birth to their daughter, Lily. Jacques was granted leave on December 30 in order to see his wife and daughter. This was the story my family always told and yet the more I thought

Mila and Lily

about it, the less likely it seemed. Why would Jacques be given leave from the camp? I suspected this to be some souped-up lore, until one day I was in the Shoah museum in Paris, looking up Jacques' records in Pithiviers, and there it was, in unarguable black and white: *"Permis à deux jours du 30 au 31 [Décembre] inclus, rentre 1ere Janvier 1942."* He really had left the camp.

"But Glass," the guards said to him before he got on the train to Paris, according to what Jacques then told his family, "if you don't return, we will kill all your friends here, and we will track you down, and we will find you, and we will kill you too."

The birth of a child was, according to Pithivier's rules, insufficient reason for a prisoner to be granted home leave. So according to Jacques' records, he had to go home because "femme gravement malade." But he'd have had to produce medical notes proving Mila was at death's door, and even then he probably wouldn't have been allowed to go. So quite how Jacques pulled off this home visit is a mystery. Perhaps Alex really did bully a guard into letting him out. Perhaps—and this strikes me as the most likely scenario—the guards just liked Jacques and knew him well enough to trust him to come back. However it happened, Nathalie Grenon, the director of CERCIL (Le Centre d'Étude et de Recherche sur les camps d'Internement dans le Loiret et la Déportation Juive), who helped me with my research into Pithiviers, described Jacques' two-day excursion from the camp as "plus exceptionnelle." It was to be Jacques' greatest piece of luck, and his last.

Jacques arrived at Mila's bedside to find Henri, Sonia, and Alex all waiting for him, along with his newborn daughter. According to Sonia and Alex, this is what happened and what was said.

Run, they told him. *This is the chance of a lifetime! You've never had any good luck, Jacques, but this is the luckiest break a man like you could have. We can help you. We will hide you. You will never get another chance like this. We are your family. They will kill you. We know what we are talking about. Listen to us. Run.*

Jacques held his tiny daughter and looked at his brothers—his brothers, with whom he'd run through the forests of Chrzanow, whom he'd lain beside while listening to the pogroms, who had always helped him fight off bullies in school and then fight off bailiffs who nearly destroyed his business before he had even started. He had relied on his brothers all his life. But Jacques had always relied on someone else more. First it was his mother, to whom he invariably deferred, and then it was his wife. He had registered his name and address in 1940 when she told him to do so, which was how Vichy knew where to send the billet vert condemning him to Pithiviers, and he would do what she advised now. They all looked at Mila. She was lying in bed, listening, her eyes shut.

"Mila?" Jacques asked.

She opened her eyes and looked around, like a queen preparing to make a regal pronouncement.

"*Mon Jacques a donné sa parole,*" she said.

My Jacques gave his word. He must go back.

Alex started shouting at her: "You stupid woman! You're going to kill my brother and I'm going to kill you!" For once, Henri and Sonia didn't try to hold him back. Instead, they just looked at her aghast.

"Mila, please, see sense, if he goes back they will kill him!" Sonia said.

Even Henri, quiet, measured Henri, joined in: "For God's sake, they're killing Jews. We can help all three of you. Think of your daughter!"

But Mila was implacable, as certain of her decision as a cow is sure that life on the farm will always be good. Realizing that there was no point reasoning with her, Henri, Sonia, and Alex turned to Jacques.

"If you go back they will kill you, your stupid wife, and your baby daughter. What kind of man are you? Stay and protect your family, for God's sake!"

"Jacques, please, we can help you. I will get you fake ID, you'll be safe here."

"If you go back on the train, Jacques, you'll never see your daughter again."

But they knew it was no use. Jacques never listened to them when Chaya or Mila was around, and he'd never had their drive, their determination to make it, to succeed, or even just to survive. He was already looking out the window, holding Lily, planning his departure.

And so, on New Year's Day 1942, Jacques got the train back to Pithiviers. He walked back into the freezing camp, his footprints in the snow the only part of him left outside in the free world. He was checked off by the guards, who either laughed at his passivity or simply took it for granted, and the gates closed behind him. They would never open for him again. His brothers were right: he had missed his chance.

Was Jacques simply a fool for returning? For so long I thought so. On the bus ride back from Pithiviers I talked with the other descendants, some of whom remembered going to the camp as a child to visit their relatives. One woman talked to me about how all the children of the prisoners knew each other, and all the men knew one another's children.

I told her about Jacques going back to the camp after his home leave to visit Mila, and I rolled my eyes—wasn't that just absurd? What an unforgivable waste of an opportunity. Surely her father would never have done that. But she reprimanded me for my callousness.

"There was a real sense of camaraderie at the camp after all that time," she told me. "It's hard for you to believe now, I know, but there was. And that's why he returned. He would never have abandoned his friends."

Jacques always had bad timing, but his decision to return to Pithiviers could not have been timed worse. Less than three weeks after he walked back to the camp, the Wannsee Conference was held in Germany, at which plans were formalized for the implementation of the Final Solution: the killing of all the Jews in Nazi-occupied Europe. As early as March 1942 more than a thousand Jews were shipped out on one train from France to Auschwitz. In early summer, German and French officials met to plan more mass deportations.

The men in Pithiviers heard the rumors from home. But on July 14, Bastille Day, they were reassured, again, by the Préfecture from Orléans that they would be protected, because they were French, and they were told not to listen to rumors. Less than twenty-four hours later they were told to pack their bags. The next day, women and children prisoners suddenly arrived at the camp, and that's when the men really started to worry, but it was too late.

On the 17th of July 1942, Jacques was ordered onto a cattle train by the French police, along with 928 other prisoners from Pithiviers and Beaune-la-Rolonde. This was convoi 6, and among Jacques' fellow prisoners on the train were ninety-six women and twenty-four children.[7] One of the women was Irène Nemirovsky, author of *Suite Française,* a series of novels about life in occupied France that was finally published in 2004, having been saved and preserved by her daughter during the war and in the decades afterward. Nemirovsky had planned to write five novels in her series, but she had only finished two when she was arrested. When the police arrived to take her to Pithiviers, she told her young daughters, "I am going on a journey now." It was one from which neither she nor Jacques would ever return. They were both thirty-nine years old.

There were a hundred prisoners in each wagon, standing pressed up against one another in the airless train.

"They won't eat us, they're just taking us somewhere to work," the prisoners muttered to one another reassuringly.

"Maybe to Drancy?" another suggested, as they'd heard about another French internment camp that had recently been opened.

In fact, the reason Jacques and the rest of the prisoners were shipped out so suddenly was that Vichy was now going after the Jews so relentlessly, and they needed the space in the French camps for the new arrests. The day before Jacques' train left for Auschwitz, French police completed the now infamous Vel d'Hiv roundup, in which more than thirteen thousand Jews, including four thousand children, were arrested, with most held at an indoor cycle track in Paris before being sent to the camps. French police had tracked them down using the 1940 Jewish census, and the man who helped to plan the roundup was René Bousquet, secretary-general of the police and close associate of Colonel Perré, Alex's friend. According to US diplomatic papers, Pierre Laval—by now the head of government—met with a group of American Quakers at this time and told them that "these foreign Jews had always been a problem in France, and the French government was glad that a change in the German attitude towards them gave France an opportunity to get rid of them." Laval, the papers add, "made no mention of any German pressure."[8] By the end of the year almost 40,000 Jews would be deported from France.[9]

For three days and nights, in the stifling July heat, Jacques and his fellow prisoners traveled in the train. There was only a tiny window, no room to sit—certainly none to lie down—no food, and no water. The only toilet was a small scrap of hay in the corner of the wagon. The smell quickly became so bad people were throwing up where they stood, worsening the stench and the misery. There was hardly even any air. Some people literally dropped dead where they stood for lack of water. At a certain point—the French/German border, it turned out—the French guards and drivers got off and were replaced with Germans. Seeing they were at a station, the prisoners cried out the window, "Water, please water!"

"None for you, Jews!" came the response, in German, from the civilians nearby. "This is hell," the prisoners wept, but it was not, because hell was still to come.

They knew now they were in Germany. And Germany, they said anxiously to one another, was a civilized country, right? Surely they were just here to work.

They arrived at Auschwitz-Birkenau in the evening. "Raus! Schnell! Schnell!" yelled the guards, hurrying them off the train, beating them with truncheons.

A lot is known about convoi 6, more than most deportation trains, because a relatively high number of people who traveled on it were still alive when the war ended—91 out of 928, and a lot of the details I've given above come from the survivors' testimonies kept at the Shoah memorial in Paris. It was still so early in the war that the Nazis needed the prisoners to help construct Auschwitz-Birkenau, so there was no selection process when the prisoners arrived in Poland—everyone entered the camp and none were sent to the gas chambers, at least not immediately. As a result, there are only two associations for descendants and relatives of victims of a specific deportation train, and one of them is the association for convoi 6. It was with this association that I visited Pithiviers in 2012. The year before, 928 trees were planted in Israel in the name of convoi 6, one for every adult and child who traveled on that train.

The tree feels like an apt memorial for Jacques, the boy who once ran through Chrzanow's silver birch tree forest and was then sent as a man to Birkenau, a camp whose name derives from the German for "birch tree." Did Jacques realize, as he walked into the death camp, that he was only about a mile and a half from where he was born? Had he spotted the thin Galician birch trees through the tiny window in the train, and did they look familiar to him? Did they make him think of his brothers and the Ornstein cousins and how they used to hide in the forests? And of his father, buried in the shadow of birch trees only a few miles away from where he was now? Did he wonder why he, alone among his siblings, hadn't risked anything to stay alive? Why he was the passive one among them and how this was the conclusion to that story? Did he think about the weird irony of his life, how he had always wanted to stay still, but was forced to travel so far, and yet ended up right back where he began? Perhaps he thought, No matter how hard a Jewish man tries, even if he fights for another country, he will still get sent back to the place of his father's grave instead of enjoying his daughter in her cot—always the past for the Jew, never the future. Never forget who you are and where you're from, because no one else around you will, and they will send you back. All that deprivation and degradation on the train, it had felt like the world was ending. Instead, Jakob Glahs walked out to find he was simply back home. Like waking from a bad dream, but the nightmare continues in real life. It had always been thus, the threat just beneath the surface. He just hadn't wanted to see it. He had crossed a continent and he hadn't seen it. But now he was back to where he started and he could see it. At last he saw it. Once again his brothers had been right.

Or maybe he thought none of these things. Maybe he was already too sick and too tired and too naturally unself-reflective to think like that at all. And who could blame him? He was always Jacques, only Jacques—why ask more of him than he was? Anyone who expected him to be other than he had been is the foolish one—Alex had learned that, and so had Henri. He had always been utterly true to himself: gentle, popular, caring, weak, trusting, loyal, unlucky, kind. So Jacques was not sent directly to the gas chambers, as so many Jews arriving at Birkenau soon would be. But according to Auschwitz's records, he lasted fewer than three months building his own tomb, so close to his place of his birth. He was killed on October 6.

On October 5, the day before Jacques was murdered, Revillon wrote another letter to the CQJD on Mila's behalf, asking for her to be allowed to stay in the apartment and stressing that she did not know where her husband was and was very anxious. Sara, too, was worried, and wrote to the Red Cross for help. She would have to wait for two years to get a reply. Henri, Sonia, and Alex did not make inquiries. They might not have known where Jacques was, but they had a pretty good idea.

Mila and Lily eventually went into hiding, almost certainly with help from Sonia as there was no way Mila could have evaded the Vichy police on her own with a newborn baby. Miraculously, they managed to survive the war, but this was to be the one miracle in poor Mila's dumb, cursed life. After the war was over, she returned to rue de la Tour, living in that dark little basement beneath the fur storage business, because it never occurred to her that she might want to do something different than what she was doing before. Sara finally received definitive proof that Jacques was dead in November 1944 from the Red Cross, who wrote her confirming his death in Auschwitz. For the rest of her life, whenever someone asked her about her brother Jacques, Sara would answer quietly, "They sent him home."

After the war, Mila was very isolated in Paris. Photos of her from that period show her with her beloved toddler daughter, holding her baby almost vampirically close to her, the only thing she had left in the world. There is never anyone else in the photo. She didn't marry again, she barely made a living trying to run Jacques' old business on her own, and in the letters she wrote throughout 1945 to the Service de Restitution des Biens des Victimes des Lois et Mesures de Spoliation, which was set up to provide some compensation to the Jews whose money and property was taken from them by the Vichy, she frequently mentions being *denue de tout* (completely bankrupt). Alex refused to see or speak to her, and whenever he heard her name he would spit and say, *"Elle a tué mon frere!"* Henri, uncharacteristically unforgiving, also refused to speak to her, furious that her stupidity had condemned his closest brother to his death. Worse, she remained unrepentant about it: Mila lived another thirty years after Jacques died, and not for a moment did she ever think she made a mistake in telling Jacques to go back to the camp. She never asked herself, if maybe she had listened to her brothers-in-law then maybe Jacques might still be alive and she wouldn't be living in penury on her own with her daughter in this dank old basement. After all, she would say, he gave his word.

Lily and Mila

Her sister Olga, who now lived in the United States, helped a little. But she found Mila such a drag, always complaining about her life and never taking any responsibility for her actions, that they hardly spoke, let alone saw one another.

The only people who helped Mila were Sonia and Sara. Both of them felt sorry for her and even more sorry for Lily. They, unlike Henri and Alex, were able to look at the truth about what happened to Jacques square in the face; they knew what he was like—had always been like—and they also knew he was a grown man who had made his own choices. Unlike his brothers, they didn't blame a foolish woman for his death. Whereas Alex in particular had always tried to make Jacques into something he wasn't by denying his true nature, and continued to do so after he died, the women accepted him as he really was. So after the war, Sara sent Mila provisions, and Sonia secretly visited her, bringing money and food, and listening silently to Mila's endless list of grievances against the world. Sonia was known in the family as a chatterbox, because she said what she thought. But Sonia was also very kind and knew when to say nothing and let others speak, and she let Mila speak.

The only other person in the family who helped her was my father, who moved to Paris in the 1960s and happened to live around the corner from Mila. He occasionally went around to her apartment for dinner—Mila was an excellent cook, and loved to make heavy Polish dishes, but my father often had to pay for the ingredients. At other times, she would come to his apartment, ringing his doorbell at odd hours of the day.

"I need to use your bath!" she would call up to his window.

There was no bathtub in her apartment and so, at the age of fifty-something, she would walk around the corner to her twenty-five-year-old nephew and beg to use his.

Lily grew up to be a sweet, quiet, gentle girl, a lot like her father in many ways. But because of the consanguinity of her parents, she was born with a hole in her heart and she was known back then as a "blue baby," because her lips purpled from oxygen deprivation caused by her weak heart. When Lily was fourteen, Sonia heard about a doctor in Denver who specialized in helping such children, and she talked her neighbor, who happened to be a radio producer, into putting on a telethon to raise money for Lily to go there. Incredibly, this worked, and Lily flew out to Denver to have her heart repaired. The operation was a success. When I was going through Sonia's belongings, two decades after she died, I found a publicity shot of Lily leaving the hospital that the radio station took. It's a very staged photo, almost comically so, with Lily sitting in a car, stiffly waving to a trio of nurses who wave back to her. But it's also an extremely sweet photo, because of Lily: she looks so happy in the photo, a typical fourteen-year-old, her tidy braids swinging gently as she waves to her nurses, a little girl about to enjoy health and happiness the likes of which she'd never before known. Before she left the hospital, her doctor told her she should be fine, as long as she never got pregnant, because her heart was not strong enough to support two lives.

A few years later, when Lily was in her very early twenties, she was walking in Paris near Luxembourg Gardens when she spotted a man sitting in a café and fell in love at first sight. His name was Victor, he came from Bolivia, and they married almost immediately. She moved with

Lily as a teenager

him to South America, and, too in love to remember or care about any medical edicts, she quickly became pregnant. About five months into her pregnancy, my father got a call at his office in New York. It was Sonia, and she had just spoken to Victor who had called her in a panic: Lily was dying.

"Should I tell Mila? She's just getting over pneumonia and I worry that she wouldn't survive the trip," Sonia asked my dad.

"Sonia, I can't tell you what to do you—you know her better than me," he replied.

"Fine, never mind!" Sonia said, slamming down the phone.

Sonia decided not to tell Mila, believing, maybe correctly, that traveling to Bolivia and seeing Lily die would kill her. But not knowing pretty much killed her, too. After Lily died in Bolivia, Mila found out that Sonia had known before and hadn't told her, thereby preventing her from saying good-bye to her daughter. Understandably, she flew into a desperate rage and refused to speak to Sonia ever again. But this meant that for the last ten years of her life she hardly spoke to anyone. Instead, she sat in the same basement flat Jacques had bought for them thirty years earlier, crying on her own, surrounded by tear-soaked photos of Lily. She herself finally died in the early 1970s, a sad and lonely life that finally came to an end. And when she went, Jacques' branch of the family tree—blighted by bad luck and bad circumstances, both of which were made infinitely worse by bad choices, from father to mother to daughter—withered away to ashes.

Chapter 10

ALEX—MYTH-MAKING

France, 1940s

In the autumn of 1940, Alex, fresh from demobilization, was in Grenoble with his fellow resistance fighters, the Sizaines, talking about how to save their now-humiliated country. Alex was keen to sneak back into Paris to see his family, save his mother, check on his business. But his close friend and fellow Sizaine, Jean Baptiste Seytour, who—unsurprisingly, given his name—was not Jewish, convinced him they would do better establishing a base in the unoccupied southern zone before making resistance runs to Paris. Alex agreed, but where should they live? Alex's money was in Paris. Seytour had the answer for that, too.

Seytour, an aspiring actor, had grown up in Nice, and, luckily for him and his fellow legionnaire, his father still lived there. So he and Alex moved in with Pierre Seytour, and for the next few years they lived a pretty fabulous life down on le Midi. Alex's friend Kiki Kisling lived nearby, and they often went to his place for dinners and drinks. Alex's former draftsman, Christian Dior, was also down in the south of France, after being demobilized from the army, and he was staying with his father and his beloved youngest sister, Catherine, in the pretty village of Callian near Grasse, about twenty-five miles from Cannes. According to Alex's memoir, when loyal friends in his salon in Paris sent him a supply of civilian clothes, he shared them with Dior because the two of them were the same size (short, in other words). Alex's other illustrator, René Gruau, was also down in the south, and it was in this period that he became friends with Dior, establishing a lifelong working relationship. It was through Gruau that Dior learned he could resume his draftsman work down in the south. He was soon even busier than he'd been in Paris because several designers had outlets in Nice, Cannes, and Monte Carlo, and they desperately needed an illustrator, as there were no photographers—or film—to take pictures of the dresses.[1] Among these designers were Chanel, Hermès—and Alex Maguy. Although Alex's salon in Paris, like Jacques' fur business, had been taken from him by the CGQJ under "Aryanization" laws, he was, in recognition of his war record, given permission in 1941 to open up a salon in Cannes. He chose an elegant little building at the plum address of Place Mérimée, on the promenade next to the seafront.

"Cannes was a refuge for Parisians in exile," Dior's biographer Marie-France Pochna wrote, describing how the bohemians would spend their days sunbathing on the beach and their nights throwing costume parties so wild the police threatened to shut these "bacchanalian orgies" down. It was a world that would have felt cheeringly familiar to Alex.

As well as height, work, and social life preferences, another connection between him and Dior was a proximity to resistance activity. Alex was working with the Sizaines and Dior's sister Catherine was about to become an important figure in the Massif Central network. Gitta Sereny later described the Massif Central as "one of the most dynamic intelligence [resistance] movements in Europe,"[2] and it had similar ambitions to the Sizaines, as it focused on gathering information about German train and troop movements for purposes of sabotage. It was also one of the most brutalized resistance networks: most of its leaders were killed by 1942, and Catherine Dior herself was arrested in June 1944 and deported to Ravensbrück.

For almost a year, Christian Dior had no idea whether his sister was alive or dead, until he got a phone call in May 1945 saying that she would be arriving in Paris the next day by train. When she came home, she had been so starved that it was several months until she could eat solid food. But no family's story was simple in occupied France, and the Diors are a neat illustration of that: whereas Catherine was in the resistance, her niece, Françoise, became a full-throated Nazi, promoting Hitler and burning down synagogues.

Dior himself would spend much of the war working as a designer for Lucien Lelong alongside another aspiring couturier, Pierre Balmain. Lelong—who would play an important part in Alex's life after the war—managed to keep his label open during the war. The few other designers who did so as well—Jacques Fath, Rochas, Maggy Rouff—did so by selling to wealthy French collaborators and visiting German officers. In fact, according to fashion historian Dominique Veillon, this proved to be such a lucrative market that collectively couturiers made 463 million francs a year, up from 67 million francs only two years earlier.[3] As much as Dior loved Catherine, he also had to eat, and so he spent the later part of the war selling clothes to the wives of men who enabled the torture of his sister. It was very hard to avoid working for collaborators if you worked in the luxury sector and lived in France during the war.

For the first few years of the war, Alex's life in the south of France was comfortable and glamorous. He was living in the Seytour family's flat and his life was as sociable as it had been in Paris, hanging around with, as he puts it, "my friend Seytour."

An obvious question about this period of Alex's life is whether he and Seytour were lovers. Certainly Alex writes about him in his memoir more warmly than he does his own family, and it's not a completely outlandish conclusion to draw about a fashion designer and an actor living together so closely for so long. According to Seytour's records he was married the whole time he was with Alex, to a woman named Caroline Antoine, whom he married in 1931, but there is no mention of her in any of Alex's records, and that marriage ended in divorce, without any children, in 1944. As far as I know, Alex never told anyone in his family about Seytour, and after he left Nice he never saw him again.

Alex's salon became so busy he had to employ twelve people to help meet the demand. But as well as being a working salon, the shop became a hangout for resistance fighters. The Sizaines would meet there often and, in the absence of having any weapons, as the British hadn't yet started parachuting in supplies, they plotted how to derail German trains coming into France. Other resistance fighters who came to Alex's salon included the French novelists Joseph Kessel, who worked as an aide to Charles de Gaulle during the war and later wrote *Belle de Jour*, and his nephew, Maurice Druon. Kessel's lover, Germaine Sablon, a singer and actress and just the kind of person Alex would know from Paris, was another frequent presence.

The question of what Alex actually did during the war only became more puzzling the more you asked him directly about it. It wasn't that Alex didn't talk about his war years; it's just that the few stories he told were disjointed, nonchronological, and utterly improbable, anecdotes so worn down with retelling they were like sea-tossed pebbles, smoothed from years of repetition, the grit long since washed away. I—and many others—suspected they were a smoke screen for something else, distractions, jimmied-up anecdotes rendered into self-mythologies. The question was what he was distracting people from.

Almost everyone who thrived and survived in France during the war later engaged in some kind of self-mythology. Once the country was liberated and the shame of France's collaboration was exposed to the world, the reality of the recent past, for many people, needed to be obscured, black covered in white. For some the motivations were obvious, for others the story was more gray.

When Alex's memoir arrived in the post, I flipped through the stories of early 1930s Paris to get to what I hoped would be the long-awaited answer of what Alex did to survive the war. There were some stories, ones my father and I had heard dozens of times from Alex himself: barely sketched allusions to arrests and brave standoffs against collaborators, more fully sketched stories about his glamorous life as a couturier in Cannes. On page 118 it looked like he was about to start detailing what life was actually like during the war. I turned the page eagerly—but there was no page 119. Nor a 120, 121, or 122. Instead, the memoir blithely skipped from 1943 to 1945 with the story resuming on page 131.

Was this just a fluke? Did twelve pages merely get lost over the years, and did those twelve pages just happen to be the ones on which Alex described his war years? Or did Alex write those sections up and then decide he didn't want anyone to read them and so threw them away? Had he, in fact, been a collaborator?

Plenty of big-name fashion designers collaborated or at least worked with the Nazi occupiers, including Coco Chanel, Louis Vuitton, and Jeanne Lanvin. Cristóbal Balenciaga designed for Franco's wife, Jean Patou made dresses for Hermann Göring's wife, and Hugo Boss—who was German and based in Germany—not only joined the Nazi party but made the Nazi Youth uniforms.[4] Marcel Rochas refused even to say hello to former customers and friends if they were Jewish, pointedly crossing the road to avoid them.[5] Pretty much the only people in France at that time who could afford high fashion were Nazis and collaborators, so the few designers who continued to work in Paris during the war would have worked with them. It wasn't impossible that Alex might have done that, too, and if so, that would have explained how he, a Polish Jew, didn't just survive the war but flourished.

Alex himself might have been opaque about what he had to do to survive the war, but the records were not. During the war he became such a person of interest that the files on him at the CGQJ could barely contain all the letters and records of his various comings and goings. Repeatedly investigations were conducted into his business affairs, and repeatedly nothing happened. This was remarkable, given how blatantly Alex was hosting resistance meetings in his salon, but it turns out there was a simple reason: in his CGQJ file there are letters from his old friend and protector, now known as General Perré, defending Alex's right to own a shop. Even more remarkably, Xavier Vallat, the Commissioner General for Jewish Affairs (head of the CGQJ), personally wrote a letter, on February 13, 1942, ordering that Alex's case should be looked at favorably and he should be left alone:

> J'ai l'honneur de vous faire connaître que les renseignements sur l'intéressé étant favorables, il conviendrait de lui faire savoir que je ne vois pas d'inconvénient à ce qu'il exerce la profession de couturier créateur modeliste. ["It is my honor to let you know that as the information we have on this particular person is positive, I do not see any reason why he should not work as a fashioin designer."]

When I found this letter in a file about Alex in a French archive, my stomach sank into my shoes. Vallat was a vicious anti-Semite who looked like a movie villain straight from central casting, having lost an eye and a leg in World War I. He was also the most important person in the CGQJ—in other words, the man in charge of all anti-Semitic activity in France. He was the man charged with the Aryanization of the French economy—conducted entirely by the Vichy government with no pressure from the Germans—and his passion was the elimination of Jewish culture from French life. All of this made his defense of Alex's shop seem especially bizarre, and the first time I read it I was sure that I'd found, at long last, confirmation of my worst suspicions: Alex was a collaborator, a spy for the enemy, and this is why he was so protected.

But the morality of French politics during the war was far too blurred to be confined by simplistic black-and-white outlines, and what this letter reveals has, in fact, little to do with Alex. Instead, it shows the changing and conflicting loyalties in the Vichy government. Yet whereas most Jews in France suffered—to say the least—from these political shifts, Alex benefited from them.

Like Perré and Pétain, Vallat was another old military vet, and while he was a massive anti-Semite, what he really was above all was a Catholic nationalist, almost as anti-German as he was anti-Semitic, one who saw the sanctity of France as his first priority.[6] So anyone who fought for France was, for him, a Frenchman of honor, even if that man was a Polish Jew. Thus, because Alex was a decorated veteran of the Narvik campaign, Vallat intervened on his behalf, which was almost like the British home secretary stepping in to adjudicate on a small local matter, but that was how much he cared about those who fought for France, whatever their religion. Vallat's priorities would soon prove to be his undoing. Within weeks of writing in defense of Alex, the German ambassador to Vichy, Otto Abetz, ordered Pétain to dismiss him, which he did. Vallat was all for the Aryanization of France, but not at the cost of turning it into Germany, and his uncooperativeness became too much for Nazi Germany. They replaced him with Louis Darquier de Pellepoix, a pro-Nazi French politician who was in Germany's pay before the war, and it was Darquier de Pellepoix who ensured the deportation of France's Jews, including Jacques, to Auschwitz. Darquier de Pellepoix definitely did not care about Jacques' war record, or that of any Jew, so for the Jews he was worse than Vallat, but in Vichy it was all relative. Vallat remained an unrepentant anti-Semite for the rest of his life, and there is no evidence he ever met Alex or that Alex ever knew he owed his wartime livelihood to him.

Even though Alex's connection to Vallat turned out to be innocent, a fog of suspicion started to form around Alex in the eyes of both Vichy and his fellow resistance fighters. He didn't especially help himself: when General Perré came to visit the shop, Alex made a big show of presenting him with a military cap. Alex didn't care that Perré was on the other side:

he saw him as an old friend and, more important, a useful connection. And when Alex went to Perré for help when he heard that his cousin Josek Ornstein had been arrested, the rumors really began.

"My Cannes branch was busy, too busy for some. People saw military officers and beautiful women there, which created doubts. Was I even kosher?" Alex wrote.

As deeply as Alex loved France and believed in defending the Jews, there was always one cause that Alex believed in above all, and that was Alex. He would do whatever it took to survive, and if that meant being friendly with some people in Vichy during the war, well, he would say, that wasn't the worst thing in the world. He was still, and would always be, the hungry little boy in Chrzanow, determined to scrape his way from the bottom of the sewer to reach the stars. He grew up thinking, "No one will help you except you." And that was the lesson he lived by for the rest of his life.

During 1941 and 1942, Alex and the Sizaines ran resistance missions to Paris. Alex was one of the few Jewish members of the group, and thus he risked more than most, as it was forbidden for a Jew to go into the Occupied Zone. For Alex, the danger was the appeal.

"I crossed the line of demarcation several times with a guide," he writes. "I was always in front to open the way. Nothing could frighten me. A rage to live burned within me. I felt invincible."

What Alex was actually doing on these missions remains somewhat mysterious. According to letters from his cousins Renée and Roger Goldberg, he was meeting up with them and his siblings, and his memoir corroborates this. Given that Roger and Renée were in the resistance, it looks like they were his main points of contact for passing information back and forth. He was, according to Sonia and Henri, at Mila's bedside when Lily was born in 1942, and he repeatedly appears at Sonia's lunches in Renée's letters of that year. He also, at some point, managed to smuggle Chaya out of Paris and down to Cannes, where she stayed with one of his fashion clients, a Madame Armande. Alex achieved an enormous amount in his life, escaping the depths of the Polish pogroms to climb to the top of the French fashion world, all thanks to his cunning and determination. But that he managed to sneak his truculent, strictly kosher, non-French-speaking mother across the demarcation line was possibly his most extraordinary feat.

He also wanted to check on his business, because it was no longer his. A man called Joseph Paquin took it over in 1941, when businesses in the Occupied Zone were Aryanized, and Alex is as vicious about Paquin in his memoir as he is about the Nazis who killed so many members of his family, describing him alternately as "a rat," "a bastard," and "the little shit." Alex would have hated anyone taking over his business, but the story of Paquin reveals something more about the world of French collaboration than Alex's ego.

Born in 1873 in the small northeastern village of Mont-Bonvillers, Joseph Nicolas Paquin also worked in fashion. He married his wife, Hélène, on December 23, 1894, and on the morning of his wedding, every newspaper had the same front page: a photo of Colonel Alfred Dreyfus, who, the day before, had been unanimously found guilty by seven judges of passing on French military secrets to the Germans. As the newly wedded M. and Mme Paquin began their married life, they did so against the backdrop of what remains a universal symbol of anti-Semitism.

Paquin was a less successful Paris couturier than Alex. As well as Alex's business, he was given the businesses of three other Jewish designers—at least one of whom was then killed in Auschwitz—and he was paid 2,000 francs a month for each. Madame Paquin certainly enjoyed the financial benefits of seizing control of Jewish businesses: during the war she enthusiastically redecorated their apartment with expensive furniture and what one fellow designer described as "bibelots anciens" (antique trinkets). Paquin protected his freebies: when Alex was given permission to open an Alex Maguy salon in Cannes, Paquin wrote a cross letter to the CGQJ, saying this would create "confusion" for customers and should not be allowed. (Thanks to Alex's high-ranking friends, this letter was ignored.) Paquin drove the CGQJ somewhat mad during the war, constantly writing letters demanding

more money, more help, and more effective measures taken against
Alex's business in the south. As I read his letters, I understood better
why Alex called him "a worm": his tone was whiny and weasely. It infuriated Alex that such a man had his hands on his beloved business in
Paris, and he vowed he would have his revenge. He would not have to
wait long to get it.

Back in Cannes, Alex's life continued peacefully, building his business, finding kosher food for his mother. In November 1942 the Italian
army invaded Nice, and, because the Italians weren't especially interested
in Germany's anti-Semitic focus, the only way Alex's life changed was
that he picked up some Italian vocabulary. But on September 9, 1943,
the Germans took over the Italian zones and Alex's life changed in the
worst possible ways.

According to Alex's official testimonies given after the war, he was
arrested three times during his time in the south of France. Twice his
powerful friends were able to help him, despite his being a foreign Jew.
The third time he pushed his luck too far.

September 18, 1943, was a warm evening, and after a long day of working in the salon Alex decided to relax in the way he'd been relaxing for
two decades, which was by going to a nightclub. This time he chose the
Pam Pam in Nice and, as usual, Alex had his own table and was drinking
with his friends, talking with the few remaining Italians left in the city.

"Suddenly, I heard a German song being played by the orchestra. My
blood rose. Disgusted and furious, I summoned the headwaiter. 'Please
ask the bandleader to come speak with me. I have something to say to
him,'" Alex writes in his memoir.

When the bandleader came to Alex's table, he loudly ordered him
to "stop playing these goddamn Kraut songs." Instead, they should play
French and British military songs, starting with *Le Boudin,* the official
song of the French Foreign Legion, followed by *La Marseillaise.*

The headwaiter begged Alex to leave, saying there were senior members of the Gestapo in the room. The Nazis had arrived in the city just
over a week earlier. Alois Brunner, the notorious Jew hunter, came to

Nice on September 10, and his police had already started conducting raids. The Germans seized control of the roads and train stations, and the Jews were now in what Serge Klarsfeld, then a child in Nice, described as "a kind of trap."[7] Even French Jews, who had previously been able to take their safety for granted, knew that the leniency they'd enjoyed under the Italians was over. What had been happening to their friends and families in the north was about to happen to them, and every Jew in the region was terrified. But Alex refused to back down.

"I'm a French soldier—I am not leaving," he replied.

"They're giving you five minutes to go," the waiter pleaded.

"Like hell will a Kraut give me orders! I'm a Legionnaire and nothing scares me," Alex replied.

He looked at the table where the waiter had run over from, and saw three members of the Gestapo sitting with a woman. One of the men took his pistol out of its holster and pointed it straight at Alex.

"Look at this coward! With a woman at his table he pulls a revolver," Alex crowed to the now-silent room, all staring at what was going on.

The Nazi got out from behind his table and walked toward Alex, keeping his gun pointed at Alex's head. When he got to Alex's table, Alex stood up.

"I am Alex Maguy," Alex shouted.

"We know who you are, Maguy. You're a Jew."

"That's right, I'm a Jew and you can go fuck yourself," he replied.

Somehow Alex managed to escape out the back of the club without being shot or arrested, but he knew he was on borrowed time now. After checking that he wasn't being followed, he went back to Cannes and to the house of Mme Armande, who was hiding Chaya for him. He left enough money for his mother to be looked after for the next year, and then hurried away before he led the Nazis to his mother. He didn't even try to hide himself, perhaps out of a sense of arrogance that he would always, ultimately, be protected. Instead, the next day he went to work as usual, and waited to see what would happen. He did not have to wait long. Within an hour, the Gestapo burst into his salon on Place

Mérimée, arrested him, and brought him to the Hotel Excelsior in Nice, Alois Brunner's headquarters.

By the time Brunner arrived in France, he was only thirty years old but was already known for being especially efficient at deporting Jews. He had worked as Adolf Eichmann's assistant and overseen the deportations in Austria, Berlin, and Greece; in Austria alone he was personally responsible for the deportation of 47,000 Jews. By the time war ended, he'd sent over 128,000 Jews to the death camps. From the moment he arrived in the south of France, he terrorized the Jews, and the raids he ordered in Nice were, according to Klarsfeld, the most brutal that the Nazis carried out in the whole of western Europe.[8, 9] They were largely carried out at night: men, women, and children dragged out of their beds, shivering in their nightclothes, terrorized and arrested. Brunner renamed the Excelsior *"camp de recensement des juifs arrêtés, dépendant du camp de Drancy"* (camp for arrested Jews going to Drancy). He ostensibly turned it into a prison where he dumped the Jews rounded up during the raids. He then tortured them, beat them, ordered them to give the names and addresses of their families under pain of death, and then put them on a train to Drancy, the French concentration camp that had taken over from Pithiviers. Brunner himself would, in a few months' time, be in charge of Drancy, and it is estimated that he sent 23,500 Jews to Auschwitz from there.

Alex was kept under arrest for four days. "The guards beat me like madmen. I did what I could to dodge the blows, like boxers do, but they held me. I never treated the German prisoners like this in Narvik," he recalled. When he asked why he was being singled out for so many beatings, one of the guards showed him the file they had on him. "It was thick like a block. The spies had done their work well. I had no illusions now. I knew I would be executed like Josek was," he wrote, referring to his cousin. But when Alex was pushed onto the train to Drancy on September 24, he realized he would not have a fate like Josek's; he would have one like Jacques'.

The story Alex always told about how he survived the war was that he was arrested but he escaped from the train. "Escaped from the train": I heard this so many times, and imagined it even more, that it became more than a story and more like a myth in my head. My brave great-uncle, bursting out of the train like a hero, running away from the big, bad Nazis! But as I grew older I learned that fairy tales aren't true and there were whispers in the family that maybe none of this had happened. Maybe he was never put on a train at all. Who knows? Only Alex, and no point asking him, you know what he's like—you'll never get a straight answer out of him. And anyway, how on earth can you prove that someone once jumped off a train?

It was easy to find the records from Drancy detailing who got off the trains from Nice in 1943, and Alex's name wasn't on any of them, which didn't prove much. But to find out who actually got on the trains, I had to go to the archives in Nice itself.

Nice is still as picturesque as it was when Alex was there—those elegant beachside boulevards, the palm trees swaying over outdoor cafes. I came to this beautiful seaside town to search through the dead. On the first day I found the work close to unbearable, especially when I'd see row after row of the same name: whole families, from grandparents to eight-month-old babies, packed off on trains that led only to death. By the third day I felt my hide getting harder, casually flicking through list after list, getting almost annoyed with the names on the list that weren't the name I wanted to see. What did I care about Gerhard Glahs? I was looking for Glass! Out of my way, Gerhard! And just as I was thinking proudly about what a tough-hearted researcher I'd become, I saw a name that undid all my efforts to stop personalizing these lists: there, listed among the Poles who were put on the train to Drancy, was "Glass, Alexandre, de 7 Place Mérimée Cannes, Juif." Alex really had gotten on the train. And he hadn't gotten off. Because he had escaped. Just as he'd always told us.

Alex was not the only person to have escaped from the train. When Klarsfeld was researching what happened to the French Jews, he noted that there were some names who got on the train to Drancy but did not then appear on the passenger lists from Drancy to Auschwitz. Some had died. Some had been released from Drancy. But in the period of September 1943–December 1943, when Brunner was at the Excelsior and sending thousands of French Jews to the camp, there were ninety-three people who got on the train to Drancy whom no one could account for. One of them was Alex.

On September 24, Alex—by now bruised and almost broken from all the beatings—was dragged out of his cell in the Excelsior along with his cellmates and pushed by the guards toward the train station. A train was waiting for them there. But they could barely see it because their senses were so overwhelmed by the noise: the whole station was filled with the sound of men, women, children, and babies screaming, crying, and begging, and officers mercilessly shouting at them in French and German. The sound was so terrifying it could stop a man's heart. But Alex marched toward the train the way a legionnaire always should, unbowed and unafraid. Alongside him was the cellmate he had become close to during his imprisonment, a lanky Frenchman called Jacques Schwob Héricourt, and the two of them got in the same train carriage together, along with eighty other men.

"Can we escape? They can't treat us like sheep. We have to do something," Alex whispered to Héricourt. But neither of them could think of anything they could do.

As the train traveled north toward Drancy and night fell, Alex thought of Jacques. At this point he didn't know exactly what had become of Jacques, but he had a strong suspicion, and after having worked so hard to not be like his older brother, were they to have the same fate after all? Had it all been for nothing? Passivity and defiance, both paths led to the same destination when chased by these persecutors. There were some demons you could not outrun. And just as Alex was thinking this, he noticed a patch of moonlight on the floor of the train and looked up to see where it was coming from. Up in the top corner of the back of the train there was a hole where two planks of wood had rotted away. He stared at it. He knew that Jacques would not have thought about the hole, and that was what had always broken his heart about his brother—

so many times he had rejected chances, offers laid out to him on a plate, often by Alex. But he always said no. Once he'd been put on the train, Alex knew, Jacques would have stood there passively and accepted his fate. Well, he was not Jacques.

He tapped Héricourt on the arm and pointed up to the hole. Héricourt looked at it, then back down to his friend and nodded, understanding. While everyone else in the carriage stared, he picked up Alex, all five feet of him, and lifted him to the opening. The train was traveling fast, about 55 miles an hour, but what difference did it make? Die trying to escape or die a passive prisoner—Alex knew which option he'd choose every time. And so, while the whole carriage watched, Alex reached toward the small opening and punched it, making the hole a little larger. He could now fit through it, just. And then, with a helping push from Héricourt, he threw himself out of the moving train.

"The shock was terrible. I landed with such force I thought at first it would kill me. And then I thought about the times I used to fall on my head out of our apartment in Chrzanow onto the rough pavement," Alex wrote.

He lay there on the side of the train track, his head bleeding, his ribs broken, barely able to breathe, let alone move. He heard the train drive off without him, and even though he was in so much pain he could hardly breathe, what he mainly felt was the extraordinary relief of no longer being a prisoner bound for Drancy. He was right to do so: almost everyone on that train, including Héricourt, would be killed in Auschwitz. But his relief turned to fear when he heard footsteps crunching toward him, and he braced himself.

"What are you doing here?"

Alex cleared the blood out of his eyes and saw a railway worker peering down at him.

"I just jumped out of a train," Alex whispered.

The man nodded slowly, looking at him.

"You're in Saint-Rambert d'Albion. Come with me, quickly. They'll be looking for you."

The railway worker and his colleagues were communists, and therefore very happy to help an escaped prisoner evade the Nazis. They took him back to their office and called a communist doctor to set his ribs and stitch up his forehead, which had torn so badly when he hit the ground that the skin flapped in front of his eyes like a veil. When the authorities came looking for Alex a few hours later, the railwaymen hid him in a large pile of manure, knowing that the Germans would be too vain about their uniforms to look for him there, and they were right. When it was safe, they brought him out of hiding, washed him, and when he was feeling up to it, taught him how to drive a train. Alex told them about how he and his cousins used to fake toothaches to take the train from Chrzanow to Trzebina, and they all laughed together. Then Alex thought more about his cousins and told his new friends his ribs hurt too much to laugh.

After a few days hiding in the railway station Alex got a message—how and from whom he never said—that he should go to Lyon, where someone would meet him and take him to a safe place. The railway workers, who presumably thought he was meeting his resistance network, gave him a lift to Lyon and wished him *bon courage*. One of them gave him his cap, small and battered and decorated with three stars. Alex kept it for the rest of his life.

At this point the story ends, at least as much as Alex ever told it, and the pages in the memoir ended here. Alex never talked about what he did after leaving Saint-Rambert d'Albion, where he went, who helped him. He made vague references to "fighting in the resistance," and that was that. I had few hopes of finding any details, but I contacted various resistance enthusiasts in central France, the area between Nice and Drancy, and asked them if they knew of any stories about a Polish Jew who had escaped from a train being hidden in their area. One, Robert Picandet, wrote back:

I am one of the heads of the Resistance Museum in St Gervais-d'Auvergne and here is some information I obtained from a former resident in Espinasse. He remembers Alex Glass very well. He lived at the home of Monsieur and Madame Aymard, who have both died, but their daughter, a Madame Gustave, remembers a sporty Israelite who lived with them and later went to Paris. She still lives in the village of Espinasse and is sure this Israelite was your uncle Alex. Perhaps you would like to talk to her?

One month later, I met Robert Picandet at the Musée de la Resistance in Saint Gervais-d'Auvergne, the town near the village of Espinasse. It was a small museum, barely two rooms large, and full of memorabilia from the *maquis*, a breakaway faction that was even more loosely organized than the resistance. The *maquis* was largely made up of French men and women who had gone underground to avoid Vichy's "Service du Travail Obligatoire," which required people to work in German factories. Some people in the *maquis* were actively against the Germans, and some were simply hiding because they didn't want to be conscripted off to Germany. Picandet explained that France was full of these renegades avoiding the French and German authorities, but the Auvergne was especially good for hiding because it was—and is still—so agricultural. This meant that there were lots of places to hide and, just as important, there was a special feeling of solidarity between the farmers and the resisters in the Auvergne. There had always been a cooperative tradition among the Auvergne peasants, and during the war they eagerly helped their undercover countrymen. Without the assistance of the agricultural workers, the resisters could not have survived: farmers and shopkeepers gave them food, local officials gave them false papers, the villagers would put them in touch with other resisters, the local gendarmerie gave them warnings if there was danger coming, and that danger usually came more from the Vichy police than the Germans.

Many Jews hid around the Auvergne, so Alex certainly wasn't unusual in coming here, Picandet told us. Several of the people hidden here were sent by a Vichy official.

"Who was that?" I asked.

"General Jean Perré," Picandet replied.

At last I found out how Alex had gotten away, and why he never went into detail about who had helped him. It wasn't the resistance that saved his life, but someone in Vichy. Things aren't always clear; they can be gray. But always a careful salesman, Alex knew that gray didn't sell, so he burnished the story.

Picandet gave me a lift in his car out to Madame Gustave's house in Espinasse. At first I insisted he not go out of his way, but I soon realized why he made the offer: the house was down long, windy paths, almost entirely hidden by surrounding forests, as far off the main road as it was possible to go. I felt like I was in a fairy tale, being taken to a magic house in the woods, and when I saw the house and Mme Gustave, I was sure of it. It was a pretty stone farm cottage in the middle of what can only be described as nowhere, with buttercup-dappled fields in front and thick woods behind it. Mme Gustave herself was the tiniest adult I'd ever seen in my life, barely more than half my height, and spry and sprightly, this tiny lone woman living all on her own in the middle of a forest.

She had lived in this house her entire life, she said, taking us into the sitting room, where she had tea and biscuits waiting for us.

"So this would have been the house Alex stayed in?" I asked.

She looked at me, surprised I hadn't already realized: "Oh yes! He was here for a long time. Tea?"

If Alex had been looking for a hiding place, he could hardly have found a better one, but had he really found this one? It seemed almost impossible. And just as I was thinking that if this had all been a wild goose chase it had been a rather charming one, I saw something that made me splutter my tea out on her floor: there, laid out very carefully on Mme Gustave's table, were half a dozen photos taken outside the house I was sitting in now. They were black-and-white, curled with age, and in every single one was Alex.

According to Mme Gustave, Alex arrived in Espinasse in the late autumn of 1943. General Perré made the arrangements. Quite how he had the time is a mystery, given that he was by this point the head of

Alex with the Aymard family in front of their house

the garde, Pétain's personal guard, meaning he was in charge of six thousand officers as well as the protection of the head of state. He had been given the job by René Bousquet, the man who organized the Vel d'Hiv. Once the Germans invaded France, the French army was almost entirely depleted, but Pétain was allowed to keep his garde, meaning they were one of the last visible signs of French sovereignty. Perré's job was to be in charge of one of the last public symbols of French pride—an apt job for a man in Vichy who put patriotism above Nazism. The garde was not exactly pro German, but it was definitely anti-resistance, as resisters were seen as upstarts against the rulers. And yet the head of the garde was stashing Jews around the Auvergne countryside. Certainly Alex was taking a huge risk, but Perré was, too.

Alex was met at the train station, probably by a farmer's wife, who brought him to the local *maquis*. Despite his injuries from having jumped off the train, he was obviously strong and in good shape, and so it was decided that Alex could pass as a farmhand. For the next five or so weeks, Alex was moved from farm to farm, as the more he moved in the first few weeks, the less chance there was that he might be denounced and caught. But Alex was always terrible at keeping a low profile, and from his first day in town he went around and introduced himself to everyone, telling them his name was Alex and he came from Cannes. He didn't even hide that he was Jewish, which made people suspect he had friends in high places protecting him. Then one day, he did something that ensured everyone knew who he was: he got in a fight outside the village bakery and knocked out someone's two front teeth. If he had wanted everyone to know that no one could mess with Alex Maguy, then he succeeded, but he also drew a lot of attention to himself, and this story is still, seventy years on, a legend in Saint-Gervais-d'Auvergne. So it was decided that he needed to be put somewhere a little more out of the way. As it happened, a friend of Alex's, called Imre, had also recently arrived in town, and the two wanted to stay together. Was there a farmhouse, a little off the beaten path, where they could both stay?

Jeanne Aymard, as Mme Gustave was known then, first learned that Alex was coming to live with her when a friend at school told her: "Hey, two men are staying at your house now!" The teacher hurriedly told them both to be quiet.

Alex and his friend, Imre, moved into the Aymards' attic—the Aymards had never taken in any lodgers before, resisters or otherwise, and they never took in any again. To this day Mme Gustave doesn't know why her parents took in Alex and Imre. In the attic they set up two small beds and a desk for them, and there was a little window with a view of the fields. The staircase to get up to the attic is behind a hidden wall in the kitchen, and there is also a second staircase from the garage so Alex and Imre could run down one if they heard the police coming up the other. The attic today is still very cozy and pretty, with slanted ceilings and only the sound of birds outside. As Alex looked around it, he must have felt the same rush of relief as when he was lying on the train tracks after making his jump. Here, at last, he would be safe. Both he and his friend.

Imre's full name was Imre Partos, and he was an aspiring fashion designer whom Alex had become close to in Cannes. They had met in Paris through Dior, and after the war Partos would work for several years with Dior, helping him create the designer's famous New Look collection of 1947 that would make the design house's name. But it was Alex who became his truly great friend. There were obvious surface similarities between them: they both loved fashion, both were eastern European Jews (Partos came from Budapest), and both were short—Imre was five foot three at a generous estimate. But Imre was more classically handsome—in fact, he had the delicate, fine-boned looks of Jacques. He was also more relaxed than Alex, and more refined, too, and was occasionally horrified by his friend's coarse manners: he often apologized to the Aymards for his friend's "piglike character."

Another difference was that Partos was openly gay, but when I asked Jeanne if there was ever any suggestion that he and Alex were in a relationship, she looked so shocked that it was clear this was the first time she'd ever even considered it.

Alex and Imre in Espinasse

"No, never, never. Of course, I was only ten. But I never heard any-thing," she said.

Whatever their relationship, the two men were extremely close: they were together the whole day, every day, sleeping together, eating to-gether, working on the local farms together. One photo from that period shows them lying together in a field, dressed for what looks like autumn, so probably quite soon after they moved into the Aymards'. They're fin-ishing lunch. Imre is looking toward Alex and Alex is looking in the distance. They are both smiling, happy.

They rarely, if ever, spoke of home. Instead, Alex and Imre spent much of their time talking about fashion: who was good, who was a hack, who knew how to sew, who knew how to style. Alex invariably won these arguments. "Alex was quite bossy, assertive. Definitely a man who got what he wanted," Mme Gustave said, squashing any tiny doubts I might have still held about whether it was actually my great-uncle Alex who had stayed in her house. Many decades later, after Imre—or Emeric, as he became known when he Anglicized his name after the war—had become a world-famous designer with a celebrity clientele that included his friend and neighbor Katharine Hepburn, Alex was credited with get-ting him interested in fashion.

"[Partos] became an operative in the French underground. There, he met Alex Maguy, a couturier who also designed for the theater.[10] Mr. Par-tos joined him as a coat designer and did an occasional stint costuming ballet," Angela Taylor wrote in his obituary in the *New York Times*.[11] (This was not entirely correct: as Alex says in his memoir, the two men had met years earlier in Paris.) And, unusually for Alex, he stayed friends with Partos for the rest of his life. Among my grandmother's shoebox pa-pers I found a letter from Alex dated December 7, 1975: "My dear sister, I've just learned with great sadness of the death of my dear friend, Imre. What a wonderful guy he was. To think that we telephoned each other several times lately and the bad weather kept me from seeing him—ah, that's life. Let's talk of nicer things . . ."

That Alex was a fashion designer was the beginning and end of all the he'd come. He could just sit still in a field, enjoying a life his father and brother Jacques would have liked for themselves, had two world wars not swallowed them up.

So was Alex just sitting in a field here or was he actually in the resistance?

"We never heard he was in the resistance," Mme Gustave insisted.

But Picandet had his theories.

"The British were very keen to hear about French people's morale, so it is likely Alex was writing reports on that and sending them to Britain."

"Perhaps he was just communicating with the Sizaines?" I suggested. But what I really meant was, maybe he wasn't doing anything at all. Maybe he was just having a nice year in Espinasse with Imre. Not every Frenchman, after all, was a member of the resistance, no matter what they said after the war.

But Picandet shook his head firmly and pulled out a piece of paper on the top of my pack of notes, which were photocopies from the various files I'd found on Alex scattered around France. This particular piece of paper was a certificate and on it was written the following:

> I the undersigned, the commanding officer of Zone 13, certify that Mr Alex Glass, an active member of the French Forces of the Interior, is allowed to move freely and for all reasons. He is entitled to any help he requires in order to do so.

It was signed, stamped, and dated September 7, 1944, meaning it was given to Alex when he was still at the Aymards'.

"This certificate proves without a doubt he was working in the resistance. Other members of the resistance in this area, zone 13, didn't have such certificates, so Alex had powerful people behind him, and he was in contact with them while he was here," Picandet said.

Alex left the Aymards in the winter of 1944 after more than a year in their attic. He first went to Cannes to get his mother, the Yiddish-speaking, kosher-keeping Polish Jew who, miraculously, had somehow survived the war. Her survival is a testament to Alex's friend, Mme Armande, who had hidden Chaya during the war, and to Alex, who had the wisdom to place his mother with her. Paris was now liberated and Alex, along with Chaya, was among the group of Jews who had managed to survive the war and now returned to the capital city. It was a shockingly depleted group. During the war, of the 300,000 Jews who were in France in 1939, more than 80,000 had been sent to the concentration camps from France, mostly, but not entirely, immigrants. Only 3% returned alive. Alex and Chaya arrived in Paris to find the wreckage of their family. Henri and Sonia were waiting for them.[12]

Alex could be a Zelig figure, slipping in and out of different social sets and leaving few ties behind him. But he stayed in touch with the Aymards for years—proof of how much he loved his time with them. Madame Aymard even worked as his housekeeper in Paris for several years, and he invited Jeanne to visit him several times during her childhood and teenage years. "But when I came, there was no more cheek pinching, no more 'ma petite Jeanne.' He was a different man in Paris—more formal, serious. Different," she recalled. There were many versions of Alex, and he left one of them behind in Espinasse. He was now back to his Parisian self.

The Germans and collaborators kept better records than the resisters, who destroyed everything as they went along for their own safety, and Alex threw away his own records later. When you've been arrested three times and lost your brother and most of your extended family to state-sanctioned murder, you tend to be cautious about what you reveal. In fact, Alex never fully trusted France again, even though he lived there for the rest of his life. When he became phenomenally wealthy later in life, he kept his money in more than two dozen bank accounts in as many different countries. France had turned against him once—how could he know it wouldn't again? So who could blame him, really, for keeping some things to himself. As I left Espinasse, I thought how even though I knew most of the story, I would never know for sure about his relationship with Perré, or even if Perré was the powerful person who saved his life. Some things will just have to stay in the shadows and be taken on faith. But when I got back home to London, I found something very unexpected waiting for me.

My uncle Rich had found another copy of Alex's memoir, which was identical to the previous one but with one crucial difference: some of the pages that were missing in my copy were present in this one. They were crumpled up, like someone had thrown them away but then (someone else?) rescued them from the trash at the last minute. And they detailed exactly what happened after Alex jumped from the train:

"Staying in Lyon was suicidal. I needed to find a place to hide. The thought that contacting General Perré in Vichy would be a good move seems quite mad today. But that's what I did because I had total confidence in Perré. He was a soldier and, although the personal bodyguard of Pétain, he could not betray a fellow soldier," Alex wrote.

According to Alex, he simply phoned Perré's house and spoke first to Perré's wife, who "couldn't believe what had happened to me," which, if true, says a lot about the Perrés' self-deluding hypocrisy, given that what had happened to Alex was what Perré was ensuring would happen to the Jews in France. Alex writes that Perré sent one of his senior officers to pick up Alex—still dressed as a railway worker—in Lyon and bring him to Vichy "in a car flying the flag of the military headquarters."

Once Alex was at Perré's headquarters, Perré offered to provide him with a military disguise.

"I told him I preferred to remain in plain clothes and rejoin the resistance," Alex told the man whose specific job was cracking down on the resistance. But Perré again agreed to help him. "Because some of his officers had contacts in the resistance, Perré had me taken to the Auvergne, where I could rejoin the resistance," Alex writes.

Everything Robert Picandet had told me was confirmed by Alex. According to Alex, he and Perré even acknowledged the danger they were both in:

"I was on the run and condemned to death if captured. Perré knew it full well, asked no questions, and saved my life. He knew how much he risked. Two or three times, he told me, the Gestapo came to his home. Because of me. He was being watched, of course."

And yet, despite this, Perré incredibly took the risk to visit Alex several times in Espinasse, and Alex would try to persuade him to flee to London with him.

"Our conversations were always very sincere. Once I dared suggest to him that we go to London together. His wife was rather pro German while he was above all a soldier. 'No, I would be unwelcome there,' he replied. 'De Gaulle is already there.' I tried to understand, but his reply pained me."

Alex and Perré had a friendship that went deeper than either ever acknowledged publicly, and although Perré's old rivalry with de Gaulle stopped him from escaping with Alex to London, it's clear from the risks Perré took how much he respected Alex, and loved him. As for what Alex was actually doing in Espinasse, all he says is that he was "a noisy recruiter for the resistance," and then the story ends again with more pages missing. Some stories are still in the shadows.

After the war finished, Perré went on trial in November 1946, not for hiding Alex but for collaborating with the Nazis. More than 300,000 people in France were investigated in the *épuration légale*—or legal purge—as part of the country's desperate attempt to maintain the myth that the majority of its citizens were part of the resistance and only the bad apples were collaborators. The people caught up in this country-wide bloodletting were, in the main, certainly guilty, but also served as convenient scapegoats for a country mortified by its collective culpability. Probably the most notorious example of this was the vilification of Frenchwomen accused of "horizontal collaboration"—sleeping with Nazis, in other words—who had their heads shaved and were marched through the streets, where they were jeered and attacked by people who may well have done a fair amount of collaborating themselves.

The trials of the high-ranking Vichy officials presented their own kind of weird hypocrisy, in that while some of the most high-profile figures were tried, many weren't, including lots of Vichy civil servants, simply because General de Gaulle, who was now in charge, knew he needed them to help run the country. Others were simply too big to convict. It would take another half century, when President Chirac was in the Élysée Palace in the 1990s, until France would truly look at its past and summon people for their long-overdue trials for their crimes against humanity.

Perré, however, had the misfortune of being prominent enough to grab attention, but not so high-ranking that he could avoid a trial in the 1940s, like his boss Bousquet. Details of his trial are kept in an archive in Poitiers, and the initial testimonies against him, from soldiers who knew him, are devastating: he was accused of sending children to concentration camps; committing war crimes against military families (sending them to the camps, in other words); punishing any officers who showed sympathy for resisters; and viciously repressing the resistance. But French historian Camille Chevallier, who helped me with my work in Poitiers, told me she was skeptical about some of the claims: "My opinion as a historian is that the accusations about General Perré are exaggerated. This is often the case with these trials with the German enemy, so that the accused are punished quickly and severely so that the French can only remember the resistance and erase all traces of collaboration. I think that the accusations are not false but they are probably exaggerated and expanded so that Jean Perré was condemned quickly. There was also a strong national desire for revenge settling of accounts between collaborator and resistance."

The testimonies in Perré's defense told a much more complex picture than the sweeping prosecutions. One man, Charles Levy, said in his testimony, "All I know is that under the German occupation, my friend Emile Perrot went to [Perré] to get me an identity card in the name of Leroy instead of Levy, which allowed me to escape the racial persecutions. I am grateful to General Perré." And then I read the testimony of Captain Dodane, made on November 26, 1946: General Perré, he said, "continued to camouflage equipment and gave many non-commissioned officers false identity cards, food to allow them to foil the Gestapo. At the same time, he hosted and concealed Mr Alex Maguy, wanted by the Germans." Alex did not give a witness statement at the trial, but he did attend it: on a small slip of paper in the archive file about Perré's trial is a list of nineteen names, including Perré's son and various military officials. Number four on the list is Alex Glass. Alex would have had to give his real name to get into court, although General Perré—having met Alex originally when he was his daughter's couturier—would have known him only as Alex Maguy, which is why he was referred to as such during the trial.

Perré handwrote his own defense, which ran to sixteen pages. He didn't mention Alex in it, and Camille Chevallier said this was prob-ably because "out of friendship, he did not want to involve Alex in his trial, and also he knew it wouldn't help him anyway." But he does men-tion that he knew that some of his men had connections with the local *maquis*. He also says that he provided "fake identity cards, food, etc to enable [resistors] to carry out their task and foil the Gestapo." He adds, somewhat improbably, that he was creating an armored division to beat the "boches" (pejorative word for Germans). Throughout his defense, Perré stresses Bousquet's culpability and Pétain's innocence, a Pétainiste to the end. But his guilt, as he knew, was a given, and on November 28, 1946, he was found guilty of "national dégredation," the most common conviction among the *épuration légale,* and almost fifty thousand others were similarly condemned. He lost his pension, was banned from living in the area for a decade, and was ordered to give up his worldly goods. For good measure, he was also sentenced to twenty years of hard labor.

In the immediate aftermath of the war, France was keen to make a show of punishing the traitors. But it was also desperate to move on and not stew over the past—forget it entirely, if possible. So in the end, Perré was punished very little. Like many other figures from Vichy who had been convicted under the legal purge, he saw his sentence commuted in the 1950s and then pretty much overturned. He died in 1971.[13]

As far as I know, Alex never mentioned Perré to anyone in his family—he knew he had to be discreet. But occasional vague allegations of col-laborationism were lobbed at him, based on misunderstood, whispered half-truths, and these continued long after he died. In 2014 he was named in a case against the Fred Jones Museum in Oklahoma, brought by a Frenchwoman called Leone Mayer, who claimed that a Pissaro painting on display in the American museum was rightfully hers as it had been confiscated from her father by the Nazis. During the trial Mayer mentioned other works owned by her late father, including a 1906 painting by Raoul Dufy, which had been sold in 1955 to Alex Maguy, who, the lawyer casually added and the stenographer faithfully recorded, "had been active with the occupying German forces during WWII in Paris."

It is entirely possible Alex handled art that had been seized from Jews during the war—a lot of art was looted. But the idea that Alex was deliberately part of some kind of anti-Jewish art scene, let alone "active with occupying German forces," is ludicrous. But it's also understandable that some sensed a gray cloud of suspicion around him because to survive, he lived in twilight, and it had long been that way. He admitted as much in his memoir when describing his too-busy salon in Cannes. Maybe Alex simply understood, better than others, that in wartime nothing is simple.

Alex spent his life spinning webs, alternately obfuscating and exaggerating. This wasn't simply to hide the truth, but to give him security and establish footholds—things he believed he needed to survive. And hadn't the war proven he was right about that? After all, he'd survived only because he had connections. He always needed to make himself look more established than he was because he knew that, in the eyes of France, he would always be a Polish Jew.

Yet for all his obfuscations, Alex wasn't a Tom Ripley—yes, he talked a lot of nonsense, but he also had the goods. He really did know this person, own that painting, escape from a train. He hadn't collaborated, but the person who saved him was a collaborator. The proof had always been in front of me—after all, against every odd, he'd survived. And like a good salesman, he took his best goods and put them in the shop window. The rest he kept in the closet.

Chapter 11

THE SIBLINGS—THE ORDINARY AND THE EXTRAORDINARY

Postwar life, France and America

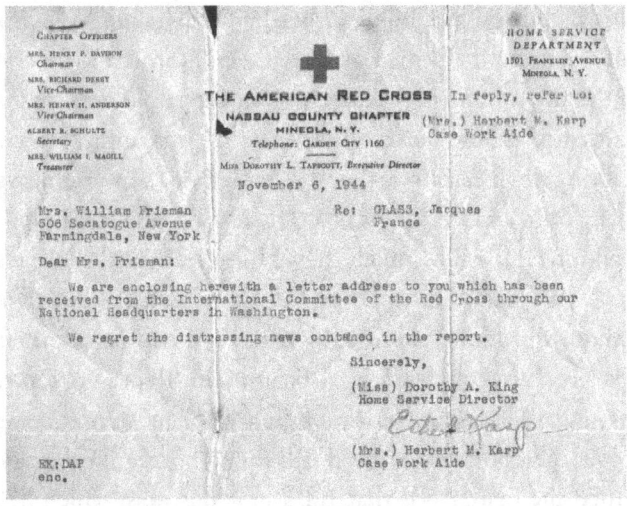

I n September 1948, Sara finally sailed back to Paris. She made and froze enough meals to last Bill for her monthlong absence, brought her two young sons, Ronald, then nine, and Richard, five, and boarded the ship. Sara was so excited that when she walked on French ground for the first time in nine years, she cried with happiness. But as she and her boys traveled by train from Le Havre to Paris, and she saw what the war had done to the country she loved so much, she cried for a very different reason. Sara had spent the war dreaming of the time when she would go home; the journey from the dock to the French capital showed her there was no home to go back to.

France was devastated after the war, physically and morally. Paris, once the grandest city in the world, was dilapidated and gray, its buildings in desperate need of repair no one could afford, its people in worse need of food no one had. In April 1945, almost a year after the city was liberated, Parisians were still living on about 1,300 calories a day.[1] When Sala took her boys to Henri and Sonia's house, Henri gave Ron an apple. Fresh fruit had only recently become available in Paris again after years of deprivation, but Ronald—raised on Long Island where fruit had never been rationed—didn't know that. So he proceeded to eat the apple the way his slightly germophobic father had taught him back home, by cutting all the peel off. Henri was horrified: "Stop that!" he cried, and he fell to the floor, frantically collecting all the apple peel. In America, Sara had tried to soothe her homesickness by imagining her family in Paris, picturing them exactly as they'd been before the war. But watching her normally calm and fastidious brother scrabble about for food scraps, Sara saw all too clearly how much they'd been reshaped by the war.

By 1944, Bill, Sara, and their two little boys had been living in a hotel in midtown Manhattan for two years. In Farmingdale their house was next to four airplane factories—Grumman, Republic, Ranger, and Fairchild—and the constant noise of fighter planes flying at very low altitudes over their house convinced Bill they'd be safer in the city. What finally settled the matter was that Bill's new business, which he started during the war, had become his most successful venture yet. Called Roxy Corporation, it made medals for the US Army. It was based in Manhattan, and because gas and coal were hard to come by during the war, regular commutes from Long Island were just impractical. And so, in 1942, Bill, a then-pregnant Sara, and three-year-old Ronald moved to a small two-room suite in the Park Central Hotel on 56th Street and 7th Avenue. Sara was thrilled: at last she was living in New York City, and she happily took her toddler son for walks up and down Madison Avenue, looking in all the fancy stores, just as she had dreamed she'd do when she had originally sailed over from France. Ronald also enjoyed living in the city, but for very different reasons from his mother. When he talks about that period now, what he remembers is how much he enjoyed roller-skating on the hotel roof and how he would tease all the nice ladies who sat on benches up there smoking all day. It wasn't until many years later that he realized they were all prostitutes.

Being based in the city proved to be a great help to Sara at the end of the war when it came to finding out what happened with her family. For three years, she'd had no contact with them, no idea whether any of them were even alive. She was frantic for news, but even after D-Day it was months before full mail, telegraph, and phone service was resumed. So word of mouth was the best source, and it was a lot easier in New York City than it was in Farmingdale to find people who knew what was happening in France. My father, then age five, remembers "a series of foreign visitors to our little two-room suite. There were intense conversations. And tears."

According to Alex's memoir, one of those foreign visitors was Yvonne Vallée, the French actress and ex-wife of Maurice Chevalier. Alex had become friendly with Chevalier before the war, and the two would remain close for the rest of their lives, even spending their final years as neighbors. (Chevalier was yet another member of Alex's social circle who lived in the gray twilight: he was accused of collaboration both during and after the war and always denied it.) Vallée divorced Chevalier in 1932, but Alex stayed sufficiently friendly with her to ask her to deliver a message to his sister while on a trip to the United States. Through Vallée, Alex reassured Sara that not only was he alive, but so were Henri, Sonia, Chaya, Mila, and Lily. No one, he wrote, had heard from Jacques for a while.

In November 1944, Sara finally got the news that Alex, Henri, and Sonia had expected. She received a letter from the Red Cross, signed by a Mrs. Ethel Karp, confirming that Jacques had been killed in Auschwitz-Birkenau. Mrs. Karp apologized for "the distressing news contained in the report." Sara had dearly loved her gentlest brother, the one who was most like her beloved father and whom she most resembled physically. She tucked the letter into her shoebox of keepsakes, alongside the photos and drawing Jacques had sent her from Pithiviers and his plaque from Cambrai. She never spoke about these mementos to her husband or even her beloved sons, but she kept them close to her for the rest of her life, carefully bringing them with her through multiple house moves, hiding them in the darkness at the back of her closet.

Compared with other families, the Glasses came through the war pretty well: they had lost Jacques and almost all of their cousins, but most of the immediate family survived. Even Chaya was fine; when Alex brought her back to Paris she was still faithfully keeping kosher, still only talking in Polish and Yiddish.

But emotionally they were in as much of a mess as Paris itself. They were deeply traumatized by the betrayal of a country they thought they could trust and in deep grief for those they had lost—Jacques, mainly. But there was no way of talking about such things then, and who had the time anyway? Everyone had suffered through the war—talking about your suffering was indulgent and unhelpful was the general attitude. Yet trauma resists repression.

Sara knew that her mother and two brothers had survived the war, but it would be another two years before she was able to sail to France to see them. So once the Freimans relocated back to Farmingdale, she busied herself by sending packages and letters to Sonia, Henri, and Alex. Because it was against the law to send food to private citizens in France, she sent them via a young soldier, named Bob Spencer, the son of her Farmingdale neighbors, who happened to be stationed in Paris near Henri and Sonia's home. Every time he received a parcel for them, he personally brought it over to their house. Until the end of her life, Sonia talked reverently about Bob Spencer and how he had saved their lives, and it's very possible that he did, because Henri and Sonia were never in greater need of food than after the war: on D-Day, June 6, 1944, their daughter Danièle was born. Henri was forty-three and Sonia forty-one, almost unimaginably old at that time to be first-time parents. But they hadn't been able to conceive before, and Danièle was like the physical manifestation of relief, or just a release: after so many years of anxiety, and four long years of living a shadowy existence, Henri and Sonia were free at last. And as soon as they could relax, out came little Danièle, their only child.

Only children started to run in my family at that point. Henri had Danièle, Jacques had Lily, and, in the 1950s, Roger and Renée Goldberg, the Glasses' cousins who almost certainly were involved in the resistance movement, had one child, my cousin Anne-Laurence. Armand Ornstein, the little boy who was hidden in the woods after his parents were shot while crossing the river, had one child, Philippe. Even Alex, who never married, eventually had a child, an only daughter.* Given that the previous generation had multiple children—there were five Glass children originally (Mindel died as a child) and seven Ornsteins—this was a marked shift, and the sharp change in the shape of the family tree is a visual representation of what fear does to the human spirit. "They never

---

* She later cut herself off from the family, and to respect her privacy I will neither name her nor tell anything of her story.

Dinner with Henri and Sonia. Renée Goldberg is smiling
at the camera with her daughter, Anne-Laurence, on her lap.

really believed they were safe again, and if they weren't, they couldn't bear to put their children through what they had been through. One child was all they would risk," was how Anne-Laurence Goldberg explained it to me. The sole Glass sibling who dared to have more than one child was Sara, the only one living in a country that had never tried to kill her.

Sara's brothers were able to write to her, thanks to Bob Spencer mailing their letters via the US Army postal service, and the surviving letters show they were responding to their postwar life in characteristic form. For Alex, that meant a combination of exuberance and fury. Ecstatic at having improbably survived the war, he was more determined than ever to seize life. In January 1945, fewer than two years after he escaped from the train that was taking him to death, Alex sent a joyful postcard to his sister from the French ski slopes: "The weather is magnificent, the sun is splendid, and the snow is great. I'm preparing my new collection for the summer season. One hundred kisses to you, Alex."

Alex's ambition was even greater after the war. As soon as he got back to Paris, he seized his fashion business from Paquin, who had tormented Alex and the CGQJ by demanding Alex not be allowed to work down in the south. But Alex definitively won that battle: on July 24, 1945, as the punishments against collaborators were really starting to bite, Paquin killed himself. He left behind an apartment full of fancy trinkets bought with the money he made from running the seized businesses of Jewish designers, and little else.

Alex did not pause to gloat, and he doesn't even bother to mention Paquin's suicide in his memoir. Instead, he desperately scrabbled around to rebuild his salon by whatever means necessary. He regularly updated Sara on his progress.

"My dear little sister," Alex wrote to her on June 8, 1945. "I once again take advantage of Mr. Bob Spencer to send you this letter. I hope you now have the press clippings that I sent you and that you like them. I'm also sending you some photographs, and I would be happy if you could have them published in American fashion magazines. I'm counting on you."

After asking his sister, a housewife on Long Island, to get his photos into US *Vogue*, Alex had another request for her:

"I must ask you to seriously look into the matter of finding Emile Best. He did much evil in France during the Occupation [and] he's hiding now in New York. He was a dealer in drawings and he was intending twelve bullets for me. I would be very happy for him to receive the fate that he was planning for me."

It's hard to say if Alex truly intended for my grandmother to stalk through New York with a Smith & Wesson, hunting a collaborationist who had escaped to the United States. But he was certainly serious when he turned his attention to Sonia, whom he loathed almost as much as he did the Nazis: "I have told you not to include the food packages for Mila and Lily in Sonia's parcels. But you recently did so again, even though you know that Mila and Lily only receive what [Sonia] doesn't want. Please address the packages separately to Mila; this way we will know she gets

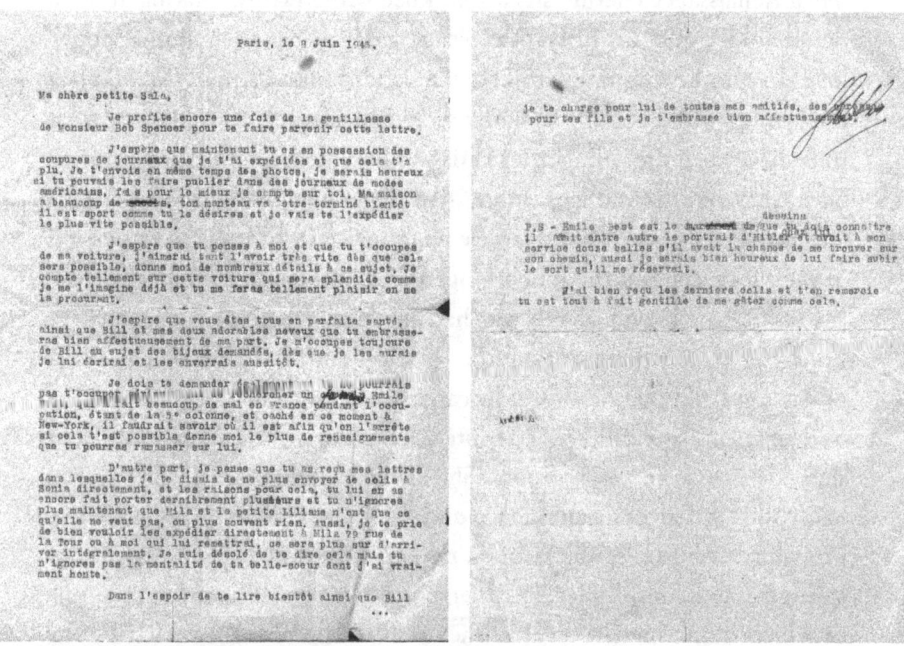

them intact. I'm sorry to have to tell you this but you know the mentality of your sister-in-law of whom I am ashamed." Alex's loathing of Sonia outweighed his hatred of Mila, even though Sonia had saved Henri during the war thanks to her black market contacts and excellent German, whereas Mila had sent Jacques to certain death by telling him to return to the concentration camp. But Sonia was smart—this meant Alex couldn't merely dismiss her as an idiot, as he did with Mila. Instead, he had to hate her personally for being unworthy of his brother. That Alex's feelings about her remained so implacably unchanged, even after all they had been through during the war, proved—as Sonia's relatives also confirmed a few years earlier, complaining bitterly about one another while in the shadow of the Nazis—that not even war can alter familial relationships.

As for Henri and Sonia, few letters from them in the immediate postwar period have survived. Instead, what has lasted are the many, many photos Henri sent to his sister of his new baby daughter. At last he had a new photographic muse. In one photo, Danièle, plump and round-eyed, like a Renaissance cherub, sits on his knee while Henri, looking about a decade older than his forty-three years, gazes at her with almost dopey love. In another, Sonia, with characteristic frankness, looks straight at the camera while holding a tightly swaddled Danièle in a park, in what must have been the winter after Paris was liberated. They had, against all odds, survived the war and, more than that, they had reproduced. As a statement of their survival, Danièle was the final word. As an expression of their love, she was the much-longed-for completion of their family.

For Sara, the end of the war had meant a reluctant move back to Long Island, but there was another change, too. For reasons I've never understood and no one alive now can explain, at some point toward the mid-1940s my grandmother's adopted French name unmoored itself and slipped back to its Polish roots. She started being referred to again as Sala, both in her correspondence and on official documents. This was probably because she, like Jacques, never officially changed her name, so it just got too complicated in America having two different names, one of which didn't match her documentation. The result was that by the end of the war she was Sala Freiman, and when she was finally able to travel to France in 1948 with her sons, her name on the passenger list appears as "Sala Freiman, h'wife." The "Sara Ryfka Glass, draftsman" who first went to America nine years earlier was long gone.

Alex met her and her two sons at the train station in Paris. Someone, probably Henri, took a photo of this meeting, and it shows Sala looking even more glamorous than usual, in a bell-sleeved fur coat made by Alex and a hat that molded itself around her perfectly coiffured hair and tied under her chin with an attached crocheted scarf. She had dressed her boys carefully for their arrival in Paris: both are in matching coats and hats, Ronald in a smart light-gray peacoat and coordinated cap, Richard in a looser checked one and checked cap. What's striking is how much the boys look like Glasses: serious Ronald is like a young Henri while Richard has Alex's pouchy cheeks and his mother's bright eyes. They all

Alex welcoming Sala, Ronald, and Richard to Paris

look happy and excited, Alex most of all, clutching little Richard in his arms. But if Sala thought this meant he would help her, she would soon be disabused of that notion.

Before the war broke out, Sala wrote to Alex that she wanted to leave Bill and come back to Paris. Would he, she asked, support her and her then-only son? The war temporarily stopped that conversation but, according to family lore passed down by Alex and Sonia, Alex made his answer very clear on this trip, and the answer was no. There was, he said, nothing for her here: France was destroyed and America was thriving. He was trying to build his business, plus he had to look after Chaya, and Henri had a new baby to look after. Sonia, for once, was in agreement with her brother-in-law: as soon as you had the second boy, she told Sala, "c'est fini"—game over.

But this was not true. Alex, Henri, and Sonia loved Sala very deeply, and they could have supported her and the boys. Alex always found a way to do something he wanted and, yes, Sonia had a new baby, but she had managed to hide Mila and Lily during the war—looking after Sala, Ronald, and Richard in peacetime would hardly have tasked her abilities. Part of their resistance to her return stemmed from their very conservative background and the time in which they lived: they believed that the mother of two boys belonged with their father, and a wife's responsibility was to her husband. But even more than that, they didn't want her to come back because they thought she was safer where she was. Even aside from France's current political and financial turmoil, Alex, Henri, and Sonia could still feel the past's hot breath on their necks. The war was over, but the memories of how their countrymen had tried, and nearly succeeded, in killing all of them were very, very fresh. None of them felt safe in France, and they never really would again, even after they all eventually became French citizens. By telling Sala to stay in New York with Bill, they were trying to protect her, just as they'd protected her by sending her to New York to marry him in 1937. It was their way of expressing love for her, but to her it must have felt like another cold rejection.

For years Sala had quietly nursed the dream that it was just the war that was keeping her from her home. But she now realized she would never live in France again, at least not while Bill was alive. Perhaps because of this, while on this trip she sent a photo to Bill of Ron and Rich in Paris, looking up at her from the street while she was apparently leaning out of a window. She wrote on it, in slightly wobbly English: "This was taken [she crossed out the word "talking," having written that initially instead of "taken"] from the 6th floor from Alex's window, and these two little Frenchmen are your sons." This could be read as either a fond message or a pointed one—a proud assertion of her children's French identity despite their American father. It was probably a mix of both. Her family would not help her if she left him, and she couldn't live without their help. So she resigned herself to wait until he died, and this was the grandmother I would forty years later meet as a child: one who was still waiting, in her seventies, for her real life to begin. And when she boarded the ship back to New York a month later with her sons, she and her brothers made what they could of their postwar lives.

Henri, after war

*   *   *

For Henri, this meant continuing to build Photosia with Marc Haenel while looking after Sonia and Danièle. The company was even busier after the war than it was before, and one of its first big jobs came in 1948, when the French government hired the company to microfilm the Marshall Plan, the US initiative to help Western Europe rebuild after the war. This commission gave Henri particular pride. Before that, he was asked to do another job: "At the end of the war, the Ministry of Prisoners and War Deportees entrusted us with the task of microfilming the Concentration Camp archives in Germany and in Poland," he wrote in Photosia's meticulous record book. Nowhere does he mention seeing— or looking for—Jacques' name in the archives.

Over the next decade and a half, Henri and Haenel built up an extraordinarily successful business, and their clients included some of the biggest companies in the world, including BP, Esso, IBM, and Renault, as well as nearly every branch of the French government. By the end of the 1960s, Photosia was worth millions. To a very large degree this was thanks to Henri's technical ingenuity, but it was also because Henri and Haenel made the perfect team: Henri the quiet but brilliant engineer, Haenel the extroverted salesman. Henri was suddenly able to keep his wife and daughter in the kind of comfort he could never have imagined during the war when he and Sonia were half-starved and fearfully skulking in the dark.

Henri and Sonia almost never spoke about what they had been through, but they were marked by the experience like a block of clay is by a firm fingerprint. Henri became even more withdrawn, and he went prematurely gray. Sonia seemed outwardly unchanged, as extroverted and forthright as ever. (When her nephew Ronald met her in Paris at the age of seven, he wrote to his father, Bill, "Aunt Sonia is like fire.") But rather than clinging proudly to their Judaism after their persecution, both she and Henri were more desirous than ever of blending in. Being Jewish was something to be endured, never flaunted. They were naturalized soon after the war, delighted to be accepted at last by the country that had tried to kill them, and they barely raised their daughter Jewish at all, never taking her to synagogue or giving her a bat mitzvah. They observed the Jewish holidays, but to those around them it seemed like this was done out of an inner compulsion that they couldn't control. They did their best to protect the next generations from it. Danièle later had children of her own, Alexandre and Natasha de Betak, whom Henri and Sonia adored and often looked after. But they would shoo their beloved grandchildren out of the house when they lit Friday night candles: "You don't need to see this, go outside," they would say, shutting the door behind them. If Alexandre or Natasha asked about Judaism, decades after the war ended, Sonia would put her fingers to her lips and say sharply, "Better not." "Don't tell people you're Jewish," they instructed Alexandre—a sad echo of their late Ornstein cousins, Maurice and Giselle, trying to protect their little son Armand when they hid him in the woods. They just wanted to be French, and for their daughter and grandchildren to be seen as purely French, because to be French was to be safe. Even after being naturalized, Henri never entirely believed he was safe, and for the rest of his life he would do anything to avoid conflict or drawing attention to himself.

So when Haenel came up with a plan in 1960, he knew he'd be able to get Henri to agree.

"Do me a favor," he said to Henri one day. "My wife, she's giving me a hard time. She says I really run the company and you're just the engineer, and so the company should really be mine. I know, I know, but you know women, right? So could you just write a letter saying that you're signing the company over to me? It won't mean anything and it will give me more peace at home. Be a friend."

One of the ironies of Henri's life is that after the war he became increasingly like the one member of this family whom the Nazis had managed to kill. He adopted some of the tendencies of Jacques that had so infuriated the rest of his family when he was alive and, ultimately, helped to get him killed. It was as if he were paying some kind of homage to Jacques, keeping his closest brother alive by reenacting him, or it might be more simple than that: Henri's nervousness was a reaction to how utterly traumatized he had been by the war. It had depleted all of his muscles and pared him back to the bare Glass bones, becoming increasingly like his father. So he didn't laugh in Haenel's face, as most people would have done. Instead he agreed to sign the letter. Sonia understood her husband and she also knew she had to protect him. So she said to Henri, "Fine, tell him you'll sign the letter, but only if he signs another letter saying that the other letter is meaningless."

Haenel agreed to this rather bizarre plan, but when he signed the second letter he crammed his signature into the bottom right corner of the letter, and made it so small it could hardly be seen by the naked eye.

Haenel died soon after signing the letters, and in 1962 his wife, in a wholly predictable turn of events, sued Henri for control of Photosia, saying that the first letter he signed proved it was now hers. Henri was terrified: he dreaded going to court up against Mme Haenel's fancy lawyers, and he had visions of ending up bankrupt, like Jacques had done. Alex, who was by now starting to become very wealthy, immediately hired one of the best lawyers in Paris for his beloved brother. *"Tout ce qj'ai est à toi,"* he told him—"All that I have is yours."

But ultimately it was Henri's wife—as had so often been the case before—who came to his rescue.

Mme Haenel insisted Henri hand over the second letter as evidence for the trial, but Sonia stopped him.

"Haenel's signature is so small, and right in the corner, that wife of his could flick it off with her thumb and then you'd have nothing," she said to her husband. So Sonia came up with a plan: she put the letter in a thick, transparent plastic envelope, sealed it shut on all four sides, and handed it over to the court like that. Mme Haenel, realizing her plan was being thwarted, was furious, and insisted the plastic envelope made the letter too hard to read and was therefore inadmissible. But the judge overruled her and Henri got to keep his 50 percent of the business.

Henri won the case, but it was now impossible for him and Mme

Haenel to run the company together. Fortunately, a large Dutch company called Van der Grinten* offered to buy it. Henri and Mme Haenel sold Photosia to them in 1966 for almost $12 million, or $50 million today.

Henri was suddenly an extremely wealthy man, one who, at the age of sixty-five, would never need to worry about money again. But the money hardly changed his and Sonia's lives at all—they continued to travel in economy class and they didn't move to a big fancy house. To become a flashy show-off like his brother Alex would have gone completely against Henri's nature. But if he had always dreamed of wrapping his entire house in gold he wouldn't have done so because, even in the 1960s, he never felt he could relax; rather, he saw the money as a way to protect himself and his family should things go bad again, as they surely would. He put most of the cash in Swiss bank accounts—away from the French, in case the country turned on him again—and invested in things such as property and art, protecting it if currency rates dropped. He and Sonia bought a small weekend house in Nauphle-le-Château, which they loved and kept beautifully maintained. A new neighbor arrived in the late 1970s who was, however, less house proud, and he let his house and lawn deteriorate badly. Sonia complained, but to no avail—her neighbor was, she later recalled, very stubborn. Newspapers from that period also described her neighbor's "unkempt" garden, because he was not just Henri and Sonia's neighbor in the countryside—he was the Ayatollah Khomeini, then in exile from Iran. He returned to Tehran in 1979, from where he launched the Iranian Revolution and founded the Islamic Republic of Iran. Many in the West at the time were nervous about Khomeini's return to Iran, and with good reason: the effects of it are still being felt today. But as far as Sonia was concerned, his departure meant that her neighborhood improved, so she was one of the very few in France who wholeheartedly celebrated his departure. Once again, by a quirk of geography Henri and Sonia had a front-row seat to some of the most formative events of twentieth-century politics.

---

* Van Der Grinten later changed its name to Oce and was sold to Canon.

Henri also allowed himself a small taste of the French style that he'd always admired: When he first got his windfall, he bought a small selection of smart suits, Charvet shirts, tailored pajamas, and custom-made shoes. He also bought an Hermès wallet and, the final treat, a Jaguar car. Henri drove that Jaguar for twenty years, only giving it up when he thought his age made him a risk on the road. He wore those clothes till the day he died, and his grandson Alexandre still wears some of them now. This was Henri's small expression of defiance: after so many years of deprivation, he at last had the money and freedom to enjoy himself, and he did. But it could also be seen as a show of submission: after all this time, Henri was still desperately keen to pass as a Frenchman, to be assimilated, to be accepted.

Sala, like Henri, also wanted to be seen as French. She never loved the country less for what it did to her family during the war because somehow she was able to separate what the country symbolized to her and what it had actually done. But Sala's deep desire to be seen as French had as much to do with America as it did with France.

Like Henri's, her postwar life was about raising her family. She made a life for herself in Farmingdale: she was polite enough to Bill's family and, in particular, helped to look after his mother, Rosy. She started painting again, and would spend the afternoons while the boys were at school working on canvases in the living room, creating beautiful French girls in the Long Island suburbs, who were perhaps an expression of her frustrated desire for a daughter, her own idealized self-image, or maybe simply a grasp at a connection to the past when she would look at such girls in the Paris museums with her older brother. She got to know her neighbors and, most of all, she threw herself into the boys' lives, always making sure they were beautifully dressed and that her home looked perfect. Dr. Brenner, her cousin Rose's husband, moved nearby, and he became the doctor for the family. Years later, Alex Ornstein came to visit and Bill drove him, along with his son Ron, to

Sara, Ronald, and Bill

Dr. Brenner's house, where Alex's sister Rose should have been living with him. My father Ron remembers watching Alex and Dr. Brenner falling into one another's arms in tears, two men who should have been lifelong brothers-in-law had the war not swept away the woman who connected them.

Sala and Bill bickered at times, and these fights were all underpinned by the central conflict in their relationship: she did not love him like he wanted her to. She started to take long naps during the day, gratefully losing the hours to unconsciousness.

"Why is your mother always sleeping?" Bill would demand of his sons, his snappishness a cover for his hurt. But there was no good answer.

Yet Sala did not succumb to the paralysis of depression. Like so many immigrants before and after her, she decided that even if she didn't understand this strange land in which she found herself, she would ensure that her children had a better life there than she ever

Sara in Long Island during the 1950s

could. She made sure they always felt not just loved but secure, as she had not when she lived in fear in Chrzanow. She spoke to them in French, raising them bilingual, and taught them about French art and food and culture, determined to expand their mental horizons beyond Farmingdale. But she also made sure they succeeded in America. She read to them often, in English and French, and even though she herself had barely been to school at all, she, along with Bill, drilled the importance of academics into both of them. The result of all this intensive home schooling was that her oldest son, Ronald, could read years before the rest of his classmates. But the teachers in Farmingdale's local school had neither the time nor the willingness to deal with students of varying abilities, so they repeatedly reprimanded him for getting ahead of the class, trying in vain to rein him back to the level of his classmates. When Ronald was seven, not long after he came back from that first trip to Paris, he was in English class and wilting with boredom as he listened to his fellow pupils slowly stammer their way through the set text, which they took turns reading aloud. To pass the time he silently read ahead in the book.

"Don't read ahead, Ronald!" the teacher barked. But Ronald was so bored he didn't listen.

"I said stop it!" the teacher said, and gave him a whack over the head.

Bill, still the fighter from the Lower East Side, had taught his boys that if someone hit them they should always stand up for themselves and hit back. He hadn't told them what to do if the person doing the hitting was a teacher, but his instruction probably wouldn't have changed that much. So Ronald, proving he really was Bill's son and Alex's nephew, pulled his fist back, and punched his teacher in the stomach.

Corporal punishment in New York public schools wouldn't be banned until 1985, so Ronald's teacher had another forty years ahead of her in which she could wallop kids as much as she desired. But while teachers hitting kids was completely fine, kids hitting teachers was considered completely outrageous. After Ronald punched his teacher the school called Sala and informed her that her son was probably "mentally retarded." They would need a psychologist to test him, and if the tests came back positive they would send him to a special school. Terrified, Sala awaited the psychologist's verdict. After a long hour of waiting outside his office, while he asked Ronald a seemingly endless series of questions, the psychologist emerged and sat beside her.

"Mrs. Freiman, there is nothing wrong with your son, except that he has the highest IQ I've ever tested," the psychologist told her. Sala began to formulate a plan to get her boys out of this small town that she knew would only stifle them.

Not long after the meeting with the psychologist, Ronald came home from school one day, went to his father, and asked, "Dad, what's a kike?" A group of bigger boys had shouted anti-Semitic abuse at him on his way home from school. It was at this point that my father, like Henri, started to see his Jewishness as akin to a club foot, something he had been burdened with through no fault of his own, and it was a feeling he would never entirely shake.

That Ronald experienced anti-Semitic bullying in Farmingdale was not a surprise: when Bill first moved there, the Ku Klux Klan was still thriving. Even in the 1940s, Jews in Farmingdale kept to themselves and were seen as separate from the rest of the town, and there was a sense of a soft segregation. "There was a level of anti-Semitism, but nothing publicly demonstrated. Just the usual thing, certain organizations not open to Jews and black people then," William Rappaport, who owned the pharmacy in Farmingdale then, told me. "Jews followed their usual ways by not doing anything that would result in problems and kept a low profile."

Bill and Sala were both much less religious than their parents, and they reflected the increasing shift toward assimilation among Jews in midcentury America: they went to synagogue on the High Holy Days, but not for Shabbat; they sent their boys to Hebrew school, but Sala's attempts to keep kosher when she arrived in America soon faded away. Bill in particular bucked against the restrictive religious binds in which he had been raised, but after the war, when the Jews of Farmingdale gathered up their courage and their money and decided to build a synagogue, despite the local bigots, it was Bill who spearheaded the fundraising for it. He even laid its cornerstone, on which his name was engraved. So although he wasn't observant, being Jewish was a central part of his identity, and while other Jews tried to keep their heads down and not stir up trouble, Bill was always more like Alex than Henri. When he heard that some anti-Semites were causing trouble in town, and even bothering his son, he didn't hesitate. During the war, he was too old to fight, so he worked as an auxiliary (or volunteer) policeman, providing support to the depleted police force, and he had kept his badge and truncheon. Bill picked up his truncheon, marched straight out the door, and, as he put it, beat the hell out of them. Bill returned home, satisfied with this outcome, but Sala knew she had to get her boys out of Farmingdale.

Bill, working as an auxiliary policeman
during the war, with Ronald

In 1952, while Bill was at work and her boys were at school, Sala got in her car and drove to Manhasset, a small Long Island town only eighteen miles away on the map but another world away socially. There, she met up with a broker and the two of them spent the day looking at houses. Sala soon found one she liked, on a broad, tree-lined street called Old Mill Road, and she took out nearly all of her and Bill's savings and paid a nonreimbursable deposit on the house. That night, back in Farmingdale, she told Bill what she had done and he hit the roof, raging at how she had spent all their money on a house they didn't need. The next morning, they all went to look at the house Sala had blown the family's savings on. It was big, three stories, and almost three times as big as their bungalow in Farmingdale. There was a drive-in garage, a pretty front garden, and a bay window in the sitting room. Just down the road, walking distance from the house, was a shopping center with designer stores lined along a promenade where people sat at outdoor tables and drank coffee. There was no John Birch Society here, no pokey little school staffed with underqualified teachers, no gangs of racist bullies in the street—and no extended Freiman family. All his life, Bill had wanted to break away from his family and move up in the world. At last, fifteen years into their marriage, Sala had helped him to do just that. He was ecstatic with the new house and the family moved in almost immediately. For the rest of his life, he proudly bragged to everyone who would listen about the time his pretty French wife went out one day and bought a fancy house.

The same year the family moved to Manhasset, Bill—at his thirteen-year-old son Ronald's urging—legally changed their name from Freiman to Freeman. It was an uncanny echo of the then-twelve-year-old Jehuda Glahs convincing Reuben to westernize their name to Glass, forty years earlier, thousands of miles away. Jehuda/Henri and Ron were so similar they were always more like father and son than uncle and nephew, and they both would always regard their Jewishness as an encumbrance, a hurdle thrust upon them on the path to a smooth and successful life. Bill's extended family was horrified and kept "Freiman," but Bill had no sentimentality about his surname, which had frequently been bastardized by census takers anyway, and he was happy to be seen as a typical American rather than an urchin from the Lower East Side who grew up speaking Yiddish. It was the definitive break from the past he had always longed for, and my family's assimilation, which began almost half a century earlier in Chrzanow, was now complete.

While in many ways privileged (in Henri's case, very privileged), the oldest and youngest of the Glass siblings led ordinary postwar lives. They raised their families, they bought property, they strove to improve their lot. They worked to make sure that their children had better lives than they'd had, and they succeeded in that, too. Theirs are stories of successful Jewish aspiration. They are also stories of assimilation: they held on to their Jewishness as a personal and private identity while sloughing off many of the outward shows of the religion. In Alex's work for the French government and in Sala's efforts to raise educated, highly ambitious American children, they also played their parts in shaping postwar France and America, respectively, which is another key part of the twentieth-century Jewish story. Jews hadn't just survived the war, they would go on to play enormous roles in the countries in which they lived.[2] There were obvious variations between their lives: Henri was very happily married, Sala was less so; Henri and Sonia went from being working class to upper class; Sala and Bill moved more incrementally from working class to lower middle class; Sala and Bill's sons went to college, Henri and Sonia's daughter did not. But in the brushstrokes, their stories are very typical of mid-twentieth-century Western Jewish lives. Successful, quiet, and largely anonymous lives.

Alex, by contrast, led an extraordinary life.

Chapter 12

ALEX—SOCIAL MOBILITY

Paris, 1940s—1970s

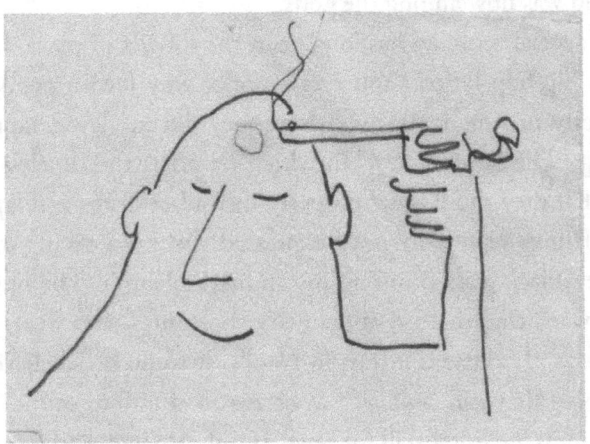

The Picasso sketch that Alex sent to Sala

In April 1961, Alex returned to Cannes, but whereas last time he went to the city in order to save his life, this time he went to change it forever. Almost vibrating with excitement, Alex walked up the driveway of the Villa La Californie and rang the doorbell, ready to meet his idol. He was shown into the house, which looked out over the Bay of Cannes, where he had worked and lived with Seytour during the war. He then walked into the sitting room, where Pablo Picasso was waiting for him.

Only two decades earlier Alex had been arrested on that bay and sent to a concentration camp; now he was having an idyllic day with the greatest artist of the twentieth century. And this was possibly the real reason Alex stayed in France, despite his fury with it: only by living alongside ghosts from the past could the triumphs of the present taste even sweeter.

"I wasn't simply happy. I was at the summit of happiness. It was the most beautiful, the greatest day of my life," Alex later remembered. The little boy who once had to steal meatballs was now friends with some of the most revered creative minds of the twentieth century, first Dior and now Picasso. Sender had brawled his way out of what was ostensibly a ghetto and was now among the gods.

Jewish social mobility has long been the subject of plays, racist jibes, and even hip-hop lyrics: "You ever wonder why Jewish people own all the property in America? This is how they did it," Jay-Z rapped in his 2017 song "The Story of OJ," in which he offers the timeless advice to his fans that they should buy property instead of drugs and lap dances.* Donald Trump reportedly once expressed shock on seeing a black accountant: "Black guys counting my money! I hate it. The only kind of people I want counting my money are short guys who wear yarmulkes every day. . . . Laziness is a trait in blacks. It really is, I believe that. It's not anything they can control."[1] Whereas an ability to count money, by implication, is a natural skill for Jews. If only Shylock had been available to do the accounting for Trump's Vegas casinos.

These stereotypes—in all their grosser permutations—have existed for centuries. And yet it is also the case that Jews in the West have experienced more social mobility than pretty much any other minority group in the late twentieth century. In his study on Jewish social mobility,[2] Paul Burstein makes this memorable point of comparison: in the 1940s, Jewish representation in *Who's Who* was lower than the overall American and the British average; by the 1990s, Jews were represented proportionally more than 4.5 times the American average and almost six times that of the British.

---

* And to think, some people argue that hip-hop has lost its connection to its young urban origins.

In America, Jews make up less than 2 percent of the national population yet account for a third of American Nobel laureates. Similarly, two out of every three European Jews were killed in the Holocaust, yet those who survived, and assimilated, were more likely to enjoy social mobility than any other minority. In Britain by the mid-1980s, for example, despite making up only 0.5 percent of the population, Jews accounted for 5 percent of the country's doctors and 9 percent of its lawyers.[3] "By the opening of the twenty-first century, it was no longer possible to find any significant area of British life from which Jews were excluded," Howard M. Sachar writes in *A History of the Jews in the Modern World*. And given how few Jews there actually are in the United States and Europe, it is remarkable how well represented they are in public, intellectual, and cultural life.

Yet there are few satisfying explanations as to why this is the case. As Burstein puts it, undoubtedly correctly, the reason there are hardly any good studies about Jewish social mobility is that Jews have resisted drawing attention to this trend, let alone explaining it, out of fear of provoking anti-Semitism. There are, after all, plenty of historic examples of Jewish success being used as an excuse for the targeting of Jews, and the Glass family experienced multiple incidents of that in their lifetimes. In the absence of proper analysis, the most popular theories range from the unhelpfully vague (they work hard, they care about education—as if other minority groups don't?) to relying on repulsive eugenics ideas and conspiracy theories.

The rise of anti-Semitism on the right* and left† in the twenty-

---

* In August 2017 a white supremacist group marched through Charlottesville, Virginia, the protesters chanting, "Jews will not replace us!" Sheryl Gay Stolberg and Brian M. Rosenthal, "Man Charged After White Nationalist Rally in Charlottesville Ends in Deadly Violence," *New York Times*, August 12, 2017.

† In April 2019 it emerged that the former Labour leader Jeremy Corbyn had, in 2011, written a foreword to J.A. Hobson's 1902 book *Imperialism: A Study*, in which he specifically praised Hobson's "correct and prescient" theories about "the commercial interests that fuel the role of the popular press with tales of imperial might." These theories of Hobson's

first century has reignited gross comments about Jewish prominence and alleged power. But it would be bizarre, and maybe even just plain detrimental, to ignore this part of the modern Jewish story when talking about Jews in the twentieth century, because pretending this truth doesn't exist merely leaves it free to be exploited by bigots and conspiracists. So when I started writing this book I knew I wanted to look at Jewish social mobility in the last century, and it didn't take me long to realize that the person in my family who best embodies this storyline, as well as the probable reasons behind it, was Alex.

The path that brought Alex to Picasso began when he returned to the fashion business after the war. Some might think that the gravity of what he'd endured during the war would have made fashion seem intolerably superficial and ridiculous in comparison. But this would be a misunderstanding of what fashion means, and has always meant, to France.

Today, Paris comes at the end of the Fashion Week cycle—the order always running New York, London, Milan, Paris—and, sure, there is usually some kind of acknowledgment in those other cities that Fashion Week was happening. A minor politician might sit in the front row at some of the shows. The local mayor will make a speech welcoming the fashion journalists, dutifully trotting out statistics about how important—meaning lucrative—fashion was to the city. But these nods invariably feel merely dutiful—halfhearted and token. You can all but hear the faint grinding of teeth as these politicians demeaned themselves to consort with the lowbrow world of fashion.

---

were that the financial system is controlled by "men of a single and peculiar race, who have behind them many centuries of financial experience . . . [and] are in a unique position to control the policy of nations." Hobson adds that the direct influence of these financial houses "is supported by the control which they exercise over the body of public opinion through the press." Just in case it's not clear who this "single and peculiar race" is, Hobson asks, in the same paragraph, "Does anyone seriously suppose that a great war could be undertaken by any European state, or a great State loan subscribed, if the house of Rothschild and its connections set their face against it?" Corbyn replied that any suggestion he was praising anti-Semitic theories was a "mischievous representation of my foreword" made by "Labour's political opponents." Justin Cohen, *The Times of Israel*, May 3, 2019.

Fashion Weeks aren't important to those cities. They are accessories rather than the main outfit, something that could easily be removed without anyone noticing the lack.

Paris is different. There, it feels like the whole city is invested in Fashion Week, as much as if a major football tournament or film festival were happening in the center of town. Taxi drivers know where the main shows happen, and waiters in cafés talk knowledgeably about whether the new designers at the big brands are living up to their hype. In Paris, fashion isn't just an add-on, it is an integral part of the city's identity; it has always been thus, and never more so than in the aftermath of the war, when Alex was reentering the industry.

In the run-up to the war and during it, while women in Britain and America were being told to make do and mend, French women were instructed it was their patriotic duty to look fashionable:

"Fashion will remain Parisienne in its most intimate fibre. You will dress yourself simply but elegantly. Those who are at the front want you to be pretty," read a fashion editorial in 1939.[4] Even the Nazis understood the importance of fashion to Paris's identity. Early in the war, Hitler set out to make Berlin the fashion capital instead of Paris, so in July 1940, Nazis marched into the offices of Lucien Lelong, a designer and then president of the Chambre Syndicale de la Haute Couture, and demanded he hand over all the records of the French fashion business. Lelong understood this was an attempt to hijack not just the French fashion industry but France's culture and pride, so in November of that year he traveled to Berlin to insist that haute couture must stay in Paris. He argued that the designers and workers wouldn't be able to produce anything if they were torn from their homes and families in France and forcibly repatriated to Germany. Surprisingly, the Nazis agreed and Lelong saved not just French fashion, but also thousands of lives, as many of the seamstresses who worked in haute couture—as well as the occasional designers like Alex—were Jewish refugees.

After Paris was liberated, some of the British and American forces were outraged at the fashionability of the Frenchwomen they saw. But as historian Anne Sebba writes, staying fashionable was seen in France as a form of resistance: "To look dowdy was a negation of patriotic duty, when by sporting extravagant costumes they could thumb their noses at the Germans. Fashion was, for the French, even after four years of occupation, anything but trivial."[5]

Fashion was considered so untrivial that the resumption of the fashion industry was seen by the French as analogous to France reemerging from the ashes of wartime humiliation. So in 1945, Lelong, along with Nina Ricci's son Robert, came up with the Petit Théâtre de la Mode, an exhibition in which French designers dressed small dolls in their latest fashions. Despite the country being pretty much broke, the French Ministry of Reconstruction supported the show, because this was an important statement about the resurgence of French industry. The dolls were placed in sets designed by French artists, including Jean Cocteau, and the designers who took part included Balenciaga, Hermès, Lanvin, Grès, Schiaparelli, Rochas, and a designer described as "Alex."

This was almost certainly Alex Maguy. "Alex's" doll, which is currently in the Maryhill Museum of Art in Washington, is wearing a loose black-and-white-checked coat with a green lining, which is very similar to Alex's designs before and after the war. More tellingly, Alex definitely contributed a design to a similar initiative, the Merci Train, also organized by Lelong, four years later, and nearly all the designers involved in the Petit Théâtre de la Mode also took part in the Merci Train. On top of that, he would certainly have known Lelong (through Dior, who worked for him) and Robert Ricci (through his mother, Nina) beforehand. "We can be almost completely sure he was also part of the Petit Théâtre," academic Ludivine Broch, who has written on the Merci Train extensively, told me.

But why would he omit his surname? Broch pointed out to me that several designers who took part in the Petit Théâtre "were going for the one-name brand," probably to make themselves sound a little more ritzy, more like Hermès or Chanel. But because "Maguy" sounded so similar to the then-popular Parisian designer Maggy Rouff—and also wasn't actually his name—he opted to use "Alex" instead. But it may also be because of a message that was being subtly pushed by the Petit Théâtre, and France itself, in the immediate postwar era. There was no reference to the resistance in the Petit Théâtre, and it's notable that various designers who had openly worked for the Nazis, such as Rochas and Maggy Rouff,[6] were involved in it. The Petit Théâtre was staged in the middle of the Épuration Légale, in which France hurriedly condemned collaborators in an attempt to banish memories of the occupation to the past. So while there was certainly appetite in the country then to punish traitors, there was also a growing desire for the country to move on from this national shame. It was this mood that would ultimately lead to Perré's quiet readmittance into society. So it may very well be that Lelong felt that Alex's full name was too closely associated with his resistance activities, or just his Jewishness, and this would serve as an undesired distraction—hence "Alex." In normal circumstances Alex would never have gone along with this, but he was absolutely frantic after the war to restart his fashion business, so it is entirely possible he would have agreed, for this one-off, to drop his surname. Alex was an extremely proud man, but if there was one quality he had in more abundance than pride, it was pragmatism.

The Petit Théâtre was hugely popular from the day it opened at the Louvre in 1945, ultimately attracting more than 100,000 visitors and raising more than 1 million francs for the war effort.[7] It was so successful it then went on a world tour, traveling to Stockholm, Vienna, Leeds, New York, and San Francisco, sending a reminder of France's superior couture culture to the world. After years of occupation and submission, France was defiantly reasserting its national pride.

Two years later, Drew Pearson, an American journalist and anticommunist campaigner, organized what would become known as the Friendship Train. This was literally a train, filled with $40 million—$500 million today—worth of donated food and similar supplies that the train collected from American citizens during the course of its muchpublicized journey from Los Angeles to New York. The train was then shipped to Europe—France and Italy primarily—and was written about by the American media as a charitable effort to help the poor and humiliated European countries, which of course it was. But Pearson had an alternative political motive for sending the Friendship Train, which was that he feared that France in particular was now vulnerable to communism. This gesture from America would, it was hoped, remind France of the benevolence of its capitalist friends. It was a kind gesture, but one with a definite political edge. France promptly responded in kind.

The Merci Train was sent to the United States in 1949 and consisted of forty-nine boxcars filled with donations from French individuals and companies as thank-yous to the American people. Each boxcar went to a different American state.* The gratitude the French people felt was real, but what they chose to send the Americans shows something was going on here beyond mere thankfulness. Church bells, French art, and World War I souvenirs were offered, all of which were very nice but possibly not that useful to, say, families in North Dakota. And as with the Petit Théâtre, there were certainly no references in the Merci Train to the Occupation and the resistance.[8] Instead it was a proud statement of France's cultural dominance and endurance, emphasizing the country's glorious military past with mementos from the first world war as opposed to the more recent one, and souvenirs from French industries, such as art, automobiles, and fashion. France was undoubtedly grateful for the supplies America had sent, but it would not be treated as a groveling peasant, thankful for crumbs. Ironically, France was a lot less bothered by the Friendship Train's ulterior motive—to save the country from communism—than it was by its more euphemistic purpose, which was to help a poor, struggling country. The Merci Train shows that even if France itself was still barely on its knees in 1949, the country had lost none of its pride.

To represent French fashion, Lelong repeated his Petit Théâtre initiative and commissioned what the Metropolitan Museum of Art in New York described as "the most talented and well-known fashion designers

---

* Washington, DC, and Hawaii shared one of the boxcars.

of the time to create mini masterpieces."[9] Alex was again one of those designers, and today his doll is in the Metropolitan Museum: she was wearing a beautiful full-length burnished blue dress with black piping around the neck and short sleeves, a cream blouse beneath, a black belt around the waist, and black stripes at the bottom, and an elegant straw bonnet, with more black piping and a long black ribbon.* Alex's inclusions in the Petit Théâtre and Merci Train were undoubtedly an honor, but they also show how France had been forced to change in the past half decade, even if it couldn't really acknowledge it openly. The former Polish refugee who arrived without a penny and unable to speak the language, whom France had tried to have killed only a few years earlier, was now seen as an integral part of the country's grandeur. Alex had been deeply hurt by France's refusal to naturalize him before the war; after the war, when he was considered an essential component to the country's sense of pride, he had his validation.

By the time Alex contributed to the Merci Train, he had fully resurrected his fashion house. This effort began in 1945 when he sold a painting by the Jewish artist Chaim Soutine[10]—which he'd bought before the war and stashed away during it, probably with a friend—for 200,000 francs. From that sale he was able to rent a room on rue Jean Goujon, just behind the extremely posh Avenue Montaigne, which he turned into his new couture salon. In his memoir Alex claims that Imre Partos and Christian Dior helped him decorate his salon, which is certainly possible as Dior was building his own salon around the corner on the Avenue Montaigne, after spending the war designing for Lelong's label. Two years later Dior would launch his New Look collection, which would both establish his name as the greatest designer of his era and confirm at last that Paris had regained its position as the capital of haute couture.

Alex had the kind of salon he'd dreamed of since he was a teenager, and he filled the room with what he had managed to save of his small art

---

* The dress worn by the doll in the museum is burnished orange, but it was originally blue. The blue dress had to be replaced due to wear and tear.

collection, including paintings by his beloved friend Kisling. One thing he did not have, however, was material for making clothes.

It was hard for all designers to obtain fabrics in France after the war, and part of the reason Lelong originally commissioned the designers to make clothes for miniature mannequins was that they wouldn't need as much fabric as actual models. Alex worked so hard—cobbling together whatever scraps of material he could find, asking friends abroad and almost certainly his sister to send over whatever fabrics they could, raising money, coming up with the designs, making them, and finding the models—that the night before his show he collapsed with exhaustion. So Lelong, as eager as Alex for this show to be a success, stepped in and presented it for him.

Lelong and Alex shared a connection that went beyond an ambition for the French fashion industry: both were suspected of collaboration. Lelong saved the fashion industry from being relocated to Germany, but his success ultimately worked against him as it suggested to some that he was not to be trusted. Surely, they said, an innocent Frenchman could not work with the Germans as successfully as he did.* Alex, who himself was the subject of whispers because of his alliance with General Perré, became one of Lelong's more vocal defenders, insistently reassuring any skeptical designers of his innocence.

Alex knew some regarded him with suspicion, but this did not put him off from dabbling in shadowy ambiguity. He himself believed, he writes in his memoir, that Lelong "was guilty of much" during the war, although there has never been any evidence he was guilty of anything. Nonetheless, Alex also believed Lelong was worth defending because "my real concern was to get my couture business relaunched."

Lelong was not the only suspected collaborator Alex worked with.

---

* Lelong's close involvement in the Petit Théâtre and Merci Train is further proof of how both of those initiatives deliberately ignored the scandals of the recent past and, to a certain degree, served to imbue political credibility on those, like Lelong and Rochas, who were regarded with suspicion.

Serge Lifar was one of the greatest ballet dancers of the twentieth century, and for three decades was the director of the Paris Opera Ballet, including during the war. After Paris was liberated he was tried and condemned as a collaborator and banned from the stage. Alex, however, took it upon himself to defend him and asked a journalist friend on *Nice-Matin* to write a piece in defense of Lifar.

"You're asking me to clear Lifar's name? Are you crazy? Especially you, Alex. I don't get it," his friend said.

"Don't think I am asking for the pleasure of it. I don't have a choice," Alex replied.

Of course, Alex did have a choice, but Lifar had commissioned him to make costumes for his ballet, for the career-saving sum of 500,000 francs. At this point, the theater was pretty much the only place where a designer could make money, as few private citizens could afford couture, and Lifar's commission was a lifeline. Once again, Alex was looking out for himself, and he won: Lifar was able to stage his ballet and Alex finally got his company off the ground by making the costumes, with the assistance of his old friend Imre Partos.

When I first read these stories I was astonished, because the image of Alex working with known collaborators was definitely not the Alex his family knew. After all, at the same time Alex was defending Lelong, he was instructing his little sister to hunt down Emile Best with a gun. Once in the 1960s, when my father was with Alex at his office, a German museum called him and asked, in careful French, if they could borrow a painting. My father watched Alex's face turning red as he listened. At last he spoke: "As long as there is breath in my body, no painting of mine will ever be hung in your country!" he shouted back in German, and slammed down the phone. In the 1980s, at a fancy cocktail party in Paris, Alex was introduced to someone he describes in his memoir as "Austria's consul general."

"Come join us, Alex, you speak German so well," a mutual friend said.

"Not German—Yiddish," Alex replied loudly.

"A chilled silence fell over the elegant room," Alex writes. "I planted myself before the consul general: 'You killed my father,' I said. 'He was a soldier in your army in 1914. He was gassed in Italy, on the Piava. He died from it. And now you have a Nazi president, Waldheim.[11] Have you no shame?' "

Even in the 1990s, when Alex was in his eighties and I would visit him in Paris, he would regularly hiss "Collaborator!" at various galleries and businesses we walked past that, he swore, had sold out the Jews sixty years earlier.

But by then, Alex had the luxury of being safe, established, and secure. In the war period and its immediate aftermath, his lifesaving pragmatism took precedence over his loyalty to a greater cause, and he worked with suspected and convicted "collabos" when he needed their help, during the war (Perré) and immediately after (Lelong, who was probably innocent; Lifar, who definitely was not). Once he was reestablished, he would rather spit on such people than talk to them, but he didn't deny his past alliances, faithfully recording them in his memoir. He might not have been entirely open about some things, but he didn't lie about what he'd had to do to survive. He was passionately proud of being Jewish, but his ultimate cause was himself, and this is why he not only survived but would, very soon, become more successful than even he could have imagined.

The most popular credible theories for Jewish social mobility boil down to four arguments: there is a Jewish tradition of valuing education; Judaism itself encourages Jews to work hard because it is a religion that emphasizes achievements in the current life as opposed to waiting for rewards in the afterlife; Jews tend to work, and succeed, in areas that have long been heavily Jewish, such as fashion, banking, and the arts; and there is something specific to the way Jews are marginalized that encourages them to succeed. The first two theories aren't relevant in regard to Alex, because he barely went to school and was not observant.

The third one is more pertinent, given how many of Alex's art friends were Jewish, although it also raises the question why certain industries were and still are so popular with Jews. In his book about how Hollywood was founded by Eastern European Jews,[12] Neal Gabler suggests that the movie business appealed to Jews because it allowed them to create an idealized view of America, even while American society denied them admission. American golf clubs might not allow Jews as members, but Jewish producers could make movies set in fancy country clubs. Connected to this was the practical consideration that moviemaking was a job Jews could actually do, because "there were none of the impediments imposed by loftier professions and more firmly entrenched businesses to keep Jews and other undesirables out." Both of these points are equally relevant to Jewish immigrants in Europe who worked in the arts, like Alex: they were able to get into that industry, and, once in, they could celebrate the beauty of a country they loved even if it had, at best, ambivalent feelings toward them. Anyone who works in a business like fashion and fine art is someone who needs to be surrounded by beauty. It is not that surprising that Eastern European Jewish immigrants, who had experienced so much ugliness in their lives, might crave a corrective.

The last theory, about the way Jews are marginalized, strikes me as being especially relevant to Alex. All minorities are, in different ways, marginalized, but Alex's specific experiences, ones that were common to countless Jews of his generation, unquestionably shaped his ambition. He was from the generation that lost ties—by choice or force—with traditional shtetl life, only then to be rejected by the country in which he'd been born. He then immigrated to another country, France, where he was reluctantly accepted, and then very much not. These events, in which he was repeatedly punished by the worlds in which he lived, encouraged Alex's strong individualism. It also, as Paul Burstein writes in his essay on Jewish success, created a marginality that made Jews like Alex "sceptical of conventional ideas and stimulated creativity that led to intellectual eminence and, often, economic success." I suspect this is also partly why financial industries have attracted so many Jews, as

Donald Trump has eagerly pointed out. Jews over the centuries experienced enormous losses, over and over again, as their businesses and homes were taken from them simply because they were Jewish. Cash, something they could hold on to and hide, was a form of protection. Even Jews, like myself, who live in comparatively peaceful times, grow up listening to stories of our parents' and grandparents' state-sanctioned bankruptcies, and so the idea of suddenly having nothing always feels very real. Money, like beauty, can feel like a protection against that, and certainly Henri and Alex felt like that. So did my father. He grew up seeing his parents often fretting and arguing over money, always feeling like they were on the verge of destitution. My father wanted a different life and to provide a different kind of life for his family, so he went into banking, and he was then able to look after his parents and his children, which was the point. He hardly ever wears a yarmulke, and he definitely never counted Trump's money, but by going into banking he adhered to a Jewish tradition as much as Alex did by going into the arts. He, like Henri and Alex, worked extremely hard, not because Jews are naturally hard workers, but because they are raised to believe they have to work twice as hard to get ahead, because they will never be entirely accepted. I doubt if my father ever consciously thought like that, but his parents did and they imbued that work ethic in him, and Alex and Henri definitely believed that. It was only by working all the time, Alex thought, that he would get anywhere.

Alex realized early on that there was no point in following rules, because the rules were made to work against him. He had learned definitively during the war that he always had to help himself, and if that meant defending suspected collaborators who would be beneficial to his career, or screaming at them in the middle of a cocktail party, he would do so without hesitation or fear. He didn't care what anyone thought of him.

Alex's acceptance and then fierce rejection of collaborationists reflects how his war experiences shaped him. Like Henri, he believed that the world would turn against the Jews again, and this led to what Howard

Sachar describes as the Jewish immigrant's "drive for entrepreneurial success."[13] But Alex's reaction to this sense of threat was the opposite of that of his older brother. Whereas Henri wanted to blend in and be unnoticed, Alex believed that the way to face this threat was not to hide but to stand out and fight, showing the world that the Jews, or at least this Jew, could not be pushed around.

This made Alex unusual, in terms of Jewish social mobility. Contrary to some ugly generalizations about Jewish success, there isn't something inherent in Jews that leads to success. If there were, then the most Jewish Jews would be the most successful, and clearly that is not the case: studies have repeatedly shown that Reform Jews earn more than Orthodox ones, and there aren't many high-profile ultra-Orthodox Jews in mainstream public life. Henri had been right from the start: assimilation leads to greater success for Jews. It contributed to Jews passing as Caucasians in a way they didn't before the twentieth century, and this in turn has helped their social mobility.

Alex was definitely not Orthodox; neither was he entirely assimilated. Unlike Henri, he never tried to be seen as French, because he learned from the war that true assimilation was a delusion—ultimately, he would always be seen as a Jew, and so he defined himself first and foremost as that instead of letting other people do it for him. His experiences—rather than any genetic tendencies—shaped his approach to the outside world and his ambition in it, and it just so happened that his unusual approach worked for him. He consciously hugged his Yiddish accent close and he loathed Germany, refusing to visit the country ever—that Sonia could speak fluent German, and continued to do so after the war, was yet another count against her in Alex's eyes.

As angry as he was at Germany, he was more furious at France for having betrayed him. Yet he never considered living somewhere else. Maybe he thought it would be too hard to start another business somewhere else, maybe he didn't want to leave Henri. I suspect there was a part of him that simply needed to triumph over France as a form of revenge on it. They couldn't throw him out during the war, and he would not be chased out afterward. But this meant that for the rest of his life, he stayed in a country that he loved dearly but had hurt him worse than any single person. He loved France, and he never forgave it.

Wounded by the French and long ago abandoned by Poland, Alex became a very vocal supporter of Israel (another common reaction among Jews of his generation, also born from experience). He and Henri bought Chaya an apartment in Haifa, and they visited her there often. Photos show them grinning happily in a Jewish homeland none of them could have imagined when they all lived in Chrzanow. "Israel is the realization of all my dreams, a dream come true after the worst atrocities which humanity has ever known. No one can doubt that Israel will become a leading country in developmental potential and the light of the Middle East," he wrote. This prediction was a rare instance of Alex being overly optimistic, but such uncharacteristic sunny hopefulness is a testament to how shocked he was by what had happened to him and his family in France, and how much he hoped—had to hope—that the new Jewish state would protect them all forever. When he was invited, as a Jewish designer, to Israel shortly after the country was admitted to the United Nations in 1949, to show his collection in Tel Aviv and Jerusalem, he was so overcome that when writing about the trip thirty years later he lapsed into near hysteria:

"Imagine what this trip meant to me. It was a matter of great pride and joy to show my people that I was a leading French couturier. All our dreams of centuries were suddenly made real. Now, I thought, our children would have a real childhood, beautiful, happy, rich. For me, whose childhood had been wounded unto death, it was more than satisfaction, it was an enormous hope."

While nowhere near as successful as his former illustrator Dior, Alex had a genuine talent for making beautiful clothes that lasted. As a child, I loved to play with the coats he had made for my grandmother, which she still had in her closet thirty, forty, even fifty years after he made them. And given that he was an independent designer with no financial backers, he did impressively well. The sleek and sporty look for which he became known before the war turned out to be a canny choice, because even if all of France had fallen in love with Dior's feminine New Look, Alex's smart coats, sharply tailored dresses, and streamlined suits were a popular look in America. Ava Gardner bought dresses from him; Marlene Dietrich bought a jacket. His friends from the Foreign Legion, including General Koenig and Lieutenant-Colonel Magrin-Vernerey, occasionally came to his presentations, and some of the most carefully preserved photos I found of Alex's salon show him proudly posing with his fellow legionnaires—all of whom look a little bemused by their couture surroundings. Sala tried to come to Paris as often as possible for his shows, and she kept several photos that show him accompanying his beautiful sister, wearing an elegant Alex Maguy dress and coat, to her seat in his salon.

His friends from the art world came, too. Kisling was by now living in the south of France, but when he was in Paris he would come to Alex's salon every day and certainly to the shows if he was in town. "Among the School of Paris, Kiki, my foster brother, emitted the greatest happi-

Chaya, Alex, a female friend, and Kisling at one of
Alex's fashion shows in Paris, 1950s

ness. While he was 100% Jewish he was the most Parisian of us all. Every Friday he would have a lunch in a brasserie and his table was open to the whole of Paris. It was the meeting place of the bohemians and beautiful women crowded round us. His love for life and for women is what I loved in his paintings. They taught me about a kind of happiness that had eluded me in childhood and which Kiki taught me to look for in paintings," Alex wrote.

Kisling felt just as fond of Alex and wrote Sala reports of their times together.

"I have made an unexpected visit to our dear brother, and you should see our Alex, how happy he is. His wit, his humor, and his life are marvelous!" he wrote to Sala on March 29, 1947.

Alex's life was glamorous, but it was not exactly marvelous. My father remembers sitting backstage at Alex's shows and watching him carefully style and dress his models, pinning this sleeve, lowering that hem. And then after the show, he would watch his uncle obsequiously thank every fashion editor and store buyer who had come to his show, bow his head humbly as American and French customers told him they liked the dress but it was in the wrong color, they liked the coat but it was too long.

"For you, madame, I will fix it," Alex would murmur.

Afterward, my father would see Alex almost prostrate with despair in his workroom, worrying that he hadn't sold enough clothes, infuriated that the designs he'd sweated over were casually dismissed by ignorant customers, terrified that he wouldn't be able to pay his seamstresses, that he wouldn't be able to eat.

Today, the big labels like Dior are awash with money (mostly from makeup and accessories rather than clothes), but in the main, it is very, very hard to be a fashion designer. When I was a young journalist occasionally posted to New York and Paris, I would often interview well-known designers who quietly spent their days shivering in underheated studios, barely keeping creditors from the door. In several cases, I'd interview a designer one day and find out he or she went out of business the next. For all the lipstick-shiny confidence fashion projects from the

A crowd at one of Alex's fashion shows

pages of magazines, the truth is not that many people have more than $3,000 to spend on a dress, and so designers are forced to give clothes to celebrities for free, in the hope of some publicity. They then have to write off the loss, hoping against all likelihood that their little gamble will pay off. As Alex's memoir makes clear, it has always been thus:

"The fame of a couturier is linked to the fame of the women he dresses. They were often more celebrities than normal clients and needed to be treated as such. They often 'forgot' to pay. It's part of the business. So a couturier has a dual responsibility: First, make women more beautiful in the great tradition of Parisian fashion. Second, support a business. To reconcile these two responsibilities is unimaginably difficult," he wrote.

Alex's clothes were regularly featured in fashion magazines, French and American, and he himself was photographed in the society pages of French papers with beautiful women, such as the French singer Luci-

enne Dhotelle (known as "la môme Moineau") and the American singer-
songwriter Betty Comden at the races at Longchamps or the Parisian
nightclubs. But despite the surface fabulousness of his life, his business
was crippled by debts, and he would go for days without eating in order
to pay his staff of 150.

In 1951, after 108 collections, Alex was invited by the French ambassador to Denmark to take part in a charity show for "the most famous haute
couturiers." By this point, his business was nearly bankrupt, so Alex hesitated to accept. But he hadn't gotten this far by being shy, and he thought
to himself: "Remember when as a child you dreamed of French couture in
your little, lost Galician village. Now, after a twenty-five-year career,
they're inviting you. Prove by your presence that you're not finished."

So Alex went, but initially felt humiliated when he saw how the other
designers had been able to bring dozens of models with them, dressed
in the most expensive brocades. He couldn't afford even a single model

Sala and Alex at a ball in Paris

or outfit. But if the Nazis couldn't destroy Alex, then certainly fashion wouldn't, so he decided to make a virtue out of his poverty. When it was his turn, he borrowed a model from a designer friend, got up onstage "taking my courage into both hands," and with only a case of pins and about seven feet of cotton, constructed an evening gown in front of the astonished audience in seven minutes. He got a standing ovation, and one Danish newspaper that covered the event described it as "a sensation."[14] A one-off dress he made with his own hands in front of the audience: it was a characteristically defiant gesture from Alex in defense of the art of couture and an illustration of Alex's refusal to give up, ever, even when the odds seemed utterly hopeless.

Alex returned to Paris and carried on as a designer for a few more years, but it was clear that couture was becoming part of the past. In 1955, *Le Monde*'s fashion critic compared Alex's classical style with the more modernist looks that would define the 1960s when the journalist reviewed his show alongside that of Pierre Cardin: "We are seeing two trends clash: some still want to reflect the female silhouette, others want to reshape it. We will soon learn who played it best," wrote the critic of the two designers.[15]

There was no competition: although the journalist praised Alex's "sylphan silhouettes" and "the astonishing and much-applauded striped pieces," Pierre Cardin's "shocking spectacle inspired by interplanetary journeys" was clearly the future.

At the same time Alex's fashion business was struggling, someone else's was taking off. His cousin Maurice's son, Armand Ornstein, was no longer the little boy hiding in the woods but an extremely handsome young man-about-town. Around this time, he teamed up with a young designer called Daniel Hechter, and Hechter's name would become as much of a byword for French 1960s fashion as Mary Quant and Biba were for British 1960s style, thanks to the extremely successful business he and Armand built together. Today, Hechter is widely credited with popularizing prêt-à-porter and helping to kill off exactly the kind of fashion that Alex made. *Prêt-à-porter* literally means "ready to wear," as in buying clothes directly off the rack, and this is how nearly everyone buys clothes today, whether they shop at Zara or at Prada. Alex, however, was firmly in the older tradition of haute couture, which means each outfit is specially created for each customer, making it extremely beautiful, but expensive and ultimately impractical. By the 1950s haute couture was already on its way out, and today, even in the big fashion houses like Dior, it accounts for an infinitesimal percentage of the company's overall sales. Alex, as a small Parisian couturier, was one of the last of an already dying breed, and while his stubbornness about retaining his independence undoubtedly hastened his end, it would have come eventually. The fashion world was changing and would soon be unrecognizably different from the one in which he trained. Alex could be pragmatic about some things, but not his art, and in this area alone he would not compromise for the sake of survival.

Alex never explicitly blamed Armand for the death of his fashion business, or even talked with Armand about fashion. In fact, he would have been furious to hear anyone suggest they were even in the same business: Armand and Daniel Hechter's clothes were intended to last just a fashion season, whereas Alex's, as he would be the first to say, endured forever. But he certainly raged against the fashion revolution Armand and Hechter inspired:

"Once there were forty great couture houses in Paris. How many exist today? Four or five at most. Ready-to-wear finally killed personal elegance and individual charm. It made Paris ugly. Today, it's the brand a woman wears that is noticed, not the woman herself. One wears Sonia Rykiel or Chanel and circulates like an automobile and its nameplate. What an absence of taste. How sad," he writes in his memoir.

Even though his business was, in part, killed by one member of the next generation of his family, Alex later managed to pass his legacy onto another younger relative: Alexandre de Betak, his great-nephew and Henri and Sonia's grandson. Almost every week through the 1970s and early 1980s, Henri brought Alexandre over to Alex's for lunch—Sonia, of course, was not invited, and nor were Alexandre's mother and sister, Danièle and Natasha—and Alex would lecture his great-nephew about art and elegance. (When I later heard about these lunches I thought of Gigi in the 1958 MGM film, adapted from Colette's novel, enduring regular lunches with her aunt Alicia, who would teach her niece about all the important things in life, like how to admire jewelry and the right way to eat an ortolan.) Alexandre resented having to get dressed up in a suit for these lunches—why did he have to spend his day all hot and uncomfortable when his sister could wear what she liked and stay home and play? While Alex would talk to the bemused little boy about fashion and all the beautiful people he knew, Alexandre would quietly wonder why, if his great-uncle knew so much about style, did he have lifts on all of his shoes? But something about these lunches stuck in Alexandre's mind, because this introduction to fashion would prove to be a formative one.

Before Alex shut his salon for good, he had one last gift to give a favored customer: a young Chinese architect called Ieoh Ming Pei, better known now as I.M. Pei. Alex and Pei met in Paris in 1951 when the latter was on the Wheelwright Traveling Fellowship, and Pei and his wife, Eileen, had been told about Alex's salon by the American architect Philip Johnson. Alex never lost his knack at spotting who was worth schmoozing, and as his alliance with Perré proved to him, befriending powerful and prominent people could only be beneficial. Alex realized early on that Pei was worth keeping in his life, and in the hope of achieving this, one of his last gestures as a designer was to send the Peis a small Modigliani sketch as a token of gratitude for their support, he wrote in his memoir. But this may have been superfluous as Pei wasn't all that impressed by the sketch. I emailed Pei's sons, Chien Chung and Li Chung, to verify this story, and initially they thought it unlikely as they doubted if their parents had ever owned such a sketch. But a few days later they emailed back. They had found the Modigliani in the back of their father's closet. Pei might have never bothered to hang it, but, once again, Alex had told the truth.

But while Pei might not have been overly awed by Alex's present, he liked Alex: whenever Pei would spot him at parties he would call out, "Shalom, Alex!" much to Alex's delight and everyone else's bemusement.

In the early 1980s, when Pei was being widely vilified for his plans to build a small pyramid in front of the Louvre, Alex was one of the very few who supported Pei, and stood up and said so. He wrote letters to Pei and about Pei to newspapers, saying that what French art needed was Pei's pyramid. Pei later returned the favor by putting Alex, by now extremely wealthy, in touch with Moshe Mayer, a real estate developer who worked with Pei, about planning the Alex Maguy Foundation in Israel, which, had it been built, would have been the ultimate proof of Alex's social ascendency. The foundation never actually materialized, probably due to cost and Alex's health, but yet again Alex was proven right about the value of having successful friends.

Alex finally shut down his salon in the mid-1950s, ending that chapter of his life. The next chapter would bring him the immortality and enormous wealth he had always longed for, and expected.

Alex's career in art began, naturally, with his friends. He first sold off his last fashion pieces, settled his most urgent debts, and with what was left, opened a small gallery on the rue Faubourg Saint-Honoré, just around the corner from Avenue Matignon, where he'd had a salon before the war. He named it Galerie d'Élysée, emphasizing its proximity—and insinuating a connection—to the Élysée Palace, the residence of the French president. Alex had always longed to be established in French society, and being neighbors with the president proved his establishment status. In characteristic fashion, he threw a glamorous opening night party for the gallery to which he invited all his old friends and colleagues, including Dior.

"I've come to wish you good luck, Alex. Have no regrets. Don't forget, I began with paintings and you will finish with paintings," Dior said to him.

"In many ways, our fates crossed," Alex writes in his memoir. "I remember Dior's beginnings, that I was the designer and he was associated with an art gallery. Now I was at a gallery and he was the designer working with Imre Partos. But I didn't hold it against Christian. It had become impossible for me to keep Imre, a truly great artist."

Another person from his fashion past who supported Alex in his move to the art world was the illustrator René Gruau. He helped Alex to decorate his gallery, and shortly afterward he painted an extraordinarily evocative portrait of Sala on one of her trips to Paris. This painting originally hung in my grandmother's apartment and now hangs over my parents' fireplace in London, and it captures her elegance and wistfulness better than most photographs. Her elbow is leaning on a table and her chin rests on the back of her hand while she gazes behind her; he immortalized her as always looking back, toward the past. In its tenderness and precision, it was clearly painted by someone with enormous feeling for the subject and her family. In 1974, almost forty years after they first met, Alex hosted an exhibition of Gruau's work in his gallery that he called "Alex Maguy Presente Son Ami Gruau." For the chosen very few, Alex could be extremely loyal and sentimental. (Kisling also painted a portrait of Sala; Alex had told Bill at that fateful dinner in Chaya's flat in rue des Rosiers that famous artists loved to paint his sister and, decades later, thanks to Alex and his extraordinary career path, that lie eventually became true.)

Alex's idea with the Galerie d'Élysée was to have shows that featured only seven paintings—seven was his lucky number, and it's also a significant number in Judaism, representing creation and fortune. Each of his shows would be centered on a theme, and his first show was called "Paris, Parisians, and Parisiennes"; his second was called "The Landscapes and Faces of France." When he was a designer he made adoring near-pastiches of French style, and as a curator he put on shows specifically celebrating French style. Little Sender was still enchanted with the fantasy of the country his father used to describe to him on Kostalista, despite everything it had in reality done to him and his family.

Over the next decade, he built up a hugely successful gallery, showing works by, among others, his old friends Chagall, Pascin, and Kisling (who sadly died soon after the gallery opened), as well as Bonnard, Renoir, Monet, Braque, Miró, Bacon, and Boudin, and sculpture by

Giacometti, Henry Moore, and Gauguin. Alex had exceptionally good taste in art, the kind only someone with a deep love of his subject can have, as opposed to someone merely chasing after the hot new thing in the art world. The gallery quickly developed a reputation for having the finest pieces from the greatest modern artists, and Alex became a name again that was cited in the gossip magazines:

"Among the many notable celebrities at the party, we saw Jacqueline Auriol [a French aviator] in the company of Alex Maguy," read a typical caption from a French magazine, which Alex cut out and sent to my grandmother and which she faithfully saved. But there was still one goal he hadn't achieved yet: meeting Picasso.

Alex had been trying to get Picasso's attention for decades. He genuinely revered him as a lover of art but he also liked him as a person: short, tough, sexual, a fighter, deeply moral but complicated, adored by men and women, one who didn't obey the rules and was rewarded for it, Picasso was an idealization of Alex's own self-image. After the war, Alex had a tangential connection with Picasso through his friends Georges and Suzanne Ramié. Like Alex, the Ramiés had been involved in resistance activity in the south of France, but now ran a pottery shop, called Madoura, on the Côte d'Azur. Fortuitously for Alex, this workshop became one of the most important centers of twentieth-century ceramics, because it was the exclusive producer of ceramics by Picasso. Alex tried in vain to utilize this connection. In 1949 he'd designed a dress covered with images from Picasso's paintings and wrote the artist to tell him, under the pretense that he was asking for permission but really just making his presence known to his artistic hero. (If Picasso did reply to that request it has long since been lost, but Alex did make the dress.) Alex became friendly with a young woman, named Jacqueline Roque, who worked at Madoura. But Alex was not the only male friend of the Ramiés to have noticed Jacqueline: in 1953, at the age of twenty-six, she caught the eye of Picasso, who was more than four decades older than her, and he embarked on a long campaign of seduction. Now Alex had yet another connection to the artist, and once he opened his gallery, he wrote to him more frequently, asking for his blessing to feature this or that painting, inviting him to his shows, even sending him birthday greetings. "Dare I ask you to do me the honor of being my guest for the baptism of my little yacht?" he wrote on April 13, 1960, referring to the boat he'd recently bought and kept moored down in Cannes. (Picasso declined that invitation.) Undaunted by constant refusals, Alex tried again almost exactly a year later, saying that he had a proposal for Picasso that involved Alex's "very, very close friends at the House of Dior." A few days later the phone in his gallery rang: it was Jacqueline, inviting him to their house in Cannes, Villa La Californie. Barely able to breathe with excitement, Alex said he would be there. Once again, a personal connection worked in Alex's favor. Eventually.

In April 1961, Picasso was eighty and a newlywed, having married Jacqueline the previous month. Jacqueline was devoted to her new husband, sorting through his correspondence, attending to the daily chores, fending off the endless stream of visitors and collectors, dealing with the lawyers, and generally arranging their lives.[16] After Picasso died in 1973,

Alex on his yacht in Cannes

the degree to which Jacqueline controlled Picasso's life would become a somewhat controversial subject, when she stopped Paloma and Claude, his children from a previous relationship, from attending their father's funeral, and was later accused of stealing their inheritance. But Picasso was besotted by her, and at the very least grateful for her attentiveness: he made four hundred portraits of her, more than of any other single person, and for the last seventeen years of his life she was the only woman the former womanizer painted.

Almost certainly, Alex's friendship with Jacqueline helped to get him his long-sought-after invitation to meet Picasso. But the artist guarded his time and privacy fiercely, and he was certainly not opening his doors to every art world hanger-on whom Jacqueline had met at Madoura. So there had been something about Alex's letter that "captured Picasso's attention," Jacqueline explained, and it turned out that had less to do with art and more to do with Alex. Picasso had lived in Paris during the Occupation and was fascinated by Alex's story of fighting in the Foreign Legion alongside Spanish Republicans in exile, as Picasso was himself a Spaniard essentially in exile. (Franco was then still in power in Spain, and Picasso was seen as an enemy.) And so he summoned him to Cannes, and that is when Alex first met Picasso at Villa La Californie.

As much as Alex saw himself in Picasso, Picasso apparently saw himself in Alex. When he entered the sitting room Picasso stood up, walked toward Alex—reaching up because, for once, Alex was the tallest man in the room—jabbed a finger into his chest: "T'es Juif, comme moi!" Picasso barked.

Alex assumed at the time that Picasso was speaking metaphorically, that he thought of himself as an outcast and a fighter, two qualities associated with Jewish resistance fighters, and that Picasso, rightly, saw in Alex. The two men talked for about half an hour. It doesn't sound, however, like Alex talked that much. Instead he listened to Picasso and didn't explain what, exactly, it was that he wanted from him after all this time: "I did not dare distract from our precious moments together to talk to you about something that is very dear to my heart," he wrote to him after the visit. In fact, Alex wanted Picasso to design a scarf for a collection Dior was putting together that year; Dior had asked Alex's assistance in contacting Picasso, and Alex realized that, if he pulled this off, it would make him look like a big player in both the fashion and the art worlds.

I couldn't find any evidence that this scarf project ever happened. But Alex got something else from Picasso even he hadn't dared to hope for: friendship. Picasso took a genuine shine to him, and they entered into an extraordinarily regular correspondence. In the National Archives in Paris there are sixty-two letters from Alex to Picasso, far more than from almost any other business associate. They are all addressed to both Picasso—whom Alex always refers to as "grand maître"—and Jacqueline, as was common with all of Picasso's correspondence, such was the degree of Jacqueline's involvement in her husband's business affairs. But they are also written with a fond familiarity unusual in both men. Among the various business discussions—Alex asking Picasso to authenticate a painting, Alex inviting him to a party at his home—are chummy postcards from Alex's trips to the United States, as well as a joint postcard, sent from the south of France, signed by both Alex and Maurice Chevalier, in which they tell him they've been speaking of him fondly.

Picasso occasionally asked Alex to check on an exhibition of his work for him, especially in Spain, as the artist was still ostensibly exiled from his home country. In April 1962, Alex went to Barcelona, as Picasso had recently donated a huge number of works to the Aguilar Palace, and he wanted to know they were hung and received properly. Alex sent back a typically effusive telegram: "Everyone from and around Barcelona is embracing your wonderful present. Even the sun shone on the party." Some of Alex's artist friends were understandably jealous of how clearly starstruck he was by Picasso. Chagall, who had known Alex for almost forty years, would make pointed comments about his constant name-dropping and ask, "So tell me, how's your Spanish friend?" But Alex couldn't be teased out of bragging about Picasso.

Shortly after returning from Barcelona, Alex's loyalty paid off. He asked Picasso to look at the selection of paintings for his next show—only seven, as usual, including a work each by Chagall, Braque, Renoir, Monet, Degas, Dufy, and Picasso—and he wanted Picasso's approval. Picasso didn't just look at the paintings: he took the unusual step of summoning Alex to his home in Mougins, where he almost never had visitors because he considered it a place of solitude and work. His attitude was so extreme that even those close to him looked at his life there as "a form of self-imprisonment."[17] For Alex, Picasso broke this self-imposed imprisonment.

It turned out that Picasso did more than approve of Alex's exhibition: he made a poster for it.

"This is for you," Picasso said, presenting him with the drawing when he arrived.

It was a detailed portrait of a face with curly hair and big eyes, on top of which Picasso wrote Alex's name, as well as the name and address of his gallery, and beneath which he wrote the name and dates of the exhibition. And then he signed and dated it April 15, 1962.

"No one can know the joy I felt. It was more than a surprise, more than a gift—I looked at the lithograph as a reward," Alex writes.

A reward for what, he doesn't say—surviving? Perseverance? Someone—Jacqueline, or more likely one of Picasso's assistants—captured the moment Picasso gave Alex the poster. Picasso is looking at the camera and Alex at Picasso, and he looks like a cat who knows he has caught the prize mouse. For the rest of his life, when he talked about the poster, he would say, "Picasso gave me my birth certificate." Reaching the zenith of the art world, through his own determination, gave Alex his identity.

But even winning the prize couldn't stop Alex from burnishing this story a little more. In his memoir he claimed that Picasso drew the portrait the first time he met him, which was not true. He also insisted that the big-eyed, curly-haired figure in the poster was a portrait of him. In fact, it is most commonly identified by Picasso scholars as Jacqueline, which would make a lot more sense: Alex had small eyes and his hair had long since given up the fight, whereas Jacqueline was a wide-eyed, wavy-haired beauty. And considering how much Picasso painted her, it seems a lot more likely that she would be the subject rather than Alex. Even at what felt to him like the summit of his achievements, Alex couldn't resist giving himself a few extra inches of height.

But whoever was actually portrayed in the poster, getting it was an enormous coup for Alex. Picasso occasionally made posters for other small galleries, particularly ones around Avignon and Arles. (He also, the year before, made one for a show in Haifa, further confirming his solidarity with the Jewish people.) But by 1962 such gestures were rare, further proving the exceptional nature of his relationship with Alex.

The two men met several times over the next decade. Photos of those meetings show Picasso talking excitedly and Alex bowing his head with uncharacteristic humility, listening to him. Picasso was always intrigued that Alex had come to art via fashion, and when Alex was one day fussing about what frames he should put on Picasso's work, the artist thought for a moment and said, "You were a couturier, and you must dress them. It is absolutely right."

Just as Alex knew it would, his alliance with Picasso gave him a new level of credibility in the art world. By the late 1960s, the French newspapers referred to him as the "célèbre marchand de tableaux du Faubourg Saint-Honoré" (the famous art dealer of the Faubourg Saint-Honoré) and invariably described him as Viennese, due to society journalists' inability to differentiate between the Austro-Hungarian Empire and Austria. He was photographed at parties, often alongside Georges Pompidou, the prime minister of France and a regular at Alex's gallery, as the Élysée Palace was just next door. In 1964, Janet Flanner, the foreign correspondent of *The New Yorker*, wrote a long and glowing review of one of his shows that featured, as always, only seven paintings: "What a joy to see so few, and those so fine!" Flanner wrote,[18] praising in particular the "superb" Cézanne painting, "unfamiliar" work by Soutine, and "immortal" Toulouse-Lautrec sketch. Her references to the paintings' buyers give a sense of how important, and global, Alex had become in the art world: a watercolor by André Derain had been bought by Brandeis University in Massachusetts, and the "Proustian interior" by Bonnard was going to the National Gallery in Washington. Alex was so proud of this praise in an American publication, he wrote to his sister and instructed her to buy every copy of the magazine she could find and send them to him, which she immediately did.

Alex's celebrity buyers were as international as his museum customers. Edward G. Robinson—born Emmanuel Goldenberg in Romania—frequently visited the gallery, and he and Alex would converse happily in Yiddish. Similarly, Kirk Douglas (born Issur Danielovitch Demsky), who, like Sala's husband Bill, grew up speaking Yiddish in New York, bought two paintings; "Actors get a better price from me," Alex told him in Yiddish, to Douglas's delight. Aristotle Onassis, Peter Lawford, Yul Brynner, Jerry Lewis, Ingrid Bergman, and Frank Sinatra all visited the gallery, and Alex's old friend Maurice Chevalier was a regular, although he never bought anything, leading Alex to gripe forever about Chevalier being cheap. Elizabeth Taylor, on the other hand, was very eager to buy from him. In Richard Burton's diary entry dated January 11, 1969, he describes going to Alex's gallery with her: "He's a tiny man who claims to be a great friend of Picasso's," Burton wrote.[19]

Despite this somewhat skeptical initial impression, Burton got on well with Alex thanks to, Burton assumes, and probably rightly, "my gift of the gab, even in French, and my fame!" Taylor wanted to buy a Picasso portrait of a woman in blue, "which made her mouth water." Burton preferred the Picasso painting of a harlequin on a horse for $40,000. "I saw many other paintings and will obviously end up buying one," he writes. "But the most impressive was two paintings by van Gogh painted on both sides of the canvas—one of a man at a loom and one (the other side) of a man sitting in a chair near a fireplace. But they are beyond even my purse."

Every New Year, Alex would send out cards to his favored customers that were actually lithographs of his latest and favorite new painting. In an undated article from the mid-1960s, *Le Figaro* breathlessly wrote about Alex sending out lithographs of *The Pétanque Players* by Cézanne to, among others, Picasso, Onassis, and President Nixon.[20] Each lithograph was worth about 15,000 francs (the equivalent of about $115,000 today), meaning Alex spent hundreds of thousands on his New Year cards. But, as the journalist added, "That is not very extravagant, if we consider the strength of his bank account."

By the late 1960s, Alex was an extremely wealthy man, thanks to his art dealing, and his own personal collection of art was at least as impressive as his bank account. The Picasso portrait that made Elizabeth Taylor salivate was part of Alex's collection at home, and although he never sold his own paintings, "Alex has promised to invite us to his home to see it," Burton writes in his diary. Alex loved to tell journalists about all the famous people he refused to sell his paintings to, from Taylor to Pompidou (a Nicolas de Staël painting, according to Le Figaro). Once French politicians had tried to kill him; now he had the power to deny them what they wanted. A particularly satisfying instance of that was when André Bettencourt, the then-future minister of foreign affairs, begged Alex in vain in the early 1970s to sell him the beautiful painting by Raoul Dufy, Le Port du Havre. Bettencourt had been decorated for his resistance work, but in 1989 it emerged that during the war he had been a member of a French fascist group and written about Jews in the most anti-Semitic terms for the Nazi propaganda paper La Terre Française. Bettencourt exemplified the moral gray shades that were all too common in mid- to late-twentieth-century French politics, and he eventually, and somewhat begrudgingly, apologized. It would have pleased Alex enormously that a former fascist had begged him for something and he'd defiantly refused.

Alex's personal art collection was as fine as any museum's. He now lived on Avenue Foch, then and still now one of the chicest streets in Paris. His ground-floor apartment was filled with, at various times, works by Monet, Renoir, van Gogh, Braque, Cézanne, Manet, Degas, and, of course, Picasso. When I would have lunch with Alex in his apartment in the 1990s, even I—a cynical, grouchy teenager—was impressed that in his bathroom, almost as an afterthought, was a Matisse personally inscribed to him. The little boy from the shtetl who had always wanted to live surrounded by beauty created a home for himself filled with the greatest treasures of the nineteenth and twentieth centuries.

When Israel won the Six-Day War in 1967, Alex donated one of his favorite Picasso paintings, *Sitting Woman* (1949), to Israel, and the Israel Museum in Jerusalem still has the work. Just as he had given his most treasured paintings, a Kisling and a Pascin, to the Tel Aviv Museum before going off to war, so he gave his most beloved one to Israel to celebrate the country's military triumph almost thirty years later. Edmond de Rothschild had a reception at his home in Paris to commemorate Alex's donation, and the guest speaker was General Koenig, Alex's general from the Foreign Legion. General Koenig talked about seeing the Jewish legionnaires carrying the Zionist flag in 1941 in Bir Hakeim in Africa, "and that immediately made me feel a kinship with them," he said. Alex was deeply moved by his general's words, which he took as proof of his "attachment to the noble and just cause of Israel," and the two men stayed close until the general's death three years later.

Not everyone from Alex's military past felt such an attachment. Alex had always been proud to have been in England alongside the Free French and de Gaulle, but that changed in 1967. In the months leading up to the war, relations between Israel and the neighboring countries of Egypt, Jordan, and Syria became increasingly strained. De Gaulle, then the president of France, warned Israel not to launch preemptive strikes against Egypt, advice Israel promptly and rightly ignored. These strikes helped Israel to win the war—as the early attacks nearly wiped out the Egyptian air force—and save themselves. De Gaulle's advice had been bad, his motives questionable, and he was so irritated that he had been ignored that he held a press conference at the Élysée Palace—five minutes away from Alex's gallery—in which he described the Jews as "an elite people, domineering and sure of themselves . . . [with] ardent and conquering ambition." *Le Monde* mocked de Gaulle's speech with a cartoon that appeared on the paper's front page, showing a skeleton behind barbed wire in a concentration camp, a Star of David on his striped pajamas, which—only twenty-five years earlier—Jews had had to wear on their clothes in Paris. "An elite people, domineering and sure of themselves," was written underneath. Others were even more cutting, such as Michel Debré, France's former prime minister, the grandson of a rabbi and once a deeply loyal supporter of de Gaulle, who said the president's comment showed "an infantile-psychological-senile" attitude.[21] De Gaulle's statement probably had a lot more to do with the hurt ego of a seventy-seven-year-old politician than any proof of long-dormant anti-Semitism within him. But Alex didn't care. To him, de Gaulle's remarks sounded like the kind of attitude he had fought against, alongside the general, an attitude that had led to his brother's death and nearly his own. It was yet another betrayal by France, and he was hurt and, more than that, furious. So he picked up the phone and called his friend and neighbor Prime Minister Pompidou to inform him he was sending back his Croix de Guerre and Bronze Star, which he'd been awarded after the Narvik campaign. Pompidou begged him to calm down and reconsider, but Alex wasn't having any of it. He boxed up his medals, addressed them to the prime minister and president of France, and had his assistant run them next door to the palace. No matter how good Alex's life became, he never stopped thinking of himself as the Jewish outsider, and he never stopped believing France saw him that way, too.

Picasso's reaction to the Six-Day War was, for Alex, even more surprising than de Gaulle's. The artist was so moved by Alex's gift of his painting to Israel that he confided in him that the first thing he ever said to Alex—"T'es Juif, comme moi"—was meant not metaphorically but literally: "You should know that my mother was a Marrano," Picasso told him, according to Alex. (A Marrano was a Spanish Jew who converted to Christianity, often by force.)

"So Picasso was one of us. And, I can add, he told me this with much pride and nobility," Alex writes in his memoir.

As far as I know, there is no evidence that this was true of Picasso's mother, or that Picasso made this claim to anyone else. Certainly no Picasso scholars I spoke to had heard it. But Alex was adamant Picasso had told him this and, if Picasso did believe it, it would explain Picasso's well-established and long-standing loyalty to Jewish people, exemplified on an individual level by his friendship with Alex.

De Gaulle and Picasso were probably the two men Alex respected most in the world, and both stood up against fascism during the war. Their opposite reactions to the Six-Day War show how two people, even those ostensibly on the same side, could find themselves so divided when it came to the subject of Jews and in particular Israel. This split arguably developed in the way we still know it because of the Six-Day War, in itself a defining part of the Jewish story in the late twentieth century and still today. Israel's victory aggravated Palestinian frustration and, in turn, nationalism. Palestinians now knew that other Arab countries couldn't and wouldn't help them regain territories now held by Israel, such as Gaza, the West Bank, the Sinai Peninsula, and the Golan Heights, and this led to an escalation of the Israeli-Palestinian conflict, which is still all too ongoing. Israel's response to this conflict has shaped its own identity and has led the country down a militaristic, far-right path that is far from the dream Alex and many other Jews harbored for it. Alex was right to take a stand against de Gaulle's cruel comments about Jews in regard to Israel's actions in the Six-Day War; how Israel reacted after the war led many others to say similar things and worse.

When I first found the shoebox at the back of my grandmother's closet, there was only one object that made immediate sense to me. I didn't know who the bespectacled man in the photos was, or what that metal plate saying "Glass Prisonnier Cambrai" referred to, or why the Red Cross was writing to Sala in 1944—but I knew exactly how my quiet, self-effacing grandmother acquired a Picasso drawing. That's because it came from the one member of the Glass family who was always happy to talk about his achievements and who achieved the kinds of things that were written about in history books. What I couldn't understand was why she had it or why she had hidden it in her closet.

Alex introduced Sala to Picasso while she was on a trip to France in the late 1960s, and she was even more excited to meet the artist than Alex was the first time he went to Villa La Californie. There is only one photo of her with Picasso and, although he is looking elsewhere while shaking her hand, perhaps for someone a little more interesting than a housewife, she is positively shining with happiness. If meeting Picasso was a kind of self-validating success for Alex, for Sala it was proof that there existed a life out there where dreams really did come true, and that life was in Paris. She never said anything, but her trips back to France, which she took every other year or so, must have been almost impossibly painful for her: yes, going to America had possibly saved her life, but she surely looked at Henri and Alex and wondered, maybe if she'd stayed, she, too, would be living a glamorous life like her brothers, instead of being a suburban American housewife. They had been able to take active control over their lives and climbed up the social ladder in ways she'd longed to

Sala and Picasso

do, too. But her role in life, as a woman from a traditional Jewish background, was to stay in the background, behind her husband.

Chaya's death in 1964 quietly devastated Sala: despite her and her mother's differences, they loved one another very deeply, and being on a different continent when her mother finally passed away, in a retirement home in France that Henri and Alex had found for her when she got too old to live on her own in Israel, must have made Sala feel even lonelier. She paid for a death notice in the *New York Times*, even though no one else in America knew who Chaya was.[22] But that didn't matter to Sala; she wanted to make a public statement of her grief and for her mother's death to not pass unnoticed. Shortly after this, Sala went through one of her periodic "blue" phases, and when Alex heard about this, he asked Picasso for a little sketch that he could send her. Picasso obliged, and he even signed it, which he often omitted to do with sketches, much to the frustration of dealers and collectors.

Until the end of her life, Alex sent Sala pictures, and she loved to brag to visitors about the priceless art her famous brother in Paris gave her. After she died and we took down her pictures and out of their frames, while some of them were worth something—some prints by Soutine, some by Vlaminck—others were worthless posters from art exhibitions. For years I assumed that my grandmother had been deceived by her brother with these posters, but after finding the Picasso in her closet, reading her letters to Alex and Henri, and spending so long in Alex's head by reading his memoir, I realized I was too harsh in my judgment, of both Alex and my grandmother. Sala was not self-deluding. She, alone among the Glass siblings, had been happy to go along with Alex's exaggerations, fudges, and self-mythologies, because she understood her brother. She knew that he loved his family, and that his ability to show it had its limits, so when Alex revealed something real, it had to be cherished and protected. That's why when he sent her something as extraordinary as a sketch by Picasso, she didn't hang it up for all to see: she kept it in her closet, where only she knew about it for the rest of her life. Here was real evidence of how extraordinary their lives were, that they had

(Left) Alex with Picasso; *(right)* Picasso presenting Alex with the poster

started in a shtetl in Poland, and now he was sending to her home in America a drawing by one of the greatest artists of all time, just for her. It was their secret and her secret, and like so many other things, she kept it that way until she died.

Chapter 13

THE END OF THE
GLASS SIBLINGS

1980s and 1990s, Paris and Miami

A s they entered their fourth decade of marriage, Bill and Sala developed a kind of mutual dependence that could, from certain angles, be seen as love. Sala in particular felt a real marital loyalty to him that ultimately meant she was never at ease wherever she was: when she was with him, she was dreaming of her family in Paris; when she was in Paris, she fretted about whether Bill had enough to eat at home. She was in a constant battle between her desires and her obligations.

A mutual respect had grown between them: they understood each other and in many ways appreciated one another's qualities as a spouse and parent. And yet, friends would say the two of them could argue over the oxygen in the air, and this was barely an exaggeration: one of their most frequent arguments was over the thermostat in their apartment. It was never too hot for Bill, whereas Sala liked it cool and fresh, and as fast as he would turn the radiator dial up, she would turn it down, horrified at how cloyingly claustrophobic he made her home. But in 1973, it looked like he had definitely won the temperature argument when he announced they were moving to Miami, Florida. The family had often gone there on holidays, and the reasons Bill loved Miami (the golf, the heat) were the same reasons Sala hated it (the lack of culture, the heat). But she went along with the move. She knew how much he wanted to go, and when he was like this there was no arguing against him. It would, after all, be better for his health than the bitter East Coast winters, and maybe there was a part of her that thought, given Bill was now in his seventies, she might not be there for too long.

Once she was there, Miami turned out to have its advantages. She loved their apartment, with the ready-made community inside the building of other older Jewish couples with whom she could play cards and go shopping, and she especially enjoyed the local Jewish deli where she could buy lox and challah. While Bill played golf all day, she made a life for herself, introducing herself to everyone in the building and teaching them backgammon on the beach. When Bill stayed home in the evenings, she went to the ballet, the theater, and every exhibition of French art. They led busy if separate lives. (She also valiantly maintained her side of the battle of the air temperature, insistently turning the air conditioner up as high as it would go in every room of their apartment, while he would turn it off behind her, barking in frustration.) She made a young friend, named Stephanie, who was the same age as her sons, and the two of them liked to go on shopping trips together, during which Sala would try on miniskirts that Stephanie would never have dared to try on herself, and she always looked wonderful. When Stephanie told her one day that she was leaving her husband, despite the disapproval of their friends, Sala looked at the ground and said quietly, "You have great courage."

Best of all, their younger son, Rich, soon also moved to Miami to work as a lawyer. Just as each of the Glass siblings reacted so differently to what they went through during the war, so Sala's sons reacted in their own individual way to their parents. Sala and Bill poured the love they couldn't give one another into their boys, but whereas Ronald found this at times overbearing and eventually moved overseas, Rich stayed close. Even as a popular bachelor-about-town, he saw his parents almost every day, and when he went to work during the day, Sala would often come to his apartment to restock his refrigerator. She loved doing this as much as he appreciated that she did it. (The Freeman boys, like the Glass siblings, are an eloquent argument in favor of nature over nurture when it comes to explaining a person's character. Despite having an identical upbringing, Ronald and Rich are in many ways as different as Alex and Jacques.)

What Sala really liked about Miami was the view from her living room. Their apartment was on the seventh floor and faced the beach. Sala could stand at the window for hours, looking out at the Atlantic Ocean she had crossed so many years ago, gazing back toward her beloved France and home. But a few years after they moved in, a developer built an identical apartment building across the street, between her and the sea, and she watched the progress of the work creeping up closer and closer to her window. One day they were at level pegging, her and the builders. Then the new building was finished, blocking her view of the ocean, and she looked out the window no more.

In Paris, once Danièle's son Alexandre de Betak was too old to be dragged to lunches with Alex Maguy, Henri and Alex saw each other less and less. Sonia and Alex, despite living just a few miles away from one another for most of their lives, never saw one another at all. It was up to Sala, far away in Miami, to hold the disparate pieces of her family together. ("Such esprit de famille," Sonia would grumble when Sala would come to Paris and insist on seeing everyone.) But by the early 1980s even Sala was struggling to hold the family together.

Sala wrote to Henri and Sonia on September 15, 1982:

Ron wants to buy us an apartment in the building opposite ours,
because that building hides our view, so it's logical. Unfortunately,
where Ron sees only the positives his father sees only the negatives and
says it would be hard to sell ours, with interest rates so high. But, I
really want it.

I just heard some terrible news. Terrorists in Lebanon. Princess
Grace. What a tragedy. So sad. And how is our Alex Maguy
behaving? He ignores me completely. Not a word since May or June.
What a disgrace. Still, I miss you all very much.

Sala lost the argument about the apartment, but she won something
more important, which was a promise from both of her brothers and her
sister-in-law that they would all take a holiday together, for the first time
in their lives. This became the trip to Deauville, which my parents and
sister went on, too, and was the first time I met Alex, Henri, and Sonia.

Not long after that holiday, the Glasses began to fall apart physically.
Henri first, when he was diagnosed with cancer. He was deep into his

Sala and Hadley in Miami in the mid 1980s

Bill and Hadley in Westchester, New York, in the mid 1980s

eighties by now, and his health deteriorated quickly. Sonia didn't want him to know what he was suffering from, so no one was allowed to mention his illness in front of him, even as Henri was visibly fading away in front of them, and he clearly knew he was dying. Finally, in 1989, Jehuda Glahs, the most studious boy in the Chrzanow shtetl, died. But he was a student to the end: on his bedside table when he died was a "teach yourself English" book, so that he could talk to my sister and me on our next visit.

The loss of her oldest brother was heartbreaking for Sala, and Alex made it immeasurably worse. When he turned up at Henri's funeral, he pushed past Sala, Ronald, Danièle, and the rest of his family, and shouted at Sonia.

"You killed my brother!" he yelled, pointing a furious finger at her, shaking off all of his family members trying to pull him away. "I'd have taken him to America where I know the best doctors, but you insisted on staying here and you killed him! He's dead because of you. I will never forgive you!"

Alex had been hating Sonia for so long by this point he probably

Henri and Sonia in Paris, 1980s
Photo taken by Natasha de Betak

no longer even remembered why. He never thought she was worthy of Henri, that was obvious, but the hate went deeper than that. Almost fifty years after Jacques' death, Alex was still blaming his sisters-in-law for taking his brothers away from him. In his mind, if these awful Polish women had just left his family alone, his brothers would have lived forever. Danièle's son, Alexandre de Betak, then just twenty-one, jumped up between his grieving grandmother and raging great-uncle. He had always liked Alex, and Alex had liked him, treating him as a surrogate son. But now Alexandre glared at him.

"Get out of here and never talk to my grandmother again. You are not a part of our family anymore," Alexandre said.

Alex only saw Sonia, Danièle, and her children Alexandre and Natasha, once more after that: at my bat mitzvah. All of them traveled to London, where I was living by then, but they studiously ignored one another all day. When the photographer asked everyone to come together for a family photo, Alex refused to pose with Sonia, so he is the absence in the middle of the family portrait in the garden. Instead, he posed for a photo on his own with me in the living room.

Sala had always assumed she would move back to Paris when Bill died, and, thwarting her to the end, he managed to stay in the ruddiest of health up until his ninetieth birthday. But just as the once strappingly athletic Bill began to weaken with age, and the life Sala had dreamed about for decades was a mere breath away, it was, once again, snatched away from her.

Sala had said to several relatives and friends over the years that her greatest fear was being physically immobile but mentally alert. This happened to a rabbi she knew, who was struck down by a cerebral hemorrhage, and although Sala often visited him in the hospital, his fate terrified her: "God forbid that should happen to me," she said to Rich. She had been trapped by circumstances for so long, the idea of being constrained even further, and all too aware of the constraints on her, must have been terrifyingly real and horrific. And with bitter inevitability, that is exactly what happened to her.

Where Bill had always been hardy, Sala was delicate, careless with her health and always happier feeding others than herself. She hated anyone fussing over her and regarded any efforts to remedy her ailments as unnecessary and embarrassing. So it was no surprise to her family that she often neglected to take the medicine her doctor prescribed for her high blood pressure. What none of us realized was that this then put her at risk of a stroke, and after a few minor ones she was finally felled by a major one. In one blow, it stilled her body and her tongue. All she could do for the rest of her life was wave her right arm and anxiously repeat the babyish sound "la." But her eyes were all too alert, and they wept in frustration.

The last time I saw my grandmother—both of my grandparents, for that matter—was in 1991, not long after my bat mitzvah. My parents took my sister and I to their Miami apartment, which I'd always remembered as elegant, decorated carefully by my grandmother and filled with her art posters. This time I walked into a modern geriatric nightmare. My once seemingly indomitable grandfather was laid out on the sofa, the muscles he'd once been so proud of all wasted away. Now it was the hard knots of his joints that bulged out, visible even through his

Going clockwise from the top: Ronald Freeman, Natasha de Betak, Alexandre de Betak, Helen Freeman, Sonia, Nell Freeman, Hadley Freeman, Ann Horowitz, Richard Freeman, Ann's partner Morty, Danièle de Betak.

Hadley and Alex Maguy

blanket. My grandmother was even more unrecognizable, her normally perfect lipstick and hair now crooked and askew. She couldn't have looked more unnervingly wrong if she'd been naked. The apartment, which she had always kept meticulously tidy, was cluttered with medical detritus: bottles, charts, packs of tubing, piles of plastic sheeting, and two wheelchairs, one for each of them. There also seemed to be about a dozen nurses rushing around, but in truth there were only two, each trying in vain to get their patients to take their pills. And while the rest of us—my parents, my sister, my uncle Rich, and I—were dazed by the chaos, my grandparents carried on as usual, which is to say they were quarreling. Sala sat in an armchair and made do with the little at her disposal, shouting, "La la la la," while pointing furiously at Bill with her one mobile arm. Bill, on the sofa, waved his hand impatiently back at her: "Be quiet, Sala!" he said.

"Look, your grandmother is pointing at your grandfather—she's saying she loves him!" my grandmother's nurse said to my sister and me with a reassuring smile. My sister Nell and I were only, respectively, eleven and thirteen, but we knew Sala was not telling Bill she loved him. She was saying she blamed him.

Sala had never exactly hidden her unhappiness, but she'd been so good at keeping it in check, ensuring the roil of emotions stayed just beneath her skin. It was terrifying to see all that now unleashed, all the anger, anxiety, and frustration that had built up over her lifetime, and not even her sons could calm her down. The only person who could soothe her was Betty, my grandparents' housekeeper who had been with them since they moved to Miami.

"Come on, Sala. Come on," said Betty, sitting on the armchair, holding her close. And Sala collapsed against her, her eyes closed, like a daughter cleaving to her much-longed-for mother.

Bill died the next year, of many things, but really just of old age. The fearsome fighter from the Lower East Side had fought until his tenth decade and, in many ways, won. Once, his mother could barely afford to give him more than a meal a day; by the time he died, he had more than a million dollars in the bank, thanks entirely to his skill at investing and indefatigable work ethic. Life had probably not worked out exactly as he wanted, but he never let it get him down. He had left behind the drag of his origins, made money, had a beautiful wife and successful sons. In his eyes he was a winner, and he was right.

I didn't go to his funeral, because by that point I was hospitalized for anorexia. My grandmother might have understood that affliction better than anyone in our family, given that her own relationship with food could be described at best as complicated. But I never spoke to her about it, because she couldn't speak then. My father, of course, went to Bill's funeral, and he and Rich brought Sala, in her wheelchair. She cried throughout the service.

"Look how sad she is that her husband died," other people whispered in awe. But she wasn't sad that Bill had died. She was sad that the day she had waited for had finally come, and it didn't matter anymore. All those fantasies of living in Paris, traveling to London, to Israel—all gone.

Two years later, she had a massive stroke and was rushed to the hospital, where doctors stuck so many tubes in her she looked more like a science experiment than the woman she was, adhering to the American medical establishment's belief that maintaining life is more important than considering what quality that life will be. Rich was at the hospital one afternoon with Betty, my grandparents' housekeeper, and the doctors said she was crashing and they would need to revive her again. He was about to sign the papers when Betty put her hand on his.

"Let her go, Richard," she said.

Rich loved his mother more than anything on earth, but he also knew Betty was right. So he went to Sala's bed and held her close. He whispered that we all knew how much she had sacrificed for all of us, that she had given up her life so that we could all live. That we loved her, and he kissed her good-bye from all of us. For the first time in God knows how long, Rich saw her make a small smile. And then she was free.

Few get good endings, and Sala definitely did not get the one she deserved. She had wanted to die in Europe, the continent of her birth and where her heart still was. Instead, she had a hideous protracted death in an American hospital, far from the place she still thought of as home, fifty years after leaving it behind. As children, my sister and I used to whisper to one another at night about how we wouldn't exist if it hadn't been for Hitler, and my father told me he used to think about that, too. Because if it hadn't been for the war, Sala would never have married Bill and the rest of us wouldn't even be cells or ether. For a while this added another dimension to my already well-hewn sense of Jewish guilt: I lived only because of the pain and loss of others, and in particular the pain of one person in particular—Sala. However, she would not have ever seen it that way. To her, our existence was what gave her loss, and her life, meaning. Her sons and grandchildren were not compensation for what she left behind; we were the explanation for it. She asked for nothing as a reward for her sacrifice, because she never asked for anything. She stayed on the side of the room, against the walls, in the shadows, loving us, erasing herself and her needs. But the one thing that she wanted, and expected, was to live one day, back in Europe, with us, with Alex, on her own. And ultimately, even that was denied to her, because after giving up her dreams to come to America, her death there was her actual nightmare. Pretty little Sala Glahs, whose father used to buy her frilly dresses from the market, who wanted nothing more than to feel well enough to play with her brothers outside on Kostalista, deserved a better end.

Sonia, on the other hand, managed to have one of the best deaths of all time.

After Henri died, Sonia proved that, despite being in an extremely close and happy marriage for more than half a century, she was more than capable of leading a contented independent life. She busied herself every day spending time with friends, walking her beloved dogs, and, most of all, playing bridge. She occasionally went on bridge cruises, boat trips where she and other like-minded bridge fans played cards all day; she sent back photos of herself flanked by the young and handsome male crew. Sonia had loved Henri dearly, but she was—as everyone knew she would be—fine without him.

Then one day in 1995, she went to her regular bridge game in Paris and brought her daughter Danièle with her. She took her seat at a card table and suddenly had a thought: "Table seven! That's my lucky number," she said, turning to her daughter. Then she turned back, keeled over, and was instantly dead. Sonia was never one for dragging things out unnecessarily.

Seven was also Alex's lucky number, of course, but he did not get quite as lucky a death. He was the last Glass standing, although by the end he was so frail he could barely stand at all. Not even those who fought against pogroms and Nazis can beat old age. The last time my father saw him was in 1999, when Alex summoned him to Paris to visit him. My father found him sitting in front of his beloved apartment building on Avenue Foch, so depleted with age he was like a balloon with half the air taken out. In order for Alex to stand up and walk around his beloved private garden, my father had to support his whole weight, and that amounted to hardly anything.

Alex died in October 1999. French death announcements in the newspapers are often written in florid and formal language, but Alex's was oddly apt. In *Le Figaro* of November 3, 1999, a small article appeared, announcing the end of Alex Maguy Glass's "tormented and ostentatious ex-

Sonia with friends

istence," summing up his beginning and his end. He'd told my father that he wanted to be buried by the Chrzanow Burial Society in Montparnasse Cemetery, alongside other Chrzanovians who had, through the twists of history and geopolitics, died in Paris. In Poland he had been landlocked in a shtetl, whereas in France he soared up to befriend the stars of the mid-century. But at heart, he was still little Sender, being cheeky to his family as they walked to synagogue together in Chzranow, and in the end he wanted to be with the people who reminded him of his father.

Chapter 14

THE NEXT GENERATIONS— AN EPILOGUE

Paris, the twenty-first century

Alex de Betak and Hadley, in Los Angeles
at a fashion event Alex produced.

The Glasses spanned the twentieth century, from Henri's birth in 1901 to Alex's death in 1999. They lived through probably the most dramatic shifts ever endured by the world's Jews, from the Holocaust to American immigration to the founding of Israel to assimilation, and their lives reflected it all. On an individual level, they took chances that are unimaginable to their children and grandchildren today, because we live in comfort that they created for us. But once they all died, whatever thin strands connected us fell away entirely: Danièle and her children seemed to drift away from us—or us from them—and I certainly didn't know anyone connected to the Ornstein cousins. Part of this was undoubtedly laziness—my father can be especially bad at keeping in touch with extended family members—but it felt also like a reaction to the Glasses themselves.

There have been many studies about inherited trauma, looking at whether children of, for example, prisoners of war die earlier than children of soldiers who evade capture.[1] One study claiming that Holocaust survivors pass on trauma to their children and grandchildren through epigenetics[2] received a huge amount of excited coverage when it was published in 2016. But it was also criticized for, among other things, its tiny sample size[3] and the shakiness of the science[4] (transgenerational epigenetic inheritance is well established in plants, decidedly less so in humans). I haven't studied science since I was sixteen, so my skepticism about the relevance to genetically inherited trauma to my family's story is based on something far more basic than epigenetics: knowing what my family is like.

The second generation—Ronald, Rich, and Danièle—grew up with an instinctive understanding that their parents did not want to talk about the past, and it wasn't genetic inheritance that gave them this knowledge. They learned it from how hastily their mothers turned off the TV when Holocaust documentaries came on, how sharply their fathers said, "Why do you ask these questions?" Many Holocaust survivors celebrated their survival by clutching their Jewish identity even closer, but the Glasses were different. Henri, Sonia, and Sala assimilated, and so did their children, because that is what their parents encouraged them to do. Even Alex, who left many of his paintings to Israel and proudly kept his Yiddish accent, was hardly religious. The only time I ever saw him in a synagogue was at my bat mitzvah. Within their lifetimes, they threw off the ties of Orthodoxy and raised children who couldn't even read Hebrew. This was as much to do with pragmatism as it was to do with trauma: they wanted their children to be safe, and they knew from their own experiences that meant not being overtly Jewish. The past to them was ugly and painful—they were too close to it to see that it was also triumphant—and therefore to be pushed to the back of the closet, like a shoebox of yellowing photos. But what binds a family together if not the past? Blood is not thick enough, especially if the extended family is scattered on entirely different continents. Shared history is the stuff that sticks.

As the Glasses themselves knew, suppressing the past does not mean you don't think about it. This is the weird irony about Jewish assimilation, and also the joke about it: all these Jews living totally Western lives, eating ham, and doing Christmas, yet always talking about the Holocaust. Well, it's a lot harder to dismiss history than religious doctrine, because one is real and one is not. I cannot remember a time when I was not aware that the only reason I am alive is that my grandmother had to give up everything to escape the Nazis, and I felt in some vague way crushed by it. There is a neat divide in my family between those who are quietly haunted by the stories in this book (my father Ronald, Danièle's daughter Natasha, me) and those who are less so (my uncle Rich, Danièle's son Alexandre, my sister Nell). Yet all of us reacted to our family's past the same way, which was to let the family drift apart. This was never the intention of the Glasses, who loved each other, but we took our cues from them: if reminders of the past should be pushed away, didn't that include our own family?

But as perhaps Jews know better than most, you can never entirely escape your past.

In the late 1990s, my parents became friends with a Jewish American woman who lived in Paris, named Flora Lewis, then in her seventies. Flora was an extremely impressive woman, a longtime foreign correspondent for the *New York Times* and the first woman to be given her own column by that paper. But early triumphs are no protection against the cruelties of old age, and when my parents met Flora she was facing eviction from her beloved apartment in Saint-Germain-des-Prés, because her building had been bought and she could not afford to buy her apartment from the new owner. So my father offered to buy it and Flora would stay on as his tenant. This arrangement lasted until Flora's death in 2002, at which point my family moved in. It wasn't until we walked in that we realized that the apartment backs onto the École des Beaux-Arts, the school where my grandmother studied textile design before she went to America.

Shortly before we took possession of the apartment, I got my first job. I'd known since I was a teenager that I wanted to be a journalist, but while I was at university a strange and more specific idea took hold.

"I think it would be fun to write about fashion," I said to my mother one morning when I was about twenty, as I read a style article in *The Guardian*.

"Mmmm, really, sweetie?" she replied uncertainly. But if my mother was surprised by my sudden interest in fashion, then I was even more so. Up until then, the only appeal clothes had for me was how much I could hide my body within them, and my wardrobe largely consisted of long black skirts and shapeless long-sleeved tops, all bought from Camden and Kensington Markets. But as I slowly began to slough off the anorexia that had dominated my teenage years and blanketed my entire worldview, I realised there was some kernel in me, that I could neither explain nor even entirely understand, that was genuinely interested in fashion. Like Sala, like Alex, I, too, wanted to see beauty.

After university, I got a job on *The Guardian*'s fashion desk and helped to cover the shows in Paris, always staying in our family apartment. Every time I walked out of the apartment to go to a fashion show, I was walking in my grandmother's footsteps, going to the same shows— Dior, Rochas, Lanvin—that she loved to read about in the magazines Henri and Alex sent to her in America from Paris.

Then one day, at the Dior show in the Tuileries, I felt a hand on my shoulder.

"Aren't you my cousin?"

It was Alexandre de Betak, now known as Alex, and he was working as a fashion show producer. He had seen my name on the list of invited press, which is how he recognized me. He gave me a hug, but I felt a little shy, self-conscious about all the big-name fashion editors watching us, wondering why the cool show producer was talking to this lowly fashion writer. He didn't seem to notice, and he took down my phone number. I watched him run around the show, making sure all the editors were happy in their seats, the lighting was right, the flowers were perfect, the sound levels were correct, the models were ready to walk on. It was like stepping into the anecdotes my father used to tell about watching Alex Maguy getting his fashion shows ready. Today Alex de Betak is one of the biggest independent show producers in the world, with clients that include Calvin Klein, Yves Saint Laurent, Nike, and H&M. But probably his closest and most loyal client is Dior, just as Alex Maguy's closest friend in the fashion world was Christian Dior. Neither Alex de Betak nor the Dior company knew of that connection until I started researching this book.

Not long after meeting Alex, I got an email at work:

I know we haven't met but I think we're cousins. Could we meet?

It was from someone called Philippe Ornstein, the son of Armand, the former little boy hidden in the woods who had grown up to help found Daniel Hechter. Philippe was then working in London at the fashion company Mulberry and he had seen my name on a list of fashion writers, which prompted him to get in touch. As soon as we met it felt like he had always been a part of my life. For hours we sat in a random bar in Soho, and there was no time for awkward pauses because we were too busy talking and laughing; it was like the best first date of my life, but it was even better because I already knew he would be in my life forever because he was family.

The third generation found one another through fashion, or the *schmatte* trade, as our grandparents would have called it when they were working for next to nothing as furriers, leather tanners, textile designers, and dressmakers in the Marais. Alex de Betak was introduced to fashion by Alex Maguy, just as Philippe was by his father and I was by my grandmother. We are living proof that the past holds on to you in ways that go beyond science, and although the Glass siblings had long since died by the time their grandchildren met, we instinctively carried on their traditions.

The more frequently I came to Paris for the shows, the closer I became to my French family and the more of them I met. As we came together, we shared what little we knew of the past, and I could see all of us getting a keener interest in it and a sharper awareness of our roots, especially as I started to know more of my Ornstein cousins, descendants of those who had escaped to Israel. Alex de Betak and I see one another especially often, and we still say how much Sala would have loved to have come to the shows with us, just as she once did with Alex Maguy.

Sala had dreamed of moving back to Paris, of being with her family, having lunches with them in cafés, reveling in the glamour of the French fashion world, walking among the boutiques in Saint-Germain. She never got to do that—but I do. Because she gave up everything, I get to live her dream. I think of her every time I walk out of my parents' apartment and down the rue Bonaparte in Saint-Germain, past the gates of her old school, to the café to have my breakfast before going to a fashion show. And I think of all of them every time my train from London pulls into Gare du Nord, how they arrived in Paris by train almost a hundred years ago, knowing almost no one and owning less. How far they went in their lives, how politics and fate and familial dynamics tore them apart, and how we came back together in the end.

Just outside Jerusalem there is a tree for Jacques. Alex and Henri planted it in his memory around the time their mother moved there. They planted it because they remembered how much he loved to hide in the woods as a boy, and how for him—and all of them—trees were a source of comfort, giving them a place to hide as children from the poverty and the pogroms. Closer to my home, and his, Jacques' name is inscribed on the wall of names outside the Shoah memorial in Paris: "Jacob Glass," it reads, changing the name of the boy born Jakob Glahs, who became the man called Jacques Glass, one final time. He is listed there alongside the 76,000 other Jews, including 11,000 children who were deported from France. "Take the time to look at a beautiful painting. Don't be afraid, just enter the painting, let it embrace you, like music. Life is worth the trouble of fighting death," are the last lines of Alex's memoir, and I try always to take the time to look at Jacques' wall. It is in the Marais, just a few minutes' walk from where Jacques lived with Alex, and where Chaya lived with Sala, steps away from where Jacques boarded a minibus and was shipped off to Pithiviers. It's a lovely, peaceful part of the city now, and I walk through it often. I stop in to see Jacques' name, maybe make a small nod, and then I'll walk out, following Henri's, Jacques', Alex's, and Sala's footsteps for a little while. Then I diverge, walking my own way as I cross the river, and go home.

Acknowledgments

I dedicated this book to my father, Ron, because he is really its coauthor. For two decades he has traveled with me around the world on research trips, acting as a tour guide in Long Island, a translator in France, a historian in Narvik, and a travel companion in Poland. He put his faith in me when I showed little evidence of deserving it to tell the most intimate stories of his childhood, enduring years of nosey questions about some of the people he loved most in his life. I hope I have justified the trust he placed in me; he has always far exceeded any common definition of fatherly support.

I am also very grateful to my uncle Rich, who was extraordinarily generous with his memories and photos. A huge thank-you, too, to his wife, my aunt Lynn, and their daughter, Gabrielle, for not just enduring my trips to Florida to pester Rich with more questions, but also for arranging interviews for me with Bill and Sala's friends in Miami, providing me with new perspectives of my grandparents.

By writing about my family in the past I got to know my family in the present. This is especially true of Danièle, Alexandre, and Natasha de Betak. Before, I hardly knew them at all; now I consider them among my closest relatives. They provided me with insights into the Glass family's life in France, and especially Henri and Sonia's lives. They have been unflagging supporters of this book, even when I felt decidedly flagged.

Anne-Laurence Goldberg is another relative I am lucky enough to have become close to through the writing of this book. She is an indefatigably cheerful travel companion—the best kind of travel companion—and her wonderful collection of letters and photos is a treasure trove of historical documents.

Armand Ornstein has been putting up with my questions about his past for so long it's a testament to him that he still agrees to meet me for dinner. I am very grateful to him for his constant support, and for putting me in touch with his sister Shoshanna and her daughter Idit Bloch, both of whom helped me to make sense of a shadowy past.

On the American side, Ann Horowitz has known me since I was born and she shared with me her thoughts and memories about the Freiman family. She put me in touch with Herb Freiman, and our time together in Long Island didn't just help me put that part of my family in context, but was a delightful experience I'll never forget. My sadly belated thanks, too, to Herb's sister, Eleanor, who spoke to me about the family shortly before she died. Charlie Reich, the grandson of Olga, great-nephew of Mila, was another lovely discovery I made through the writing of this book, and I am grateful to him for his kindness and insights.

Aside from my family, there is no one who has contributed more to this book than the brilliant academic Daniel Lee. I met Daniel at a conference about the resistance in London, and I don't know what good deed I did in a previous life to deserve this stroke of luck, but there is no question that this book would not have been written with him. He traveled with me around France, gave up his holidays to research my family in dusty archives, put their story into historical context for me, and, of course, made the great discovery about where Alex Maguy spent the war. More than that, he became a true friend, even though I consistently failed to live by his dictum: "Historians don't stop for lunch."

Jona Cummings, aka the Jew Whisperer, who coaxes memoirs out of neurotic Jews, helped me enormously with my research and, at least as importantly, gave me the confidence I actually had a book here when I tortured myself with self-doubt. My friend and colleague, Jonathan Freedland, introduced me to Jona, and for that, and much more, I thank Jonathan.

I was inspired to write this book after writing an essay about my grandmother for American *Vogue*, at the encouragement of my editor there, Eve MacSweeney. I thank her and Anna Wintour for editing and publishing it.

The people in this book had a great number of friends, and I am very grateful to those I spoke to during the writing of this book, some of whom have since passed away: William and Marcia Rappaport, Sue Guiney, Betty Laster, Dorothy Berger, Stephanie Freed, Nicole Rivoire, Ilie Wachs, Catherine Amidon, and Jeanne Gustave. Chien Chung Pei and Li Chung Pei were very generous with their time in helping me to establish Alex Maguy's friendship with their father, I.M Pei. My thanks to Emma Cobb for her help in contacting them.

I made use of many researchers and translators around the world and shamelessly pillaged the minds of academics far more brilliant than me. These include Simon Kitson, Matthew Cobb, Martin and Aga Kahn, Ludivine Broch, Agata Jujeczka, Camille Chevalier, Jane Winfield, Hugo Sharp, and Beate Rozek. Thanks to Oriole Cullen for her insights into the life of Christian Dior, and for Laura Mitchell at the Victoria & Albert Museum in London for putting me in touch with her. I also owe a debt to Callie Adams at the Christian Dior press office in London. Isabelle Rouge-Ducos, Violette Andres, and Emelie Bouvard at the Picasso Museum in Paris talked to me about Picasso's life and kindly arranged for me to look through his correspondence with Alex Maguy. Robert Picandet at the Resistance Museum in Saint-Gervais-d'Auvergne (Puy-de-Dôme) opened up a window into a part of Alex's life he had always kept shut to the rest of us. The Tenement Museum in New York helped me to understand the Lower East Side when Bill lived there, and the museum's director of curatorial affairs, David Favoloro, patiently explained to me what the Freiman family's day-to-day life was like. Alex Maws and Martin Winstone from the Holocaust Educational Trust talked to me about the evolving attitudes of different countries toward the Holocaust, and Alex especially has been a source of support and encouragement. Alisa Friedman, Noa Rosenberg, Yafa Goldfinger, and Sophia Berry-Liftshitz at the Tel Aviv Museum, and Michal Marmary and Dr. Adina Kamien-Kazhdan at the Israel Museum in Jerusalem kindly tracked down for me the paintings that Alex donated in his lifetime. Joshua Rothman at the *New Yorker* dug out an archival article about Alex for me, despite having more than enough to do in his full-time job. Richard Nelsson and Luc Torres at *The Guardian* were similarly patient with my bizarre requests (a review of a fashion show from seventy years ago in Denmark? No problem!). For archival research, I relied on the Memorial de la Shoah, L'École des Beaux Arts, Les Archives Nationales in Fontainebleau and Pierrefitte, Les Archives de la Ville, and La Fondation pour la Memoire de la Déportation, all in Paris, as well as Les Archives Departmentales des Alpes Maritimes in Nice, Yad Vashem in Jerusalem, and the British Library in London. I am indebted to the archivists at CERCIL in Orleans, especially Nathalie Grenon, for providing me with details of Jacques' time in Pithiviers.

The following people provided invaluable support, advice, and friendship during the writing of this book: Helen Freeman, Nell Freeman-Romilly, the Macrae family, Carol Miller, Jonathan Freedland, George Morton-Jack, Jess Cartner-Morley, Alex Needham, Oliver Wainwright, Jon Henley, Marina Hyde, Roland Woodward, Lauren Collins, Ruthie Rogers, Hugh Hamrick, Adam Phillips, and Arthur Ferdinand Freeman. My agent, Georgia Garrett at RCW, and my editors, Louise Haines at 4th Estate in London and Emily Graff and Lashanda Anakwah at Simon & Schuster in New York, never lost faith with this project, or with me. I am extremely lucky to have such wonderful women on my team.

My editors, past and present, at *The Guardian* have long since learned to tolerate my wild-goose projects and pet obsessions. I am especially grateful to Katherine Viner, Melissa Denes, Kira Cochrane, Malik Meer, Catherine Shoard, and Ian Katz for their enduring forbearance.

My partner, Andy Bull, was almost certainly the only sportswriter at the US Open in 2019 doing line edits on a chapter about Auschwitz. More than anyone, Andy made me believe I could do this, and he provided not just emotional encouragement but practical support, too, not least looking after our children while I ran off again to spend my days with the dead. He edited every draft line by line and solved all my seemingly unsolvable structural problems. His love—and willingness to shoulder the domestic duties—made this book possible.

And finally, I thank my children: Felix and Max, who always know exactly when to come into my study and tell me it's time to stop working, and Betty, who was my in utero companion during much of the writing of this book and, with perfect timing, arrived the week after I finally finished it. This is the story of your past. You will write the future.

Notes

Introduction

1 Richard Allen Greene, "A Shadow Over Europe," cnn.com, November 2018.
2 Elian Peltier, "Sharp Rise in Anti-Semitic Acts in France Stokes Old Fears," *New York Times*, February 12, 2019.
3 "Anti-Semitic Incidents Remained at Near Historic Levels in 2018; Attacks Against Jews More Than Doubled," press release, Anti-Defamation League, New York, 2019.
4 Maggie Astor, "Holocaust Is Fading From Memory, Survey Finds," *New York Times*, April 12, 2018.
5 Greene, "A Shadow Over Europe."

1. The Glahs Family—The Shtetl

1 Chrzanower Young Men's Association, *Chrzanow: The Life and Destruction of a Jewish Shtetl*, Mordechai Bochner (Roslyn Harbor, NY: Solomon Gross, 1989).
2 Lukasz Dulowski, "The Jewish City of the Dead," *Przelom*, March 28, 2001.
3 Ibid.
4 This is from a translation of *Sefer Chrzanow: lebn un umkum fun a yidish shtetl*, Mordecai Bochner, ed. *Chrzanow: The Life and Destruction of a Jewish Shtetl*, Jonathan Boyarin, trans. (Roslyn Harbor, NY: Solomon Gross, 1989 [Y,E]).
5 Ibid.
6 Schwarzbart, *Chrzanow*.
7 Reb Moyshe Bochner, *A Tear for My Father*, jewishgen.org.
8 Schwarzbart, *Chrzanow*.
9 Harrison Fluss and Landon Frim, "Aliens, Antisemitism and Academia," *Jacobin*, March 2017.
10 Alphonse Tousennel, *Les Juifs Rois de L'Époque*, 1845.
11 On October 5, 2018, President Trump tweeted that the women protesting Brett Kavanaugh's nomination to the Supreme Court were "paid for by Soros and others."
12 Peter Walker, "Nigel Farage Under Fire Over 'Anti-Semitic Tropes' on Far-Right US Talk Show," *The Guardian*, May 6, 2019.

13 The source here is an academic paper supplied by its author: Agnieszka Cahn, "A Critical Analysis of Adam Doboszynski's March on Myslenice in 1936."

14 The source here is information provided by the two cited European universities: Between 1921 and 25, Jews made up 26.9 percent of the German Polytechnic in Prague and 3.1 percent of the Czech Technical University, both of which Jehuda attended.

15 Paul Hanebrink, *A Specter Haunting Europe* (Cambridge, MA: Harvard University Press, 2018).

16 Yizkor Book Project, jewishgen.org.

17 Schwarzbart, *Chrzanow.*

18 Yizkor Book Project, jewishgen.org.

19 Ibid.

20 Schwarzbart, *Chrzanow.*

21 Alex Duval Smith, "Polish Move to Strip Holocaust Expert of Award Sparks Protest," *The Observer* (London), February 14, 2016.

22 Associated Press, "Holocaust Scholar Questioned on Claim That Poles Killed More Jews Than Germans in the War," *The Guardian,* April 14, 2016.

23 Edna Friedberg, "The Truth About Poland's Role in the Holocaust," *The Atlantic,* February 6, 2018.

24 "The European Union Must Stand Up to Polish Nationalism," editorial, *New York Times,* February 28, 2018.

25 Tom Porter, "Polish Official Claims Jews Were Passive in the Face of Nazi Violence," *Newsweek,* February 10, 2018.

26 Christian Davies, "Poland's Holocaust Law Triggers Tide of Abuse Against Auschwitz Museum," *The Guardian,* May 7, 2018.

27 James Masters, "Polish Prosecutor: 'Auschwitz' Football Chants Are Not Anti-Semitic," cnn.com.

2. The Glass Siblings—Immigration

1 Of the rest, 112,000 went to Canada, 150,000 to Argentina, 210,000 to England, and 2.65 million to the United States. Ioan Mackenzie James, *Driven to Innovate: A History of Jewish Mathematicians and Physicists.*

2 Jacques Adler, *The Jews of Paris and the Final Solution* (New York: Oxford University Press, 1987).

3 David H. Weinberg, *A Community on Trial* (Chicago: University of Chicago Press, 1977).

4 Vicki Caron, *Uneasy Asylum: France and the Jewish Refugee Crisis.* The Aliens Act 1905 was written specifically to curtail eastern European Jewish immigration into the United Kingdom. It was amended in 1914 and 1920, imposing even more stringent restrictions that were only partly lifted in the 1930s. The 1924 Immigration Act was conceived for the same purpose in America. Vicki Caron, *Uneasy Asylum: France and the Refugee Crisis* (Stanford, CA: Stanford University Press, 1999).

5 Weinberg, *A Community on Trial.*

6 Green, *The Pletzl of Paris.*

7 M.K. Dzrewanowski, *Poland in the Twentieth Century* (New York: Columbia University Press, 1977).

8 Green, *The Pletzl of Paris.*

9 Vicki Caron, *The Path to Vichy: Anti-Semitism in France in the 1930* (Washington, DC: The Center for Advanced Holocaust Studies, 2005).

10 Ibid.

11 Paula E. Hyman, *The Jews of Modern France* (Berkeley: University of California Press, 1998).

12 Green, *The Pletzl of Paris.*

13 William Wiser, *The Twilight Years: Paris in the 1930s.*

3. Henri—Assimilation

1 Caron, *Uneasy Asylum.*

2 Ibid.

3 Weinberg, *A Community on Trial.*

4 Hyman, *The Jews of Modern France.*

5 Adler, *The Jews of Paris and the Final Solution.*

6 Weinberg, *A Community on Trial.*

7 Ibid.

8 Adler, *The Jews of Paris and the Final Solution.*

9 Hyman, *The Jews of Modern France.*

10 Ari Yashar, "Shocking Figures Cite 85% Assimilation in Europe," israelnationnews.com.

11 In 1939, 9.5 million Jews lived in Europe. In 1945, the Nazis had shrunk this number down to 3.8 million. Today, it stands at about 2 million (Pew Research Center).

12 Per records at the Sorbonne, a foreign Jewish woman studying at the university in this period wasn't as unusual as it might sound. In the early 1930s, the Sorbonne had 14,500 students, 41 percent of whom were women and 30 percent of whom were foreign.

4. Jacques—Passivity

1 *The Times of Israel,* February 10, 2018.

2 In 1976, an Air France flight 139 was hijacked mid-journey between Tel Aviv and Paris by members of the Popular Front for the Liberation of Palestine and the German Revolutionary Cells, and diverted to Uganda. Michel acted as the translator and mediator between the hostages and captors. He persuaded the main hijacker, Wilfred Bose, to start releasing hostages, including Michel's own son, Olivier, then twelve years old. When Michel himself was eventually released, he was able to give Mossad details of the hijackers' compound and their daily habits, all of which was invaluable to the rescue mission. Michel wrote about this in his autobiography, and Saul David writes about it in more detail in his book *Operation Thunderbolt* (London: Black Bay Books, 1982).

3 Michel Cojot-Goldberg, *Namesake* (New Haven, CT: Yale University Press, 2017).

4 Caron, *Uneasy Asylum.*

5 Weinberg, *A Community on Trial.*

6 Marlise Simons, "Chirac Affirms France's Guilt in Fate of Jews," *New York Times,* July 17, 1995.

7 Albert Saurrat was prime minister of France for, first, one month, October–November 1933, then again for the slightly longer term of five months, January 1936–June 1936.

8 Caron, *Uneasy Asylum.*

9 In 1940, Saurrat would vote in favor of allowing Marshal Pétain's government to draw up a new constitution, thus helping to establish Vichy France.

10 Caron, *Uneasy Asylum.*

11 Weinberg, *A Community on Trial.*

12 yadvashem.org.

13 Combattantvolontairejuif.org.

14 Sergeant-Major Frederick Read, *A War Fought Behind the Wire: A Soldier's Tale of Life in the British Army, 1925–1947*

15 Richard Satloff, *Among the Righteous*

16 Jean Edward Smith, *The Liberation of Paris: How Eisenhower, de Gaulle, and von Choltitz Saved the City of Light* (New York: Simon & Schuster, 2019).

17 Michael Marrus and Robert O. Paxton, *Vichy France and the Jews*

18 Ibid.

19 Ibid.

20 Sharon Waxman, "1940 Jewish Census Reopens French Sore," *Chicago Tribune,* December 30, 1991.

5. Alex—Defiance

1 Marie-France Pochna, *Christian Dior: The Biography* (New York: The Overlook Press, 2008).

2 Christian Dior, *Dior by Dior: The Autobiography of Christian Dior* (London: Victoria and Albert Museum, 2007).

3 Drusilla Beyfus, "René Gruau: A New Look at the Influential Dior Illustrator," *Daily Telegraph,* October 23, 2010.

4 Although both Dior and Gruau worked for Alex in Paris, according to Natasha Fraser Cavassoni's book *Monsieur Dior: Once Upon a Time* (Painted Leaf Press, 2014), they didn't actually meet one another until all three of them fled down south during the war.

5 Weinberg, *A Community on Trial.*

6 Richard D. Sonn, *Jews, Expatriate Artists, and Political Radicalism in Interwar France* (Fayetteville: University of Arkansas Press, 2009).

7 Douglas Porch, *The French Foreign Legion: The Complete History of the Legendary Fighting Force.*

8   Robert Gildea, *Fighters in the Shadows: A New History of the French Resistance* (Cambridge, MA: Harvard University Press, 2015).

9   Andre-Paul Comor, *L'épopée de la 13ème Demi-Brigade de Légion Étrangère 1940–1945* (Paris: Nouvelle Editions Latines, 1998).

10 Commendation signed by Charles de Gaulle, April 6, 1945.

11 Oddmund Joakimsen, *Narvik 1940: Nazi Germany's First Setback During World War Two*, Nordland Red Cross War Museum.

12 Ibid.

13 Ibid.

14 Gildea, *Fighters*.

6. Sara—Emigration

1   http://www.worldfuturefund.org/wffmaster/Reading/Hitler%20Speeches/Hitler%20Speech%201937.01.30.html.

2   Caron, *Uneasy Asylum*.

7. Bill—America

1   Annie Polland and Daniel Soyer, *Emerging Metropolis: New York Jews in the Age of Immigration, 1840–1920* (New York: New York University Press, 2012).

2   Ande Manners, *Poor Cousins* (Coward McCann, 1972).

3   Ibid.

4   Polland and Soyer, *Emerging Metropolis*.

5   Rose Cohen, *Out of the Shadow: A Russian Jewish Girlhood on the Lower East Side* (Ithaca, NY: Cornell University Press, 1995).

6   Polland and Soyer, *Emerging Metropolis*.

7   The Triangle Shirtwaist Factory fire of 1911. David von Drehle, *Triangle: The Fire That Changed America* (New York: Grove Press, 2004).

8   *New York Times*, January 6, 1900.

9   *Mail and Express*, October 1, 1900.

10 Arthur Minturn Chase, "Children of the Street," *Outlook*, July 27, 1912.

11 Deborah Dash Moore, *At Home in America: Second-Generation New York Jews* (New York: Columbia University Press, 1980).

12 Madison Grant, *The Passing of the Great Race*, 1916.

13 Hate Crime Statistics, FBI, https://ucr.fbi.gov/hate-crime/2016.

14 Suman Raghunatham, "Trump's Xenophobic Vision of America Is Inciting Racist Violence," *The Nation*, January 27, 2018.

15 Pankaj Mishra, "Watch This Man," *London Review of Books*, November 3, 2011.

16 Polland and Stoyer, *Emerging Metropolis*.

17 Jedediah Purdy, "Environmentalism's Racist History," *The New Yorker*, August 13, 2015.

18 Alex Ross, "How American Racism Influenced Hitler," *The New Yorker*, April 30, 2018.

Ross also writes about how "America's knack for maintaining an air of robust innocence in the wake of mass death [during slavery] struck Hitler as an example to be emulated."

19 Polland and Soyer, *Emerging Metropolis*.

20 Howard M. Sachar, *A History of the Jews in the Modern World* (New York: Vintage, 2005).

21 It was thanks to certain individuals that the rot was, if not entirely reversed, then at least slowed. One especially notable individual was Franklin D. Roosevelt, who became president in 1933 and had no tolerance for old bigotries. To head up his New Deal program, FDR installed two sons of Jewish immigrants, Louis D. Brandeis and Felix Frankfurter, who themselves then helped to find other Jews who worked to implement the New Deal. Roosevelt believed that no person of talent should be overlooked, and especially not in the early 1930s, when the country was so desperately in need of help. Around four thousand Jews worked in the US government in the 1930s, "an unprecedented number for any Western government" (Sachar, *A History of the Jews*), and for his reelection campaign in 1936, FDR got 86 percent of the Jewish vote.

8. Henri and Sonia—Denounced

1 Adler, *The Jews of Paris and the Final Solution*.

2 Ibid.

3 Jean Guehenno, *Diary of the Dark Years: Collaboration, Resistance, and Daily Life in Occupied Paris* (Oxford: Oxford University Press, 2014).

4 Ibid.

5 Marie-Madeleine Fourcade, *Noah's Ark: The Secret Underground* (New York: Zebra Books, 1974).

6 Ibid.

7 Bousquet enjoyed a heady career after the war. Initially he was, like most Vichy officials, convicted of "Indignité national," and sentenced. But—also like most Vichy officials—that sentence was soon reduced as France tried to move on as quickly possible and pretend no Frenchmen had committed any actual crimes. Bousquet went on to make a name for himself in journalism, and he became especially close to François Mitterrand. But the then president of France was forced to end that friendship when some rather inconvenient allegations about Bousquet's past came to light. Thanks to Serge Klarsfeld's tenacity, the myth that Bousquet was merely an innocent official in Vichy was shattered in the 1980s when evidence was produced that he personally had been in charge of deporting Jewish children to their death. Before Bousquet stood trial, he was shot and killed in front of his home in 1993 by Christian Didier, who proudly took credit for the murder. Didier was sentenced to ten years in prison for the killing, but his real crime was scuppering what would have been the first trial of a French citizen for crimes against humanity. Bousquet's trial would have been an extraordinary beginning to France reckoning with its Vichy past. "Serge Klarsfeld: Nous n'attendons rien de ce process," *L'Humanité*, November 6, 1995.

8 http://maitron-fusilles-40-44.univ-paris1.fr/spip.php?article166449.

9 Fourcade, *Noah's Ark*.

10 Ibid.

11 Shannon L. Fogg, *Denunciations, Community Outsiders, and Material Shortages in Vichy France* (Columbia: University of Missouri Press, 2003).

12 Andre Halimi writes more about this in *La Délation sous l'Occupation* (Paris Edition: Alain Moreau, 1983).

13 Henry Samuel, "Petty Disputes Led to Nazi Denunciation in WWII France," *Daily Telegraph*, December 2, 2008.

14 Ibid.

15 Serge Klarsfeld, *Memorial to the Jews Deported from France, 1942–1944*, B. Klarsfeld Foundation, 1983.

9. Jacques—Captured

1 "Premières Rafles et Camps d'Internement en Zone Occupée en 1941," www.cercleshoah.org.

2 *L'Écho de Pithiviers*, May 24, 1941.

3 Sean Hand and Steven T. Katz, *Post-Holocaust France and the Jews 1945–1955*.

4 yadvashem.org.

5 CERCIL (The Study and Research Centre on the Internment Camps in the Loiret).

6 There is an interesting contrast between France's attitude toward its concentration camps and that of Poland. Auschwitz-Birkenau are, famously, carefully preserved, whereas Pithiviers, Drancy, and Beaune-la-Rolonde have long since vanished. The only concentration camp in France that was really preserved was the Natzweiler-Struthof concentration camp, and that's because it was run by the Germans and was in Alsace. But whereas France has increasingly acknowledged its culpability, Poland, as I discussed in chapter 1, is now doing the opposite. "It's only since the 1990s that camps in France started being commemorated," Martin Winstone from the Holocaust Educational Trust told me. "That comes from the state on some level, but it's also a generational shift. People begin to question their parents' and grandparents' historical myths."

7 Again, it was entirely Vichy's idea to arrest and deport Jewish children—the Nazis never demanded this. Michael R. Marrus and Robert O. Paxton, *Vichy France and The Jews*.

8 https://history.state.gov/historicaldocuments/frus1917v01/d393.

9 Smith, *The Liberation of Parish*.

10. Alex—Myth-making

1 Pochna, *Christian Dior: The Biography*.

2 Gitta Sereny, *The German Trauma: Experiences and Reflections 1938–1999* (London: Penguin Press, September 2000).

3 Anne Sebba, "How Haute Couture Rescued War-Torn Paris," *Daily Telegraph*, June 29, 2016.

4 In 2011, Hugo Boss issued a formal statement expressing "profound regret" for its wartime

activities (*Jewish Chronicle*, September 22, 2011). Admitting regret takes a long time sometimes.

5 Anne Sebba, *Les Parisiennes: How the Women of Paris Lived, Loved and Died in the 1940s* (London: Weidenfeld & Nicolson, 2016).

6 Marrus and Paxton, *Vichy France and the Jews.*

7 Serge Klarsfeld, *Les Transferts de Juifs de la Region de Nice Vers le Camp de Drancy en Vue de Leur Deportation 31 Aout 1942–30 Juillet 1944* (Association "Fils et Filles de Deportées Juifs de France," Paris, 1993).

8 Ibid.

9 Klarsfeld has first-hand knowledge of the brutality of the raids. When he was eight, his family home in Nice was raided, just a week after Alex was arrested. Serge, along with his sister and mother, managed to hide. His father, Arno, sacrificed himself to save them and was sent to Drancy (Klarsfeld, *Les Transferts de Juifs*).

10 As far as I can tell from his memoir, Alex did not start designing for the theater until after the war.

11 Angela Taylor, "Emeric Partos, 70, Fur Designer Noted for Innovative Flair, Dead," *New York Times*, December 3, 1975.

12 Smith, *The Liberation of Parish.*

13 https://www.saint-cyr.org/medias/editor/files/1912-1914-97e-promotion-de-montmirail.pdf.

11. The Sibilings— The Ordinary and the Extraordinary

1 Antony Beevor and Artemis Cooper, *Paris After the Liberation* (New York: Penguin, 2007).

2 Jews make up less than 1.4 percent of the American population, yet in polls Americans continually overestimate this to 20 percent "because of our disproportionate visibility, influence and accomplishments" (Alan Dershowitz, *The Jewish Question for the 21st Century: Can We Survive Our Success?* [Boston: Little, Brown, 1997]).

12. Alex—Social Mobility

1 John O'Donnell and James Rutherford, *Trumped! The Inside Story of the Real Donald Trump—His Cunning Rise and Spectacular Fall* (New York: Simon & Schuster, 1991).

2 Paul Burstein, "Jewish Educational and Economic Success in the United States: A Search for Explanations," *Sociological Perspectives* 50, no. 2 (Summer 2007).

3 Sachar, *History of the Jews in the Modern World.*

4 "Le Jardin des Modes," September 1939, via Sebba, *Les Parisiennes.*

5 Ibid.

6 Sebba, "How Haute Couture Rescued War-Torn Paris."

7 Sebba, *Les Parisiennes.*

8 Ludivine Broch, "The Merci Train: Remembering the World Wars in 52,000 Objects," https: blogs.kent.ac.uk (2017).

9 metmuseum.org.

10 Like Alex, Soutine was an eastern European refugee in Paris, having emigrated from what is now Belarus in his twenties. But he was less lucky than Alex: during the war he tried to go into hiding but had to emerge when he desperately needed surgery for an ulcer. The surgery failed to save him and he died in 1943, something Alex does not mention in his memoir, probably because so many people in his circle died during the war that it became almost a given for him.

11 Kurt Waldheim, president of Austria 1986–1992. He repeatedly lied about his Nazi past, but during his campaign for the Austrian presidency it emerged that he had been involved with Nazi youth groups as a teenager, and then during the war had been affiliated with German military groups that deported thousands of Jews. Both despite and because of this, he was elected president. Jonathan Kandell, "Kurt Waldheim, Former UN Chief, is Dead at 88," *New York Times,* June 15, 2007.

12 Neal Gabler, *An Empire of Their Own: How the Jews Invented Hollywood* (New York: Anchor Books, 1989).

13 Sachar (*History of the Jews in the Modern World*) also writes that this drive "stabilized" by the late twentieth century, and the children and grandchildren of Jewish immigrants now had the "leisure to seek new outlets in the liberal professions." This is certainly reflected in my family: while both my father and uncle worked in banking and the law, I was lucky enough to have the financial security to pursue my dream of being a writer and journalist.

14 *Aarhaus Amtstidende,* April 14, 1951.

15 "Les Premières Journées," *Le Monde,* February 3, 1955.

16 John Richardson, *The Sorcerer's Apprentice* (Chicago: University of Chicago Press, 2001).

17 Pierre Daix, *Picasso: Life and Art* (London: Thames & Hudson, 1994).

18 Janet Flanner, "Letter from Paris," *New Yorker,* June 17, 1964.

19 Richard Burton, *The Richard Burton Diaries* (New Haven, CT: Yale University Press, 2013).

20 "La Semaine d'Edgar Schneider: C'est son Cézanne-ouvre-toi!" *Le Figaro,* undated article.

21 Jonathan Fenby, *The General: Charles de Gaulle and the France He Saved* (New York: Simon & Schuster, 2010).

23 Deaths, *New York Times,* July 20, 1964.

14. The Next Generations—An Epilogue

1 *Proceedings of the National Academy of Sciences,* National Bureau of Economie Research, 2018.

2 Rachel Yehuda, et al., "Holocaust Exposure Induced Intergenerational Effects on FKBP5 Methylation," *Biological Psychiatry Journal,* September 1, 2016.

3 Olga Khazan, "Inherited Trauma Shapes Your Health," *The Atlantic,* October 2016.

4 Ewan Birney, "Why I'm Sceptical About the Idea of Genetically Inherited Trauma," *The Guardian,* September 11, 2016.

About the Author

Hadley Freeman grew up in New York City and London. She has been a staff writer at *The Guardian* newspaper for two decades and her work has also appeared in many other publications, including *Vogue* (US and UK). This is her fourth book. She lives in London with her partner and their three children.

further when he looked at me. "Clean it!" he grunted through his teeth as he clomped past me. He disappeared down the passageway.

I picked up the ceramic shards carefully, gathering them in my skirt. From beyond the pantry came murmuring, and the rant began again, only to be cut short by violent coughing. The coughing too ended abruptly. After a moment, the door creaked open, and the chamberlain's uneven step echoed down the hallway. The lash wounds on my back prickled as I heard him round the corner behind me. I turned and stood, holding the broken cup in the folds of my dress.

The chamberlain's hands were now empty, and he rubbed his palms forcefully over his sparse, greasy hair. He looked like someone whose best cow had been seized by the tax collector.

Geoffrey's eyes darted to the bucket beside me, and his expression lightened. "I have a job for you," he said. His lips thinned, baring more of his crowded yellow teeth.

I waited to hear what new trial he had devised.

"In the great hall, you will find your *master*," he drew out the word scornfully, "sprawled upon the floor, lounging in a pool of his own vomit. You will clean Sir Emont, the floor, the chair, and anything else befouled by his stinking spew."

I was shocked by his disrespect for the lord of the manor.

"He won't remember that we sent a dirty runt like you to clean his mess. He won't remember anything when he wakes in the dead of night with a mouth full of sawdust and a hatchet through his head."

After a momentary panic, I realized that he was speaking of a headache.

"When you finish, report to me." He limped back toward the kitchen.

Any satisfaction I had felt about making progress on the laundry evaporated. I did not want to go down that hallway to a part of the house where I knew I did not belong. It was wrong of Geoffrey to send me there. A laundry girl could not tend to the lord of the manor. The situation amused Geoffrey, though whether it was my discomfort or Sir Emont's debasement that pleased him, I could not tell.

With a sigh, I returned to the laundry room to find a rag and a brush, and then I fetched fresh water from the rain barrel. I had to do as I was told.

I crept down the dark corridor leading to the great hall and opened the door into the screens passage, the area under the minstrels' gallery that divided the service quarters from the living quarters. The back of the decorative wood screen was rough and plain, and bright light sliced through the arches facing the great hall, making the shadow at my feet a straight, sharp edge. I took a deep breath before stepping across it into the light.

The room was cavernous, with the same high-pitched roof as the kitchen. A long row of giant arch-braced trusses made of dark oak lined the ceiling. Their right lines had been softened by ornamental curls and long sweeping curves, but that made them no less imposing. The ceiling itself had been painted with a pattern of red and gold lozenges surrounded by a band of stars that encircled the whole of the hall, blurred by peeling plaster and a coating of dust and soot. Brilliant sunshine spilled from grand mullioned windows, dulling the firelight that writhed and flickered on a hearth larger than the sleeping loft of my father's cottage. The massive overmantel was engraved with four different coats of arms, and

it was supported by lions carved from the same blue-gray stone, gazing with fierce pride at something only they could see.

The great hall was occupied by a single individual. He was not sprawled on the floor, as described by the chamberlain, but he was slumped forward and unmoving at the end of one of the trestle tables nearest the fire. As I approached, the rancid smell of vomit stung my nose and caused my empty stomach to churn.

Emont's leonine head was cradled in the crook of his elbow. He had the apple cheeks of a boy, but a regal forehead. His sparse whiskers were in need of a shave. Hair spilled over the embroidered sleeve of his white shirt, the ends curling in a puddle of maroon vomit, and his mouth hung slack. The table had been cleared after the meal, but several carafes remained, along with cups that must have belonged to other guests. The lord of the manor still held a cup in his hand, ready to toast the empty benches. He snorted, startling me, and then sank back into a soft, rhythmic snore.

Dark red stains spread over the underside of Emont's sleeve, making it look as though his arm was bleeding. He had obviously been drinking wine. I would need to move him in order to clean the mess. I sighed again and set my bucket of water on the table next to his elbow. A giant baby, vomiting on himself and falling asleep.

I did not want him to wake and find me there, but I did not see how I could move him on my own.

"Sir?" I said tentatively, next to his ear. The fumes were sickening.

He did not stir.

"Sir?" I said again, shaking his shoulder lightly.

He snorted but did not wake up. I decided to start cleaning; maybe the cold water would rouse him enough to move. I started

with his hair, taking the ends in my hand and rinsing them with a dripping brush. His hair felt silken against my fingers, and the firelight burnished its red and gold hues.

I smoothed his damp hair carefully over his doublet so that it would not fall forward again, and I lifted his heavy head by pushing the flat of my hand against his forehead. This, or the damp cold rag over his mouth, finally caused him to stir.

"Hmmmph!" He pulled his head back from my hand and looked up at me from under drooping lids. He had a weak, dimpled chin and a small round nose that would have been pretty on a girl, but his broad face was as bland as pottage. His head wobbled, and I feared that he would fall forward again, so I reached for his shoulders. He seized my wrist so suddenly that a startled cry escaped my mouth. His grip was surprisingly firm.

"Who are you?" He spoke slowly, as though it took great concentration to form the words.

I wanted to squirm away and hide. "Agnes, sir."

"What are you doing here, Agnes?"

"I have come to clean up, sir."

His eyes drifted to the table, and then down to his soiled doublet. He snorted, and the ghost of a smile crossed his lips. "This is most unfortunate for you, isn't it?" He squeezed his eyes shut as if pained. I wondered if he felt embarrassment. He certainly did not seem as discomfited as I felt.

"Why don't you move aside, sir, and I shall get this finished."

He slid down the bench toward the fire, using his hands to steady himself. I quickly washed the table, bench, and floor. When I stood again, he was watching me blearily. The bloodshot whites of his eyes made the peculiar violet-blue of his irises more vivid.

I stacked the cups from the table and placed them on the tray that the chamberlain had left behind.

"Leave the carafe!"

"Yes, sir." I placed the full carafe and a clean cup beside him. Nervously, I said, "Sir, I should clean you up a little." The wet cloth dangled from my hand.

He grabbed the rag and dabbed ineffectually at the front of his doublet and the sleeve of his shirt. "Don't worry, the laundress will get these."

I blushed deeply. He was obviously confused.

"Just help me with the belt and buttons. I am no good with buttons."

I should have made an excuse and left to find the chamberlain, but he seemed so helpless, swatting intently at his waist and fumbling with the buckle. I felt a pang of pity, maybe even tenderness. I helped him with his buckle, followed by the rows of buttons on his doublet and shirt. He thanked me earnestly and struggled to remove his clothing. I quickly picked up my bucket and the tray of cups, made a hasty curtsy, and escaped while his head was still bent, before he could ask me to help any further.

After reporting to Geoffrey and begging one of the scullions to find me some food, I returned to the laundry room for another long night. The laundress did not come again, though I noticed that she had taken the chamber pots away.

When it was time for bed, I lined up my stones. It was too dark to tell whether there was blood on the back of my dress. The pain would cause me to sleep on my belly that night.

Gratefully, I pulled the heavy horse blanket over me. The scent of the stable was comforting. From the darkest corners of the room came the soft scratching and scrabbling of rodents, but I told myself that my stones would protect me from them. Children's thoughts incline toward magic and superstition, and mine were no exception.

THE LORD'S CHAMBERS

Those first days at the manor formed the pattern for my next four years as a laundry girl. In some ways my life improved, but in other ways it did not. I worked harder—and longer—than at any other time in my life. Even when I started the brewery as a young mother, I did not experience the kind of exhaustion, the bone-deep weariness that I did at the manor. There were times when I did not think that I could lift the kettle one more time, though necessity drove me to lift it anyway. I was habitually dark with ashes, and the harsh soap caused blisters on my hands.

I did discover efficiencies that allowed me to keep up with the endless round of laundry. John found a ladder for me so that I could dump dirty water more easily out of the window, and he placed a rain barrel just outside so that I could lower the bucket for fresh water during the rainy seasons. I learned how to keep all of the laundry stages operating at once, so that no time was wasted in idleness. I also learned which fabrics required the most thorough bucking and which did not, and I batched my laundry accordingly.

While I was never truly happy during those years, small com-

forts cheered me. I looked forward to Mass every week in the manor's chapel, where I was transfixed by the stained-glass window behind the altar. I paid no attention to the priest's Latin murmurs and chants but allowed myself to be transported by the jeweled perfection above his head.

The window depicted the Holy Spirit in the form of a dove, diving from heaven on rays of golden light, luminous golden swords that pierced the head and breast of a kneeling Virgin Mary. The Virgin was so white, paler than death, or snow, a sapphire cloak over her shoulders and honeyed hair tumbling to her waist. A book had fallen to the floor, leaves fluttering, and the Virgin clasped her hands to her heart. She was not looking at the dove. Her downcast eyes, profoundly sorrowful, seemed blind. I would close my own eyes and imagine swords of light; the urgent beating of great wings; a turbulence of draught and feathers, sharp claws sinking into my wrist, foreign, soft, insistent writhing against my breast.

I found ways to improve my creature comforts at the manor. I kept (and mended) the horse blankets until I met my family again at the parish church on May Day, when I asked my sister for a blanket from home. She ran to fetch it right away, my sweet, stern Lottie. I added straw to my pallet and placed a sock filled with oak ash near my bed to keep the rats and mice away.

I looked for allies in the kitchen, and the most elderly scullion, William, became a valuable acquaintance. He seemed lonely, and I think that he enjoyed my chatter and occasional sour remark. He would smile widely in appreciation, exposing the gaps in his rotting teeth, and pat my arm softly with his chapped and calloused hands. When I did not appear at meals, he was careful to set aside

food for me in a basket in the larder. If there was meat, he saved me a generous portion, and he always managed to secure a piece of bread, even when there was none for the other servants to eat. It bothers me to this day that I did not have the means to repay him for his kindness.

Neither John nor William could protect me from the laundress, who was an unpredictable bully. On the best days, she helped me with the fire or folding linens and chatted. She told me about her time as a laundry girl, how hard she had worked and how often she had been thrashed by the laundress. Elisabeth claimed that she had less appetite for the whip than her own overseer, that I was fortunate. It was true that she had whipped me only thrice in four years, and though she sometimes whacked me with the dolly stick, that was far more bearable.

Elisabeth's favorite subject was her former sweetheart, a young swain who had died many years before in a fire at the mill. By her account, he was the most handsome, strong, courageous, clever, and pious man ever to have walked God's green earth. She said that she had been the prettiest girl in Aviceford, and I believed her, for despite sagging jowls and the coarsening of age, evidence of fine features remained, as well as clear gray eyes and masses of ill-kempt fair curls. Beauty notwithstanding, she would likely not have married her beau without a dowry. I was tempted to say that his death was providential; otherwise, she would have suffered through his marriage to the second-prettiest girl in the village. I knew what was good for me, so I held my tongue.

Most days, Elisabeth ignored me, but on the worst days she toyed with me, making arbitrary demands, forcing me to work through meals or stay up through the night. She might decide at suppertime that all of the bedsheets needed to be washed and

pressed by morning, or that the whites were not clean enough, and I had to start again.

It puzzled me that Elisabeth remained in the manor's employ when she did so little work. There was too much laundry for one person; on holidays I would usually fall behind if the laundress refused to help, but the chamberlain never intervened. Since there was no lady of the house to supervise the servants, and since Emont took no interest in the management of domestic affairs, Geoffrey Poke acted as the final authority. He was not a person to whom I could appeal for justice, particularly following some turns of event that solidified his dislike for me.

Geoffrey himself heralded the first incident. He appeared in the laundry late one night, giving me a terrible fright. I was in the habit of being alone, as the laundress usually only came to drop off washing or chamber pots, or to nap in the afternoon. I did not hear him approach, as I had been thrashing the clothing vigorously with a dolly stick. I looked up to find a looming, skeletal figure holding a flickering candle. The flame illuminated Geoffrey's countenance fitfully, creating deep shadows where his eyes should have been.

I could tell that the chamberlain was furious. He uncurled his long fingers, dragged his palm across his shining pate, and clenched his fist again. "Come with me," he said.

I did not ask why. I removed the apron that I had learned to wear over my dress to keep it clean from ashes, and I used the inside to wipe my hands and face.

The chamberlain said nothing as he led me down the corridor. The clomp and drag of his feet filled the silence. As he did not hold the candle aloft, I was forced to wade through thick shadow

behind him, lifting my feet carefully so that I would not stumble on an uneven flagstone. When we turned down the passage to the great hall, I assumed that this was going to be a repetition of my last encounter with the manorial lord. I wondered why I had not been told to bring a bucket.

To my surprise, the great hall was empty. The fire had died to embers, and the room was dimly lit by guttering candles in sconces bolted to the wall. Flickering shadows from iron fleur-de-lis crenelations made jagged teeth across the floor.

Geoffrey crossed to the dais and climbed stairs to an entrance that I knew must lead to the manorial lord's private quarters. I followed stupidly, unable to conceive of a reason why I might be brought there. We traversed another cold, dark passageway, approaching a door surrounded by a halo of light. The chamberlain knocked and pushed forward without waiting for a response. The heavy door creaked reluctantly open. Geoffrey's stooped shoulders obscured my view of the room, but I could tell that a fire was lit, and an emerald and gold canopy confirmed that we were indeed entering a bedchamber.

Coldly, the chamberlain said, "I got the girl like you asked." He pulled me out of the dark doorway and gave me a shove into the room, causing me to lurch and nearly fall into a short man with a bulbous nose and a red cap. He took a quick step back, squinting and blinking.

With a shiver, I recognized the man as the apothecary from Waithe, the town nearest Aviceford. When wealthier villagers became ill, the apothecary was called, as there was no physician within many miles of the village. Our family could not afford the apothecary, but I had seen him at the home of the reeve, when the reeve's wife fell sick with childbed fever. The poor woman died

despite the astringent poultices and medicinals concocted by the apothecary. I shared sickbed vigil with some other girls whose families could spare them from home, and the sad reeve paid me a few coins when it was all over. I was glad for the money, but I did no more to earn it than mop the good wife's brow.

A violent fit of coughing came from the bed, and I realized that the chamberlain had been addressing the patient, not the apothecary. Emont was propped on his elbows, facing the firelight, his broad chest heaving violently with each cough. When he recovered from the fit, he looked at us vacantly. His face glistened with a film of sweat, and his eyes were glassy.

Geoffrey said, "I don't know what you want with the girl, my lord." He flung the last word like slop to a pig. "The chamber servants, including myself, are more than capable of caring for you. The laundry girl does not belong here."

Emont shook his shaggy head, then moaned and slumped onto his back. Geoffrey's eyes narrowed, and his thin top lip tightened in a snarl. He spun and clomped away, pausing to spit on the floor before leaving the room.

I approached Emont, who lay with his eyes closed. The flush of fever and his rapid breathing made him look like a ruddy-cheeked boy who had been playing in the snow. The apothecary removed a cup from Emont's hand and brought it close to his face so he could peer inside. "You must make sure that he drinks his medicine." He squinted at me again, frowning.

I nodded. I did not want to be there, and a wave of anxiety washed over me when I thought about the laundress. I should have been more frightened about being left in charge of a sick nobleman, but for some reason, I was not.

The apothecary carried his brown leather bag to the fireside,

where he riffled through its contents, lifting out one bottle and then another for close inspection. When he found the medicine he was seeking, he brought it to me. "Give him a half-filled cup of this horehound and coriander elixir three times each day. He needs to finish what is in this cup before he sleeps. If his fever does not break within two days, you should send for a surgeon, as he will need to be bled."

I wondered how far a messenger would need to travel to find a surgeon. I fervently hoped that Emont would recover quickly, not least because I needed to get back to work. I took the bottle of medicine from the apothecary and thanked him.

After the apothecary left, I drew a stool to the bedside. The floor had been strewn with meadowsweet and lavender, and the herbs crushed under the feet of the stool released fresh fragrance. Emont appeared to be in the shallows of a fitful sleep. His eyes flicked erratically beneath purple-veined lids, and his breathing was ragged. He did not wear his nightcap, and his damp, greasy hair splayed out on the pillow like a ratty halo. I had never seen a feather bed before, and I pressed lightly on the edge of the mattress, feeling its softness. How glorious it would be to sleep in such a bed every night.

Emont did not wake even during his coughing spells, and I grew stiff from sitting still. I leaned my forehead on the corner of the mattress and dozed. When I opened my eyes again, the room was dark and cold, and my neck was sore. The fire had died to an orange glow, and the candle was half spent. All was silent except for the distant hoot of an owl. As I stirred the embers, they sparked and smoked, so I put fresh wood down, coaxing the flames back to life. Although I was unsure of the hour, I thought that it must be time to rouse the master for his medicine. I shook him gently, and his eyelids fluttered. He coughed and turned onto his side.

"Sir, you must wake and take your medicine. Wake now."

He opened his eyes, still coughing, and looked at me, confused. "What is it?" His voice was croupy and weak.

"I am Agnes, sir, and I have your medicine."

For some time, he stared at me blankly. Then, narrowing his eyes, he said, "You despise me too, don't you?" His cough was a wet rattle. "Contempt. I see it."

"Sir, I am sure that no good Christian holds you in contempt. Now it is time to take your medicine, sir."

He nodded docilely. He drank from the cup that I handed him, and though he grimaced, he finished the draught. He lay back and closed his eyes.

"I hate this place," he rasped, coughing again. "Would that my father had never bargained with that woman." He made no more sound, and soon fell back asleep.

I nursed Emont for two days, after which his fever subsided. He continued to speak and sometimes cry out in his delirium, and I was never sure whether he was aware of my presence or not. When his eyes did focus on me, he seemed content to have me there. Though much of what he said made no sense, I suspected that his unhappiness ran deep. I was too young to understand how a wealthy man could be sad, but I perceived bleakness in him.

Elisabeth did no laundry while I was gone. Upon my return, she ordered me to work through the night to catch up, and when she found me asleep in the morning by a dying fire, she beat me with a dolly stick.

A fortnight later, when Emont requested my aid again, Elisabeth was in the laundry with me.

"What does the master want with this gormless girl?" she snapped at the chamberlain.

"Shut your gob," Geoffrey replied.

"You can't take her from me. I've only got the one."

"Are you telling me what I can and cannot do?"

Elisabeth seemed to catch herself. She pressed a hand over her eyes, and when she lifted it, her brow was smooth and her lips curved in a coy smile. "I never tell you what you *cannot* do, now do I?" Her tone was one I had not heard before.

To my astonishment, Geoffrey smiled too. "The girl will be back before you notice her gone," he said.

Elisabeth's laugh was edged with frost.

I followed Geoffrey back to Emont's chamber. The shutters were closed, and the light from a low fire imparted a desultory, reddish glow. An iron candelabrum hung from a ceiling beam, and though it was daytime, the candles were lit, slumped and melted, lowering stubby fingers of wax drip by drip. The master slouched in a chair by the hearth and motioned me over when I entered. I curtsied and waited expectantly, but his head remained bowed. He tapped an empty cup against the armrest; the metallic clank rang loud in the silence.

"Geoffrey," he said without turning his head. "Leave my wine. You may go."

The chamberlain set a flagon on the floor beside Emont. "The laundress needs the girl back tonight," he said.

Emont mumbled something unintelligible and waved the chamberlain away. Geoffrey pressed his lips together; a crooked tooth poked out, which made him look more like a grizzled old hound than the tyrant I feared. He slammed the door, which made me jump, but Emont did not react. He turned his head slowly to look

at me. His eyes were sunken, and the shadows made his gaze baleful. He extended the hand that had been curled in his lap, and I saw the glint of a blade.

"Can you help me?" He held out the knife. The handle was made of smooth bone with a gold tip. A silver cross had been inlaid where the handle was widest.

"Sir?" My thoughts darted like rabbits, trying to divine his meaning.

"Oh, ah, if you would be so good as to trim my nails. I can manage the left hand but not the right."

I had not been aware of holding my breath, but it came out in a rush. "I should open the shutters so I can see." I bustled to the window. Though the day was overcast, I was momentarily blinded by the flood of light.

In ordinary sunlight, the room and its inhabitant looked shabby and forlorn. Dark patches of soot on the walls and ceiling appeared to be centuries old, as did the faded tapestry and drapes. Wine had been spilled on the bedclothes. I wondered if they had been changed since I last stripped the bed. Emont's fine silk robe bore stains, and his stockings were crumpled around his ankles. Scraggly whiskers fuzzed his cheeks and hid the dimple in his chin; his long hair was tangled and matted.

The fire flared and spat when I fed it a log sticky with pine sap.

"Let me have the knife," I said. After the words left my mouth, I feared that I had been rude, but Emont held the knife out obediently. I never trimmed my fingernails; mine broke or I bit them off. I decided to approach the task like whittling, aiming the blade away from the fingers. I took his hand, which was small for a man, soft and pale as pastry dough. It looked dainty in my rough, blistered paw.

"No," Emont said. "Not like that. Use the knife to curve." He placed his other hand on top of mine to demonstrate. His palm was warm.

The sharp blade peeled the nail away like bark from a tree. When I had finished cutting the nails on his right hand, I said, "Should I help with shaving, sir? Or perhaps your hair?"

"I could use some tidying, couldn't I?" He raked his hair with his fingers. "Perhaps you could assist, thank you." He filled his cup with the wine Geoffrey had left and took a great swallow. He coughed and then said, "You have eyes like a cow."

"Sir?"

"Your eyes. They are soft and brown and solemn. Just like a cow."

"Oh." I wasn't sure how to respond.

"Not that I am comparing you to a cow. You seem like a clever girl."

"Cows can be clever too, sir."

He seemed to find my statement amusing, though I had meant it sincerely. Emont laughed heartily before draining the rest of his cup. "Get on, then," he said. "Make me beautiful."

I brushed his hair first, as I was confident that I could do it well. Untangling snarls and smoothing his curls made me homesick, not only because it reminded me of brushing my sister's hair, but because it had been so long since I had felt a tender touch. Loneliness lodged in my throat like a piece of gristle.

I fetched a bowl of water and the razor. Emont closed his eyes and tipped back his heavy head while I scraped at his whiskers. A contented smile made his appearance more youthful. "You have the touch of an angel, Agnes," he murmured.

After I patted his cheeks dry, Emont thanked me distractedly

and poured himself another cup of wine. He propped his stock-inged feet against the hearth. "Shut the window before you go," he said.

I walked slowly back to the laundry. Nothing good awaited me there.

Elisabeth was stirring the fire; a shower of orange sparks turned to gray ghosts. "The sun is already setting," she said. "You had better hustle. I wouldn't like to have to punish you." She held the poker aloft and waggled it, as though mocking the threat implied by the gesture.

"The master asked after you," I said.

The laundress's expression went blank.

"He wanted to know how I like my position." I paused. "He said I looked tired and asked if I was overburdened. I told him you had been feeling poorly and so hadn't been able to do your duty of late."

Elisabeth lowered the poker in a leisurely fashion, but I could see her jaw working as she clenched and unclenched her teeth.

"I am to report back to him. He is a most considerate master."

The laundress did her part with the laundry that night, and she never beat me again for the offense of being called into the master's service. I wish that the same ruse could have fooled Geoffrey, but he knew the master intimately. Geoffrey understood that Emont had only the murkiest idea of how the manor was run and that Emont depended on him completely to maintain a facade of re-spectability. Moreover, love of drink breeds a sort of blindness to other people, and Geoffrey knew that our master would not take a real interest in my life. The chamberlain sharply resented my in-

cursion into his territory, but he did not feel threatened by me. He knew that his power over Emont far exceeded any small influence that I might have.

A second event that increased Geoffrey's dislike for me might have yielded an advantage had I known how to use it. This happened on a day when there was a large party of visitors, and I had a heaping basket of white linens to clean. The guests and Emont were presumably at dinner in the great hall, but the laundress had not brought the chamber pots as usual. I was frustrated with the stains, and I decided to fetch the chamber pots myself.

I had by that time visited the sleeping quarters and solar on several occasions when my help was requested by Emont, and I knew how to access that part of the house while avoiding the great hall. I went out the back entrance near the kitchen and circled the manor house, past the garden and dovecote. I squeezed through a thicket of holly bushes that crowded the windowless base of the west wall and there mounted a neglected staircase that led to the second story. I had to tread carefully on the weather-worn steps as the mortar was crumbling and stones sometimes came loose underfoot. The oak door at the top of the stairs was never barred; it opened onto a landing that looked down on the great hall. Three long tables had been covered with white linens and set with silver; the guests in their finery were colorful and raucous, out of place in somber Aviceford Manor. As I ducked down the corridor, I heard an explosion of laughter and wondered what grown men and women found so funny.

I made quickly for Emont's sleeping chamber, because that was the room I knew the best. When I opened the door, I saw two fig-

ures moving on the feather bed, and an unpleasant sensation trickled down my spine. The laundress was entirely unclothed, swaying on all fours, like a child pretending to be a horse. Her pendulous moonlike breasts were blotched with red; they swung heavily as her head reared back, yanked by the chamberlain, who had one hand wrapped in the nest of blond curls at the nape of her neck. Elisabeth held her eyes closed and bared her teeth in a grimace.

The chamberlain was a more unsettling sight still, as he was clothed from the waist up like an aristocrat dressed gaily for a hunt. He wore a velvet and gold doublet with a fur collar and a hat with a long curving feather that bobbed violently by his ear. With each low grunt, his naked hips and sagging bottom thrust energetically at the laundress's jiggling rear, which he observed with intense concentration.

I might have escaped unnoticed had Elisabeth not turned her head to the doorway at that moment, just as I pulled it shut. Her face was half veiled by tangled hair, but I caught her look of unalloyed hatred before she disappeared behind the reassuringly solid surface of the closing door.

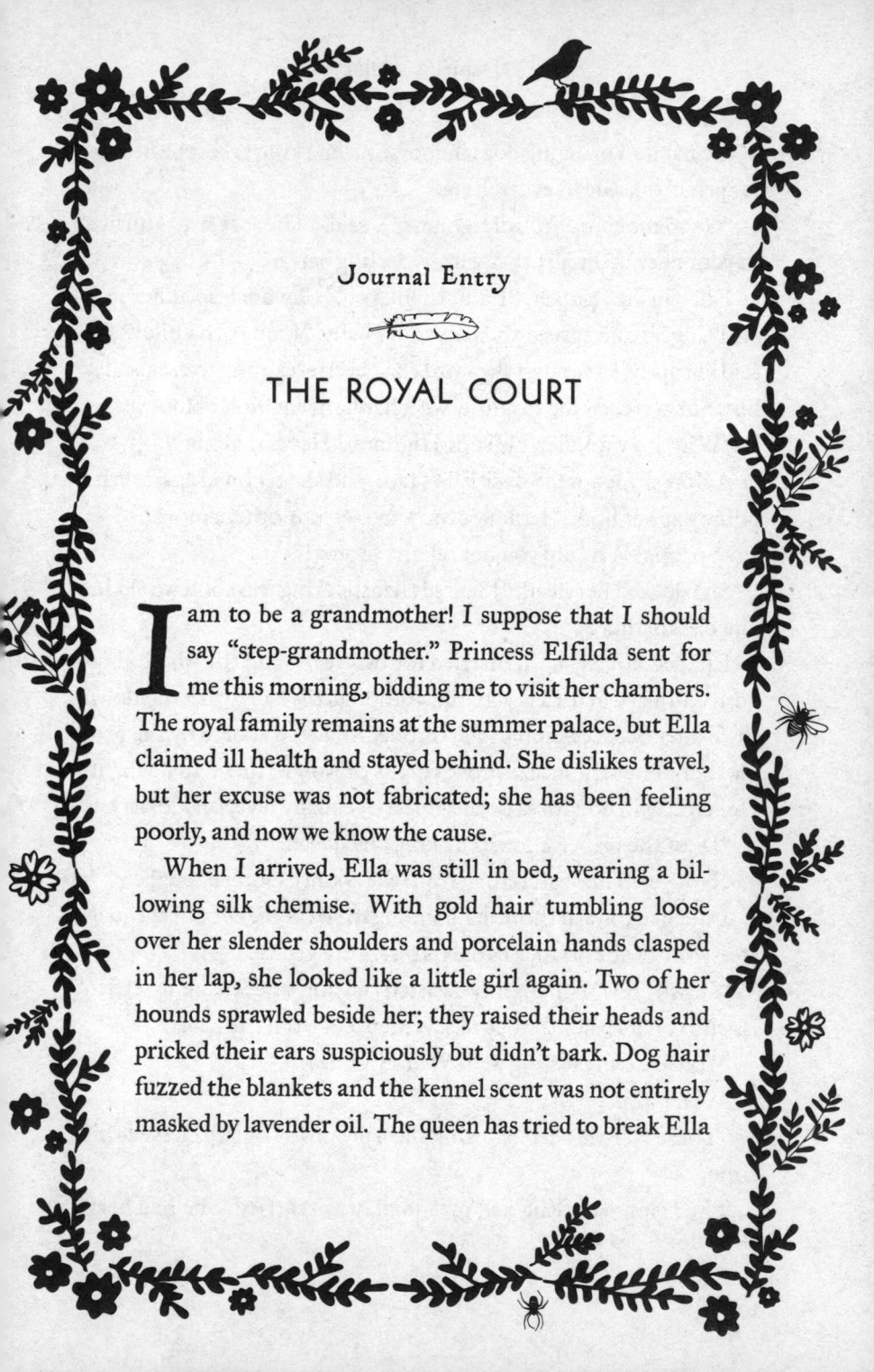

Journal Entry

THE ROYAL COURT

I am to be a grandmother! I suppose that I should say "step-grandmother." Princess Elfilda sent for me this morning, bidding me to visit her chambers. The royal family remains at the summer palace, but Ella claimed ill health and stayed behind. She dislikes travel, but her excuse was not fabricated; she has been feeling poorly, and now we know the cause.

When I arrived, Ella was still in bed, wearing a billowing silk chemise. With gold hair tumbling loose over her slender shoulders and porcelain hands clasped in her lap, she looked like a little girl again. Two of her hounds sprawled beside her; they raised their heads and pricked their ears suspiciously but didn't bark. Dog hair fuzzed the blankets and the kennel scent was not entirely masked by lavender oil. The queen has tried to break Ella

of the habit of bringing dogs indoors, but the king takes the beautiful princess's side in everything.

"Good morning, Your Highness," I said. "The rose has returned to your cheeks. I trust that you are feeling better?"

Ella flushed pinker. "I am, thank you." She unclasped her jeweled fingers and spread them over her belly. "I am with child!" she said abruptly, as though the words had been straining to escape her lips. She watched me carefully with her lambent violet-blue eyes.

"Why, how wonderful, Your Highness! How far along?"

A slow smile spread over Ella's face, and she reclined against the pillows at her back. "I am not certain——four or five months."

"So long! Why did you not tell me sooner?"

She ducked her head. "I feared that speaking too soon would invite bad fortune."

Ella has already been married for two years, and the whole kingdom is impatient for a royal child. Although the baby will be far down the ladder of succession to the throne, Ella is so adored by the people that her every sneeze provokes fits of wonderment and delight. Her child will doubtless be the object of equally feverish idolatry.

"Does the prince know? The king and queen?"

"Not yet. They will return from the country soon enough."

I stepped toward the bed, intending to sit on the edge of the mattress; one of the hounds bared its teeth and growled.

"Down, Bo!" Ella lightly swatted the dog's neck, and it settled its chin on its paws. I stopped several paces from the bed.

"You are truly feeling well, Your Highness?"

"Yes, I am."

"There is little peril of losing the baby now. You are blessed this time."

The prior year, Ella had presumably miscarried. She had been

sick, with vomiting, and she confided to me that her monthly bleeds had ceased. Then one morning, I was called to her chambers to find her in bed like today, but pale and trembling. She pulled back the covers to reveal blood-soaked linens; the nightgown she wore was stained scarlet from the waist downward. She swore me to secrecy, and I arranged for the bedclothes to be smuggled to the laundry without the knowledge of the ladies-in-waiting. I sponged her clean and helped burn her nightgown in the fireplace. There was little call for such furtiveness——miscarriages are commonplace, after all——but the princess has always been uncomfortable with matters of the flesh. I told no one of the incident, not even Charlotte or Matilda.

"Are you sure that the danger has passed?" Ella twisted a lock of hair through her fingers and brushed the ends against her cheek, as she used to do when she was a child. I have always found the gesture annoying.

"Nothing is certain, Your Highness, but it is highly auspicious that you are so many months along and healthy. Have you felt the baby quicken?"

"No . . ." Ella frowned. "How does it feel?"

"You will know soon." I smiled at her concerned look. "It is a lovely fluttering."

"How much did the birthing hurt?"

I thought about how to respond. I wanted neither to frighten nor mislead her. "It is bearable, Your Highness, and it ends in the greatest joy you can know."

Ella looked unsure but asked no more questions. She cradled the head of one of the hounds with both of her hands and kissed its nose repeatedly, making little cooing sounds. Then she smiled and said, "I hope it will be a boy!"

Charlotte and Matilda will be delighted to know that their step-sister is with child. I hope that they will be given some role in the upbringing of their niece or nephew; sadly, this is likely to be the nearest experience they will have to motherhood. It is not only their lack of beauty that prevents marriage: Though we live like aristocrats, we are penniless and depend upon the generosity of the king for every scrap of clothing and food. I have no dowry to set-tle on my daughters. Being aunts would give them joy and a much needed wholesome pursuit away from palace intrigue.

As I reflect on my recent writing about Elisabeth, I wonder whether she ever miscarried or gave birth in secret. I would guess that she had congress with the chamberlain for years, and she was not yet too old for childbearing when I arrived at Aviceford Manor. With her large girth, a pregnancy may have gone unnoticed, and I do recall at least one mysterious absence, when she left the manor for more than a week.

Perhaps the devil's bargain she made, trading her chastity for comforts Geoffrey Poke could supply, seemed like a good bargain to Elisabeth. Nothing, however, could make up for the pain of giv-ing away a child.

The laundress gave me ample reason to hate her, and I used to think that she had been born without a single virtuous bone in her whole body. Now that I am older and have seen so much more of mankind, I no longer believe that people are born without virtue. It gets beaten out. Misfortune threshes our souls as a flail threshes wheat, and the lightest parts of ourselves are scattered to the wind.

THE MESSENGER

I was fourteen when there came an opportunity for me to escape the manor house, at least for a short time. I was by then desperate for any change. I had grown increasingly lonely, not only because I felt my isolation more keenly as I grew older, but because I lost my only friend. John was killed one snowy winter morning by the collapse of a barn roof. He had been the person I sought the moment I entered the kitchen for meals, the audience for stories I rehearsed in my mind, my guide for navigating the alliances and enmities of other servants. He taught me how best to stay out of the chamberlain's way and where to stash the apples he brought me from the orchard. Most of all, John pulled me back from my tendency toward melancholy. Whenever tears threatened, he had some witty words or humorous antic at the ready. I did not know how much I relied on him until he was gone.

After John died, I fell into a deep sorrow. I received news of the barn collapse from Elisabeth. I do not think that she relished my pain; even she seemed sad about John's death. For the first time since my arrival at the manor, I broke down and sobbed in front of

the laundress. She said nothing to me, but let me exhaust myself, and when I returned to the bucking tub with sore eyes peering from swollen slits and a trail of snot and tears down the front of my gown, she did not chastise me.

From that day, my time at the manor was almost unbearable. I sat alone at supper and listened to my heart thunder as I lay awake each night. I had no appetite, and the frocks that had become too tight across my growing bosom and hips hung loose once more. I sleepwalked through my duties in the laundry, hardly bothering to acknowledge the laundress on the rare occasions when she was chatty. I felt invisible.

On saints' days and other holidays I was allowed to leave the manor, and I saw my family then, usually at church. It should have made me feel better, but somehow it made me feel even more alone. Everyone in my family had married, and Lottie already had two babes, though one of them died in the cradle. My father married a widow from the village, a sharp-tongued gossip. My brother and his wife still lived at Father's house, and Lottie lived in Nether End, nearer the church. Without a dowry, Lottie had been unable to do better than a villein as poor as our father, and while her husband was a godly man, I doubt that she loved him.

Elisabeth was a constant reminder to me of what my life would become if I did not find a husband. She never spoke of the bedchamber scene I had witnessed, but it became evident to me that she had chosen harlotry over the drudgery of being a laundress. Even at the age of fourteen, I understood that slothfulness could not account fully for such a choice; she must also have been driven by despair, the same shadowy desolation that closed on me. Blistered hands, an aching back, endless toil, unremitting loneliness shaped my days and nights and every day to come, a

gloomy blur of sameness that stretched nowhere except to its own pointless end.

As I teetered on the brink of marriageable age, I was too conflicted to truly mourn my lack of prospects. Even wedlock, while preferable to life at the manor, did not represent escape. The best that I could hope for was the life my sister lived, a smoke-filled house of dirt and straw, an empty belly, dead babies. I was a mouse trapped in a corner, looking for a crack to flee through but despairing of finding one.

It is said that clouds may turn forth a silver lining, and indeed, if Elisabeth had been less spiteful, I might never have found out about the opportunity at all. She taunted me one hot afternoon in August, as I was kneeling on the lip of the laundry basin scrubbing shirts. Sweat slid from under the band of my bonnet, trickling to the tip of my nose or the edge of my jaw before splashing into the tepid pool. Elisabeth had come to recline in the relative cool of the dark laundry room; she lay on a pile of linens, wearing only her chemise, fanning herself with the lid of a rush basket.

"I heard something from Geoffrey."

I swatted at a fly that droned in erratic circles around my head and then returned to scrubbing, not caring what she had to say.

"I heard that Abbess Elfilda requested a girl to help with her mother."

Her tone of voice told me that she was up to no good, but she had piqued my interest. I took her bait. "What do you mean, miss?"

"I mean that the mother of the abbess had a lady's maid who took ill. It will take some time to get a new one, and so the abbess asked for a loan of a girl from our manor. I told Geoffrey that of course we couldn't spare you."

My mouth felt dry. "I am not sure that I understand, miss."

"I mean, you dimwit, that you might have gone to the abbey to play lady's maid for the old woman. But you shan't." Her fleshy underarm jiggled like a pale fish on a hook as she fanned herself. "They'll find a girl from one of the other manors. Anyway, we have only you." She wrinkled her nose. "Cothay Manor has a goose girl and chambermaids for the lady, besides two laundry girls. The abbess only wants to take from our manor because she knows the souse won't complain. Besides, Geoffrey says she wants to punish us for poor revenues. God's bones, we can barely keep up as it is."

I struggled to control my voice. "When did the message arrive, miss?"

"This terce. The abbess's messenger is still in the kitchen, waiting for supper. A dark-skinned devil."

I returned to scrubbing, trying to ignore the roaring in my head. I could not stand that the possibility for liberation had miraculously appeared, only to be snatched away by the person I most wanted to escape. Although I was no longer a child—in fact, I stood a full head taller than Elisabeth, and I was as strong as any boy—the laundress made me feel powerless.

Sharp pain sliced neatly through my self-pity. I had scraped my knuckles against the rough stone at the edge of the basin. For a moment my fingers went limp; I watched as the new pink furrows I had dug began to slowly fill with red. Sitting back on my heels, I sucked the blood away. It tasted of metal, like the blade of a knife.

Pain calmed the ferment in my mind. There had to be a way to circumvent Elisabeth; I could not sit idly by as she closed the door to my escape. I had to find some way to approach Emont. Even if I failed, I would have the comfort of knowing that I did not just lie down and let Elisabeth wipe her feet on me. I went back to work, nurturing the seeds of my new resolve.

When suppertime arrived, I spread the ashes on the bucking cloth, wiped my hands, and walked slowly toward the kitchen. The usual chaos awaited me there. The serving staff was just finishing with the lord's supper in the great hall, and many of the other servants were gathering at the trestle tables in the kitchen for their own suppers. It was hotter in the kitchen than in the laundry, and the men were red-faced and sweating. We were not supposed to eat the leftovers from the master's table, but as Emont employed no almoner to supervise the table scraps, and as tonight there were no guests, the serving boys brought back a plate of sturgeon with pear and raisins and a pigeon pie. On the kitchen tables were trays of pork roast, carrots, turnips, and ceramic jugs of ale.

The abbess's messenger was seated near the door, enthusiastically tearing into a piece of pork. I had noticed him before when he had stopped in for meals at Aviceford Manor. He looked different from anyone I had ever seen; his skin was chestnut, as though he spent every day of his life in the sun, but his face was smooth, not rough and wrinkled. He always seemed to be in good humor, joking with the kitchen staff. He carried himself with confident grace, but he did not behave haughtily toward the servants, even though they were beneath his station.

On an impulse, I walked over and stood in front of him on the opposite side of the table. When he looked up, I curtsied. "Greetings, good sir. I am Agnes." I did not have a plan for what to say next.

The messenger leaned back, stretching his long legs in front of him, and he beamed at me. His teeth were white and straight as a string of pearls, and his smile could have lit a cathedral. "Good

evening, Agnes. My name is Fernan. I am pleased to make your acquaintance." He spoke with a slight accent, the result, I would later learn, of a childhood in Aquitaine.

"I have heard that you brought a message about a position at the abbey."

He arched his black eyebrows. "Why does a laundry girl know the content of a message intended for her master?"

"How do you know that I am the laundry girl?"

"Either you are a laundry girl or you have been cleaning chimneys, cinder wench!" He laughed, and I blushed deeply. I had forgotten to wipe my face before coming to supper.

"Did you already deliver the message to the lord, then?" Despite my embarrassment, I looked him steadily in the eye. I knew from what the laundress had told me that the message had been delivered to the chamberlain instead.

His smile wavered. He opened his mouth to say something, and then closed it again. It was my turn to raise my eyebrows, which made him laugh again. "I suppose that I did not deliver the message directly to the intended recipient, no, but not everyone reads his own letters." Fernan waved genially at the bench in front of me. "Sit, sit! Join me. I have a weakness for cheeky lasses."

"I cannot sit here, sir. This table is for the highest rank." He should have known that. He was making fun of me. Already, I was getting sidelong looks from the menservants gathering at the table. When the chamberlain arrived, I would be in trouble.

"Nonsense! You are my guest."

"Really, I cannot." His flippancy irritated me. "I have a favor to ask of you." I was surprised by my own temerity.

"What might that favor be?"

"Can you speak with Sir Emont about his response to your message before you leave? Can you call on him after supper?"

Fernan wiped his sweaty brow with his sleeve. "I think that I can guess the reason for this strange request, and I don't object to helping you. I still need Sir Emont's signature on the response that I have drafted." He patted the satchel by his side. "However, your master is not likely to go against Geoffrey's recommendation."

"I know, sir. But I would appreciate it all the same."

He shrugged his shoulders and smiled. "Very well! I wish you luck, laundry girl."

My heart pounded as I walked to my usual seat near the other end of the kitchen. I used to eat with John and old William, the scullion who rewarded my chatter with treats that he secreted away during the course of his day in the kitchen. Poor, frail William got no break from his labors, and by the time I was fourteen, he had died of brain fever, the result of overwork. My supper seat was now between a chitty-faced, sullen youth who ignored me and an oily scullion who pressed his skinny leg against mine at every opportunity. As usual, we made no conversation. I was too nervous to eat, but I had to bide my time until all of the servants were finished in the great hall. I pushed my food around my bowl, watching the traffic through the kitchen doors carefully, because if I waited too long, the chamberlain would be finished with his own supper and roaming again. When I judged it to be safe, I bade my tablemates a good night and slipped out of the kitchen. Fernan was still at supper; as I passed behind his broad back, his animated story provoked a roar of laughter from his neighbors.

My life would have turned out very differently had I not found Emont still sitting in the great hall that evening. The red sun

lay low on the horizon, lighting the room with a fiery glow. As I passed the series of diamond-paned windows, the warp of the glazing made the sun look like a rosy apple bobbing in a rain barrel. Emont stared into his cup, paying no attention to the sunset. I approached from the front so that I would not startle him, but it still took a moment for him to notice me.

"Agnes. Why are you here? You're filthy."

I blushed for the second time that evening. I had forgotten about the soot on my face. "I have heard, sir, that Abbess Elfilda needs me to fill in for her mother's lady's maid until they can find a suitable replacement from the castle."

He narrowed his eyes. "So Geoffrey told me. He also told me that he cannot spare you."

I gathered my courage. "Sir, might not a refusal to send me to the abbey anger the abbess further?"

"Further?"

"Oh . . . It is not my place to say, sir . . . I should not have come to you. It is only that the laundress seemed so afeard that if I did not go to the abbey, Mother Elfilda would punish us. She said small remittances from Aviceford displease the abbess, and she will be furious if we refuse this request as well. I only came because the laundress was so troubled. I mean no impertinence, sir."

Emont scowled. He took a long draught from his cup and set it heavily on the table.

"Sir, if you had sent me, I would have been diligent and godly, but I can see that I should not have bothered you with things that I cannot understand. I am most contrite." I curtsied and lowered my gaze, waiting for him to dismiss me.

Emont might not have had much stomach for arguing with Geoffrey, but I could tell that my words had reached their target.

He groaned with irritation and released me with a gruff command. I flew from the room, seeking familiar, safe territory before the chamberlain could overtake me.

I learned of my success in the very early morning when the tip of Fernan's boot jostled my elbow. I had been sleeping prone on the kitchen floor, and it took some moments for the sticky cobwebs of slumber to clear from my head.

"Up you get!" he whispered. "We have a long road ahead!"

When I realized that he was taking me to the abbey, my heart leapt into my throat, but I was careful not to show my excitement. Fernan turned his back while I took off my nightcap and pulled a dress over my chemise. I silently gathered my few belongings, including the stone collection, and placed them in my bag. The morning was mercifully cooler than the day before, but there was no need for a cloak. I pinned my plaits together and covered my head with the gray coif that I reserved for rare trips outside the manor.

As we left the kitchen, I cast a glance at the bulky form of the laundress, who lay sprawled in her scant underclothes, glistening with sweat in the weak light of dawn that filtered through the skylights. I prayed that I might not meet her again.

6

ELLIS ABBEY

Fernan led me silently to the stable. His demeanor was less friendly than the night before, but I didn't care. Everything made me want to sing for joy: the rosy dawn giving way to the brilliant light of day, the dew that soaked my shoes, the sweet scent of woodbine. I stopped at the rain barrel to rinse my face and ran to catch up to Fernan, who strode ahead. He walked with a springy lope, leaving dark imprints in glittering patches of sunlit dew. It pleased me that I could copy his long stride, for I nearly matched his height. I imagined that we were a pair of wolves slinking over the dappled grass.

The stableboy had already saddled Fernan's rounsey, a silvery gray mare named Perla. I was to ride pillion behind Fernan, and there was a moment of awkwardness when it became apparent that I did not know how to mount a horse. There was no resemblance to a graceful wolf in the way I struggled to get my leg over the horse's back. Through some combination of Fernan pulling and the boy pushing, I was finally settled with my bag in front of me, gripping the back of Fernan's saddle.

Fortunately, Perla was a good ambler, and though Fernan told me that I rode like a bag of barley, I was soon able to relax my grip and take in my surroundings. Fernan rarely spoke, and I tried to ignore his broad back in front of me; something about the way his thin tunic rolled across his shoulders and clung to his skin as the morning grew warmer made me uncomfortable.

August is a busy month in the countryside. Fruit pickers swarmed the orchards, and the boughs of trees trembled under the weight of climbers. Women and children milled among the stands carrying baskets, yelling objections when they were struck by apples falling from above. The fields too were humming with industry, as every available pair of hands had been conscripted for the wheat and rye harvest. Teams of reapers crept alongside golden palisades of grain, felling stalks with flashing sickles, while binders followed behind, gathering swaths into bundles. The weather had cooperated that year, remaining dry and unusually hot for the whole week, and while the harvesters no doubt cursed the heat, they would be grateful for an easy harvest. I knew that my father and brother would be somewhere among the workers in the fields, but I could not make them out that day.

The dry weather sped our travel, and we were soon beyond the boundaries of Aviceford Manor's demesne. As the sun climbed steeply overhead, we entered a small market town, which Fernan told me was called Old Hilgate. It was a rank and cheerless place, with rickety market stalls made of wood and cob, some of them three stories high, crowding the narrow, rutted street. Perla had to pick her way through streaks of rubbish strewn from doors and windows, and entrances to side alleys were choked with barrels, broken crates, and other detritus. Few townsfolk roamed the streets, because it was not a market day, and shops were closed.

Fernan told me that on market day, the town would be transformed as people from the countryside and manors poured in. The shops were thrown open, the streets teemed with bustling crowds, and the alehouse filled to overflowing. Music and banter enlivened the now quiet marketplace as goods were bought and sold, gossip exchanged, news delivered, flirtations traded. "Even a serious girl like you might find it to your liking," Fernan said. Though I couldn't see his face, I knew that he was smiling.

When we reached the market cross, Fernan pulled Perla to a halt. "We should stop here to eat," he said, pointing to a squat building; a garlanded alestake jutted from the thatch roof. "The ale is usually watery, but the food is not too bad." He held out his hand to me, but I did not immediately understand that he meant for me to dismount. He heaved a sigh, and turning in his saddle, grasped me around the waist. I yelped with surprise as he hoisted me from my perch and slid me halfway down Perla's flank before dropping me to the ground. I landed unharmed, though his grip had been disagreeably firm. More than anything, my dignity was bruised.

"I do not enjoy being treated like a child!"

"Then dismount like a lady next time. Do me a favor and hold the reins."

I took the reins grudgingly while he jumped down and strode into the alehouse to find someone to feed and water the horse. He brought back an urchin with a dirty face and a runny nose, and we left Perla in his care.

The alehouse, which was smoky and poorly lit by a few tallow candles and a halfhearted fire, was furnished with four long tables, all empty except for a clutter of flagons at the farthest ends. The straw on the floor was moldering and matted down, littered with food scraps that had been left untroubled for some time.

We took seats nearest the only window, hoping that a breeze would diminish the stink of tallow and rot, and a stout alewife came to take our order. Her surly expression softened as Fernan chaffed her good-naturedly. The ale she served us was indeed watered down and had a bitter taste, but the meat pie was decent, as was the applemoyse. Given the uncleanliness of the alehouse and the poor quality of the ale, it did not surprise me to discover that the alewife's daughter did the cooking. She should have done the cleaning as well.

Fernan jollied me as he did the alewife, and I soon forgave him for shoving me from the horse. As we finished our dinner, I asked him how he had learned to read and write. I had never known anyone but priests and noblemen to be lettered, and I felt the prickings of envy. Fernan did not object to answering my question; indeed, he seemed to relish the sound of his own voice.

"I learned to read Latin when I was a child in Aquitaine. I grew up on the fringes of the court of Edward of Woodstock, Prince of Wales . . . He was Prince of Aquitaine too, of course."

I knew nothing of Aquitaine or princes, so I held my tongue.

"When my father was a young knight living in Castile, he was conscripted into service by the prince. As he told it to me, my father took no notice of the quarrel over the Castilian crown, as he had not a drop of Castilian blood in his body. He was a heathen from Granada."

My spine stiffened at the word "heathen."

"My father was a mercenary. He was a skilled knight, and he served the prince well. Edward of Woodstock was a fierce warrior—as well as a fine leader—and my father admired him." Fernan paused and glanced out the window. The sunlight made

his amber eyes glow bright. When he looked back down at his cup, his eyes seemed an ordinary dull brown, like tiny lanterns that had been extinguished.

"My father pledged fealty to the prince. He followed Edward to Aquitaine and converted to Christianity. That is how I came to be born in Aquitaine. My father taught me horsemanship and swordsmanship, and the prince allowed me to be educated with boys in his court." He grinned at me, perhaps aware of both my awe and my defensiveness about my ignorance. "That, laundry girl," he said, "is how I learned to read and write."

"What of your mother?"

"I never knew her. My father told me that she was godly and fair."

"Have you any brothers or sisters?"

"Nay, none."

"How did you come to England?"

"My father died of consumption. When the prince moved back to England, he brought me with him and left me under the authority of Mother Elfilda, his father's second cousin."

"Why are you not a knight?"

Fernan smiled and leaned back against the wall, swinging his legs onto the bench. "Is this an inquisition? You should tell me about how you came to be a laundry girl at Aviceford Manor."

"I was the second daughter, my mother died, my father couldn't keep me. I needed to eat."

"You might consider embellishing your story just a trifle for the sake of the listener."

"I don't like embellishment. Why are you not a knight?"

"Being a knight is not just about being able to ride a horse and fight, Agnes. The English consider me to be lowborn."

"Even though your father was a knight?"

"He was not an *English* knight."

"I see. Well then, how did you become a messenger?"

"Mother Elfilda decided that since I can read, write, ride, and handle a sword, I would make an excellent messenger. And I am good, if I dare say so. I like it too. The work pays well, because of the danger. And I meet so many pretty girls."

"Don't tease." My voice sounded severe to my own ears. "What danger?"

"I could get saddle sores."

"A tender arse is indeed a handicap."

"Whatever happened to 'yes, *sir*' and 'no, *sir*'?"

"I am a lady's maid now. And you are not so much older than me . . . *Sir*."

He laughed, baring his gleaming teeth. "You are not as staid as you pretend!"

I opened my mouth to ask another question, but he cut me off, saying, "We should be going. We have hours yet to ride, and you don't seem to run out of questions!" When he slapped tenpence on the board, my expression must have betrayed my thoughts, for he laughed again, saying, "I told you that I am well paid!"

We rode the rest of the way mostly in silence, and I was content to be left to my own happy thoughts. God had opened a window for me, and I flew forth like an arrow, growing dizzy with my rise. Already the manor seemed like a dark blot far beneath me.

As we neared the abbey, the trees grew thicker and more wild. Ellis Abbey was built on Ellismere Island, which was not truly an island, for it attached to the shore of the lake by a thin isthmus.

The island was thickly forested, an empty wilderness except for the abbey and a hunting lodge owned by the king.

We were nearly upon the abbey when it came into view. The entire compound was enclosed by a massive stone wall that could have served as fortification for a castle; beyond the enclosure, alabaster spires soared to the sky like pale fingers stretching toward heaven. The lake was a dark mirror, a reflection of the blue sky and soft clouds, and it seemed that the Kingdom of God was everywhere around us, just beyond reach.

My heart quickened as we passed through the shadow of the open gate. Over the crown of the arch, three words were carved deeply into the moss-blackened stone.

"What is written there?" I asked.

"It says, 'Welcome, Cinder Girl!'"

I didn't gratify him with a laugh, and he couldn't see my smile.

The abbey was built so that the first view encountered by a visitor was of a road, perfectly straight, flanked by rows of magnificent elm trees. At the end of the road, framed by the elms, was the ghostly face of the church. High walls and a vaulted stone roof were supported by swooping flying buttresses, giving the appearance of a white bird about to take flight. The outside wall of the nave was adorned with a rose window and steeply pointed lancets alternating with decorative arcading. The church did not seem high-wrought, but airy and graceful, aspiring skyward.

We did not take the road toward the church, but turned aside, toward the stable. We passed a rose garden and a fishpond, and then a field of brilliant purple lavender. My most fevered imaginings could not have matched the beauty of the place.

Fernan left Perla with the stableboy and ushered me with my small bundle toward the dormitory, a long building that enclosed

one side of the cloister behind the church. "You had better clean yourself while I inquire about whether Mother Elfilda might receive you," he said.

I had washed my face in the rain barrel that morning, but no matter, I was not going to argue. Fernan left me at the entrance of the dormitory and told me to wait while he sent one of the sisters to help me. I sat on the stoop, inhaling the sweet, hot scent of summer, watching bees drone drunkenly from one clover to the next. The queasy fluttering in my stomach settled; I was too happy to be worried.

I took the stones out of my bundle and held the most treasured ones in my hand. I thought of myself as grown up, but I had yet to put all childish things aside. I had not added to the collection since the day I left home, as any association with the manor would only tarnish it. While the green stone was always my favorite, on this day the white stone seemed almost as precious. It was small and many-faceted, and it glittered in the sunlight. The stone, in its simplicity and inconsequence, seemed as much an inspiration to modesty and purity as the abbey itself.

I nearly fell backward when a nun opened the door behind me; my pebbles clattered on the flagstones as I hastened to kneel.

"Get up, then. I've come to give you a bath. I am Sister Marjorie." Her voice rasped like dry leaves. "Follow me."

I scrambled to gather my belongings and followed the shuffling nun into a sunlit arcade. The stone floor was worn to a smooth polish in the most trafficked areas; to one side stood a wall of columns, clusters of slender, dark marble stems surrounding fluted central pillars. Slanting shafts of light created shadow doubles of the columns on the floor separated by bright arches. Sister Marjorie's white veil glowed when she passed through the luminous half-moons.

The sound of falling water came from the cloister, and I glimpsed a fountain and a profusion of flowers before we entered the dormitory. I wondered why such a magical place would be deserted.

Sister Marjorie led me slowly from one end of the long dorter to the other. She was so short that from the back, she would have looked like a child were it not for the stoop of her shoulders. Besides mattresses lining each wall, the enormous room was empty of furniture and clean as a pin. The floor was strewn with fresh rushes, the walls were free of black woodsmoke stains, and sweet air blew from open windows. Trees growing near the casements dappled everything with light and pearl gray shadow that shimmered when the wind blew. The dormitory seemed a comfortably cool place to sleep, though I would discover in winter that the cold could bite, for there was no fireplace.

At the far end of the dorter was the warming room; fires were allowed there, but none was lit on such a warm summer day. The windows were mere slits near the ceiling, better suited to letting smoke and steam escape than allowing sunlight to enter. Whitewashed walls, the scent of rosewater, and two fat, gleaming copper tubs made the room inviting despite the dim light. One of the tubs was still filled with unheated gray water; on the surface, a film of soap scum made lazy swirls.

"Leave your dress on the floor. I shall bring you a clean frock." The nun handed me a lump of soap and padded slowly to a linen chest.

With a shiver of pleasure, I remembered that I would not have to do the laundry. I said a silent prayer of thanks, for I could scarcely believe my good fortune. I tossed aside my clothing and climbed into the tub; I was too tall to fit properly, and with my knees folded near my ears, I must have looked like a giant cricket.

A few rays of sunlight angled steeply across the warming room, plucking golden notes from the burnished belly of the empty copper tub next to mine. I watched as a spider lowered itself toward the tub on a wisp of thread. It became transfixed in the path of a sunbeam and froze, spinning perilously, so I reached over and broke its web with my finger, lowering it safely to the floorboards. "Godspeed!" I whispered as it darted into the shadows.

Sister Marjorie returned carrying a scrub brush and a gray woolen gown very like her own habit. I did not like the idea of being scrubbed or having to wear such a hot, itchy frock, but I was too happy to really mind. Frail as she appeared, the nun was plenty strong enough to scour me to a bright pink. She informed me that weekly baths were expected at the abbey. This was not as bad as it might sound, for in the winter, though the water in the tub did not stay hot for long, the warming room was cozy with a cheerful fire. Also, once the sisters trusted me to clean myself properly, I was allowed to scrub myself.

Sister Marjorie spoke little; she did not even ask my name. I imagined that at her age, her thoughts were drawn toward the world to come. I dressed in the clean linen chemise from my bundle and the gray frock, which was as disagreeable as it looked. The elderly sister then took me back through the dorter and into the cloister.

The cloister was no longer deserted. A dozen nuns sat upon stone benches or strolled silently along the paths that separated four flower gardens. The paths met in the center of the cloister, where a three-tiered fountain splashed water into a quatrefoil basin of polished black stone. The gardens were full of color at that time of year, flush with pink roses, yellowwort, purple foxglove, mauve centaury.

The ebb and flow of gray-clad vestals in the cloister would become familiar to me in time. Their days, like the phases of the moon, slipped by with quiet regularity. Each nun was assigned her own work to keep the abbey functioning, but everything, even sleep, came second to prayer. Matins, lauds, prime, terce, sext, nones, vespers, and compline were divine duty, prayers that marked the passage of the hours and gave meaning to each day. When the bell sounded its sonorous peal, the abbey, like a beast with one single heart and mind, fell at once into worship.

Sister Marjorie approached one of the other nuns in the cloister. They murmured quietly, the taller nun bending to hear, their veils drooping together, hiding their faces. Sister Marjorie pointed at me and then beckoned me to approach. The other nun had a round face, and her smooth cheeks dimpled when she smiled at me. "My name is Sister Marjorie also," she said. "That will make it easy for you to remember. The sisters call me Marge. What is your name, dear?"

"My name is Agnes, Sister."

"That is a lovely, holy name. Sister Marjorie tells me that I am to take you to meet Mother Elfilda in the chapter house." She looked at me appraisingly. "Do you know proper manners for an audience with the abbess?"

"No, Sister." I swallowed nervously.

"Come with me. We shall wait in the vestibule of the chapter house, and I shall explain what you need to do."

We crossed the cloister to a faceted round building with a vaulted roof. It was nearly as ornate as the church, with towering stained-glass lancets and decorative moldings. The nun ushered me into a dark, cool anteroom and indicated that I should sit on a stone bench that jutted from the wall. Low voices from the inner

chamber drifted toward us, but I could not make out any words. While we waited, several laymen wearing country clothes arrived and sat in patient silence across from us. I recognized one of them as the reeve from Aviceford Manor; he must have had a special petition for the abbess.

Sister Marjorie bent her freckled face toward me and instructed me in a barely audible whisper. "When you enter the chamber, kneel in the doorway, and then progress to the middle of the chamber, where you must kneel again. Do not move unless Mother Elfilda beckons you forward. When the prioress tells you to stop, kneel again and wait until you are spoken to. When you are requested to speak, always begin with a greeting. Bow on each occasion you are asked to speak. Do you understand?"

I felt a stab of doubt; I was not sure that I had followed what she had said, and it was all foreign to me, but I nodded anyway.

"Now, sit quietly," she whispered. "Someone will come for you when they are ready. The prioress is fitting you in between appointments, so it will be a quick audience." She smiled at me encouragingly and then crept away, leaving me alone.

It felt like hours before the heavy chapter house door swung open and a group of sisters swept out, their white veils billowing behind them. One of them signaled to me that I should enter, so I edged uncertainly toward the door as they filed past. When I reached the threshold, I knelt and looked up. I had a fleeting, fanciful idea that I had entered a jeweled forest. Colors from the stained glass mixed with shadows in a way that reminded me of light filtered through a canopy of trees, and the ceiling was so distant and dark that it might not have been there at all. At the far end of the room was a dais, and upon the dais, in an ornately carved chair, sat the abbess. The prioress stood stiffly next to her, vigilant and obe-

dient. Over the top of a brass lectern in the shape of an eagle, the tip of a quill bobbed; the nun who wrote with the quill was short enough to be invisible to me.

Mother Elfilda motioned to me with her hand, and I moved to the center of the chamber and knelt again as I had been told to do. The prioress clucked impatiently and said, "Come here, girl! You are not a tortoise."

I approached the dais, kneeling for the third time. Mother Elfilda was tiny and delicate, like a child pretending to be king on her father's throne. Her exquisite features might have been carved from alabaster, so white and still was her face. She wore the same gray habit and spotless wimple as the other nuns, though her veil was longer, and a heavy gold cross hung from her neck. I could tell from the fine, pale arches of her eyebrows that she was fair, and her eyes were the color of robins' eggs.

"Who might this be?" Mother Elfilda's voice had the pure timbre of a Sanctus bell.

I was not sure whether she had addressed me, but as the prioress glared at me with her close-set dark eyes, I croaked a nervous reply. "God bless you, my lady, I am Agnes come from Aviceford Manor to work as a chambermaid."

"Chambermaid? But there are no ladies' maids at Aviceford. Oh—you must be the one sent to help Mary with Rose House. You know how to clean properly, I hope? The work at Rose House is not heavy, but you can help in the laundry if you have spare time."

That I was not to be a lady's maid felt like a truth I had known all along but had been too stupid to acknowledge. Of course the laundress had exaggerated the desirability of the post in order to make me feel worse for not being able to take it. Why had it not occurred to me before? She would have wanted the post for herself

if it had truly been so good. I had come to the abbey to do the same sort of work that I had done at the manor, and the laundress would know it. The cow.

"Take her to Mary so that she can be settled. God be with you, Agnes."

I bowed and took several steps backward before another nun grasped my elbow and escorted me outside. Why had I made such a stupid presumption? Worse, why had I made my presumption known? The abbess seemed to have disregarded my ignorant comment, but I wanted to reach back through time and snatch my words from the air. I cringed when I imagined Fernan discovering my mistake, and then I cringed again when I realized that he had already known the truth when I boasted about being a lady's maid. He had, after all, been the deliverer of the message.

Humiliation is felt most sharply in youth, and it is hard for me now to understand why Elisabeth's deception was so painful to my young self. I did suffer. Eventually, I consoled myself that I was out of the manor, and the abbey was near to paradise itself. I decided that humiliation was my punishment for the sin of pride, which I should tear from my soul by its roots.

ROSE HOUSE

Mary was in charge of maintaining the residential building, otherwise known as Rose House, one of many outbuildings in the abbey's compound. Due to its isolation, the abbey had to be self-sufficient, and the outbuildings included an infirmary, a guest-house, a bakery, a brewery, workshops, a laundry, and, of course, barns, stables, a henhouse, and a pigsty. Beyond those buildings lay vegetable gardens, orchards, modest grain fields, and a mill where the nuns ground their own wheat.

Rose House could accommodate up to four residents, and it was usually populated by affluent pensioners. During the time that I worked at the abbey, however, the whole building had been turned over to the abbess's mother, the dowager countess of Wenslock. Lady Wenslock was cousin to the former king, and she was exceedingly wealthy in her own right. It was gossip among the servants that she chose to live at the abbey in order to atone for whatever sins had led to her eldest daughter's madness. Providence had marked very different fates for the two living fruit of Lady Wens-lock's womb. Abbess Elfilda had become a powerful instrument of

God, a mystic and philosopher, whereas Lady Alba had fallen prey to the devil, descending into lunacy and delirium. Had I foreseen the hand that Lady Alba would eventually play in my own fate, I might have listened to the gossip with more interest.

While Rose House was beneath the means of its noble denizen, it was not rustic. Each of the four apartments boasted a sizable hall decorated with tapestries, carved panels, and moldings, and Lady Wenslock had brought furniture, statuary, and silver with her. There were separate solars for sleeping and sitting, and the garderobes were comfortable. Because Lady Wenslock had claimed the largest apartment and made annexes of the other three, she dedicated chambers for music, embroidery, reading, dining, and receiving guests. Many times each year, visitors made the trip from the city to stay with her and enjoy a quiet retreat. For the wealthy, this was a pilgrimage to a holy place, as Ellis Abbey was a sanctuary where God's presence could be felt most powerfully.

Although Lady Wenslock did not live like an anchoress, she did not have all of the comforts customary to a woman of her rank either. Her needs were attended to primarily by Mary, a young woman who had graduated from the nunnery's school. Mary, in turn, had but one servant working exclusively for her—the position that I would fill—though she could borrow from other parts of the abbey when necessary. Visitors to Rose House brought their own servants, and all of the cooking took place in the abbey's kitchens, but due to the fluctuating number of visitors, the amount of work necessary for upkeep of the residential building was unpredictable from week to week.

I met Mary in the main hall, which, despite its grandeur, was almost cozy, as it was crammed with draperies, decorative furniture,

artwork, and bagatelles. I wondered whether Lady Wenslock had tried to stuff the furnishings of an entire castle into Rose House.

Mary herself was a far less interesting sight. She was angular and thin, with a wan, pinched face and furrows between her brows that belied her years. Her gray frock flapped loose, and the way her pointed chin jutted forward on her long neck made me think of a chicken. She greeted me politely enough and asked about my experience.

"I did all manner of work at Aviceford Manor," I lied. "I can do whatever is needed, be it cleaning, polishing, provisioning, tending the fires, smoothing or repairing her ladyship's garments, or running errands." Anything Mary asked me to do would be better than working in the laundry.

"My lady countess is exacting. She has requested a new servant from Wenslock Castle; the girl will come next month when her ladyship's niece visits the abbey. In the meanwhile, I expect you to do the cleaning, keep the buttery and woodpile stocked, and tend the fires if the evenings and mornings become cooler. I tend to my lady's person and wardrobe." She sniffed. "Your duty is to stay out of her ladyship's sight."

Mary stiffened as the dowager countess herself entered the hall. Despite a slow and faltering step, she looked like a galleon, her ample bust leading the way, her gauzy white wimple tented on both sides of her face like sails. She wore a green velvet gown embroidered with gold thread, but no jewels save a brooch in the shape of a cross. To my astonishment, she made straight for me. I knelt hastily, bruising my knee. Lady Wenslock took a wheezy breath, saying, "You must be the one come to fill in for poor Lizzie. I hope that you will find Rose House to your liking. Mary will help you."

As I stared with round eyes, Mary said, "I was just going to explain her chores, my lady." Her expression was sour.

The countess lowered herself carefully into a chair, deflating like a bread loaf taken out of the oven on a cold day. "First, fetch my Book of Psalms, and bring that stool closer so that I can raise my feet." She looked at me and smiled, the wrinkles on her face rearranging themselves; tiny sunbursts appeared in the corners of her eyes. "Stand up, child. What is your name?"

"My name is Agnes, my lady. God bless you, my lady," I added quickly.

As Mary left to find the psalter, Lady Wenslock sighed, saying, "I don't suppose that you can read, young Agnes."

"No, my lady."

"Mary can read, but she has no feeling for it. She makes prayers sound like an accounting of the wheat harvest. I have asked my niece to find me a girl who understands the words she reads. Of course, such a girl would refuse to work for Mary, and Mary is such a good girl."

I shifted my weight from one foot to the other, wondering what I should do.

"I believe that girls should be taught to read and write. My daughter's treatise on the spiritual weapons required to defeat evil is considered as wise and important as any recent written work. Perhaps even divinely inspired. Imagine what ideas are locked up in the hearts and minds of women who simply lack the tools to express them."

Mary had returned, carrying the book.

"Do you not agree, Mary?"

"My lady, your most holy daughter is a marvel and a gift to us all straight from God," Mary said with sudden passion, "but I

know my place at your feet and at Mother Elfilda's feet as sure as Agnes knows hers."

"Your humility does you credit, Mary. True nobility comes from being humble, benign, and courteous. Without these key qualities, all other virtues are worthless." She took the psalter from Mary and opened it, holding the book at arm's length and tilting her head back. We waited several moments, but she ignored us, so we curtsied and Mary led me away.

"My lady countess is most devout."

"She is kind."

"Yes," said Mary acerbically, "he that hath pity upon the poor lendeth unto the Lord. This is one of her many favorite sayings."

"What happened to Lizzie? The girl who was here before me?"

"Lizzie got herself with child."

"Lady Wenslock must have been greatly aggrieved!"

"Quite the contrary. It was Mother Elfilda who threw her out. Lady Wenslock would not throw a stray dog out of the house."

I had the impression that Mary did not approve of Lady Wenslock's lenience. She showed me the rest of Rose House, which was equally crowded with furniture and decorative objects, some beautiful, some strange. I wanted to pause to admire each one, but Mary kept a brisk pace.

The room that impressed me most was the library. Mary explained that the countess had collected over two hundred books in her lifetime, a sum that was incomprehensible to me. She had donated most of the books to the abbey's large library, but she kept some of her favorites at Rose House, heavy leather-bound tomes chained to lecterns. The library was the brightest room in the building and also the most spare. White damask embroidered with *W*'s encircled by gold crowns draped the lecterns, and the walls

were lined with matching simple white tapestries, showing what I assumed to be the arms of the late Count of Wenslock and edged with the same crowned initial. The room was otherwise bare of furniture and art.

"Can you read those books?" I asked, delighted by the romance of the room.

"Nay!" She looked shocked. "I am not allowed to touch them! And you may not enter the library except to dust."

She pointed out the buttery, and then we left Rose House to visit the brewery and the kitchen where I would fetch Lady Wenslock's meals. Mary explained that the nuns took their meals in silence, and the countess preferred to eat alone or with her guests when she had visitors. I would have to bring the tray of food to Rose House and then dash back to the dining hall so that I could partake at the servants' table. Although not bound by vows, the servants were not allowed to break the silence either. This sounded dreary to me, but Mary did not seem to mind. I suppose that she was used to it from her years at the convent school.

I came to find out that Mary was the daughter of a baronet, and she had been sent to the abbey as a child, biding her time until her parents could find a suitable husband. Since the baronet was not exceptionally rich, and since Mary did not possess beauty or charm to overcome her lack of a fortune, eligible men proved elusive. As the bloom of youth fell away, her prospects dimmed further. She was content to become a nun, but her father had not yet given up his ambition of finding a match that would elevate the family's fortunes, and so she waited patiently, caring for Lady Wenslock.

Though Mary was gentle born and austere by nature, she did not treat me unkindly. To my relief, even though I sometimes finished my work early, Mary never sent me to help in the abbey's

laundry. I discovered in those first weeks that she preferred me to do my work without consulting her, and as long as we did not have guests, she did not mind me visiting the cloister or the rose garden if I had time.

Rose House was named for the adjacent rose garden, and I had a favorite spot, a sun-warmed stone bench facing a bowered path to the fishpond. I liked the chatter of birds and shimmer of water through the tangled vines. As summer drew to an end, there were few blooms left, but the air still held the lingering scent of roses. Sometimes I collected fallen petals for the sisters who made aromatic water and salt paste. To this day, the smell of roses transports me back to a time when the breeze, the sun, the reflections of water on a bowered path were an unspoken promise from God.

One day Fernan's silhouette blackened the arch of the bower; I recognized him by his broad shoulders and easy lope. The gravel crunched under his heavy boots as he approached, flashing his bright smile.

"How goes the life of leisure for the new lady's maid?"

I colored, remembering my mistake. "You know perfectly well that I am not a lady's maid. But I am doing fine, thank you."

He threw down his satchel and sat beside me on the bench. "I am very glad to hear it. You look well. Now I can see your pretty face without the soot. You look rested. And your hands are no longer blistered." To my shock, he took my hand from where it rested on the bench and stroked it lightly. I snatched it back without thinking, as though his touch burned. He paid no attention.

"How do you find life at the abbey?"

My mouth was dry. "It is heaven. Mother Elfilda is a saint. Lady Wenslock is too." I wanted to slide farther away from him, but it seemed like an awkward thing to do. The flesh on my hand tingled.

"Have you figured out yet how to make your post permanent?"

"No. A new girl is supposed to come next week. I had managed to put out of my mind the knowledge that I would be sent back to the manor. I did not want to think about it. Frustration rose like gorge to my throat. "You are so fortunate! You can come and go as you please. I . . ." I lowered my voice. "I am not free."

Fernan looked at me thoughtfully. "Maybe it is unjust that my father was a knight and yours is a peasant. But you were born with some advantages. You are smart and pretty. And resourceful. Your life is only beginning."

Nobody had ever described me as pretty before. I looked at him to see if he was making fun of me, but his eyes were serious.

"You really don't know that you are beautiful, do you," he said.

I looked down at my big hands and long, tapering fingers. "My father always called me an ox. He told me that I wouldn't need a dowry because I could pull a plough as well as any team."

"Being strong does not disqualify you from being beautiful."

"Beautiful for a plough-beast." I ducked my head, but I felt a flush of pleasurable warmth, along with a tangle of feelings that I could not identify. "I have to get back to work."

I stood abruptly, but he rose at the same time, very close to me, so that my eyes were level with the opening of his collar and the hollow at the base of his brown neck. I could not breathe until he stepped away with a small bow. He picked up his satchel and adjusted the strap across his chest. "I hope to still find you here after next week. I shall look for you here in the garden whenever I pass by on my way from the stables."

As I watched him walk away, I resolved to never linger in the rose garden again. A moment later, I wondered how often he visited the abbey.

Mary and Lady Wenslock attended Mass daily, and Mary did not mind if I did too, as long as we were not too busy. Mary and the countess set out much earlier than I, for Lady Wenslock walked slowly, and she preferred to arrive and settle herself before the gray flock of sisters rushed silently into the church.

Mass was my favorite part of every day. The church building itself was enough to induce rapture; I believed that no heathen could enter it without being compelled to fall immediately on his knees and praise God. The sheer height filled me with awe. The walls ascended like cliffs to the dizzying apex of the vaulted roof, the columns virtually disappearing into the shadowy reaches. Gold stars had been painted between the ribs of the vaulting, adding to the illusion of infinite distance, and jeweled rose windows floated mysteriously in the blackness, seemingly without support. During the Latin Mass, I would gaze at the paintings of the stations of the cross, or at the scenes depicted in the lancet windows, their brilliant images arranged in panels one above another, and try to imagine what it would have been like to have lived in the time of Christ.

The part that I loved most was the sermon by the abbess at the end of Mass. After the priest said *"Benedicamus domino,"* Mother Elfilda would climb the spiral stairs to the pulpit, regal and light as an angel, to address the congregation. She held us in thrall, her command so profound that no cough or rustle could be heard until the last word dropped from her mouth. Her voice would rise, clarion clear, echoing through the nave and choir, and then it would fall to a hush so intimate that I felt she was speaking only to me. It was not only her otherworldliness that held us spellbound, but

the wisdom and dazzling truth of her words. When she reached the most stirring parts of her sermons, her white hands would sometimes lift from the lectern like doves taking flight, but her pale face always remained still and saintly, like the image of the Virgin in the manor's chapel.

In one of the sermons I remember best, Mother Elfilda compared the Virgin Mary to an onyx, the precious stone that opens up to receive a drop of dew when the sun shines on it. After nine months it opens again and another onyx falls out, leaving the original stone unchanged. Mary remained pure, untouched, even as God forced Joseph to wed Mary.

Mother Elfilda did not dwell on Joseph's reluctance, a story I had heard many times, but rather on Mary's reasons for needing to wed Joseph. Marriage was protection against being stoned for adultery, and she needed help for the birth and flight into Egypt. A painting in the church depicted a beatific Mary and baby Jesus on a donkey, the baby's tiny fist clutching at her cloak, and Joseph walking beside them with an expression of grim determination. He was a guard for the Holy Family and a decoy to prevent the devil from identifying Christ.

Another of Mother Elfilda's sermons that affected me deeply was a reminder to the sisters of the symbols that their ordinary clothing represented. Even more than paternoster beads represented prayer, a habit represented contrition and confession, a kirtle trust in God, boots two desires, to amend and to abstain from evil, a girdle restraint of one's will, a wimple abstinence, and a veil obedience. Every part of the sisters' lives perfected the bending of human desire toward God.

Although I was not allowed to quit my duties in order to observe the liturgy of the hours, I began to observe them in secret.

As long as I was alone, when the bell tolled, I knelt wherever I found myself, usually on the cold stones. The ache in my knees caused me to stagger when I tried to stand. At matins, when the sisters slipped quietly from their beds in the dark of night to go to chapel, I rose and knelt beside my mattress, in winter shivering so violently that my teeth knocked together. I willed my soul to forget about its cage, unleash itself, swell past the boundaries of my flesh, and open itself utterly to the Holy Spirit. Sometimes I felt an answer, a warmth blooming deep inside me, a soft unfolding of unspeakable tenderness. When the susurrus of leather-clad feet in the arcade warned of the sisters' return, I was reluctant to crawl back into the cocoon of my blanket.

I did worry that God would be displeased with my unorthodox observance of the hours, or that someone would catch me kneeling alone and accuse me of Lollardry or some other form of heresy. Yet my devotion suffused me with peace and quiet joy, a bright clarity of mind. I began to see tiny pieces of the Kingdom of God all around me, and something as ordinary as the song of a lark could bring tears to my eyes.

ENLIGHTENMENT

A few days after my conversation with Fernan, Mary informed me that Lady Wenslock's niece had delayed her visit until after Michaelmas. I rejoiced in my reprieve, and I did all that I could to make Mary happy. I did not know whether she had any influence over my staying or leaving, but it would do no harm to have her on my side. I made sure that she always had ale on hand from the most recent batch, and I strewed fresh herbs or made bouquets every day. I anticipated where the countess and Mary would sit in the evening, and I prepared a fire ahead of time. In every way, I tried to be helpful but invisible.

Mary spent most of her time with the countess, scribing letters, helping in the dressing room, or, most often, reading to her. She was also responsible for taking her ladyship's gowns to the laundry and arranging her wardrobe. She devoted little time to inspecting my work and even less to telling me how to do it. I liked to plan my own days and keep my own counsel.

One day, when Mary was away, I came upon Lady Wenslock sitting alone. She wore a glossy marmalade gown that swallowed

the chair beneath her, and her hair was covered as usual by a wimple that flared like wings, maintaining its complex structure by means I could not fathom. I was hoping to leave unnoticed, but she looked up from her book and beckoned to me.

"Come here, come here. I need someone to read to me." Her loose jowls trembled when she spoke.

I curtsied, bowing deeply. "I beg your pardon, my lady, but I cannot read." I wondered if she was touched.

"No matter, come here."

I walked to her side and stood obediently.

"Do you know what book this is?"

I had heard Mary reading to her from it many times. "Your psalter, my lady."

"Very good. What psalms do you know?"

"I know several by heart, my lady. I do not know the numbers."

"Recite one now for me."

I began with the first one that came to my mind. "'By the rivers of Babylon, there we sat down, we wept, when we remembered Zion. We hanged our harps upon the willows.'" I relished the words that tumbled from my tongue, a long string of ancient and perfectly polished phrases that belonged to other people, in other times, and yet lived somewhere inside me. As I spoke the last line, a chill trickled down my spine: "'Happy shall he be, that taketh and dasheth thy little ones against the stones.'"

"Wonderful! That is not a psalm for the faint of heart. You have remembered nearly every word correctly, and you spoke them with feeling. Well done. Now, that is Psalm 137 . . ." She opened the book to a page illuminated with angels, trees, flowers, and a river of turquoise and purple.

"These are the words you spoke. Do you know this letter?" She

pointed to a bulbous, richly colored rendering of the letter *B* encircled by gold filigree. The figure of Christ crouched in the emptiness created by the top half of the letter, and he reached down to men in the lower half, while they raised their arms longingly toward him.

"That is the letter *B*, my lady." My brother had learned his alphabet at church, and he had taught me most of the letters.

"Good!" Under her drooping lids, her eyes were bright and clever as a raven's. "Then what does this first word say?"

"By?"

"Yes, of course! By. And the next?"

"The."

"Yes!"

"Rivers."

"Yes! Now, if you know your letters, you can tell when you have a word wrong, because you will know that the sound at the beginning of the word is incorrect."

My heart beat like a rabbit's. She smiled at me, pleased. "Go to the solar with the blue canopy and hunting tapestries. You will find several old psalters in the chest there. Bring one to me."

I flew to the room and opened the chest. Something made of gold brocade lay on the top, but when I lifted the folded cloth, I found five books beneath. The covers were worn and undecorated, and when I leafed through the first one, I found the inside plain as well. I brought it back to Lady Wenslock, and she nodded with satisfaction. "I shall mark the pages of the psalms you know so that you may study them. Hand me my embroidery, there."

I lifted her embroidery from the floor, and she cut several lengths of thread. "This first long one marks Psalm 137. Which other psalms do you know?"

"'In the Lord put I my trust. How say ye to my soul, flee as a bird to your mountain . . .'"

"Ah, Psalm 11. 'Upon the wicked he shall rain snares, fire and brimstone, and a horrible tempest: this shall be the portion of their cup.' Very good." She marked another page with a shorter thread. "One more?"

I could not think of another in that moment and shook my head, looking at the floor. "No, my lady."

"No matter, no matter. Take this psalter, child, and study those two psalms. When you have made out all of the words, come back to me, and we shall find two more."

I took the book from her, and she patted my hand; her wrinkled skin was surprisingly soft. Gratitude welled in my heart. *A price far above rubies,* I thought. I could not recall what those words described, but I knew that what she had given me was precious beyond measure.

From that day, I took my psalter with me to the rose garden at every chance. The last blooms had fallen, and the purple lavender was gone, but the trees were beginning to dress for autumn, and the sun on the pond seemed even more brilliant through the thinning vines. I studied the psalter and listened for Fernan's step on the gravel, and after some days, I heard it again. I felt an irrational urge to hide at the sound of his boots. I steadied myself, and he joined me on the bench.

"Agnes, I am glad to see that you are still here."

"Her ladyship's niece delayed her trip until after Michaelmas."

"And what do we have here?"

"A psalter. Of course."

"Of course? But I thought that you could not read!"

"Nor can I. I am learning."

He leaned over my shoulder to look at the page. He smelled of woodsmoke and something foreign, not disagreeable, but earthy. "'For the righteous Lord loveth righteousness; his countenance doth behold the upright.'"

"Can you read it for me? I want to be sure that I have the words right."

He smiled and read the psalm to me. His voice had a pleasant timbre, and his light accent made the words exotic. Desert, mountains, rain of brimstone, tempests of fire, he made these as real as the garden around us.

"Shall I test you? What does this say?"

He pointed to words on the page and I read them. I had been studying the psalm for some time.

"You are a scholar, cinder girl." He regarded me warmly. His eyes were a deep amber-flecked brown, fringed with long black lashes that would be the envy of any woman. "Do you want me to help you with your reading?"

I nodded.

"I shall give you a parchment," he said, removing a sheet no bigger than my hand from his satchel. "You must find a quill and ink. We shall make it a game. As you learn words from your psalter, you can use them to write a letter to me. When you have filled this parchment, give it to me, and I shall check it for errors." He leaned close, and I could feel his warm breath as he murmured, "Write something nice. At your core, you are soft and sweet." He ran a fingertip lightly over the gooseflesh on my neck before getting up to leave.

I stayed rooted to the bench, clutching the parchment in my lap,

as the crunch of Fernan's boots grew fainter. My stomach tumbled. I could not tell dread from longing. The sliver of space that had separated his shoulder from mine as we sat together on the bench had pulsed with warmth, and just as when a cat jumps down from your knee, the cold that replaced it was made more profound by its emptiness.

I did not move for a long time, letting the chill of the autumn breeze blow away the memory of his touch. I wanted him to come back; I wanted to lean against his broad chest, feel his warmth surround me. I wanted him to never return. Something about him sickened me. He made me feel as though I were descending to a dark place, as though he were choking off the light and air above me.

After more than an hour, the church bell tolled for none. I rose stiffly from the cold stone bench to kneel on the gravel. I closed my eyes, welcoming the cleansing pain. I let it wash over me, purify me. Roiling excitement and disgust thinned and parted like clouds revealing a patch of blue sky. With growing clarity of mind, I realized what I had to do.

The Holy Spirit was telling me to devote my life to God. This was why I had been sent to the abbey, why the countess was teaching me to read psalms, and why Fernan filled me with confusion. My heart yearned for the pure, celestial element of air, not the base, dark element of earth. Every sign pointed in the same direction, toward God, only I had been too blind until now to see it.

I would become a bride of the Lord, a maidservant, allow myself to be absorbed into the body of the church. I would never be parted from Mother Elfilda, who was as beautiful as an angel and as wise as a saint. I would do anything she asked of me. Being near her was more worldly reward than I deserved.

My heart grew wings as I thought about spending my life at

the abbey, learning, praying, devoting my body and soul to God. When I stood again, I felt a new peace and sense of purpose. I tucked the parchment into my pocket and returned to Rose House.

September passed swiftly. I did not spend time in the rose garden anymore, but I continued to study my psalter when time permitted. I convinced Mary to teach me new psalms; though I was too timid to admit to her that I was trying to learn how to read, Mary soon found out. Lady Wenslock had me recite psalms to her on occasion, and she marked new ones in my psalter, which slowly filled with colorful embroidery thread. The more words I learned to read, the easier it became for me to memorize new psalms, and the countess was pleased with my progress.

I told no one about my plan to join the nunnery. I was most frightened of telling Mother Elfilda, but the idea of returning to the manor was unthinkable, and so I requested an audience with the abbess. I received no response, and as Michaelmas approached, I became increasingly nervous. I prayed and prayed. The Holy Ghost whispered to my heart: an audience would come.

On the eve of Michaelmas, I had to accept that I was not going to have the opportunity to speak with the abbess. I told myself that I should not have expected an audience; Mother Elfilda had great responsibilities. She had authority not only over the convent but over the abbey's vast holdings, which meant that except for the king and the bishop, there was no higher ruler, judge, or spiritual guide for the souls occupying the abbey's lands. A request from a domestic servant was doubtless of lowest priority on a long list of petitions she received daily. Still, I had been so certain of an answer. It had seemed like divine will.

It was with great heaviness of spirit that I readied Rose House for Lady Wenslock's guests. After days of preparation, only the finishing touches remained. I found bright yellow hawkbit growing near the fishpond, and I mixed these with lacy hogweed to decorate the bedchambers. I put fresh linens on the beds, replaced every candle, and burnished the countess's silver ornaments one last time. Finally, I fetched barrels of fresh ale from the brewery and arranged them in the buttery.

The outriders arrived near noon and alerted the grooms to be ready to receive the horses. Mary ordered me to fetch four more servants from the abbey to help with unloading. I was taken aback, because I had been told to expect only three guests, the countess's niece and two other ladies. Mary smiled cynically. "An honorable life may not consist in the abundance of one's possessions, but status certainly does. You are not used to the ways of the wealthy. Next to her peers, my lady countess lives like a pauper."

I could not imagine any pauper living like Lady Wenslock, but when I saw the packhorses, carriage, carts, and wagons, I understood the need for many hands. A uniformed guard opened the door of a peculiar bulbous carriage emblazoned with the royal arms, and three ladies in rustling silks stepped down. Six other guards waited idly for grooms to take their horses, while the ladies' servants and I bustled in and out of Rose House, carrying chests, trunks, carpets, and trundles, listening carefully for Mary's instructions. I looked around, wondering which of the women was to be my replacement.

The week after Michaelmas was a blur for me. There was much to do to keep the guests comfortable, and I was busy from dawn

until long past dusk. I could not even take time to attend Mass, and I was tortured by the thought that I was missing Mother Elfilda's sermons during my last days at the abbey. Even when I had time to eat, I hardly touched my food. I receded from the world like a wave sliding back along the shore.

Then, one day, the guests departed, and life at Rose House returned to normal. Nobody told me to leave, and no new servant appeared. When I asked Mary about it, she merely shrugged and said, "I told you that my lady countess would not put a stray dog out of the house."

This was how I learned that I would be allowed to stay on at the abbey. I would like to say that I felt overwhelming relief, but for some time I felt only disorientation. Never before had the complete absence of an event changed my life so profoundly. It was as though I had prepared for a blow that never came, but I was unable to let my body unclench. I went about my life as before, not quite believing that any of it was real.

I immersed myself more than ever in my psalter. To supplement my reading, I began to write on the parchment that Fernan had given me, using a quill and ink that the younger Sister Marjorie took from the abbey's scriptorium. I told her that I was copying psalms, and she said that God would approve of that use of the abbey's writing supplies. I wrote slowly and awkwardly, sometimes hunting for days for a single word. My choice of words was limited to those that appeared in my psalms, and I had only a small piece of parchment to record them, so I had to choose and scribe with care.

I did not see Fernan anymore, and I had no intention of showing him my work. Nevertheless, I would be lying if I said that I had not

been writing for him. In a childlike way, I imagined him finding the parchment. He would read the painstakingly selected words, and his eyes would widen in wonder. He would shake his head in disbelief that an uncouth maid like me could produce such radiant sentences. Sometimes in my imagination, I would be standing before him, and he would take my hand and tell me that I was clever. The image caused a pleasurable flutter, but I never imagined him doing more than taking my hand.

Autumn grew colder and darker, and the first snow fell. I found it difficult to sleep at night, for even with the shutters closed, the frigid wind whistled through the paneless windows of the dorter. There were moans and grumbles throughout the long night, as the nuns also slept poorly. In the gray dawn, our breath became fog, and sometimes our coarse wool blankets were white with hoarfrost. Nature compensated for its cruelty, however, when the sun rose full on pristine snow. I liked to kick the glinting powder in the air on my walk to Rose House, keeping my cold fingers tucked under my arms and thinking about the fires I would soon have crackling. The countess spared no expense when it came to keeping our woodpile stocked.

During Christmastide, the nuns spent less time attending to their duties and more time in church. After nones, the sisters forewent their usual administrative meeting in the chapter house and met instead to sing. Music wreathed through all twelve days of Christmas, culminating in a service on the Feast of the Epiphany. No words could describe the music. The voices of the sisters rose toward heaven, revolving around one another in a slow dance, echoes weaving back through the original melody to create sound that was both complex and ineffably pure. When Mother Elfilda sang alone, the beauty of her voice pierced me like the sword of Saint Michael.

The food of Christmastide was less wonderful than the song, but far richer than the usual fare at the abbey. We ate goose cooked with butter and saffron, and after the Mass of the Divine Word, we even ate roasted swan. The king sent venison from his hunting lodge, and of course there was mince pie and frumenty with cinnamon, nutmeg, and dried currants. I was sorry to return to our usual bland diet when the holidays were over, but that was a reminder to me of how blessed my life had become. I did not like to think of my sister cooking pottage over a meager fire, worried that the barley might not last the winter.

It was not until the eleventh day before kalends of February that the prioress finally granted me an audience with Mother Elfilda. I felt less urgency for the meeting than when I had first requested it, but that did not diminish my nervousness. In fact, the long wait for an audience made it seem even more important and valuable.

I had not returned to the chapter house since my first meeting with Mother Elfilda. Before entering the foyer, I stomped the snow from my shoes. My throat had been sore since morning, and now my stomach hurt as well. I pushed back my hood and fidgeted with my coif, rehearsing for the thousandth time the words that I would say to Mother Elfilda.

I watched the other petitioners as they were ushered one by one into the chapter house, wondering what business brought them to the abbey. After some time, the door opened again and a sister motioned to me silently. The chapter house looked just as it had when I was last there, with Mother Elfilda on the dais and the prioress standing at her side. I knelt in the doorway, and the prioress said brusquely, "Come here, child."

Kneeling before the dais, I was closer to Mother Elfilda than I had been in months. I was struck once again by the abbess's small stature and icy fragility. Her face was unlined, though she must have been nearly beyond childbearing age, and her features were perfectly still, barely inhabited. She turned to the prioress, who looked down at her scroll. "This should be Agnes, Mother, the girl who works for Lady Wenslock. She came from Aviceford Manor after that problem with the other servant. Lady Wenslock asked that she stay on. The girl requested this meeting."

Mother Elfilda looked back at me. "Yes, Agnes?"

The words that I had practiced for months caught in my raw throat. The solemnity of the chapter house, the regal bearing of the abbess, the impatient stare of the prioress, these brought the abbey into clear focus, as though I were seeing each stone and glass pane in detail for the first time. It was like waking from a gauzy dream to see the mold and soot stains on the ceiling, reminders that snapped me sharply back into the real world.

"God save you, Mother." My voice sounded strange to me.

"Yes?"

"I have prayed . . ."

She gazed at me blandly.

"I have prayed, and I think . . . I think that perhaps . . . perhaps the Holy Ghost is guiding me toward a new fate."

"Ah." Her voice was clear and brisk. "You would like to get married, and your father is not free. You should return to Aviceford and arrange the terms with Emont. We shall find a replacement. What are you, sixteen?"

"Nearly fifteen, Mother. But I do not wish to marry. I wish to be a nun!" There, it was said.

A crease appeared between her brows, and she pulled her head

back as though she had smelled something foul. "You are a servant. You are not even free."

The prioress scowled and banged her staff on the wooden dais. "You are wasting the abbess's time with your nonsense!"

I lurched forward, holding my stomach. I could not catch my breath. Seeing the expression on Mother Elfilda's face, I realized with horror the extent of my delusion. To the abbess, I was a pack-horse, an animal that has value as long as it can work, nothing else. She would no more invite me to become a novice than she would invite a horse to the dinner table. I had made a fool of myself a second time, only this time, the humiliation was nearly too much to bear. A nun tugged at my hood. The door creaked as the next petitioner entered. I managed to croak some sort of blessing, though the abbess and prioress were already conferring about the next meeting, and they did not turn to see me go.

Once I was out of the chapter house, I could no longer control the waves of sickness. I ran out of the cloister, and the vomit came up, burning my sore throat, staining the snow an ugly yellow. I wanted to run to the woods and keep on running. I wanted the earth to swallow me. I wanted to lie down and never rise again.

Instead, I covered up the dirty snow as best I could and went back to work. When the church bells rang, I did not stop to pray, not then and not ever again.

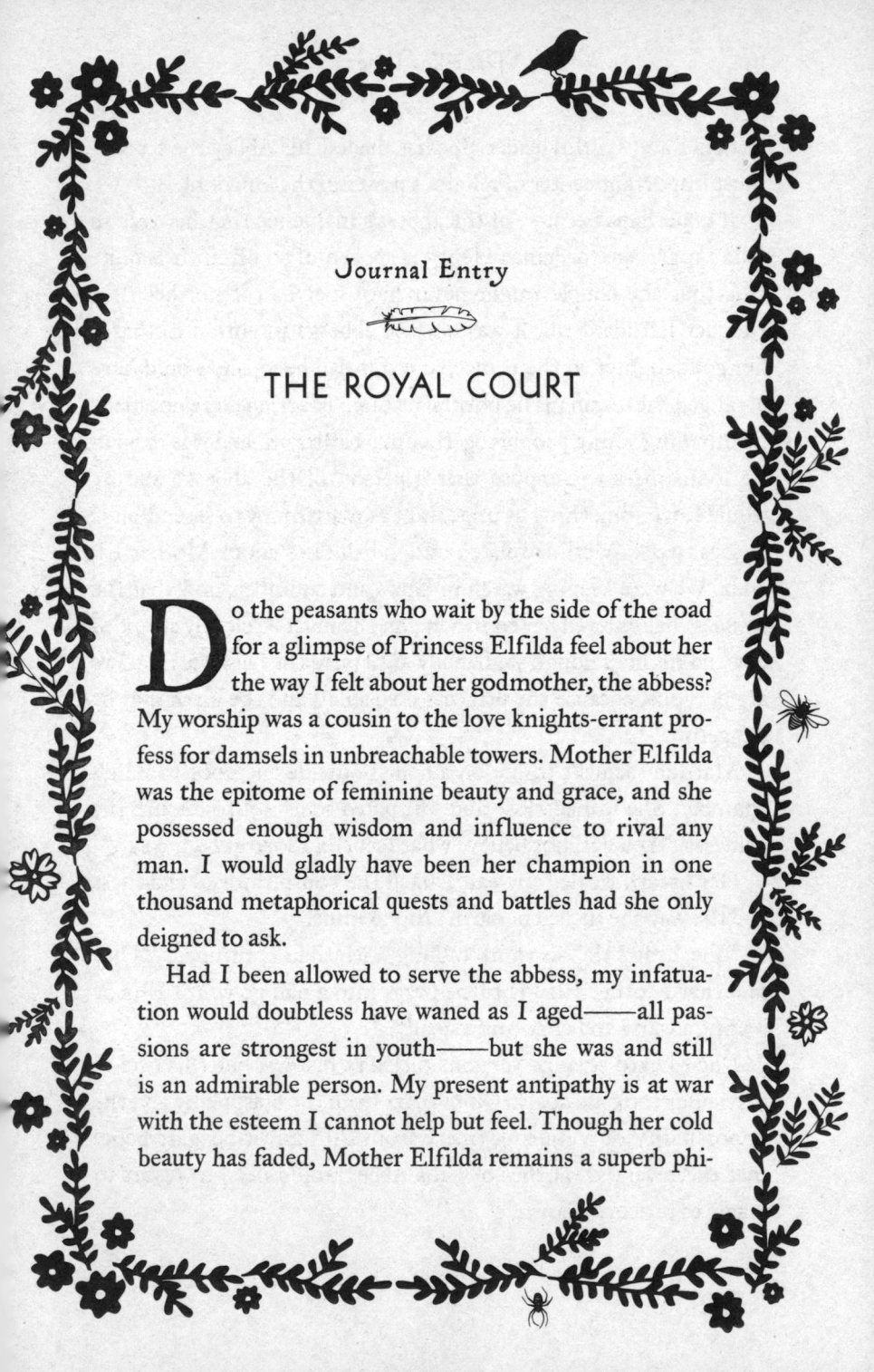

Journal Entry

THE ROYAL COURT

Do the peasants who wait by the side of the road for a glimpse of Princess Elfilda feel about her the way I felt about her godmother, the abbess? My worship was a cousin to the love knights-errant profess for damsels in unbreachable towers. Mother Elfilda was the epitome of feminine beauty and grace, and she possessed enough wisdom and influence to rival any man. I would gladly have been her champion in one thousand metaphorical quests and battles had she only deigned to ask.

Had I been allowed to serve the abbess, my infatuation would doubtless have waned as I aged——all passions are strongest in youth——but she was and still is an admirable person. My present antipathy is at war with the esteem I cannot help but feel. Though her cold beauty has faded, Mother Elfilda remains a superb phi-

losopher and skillful leader. She has made Ellis Abbey the second-most important center of religious power in the kingdom.

It is perhaps because of the abbess's influence that her role in Ella's marriage to Prince Henry is spoken of so often. It is quite true that the couple might never have met had it not been for Mother Elfilda. Still, it was not the abbess's intention to marry her goddaughter to the prince, and if it had been, she would have arranged the union in the normal fashion. Marriages are not made by throwing young people together in a ballroom, and it is romantic foolishness to suppose that a person of the abbess's stature would leave something as important as matrimony to serendipity.

Last week, Matilda related outlandish tales about Mother Elfilda. We were keeping watch in Ella's antechamber; now that the princess has entered her confinement, she must be closely attended day and night. Though we happily anticipate the baby's arrival, we are nervous, because the princess is so small and the birth may be dangerous.

Matilda sat next to me on a bench outside the door to Ella's chamber. She leaned close and whispered so as not to disturb the princess. "You will not believe what Isabella Florivet had to say."

Her breath tickled my ear. I liked the conspiratorial closeness and the way she tucked her arm around mine.

"She heard the servants talking," Matilda continued. "They said that Mother Elfilda turned rags into a ball gown for Ella by waving a wand and chanting a spell!"

I had heard strange versions of Ella's history, but this one in particular took me aback. Quite apart from the blasphemy and the impossibility of conjuring finery from thin air, it beggars belief that the reverend mother of Ellis Abbey would need to resort to magic to procure a gown.

"Nonsense! Do they dare to call the abbess a sorceress?" I asked incredulously.

"No, Mother." Matilda stifled a laugh. "Apparently, she's a fairy! A *good* fairy, of course, not one of those baby-snatching sorts." She covered her mouth with her hand and glanced guiltily toward Ella's chamber, worried that she had invited bad luck.

I patted her arm and said, "Not to worry, dearheart, we won't let any fairies near our princess."

I suppose it is easy to believe that the otherworldly abbess is not a mere mortal like the rest of us. I used to take her for an angel, but I too would now rather prefer to think of her as a sprite.

9

FERNAN

The abbey never lost its beauty for me, but once I no longer felt a part of it, the beauty turned cold. Timeworn saints with storm-blurred faces stared blindly from arches and doorways, and stone after pale stone climbed mutely toward the sky, monuments to dead days, refusing to divulge their secrets. I thought of the hands that had raised the buildings, carved the stone, assembled the stained glass. I wondered how many workers had died during the construction of the church and how they had been paid for their labor.

I continued to attend Mass, but I sat as far from the pulpit as possible. When Mother Elfilda climbed the spiral stairs to give her sermon, I opened my psalter to read. She was not addressing me, so I was not obliged to listen.

Despite my disillusionment, my feelings toward the countess did not change. She might have been eccentric in the attention she paid to a servant girl, but I remained grateful. We did not speak often, and Lady Wenslock never offered me the same familiarity she did to Mary, but she treated me with the respectful condescension of a superior, not the disregard of an animal husbander.

Spring breezes caused the snowdrifts to round and slump, wearing them thinner until yellow grass and mud showed through. The
longer days tempted me back to the rose garden, where buds were
beginning to form. Bright green haloes softened the skeletal angles
of branches, and then one day, the trees burst into full leaf. Swal-
lows darted and swooped in the fresh-scrubbed spring air.

I had not seen Fernan since early autumn, and I did not doubt
that he had given up looking for me in the garden. One day, however, he appeared, whistling through his teeth and looking as
carefree and handsome as ever. I had been walking toward the
fishpond, and he joined me on my stroll.

"Well, well, if it isn't Miss Agnes. I thought that you had gone
back to Aviceford, but I didn't find you there either."

Although not even a year had passed, my decision to avoid Fernan seemed to belong to a much younger version of myself. I could
not explain the reason for my absence without also exposing my
callowness, and so I merely told him that I had been busy.

"I am glad to see that they have let you out for some sunshine,
finally," he replied. "You look well. You seem to have grown even
taller, and it suits you."

I kicked at the gorse beside the pond.

"You wear the most dismal clothing though. You look like one
of the nuns."

"Well, I'm not. Anyway, you are hardly in a position to throw
stones."

"True enough," he said, looking at his coarse, mud-flecked
cloak. "I don't want to call attention to myself. Besides, I'm not as
pretty as you."

I made a face.

"Tell me, what is the news at Rose House?"

I informed him about the latest visitors, and about Lady Wenslock's health. She had not much appetite, and her cheeks were hollow. "I am worried that she is ill, although she complains of no fever, nor cough, nor stomach trouble. She is more fatigued than she used to be."

"Well, she is a very old woman. Frailty is to be expected. How goes your reading?"

I blushed and looked down at my psalter full of threads. "It is improving."

"Did you write me a letter? I have been waiting for it."

I had the parchment tucked into the back of the book, but now I was too shy to show it to him. "I could think of nothing to say. Anyway, I don't know how to write very many words. I just copied down some things. It isn't for you."

"Let me see it anyway. I told you that I would correct your writing. I don't mind if you had nothing nice to say to me."

"It wasn't that! It was hard to find words."

"So show me what words you managed to learn."

He stopped walking, and I realized that he would not take no for an answer. Reluctantly, I handed him the parchment, and he read aloud:

"'When I consider the silver face of the moon that waxeth behind thick clouds of night I ask if she knoweth any thing seeth she a man on a horse a shadow small as dust driven by the wind or the foolish young woman who looketh upon her in wonder the light of her countenance revealeth all that liveth what then thinketh the moon of man and woman who dwelleth in her light joined by her regard from the heavens.'"

His voice trailed off at the end. He read it again, in silence, and then he looked at me as though I had grown donkey ears. "Did you write this?"

"Yes . . ."

"By yourself?"

"Well, I copied the words . . ."

"This is not from any psalm."

"No, no, I mean that I took words from different psalms."

"I cannot believe that you wrote this. Are you a witch?"

I laughed, and after a moment, he laughed too. I wondered about his hesitation. He handed the parchment back to me and frowned. "You should be a nun, not a servant."

"Well, I am not."

As we completed the loop of the pond, he motioned toward the stable.

"I should be going."

"I didn't hear your news."

"I shall come back tomorrow. Can you meet me? Same time?"

I nodded.

"Very well. Good evening to you, witch, or marvel, whatever you may be."

The following day, I found myself looking forward to seeing Fernan again. My thoughts about him were no longer darkened by queasy apprehension; whereas before he had seemed foreign or unwholesome, our stroll around the pond had made him seem quite ordinary. I was in need of a friend, and I did not see why that could not be Fernan. The churnings of my mind had unnecessarily complicated what should have been simple. I decided to be more blithe, more like Fernan. I finished my work quickly so that I could get to the rose garden on time.

Fernan was already waiting for me when I arrived at the garden. He was not wearing his usual traveling clothes, but a white shirt that contrasted sharply with the deep bronze of his skin and a neat, fitted doublet. For once, he was not carrying his satchel. He gripped a drooping bunch of bluebells in his hand. When he smiled and waved, my heart made a sudden leap.

Fernan offered the flowers to me with an exaggerated bow and suggested another stroll around the pond. I liked that his long stride matched my own, and I was reminded again of two wolves loping through the woods. We tarried by the water while he told tales from his travels. One story about a hare that got loose in an alehouse caused me to laugh until tears streamed down my cheeks. We saw the occasional worker or servant pass by, but they were far away and paid us no heed. It seemed as though we were alone in the world.

Except to hold my elbow on a muddy incline, Fernan did not touch me until we said good-bye. He tucked a bluebell under the edge of my coif and asked me to meet him again the following afternoon, which was to be his last day at the abbey for a fortnight. I savored the memory of the warm brush of his fingers on my brow as I returned to Rose House with a light step.

I woke, crestfallen, to the sound of rain. In the fog of sleep, the reason for my heavy heart was at first elusive. It had something to do with dark leaves shaking under the assault of raindrops in the empty rose garden. Fernan would not come.

All morning, I watched the sky anxiously; by dinnertime, the rain had stopped, but the clouds had not lifted. My chores stretched to eternity. When Mary asked me to restock the wood bins, I could

not hide my impatience. "Can I not do it later? I would like to go out for a bit."

Mary looked at me suspiciously. "Why are you so eager to go out on a day like this?"

"I want to take a stroll before the rain returns." I knew that she found my preference to be outdoors peculiar but not objectionable.

"Restock first. Then you may go out."

Though I resented the delay, her question had awakened my guilt. Was it appropriate for me to spend time alone with Fernan? I wondered what Mary would think if she knew that I was not taking my stroll alone. I did not want to think about it, and I swatted the worry aside with annoyance. The wood made a satisfying clatter as I released it into the metal bins. I liked the sharp smell of pine on my hands.

The rain held off until I got to the rose garden, although the sky was eerily dark. Fernan did not remark upon my tardiness. He had brought bluebells again, and he carried a cerecloth cape.

Perhaps because of the weather, or Fernan's imminent departure, or Mary's question, I was in a somber mood. Fernan first tried to jolly me, but I resisted. Finally, he said, "What is wrong?"

I shrugged. "I guess that I am not much good at conversation today."

There was a slow beat of raindrops, and the tempo quickly increased. Fernan lifted his chin toward the sky, letting fat drops splash against his face, and then he opened his cape, pulling the hood over my head and wrapping the cerecloth around both of us. He snaked his arm around my shoulder and pulled me toward him. "A little rain won't hurt us, will it?"

Rivulets were beginning to form under his glossy black curls,

and water dripped from the tip of his nose. His smile was fierce. "There is shelter close by. We can wait out the worst of this torrent."

He led me not toward the stable, which was closest, but to a barn just beyond the pond. By the time we reached it, the rain was hammering hard, and it was a relief to find refuge. Fernan pulled the heavy door shut behind us, leaving us in the dark, surrounded by small piles of hay, withered dregs of the winter supply. Rain beat thunderously on the roof. I shivered with cold. I thought about running back to Rose House, where the fires were lit.

"Take off your wet cloak," Fernan said. "I shall cover us both with the cape, and you will feel much warmer." I could not make out Fernan's features well in the dim light, but I could hear affection in his voice.

I dropped my sodden cloak on the floor and hesitated.

"Come on," he said, patting the hay beside him. "I promise not to bite."

I crouched next to him, and he put his arm around me again, pulling the cape up to my shoulders.

"There, isn't that better?"

I was warmer, but my body still shook, echoing the pounding of rain above us. I tried to calm myself by counting the slats in the door.

Fernan tugged at my coif. "You should take this wet thing off and let your hair dry." He jostled my shoulder playfully. "I won't watch."

Out of vanity more than anything, I welcomed the suggestion. I had beautiful hair like my mother's, mahogany and thick. I had taken to sprinkling it with rosewater, and the scent was lovely

when I let my hair down. I pulled my plaits from their crisscross and shook them loose. My tresses fell nearly to my waist, brushing against the hay at our backs.

Fernan whistled. "Who knew that the cinder girl had such a magnificent mane?" He ran his fingers through my hair, and I did not pull away. "So soft too." He continued to stroke my hair meditatively, and after some time, his hand caressed my face as well. "You are so beautiful, Agnes." His voice sounded tight, constricted.

I was used to the dark by then and could see Fernan better. He gazed at me with great concentration. I thought it strange and wonderful that such a strong, handsome, intelligent man should be interested in me. It made me feel powerful and weak at the same time.

When Fernan bent to kiss me, I lifted my face toward his. I was shocked to find myself melting into him; I was a candle that had never known a flame, and now that the flame was lit, I softened and glowed in a way I had not known was possible. Our lips touched gently at first, and then more forcefully. I put up no resistance when he pushed me back into the hay, nor when he nuzzled and touched every part of me, lighting fires wherever he went. I should not have been surprised when I felt him pushing between my legs. I tried to sit up, but he leaned heavily on my chest, murmuring my name, telling me that everything would be fine. I struggled feebly against his weight, but he entered me with a tearing flash of pain.

It was as though I had been struck hard across the face. I woke from my languorous torpor to find a man jerking and jiggling on top of me, an ache between my legs, sharp bits of hay poking my bare skin. I had been bewitched, and the spell was broken. Fernan was lost in his own world, panting, eyes shut. After some time, he moaned loudly and collapsed over me.

I watched the brightening light between the slats of the barn

door and listened to the rain slow and stop. Fernan's breathing eased. He seemed to have fallen asleep. When he did not move, I tried to shift him off of me. This woke him; he smiled and tried to kiss me, but I turned my head.

"Oh, Agnes, it is too late to be reticent now. Kiss me."

I refused, so he rolled away. "It is not always so nice for maidens the first time. You will get used to it." He smiled. "You were sublime." He stroked my hair, but I cringed. "You should not feel guilt. You are not a nun, after all."

Everything he said only made me feel worse. I stood and pulled down my skirts; something sticky oozed down my leg. There was blood on the floor. My only thought was to get out of there, back to something familiar, back to Rose House.

Fernan escorted me as far as the garden. I did not want him to come any farther, lest we be seen together. I had not worried about being seen the day before, but everything seemed different now, dirty.

"I shall be gone for a fortnight, Agnes, but I shall look for you when I return." He picked up my hand and kissed it gently. "Do not break my heart, lovely lady."

Before returning to Rose House, I walked to the stream. I was still sore, and every step was a reminder of what had transpired. I followed the brook into a small thicket where I could be concealed, and there I cleaned myself in the frigid water. I lifted my skirt and knelt in the water until I was numb. I wanted to wash away the last hour of my life, go back to a time when I felt whole. I knew that something fundamental within me had changed, though I did not yet know what.

I lay sleepless all that night, buffeted by warring emotions. I did not want to think about what had happened, but I could not put it out of my mind. I felt sick when I remembered Fernan on top of me, his eyes closed like a newborn kitten, making sounds that were not quite human. It was an unholy fire that he had awakened in my body, but my heart quickened as I remembered how deliciously it had licked the marrow of my bones. His stories by the pond, the sunlight on his face, his soft kiss on my fingers, those were memories that did not belong to the dark barn, the smell of damp wool and moldering hay. One Fernan I loved, the other revolted me.

In the days that followed, I could think of nothing but Fernan. I changed my mind one hundred times about whether I would return to him, but long before a fortnight had elapsed, I began to frequent the rose garden again.

Fernan reappeared on a summery afternoon. He was as cheerful and jocular as ever, and we fell easily back into conversation. He did not act as though anything had changed between us, and I wondered whether I had dreamt the time in the barn. He remained at the abbey only two days, and on the second day, he brushed his lips softly against mine, telling me that he would return in one week.

I waited eagerly for his return. This time, Fernan brought me a gift, a dark green gown that he had bought in the city. I gasped with pleasure when he unfurled it and held it against my shoulders. The fabric shimmered, and there was gold embroidery over the breast. It was nearly as beautiful as one of Lady Wenslock's gowns.

During our stroll, Fernan linked my arm with his, so that I held his forearm. When he covered my hand with his, I felt safe. Under the bower in the rose garden, he pulled me to him and kissed me tenderly. Then he looked earnestly into my eyes, caressing my

neck with the tips of his fingers, and asked me to sneak away in the night to meet him in the barn. To my surprise, I agreed.

The moon rose nearly full that night and peered into the dorter, illuminating the long row of sleepers with eerie yellow light. I lay awake, studying the stars in the nearest window, my chest thrumming with the pounding of my heart. Sounds of coughs and shifting bodies gradually quieted. Once I judged that everyone was asleep, I rose and removed my nightcap. I had hidden the gift from Fernan beneath my bed during evening services, and now I slid it out, folded it over my arm, and crept silently toward the arcade. In the shadow of the pillars, I pulled the gown over my thin shift and shook my hair loose. I did not pause to think again, but flew barefoot over the darkly lit paths to the barn.

Fernan opened the door when he heard my footstep. Yellow pools of candlelight flickered where he had arranged candles on the floor, and the hay had been moved to one side of the barn and covered with a blanket. Fernan smiled broadly and took my hand, guiding me over the threshold. "You look like a princess, my sweet," he said, kneeling to kiss my hand. "Will you dance with me?"

"I do not know how to dance."

"I shall teach you." He stood facing me. "You will move past me so." He put his hand on my waist and guided me across the rough floor. "Turn away, now spin and face toward me."

I did as he asked.

"Now take my hand and we shall take one turn together."

My hand felt small in his. He looked happy. Soon, I was happy too. As we danced without music, he drew me close at every opportunity, making a game of kissing me when we passed each other. After some time, we were not dancing anymore, only kissing, and I did not want him to stop. Like a plum, I had ripened as

spring turned to summer. I was filled with sweet nectar, heavy on the branch, loosening for the fall. He had only to cup me in the palm of his hand and pull ever so gently, and I was his.

There was nothing logical about the way I behaved that summer. I knew that Fernan would never marry me, but I continued to meet him at the barn when he asked. I had no hopes for my future, and that made me reckless. Deep down, I knew that I was careening on the brink of a precipice, but loneliness, love, and the impetuousness of youth drove me on.

It was simple to slip away at night, because anyone who saw me would assume that I had failed to properly take care of my needs at the rere-dorter before bed. The ease of our trysts lulled me into complacency. During daylight hours, Fernan and I rarely met anymore, so my life was sliced sharply in halves by the setting of the sun. In my real life, I was a dutiful servant who was increasingly worried about her ailing mistress. In my dream life, I was the desirable young lover of the handsome, charming son of a knight. I saw myself reflected in the hunger in his eyes, and I liked what I saw. I admired the creamy whiteness of my skin against his, the perfection of my pear-shaped breasts in his hands, the coltish sleekness and strength of my body under him, my long legs wrapped around his waist. Fernan was the blank parchment upon which my dream self was illuminated, and his desire made me wondrous.

Like all idylls, ours had to come to an end. In early autumn, Fernan's mood changed. He became distracted, testy, and his teasing took on an edge of cruelty. At first, I did not understand what was wrong. I tried to please him, but that only made him withdraw fur-

ther. He spent less time at the abbey, and our trysts became rarer and more brief. As I felt him slipping away, my desperation grew. My dream life had become the only life I wanted to live, but it was not mine to choose. Only Fernan had that power.

One night, Fernan was late coming to the barn, and when he arrived, I rushed to him and threw my arms around his neck, crying, "What happened? I was so worried!"

He peeled my arms away and then released me. "I am here now."

"But why are you so late?"

"Why do you pick at me like a villein's slut?" He began to pace.

"You kept me waiting. I was not sure that you would come."

"I should not have come!"

My desperation was unbearable. I took his hand. "Lie down, my love, and I shall stroke your brow. I did not mean to upset you."

"Is going to bed all you can think about? As though you were a common whore?"

"I love you, Fernan!"

"You are not going to trap me by speaking of love or by having that child. You came to me willingly. You threw yourself at me!"

I was bewildered.

"You mean to tell me that you do not know that you are with child, with your swollen belly and breasts like melons? You can hardly fit into your shift!"

It was true that I had grown rounder and that I had not felt well. I was vaguely aware that I had not had a monthly bleed in some time. My hands instinctively covered my belly. As the truth revealed itself, I began to sob.

"Come on now. Stop your crying." Fernan's voice softened. "Come here, Agnes. Come here."

He put his arms around me, but I could not stop my pitiful

display. Convulsions shook me as I tried to keep from making a sound. I cowered in his arms.

"I did not mean to be so cruel. Perhaps there will be a miscarriage. Such things happen."

I pressed my face into his shoulder and tried to shut out the waves of panic. I had felt trapped before, and I had thought that the world could take nothing more away from me. I now understood that I had been mistaken.

The months that followed were bleak. I was fatigued and sore, and I battled an agitation that kept me from sleeping and eating. I had been so blinded by the metamorphosis of my body from child to woman that I had not recognized the signs of pregnancy, but now that I knew I was with child, I could not ignore the relentless swelling of my belly. I wondered how Fernan had noticed the change when there was only a modest hillock below my waist, but now the bulge was undeniable. I did not imagine a babe within, but a tumor or bubo. If I could have sliced my belly off with a knife, I would have done so.

Lady Wenslock's health continued to worsen. A physician now resided at Rose House, and nuns from the infirmary had been brought in to tend to the countess at all hours of the day. She rarely rose from bed, which meant that I did not see her anymore. It was whispered that Lady Wenslock would soon die.

Whereas the prospect of her death used to cause me worry about my own security, now I only felt sad that she suffered. Lady Wenslock's death could no longer alter my fate. Once it became apparent that I was with child, I would be forced to leave the abbey. I had nowhere to go.

I had no more trysts with Fernan, and I mourned him. There were times when I hated him, to be sure, for the part he played in my predicament. Yet I also remembered moments of great tenderness. His eyes had shone when he gazed at me, and I had felt safe in his arms. I thought that he loved me, even while I understood he needed to marry a person closer to his own station.

I believe that it was Mary who made the abbess aware of my condition. She asked questions about my ever rounder figure, and then I was told to report to the chapter house. I was seized by a foolish impulse to run away, but I set it aside. In any event, I was not sure that I had the energy to do such a thing. A terrible lassitude had entered my body, turning my limbs to lead. Even my heart was invaded by metallic coldness. I imagined myself transfigured piece by piece into a statue of dull gray ore, my heartbeat slowing until it stopped altogether and I remained frozen, a parable for future generations, an eternal warning.

Two nuns were sent to escort me to the chapter house. Like a condemned prisoner flanked by guards, I walked with my head bowed in shame. The first snow of the year had fallen earlier in the day, and a few stray snowflakes still floated down. I marveled at the perfection of a delicate flake that landed on my sleeve. Why had God made nature so perfect and humans so flawed?

One sister entered the building ahead of us, presumably to announce our arrival, and there followed an exodus of nuns and laypeople. My remaining attendant then guided me into the nearly empty chamber. I could not look at the prioress or abbess as I approached. Once I was kneeling before her, Mother Elfilda spoke to me in a cold voice. "Is it true what I have heard about your condition?" Her face was a mask.

I could not speak, but I nodded.

"Speak louder. We cannot hear you."

"Yes, my lady."

"You are aware that fornication is a mortal sin."

"Yes, my lady."

"Did you commit this grievous sin with full knowledge of the gravity of your offense?"

"Yes, my lady." No amount of blinking could prevent my tears; they splashed onto my bodice, leaving ragged blotches on the gray wool.

"Were you coerced into this sin?"

"No, my lady." A loud intake of breath, an aborted sob, escaped my throat and echoed like a thunderclap in the silence.

"Did you commit this sin more than once?"

"Yes, my lady."

"This is a very grave matter. Your soul is not merely weakened, but dead to God. Your bond to God's saving grace has been most monstrously ruptured."

I focused on her white slippers, willing my breath to slow.

"With whom did you commit this sin?"

My gaze snapped to her face, and fear replaced self-pity. I had not thought about what this would mean for Fernan. Mother Elfilda's face remained expressionless.

"Mother . . . I . . . I do not know his name."

A flash of anger contorted her lovely features momentarily. "Do not play games with me! What is his name?"

"My lady." I swallowed hard. "He did not tell me, my lady."

"Nonsense! Is it not enough that your soul is in mortal peril? Must you compound your shame with dishonesty? I shall discover who committed this grotesque sin with or without you. Tell me his name!"

"Fernan, Mother."

"I cannot hear you! Speak louder."

"Fernan, Mother."

"I thought as much." She sighed, then turned to the prioress and spoke irately. "This cannot continue. My abbey cannot be responsible for situating every servant girl he beds and gets with child!" The abbess then lowered her voice, and I could hear no more of what she said.

The prioress waved my dismissal as she bent to catch the words of Mother Elfilda. A gray veil dimmed my eyesight as a nun escorted me out of the chapter house and into the gathering dusk. She left me in the cloister, which was crowded with sisters hurrying to supper. The dusting of snow on the ground was now crisscrossed with lines of dark footprints.

After some time, the cloister emptied, and darkness drew closer. The night was moonless, but stars appeared through rents in the scudding clouds. My dizziness passed, leaving emptiness in its wake. I sat on a snow-covered bench, waiting for tears to blur the stars and set them swimming. The sharp pinpricks of light remained, distant and immovable.

OLD HILGATE

Like a prisoner, I was outwardly passive, but my soul could find no peace. I had fooled myself into believing that I was important to Fernan, that he loved me, that his love elevated me beyond what Abbess Elfilda could see: an ignorant, cringing servant, a stain upon the earth. I blamed myself for my situation more than I blamed Fernan. My self-deception had been willful. Even then, as I waited to be cast out of the abbey, I recalled the tenderness in Fernan's voice and touch, not the way he discarded me once his desires were satisfied.

I would be sent back to my village, and Emont would ask the reeve to find a husband for me. Every child was a potential asset for the manor, and if I could not be put to use as a servant, I would be put to use as a breeder. The pregnant daughter of a penniless villein is not a wife any man desires, however. I would be given to someone with no better prospects. Someone poor, probably an old widower who needed a woman to raise his children. I hoped that he would not be cruel or violent.

At least I would see my sister again. Lottie would never turn her

back on me. In the past, I had felt sorry for her, but now she would
feel sorry for me. Her husband was poor, but he was young and
decent. I wished that I had never been sent to the manor, that my
father had found a husband for me as he had for Lottie.

I did not want to think about feeding someone else's starving
children with the scant, spoiled remains of winter oats, or giving
birth to my child on some stranger's dirt floor amidst rodent and
chicken droppings. Still, that fate would be better than finding no
husband at all.

My purgatory ended when Fernan himself came to Rose House
and asked to speak with me. Mary looked as though she might
faint. I was taken aback, but days of stewing in dread and remorse
had dulled my feelings. When I asked Fernan to follow me to the
library, Mary was too astonished to raise an objection. I knew that
she would not bother us there.

The white draperies and tapestries were blinding in the sunlight
that poured through the arched windows. I adored the library,
and I had cleaned it until it was as spotless as a shrine. In all that
time, I had never dared to do more than hover near the mysterious
leather-bound tomes, inhaling their musty odor. The books now
reminded me of the whole world beyond my petty heartache, and
that thought made me calm.

Fernan was unshaven and subdued. He seemed smaller than
the last time I had seen him, as though he had shrunk, or I had
grown. For the first time, I noticed that his thin wrists dangled
foolishly from his too-short sleeves, and his face contorted in an
unattractive grimace when he was distracted by thought.

"You wish to speak to me?" The coldness in my voice was foreign to me.

"Yes, I . . ." Fernan looked around, disoriented. "Mother Elfilda is displeased, as you might imagine."

"I am aware of Abbess Elfilda's displeasure."

"She has threatened to end her patronage of me if I do not take responsibility for the baby." He winced as though the words caused him physical pain.

After a long pause, I threw my words at him. "You have to marry me?" I meant to hurt him with my sarcasm, but the words hurt me instead.

"I have to take you away from here."

"And leave me?"

"No . . ." He looked miserable. "The last girl, Lizzie . . . They found her a husband. Mother Elfilda refuses to do it again."

At the mention of Lizzie, I felt a surge of disgust. It was doubly humiliating that I had been lured into the same pitfall as the girl before me. "Where do you plan to take me?"

"Old Hilgate. I shall rent you a room at the alehouse."

"What about you?"

Fernan narrowed his eyes. "I am a messenger for the church. My life is on the road. I shall give you the money you need, but do not expect me to keep you company."

I searched his face for some trace of the old Fernan, the man who had teased me, stroked my hair, taught me to dance. This Fernan looked sullen, like a child denied his supper. It struck me that he had always been like a child. He was charming and flirtatious when he wanted something, but frustration made him petulant. He had scooped my heart from my breast to use as his plaything, but

now he was tired of it, and he was angry that he could not move on to other entertainments.

"I understand, Fernan. I shall impose on you as little as possible." He looked relieved. "We leave at noon."

After packing my few belongings, including the green gown that could no longer stretch over my tumescent belly, I left the abbey as I had come, riding pillion behind Fernan on his pretty rounsey. The air was cold but still, the sky a flat, featureless gray that portended snow. I did not look back until we rode through the gate in the outer wall. There, I glanced at the words carved so deeply into the weather-worn stone at the apex of the arch. I could read them now: *Ecce ancilla domini*. Behold the handmaid of the Lord.

Fernan brought me back to the market town, Old Hilgate, and there he rented a room at the alehouse. The building was as grim and filthy as I remembered, and the room above the brewery was draughty and dark. The first night, Fernan slept beside me, his arm around my thick waist. The wind whistled through cracks in the daub, and our blankets were rough and foul smelling. I lay awake long into the night. The warmth of Fernan's body against my back and the soft rumble of his snore made me feel lonelier than I had ever felt before.

In the morning, he was gone. Fernan left a bag of coins next to the bed, and I was grateful for it. Downstairs, I found the alewife sleeping by the fire, and I roused her to ask for a drink. She had grown gaunt since I had last seen her, and her cough was ominously deep, a wet rattle. The woman gazed at me blankly with bloodshot eyes but did not stir. I told her to go back to sleep and helped myself to the bitter ale.

Snow had fallen in the night, and the sky was an empty blue. I ventured out for a walk and found the town to be more pleasant than I remembered, if only because its squalor was tucked neatly under a clean white blanket. Flags of bright blood on the snow advertised the fleshmonger's shop; a gabble of trussed poultry floundered nearby. Chimneys puffed cheerily, and children tromped through fresh snow in the streets, shouting to one another as though every one of them were deaf. It was near Christmastide, and doors were decorated with pine boughs and bright ribbons. Few townsfolk were out, but those who were greeted me civilly. I took a deep breath of the wintry air. I could make a fresh start in Old Hilgate for myself and for my child.

When I returned to the alehouse, a plump, ruddy-faced woman was plying the alewife with a bowl of stew. She paused with the spoon in midair and squinted at me. "Good day to you. Are you the renter Alice was telling me about?" Her gaze swept from my head to my toes.

"Yes, my name is Agnes, Goodwife." The woman was dressed in costly velvet, and I was acutely aware of my rough woolen dress and ratty cloak. At least the cloak hid my swollen belly. I was about to duck my head and curtsy, begging her pardon, when it occurred to me that she knew nothing about me. I stood tall and lifted my chin. "My husband and I just arrived. Forgive my appearance, I have not yet unpacked." I gave her what I hoped was a charming smile.

The alewife turned her head, refusing the spoon. She moaned softly and slumped back into her chair, closing her eyes. The other woman set the bowl down.

"Welcome, then. I am Henny, the blacksmith's wife. I am trying to get Alice here to eat a little dinner. Will you be staying long in Old Hilgate?"

"I am not sure how long." I hesitated. "My husband is a messenger, and we were just married, so we have not yet decided where to settle."

"A hearty congratulations on your marriage, and God bless! From where do you come?"

My heart raced. "Ellis Abbey, most recently. My husband is a ward and agent of Abbess Elfilda."

Her broad face lit up. "Oh, were you a pupil at the abbey, then? That would explain it," she said, presumably referring to my attire. "And you fell for the abbess's ward!" She winked at me. "How wonderful! Who are your parents, dear?"

The woman had unwittingly helped with my deception, but I did not have a ready answer to her new question. I said the first thing that leapt into my mind. "They are Sir Roger Thorpe and Lady Thorpe of West Chillington." These were Mary's parents.

Henny's eyes widened, and her hand flew to the base of her throat. "Oh! So you come from nobility, then!"

I blushed at my poorly chosen falsehood. "Nay, Goodwife, my father is but a baronet, so I am an ordinary commoner." For good measure, I added, "My parents will not acknowledge me now that I have married in secret without their consent. They have cut me off entirely."

"Oh, my poor dear, that is terrible!" She bustled over to where I stood and took my hands, looking at me earnestly with her watery blue eyes. "You are such a dear, modest girl. Look at you blush! If you need anything at all, you just ask me. You are most welcome in Old Hilgate!"

I squirmed and endeavored to direct her attention away from me. "How is the alewife?"

Henny shook her head somberly and dropped my hands. "Alice does badly." She returned to the alewife and stroked her cheek. "You are going to eat the last few bites for me now, aren't you, sweeting? We need to get you stronger."

Alice opened her eyes and mumbled something that I could not hear, and Henny let out a barking laugh. "There is the spirit! We shall have you back on your feet by next week."

Alice was not, in fact, destined to get back on her feet. Henny told me later that Alice had a wasting illness, consumption. The woman's misfortune was compounded by the loss of her business, for the aleconner had barred the sale of Alice's thin, vile-tasting brew. Worse, her only daughter had died the year before from drowning in the river, so she had no family to care for her. Without income from food or ale, poor Alice relied on the charity of her neighbors and the occasional room rental for her living.

Henny brought daily meals for Alice, though she had a large brood of her own to feed. George, her husband, was the only blacksmith for many miles, and he did a brisk trade. They were one of the wealthier families in Old Hilgate, and George was both an alderman and a leading delegate of the parish guild. Both husband and wife were respected in town for their acts of charity. I came to know Henny as a genuinely good and generous person, and it pains me to remember that her knowledge of me was based in a lie.

I used most of the money that Fernan left me to buy three new gowns and a cloak. There was not much to choose from at the weaver's shop, but I found serviceable wool. I instructed the tailor

to create long, vertical seams and wide necklines, the sort of cut favored by guests at Rose House. The wool fabric was wrong for that style of dress, but the townsfolk of Old Hilgate knew nothing of the latest fashions. I paid for rabbit-fur trim on the hood of the scarlet cloak, which was an extravagance, but it seemed like the sort of thing a well-bred woman would do. Looking back now, from my place at the royal palace, I know how rustic I appeared, but at the time, I thought the clothes exceedingly fine.

To complete my transformation, I learned to wear my hair like the ladies from the city who visited Lady Wenslock. I folded my plaits on each side of my face and tied them with ribbons, or sometimes I bound them with crespinettes. Of course, unlike the ladies at Rose House, my crespinettes were unadorned by jewels. When I went out, I always wore a plain wimple, as would any respectable married woman.

By the time Fernan returned, I had already been introduced to a number of townsfolk as the newly married, estranged daughter of a baronet.

"My, my," he said, dropping his snow-dusted cloak on the floor of our room. "I hear that you have come up in the world!"

"I did not intend to deceive everyone. It just came out that way."

"Really, now, you just couldn't stop yourself from lying?"

I felt my face grow hot.

"I don't care. It makes things easier for me, actually. Where did you get the gown? It is rather . . . unusual." He put his hands on my shoulders, forcing me to turn in a circle. He flipped the plaited loops of my hair playfully as I spun.

"I had it made. I couldn't afford better fabric."

"*You* couldn't afford? It isn't your money, is it? How much did you spend?"

"Not much. I needed clothing."

"Don't think that you have landed in the lap of luxury. The coins I gave you must last the month. Use them to feed yourself, not to buy fripperies."

I had only a few pence remaining, not enough to get by for weeks longer.

"What do you care about appearances anyway?" he continued. "The only reason the townsfolk believe you is that they are cloddish louts. I could pass off Perla as the king's finest warhorse here. You have aspirations to climb to the lofty heights of Old Hilgate society? I suppose that *is* a grand aspiration for a laundry girl."

I chafed at his harshness, but there was no advantage to provoking him.

"Have you had supper?" I asked.

"Yes, and I am spent." Fernan sat heavily on the bed and flopped back, his arms outstretched. He hadn't bothered to remove his boots, and dirty meltwater dripped from his heels, collecting in brown puddles on the floor.

"I shall bank the fire then and help you to bed."

Fernan lay with his eyes closed while I readied the coals. Flickering tongues of the dying fire illuminated his handsome profile and lent his skin the rich luminosity of polished bronze. Whereas once his appearance would have stirred up a whirling cloud of trembling butterflies in my belly, I couldn't help but notice that his top lip was too thin, the angle of his jaw too soft, his brow too prominent.

After undressing, I brushed my hair with lavender water and loosened my shift so that my swollen breasts swayed and strained against the sheer linen. Fernan did not open his eyes when I removed his boots, but when I pulled at his breeches, he propped

himself up on his elbows. In the dim light, I thought that I detected hunger in the gleam of his eyes, and when he reached for my face and pulled me toward him, I knew for certain.

His desire ignited my own lust briefly; the response of his body to my touch was affecting, and his gaze told me that he wanted me. Still, his rough hands hurt my breasts, tender with ripening milk, and when he closed his eyes, he receded from me like the sun slipping below the horizon. It was not long before he gasped in a helpless spasm and lay heavily over me, panting, his breath hot against my skin. I pushed him away before he fell asleep. He left me slick with his sweat; I shivered and pulled the blanket to my chin.

When Fernan left again the next morning, there was a new bag of coins by the bedside.

After I whitewashed the walls of our chamber and bought a trunk to store our few belongings, I had little to keep me occupied. At first, I was elated. I had not often been bone-weary at Rose House, but my time had not been my own. Like the stones in the church walls, the sheep that gave wool, and every blade of grass underfoot, I had been the property of the abbey. To wake in Old Hilgate with no master, no duties, to be entirely unaccounted for—it was a miracle.

The joy of idleness wore thin after a few lonely weeks. I spent some time with Alice, helping her to bathe, emptying her bedpan, laundering her linens. The woman's caustic humor and lack of self-pity appealed to me, but she hadn't the strength for company. I couldn't even interest her in my cooking, which was understandable, since my pottage was barely edible, and Henny brought such delicious food.

Restless one day, I decided to visit Henny at her home, a half-timbered house remarkable for its large size and costly tiled roof. She greeted me at the door with a child on her ample hip and a sword in her other hand.

"Oh, Agnes, come in!" Henny said. She had to raise her voice to be heard over shrieking children and clanging from her husband's smithy, which was located directly behind the house. A wave of heat spilled from the doorway into the wintry air.

I must have looked startled by the sword, because Henny held the blade out for me to inspect the decorative work and said, "I do the etching for George. Isn't this coming along nicely? This is meant to be a vine of roses here, around the feet of the lion. Come in, come in!"

Shyly, I stomped the snow from my boots and stepped inside. Fires crackled in two hearths at opposite ends of the expansive hall. The warmth was welcome after a frigid morning above the alehouse. Alice's fires often died, and I did not want to spend money to keep one lit in my chamber.

"We are always in the midst of shambles," Henny said. "It must seem like a sty, but our humble home welcomes you. Here, sit!" She dropped the sword on a table with a clatter and patted the bench. It had apparently been her workstation before I arrived, for there were bowls of acrid liquids, rags, brushes, sharpened sticks, and globs of half-melted wax crowding the table's surface.

"Take off your cloak," Henny said. "You may leave it anywhere."

The tot on Henny's hip patted and poked at her mother's large breast.

"You had your milk for today," Henny said, though the child was too young to understand. "It's time you learned to eat meat!" To me, she said, "I'm too old for babies. Thought little Tom was

the last, then this one came along. But you are the sweetest faunt-kin, aren't you, lovey?" Henny kissed the girl's plump cheek and sat beside me with a sigh. "You look like you've got one on the way. Say good-bye to that pretty figure. This is what a dozen childbirths will do to you." She pointed at her broad waist. "Have you had dinner? Stay, and I shall feed you with this horde of savages."

"You are too kind," I said. "You have enough mouths to feed."

"So one more makes no difference. Besides, you should enjoy Bessie's cooking. She's my eldest. Deaf and dumb, but cleverness in the kitchen will get her a husband someday, I don't doubt. Her black pudding is the best you will ever have. She is such a good girl. Marion, have you met her? From the house on the corner? Her daughter is Bessie's age and gives her no end of grief. Lazy as an old sow. An old sow in heat. She goes snuffling after boys when she should be minding the shop."

"It seems that everyone in town has a shop."

"A body has to make money. I suppose you have a dowry and your husband's income." She lifted a reddened, chapped hand and examined her broken nails. "I wish I could be a noble lady, just for a day."

I folded my own hands in my lap so as not to draw attention to them.

Three little children dashed into the hall and chased one another around the table, yelling and laughing.

"Quiet!" Henny shouted. "Charlie, I will box your ears if you knock over my supplies!"

They continued to yelp but ran away again. Henny sighed. "Savages, truly."

"Do you have a stall on market day?" I asked.

"No, dove, my Georgie works on commissions," Henny said proudly. "I miss shop work sometimes. My father was a fish-monger, and I liked seeing customers. Father said a blatherskite like me was bad for business; I kept people chatting too long. I have always had a mouth on me. You seem like the quiet sort, dig-nified. Sometimes I wish I were like that too, but you can't change how God made you."

"Perhaps I should open a shop." A thrill ran through me as I said the words. The idea of making my own money was intoxi-cating.

"It's not easy work, child," Henny said doubtfully. "And there isn't much a lass can do. Become an alewife like Alice, that's about the only choice. Mind you, we miss having a real brew house in town. There's old Hal's place, but he just brews on the side, and he charges a king's ransom for the stuff. I'd rather make my own. Or rather, Bessie and Meg make our own. Such good girls." Henny absentmindedly shifted the whining baby to her lap and bounced her. "There was a young widow, years ago, who made a delicious brew. Alice, bless her heart, never came close to as good. She al-ways charged a fair price though. Alice may speak sharply, but she is virtuous, and under her rough ways is a heart of pure gold. The widow I told you about, well, she was a pretty one, and the men nursed their ale all night and mooned after her. Now that I think of it, you look something like her, though you are much taller, and your hair is more of a mousy color. She ran away with a carpen-ter from the city. It was quite a scandal, for they said he had an-other wife. You should have heard the gossip! The wives here were happy enough to say Godspeed to that little vixen. Though I don't know. Wasn't her fault she was so pretty."

I let the subject fall, but the thought of making money consumed me after our conversation. Brewing could give me freedom

When Fernan returned, I presented my plan casually while I bathed his feet. "How would it be," I asked, "if I earned a few shillings while you travel?"

Fernan's leg jumped involuntarily as I scrubbed a sensitive spot on the sole of his foot. He liked me to scour his callouses, but he was ticklish.

"What?" he said disinterestedly.

"I thought that perhaps I could convince Alice to let me revive the idle brewery and regain the license to sell ale."

"Mmm." He closed his eyes, and after a pause he murmured, "Brewing is bad business. Prices are fixed by the king. When the cost of ingredients gets too high, brewers lose money."

"Alice made it work."

"Barely, by the look of things."

"I wish to give it a go."

"Hire yourself out. That would be secure income."

"My labor would pay mere pennies. If I had my own shop, I could make this a real home for us."

Fernan snatched his foot from my hands impatiently and sat up. "If Alice wants to put you to work, that's fine with me. Just don't expect me to subsidize your little adventure."

I remained kneeling, expecting him to return his foot to the basin, but instead he looked at me in silence for a moment and then grabbed the hair at the back of my head. With a firm hand, he dragged my face close to his. "Don't look at me like such a worried rabbit," he said with a smile. He bent closer and kissed me. Even

as I felt smothered by his wet, demanding mouth, his familiar scent drew me in. I was not sure that I wished to be free of him.

Alice was easily convinced to let me try to reclaim a license to sell ale. Her life had become a trial, and she relied on the aid of friends and neighbors to get through each day. A tenant who could keep a roof over her head was welcome. "The work is unpleasant, unblessed, and unprofitable," she told me, "but I am exceedingly glad to have you pay the rent, lass." There was fondness in her voice if not in her words.

The difficult part of my scheme was learning how to brew. Even with instructions from the alewife, it took me some time to make a passable batch of ale. The malted grains left in the brewery had gone to rot, and she did not have a kiln, so I was forced to buy expensive barley that had been malted at Cothay Manor. Fernan would be angry, but I planned to make the money back. I could not rebuild Alice's business without spending some money first.

When I tried the hand quern, it took me a whole day to grind enough grain for one batch, and then Alice told me that I had damaged the husks too severely, so I had to begin again. The mashing, however, was the hardest part. Knowing how much scalding water to add to the mash and how long to continue mashing is something that can only come from experience. The first four batches I made tasted nothing like ale, and the fifth was oversweet. By the sixth batch, however, I had a decent drink.

Through my trials and failures, I began to understand why Alice's brew had been so unpalatable. The ingredients for ale were not cheap, and her equipment limited her production to small batches. Since the royal assize set the price for ale so low, Alice

chose to cut corners in order to increase her profit. She added oats
to the barley, and she saved fuel by not boiling and skimming her
wort. Then she added extra water to the grain, making three or
four infusions, which she mixed together to produce a dilute ale
that soured quickly.

I decided that a new approach was needed. After the aleconner
declared my drink to be fit for sale, I swept and scrubbed the alehouse, cleared out the filthy rushes, polished the flagons until they
shone. I replaced the alestake and made merry garlands of holly
to decorate it. I had already spent most of Fernan's money on barley, so I decided that there was little additional harm in spending
my last shillings to buy a large stack of firewood from the wood-
monger and replace the rank tallow with fine beeswax candles.
The plaster on the walls was still blackened and grimy, and the
window could not be opened in winter because it lacked glazing,
but the room was nonetheless transformed. The sight even coaxed
a faint smile from Alice. "You have worked a small miracle here,"
she said. "A pig would no longer feel at home!" Speaking brought
on another paroxysm of coughing, and she spat dark blood onto
her sleeve.

Despite her weakness, Alice wanted to be in the thick of things
as the alehouse reopened, so I bundled her in blankets and sat her
by the fire. She had lost so much weight that I could lift the tiny
woman as easily as I could lift a child. As time passed, I grew large
and rosy with new life, while Alice dwindled. Sores appeared in
those places where her sallow, sagging skin was an insufficient
cover for the sharp bones beneath. Her breath smelled of rot. I did
my best to make her comfortable, but I could see that she suffered.

On the first day that the alehouse opened anew for business, I
made only two sales, and I began to panic. The next morning, I

brought gourds of ale and cups to nearby shops and offered free drinks to anyone who would try. Most of the townsfolk had tasted Alice's ale previously, and they said kind things about the quality of my brew. I also visited the homes of townspeople I knew, including Henny, and I invited them for a free drink that evening. I could not afford my generosity, but I had to do something to bring in customers.

That night, the alehouse was full to overflowing, and everyone seemed to be in the mood for a wassail. The crowd was raucous; men joked and guffawed loudly, and spirited songs broke out within and without the building, as some revelers even sat in the snow to drink their free ale. At one point, someone stumbled or was pushed into a table, and all of the flagons landed on the floor with a mighty crash, provoking uproarious laughter. Alice sat serenely by the hearth in the midst of the tumult, her eyes closed, a slight smile on her lips. The fire and the warmth of many bodies made the room so hot that I felt faint; I welcomed the blasts of cold air that swept in every time the door was opened.

Henny and George arrived toward the end of the evening. They knew all of the townspeople, and they made a point of greeting each and every one of them heartily, infusing the room with even greater cheer.

"We always liked to come here when poor Alice was brewing," Henny told me, "though I confess we liked the kidney pies better than the ale." She wrinkled her nose. "Look at this crowd! It is so nice that you have brought good ale to Old Hilgate. We will stop brewing our own now! It must be hard for you, raised as you were, to do the work of an alewife. It is good, honest work, and I greatly admire you for not being above it. It does nobody credit to be all high and mighty. Christ Himself associated with the lowliest

of people. I met Mylla Ainsley on the way, and she said that you should quit your husband and go home if he is so poor and your parents are so rich. I told her she knows nothing of young love! Not to mention Christian humility. Where is that husband of yours?"

I escaped Henny's patter to check my stores in the brewery. Only a few gallons remained. Though I had started to charge customers after their first drink, the income was not enough to buy all of the new brewing supplies I would require. I shuddered, realizing that I would have to ask Fernan for more money.

As though he had been conjured by my thoughts, Fernan was at the door when I exited the brewery with the last of my ale. He looked around the crowded room, startled. I grabbed a flagon and threaded my way to him.

"Would you care for a drink?" I did my best to smile flirtatiously.

"What is this?"

"An alehouse."

"Yes. I know."

"We spoke about this. I got the license. I thought you would be pleased to see me earn a few shillings."

A slow smile spread across his face. "Really? Is that so?" He tipped the flagon as though examining the contents. "Let me taste your wares, then." He drained the flagon in one long draught. "Not bad! Not bad at all. A refill!" He handed me the empty flagon and pushed even closer to me than was necessary in the crowded room. "You look lovely tonight. A little plumpness suits you." He patted my round belly.

I hurried to fetch more ale. When I turned away other requests, explaining that the stock had been drained, the alehouse began to empty. I kept Fernan's cup full, however. Henny was kind enough

to put Alice to bed, and George clapped Fernan on the back before leaving, declaring Fernan to be a right lucky fellow.

There was much cleaning to be done, but I left it for morning so that I could go with Fernan to bed. I brought up one of the new beeswax candles and helped Fernan to undress. He sighed as I stroked his back. "How much money do you expect to make from your new enterprise?" he asked.

"If I sell my regular ale at two pence per gallon and spiced ale at three, I could make two or three shillings each day easily. It costs twelve pence for a bushel of malted barley, but I can malt my own come summer. After I pay for firewood and sundries, I could earn more than a crown each week." I was making most of this up, because I did not know how much I would sell each day, nor whether I could continue to get away with charging more than the one and a half pence for ale allowed by law.

Fernan whistled between his teeth. "That is a tidy sum. How much did you make tonight?"

I would have to ask for more money eventually, and he was in a good mood. I decided to seize an opportune moment. "I had to give drink away in order to get word out about the alehouse. I need to brew even faster, and I am almost out of barley. I shall need another couple of shillings, but I promise that this will be the last time."

The words had hardly left my lips when his fist slammed into the side of my head. The floor tilted ominously. I had not regained my balance when he hit me again, and I fell to the floor. There was a loud ringing in my ear, and though he shouted something at me, I could not make out the words. I crawled to the door, and he did not try to stop me.

I spent the night by the hearth in the alehouse. At dawn, the clomp of Fernan's boots on the stairs woke me. He was dressed in

his cloak, and he carried his satchel. I feigned sleep, so when his footsteps stopped near me, I do not know whether he looked down at me or merely paused to adjust the strap of his satchel. After I heard the door slam, I rose and began the long task of cleaning up from the night before.

I managed to borrow enough money from Henny to get me through the next week, and after that, I did not have to ask for money again. I created new spiced ales, using combinations of juniper, apples, laurel, cinnamon, and lavender, and these were enormously popular. Increasingly, townspeople bought their home supplies from me rather than brewing ale themselves, and I had trouble keeping up with demand. I hired a girl to help with cleaning and serving so that I could devote all of my time to brewing. I knew that soon I would have to find ways to increase my production. I would also have to think about what would happen when Alice died. I could not afford to buy the alehouse from her, and as Alice had no living kin, Ellis Abbey would repossess the alehouse, and I would be without a home or source of income.

The next time Fernan came home, he acted as though nothing had happened between us. He had, after all, merely disciplined his wife. He did leave me an allowance when he departed, so perhaps he meant to make amends, but I did not want his offering of peace. I bided my time, and when I had saved enough money, I filled two bags with coins and placed these, along with the unopened sac he had given me, on a trencher meant for his supper. The alehouse was busy that evening, and some eyebrows rose when I placed a plate full of money in front of my husband. Fernan said nothing about it, but he never offered me another penny of allowance.

MOTHERHOOD

As weeks passed, I became increasingly aware of the babe that grew inside me. When I lay still, I felt a queer fluttering, as though a creature covered in softest eiderdown were circling, trying to settle itself for sleep in my belly. In those quiet moments, joy would thrill in little waves from my heart to my fingertips, sweeping away foreboding about the birth. A restless excitement grew in me too. For the first time in my life, it seemed that something important would belong to me.

Fernan spent more time at the alehouse as the baby's time drew near; he seemed intrigued about the idea of becoming a father. I had not forgiven him, but I decided that it would be better for me to keep him close than to push him away. I fed him, washed his feet, encouraged his self-pride, and made myself available and receptive to him in the night. He began to tease me sometimes as he used to do, and he joked about how strong our son would be—for he was sure the child was a boy—given the mighty kicks he could feel when he rested his hand on my belly.

Despite his more frequent visits, Fernan was away the evening

my lying-in began. When the cramping started, I wondered if I had eaten something gone foul, but at the iron-fisted grip of the first real pain, I knew to send the neighbor to fetch the midwife.

The midwife arrived at dusk to find me crouched in a corner, gasping with each new paroxysm of pain. She was a frail woman with a stooped back and chilblains on her crooked fingers, and I wondered if she was fit for the task. She got me into bed, gave me vinegar and sugar to drink, and opened the window to let in the frigid air. I was grateful for the cold, as it took my mind away from the pain. When I lay back in bed, I felt a warm gush of fluid on my legs and cried out with fear. The old woman clucked and brought some rags.

"This is good, very good. Now that the water has broken, things will go quickly."

"How quickly?" I squeezed my eyes shut as another wave of pain flowed over me.

"Who is to say, dear girl? It is up to Saint Margaret. Before sunrise, I am sure. Let us say a prayer to Saint Margaret now."

She placed an amulet on my belly and began to murmur and chant. I closed my eyes between the pains. When she finished her prayers, she rubbed my flanks with strongly scented rose oil. My throat constricted as the image of the rose garden at the abbey floated unbidden to my mind, but a fresh wave of cramping overpowered the remembrance.

The midwife's granddaughter arrived near the middle of the night and started a fire to heat some water. The midwife napped in a chair as her granddaughter took over the vigil. She was a pretty girl, younger than me, but obviously used to attending at births. She tried to get me to drink more vinegar with sugar, but I could not. I felt as though a beast had clamped its jaws around my middle

and was shaking me, trying to tear me in two. Just when I thought I could bear it no longer, the girl called to her grandmother. The old woman sprang up surprisingly swiftly.

"Is the babe come to meet us finally?"

The girl pointed to what must have been the evidence between my legs.

"Bring more rags, and warm the water. Good, good. I can see the head. Your babe is behaved. Coming out just right. It will be over soon, and you can rest."

There was a slither and another rush of fluid, and then the midwife held a slimy, dark creature in her hands. She deftly flipped it over her forearm and swept her finger in its mouth. A loud wail ensued, and the midwife heaved a sigh of pleasure. "You have a big, healthy baby girl, dearheart. Thank Saint Catherine. She is a dark one, but babies lighten up. I bet this one will turn out as fair as my Maggie here."

The midwife severed the cord, and then she helped her granddaughter to wash and swaddle the baby snugly in strips of linen. She set the cocooned bundle on my chest and busied herself between my trembling legs with a new mess of sticky afterbirth.

The babe's eyes were shut behind swollen lids, and her black hair was matted to the top of her skull, where her skin fluttered and pulsed. She seemed alien, a pupa that had pushed her way out of her casing. I lifted her so that I could see her face better and found that my arms were shaking too. Though her skin was flush with blood, I could tell that her complexion was nut brown, like Fernan's. Her lips were a delicate bow, tiny and perfect. I traced her mouth with my finger, and she opened her eyes, little slits filled with the softest glisten of black, a gaze that was placid, wise, distant. She stared at me as though she could see through me, or as though she knew

me entirely. I could scarcely believe that this strange creature belonged to me.

"There now, mostly clean. Give your bantling aught to drink. We are going to get some sleep, but Maggie will come back at sunrise. Here is a pitcher of ale and a bowl of fresh water. Maggie, dearheart, close the window and bank the fire."

"I have already finished with the fire, Grandmother!" Maggie pulled the shutters closed, and they departed.

I had seen women feeding their babies in the village, but I felt awkward and uncertain. I pulled up my shift and held it bunched around my armpits, exposing my breasts to the cold air, and I brought the baby's face toward one of my puckered nipples. Immediately she parted her lips and clamped her warm velvet mouth on my breast. Her dark cheek pressed into my pale goose-flesh; she sucked with controlled urgency, as though drinking were the only thing in life that mattered, and she was the master of this important task. It was a marvel that she knew exactly what to do. I was not expecting the shock of pleasure, nor the wonder I felt then. After some time, her rhythm slowed, and the grip of her mouth loosened. Her lips made a soft smacking sound as she released, and all of the tension left her little body. Her head lolled back as sleep overcame her.

As I watched her drowse, tears filled my eyes. I was seized with the fear that she would die, that I would lose her. Angels are not meant to dwell in the world of men. I was never meant to have anything so good.

✳

Through the night, the baby woke me with her cries, and each time I pulled her close, I felt a queer sorrowful joy. She was a piece of me that had broken free to become her own person, a stranger. We did not know each other, and yet in the instant I first beheld her, she became everything to me. As long as we both lived, I would never truly be alone again.

When Maggie came again the next morning, she was as cheerful and energetic as she had been the night before. She brought with her a cradle that she had borrowed from the Dryver family; it had been well used by their six babies, but Sara Dryver was not expecting another soon. Maggie fed me bread and milk, and I felt well enough to get up. I was tired and sore, but much of my strength had already returned.

Fortunately, I remained healthy, and I went back to brewing and cooking. Though new motherhood prevented me from sleeping well at night, my heart and my step were light. I swaddled the baby and carried her everywhere with me. When I had to serve drinks in the alehouse, she stayed in her cradle by the hearth. Customers took turns picking her up when she fussed, even a few of the men. Some commented on her dark complexion, but most just cooed and smiled.

I looked up every time the door let in a gust of cold air, hoping that Fernan had returned and we could have the baby christened. When he finally did arrive, he was in a foul mood, for he had heard from one of the townspeople that the baby was a girl. It was evening, and the alehouse was crowded. In winter, there was little to do after the sun set, and the men liked to gather together by the fire and drink spiced ale. Fernan took off his cloak and found a spot on one of the benches nearest the door. I brought him a tankard, and the fleshmonger sitting next to him made a joke about new parents.

Fernan just scowled and swallowed a long draught. He thumped the tankard on the board and did not meet my eye.

Later that night, I brought the baby to him and placed her in his arms. Fernan did not smile, but his expression softened. He put his smallest finger in her mouth, and she sucked eagerly for a moment before she realized that there was no milk to be had. She cried and waved her arms in wide, uncoordinated jerks until her tiny paw found Fernan's finger, and then she settled again.

"We have to choose godparents and have her christened."

Fernan shrugged irritably. "You choose."

"I want my sister to be the godmother."

"Don't be stupid. A peasant sister would ruin your story. Anyway, I shan't travel half a day for a christening. You should ask Henny and George to be godparents."

I knew that he was right. It was impossible for my sister to be the godmother. Even if it were not for the fiction I had created about my life, it would have been an unwise choice, because Lottie had nothing to offer our daughter, whereas Henny and George had wealth and influence in Old Hilgate. I longed for my sister though. The bonds that had closed around my heart when I left the abbey had sprung open again at the birth of my daughter, and I felt the ache of Lottie's absence as though for the first time.

"We can make George and Henny godparents, but I want to name her after my sister, not after Henny."

Fernan sighed loudly. "Henny will be offended, but do what you want. It is on your head."

I lied to Henny, telling her that my sister had died years before, and that I wanted to name my child in honor of the only family

member who had ever truly cared for me. Henny, God bless her, was a sentimental creature. She looked as though she were going to weep over my long dead sister. George grumbled about the irregularity, but Henny told him to mind his own business. Her large extended family lived in Old Hilgate or the immediate environs, and she pitied me for my isolation. The least she could do was to not make a fuss about her goddaughter being named for my dear departed sister.

A dozen parishioners joined us at the church door for the christening. They gathered in the thin midwinter sunlight, stomping their feet and flapping their arms to keep warm. It was a bitterly cold day, and the priest's words hovered in a fog above his head as he muttered his blessing through frozen lips. Father Michael placed salt in the baby's mouth, provoking an indignant howl. George and Henny quickly recited the paternoster and credo, while the priest snuffled and wiped his red nose on the edge of his stole.

We were relieved to proceed to the baptismal font; it was no warmer inside, but at least we were sheltered from the wind. Henny undressed the wailing infant and handed her to Father Michael. Watching my naked child tremble and shriek with panicked incomprehension caused my hands to shake; I willed them to be still. The priest plunged her into icy water for one brief, cruel moment, and then it was mercifully over. Henny wrapped the newly baptised Charlotte in a white gown and delivered her to my waiting arms.

We threw a party for the christening at the alehouse, but Fernan did not even stay until the celebration ended. He said that he had to return to the abbey before sunrise, but I suspected that he wanted to avoid another night of broken sleep. After everyone left,

I banked the fire and took the exhausted Charlotte to bed with me, tucking her little body into the crook of my arm and covering her with warm blankets. Charlotte was my family now.

Alice died quietly one night during Pentecost, and most of the townsfolk attended her funeral. Despite her sharp tongue and bad ale, Alice had been well liked. She had always been willing to help a neighbor in need, and she had provided free food to those who could not pay. I too had developed an affection for Alice, but during her funeral Mass, I was preoccupied by my own fears.

I looked around the church and reflected that I now recognized most of the parishioners. Children shifted from foot to foot, their faces masks of boredom. Some of the girls wore bright ribbons and daisy chains. It had been a long winter, and everyone was grateful for spring.

I rested Charlotte against the swell of my belly, an early sign of the new baby already on its way. It was too soon. My Charlotte would just be learning to walk when this second one arrived. I wondered how many children my sister had, and how they fared. Then I began to worry again about how I was going to manage with Alice gone.

I had to appeal to Fernan for help. I was not sure that he could afford to buy the alehouse back from Ellis Abbey, and even if he could, how would I convince him to do so? He was miserly, and he would think only of the risk of losing money. My roaming gaze slid past the altar and paused on the back of George's balding pate, which dipped slowly forward and then jerked upright as he struggled to stay awake through Mass. His family took up the whole

front pew; Henny hissed like a mother goose at their wiggling, whispering children. George was a businessman. I decided to approach him for advice when church let out.

George set a time to visit me the next morning, but he surprised me by arriving earlier than planned. I was just finishing Charlotte's feeding, and I hastily laced my gown. He did not apologize. Instead, he took a seat atop a table and planted his dirty boots on the bench in a wide stance. George was a short, thickset man, but he took up as much room as a man twice his size.

"So, you want to buy Alice's alehouse?"

I lowered the sleeping Charlotte into her cradle. "Yes. I need to convince Fernan that it would be a sound investment. Business is good, and I am making nearly a pound each month after expenses. What do you think it would cost to buy this building?"

George looked around, frowning. "The alehouse is in poor condition. It needs work. The steward could probably be talked into selling it for twenty pounds."

"If I am careful with my money, I could pay that back in three years."

"I can offer you the money at an interest rate of fifteen percent."

I had not expected this. "Usury is against the law."

George laughed. "Nobody gets arrested for loaning money. Anyway, it would be between you and me. Nobody else need know. And if you cannot make a payment on time, you can find other ways to compensate me. It must get lonely with your husband away so much of the time." He jerked his hips forward suggestively, and his potbelly jiggled. Then he smiled down at me as though he had made a funny joke.

I felt a wave of nausea, then anger. I had not expected this from

George either. "I shall consider your generous offer of fifteen per-cent interest," I replied evenly. I looked him in the eye, unsmiling.

George pouted about my coldness, but he made no further advances. After he departed, I scrubbed away the muddy foot-prints that he had left on the bench and floor.

Despite the unpleasantness, George had been helpful. I had an estimate for the price of the alehouse, and he had given me the idea of offering to pay Fernan back with interest. When I made my proposal to Fernan, he did not blink at the price of twenty pounds. I realized then that I had underestimated both his wealth and his desire to be free of me.

In the end, Fernan managed to negotiate a price of fifteen pounds for the alehouse with the abbey's steward, and I was elated. Though I knew that Fernan had helped me with his own best in-terest in mind, I felt a new warmth for him. He had negotiated skillfully, and he had taken on the encumbrance of purchasing the alehouse without complaint. He was not a toad, like George, and he had remained faithful to his promise to Abbess Elfilda to sup-port me. He did not love me, and I did not love him, but after Fer-nan purchased the alehouse, I found the burden of being a good wife less onerous.

In spring and summer, my ale sold more quickly than ever be-cause of frequent market days, but regular evenings were slow. Long hours of sunlight kept people at work, and cold did not chase them indoors at the end of the day. When it was quiet, I liked to open the window upstairs and lie in bed with Charlotte, watching the colors of the sky change with the sunset. The night winds that sent inky clouds scudding across the square of pink sky framed by our casement also breathed delicious cool air into our cham-ber, waking orange tongues of flame in the fireplace, billowing the

makeshift bed curtains I had hung from one of the ceiling's rough wooden beams. The breeze flowed over our bare skin with a caress that was both voluptuous and pure. Sometimes Charlotte nursed lazily, twining her little fingers in my hair, pulling soft strands against her cheek and holding them there with surprising force. Other times I rocked her in my lap, singing to her. She would look at me with a serious expression, a tiny furrow in her brow, as though she were trying to understand the words of the lullaby. Some nights, she cried inconsolably, though I never knew the reason. When that happened, I walked with her, bouncing, telling her stories she could not understand. Charlotte's wailing would fade to mewling and then snuffling, and if I nuzzled and kissed her smooth skin, she would smile. After she fell asleep, I watched the rapid rise and fall of her tiny chest and drank in her sweet milk scent, wishing that I could see inside her dreams.

Fernan warmed to Charlotte as she grew. Along with his coloring, she inherited his bright smile and liveliness, though not his gregariousness; as a baby, just as now, Charlotte was cautious with strangers. I think that Fernan saw his own reflection in his daughter's face, and that made him happy.

Just before Matilda was born, Charlotte learned to totter around on her sturdy legs, and Fernan liked to chase her with a feather or fuzzy blade of golden sedge, tickling the back of her neck until she laughed with delight. When she lurched too close to fires and hot cauldrons, he snatched her back, but one afternoon he was too slow, and she knocked into a boiling kettle that I had left on the hearth. She burned her arm, and her neck was scalded by water that sloshed from the spout. She still has a rose-colored scar that snakes from the base of her throat to the edge of her jaw, which is why she wears only high-collared gowns.

Charlotte's shrieks reverberated through the kitchen; Fernan scooped her up in his arms and plunged her into an open barrel of ale to cool her skin, but her agonized cries did not abate. I dashed across the room more swiftly than I would have thought possible in my ponderous state, and when I reached out to help him hold the thrashing child, I felt Fernan trembling.

We wrapped Charlotte in soft cloth, and Fernan paced in circles, cradling the whimpering baby, a look of anguish on his face. When she finally settled, I sat beside Fernan and leaned my head against his shoulder. He laced his fingers through mine, and I whispered a prayer as we watched our injured daughter drift into a fitful sleep.

It is said that mothers' remembrances are all about the firstborn, and that is true for me. My memory of Matilda's infancy is a warm-hearted haze punctuated by fleeting images: her downy head nestled against my neck, her clinging to my chest, naked and froglike, in the last warm days of early autumn, her snuffly breathing when she nursed. Matilda was a sweet, quiet baby who never demanded much.

Fernan was unhappy that I bore another girl, and he hated to be kept awake by crying, so he stayed away from Old Hilgate for increasingly long stretches of time after Matilda's birth. I do not doubt that he kept another woman, or women. When he was home, Fernan was mostly cheerful. I paid my debt to him regularly, with interest, and I made him comfortable at the alehouse. He sometimes cuffed the children, but he did not hit me again. I was grateful that Fernan mostly left us alone, and I prayed that I would not become pregnant again for some time.

We chose Matilda's godparents well. John and Matilda Lothrop

ran the town's mill, and after they became her godparents, they crushed my malted barley at no expense. John adjusted the grinding plates to just the right distance apart, so that he did not turn my grain to flour. I gave them free ale in return, but the better end of the bargain was mine, as they saved me many hours of hard work with the hand quern.

It took me two years to repay Fernan, and then I had a third story built on the alehouse, replaced the old daub, plastered the walls, and added glazed windows. The building became one of the finest in town. Old Hilgate was not a great center of commerce, but it had its own bourgeoisie, and I was welcomed into their ranks. I solidified my social position by offering help to merchants with simple reading or writing; I even sometimes helped with accounting. They thought that I had received a rarefied education at the abbey, but in truth, I had only a small amount of knowledge; it was just that their knowledge was even less than mine.

Once Matilda learned to walk and talk, the girls became thick as thieves. Charlotte was practical and inventive, whereas Matilda was both soulful and fierce. Between the two of them, they concocted elaborate schemes, such as the time they created dyes from berries, flowers, and mud, and they used them to paint pictures on the outside wall of the alehouse. They looked nothing like sisters, as Matilda was fairer, with a tawny complexion, hazel eyes, and auburn hair, whereas Charlotte had her father's brown skin, big dark eyes, and a mass of glossy black curls that sprang out from the tight plaits I wound around her head. Yet the two were always together, like peas in a pod, arms circling each other's waist, whispering little-girl secrets in each other's ears.

At the end of each day, Charlotte and Matilda tumbled like pup-

pies into bed with me and demanded a story. I have never possessed much imagination, but I made up stories as best I could. They only liked happy endings, and their favorites involved castles. I talked or sang to them until they fell asleep, their small limbs draped over me. Even at the time, I knew that those were the happiest years of my life.

MISFORTUNE

lthough the four years following Matilda's birth were golden, they were not perfect. There always seemed to be some problem with the brewery; rodents eating the grain, the ale spoiling too soon, the abbey's sergeant imposing unreasonable fines. What made me most unhappy during that period, however, was watching Charlotte awaken to the fact that she was ill-favored.

It is said that beauty is in the eye of the beholder, and while I believe that to be true, it cannot be denied that society has strong opinions about what is beautiful and what is not. My Charlotte was unacceptably dark skinned. It did not matter that she was strong and lithe, or that her shining brown eyes were large and soft as a doe's. It did not matter that she had inherited her father's dazzling smile. To other children—and to many adults—she was ugly, and to them, her outward appearance reflected darkness in her soul.

In her sixth year, at midsummer, Charlotte was attacked. The Saint John's Day celebration was just getting under way in a meadow outside of town. It was a hot day, and I was helping to move a food table into the shade of a tall oak when little Matilda

came pelting over the riverbank at a furious pace. She grabbed my wrist and pulled me away with all of her strength, sobbing. I could not understand what she was trying to tell me, but she pointed toward the river, and I ran in that direction, terrified.

When I crested the riverbank, I saw that a half dozen girls had surrounded Charlotte, shouting names like "witch," "blackie," and "devil's daughter." Their voices were shrill and edged with spite. I recognized three of them as Mylla Ainsley's children, our near neighbors. Charlotte's gown was torn and covered in mud; she had fallen or been pushed to the ground several times. Blood trickled from a gash in her forehead and another on her arm. The girls picked up stones from the bank and launched them forcefully at Charlotte, pushing her farther and farther into the river. Charlotte, wild-eyed, struggled to keep her footing in the rushing water while raising her hands to deflect the stones.

Fury swept me down the bank with such speed that I might have been flying. With strength fueled by rage, I seized the nearest girl by her shoulders, lifting her high into the air. She seemed to weigh nothing at all. I shook her much harder than I intended, and her head wobbled and snapped back and forth as though she were a dead rabbit in the jaws of a dog. The other girls stood frozen, staring. I wanted to throw the evil child into the river, but I released her instead and let her fall to the ground. Charlotte whimpered and waded unsteadily toward me through the current. I scooped her from the water and held her tight, murmuring soothing words, wiping the blood from her brow until she quieted. By the time I looked again, the girls had fled.

Charlotte was afraid to go outside after that. The Ainsley brood lived in our row; there were seven or eight of them, and they roamed like savages. John Ainsley was a master carpenter, and though he

provided well for his family, he traveled for work, leaving his wife, Mylla, alone to manage their children. Mylla was a pious and opinionated woman who could not keep her own home in order, but she always had time to pry into the affairs of other people.

I called on Mylla to let her know what had happened and to enlist her help in making sure that it never happened again. She came to the door wearing a prim gown with an unfashionably high collar. Her face was still lovely, but there were deep creases between her brows, made permanent by age. Her graying hair was pulled back severely and covered by a veil, though her bare feet indicated that she had no immediate plan to leave the house.

"Yes?" She eyed me suspiciously.

"Good morning to you, Goodwife. I have come to tell you about something that involves your girls and my Charlotte."

"The darkie?"

I flushed. "So your daughters called her. They threw stones at her and tried to push her into the river. She could have drowned."

"My girls would know when to stop. They would never have let her drown."

I bit my lip, trying to keep my temper in check. "Stopping just shy of murder is not a demonstration of Christian charity. Your girls were not only calling names, they were throwing stones. Charlotte was terrified."

Mylla glared at me. Her eyes were green and gold, beautiful, but filled with hostility. "True Christians are not just fair of face but fair of spirit. I was not there to see what happened, but I know my girls would never hurt any good Christian girl who was minding her own business."

"Well, I was there, and I am telling you that your children attacked my Charlotte."

"That seems unlikely to me."

"I saw it with my own eyes!"

Mylla shrugged her angular shoulders. "I don't know anything about it."

I stood helpless before her, trembling with fury. Mylla's lips twisted in a smug smile. I yearned to remove the smile with a sharp slap across her face. Instead, I did the only thing I could, which was to bid her good-bye and walk away.

After Saint John's Day, Charlotte clung to my skirts, refusing to go out. I had hoped to tell her that the Ainsley children would leave her alone, but I could not even offer that assurance. I tried to convince her to go out anyway. I did not want my daughter to live her life in fear, and I did not believe that children would bully her too badly in town, where adults were watching. Matilda joined me in trying to convince her, tugging on Charlotte's hair and scampering about, teasing, but Charlotte still refused. Matilda would go outside alone, her head hung low. She was a quiet girl, but determined, and she was not going to let her fearful sister keep her cooped up indoors.

I put Charlotte to work in the brewery; she helped me to sort through the old barley or stir the mash when I had to tend to customers. She was diligent and focused for such a young girl, and I was proud of her. Still, I could tell that she was wistful; she wanted to be in the sunshine with her sister, and I wanted that for her also.

One day, Matilda succeeded in convincing Charlotte to leave the house to play. God help me, I encouraged her to go. I knew that something was amiss when I heard the screaming. Children were always shrieking outside, but this was a sustained keening, a formless wail of distress. I rushed into the street in time to see

that the noise came from one of the Ainsley girls; she ran past me, a flurry of pale blue petticoats, her face contorted in a howl. I did not see Charlotte and Matilda, so I ran in the direction from where the girl had come.

As I passed the first alley, I spotted my daughters. Matilda was helping Charlotte to stand; it looked as though she could bear no weight on her right foot. Charlotte's hair was disheveled, standing out in a wiry halo around her head, and her dress was completely torn from the neckline to the waist. Both girls looked grim. Matilda was muttering something to her sister, and Charlotte was crying.

I stopped in front of them, panting. "What happened?" I asked. My voice sounded too sharp; I had not meant to bark at them.

"They hurt Lottie." Matilda was nearly four, but she still lisped like a baby. There was a smear of blood on her chin.

"Who hurt Lottie?"

"The girls."

"What girls? The Ainsley girls?"

"And others," said Charlotte.

"They said she was a witch. They pushed her."

"My ankle is twisted."

"They said witches get pulled on a rope, and they are naked. And people throw stones."

"Why did the girls run away? Why was the girl screaming?"

Matilda looked at me slyly. "I bit her."

"You bit her?"

"Tilly jumped at the big girl and knocked her over too." Charlotte wiped her tears, leaving a long streak of dirt across her cheek. "Then she bit her. Hard. The girl tried to get away, but Tilly hung on with her teeth. The girl got mad, and then she got

scared because she was bleeding and Tilly wouldn't let go. I was scared too, I thought Tilly would kill her. Then she got her off and ran away, and the others ran too."

Matilda tilted her round face toward me with an expression of defiance mixed with apprehension. She set her mouth in a grim line, waiting for the blast of my anger and her punishment. I wanted the girls to have the appearance of being high born, and they were used to me reacting furiously when they behaved badly. I was not qualified to teach the nuances of manners, but I routed out coarse behaviors by whatever means were necessary.

Matilda held Charlotte's brown arm protectively over her narrow shoulders. A dark bruise was blooming under her eye, and I realized that the blood on her chin belonged to the girl she had bitten. She looked fierce, barbaric. As I watched them, these mysterious creatures who came from my womb, I felt my determination, my certainty, sag and collapse. I did not know what was best for my daughters.

I lifted Charlotte; she was heavy, but I was big and strong enough to cradle her in my arms still. I kissed her forehead. She still had a raw scar there from Saint John's Day. I sighed and said, "We should go home, girls."

This time, it was Mylla Ainsley who called on me. She never frequented the alehouse as a customer, and she looked about the empty room awkwardly, as though she had entered a foreign country. It was clear that she did not want to be there. She wasted no time in getting to the point; her voice crackled with anger. "Your beastly urchin bit my Ann. If I *ever* see either of those animals again, I shall personally whip them to a bloody pulp. We are God-fearing

citizens in this town! You don't belong here. None of you. Not you or your heathen husband or your heathen children. Go back to where you came from!" Her eyes bulged, and taut cords appeared on her neck.

"You cannot come to my home and threaten my children."

"Home? This is no home. This is a nest of sinners!" Her eyes were wild. "I shall threaten if I like. My family has been in Old Hilgate for five generations, and we do not tolerate heathens here, or witches."

My blood turned cold. It was one thing for children to call one another witches, but it was something else entirely for an adult to use that word. Although I had never heard of a child being put to death for being a witch, it was a dangerous accusation.

"What do you mean, 'witch'?"

A glint of triumph shone in Mylla's eyes. She had seen my fear.

"You know exactly what I mean."

"Take that back, or you will regret it."

"Take what back? That your ugly daughter is the result of congress with the devil? That she is marked?" She said this with a sneer, taunting me.

"If you say one more blasphemous word about Charlotte, you will regret it."

"Ha! Who knew that you could be so funny? *You* listen to *me*. I shall say whatever I want. If your brats come within fifty feet of any of my children, I shall flay them. Nobody would stop me, not after what happened to my Ann today. They are animals. You keep them away, or *you* will be sorry!" She left, slamming the door behind her for emphasis.

With trembling fingers, I poured myself a cup of ale, and then another. I could not rid my mind of the image of myself as a young

girl, helpless, unable to defend myself against the laundress who mocked me, I felt the full force of my hatred for Elisabeth, but she now wore the face of Mylla Ainsley. It was worse that the victims were my own daughters; I would have suffered any injury or indignity if my suffering could have spared them theirs. I could not stand having failed Charlotte and Matilda.

After some time, and yet more ale, I grew calmer. My girls were healthy, and they were fortunate to have been born into better circumstances than me. Snot-nosed bullies would not determine their fates. The extent of Charlotte's success in life would be the true measure of whether she had won against Mylla Ainsley and her ilk. In the meanwhile, I would find a way to shut Mylla up about Charlotte. I was determined to give her a taste of her own medicine.

My plan proved easier than I had anticipated. While I chatted with customers in the alehouse, I mentioned that Henry, the itinerant tinker, had seen an unusually large black cat on Mylla's roof, and I asked whether anyone had noticed a strange number of dead rodents and birds on our street. Townsfolk disliked Mylla; some were envious that she had been a great beauty in her youth and had married well, others resented her sanctimoniousness, but all seemed eager to see her brought down a peg. Soon, gossips were asking why the smoke from Mylla's chimney had a greenish tinge, and why she always kept her shutters closed. There were sightings of a mysterious cloaked figure slinking toward the river at night; I even heard claims that a naked woman was seen in the embrace of a shadow at the edge of the woods. It was not in the least believable that a woman as pious and rigid as Mylla would turn to witchcraft, but the story was titillating enough to spread like fire on a thatch roof. To encourage the conflagration, I reported that Maggie, who had taken over most of her grandmother's midwifery practice, had

noticed an unusual number of miscarriages in Old Hilgate. I had even suffered two miscarriages myself.

Eventually, the rumors made their way to Mylla's ears. She did not have to be shrewd to realize that I had something to do with the gossip, and she paid me another visit. This time, I was ready for her.

Mylla threw the door open with a bang, startling a party of travelers who were supping at the alehouse. I was in the brewery, but if I had any doubt about who had slammed the door, it did not last long. Mylla shrieked, "Agnes! Agnes, you rump-fed hag, get out here!"

I straightened my skirts and went out to meet her. "Why, Mylla!" I said. "What a pleasant surprise. What can I do for you? I have some new lavender ale that is fresh and not too sweet if you would like some."

She flushed even more deeply. The travelers had stopped eating and watched with interest, doubtless hoping for an entertaining catfight.

"I know that it is you spreading scurrilous rumors about me!"

I raised my eyebrows. "Rumors? What sort of rumors? You know that I am too busy for gossip."

"You are trying to get me accused of heresy!"

"Oh my. Such a thing would be very dangerous."

Her eyes flashed murderously. "Nobody will believe your villainous lies. Everyone in Old Hilgate knows the godly life I have lived!"

"Oh. Well then, you have nothing to worry about."

"Do not pretend to me that you are not behind this!"

"Maybe if I did hear such a rumor, I could try to squelch it the way you try to squelch lies about my children. You know that all

of Old Hilgate drinks and sups at my tavern. They listen to me. Or maybe you could spend some time here yourself. Get to know people better. They find it strange how much you keep to yourself."

Mylla glared at me, breathing hard. She must have realized that it was a fight she could not win, for she picked up a full flagon from the table and threw it in frustration. It clattered on the sideboard, splashing an arc of ale onto the wall. The man whose ale it had been yelled "Ho!" but Mylla paid him no heed. She spat on the floor and left without saying another word, but I knew that things would get better for Charlotte after that day.

Although Charlotte's troubles caused me pain, we had plenty to eat, a comfortable home, and a community that mostly welcomed us. Fernan remained distant but constant. We had no more children for a time, partly because Fernan was so often absent and partly because of my miscarriages. Fernan still hoped for a son, but I eventually gave him another daughter, which was when our real misfortunes began.

Matilda was four years old when I was pregnant with Catherine, so I was glad to welcome a new baby. She was born healthy, but Fernan came home with a fever one day, and the baby sickened a fortnight after he left again. In the beginning, Catherine was colicky and restless, and she refused to nurse, but this was soon followed by a high fever and flux. I called on Maggie, who gave me some poultices. It seemed at first that Catherine was improving, but then, to my horror, I noticed small reddish spots in her mouth and on her forehead.

Maggie brought her elderly grandmother to see the baby, but by then the rash had spread over Catherine's entire little body, form-

ing flat, velvety patches. Matilda also developed a fever. I did not need a midwife to tell me that this was the pox.

I sent Charlotte to stay with her godparents, and I asked Maggie to fetch medicine from the apothecary. It was of no use, because Matilda vomited every hour, and she could not keep the tonic down. I closed the alehouse so that I could tend to the children day and night.

Catherine whined and fussed, but Matilda's suffering seemed worse. She heaved and choked when there was nothing in her stomach left to come up, and she drifted from fitful sleep to confused delirium. The shivering that racked her body was so violent that her teeth chattered. She sat up in bed once, her eyes open but unseeing, and cried out. Most of the time, I lay helplessly beside her, stroking her back or singing softly. I could not understand how she shivered when her skin was as hot as a cauldron on the fire.

I wondered how Fernan fared, and too soon the news came to find me. A pounding on the door woke me just before dusk; I had nodded off beside the children. I left Matilda sleeping and carried Catherine with me to answer the knock. Catherine had become quieter, and I did not know whether to be glad or worried. She slept most of the time, and I had to rouse her to nurse. The rash on her skin did not seem changed.

At the door stood a burly young man who introduced himself as Ralf, the sergeant for Ellis Abbey. He took a step back when he noticed the rash on Catherine's face.

"Sorry to bother you, Goodwife, but I have brought bad news. The man who owns this alehouse has died, and I am here to evict any tenants."

"Fernan is dead?" My head hurt, and my heart began to pound.

"Was he a relation?" The sergeant asked this reluctantly, not

wanting to hear the answer; he had already guessed that I was not a renter. He scuffed the dirt with his toe. The weather had been dry, and a cloud of fine dust rose.

"He was my husband . . ." I was used to Fernan being gone, and we had shared little genuine intimacy, but the knowledge of his death brought real grief. I thought of the day before his fever, how he teased Charlotte and Matilda, dandling them on his knee just as he had when they were babies. He bounced them high into the air, much to their delight. I couldn't imagine his powerful limbs stilled, his eyes sightless globes, his familiar face a mask of death.

"I am sorry to hear it, madam. I am also sorry to tell you so, but you will have to leave." He looked embarrassed.

"But it is my alehouse! I own it. I have paid every cent for it."

"I don't know anything about that. I was told to come here and make sure there are no squatters."

"How did Fernan die?"

"Pox. He was at the hospital at the abbey, but the nuns could not save him." Ralf crossed himself quickly.

Tears rose to my eyes. I was so tired. "I need to tend to my children, and when they are better, I shall visit the abbey to sort this out. The alehouse is mine."

He looked at me dubiously, unsure what to do.

"Please. I need to go back to my daughter. Tell the reeve, or the steward, that I shall come as soon as I can to sort this out."

The sergeant hesitated. He looked at Catherine, and then he glanced over his shoulder to where his horse was tied. When he looked back at me, his expression was troubled, but he said, "Very well."

I waited on the threshold until he unhitched his horse and left.

Matilda continued to sleep. The vomiting seemed to have

ended, and she felt less feverish to my touch. I searched her face and breast anxiously, hunting for the first red spots, but her tawny skin remained flawless. My lips moved in a whispered prayer to Saint John that Matilda be spared.

I lay back down and arranged Catherine beside me. Her eyelids fluttered faintly, but she did not otherwise stir. I wondered whether I should wake her for a feeding, but she seemed so peaceful that I did not want to disturb her. I watched her little face in repose until the last light from the window died. In the gloom, the rash hardly showed. Her breath came quick as a rabbit's. I settled my head next to her so that I could feel her little belly press up against my cheek with each rapid breath, and I fell back asleep.

In the morning, I woke to find Catherine's body cold. Her lids were open, and her glassy eyes stared sightlessly at the ceiling. As though falling from a height, I watched the pain rush toward me without feeling it. When it hit, the breath left my body soundlessly, surging from my mouth like my soul escaping. My baby was dead. My Catherine.

No tears came, and my body ached with the effort to expel some part of my agony. I dug my fingernails into my arms until bright spots of blood appeared.

I could not leave Matilda, who still slept, so I cradled Catherine's body all morning, kissing her cold brow and praying for her soul. I told myself that she was already with the angels. But who in heaven would comfort her when she was alone and frightened? At the thought of Catherine forsaken and afraid, my tears finally came in great racking sobs.

Matilda woke, and I struggled to compose myself. She looked at me, confused, trying to make sense of what was happening. "Mama, what is it?" Her voice was weak and thick with sleep.

"It is nothing, sweetheart. I am just worried for Catherine." I hid the baby's face from Matilda. "You must be thirsty! I shall fetch you a cup of water."

I went downstairs and placed Catherine's body in her cradle, covering her entirely with a blanket. I felt sick. I wished that Fernan would come home. As soon as the wish flitted through my mind, I remembered that Fernan too was dead, and a new wave of grief threatened to overwhelm me. I could not think about that now. I had to tend to Matilda.

Matilda drank the water I brought, but she ate nothing. "Where is Catherine?" she asked.

"In her cradle. I thought that she would be better there."

"Where is Lottie?"

"With Henny and George. She will come home soon. I have to go out for a little bit. If Henny comes by, tell her to wait for me. I shan't be gone long."

I carried Catherine's body to the rectory and found Father Michael. He had been eating bread and cheese, and he wiped crumbs from his black beard with a bony wrist. I told him numbly about Fernan as well. He blessed the bundle in my arms and said that he would pray for both of their souls, and he would prepare a funeral Mass for Catherine the following day. I am sure that he pitied me, but I could not help but feel that it was only another day's work for him.

When I returned to the alehouse, I saw a pot of steaming stew on the table by the door, and I knew that Henny had come to visit as she did nearly every day. I found her upstairs, laying fresh blankets on Matilda and piling the soiled clothing for washing. When she saw me, she looked concerned; I shook my head, warning her not to ask in front of Matilda.

"We are enjoying having Charlotte with us," Henny said cheer-

fully. "She is a helpful child. She misses you though. She would like to come for a visit. Might do all of you some good!"

"I am not sure, Henny. This air is corrupted. Let her bide with you a bit longer."

"I am glad to see that Matilda looks better!"

"She does. I pray that . . ." My voice trailed away. I avoided meeting Henny's eyes.

"Well, now that I have tidied up here, let's get you some supper. You are too thin!"

Downstairs, I told her about Fernan and Catherine. She embraced me warmly, exclaiming, "Oh, you poor dear girl! You poor, poor dear!"

Her kindness provoked a new flood of tears. When I could speak again, I said, "Henny, I could not manage without you. You are an angel."

"Tut, tut, no talk of angels. Someone up there might hear you. Your job is to care for your little one. Charlotte is fine, and I shall see to the funeral arrangements. All you need do is show up. I shall fetch you tomorrow. Now eat up!"

I thought about Alice sitting in the same spot while Henny spooned food into her mouth, and how strange it was that I had taken her place. I had become an alewife, and like her, I had lost a daughter and a husband. Henny now brought dinner for me as she used to do for Alice. Like the seasons, the cycle of life and death rolls relentlessly forward, grinding our selfhood, those treasured sentiments and aspirations that distinguish each of us, into a handful of dust. Once I am dead, nobody will remember Catherine. Apart from a faint echo in the depths of her sisters' memories, it will be as though she never existed.

*

Spots appeared on Matilda's face the following morning. Though I knew to expect the worst, I had allowed myself to hope that she would be spared, exposing myself anew to the grip of despair.

Matilda looked deathly ill. Although her fever had not returned, she whimpered that her whole body hurt, especially her head. She lay unnaturally still, her limbs limp, her eyes closed. I held her hand, not knowing what else to do. Her fingers did not grip mine in response, and her skin felt clammy and cold.

I left Matilda briefly to attend Catherine's funeral; I do not remember the Mass, for while I mourned one daughter, I battled the terror that I was about to lose another. Even after that short absence from home, I was shocked by Matilda's appearance when I returned. Her face was entirely covered by angry pox, now swelling into discrete mounds, as though a horde of red insects swarmed over her skin. Her eyelids were thick and purple, and her mouth hung slack.

I propped Matilda against my arm and tried to feed her broth, but it trickled down her chin. She was not asleep, but profoundly lethargic, and she seemed unable or unwilling to swallow. Most of the bowlful soaked into her shift.

To quell my rising panic, I kept busy. I brushed Matilda's soft hair, rubbed her skin with ointments from the apothecary, gave her sips of water when I thought she could manage. I washed her clothes and blankets, and I changed her shift. When Henny brought supper, I tried to get Matilda to eat, but it was no use.

For eight days, Matilda languished. Horrific pustules on every part of her body grew to the size of berries, then burst, releasing a foul fluid. Her features became distorted beyond recognition. I plied her with broth and water, but she wasted before my eyes. I cradled her in my arms and prayed to God and to every saint

in heaven to heal my daughter, my fierce, loyal, clever Matilda. I begged God to take my life instead, to let innocent Matilda be raised by her godparents, good people who had lived a better life than I had. At night, Matilda twitched and moaned and kept me from sleeping, but I held her close, wishing that I could somehow bring her spirit inside me, so that I might shelter her and give her a new birth.

On the ninth day, Matilda sat up in bed and asked for a cup of water. My heart leapt with joy; I would have walked all of the way to Saint Augustine's well to fetch her a drink if she had asked me. Matilda's strength returned quickly after that, though her skin remained hideous. The pustules turned purple and black, and some became open sores. The apothecary made new ointments to soothe her pain and promote healing.

I brought Charlotte home, and although I tried to forewarn her, she cried out when she saw Matilda's face. Charlotte quickly regained her composure and kissed the top of Matilda's head, telling her sweetly how much she had missed her, but Matilda began to sniffle. "Does my face look so bad?" she asked, her voice trembling. She looked at the macerated skin of her hand, doubtless wondering if her face looked the same. In truth, it looked worse.

"No!" Charlotte and I said in unison.

More softly, I said, "No, sweetheart. You are my beautiful princess."

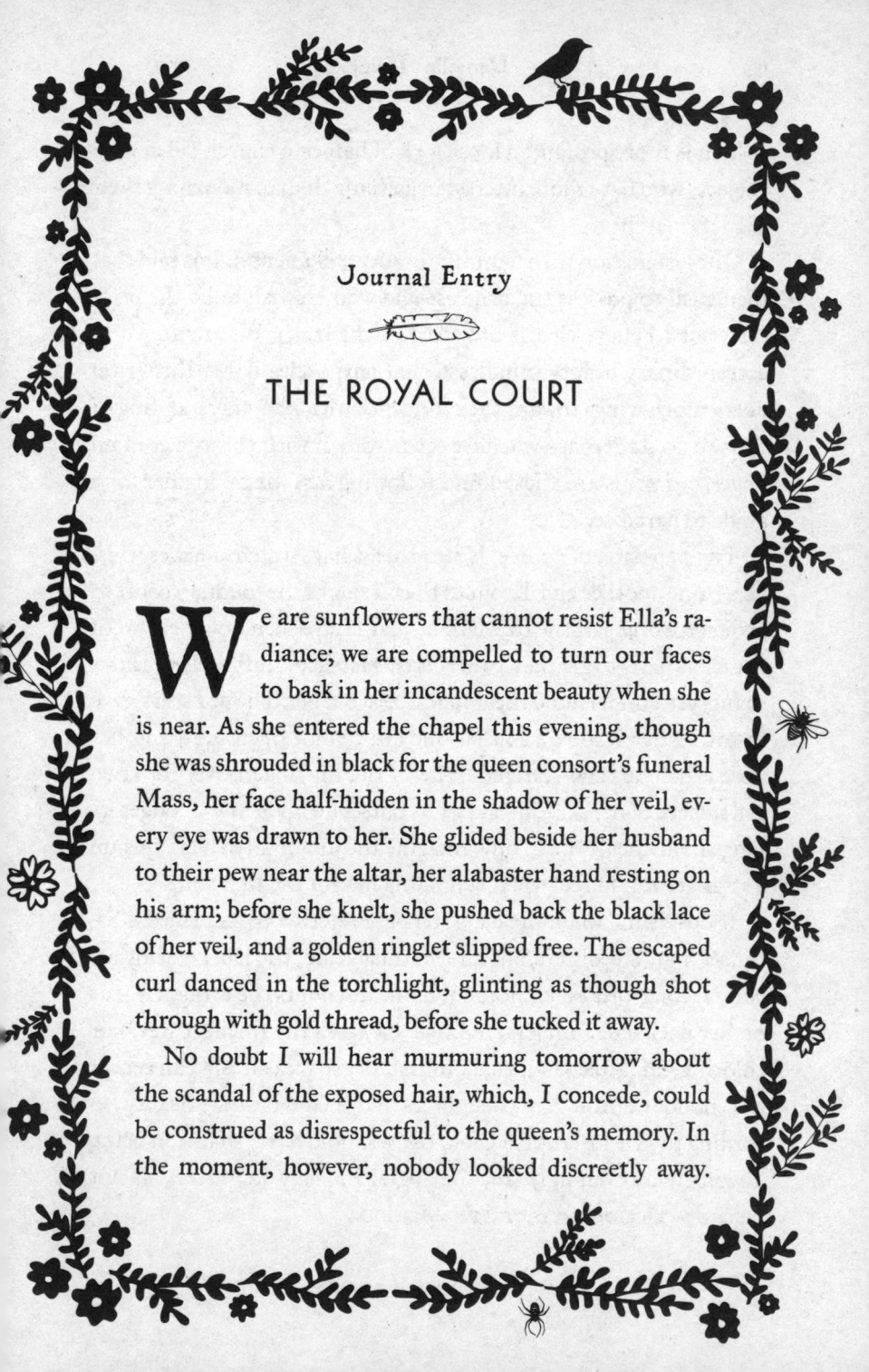

Journal Entry

THE ROYAL COURT

We are sunflowers that cannot resist Ella's radiance; we are compelled to turn our faces to bask in her incandescent beauty when she is near. As she entered the chapel this evening, though she was shrouded in black for the queen consort's funeral Mass, her face half-hidden in the shadow of her veil, every eye was drawn to her. She glided beside her husband to their pew near the altar, her alabaster hand resting on his arm; before she knelt, she pushed back the black lace of her veil, and a golden ringlet slipped free. The escaped curl danced in the torchlight, glinting as though shot through with gold thread, before she tucked it away.

No doubt I will hear murmuring tomorrow about the scandal of the exposed hair, which, I concede, could be construed as disrespectful to the queen's memory. In the moment, however, nobody looked discreetly away.

Which is more profane, a loose lock of hair or a church filled with subjects who have more interest in gawking than in mourning their dead monarch?

Our fascination with feminine beauty is elemental. It is said that men wish to possess the princess and women wish to be the princess, but I believe that is only part of the truth. We are drawn to extraordinary beauty mindlessly and purposelessly; we flutter on dusty moth wings toward the effulgence with no understanding of why we do it. Perhaps when we see a woman with the aspect of an angel, our souls are tricked into following her, mistaking her for a guide to paradise.

The opposite, of course, is also true. I have watched ladies whisper to one another and detour to the far side of the fountain court to avoid crossing paths with Matilda, and I have seen how a crowd of courtiers parts to give her a wide berth. Her face is infinitely precious to me, yet I understand the impulse to avoid her. The pox scars have distorted her features, so that one eye cannot open fully, and her nose is bulbous and cratered. When I run my fingers over the cragged surface of her skin, an odd pain courses up my arm and lodges its fangs in my heart. I can only imagine the jolt of pity and revulsion a stranger might feel when beholding her for the first time.

It upsets me when my daughters are referred to as Princess Elfilda's "ugly stepsisters," but in Matilda's case, the label is sadly accurate. Charlotte is not homely, if one discounts the unsightly scar on her neck, but I understand that she lacks the fine features, fair coloring, and silken hair that our nobility so treasures. I can accept that nobody admires my daughters, but if God bestows beauty according to His inscrutable plan, there should be no shame in being uncomely or even ugly. Yet the "ugly" in "ugly stepsisters" is not mere description but moral repudiation.

I had hoped that Charlotte and Matilda could participate in the care of young George, Ella's son, but his nurse is frightened of them. She seems to believe that their ugliness will contaminate the little boy, or that their appearances are the result of inner corruption, an indication of wicked intent. She refuses to let Charlotte or Matilda hold their nephew, and when they try to play with him, the nurse hovers nearby, squawking and interfering. When George visits with his mother, my daughters have more freedom to engage with him, but those occasions are rare.

I am not ungrateful for our miraculous good fortune, but this is the sort of injustice that makes me wish that we could flee this gilded cage, just the three of us, to live in peaceful seclusion. Despite our rarefied circumstances, we have no control of our destinies.

RETURN TO AVICEFORD MANOR

Workers from the manors traveled to Ellis Abbey every autumn to harvest the grain, and I decided to take advantage of their migration for an escort on my way to petition the abbess. The road to the abbey passed through Old Hilgate, and near Michaelmas each year, workers flocked to the alehouse for a drink. I hungered for tidings of my family, and whenever I discovered that one of the workers came from Aviceford, I plied him with free ale in exchange for news. In this way, I learned about my father's death and about my brother's modest success. Thomas had inherited our father's half-virgate and had painstakingly expanded his landholdings, first through hard work and clever alliances, and then through marriage to his second wife, who was a daughter of the reeve.

Few women traveled for the harvest, and the men knew nothing about Lottie, except that she was still alive, as was her husband. They could not tell me how many children she had, whether she had enough to eat, or whether she was happy. Such details do not interest menfolk.

I did not recognize most of the villagers from Aviceford, and none of them recognized me. My transformation into the daughter of a baronet would not have fooled gentry, but the villagers doffed their caps and called me "m'lady." They gave me curious looks when I asked after Lottie and Thomas, but they were too respectful to question me. It was not that they had heard the false tale of my parentage, but that I dressed in silks and imitated the diction and conduct of my betters. Rose House had provided my first template of gentle manners, and I had learned to emulate Fernan's court-bred speech and bearing. Even though I worked as an alewife, the peasants assumed that I had been born into a respectable family.

When I requested an escort to Ellis Abbey, a group from Cothay Manor accommodated me willingly. I left Charlotte and Matilda with Henny, promising to return within the week. The workers made space in their cart and laid down rough woolen blankets so that I would be comfortable. To reward their kindness, I brought loaves of bread, cheese, and two cold legs of mutton to supplement their suppers.

As we pulled away from the alehouse, I examined its familiar facade; the upstairs windows looked back at me like a pair of consoling eyes. I had known that building in so many moods. The old hunched thatch roof, damp and disheveled in gloomy drizzle, had given way to a smart new slate roof that the alehouse wore like a jaunty hat. In autumn, crimson ivy wrapped the walls in flame, and in summer, misty clouds of miniature white roses climbed the trellises. I had lifted the children on my shoulders to pluck gnarled icicles from the lintel and sweep away the snow that crouched plumply above our heads, waiting to drop. It did not seem possible that we could be evicted from our home.

The villeins had been on the road since first light, but they main-

tained a good pace; we left Old Hilgate in the late morning and arrived at our destination before dusk. When the white spires of the church came into view, time melted away, and I felt the same awe that I had a decade earlier. We made our way up the tree-lined avenue to the road that led to the stable, and when we passed the rose garden and the pond, I had a fleeting urge to jump from the cart and run to Rose House. I wondered what had become of Mary since the countess's death and whether anyone lived at Rose House now.

The party left me at the guesthouse and went on to the barracks at the edge of the compound where they would spend the night. I could not find an empty room, but a woman from Healdshead Manor offered to share hers. It was a tidy, narrow chamber with two simple pallets and a basin, a palace compared to the housing for the workers.

I could not sleep that night. It was not only that the other woman snored and that I was away from my daughters for the first time. It was that I could no longer shut my mind to the worry that the abbess could deny my claim to the alehouse. What future could I offer to Charlotte and Matilda if my living were taken from me? It would not be easy to find Charlotte a husband even with a dowry, and it would be even harder for Matilda if her pox did not heal well. Without either money or beauty, they would have to become servants or settle for a husband nobody else would want.

Lying awake, I thought of my stone collection. The stones had sat for years on the lid of a chest at the alehouse, where the girls liked to sort them by color and size or arrange them in patterns. Though I was a grown woman, a stone in my palm would have calmed me that night.

I had to wait two days for an audience with Abbess Elfilda. The overcast sky sent down a constant, halfhearted drizzle, but I spent my time outdoors, walking restlessly around the compound. As I passed close to the fishpond, sleek frogs leapt from the grass by my feet and splashed into the jade water. The lavender had gone to seed, but there were frowsy blooms left on the rosebushes, nodding their heavy heads in the wind and rain.

I had been little more than a child when Fernan and I had strolled through those grounds and flirted in the garden. I had allowed his brown eyes to become the whole of my world, allowed myself to believe that I would be there to witness the blooming of roses every spring and to collect petals from their fading coronas every autumn. Since then, eight years had passed, more than a third of my life. I was a mother, a widow, an alewife. I felt incomparably older, but the gardens that had bloomed in my absence still beckoned to me. My romantic vision had shifted: I wanted to hold my daughters' little hands and show them the frogs and flowers, hunt for wild strawberries, recline on the grassy banks of the pond to sing songs. The nobility imagine that we peasants are too brutish for fanciful dreams. They should ask themselves why, then, are fairy tales so popular with the masses?

I saw Sister Marjorie, and a few other familiar faces, but they did not recognize me. My sorrow made me shy and apathetic, and I could not bring myself to approach them. Besides, I did not want to answer questions about my years in Old Hilgate. I had built my life on lies, and I was not proud of it.

The sun broke through the clouds as I made my way to the chapter house on the third day, and I chose to see the change in weather as a good omen. I fiddled with my veil, hoping that I had selected the best clothing to project competence and respectability.

Although my name was toward the end of the list of petitioners for the day, I arrived early, having nothing else to keep me occupied. I watched the anxious faces of other petitioners in the anteroom, wondering who would leave successful that day. The expressions on their faces as they left the chapter house told me who had received a favorable response and who had not. I prayed silently that I would be smiling when I left. The afternoon stretched on. My stomach grumbled and I felt light-headed, for I had been too nervous to eat.

When my name was called, I squared my shoulders and forced myself to walk with a firm step. The chapter house had not changed, except that there was now a desk beside the lectern, and this was occupied by an officious-looking nun with a scroll and quill. Jeweled light splashed momentarily across her parchment as the sun darted from behind a cloud and disappeared again. She read out my name and the reason for my visit as I curtsied to Mother Elfilda. I did not recognize the new prioress who stood next to her on the dais. She was younger than the prioress I had known, but she had the same rigid posture and stern face; doubtless she also had the same talent for enforcing discipline.

The abbess was even slighter than I remembered. She could not have been much taller than my Charlotte, and I doubt that she weighed as much. She turned her tranquil gaze toward me. "You are the girl who left with Fernan." It was not a question.

"God be with you, Reverend Mother." I noticed fine lines at the corners of her eyes, radiating like spiderwebs. It struck me as an odd placement of wrinkles, since I had never seen her smile.

"And you are here because you claim that his alehouse belongs to you."

"I bought the alehouse from him, Mother. I paid every penny."

"I suppose that you have brought the new deed?"

I flushed. "We did not sign a deed, my lady. He was my husband."

"Then according to our documents, the alehouse belonged to Fernan. After his death, the property reverts to Ellis Abbey."

"But I am his widow! I am at least due my piece of the inheritance, my lady!" I curtsied low to apologize for the forcefulness of my statement.

The abbess beckoned to the prioress, who stooped toward her. They conferred in low voices, and then Mother Elfilda said, "I am told that we have no record of your dower either. In fact, we do not have a record of your marriage."

"God bless you, Mother, it is true that I had no dower. I was penniless. There may be no record of the marriage, but that is not uncommon. We lived together as man and wife. Surely, my lady, the abbey's court will recognize the law of inheritance for widows!"

The abbess's blue eyes were cold. "The law specifies no such thing. It may be customary for widows to inherit, but in a case where there was no dower—and I suspect no wedding—nothing is owed to you by law. *Vir caput est mulieris.* Man is head of the woman."

"Forgive me, Mother, but I have two young children. What will become of us?" My voice shook with frustration and fear.

"You will return to Aviceford, and Emont will find you a new husband."

"No! Pardon me, my lady. I cannot. Please. I am begging you. Please give me the opportunity to buy back the alehouse from the abbey. I can pay for it in less than two years!"

Abbess Elfilda looked to the prioress, who asked sharply, "What can you offer for it now?"

"I have two pounds in savings. I shall have more soon!"

"This girl is wasting our time, Mother!"

I thought of George and his offer of a loan. "I can get twenty pounds!"

The prioress sighed impatiently. "Where will you find such money?"

"A friend."

She narrowed her eyes at me, but Abbess Elfilda held out her hand and spoke mildly. "Usury is prohibited, and I weary of this discussion."

Not knowing what else to do, I prostrated myself on the stone floor. "Mother, I am begging you, in the name of Jesus our Lord, please help my daughters! They are innocent. I have raised them to be courteous and godly, and their father was the son of a knight. Surely God's plan is not for them to be the wives of coarse and brutish peasants!"

"Get up!" the prioress snapped. "Mother Elfilda is finished with you!"

"No, it is all right, Eleanor." The abbess sounded tired. "They are the daughters of my ward, after all. What do you request on their behalf?"

Much as I had hoped to keep the alehouse, I had prepared myself for rejection during my lonely walks around the pond. I knew what to ask next. "My lady, Charlotte and Matilda would be ideal students for your convent school. They are good girls. They are clever, obedient, and devout."

"How will you pay for their education?" demanded the prioress.

"With respect, Mother Prioress, the abbey's coffers were enriched once when Fernan bought the alehouse, and they are being enriched again now because of his death. I have improved the

building, and it will fetch far more than the last time. These monies, along with Fernan's savings, will pay for his daughters' educations many times over."

The prioress seemed unaffected by my words, but I detected a softening in Mother Elfilda's voice when she said, "This is a just argument. It would be the right and Christian thing to do to bring the girls into our school."

I sagged with relief. All was not lost. "Thank you, my lady! You will find them to be excellent students."

"You still must return to Aviceford."

"Yes, my lady."

She looked at me steadily. "You have genteel manners and speech. You might make a fine lady's maid. My sister now lives at Aviceford Manor, and she is expecting her first child. I shall send you to help."

The days following my audience with the abbess were an agony. I was frantic to return to Charlotte and Matilda, but once I arrived home, I was equally frantic at the thought of losing them. I lay awake at night, listening to their snuffly breaths, resting my fingers lightly on their slender chests to feel their warmth and the movement of the sweet bones beneath their skin. To please them, I made their favorite foods, and though queasiness and the lump in my throat kept me from eating, I watched hungrily for their bright smiles. At times my despair overwhelmed me, and I slinked into the brewery and muffled my sobs in a towel. I tried to feel grateful for their opportunity to attend the convent school, but I was too absorbed by my own selfish pain. When my daughters left my body at birth, their roots remained behind, entwined in the flesh of

my heart, wrapping tighter and deeper as they grew tall and strong in the light of the world. The blood in my veins sang their names with each heartbeat, and I did not know how to survive being torn from them.

Matilda's pox had blackened and were beginning to heal. Scarring was inevitable, but I still prayed back then that some of her beauty would return. Her health had certainly been restored, as had her spirits. It broke my heart to see how happy it made her to have me home again. She gamboled about the alehouse like a spring lamb.

Charlotte, on the other hand, sensed my distress, and she followed me everywhere with a furrowed brow. I knew that I had to tell them of what would come to pass, but I put it off, hoping that I would think of some new solution. When the abbey's sergeant returned with a notice of eviction, however, I knew that I could delay no longer.

I sat with Charlotte and Matilda on the bed and told them that they were to go to school. While they looked at me with wide eyes, I described for them the beauty of Ellis Abbey and the wonder of the library and scriptorium. I told them about the rose garden and the fishpond. When I finished, Matilda said, "But, Mama . . . we want to stay here."

"Yes!" Charlotte agreed. "We never want to leave!"

"I would also like to remain here in Old Hilgate," I replied. "We do not have a choice in this."

They looked alarmed, and Matilda asked, "But why?"

"Because your father is gone, and we are not allowed to live here anymore."

"Where will you go then?"

"I must go to Aviceford Manor."

"Where is that?"

"Not far," I lied. "I shall visit you as soon as I am able."

"But I cannot bear to be without you!"

I sensed Matilda's rising hysteria. Though I had tried to keep the sorrow from my voice, I had not done well. To distract them, I gathered the stones from the chest and handed half of the collection to each girl, saying, "When you miss me, take one of these stones into the palm of your hand, like so. Then close your eyes and concentrate on one of your happiest memories from Old Hilgate. When you do that, God will whisper in my ear, and I shall send you the softest kiss on your cheek. You will feel it, I promise."

The girls were not mollified and would not be turned back from their grief. They were so desolate that I nearly changed my mind in that moment. If I accepted a new husband, no matter what deprivations they would suffer, we would at least stay together as a family.

I knew that their only opportunity for a life of peace and comfort lay in the church. As nuns, they would have a far better life than I could give them. I held my daughters as they wept long into the night.

I sent Charlotte and Matilda to Ellis Abbey with Mylla Ainsley's husband, John. Much as I loathed Mylla, John was a good man, and he was kind to my daughters. He needed to lug his carpentry tools to the abbey, and he was glad of an excuse to ride in a coach.

After we loaded a trunk full of clothing into the carriage, the girls would not say good-bye. Charlotte clung to me and refused to let go. I kissed the top of her head; the frizz of hair that had come loose from her braids tickled my chin. Her familiar scent, like spring grass and fresh-baked bread, brought more tears to my eyes. I knelt awkwardly, still holding Charlotte, and I begged

Matilda to kiss me, but she clutched her doll and turned her face away. Finally, John had to pry Charlotte from me and force them both into the coach; Charlotte tried to twist away, so he cuffed her sharply, and she stumbled into the bench with a dazed look. John swung himself up and gave the horses a smack with the reins. As they pulled away, Matilda watched me with frantic eyes, her arms outstretched, wailing "Mama! Mama!" until her voice was mercifully drowned by the wind.

I told myself that I had done the right thing, that my daughters would be happy, but I was plagued by doubt and by my own excruciating loneliness. Nothing gave me comfort, and I could find no respite from the emptiness. I drank ale to excess, hoping that it would usher in oblivion, and so it did, for a brief while. Then I would wake, dizzy and sick, staring into blackness, startled by a scrabbling rat or wind-rattled shutter. More tankards could hurry the endless blank hours of darkness before dawn, but morning brought nothing but more sickness and another long string of creeping, desolate hours until dusk.

By the time I returned to Aviceford Manor, I had wrung out all of my tears, and I felt as insubstantial as the dry autumn leaves that drifted and crunched underfoot. I paid little attention to the exterior of the manor. Ivy grew thicker than I remembered; the gargoyles were draped with creepers, and inky stains of lichen nibbled at their heads. They leered blindly at me through broken eyelids as I passed through the front entrance. I noted with numb indifference how much the interior had been altered. The austerity of the manor had given way to jumbled, extravagant domesticity. Even the corridors were choked with a hodgepodge of rugs, tap-

estries, carved furniture, and statuary. As the new chamberlain led me through the foyer, I recognized one of the statues, a bronze cerf that held its head cocked to one side, as though listening. My fingers remembered the contours of the smooth flanks and sharp antlers that I had once dusted at Rose House.

In my absence, Emont had taken a wife, Lady Alba, the daughter of the late Count and Countess of Wenslock and sister of Abbess Elfilda. Emont's wife had apparently inherited not only her mother's belongings but also her mother's taste for miscellany and tolerance for clutter.

I had heard tales of Lady Alba when I lived at Ellis Abbey; it was said that she was even more beautiful than her sister, but that she had caused her mother much heartache. As a young woman, Lady Alba had visions and heard the voice of God, and it was said that she was destined to become a great mystic. While her older sister rose in the church to the position of abbess, however, Lady Alba's behaviors became increasingly strange. She stopped eating because she believed that her food was poisoned, and nobody could convince her otherwise. She became so thin that her clothing hung off of her like rags, and she wore the same loose gown every day and night until she smelled like a beast of the woods. After she proclaimed herself to be the Virgin Mary, she was sent to the archbishop for a cure of the evil spirits that had invaded her body. It was even whispered that she bore a demon child.

When Lady Alba reemerged into society, near the time that I moved to the abbey, her mind and beauty had been restored, but her mother could not find her a suitable husband. According to Mary, Lady Wenslock was greatly aggrieved by this problem. She died without seeing her youngest daughter wed, but somebody else had succeeded in finding a match, probably Abbess Elfilda. Emont

could not have been the first choice, but then the trouble of finding a husband grew worse with time. Lady Alba must have been at least a thirty-year-old bride, what Fernan used to call "winter forage."

The new chamberlain introduced himself as Wills; he appeared to be far more pleasant than his predecessor. When I asked what had happened to Geoffrey Poke, Wills replied merely, "He died." Wills had a large round face topped with ginger curls that made me think of a pumpkin, and though he was twice my age, approaching fifty years, his manner was oddly hesitant. I wore fine clothing, my best scarlet silk and a lace wimple that Henny had pronounced perfect for setting off my fair skin and brown eyes. I spoke with a cultured accent, affected a stately bearing, and stood a full head taller than Wills. I expect that he did not quite know what to make of me.

Wills led me through the great hall, which was brightened by white tapestries brought from the library at Rose House, the ones showing the arms of the late Count of Wenslock. I was so used to seeing the tapestries in the smaller chamber that they seemed dwarfed by the great hall. The effect was vaguely comical, like seeing a grown man dressed in clothing meant for a child.

We mounted the stairs to the family's quarters, and Wills knocked lightly on the door to Lady Alba's chambers. A young woman with a worried expression and dark circles under her eyes answered the door. She looked at me suspiciously, and then asked, "What is it that you want, Wills?"

"Not even a hello, Joan? I have brought a new maid sent by the reverend mother. Her name is Agnes."

"You are a maid?" She looked shocked.

"Yes, I am. I am pleased to meet you, Joan."

The woman gaped at me, and then she recovered and smiled

shyly. "Between Gisla and me we've got our hands full, so I'm not sorry to have you join us. Why don't you come in and meet Lady Alba and her new babe. Gisla will figure out how you can best help."

Wills left us, and Joan stood aside to let me into the anteroom that adjoined the main chamber. There was a canopied bed on one side of the room and an imposing armoire on the other. On the wall beside the armoire was a painting of a pretty blond girl seated on a horse. Except for a braid encircling her pale forehead, she wore her hair loose, and it cascaded nearly to her booted foot. I wondered if it was a portrait of a young Lady Alba.

When we entered the large inner chamber, it took a moment for my eyes to adjust to the gloom. Though there were two large windows, the shutters were closed fast, making the room airless and dark. Narrow strips of sunlight squeezed through thin cracks, illuminating dust motes but little else. An enormous bed hulked in the middle of the room; it was raised on a platform beneath a frame draped with hangings. Thin bands of moted light slashed the drapes with the radiance of a cloudless afternoon. As my eyes grew used to the shadows, I could make out the *W*'s encircled by gold crowns embroidered on the canopy and bed curtains. A silvery voice called from behind the drapes. "Joan! Did you fetch my wine?" The familiar clear timbre of the voice made me shiver.

"No, my lady, I am going to fetch it now. I have brought a new maid sent for your comfort by Mother Elfilda. She is called Agnes."

"My sister sends a maid; should I be afraid? I think not, she has brought ought that is sought. That is a new . . . thought? . . . Spot?" There was a long pause and then a giggle. "What rot!"

Joan pulled back the curtain as Lady Alba made blowing sounds with her lips. She lay sprawled on the feather bed, dressed only in a

gossamer shift, her back resting against a pile of satin pillows. Like her sister, she had the delicate features of a doll, and her skin was so pale that she glowed like the moon in the dim light. Lady Alba did not otherwise share the abbess's ethereal quality, however. She was plump, with dimpled cheeks and a jiggling bosom that overflowed her bodice. Her teeth were discolored, giving her a slightly sinister air when she smiled, but it was easy to see why she had been considered such a beauty when she was younger.

An elderly woman—Gisla, I assumed—sat on a stool next to Lady Alba, holding the ends of her corn-silk hair in one hand and a brush in the other. "Welcome, Agnes." Her voice creaked like a door on ancient hinges. "We will be glad of your help."

I was startled by the wail of an infant; only then did I notice the cradle beside the bed. The cry wrought its work on my breasts; I felt a painful tingling, and then milk gushed from my stiffened nipples, soaking through my gown. Gisla's eyes widened.

"You have milk! Where is your baby?"

My arms ached for Catherine as though she had just that moment been torn from me. "She is dead."

"I am so sorry, dear. But I must say, you have come at a good time! We are looking for a wet nurse for the little one."

I did not know what to feel. The infant's cry had made the pain of Catherine's death fresh and sharp, but at the same time, I longed for the comfort of a baby in my arms.

Joan picked up the crying infant and rocked her gently. Lady Alba paid no attention; she flicked impatiently at some invisible lint on her sheet and asked Joan again to fetch her wine. Gisla rose stiffly from her stool and shuffled around the bed. "Hand me the babe, Joan. You go and fetch the mistress her drink." She turned to me. "Come with me; let's see if you can quiet this little thing."

I followed Gisla to the anteroom, where she bade me to sit on the edge of the bed. "It would be a shame for your milk to go to waste. And you will feel better to get rid of some of it." She handed me the baby, who weighed nothing at all. My daughters had all been big and sturdy; Lady Alba's baby was a mere wisp by comparison.

"What is her name?" I asked.

"Elfilda, after her godmother. But we call her Ella."

14

ELLA

Ella and I had problems from the beginning. Nursing was difficult for both of us, because Ella could not abide the rapid flow of milk, and yet she was hungry. She latched eagerly to my breast, but within moments she would begin to thrash her head from side to side, pulling painfully on my nipple. She would then release with an angry cry, jerking her fists in the air while my milk sprayed against her reddened cheek. I would settle her by walking and singing, but the sequence inevitably repeated until my milk had been drained to a slow trickle.

I worried about Ella's feedings because she was so tiny. I could cradle her head in one hand and easily support her entire body on my forearm. By her age, Charlotte had already weighed a stone, but Ella must have weighed less than half that. She was slim and long limbed, with skin so translucent that I could see the blue veins snaking across her scalp. Her little body thrummed with nervous energy, and her voice was high pitched and eerie, like a lute strung too tight. She had the alert look of a wary bird, and her eyes were

a dark slate; it was only later that the color faded to the peculiar shade of violet she is so famous for now.

Lady Alba did not like to be woken by the baby, so I slept in the anteroom with Ella and Gisla, while Joan used the trundle in the main chamber. Ella woke every two hours through the night, and I passed my days in an exhausted fog. Remembering the sweet, idle first months of my own daughters' lives made me miss them all the more. My babies had nursed with calm earnestness, their eyes unfocused, their expressions entranced, as though they were gazing into the heavens. My milk made them drowsy and content, and they drifted into sleep like a skiff pushed along by a light breeze.

With Ella, feeding was a battle that was never won nor lost, only punctuated by armistices when both sides were too spent to continue. I got to rest when Lady Alba took the baby, but that was often only once each day. Sometimes Lady Alba played with her daughter's fingers and toes and spoke to her in singsong nonsense rhymes. Other times, she placed her in the cradle and ignored her completely. Whenever Ella cried, Lady Alba gave her to me to take away.

Because my entire responsibility was to care for the baby, I enjoyed far greater freedom than I had during my previous time at the manor. I was not officially permitted free rein of the house, but in practice nobody checked my movements. Lady Alba left her chambers only for supper, and sometimes not even then. If she was not in the mood to dress, she would have Joan bring her food on a tray.

When Ella was awake, I swaddled her and carried her with me to wander the corridors and grounds. She liked to be walked, and I found Lady Alba's chambers suffocating, so I was glad for an escape. Though I usually skirted the great hall by taking the outside

staircase and reentering by the back foyer, on a particularly rainy autumn day, I decided to stay indoors.

The great hall seemed to be unoccupied. A fire roared in the giant hearth, its crackling drowned by the torrent of rain that battered the windows. The air was chill, and though I disapproved of the wastefulness of a large fire, I was tempted to warm my hands for a moment.

Two imposing high-backed oak chairs flanked the fireplace, new additions since the arrival of Lady Alba. I had almost traversed the long shadow of the nearest chair when I glimpsed a hand on the armrest. I froze, realizing that the room was occupied after all. I meant to creep along the wall and leave undiscovered through the screens passage, but fate would not have it so. A puddle of water had formed at the base of one of the windows, making the floor slick. My fall was swift and silent. Instinctively, I twisted my body in midair, so that my back struck the floor, followed by my head. My ears rang from the thud of my skull against the stone, but I succeeded in holding Ella away from my body, unscathed. For a moment, we remained an inert tableau, my back to the floor with Ella suspended above me, her face toward the roof. I wondered if she miraculously still slept, but then came a piercing shriek. The cry continued until she had squeezed every shred of breath from her tiny body; she fell silent as she choked and struggled to fill her chest anew, and then she let loose another shrill wail.

I rose awkwardly to my feet, hushing the baby. My head throbbed. Standing before me was Emont, arms crossed, frowning. I curtsied and apologized for the intrusion.

"You must be the nurse." His words were rounded by a soft slur. From his silhouette, I could see that he had grown heavier.

"Yes, sir." I jiggled Ella, whose cries had begun to subside.

"How is my daughter?"

"She does well, sir." On an impulse, I added, "Would you like to hold her?"

He looked at his child dubiously. I thought that he would say no, but he surprised me by reaching out his arms. His hands were steady. I gave him the little bundle, and he retreated to his chair by the fire, murmuring. I followed him, saying, "She knows her father. She is quiet in your arms."

He smiled up at me, pleased. Age and paunch had not improved his looks, but his smile was charming. "You seem familiar. What is your name?"

"Agnes, sir."

"Agnes. Do I know you?"

"I worked here years ago. As a laundry girl."

His gaze swept over me quizzically. "You were not the girl who looked after me when I was ill?"

"I was, sir."

"My. Yes, I recognize your eyes. You were always so grave."

"My cow eyes, sir? I believe that is what you called them."

Emont snorted. "Yes, I recall that you were always direct too. I see that you have grown up. You seem quite . . . elegant." In the firelight, I could see that his coppery hair was now streaked with white. He had pouches under his eyes, and one of his lids drooped, but the irises were a more startling blue than I remembered.

"I had the benefit of some education, and I married well."

"What happened to your husband?"

"He died of the pox."

"Ah." He looked down at Ella, who had fallen asleep again. He rocked her gently. "I am sorry."

My throat tightened in response to his solicitude.

"What is that by your ear? Are you bleeding?"

I lifted my hand to my temple, and my fingers came away sticky with blood. Emont rose and handed Ella back to me. I realized that I had grown taller than him. He pulled an embroidered handkerchief from his pocket and reached for my face. I flinched as he leaned close and dabbed softly. His breath smelled strongly of wine. I stood stiff and ill at ease, but he seemed to find nothing strange about the situation. After a moment, he gave the handkerchief to me, saying, "I think that the bleeding has stopped, but keep this in case you need it."

"Thank you." I stepped away from him.

"You must bring Ella to see me every day."

"Yes, sir."

"I am glad that you are back, Agnes."

"Thank you, sir."

He smiled at me and then sank back into his chair, closing his eyes wearily.

It became my routine to bring the baby to the great hall each day at dawn, after her morning feeding. Ella and her father were both early risers. Emont was occasionally surly, but he took only ale before noon, so he was not drunk in the mornings. In the hour or two before the chamberlain or the reeve arrived to discuss manorial business, Emont held his daughter, cooing like a grandmother. I was beginning to notice how peculiar he was, how bumbling and unrefined, something that I could not see as a child. He paid little heed to social convention, but I do not believe that he rebelled against it; he was simply oblivious.

Emont conversed with me as though I were his equal. He asked

about my experiences, and he was particularly interested in my time at the brewery. The first morning, he asked how I learned to brew ale.

"Alice, the former alewife, gave me lessons."

"Was it difficult?"

I laughed. "Yes, sir. The first six batches were awful! I thought that I would go out of business before I even got started."

"What did you do wrong?" He sounded genuinely curious.

"Well, first I damaged the husks of the barley, and then I ground it to too fine a flour. Then I mashed too long, then too short, then too hot, then too cool. Then I boiled it too soon and the head fell." I smiled. "There are so many ways to ruin a batch of ale!"

Emont handed me his cup. "Taste this and tell me what the brewer could do better."

I took a dainty sip. "Better is a matter of taste, sir. I find this overly sweet. I would have added more gruit. I would have let it stand longer before straining."

Emont looked delighted, as though I were a juggler who had performed a difficult trick. After that, he made me taste his ale nearly every day and give him a critique. It became a sort of game for him to predict what I would say when I did my tasting.

As the time for manorial business approached, Emont became restless and irritable. He complained about the difficulties of administration and the demands of the abbey. He particularly disliked court days, when he had to preside over disputes and disciplinary actions for wrongdoers. On those days, he yelled for more ale, and the serving boys could not bring it fast enough. By the time the first petitioner arrived, Emont was often soused and completely ineffectual.

One morning, when I prepared to take Ella away, Emont re-

quested that I stay. The baby had fallen asleep, so I remained in my chair. Emont fidgeted with his cuffs and pushed stray hairs back from his brow. His hair had thinned, and he wore his curls pulled back in a scraggly tail. He rose and paced by the fireplace. When the bailiff arrived, he scowled, saying, "I was rather hoping you might have found something else to do with your morning."

The bailiff, a bearded bearlike man with a gruff demeanor, did not look amused. He carried a roll of parchment under his arm, and his face became grimmer when he saw me. He turned to Emont. "Sir. What is the woman doing here?"

"I asked her to stay."

The bailiff opened his mouth to reply but then seemed to change his mind. He shook his head in disapproval as he spread the parchment on a trestle table, weighing the edges down with Lady Alba's bronze candleholders. "We have some problems, sir."

Emont shrugged impatiently. "We always have problems."

"We could barely make our payment to the abbey. But now the mill needs a new millstone, which is probably coming at a good time, since one of the horses that's used to run the mill is lame. We have brought in no new fines this month, and we have lost three villeins to fever."

I shivered as I thought of Lottie and Thomas, hoping that they were not among the dead. I was anxious to visit the village, but there was not enough time between Ella's feedings.

"Also, we are losing our second girl this year to Cranfield Hall. We need to make these girls marry Aviceford boys or raise the price for leaving. We are short enough of hands as it is."

"What is the fee that we have levied?"

"One ox."

"That does not seem too low a price."

"And yet it is, apparently, because they keep leaving." The bailiff's tone was biting.

"Who decided that it should cost an ox?"

"You did, sir."

"Well, what should it be?"

"Is it not up to you to decide, sir? An ox does not seem to be sufficient."

The exchange continued in this manner for some time, with both men becoming increasingly frustrated. When Emont ended their meeting, it seemed to me that nothing had been resolved. Emont flopped heavily into his chair and bellowed for some wine. A serving boy scurried in, carrying a carafe and a cup.

"I hate this place." Emont rubbed his eyelids and blinked. I wondered whether Ella would inherit his long lashes. "It gives me a headache."

"Why do you use horses to run the mill?"

"Why not?"

"Because oxen are cheaper. They eat less and do not need to be shod. But the way the abbey's mill works, using wind, is cheapest of all. You do not have to feed a windmill."

"The mill has always been run by horses."

I shrugged. "That does not mean that it must always remain so."

Emont looked annoyed. Perhaps my presence had been a comfort to him, but it was not anymore, so I prepared to leave.

"Good day to you," he said wearily.

I tucked Ella closer and curtsied.

"I shall see you in the morning, sir."

"Yes, see you in the morning."

I took most of my meals in the family's quarters, along with Joan and Gisla. They were pleasant companions, though Joan could be testy when Lady Alba was giving her trouble. The mistress was capricious, and she sometimes made unreasonable demands. On one occasion, she got it into her head that we were all living inside her looking glass, and that the image in the looking glass was the real world. She had Joan turn everything in her chamber backward, including the bedclothes.

On a more frightening occasion, Lady Alba decided that Ella was a changeling. I had left the baby in her mother's care, and Joan caught her dangling the squalling Ella by her legs over the fire, shrieking, "Tell me your name! Tell me your name!" After that day, we made sure that Lady Alba was never alone with her daughter, although to my knowledge, she never mentioned fairies or changelings again.

Rarely, I took a meal in the kitchen with the other servants. The atmosphere was more relaxed since Wills took Geoffrey Poke's place as chamberlain; seating by rank was no longer strictly enforced, and the chatter was louder and more jovial. Many of the servants were new to me, but the one person I would gladly have missed was still there. The laundress had grown even fatter since I had last seen her, and the lines on her face gave her an expression of perpetual sourness.

The first time that I noticed her, my heart quickened, and my palms began to sweat. I forced myself to walk slowly to her table and take a place across from her, where I sat with my hands neatly folded until she looked up. I expected her to be startled, but she merely narrowed her eyes suspiciously.

"Huh? What do you want?" As she spoke, she opened her mouth wide, affording me an unpleasant view of the food she was chewing.

"I just stopped by to say hello, Elisabeth."

"Do I know you?"

"You don't recognize me?"

I was gratified to see her eyes widen.

"What are you doing here?"

"I am the nurse for Sir Emont and Lady Alba's baby."

The laundress looked around uncomfortably. "You have come up in the world, haven't you?" She gave me a treacly smile. Her teeth were rotting.

"Yes, I have." I reached across the table and took the bread from her plate, and then I smiled back at her. "It is so lovely to see you again."

I walked away. Elisabeth was worried, and that was enough for the moment.

It was not until Saint Crispin's Day that I had an opportunity to visit Aviceford Village. Both Sir Emont and Lady Alba had fallen ill with flux and vomiting, and I offered to keep the baby away for the day. Joan and Gisla were so busy caring for the mistress that they did not ask what I would do. I doubt that they would have approved of my plan to take Ella to the parish church with me, so I did not mention it.

Ella was a fussy baby, but she was most settled when we walked. Her watchful eyes stayed open, and I chatted to her along the way. I pointed out a squirrel and a sparrow, and I sang a song about a robin that my mother used to sing. I could only remember a single verse, which I repeated over and over, but Ella did not seem to mind. She frowned at the sky or stared at my chin with a serious expression on her face.

Arches of crimson and gold branches over the road were made brighter by vivid patches of cerulean sky. There was not a breath of wind, but the occasional leaf came loose and floated down. One landed on Ella's head, and she responded with such wide-eyed shock and consternation that I had to laugh.

We came upon the bridge by the church far sooner than I expected, for I remembered the walk as being much longer. The river was no more than a stream, and the span of the bridge was so short that I could cross it in five strides.

When the church came into view, I was seized by shyness. Clusters of villagers sauntered down the lane opposite me, collecting in the churchyard; over the hubbub of conversations drifted the laughter and shrieks of young children. The church, which once seemed so magnificent, looked dingy and inconsequential to me now. Some of the villagers glanced at me curiously.

I had not seen my sister and brother since they were youths, but I recognized Thomas in the crowd right away. His head was uncovered, and he wore his wavy brown hair the same way he had as a boy. Though his shoulders had broadened, he still slouched as he used to. He was engaged in conversation with an older man when I tugged on his sleeve.

"Yes?" He took a step back.

"Thomas! I am your sister Agnes!"

"Agnes?" A look of surprise came over his face. "Not little Nessie who went off to the manor house?"

He regarded me from head to foot, and I realized that my fashionable wool dress and wimple were foreign in the village. I touched the edge of my veil self-consciously. "I am. I went to Ellis Abbey for a time, and then to the town of Old Hilgate. I worked as an alewife."

"You sound mighty fancy. Where did you learn to talk like that?"

"The abbey, I suppose."

My brother was like someone from a dream. He was both familiar and entirely alien. His placid brown eyes were the same, but his face was bronzed by the sun and deeply creased, ancient. Like the bridge over the stream, and the church, he had shrunk. I remembered a strapping youth, clever from his lessons at church, seasoned and wise from his work in the fields. Before me was a tentative, uncouth peasant with stooped shoulders and gnarled hands, a gap where his front tooth had gone missing, cheeks hollow from privation.

Thomas turned back to the man whose conversation I had interrupted. "Can you believe this is my little sister?"

"I would've guessed she was lady of the manor!"

"Where are you living now, Nessie? Look at your sweet babe!" Having recovered from his surprise, Thomas seemed pleased to see me. He peered at Ella.

"Oh—" I felt disoriented and unaccountably miserable. "Nay, this here is the daughter of Lady Alba. I am her nurse."

"So you are back at the manor!"

As Thomas spoke, a small, meek woman approached. She had a purple bruise on her weather-worn cheek, and she held the hand of a boy of about three years.

"Lottie! Would you believe it . . . Here is Nessie!"

The woman stiffened and looked at me warily.

"Lottie?" My voice caught in my throat. She looked nothing like the sister I remembered. "Why— Why, I wouldn't have recognized you!" I had tried to sound cheerful to cover my confusion, but I realized that my words might have been hurtful. I paused lamely, searching my tumultuous mind for better words. We both remained rooted in place.

"Nessie was just telling me that she is the nurse at the manor. This is the new baby."

"Her name is Ella," I volunteered, my voice too bright.

As though woken by her name, Ella began to wail. I jiggled her while Thomas and Lottie stood awkwardly by.

"Do tell me your news, both of you! Thomas, I have heard that you are doing well. And, Lottie, how many children do you have? Where is your home?"

"I've got three. This one's Hugh. I lost four. My Margaret drowned last spring."

I could barely hear her over Ella's crying. "Oh, Lottie, I am so sorry. I hope the others are well?"

"Well enough."

"How is your husband? Aldred?"

Thomas crossed his arms and frowned. "His name's Aldrich."

Lottie shot a worried look at her brother.

Ella continued to cry, and little Hugh pulled on his mother's arm.

"What celebrations are planned for Saint Crispin's Day?"

Thomas gestured to women setting out food on a table next to the church. "Mass. Then we eat, as usual. That woman on the end with the green hood, she's my wife, Matilda."

"Matilda! That is the name of my daughter." I looked at Lottie expectantly, but she did not ask about my children. She swatted her son to stop him from tugging on her. Her gaze darted around the crowd.

"A well-chosen name," Thomas said.

We all fell silent except for Ella. I groped anxiously for something to say, but my mind had been swept clean. The baby's piercing cry nettled me. Finally, Thomas said, "Looks like time to go in for Mass. You coming, Nessie?"

"I'll try to settle the baby, and then I may come in."

"Well, sure is a surprise to see you. I hope we shall see more of you, now that you are back. We heard that you left, but then nothing more. I feared you died." He looked to Lottie. "Are you coming in?"

Lottie nodded to him and gave me a weak smile. "There has been a Christmastide celebration at the manor since Lady Alba came." A bit of warmth entered her voice. "Maybe we shall see you there."

I watched until they disappeared through the church door, but Lottie never looked back. I walked back over the bridge as quickly as I could while comforting Ella, ashamed by how relieved I felt to be returning to the manor.

MANORIAL BUSINESS

Christmastide was a sad time for me. I longed to return to my life in Old Hilgate with Charlotte and Matilda, or even to hear news about how they fared at Ellis Abbey. I consoled myself by remembering the roasted swan and pudding that the nuns had served at the Feast of the Epiphany. I could imagine the delight on my girls' faces when they tasted the first succulent bites. Charlotte would nibble daintily, luxuriating in new delicacies, while Matilda would wolf down her meal and then sneak her little fingers onto her sister's plate, crawling her hand forward like a clever spider. I imagined them hale and smiling; I could not bring myself to consider any other possibility.

Lady Alba worked herself into a state of high excitement before the holidays as she planned for banquets. She usually lost interest in new pursuits within hours, but Christmas held a particular fascination for her. She emerged from the cocoon of her chambers to give servants orders and supervise their preparations. It was the only time of year that she undertook any of her duties as lady of the manor, and she did a poor job of it, not knowing how the manor

functioned. Some of her dictates were nonsensical, and some re-sulted in needless waste, but nobody was brave enough to gainsay Lady Alba when her blue eyes were flashing and her rosy lips were parted in a fierce smile. The servants grumbled, and Emont was even more mercurial than usual. In the mornings, when I brought Ella to him, he bellyached about his wife's intention to invite every soul in Aviceford for Twelfth Night.

"It is good for you to be charitable," I told him. "Loyal villagers make better workers than unhappy ones."

"Maybe it is good to be charitable when you are rich, but it is a right foolish thing to be when you cannot afford it!"

I had sat through enough of Emont's business meetings to know that his statement was true. "Perhaps you could reason with Lady Alba? Tell her to bring some provisions to the parish church instead?"

"Reason?" Emont snorted scornfully. "One does not reason with Lady Alba."

It was not proper for him to speak to me so familiarly, but it was not unusual either.

"Why not hunt for venison?" I was still thinking of Christmas-tide at the abbey.

"I have no license, and this land is all royal forest hereabouts."

"Lady Alba could ask her sister. The king is generous with the abbey. And he would not deny a license to his cousin, particularly not at Christmas."

"Second cousin. You do not see us getting visits from the king," he said dryly. "But it is a good suggestion. That might suit my lady very well. She is an excellent horsewoman." Emont smiled for the first time in days.

🐝

Lady Alba did organize a hunting party, and I observed their return through the warped glazing of a window in the great hall. I was taking advantage of the master and mistress's absence by walking with Ella through the empty house when a wavering blotch of color crested the brown hills near the orchard. A fragment of scarlet streaked away, and quite suddenly Lady Alba was galloping toward me at full speed, a mere stone's throw from the window. She pulled her horse up sharply just in front of the manor; the bay mare reared, beating the air like a charger in battle. Tendrils of pale hair whipped in the wind, and the lady's red cloak billowed and fluttered behind her. Her face was flushed, and her smile was wild and triumphant.

When Emont plodded into view, he looked stodgy and grim in comparison. His wife tossed some words to him over her shoulder, and then she threw her head back in laughter. Emont's countenance soured further.

I did not wait to see what quarry they had caught, because I had no invitation to be in the great hall, and I did not want to be discovered. I later heard that they had killed two small red deer. Much of the meat was preserved for Sir Emont and Lady Alba, but there were plenty of leftover innards to make pies for the villagers.

The banquet at Aviceford Manor was a strange affair. The great hall was decorated with garlands of holly, ivy, and bay, and scores of candles glowed in the wall sconces and on the tables. These, along with a hearty fire, made the room festive and welcoming. The people of Aviceford were not used to such finery, however. They entered bashfully, hesitating before taking a place at the long tables, and then they whispered or sat in silence, as in church.

Lady Alba wore a green silk kirtle of a hue that flattered her milky complexion; jewels sparkled at her throat and on the gold

net caul that bound her fair hair. She swept through the aisles that divided the long tables, loudly commanding the villagers to eat more and be merry. Every man, woman, and child paused with head bowed as she passed by, in direct opposition to her bidding. She continued to bawl cheerfully, unobservant, stopping every now and again to take some wine. Emont sat alone at the oak table on the dais, sipping his drink and pecking at his food, ignoring his wife's behavior.

I left Ella with Joan in the solar so that I could find my brother and sister. After taking in the scene from the top of the stairs to the great hall, I descended nervously. My mind had recoiled from thoughts about Thomas and Lottie since our awkward exchange at the church, and I was reluctant to touch a wound that had not yet healed. Though we were bound by blood, we had grown so far apart, as though we no longer spoke a common language.

I closed my eyes to be rid of the image of Thomas and Lottie walking away from me, but the devil played a trick. Behind my eyelids, I saw not my brother and sister, but Charlotte and Matilda, their backs to me, receding in the distance. My heart pounded and my hands grew slick. My children were younger than I was when I left home. Would they become estranged from me too? I had feared never being reunited with my children, but to lose our attachment would be a worse fate, one I could not bear.

I found Lottie when I reached the bottom of the stairs. She was sitting halfway across the room, her head bent low over her plate, eagerly shoveling food into her mouth. Next to her sat a tall, spare man, her husband. He was feasting with as much determination as Lottie; I could not make out his features well, except for a beaklike nose that pointed toward his trencher. A skinny girl of about six years sat next to him, and while I watched, she dropped her spoon

on the floor. The man cuffed the back of her head so hard that her chin crashed against her breastbone. She did not cry out, and the man resumed eating.

I looked back at my sister. What did that sallow-faced woman have to do with me, or with the Lottie I remembered? She had been depleted, used up by the exigencies of her family and the costs she had paid for mere survival. Her life had unwound too quickly, and there was nothing left to look forward to other than the gnawing hunger of winter and more children who would die before they were grown. The same would have been true for me had I stayed.

I made my decision swiftly, strangling a nascent bloom of horror. I ran back up the stairs, knowing that I would not see my brother or sister again.

Joan sat in the anteroom to Lady Alba's apartment, braiding her hair by the light of a guttering candle. She was surprised that I returned so soon. "Did your family not come?" she asked.

"Nay, they did not come. You should go down now and eat some food. I shall watch over the baby."

"She will sleep now through the night, I expect. You could come too. I heard that there will be a minstrel after supper."

"I am tired, and I have heard minstrels before."

Joan, who was still a little bit in awe of my former life, did not attempt to persuade me further. She finished braiding her hair and left for the great hall. I checked on Ella in her cradle and then sank onto the bed in the anteroom. By the light of the candle, I could dimly make out the painting beside the armoire. Gisla had confirmed that the portrait was of our mistress as a child, seated on her favorite horse. The girl in the painting had a serene expression, so

different from Lady Alba's today. I wondered whether the demon that had possessed her as a young woman had been only partially exorcised, whether the shadow still lived within her.

My mind pulled at its traces like a stubborn mule, trying to turn my thoughts back to Lottie or my daughters, but I would not allow it. I carried the flickering candle into Lady Alba's chamber, treading cautiously in the weak aura of light cast by the flame, for there were often unexpected obstructions where the lady had tossed some garment or bauble on the floor. A movement by the bed startled me, and I spilled a blob of hot wax on my wrist; as I choked back my cry, I realized it was only a looking glass that had been propped against the trundle. At the bedside, I found the object of my search, a carafe of wine that was still half full. She would not remember in the morning how much had been left. I poured myself a large cup and then settled back on the bed in the anteroom, pulling a blanket over my shoulders. A strain of flute music drifted up from the great hall below. The minstrel had begun the evening's entertainment. I gulped the wine, hoping to escape into sleep. Ella would be up before dawn, demanding her breakfast.

When the door swung open, I knew that something was amiss. Even Lady Alba would not bang the door so loudly, for fear of waking the baby. Emont stood on the threshold, swaying slightly.

"Won't you invite me in?" His voice had a bitter edge that he had not used with me before.

"Of course, my lord, you are at home," I said soothingly, rising from the bed. "But your lady has not yet returned."

"I know. She is dancing with the whoresons she invited into my home."

"It is not unusual for the lady of the manor to organize a Christmas feast for the villagers."

Emont raised his voice. "She is debasing herself and my name by mingling with rabble and scum!"

I did not point out that he was associating with a servant.

Emont stepped close to me after closing the door behind him. He smelled of cloves and sweat and the bilious sour-sweetness of drink. He pushed his flat, leonine face nearer to mine. "You are beautiful," he said more softly. He reached for me and wrapped his hand around my neck, trying to pull me to him. I resisted, stepping backward, which caused him to stumble sideways into the armoire. There was a loud crack as his shoulder struck the door of the armoire heavily, and then he heaved himself upright again. I held my breath.

Emont glared at me with his fists clenched. Though I had heard nothing from Lady Alba's chamber, I said, "I think I hear your wee daughter crying. I must see to her."

I took the candle and ducked into the other room. My breath came quickly, and my hands were shaking. I had the urge to smash my fist into Emont's face, but that would cost me my position, and I had nowhere else to go. Acceding to his advances could be just as disastrous for me, and the idea of letting him paw me was revolting.

I went to the cradle, where Ella still slept. Resentment surged as I looked at her. She was so scrawny and strange. She turned her head away from the light and mewled. I would take her with me, because Emont would not trouble me if I was holding his precious daughter.

The moment I picked her up, Ella began to cry. I brought her to Emont, and I was surprised to find him sitting on the edge of the bed with his head in his hands. His tangled hair hung forward and hid his face from my view. When he looked up, his expression

was sorrowful, and a little bewildered, and I pitied him. He was the same awkward Emont who begged for my company daily. I sat beside him and shifted the baby onto his lap. She reached for the tips of his curls and quieted.

"You see how she adores her father. She is always content with you."

I could hear the trace of a smile when he answered, "She is an angel come down to earth to comfort me." He caressed his daughter's cheek. "You take good care of her."

I thought guiltily of how roughly I had just pulled Ella from her cradle. "I do try."

"Her mother is not suited to the task." He paused, and then sighed. "Neither am I suited to be a father."

"You are more devoted than any father I have known! You visit with her every day."

"Her mother is busy spending Elfilda's dowry on silk gowns and trinkets, and I can barely furnish the food for a Twelfth Night celebration from the money we bring in for the manor. What kind of life am I going to give my daughter?"

Emont was so wealthy by the standards I had known that I was appalled by his self-pity. "Your daughter has her mother's beauty, the good name of her father, the blessings of her godmother, and she will never want for food," I said curtly.

He looked up at me, blinking, as though dazzled by a sudden light. "I must seem ridiculous to you."

"Oh! Not at all, sir, not at all."

"You know what it is to be hungry, don't you? To work for your living. Not to be free. You must think me so ungrateful."

I squirmed, not knowing how to respond. Emont took an eccentric interest in my brewing experience, but I had never before had

the impression that he viewed me as a fellow mortal. No master does.

"I hope you don't think me a drunken popinjay. I suppose I'm not dressed well enough to be a popinjay. And I am drunk." He snorted softly. Emont kept his head bowed for a moment and then handed Ella back to me, saying, "I should go."

When I took the baby from him, she began to cry again. I bobbed in a shallow curtsy. "Good night. I shall bring Ella to you tomorrow."

On his way out, Emont staggered and took a bruising knock against the door frame. As I closed the door behind him, I felt a measure of disgust, but I also had an urge to call out to him, to say something that would ease his mind or provide some small comfort as he fell asleep.

The next morning, Emont did not acknowledge our meeting in Lady Alba's chambers. The pouches under his eyes were pronounced, and he was more disheveled than usual, but he chatted as though nothing had happened. I had expected him to be embarrassed and to treat me coldly, but the opposite was true. From that day forward, Emont took me into his confidence more than he ever had, sharing his frustrations with the manor and the demands of the abbey. I came to understand that he relied entirely on the information and advice of the chamberlain, the bailiff, and Mother Elfilda's steward, and that he did not review the books himself. He was like a boy who had not memorized his Bible verse and hoped nervously that the priest would not call on him. Although he had authority over all but the steward, he lacked the confidence to gainsay their decisions, possibly because he feared being discovered as ineffec-

tual. He pretended to grasp the details of the manor's finances, but he had never applied himself to learning them. I wondered whether he had the capacity to learn them even if he was willing to try.

I knew enough from running a brewery to be able to understand household accounting, and I was frustrated with Emont's lack of insight. I asked him to show me the books, and he seemed eager to accommodate my request. Days went by, however, and the chamberlain did not bring the accounts for me to review. I asked Emont again, and he told me that he would remind Wills. Finally, I grew tired of waiting, and I approached Wills myself.

I found the chamberlain in the kitchen, upbraiding a scullion. I waited until the end of his harangue, and then I called to him. Wills's eyes narrowed when he saw me. "Yes?" he asked.

"Sir Emont has asked me to review the household books."

His round face colored. "What business is it of yours? Since when does a nurse review household accounts?"

"Since our master asked me to do so," I replied mildly.

"I don't have time right now."

I stepped closer, so that he had to lift his chin to look up at me. "If there is something that you would rather I did not see, then it is not a good idea to play games with me now. I shall see those books sooner or later, and when I do, you may wish for me to be pleasantly disposed toward you. I suggest that you get them now."

The red in his face spread to the roots of his ginger hair. He glared at me and then turned away. "Very well," he said, "I shall bring you the scroll for the past year."

It took me three days to finish combing through the accounts while Ella took her naps. The pattern that emerged was of incompe-

tence more than petty thievery. While Wills had probably padded some of the expenses in order to set aside an income for himself, his greed was not the biggest problem. There was obvious waste in purchasing items that could have been produced at the manor, overstaffing the kitchen, failing to make use of animals that had been confiscated from tenants or collected as heriots. There were senseless extravagances, most likely at Lady Alba's behest. Taxes and fines were not being consistently levied, and when they were, they were not always being collected. I did not have details from the bailiff about sales of grain and produce, or about fees collected for use of the mill or ovens, but I could see from the income column that whatever it was, it was not enough.

I spoke to Emont about my findings, and he asked me to join his meeting with the chamberlain and the bailiff, who was known among the villagers as Black Bear, or simply Black, for his large size and dark hair. They were already at the table when I arrived carrying the scroll; Wills shot me a glance that was both worried and hostile, and Black tipped his head almost imperceptibly in greeting. A woolly beard partially concealed the bailiff's expression, but there was no mistaking the coldness in his eyes.

"I invited Agnes to point out some unnecessary expenses she discovered in our accounting," Emont said apologetically.

"How could she possibly know what is necessary and what is not?" Wills said.

I opened the scroll and smoothed it over the table. "Let me show you some ways you might save a few shillings," I said briskly. "Then you can get on with more important matters."

The bailiff grunted, and Wills crossed his arms, frowning at the parchment.

"You see what you have spent on flour just for December?"

"We had the whole village here at Christmastide," Wills said, "of course we needed flour!"

"Look at November, then. It was no better." I turned to Black. "How often do we accept promise of payment for use of the mill?" I knew from Matilda's godparents, who ran the mill in Old Hilgate, that debts did not always get paid.

"What does that have to do with anything?" Wills asked peevishly.

I ignored Wills and kept my gaze on Black, who shrugged his broad shoulders and said, "I don't know. Perhaps four or five times each month."

"Those people haven't the money to pay. What if they don't have money the next month either? Do you let them use the mill?"

The bailiff glanced uncomfortably at Emont. "Sometimes."

"They have no money, but they do have wheat or barley. What if you took a portion of their milled flour?"

"The villagers already harvest grain on manorial land."

I pointed to the ledger. "And this is what you spend to buy your grain back from the abbey. If you take flour as payment from the villagers' allotments, you can bypass the abbey altogether." I turned back to Wills. "How much flour do we lose to mouse infestations and rot?"

Wills reddened. "I don't believe that is a problem."

"Have you not seen how much the scullions throw away? If you had mouse-proof containers built and kept them nearer the fire, where it is dry, you would suffer far less waste."

"Even if we eliminated the cost of flour altogether, it would make no real difference to our monthly expense."

"I beg to differ. Every line on this sheet is important. What about this one? Twenty crowns for ale? A royal fortune! We could

make our own for a few shillings. Why do we not make our own soap too? And why do you have so many kitchen staff? You have three paid servants and a half dozen villeins who must be fed from the manorial larder. They sit idle when there are no guests, which, as far as I can see, is nearly always. They could be working the land instead of sitting on their thumbs."

It was the first time I saw the bailiff smile. "The lass has some sense in her pretty head," he said to Wills. "I could use some of those idle hands to repair the church roof."

A loud snore caused me to start. Emont had fallen asleep beside me, sprawled on the table. He stirred, and his arm flopped over a portion of the parchment. I stood over him, unsure how to proceed. He let out a long, whistling breath that ended with a comical vibration of his lips, not unlike the sound of escaping flatulence. The bailiff chuckled, and when I looked at Wills, he was having trouble suppressing his own smile.

"I suppose this concludes our session," I said.

"Yes," Wills said stiffly, his smile snuffed out. He tugged the ledger from under Emont's arm. "We cannot continue without the master."

The bailiff bade me good-bye politely, but Wills left without a word. I found him later, in the kitchen.

"Would you like me to show you the problem with the flour?" I asked.

"I have eyes in my own head."

"I am not your enemy, Wills. I would like to be of assistance."

Wills looked at me skeptically.

"I cannot say why I have the master's ear, but I have it—"

"Yes, why?" he interrupted. "I bet you lift those fancy skirts for him."

I stared at the chamberlain until he began to shift uncomfortably and dropped his gaze. "You have not only insulted me grievously, you have insulted the lord and lady of the manor," I said. "Would you stand for any of your staff to say such a thing?"

"I shall look into the grain and flour storage," Wills said by way of apology. "You had best get back to work."

Though he said no more about it, Wills did follow my advice about the flour. I became a regular attendee of business meetings, and Wills grudgingly accepted some of my suggestions. Once the resistance of the bailiff and chamberlain had worn down, Emont began to wander away partway through meetings, leaving me to finish for him. As the lord's tacit representative, I took over, in one small way, the duties of the lady of the manor.

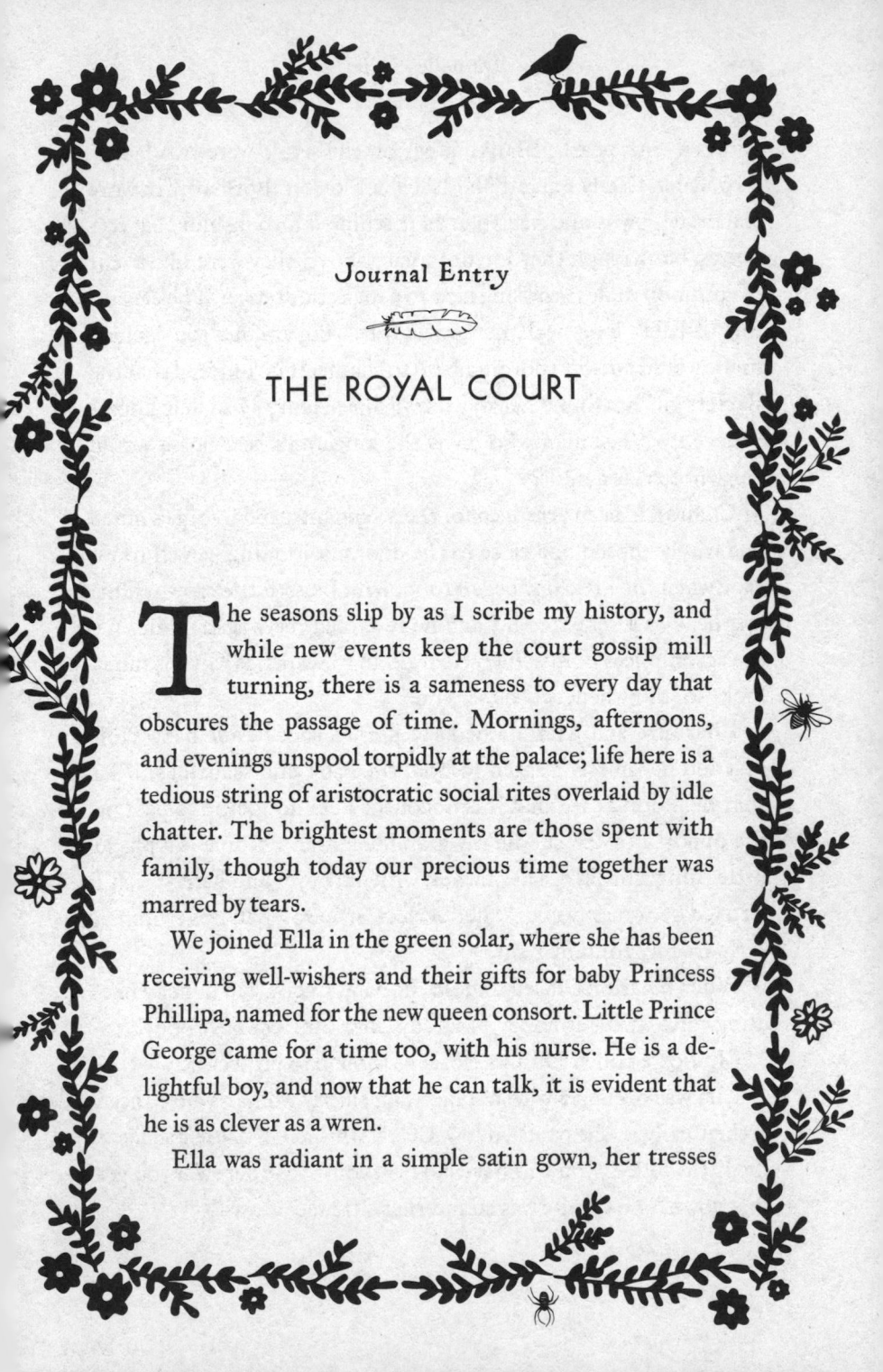

Journal Entry

THE ROYAL COURT

The seasons slip by as I scribe my history, and while new events keep the court gossip mill turning, there is a sameness to every day that obscures the passage of time. Mornings, afternoons, and evenings unspool torpidly at the palace; life here is a tedious string of aristocratic social rites overlaid by idle chatter. The brightest moments are those spent with family, though today our precious time together was marred by tears.

We joined Ella in the green solar, where she has been receiving well-wishers and their gifts for baby Princess Phillipa, named for the new queen consort. Little Prince George came for a time too, with his nurse. He is a delightful boy, and now that he can talk, it is evident that he is as clever as a wren.

Ella was radiant in a simple satin gown, her tresses

adorned with pearls. Flanking her on the settee were two ladies-in-waiting, Cecily Barrett and Isabella Florivet. Both women wore elaborate gowns and had their hair sculpted into fashionable cornettes, but though they are not unattractive, they were like a pair of common mules browsing next to a majestic destrier. The elegant line of Ella's long neck, her graceful bearing and lustrous golden mane would put any thoroughbred to shame. It is rumored that the Barrett girl has found her way into Prince Henry's bed, but I don't believe it. What man who owns the kingdom's best horse would consent to ride a mule?

Chairs had been arranged for the attendants, and George's nurse had wisely chosen one close to the door, positioning herself to escape when the little boy began to squirm. I kissed the crown of his fair head as I squeezed by, and he rewarded me with a smile. We are accomplices in mischief, Georgie and I, which is why his nurse looks so sour whenever she sees me.

Charlotte and Matilda had saved me a spot beside baby Phillipa and her nurse. I asked to hold the baby, and Isabella sniffed sharply. I don't care that it is uncouth; I am not going to pass up the opportunity to cuddle my granddaughter. Phillipa is a placid little thing; she favors her father, with dark eyes and hair. When I stroked her creamy cheek, her perfect little rosebud lips twitched with dreamy contentment.

When Charlotte asked to hold the baby, Cecily said in her wheedling voice, sweet as honey, "Is Lady Charlotte feeling broody?"

Charlotte pulled Phillipa closer as though to protect her.

Ella was occupied with a subject, an elderly woman who winced arthritically as she curtsied low. Cecily whispered, "Don't squeeze the little doll, or you will have puke on your . . . Where *did* you get that gown?" Her smile was counterfeit. "It is so . . . rustic."

Isabella giggled and said, "I have heard that a certain courtier has taken a keen interest in Lady Charlotte. Perhaps there will be babies in her future after all."

I was surprised to see a faint flush in Charlotte's cheeks. She is usually dismissive of these cruel girls, but her look was one of embarrassment tinged with self-conscious pleasure.

"What sort of interest do you mean?" Matilda asked sharply. She put her arm around her sister.

"Oh, well, you should ask Charlotte, shouldn't you? Perhaps I have said too much." Isabella lowered her chin and widened her eyes, parodying a child caught in a fib.

"What is she saying, Lottie?" Matilda asked.

"It's . . . It's probably nothing."

Charlotte's discomfiture was difficult for me to watch.

"Your 'probably nothing' seems to be provoking a good bit of amusement," Matilda said dryly. She is never afraid of speaking her mind, which may be a silver lining to her disfigurement. She doesn't care a whit what anyone thinks of her.

"There have been letters . . ." Charlotte's voice was so low that I could barely hear her. "And a gift. A trinket, really." She pulled a ring from her pocket. It was cheaply made and obviously too small for her fingers.

"Oh how adorable!" Cecily said. "She carries it with her!" She winked at Isabella behind Ella's back.

"Who sent the letters?" I asked cautiously.

"I have not met the gentleman," Charlotte responded, her eyes downcast.

"Do tell us his name!" Isabella said.

The well-wishers had cleared out, and Ella turned to face us. "What is so funny?" she asked.

"Charlotte has a secret admirer!" Cecily said. "Tell us his name!"

"Sir Blakely Snoodgrum," Charlotte whispered.

Isabella tittered and Cecily covered her mouth with her hand. Ella looked from one to the other with her lovely violet-blue eyes. "Isn't that what you call his majesty behind his back?" she asked.

Cecily frowned.

"See, now you've ruined their fun, Princess." Matilda's voice was harsh, and Ella flinched.

"They were making sport of Charlotte," I explained. "Tell me, Cecily, how many marriage proposals have you received? And you, Isabella, you must have been heartbroken when the baron married Lord Geraint's daughter. Her fortune is so much smaller than yours! I wonder why he chose her?"

Matilda snorted, Charlotte blinked back tears, and Ella watched us with a puzzled frown. She is bright, but she has never been able to discern oblique messages concealed behind ordinary words. Cecily opened her mouth to deliver what I don't doubt was to be a nasty retort, but Matilda cut in, saying, "Isn't Phillipa lovely? It brings tears to my eyes just to see her so happy in your arms, Lottie. She is a sweet lamb and beautiful like her mother." She made as though to brush away a tear, and Charlotte glanced at her gratefully, her eyes brimming.

"Our poor princess looks exhausted," I said. "Would you two ladies be so good as to inform the chamberlain that she needs to rest and see her back to her chambers?"

Ella looked relieved.

"You have no standing to tell us what to do!" Isabella said crossly.

"Of course, it was only a suggestion. Your Highness, are you weary?"

"Yes, very much."

"So, I shall find the chamberlain myself. Come, Charlotte, give Phillipa back to her nurse and help me to find Aleyn."

We left Matilda to contend with the other two ladies-in-waiting, which I am sure she did ably. I wish that our lives were not filled with people such as these, that we could live like a real family. I miss the intimacy, the warmth, the simplicity that we captured so fleetingly in those tender days that are more dream than memory for me now.

VALLEY OF THE SHADOW

By the age of three, Ella had become a child of breathtaking beauty. Every time I glanced at her, I found her even more exquisite than she had seemed the moment before. Her hair grew in silken curls like her father's, but the color was pale gold, like her mother's. She had eyes too big for her small head, liquid pools of amethyst fringed by long, sweeping lashes. While most children have sturdy, chubby limbs, Ella's were the slender and graceful limbs of a fawn. Lady Alba dressed her in light-colored satins that suited her fair skin, but the gowns were impossible to keep clean. I took to dressing her in serviceable wool whenever I knew that her mother would not see her.

Like other children, Ella learned to walk on her first birthday, but she did not begin to speak until her third. Until then, she had been able to follow instructions, but she mainly got by with pointing, grabbing, or crying to communicate what she wanted. Emont worried that his daughter was simple, and he sighed with relief when, seemingly overnight, she learned to chatter and sing. Her

voice was pitched high, the droll but charming warble of a sparrow. When she shrieked, however, her voice pierced like a dagger.

Ella did not like stories or pretend play. What she liked best was sorting and arranging. I remembered how much I loved collecting stones as a child, and I tried to interest her in searching for a new collection with me, but she did not care for the outdoors. Gisla suggested that I try buttons, and that was more successful. Ella could sit for hours, lining up the buttons in neat rows from largest to smallest or sorting them by color and shape.

Emont was smitten with his beautiful daughter, and he denied her nothing. He requested treats from the kitchen every morning, so she was anxious to go to him as soon as she woke. Ella still slept beside me when she was three, and she would prod me awake with little kicks and pokes, telling me to hurry. It was a struggle to get the child properly clothed and her hair brushed; she squirmed and complained, and if she saw an opportunity to escape before her toilette was complete, she would invariably take it. Emont seemed not to care whether her hair was a squirrel's nest, and if Ella managed to elude me in the morning, she would peer at me triumphantly from behind the safety of her father's legs. Gisla was the only one who could convince the girl to sit docilely for a brushing; the old woman had infinite patience and a soft touch.

Once Ella was clothed, she would race downstairs singing "Treats! Treats!" Emont hid the sweets, pretending that he had not brought any. Ella searched the hall and Emont's pockets until she found her reward, and Emont allowed her to curl in his lap like a cat while she nibbled.

Ella preferred her father's company to anybody else's, I believe because he demanded nothing from her. He did not insist on good manners, like I did, or dress her up like a doll, like her mother. He

did not try to draw her into conversation like Joan and Gisla. He simply let her abide in his presence, and she was content.

Toward the end of Ella's third year, Lady Alba changed in some fundamental but inexplicable way, as though a part of her went missing. She had never gone out much, but during that period, she withdrew almost entirely from the world. She refused to leave her chambers, and I never saw her fully dressed anymore. A light within her was snuffed out. Whereas she used to vacillate between fevered intensity and the charming whimsy of a mischievous child, she became listless and indifferent. Her eyes were dull and her face slack. Night and day, she huddled on her bed wearing the same dirty shift, refusing to let Gisla or Joan bathe her.

I often found Lady Alba muttering to herself when I brought Ella to visit. She paused with her head tilted to the side as though listening for a response, though nobody else spoke. If I tried to get her attention, she usually ignored us or feigned sleep. Ella sang little ditties, hoping that Lady Alba would join in as she used to. When she got no response, she settled for lying next to her mother on the bed, playing with her limp white fingers. The sun burned through the shutters, laying stripes across the accumulation of discarded toiletries on the floor. The rosewater that Joan sprinkled on the bed could not hide the stench of Lady Alba's unwashed body, but Ella did not so much as wrinkle her little nose.

Emont had been a rare visitor to his wife's chambers, and after one particularly bad evening, he stopped visiting altogether. Ella was asleep when Emont knocked on the door; Joan vacated the chamber to give the master and mistress their privacy. After a silence, we heard an incoherent scream and then loud cursing

from Emont. He banged the door open, holding the palm of his hand over his eye. Streaks of blood ran down his face. He lurched rapidly through the antechamber, like an injured hart fleeing from hunters. That was the last of his nocturnal appearances.

Gisla wrung her knobby hands, worrying for Lady Alba's soul. She brought the priest to give her mistress communion and hear her confession, but Lady Alba turned mute as a stone. Gisla told me that when the priest blessed her forehead with holy water, the lady recoiled from his touch. This convinced the loyal servant that the devil had invaded her mistress's body, and she resolved to speak with Sir Emont about sending Lady Alba to the bishop.

Whether the bishop could have saved Lady Alba, we cannot know. What transpired was so dark that nobody has spoken of it since. One day at dawn, as I floated in the shallows of early-morning sleep, Joan burst from Lady Alba's chamber, wailing and sobbing. Gisla was already out of bed, and she asked sharply, "Whatever is the matter, girl?"

"The mistress!" Joan wailed. Her face was a mask of anguish.

Gisla's eyes widened in alarm. She marched briskly into Lady Alba's chamber to investigate. Ella, who sat up straight in bed beside me, stared after the old woman, her face blank. I pulled the child protectively toward me, and though she did not resist, she did not yield either. She remained silent and inanimate as I kissed the top of her head.

Gisla shouted my name, and Joan collapsed against the wall, mewling helplessly. My legs refused to run. Fear and duty struggled for control of my limbs, and though duty won, I moved toward Lady Alba's chamber with leaden footsteps.

I could not make sense of the sight that greeted me. Gisla, her wrinkled face red with strain, gripped Lady Alba's thighs, holding

her aloft as though she were tossing her into the air. Lady Alba slumped to one side; her corn-silk hair cascaded over her shoulder, dancing slowly back and forth over the top of Gisla's black nightcap. She swayed gently, like a stalk of wheat in a light breeze.

"Come here!" Gisla wheezed. "Take her legs!"

Lady Alba's face turned slowly toward me like the moon waxing. It was purple and swollen beyond recognition. I swallowed the gorge that came to my throat and relieved Gisla of the task of supporting our mistress's weight. My strength fed on fear and revulsion. I lifted Lady Alba effortlessly, high into the air, so that the cord around her neck slackened, and she slumped farther sideways. Her cold body pressed against my cheek; the foul smell sickened me. Gisla righted the overturned footstool and stepped up to untie the noose from Lady Alba's neck. This attempt was unsuccessful, but she retrieved a knife from the side table to slice through the silken tie. Lady Alba must have used the same knife to cut a length of cord from the bed hangings.

I laid the body awkwardly on the bed. Joan still moaned in the anteroom. I went to the door and saw that Ella was on the bed where I had left her. She watched her hands intently as she waved her fingers sinuously in front of her eyes, something she did to calm herself. I closed the door softly, hoping not to disturb her.

Gisla worked to remove the noose from Lady Alba's neck. It had bitten deep into her flesh, and the swelling nearly swallowed the cord, leaving only a thin sliver visible in the channel it had cut. Lady Alba's eyes were slits between her puffy, violaceous lids, and the whites had turned a satanic red. I tried to close her eyes, but they would not remain shut.

"Agnes, try this knot. My old hands are no use." Gisla's voice shook.

I worked on the cord until I loosened it, and then I pulled it as gently as I could from the furrow in Lady Alba's neck. It was dark with blood, but nothing fresh oozed out.

"She has been dead some hours."

Gisla nodded and winced as though it hurt her. "The stupid sow slept right through."

"It was not Joan's fault."

Gisla did not answer. When she looked at me, there were tears standing in her eyes. "Help me to wash her. Fetch some water."

"No amount of water is going to hide what she did."

Gisla struck me across the face with shocking ferocity. I brought my hand to my stinging cheek.

"Fetch the water."

The slap woke my anger, but I also saw too late how traitorous my words had sounded to the old woman. I did as she bade me.

We stripped away Lady Alba's shift and gave her the bath that she had so badly needed but refused. It was a strange intimacy with her body, greater in death than it would have been in life. She could not flinch or pull away, and we could not mount a wall of words between us. The absence of her soul made her nakedness stark, and I did not want to touch her. Gisla tended to her with a quiet tenderness that made me feel ashamed.

The color drained from Lady Alba's face as we cleaned, leaving her pale except for delicate blooms of red on her cheeks and nose. The whites of her eyes remained discolored, but as the swelling subsided, we managed to close them. In silent collusion, we dressed her in a high-necked gown that hid the wound on her neck. Gisla's hands trembled as she fastened the buttons.

Gisla took her mistress's jeweled brush and worked through the tangles in Lady Alba's hair as she had done so many times before.

She looked at me, her face grim, and spoke for the first time since we began the bath. "You had better go and tell Sir Emont."

I dressed quickly in the anteroom. Joan had ceased her moaning, but she remained crumpled against the wall. I asked her to stay with Ella before I left.

Emont was still in his bedchamber; as he did not like to have an attendant sleep with him, he answered the door himself. His reddish curls hung in greasy ropes from beneath his nightcap, and his white, hairy legs poked out from beneath his gray undertunic. I would have felt more comfortable delivering bad news in the great hall, when he was fully dressed, but I could not delay. I took a deep breath. "I am sorry to bring you bad news, sir, but Joan found Lady Alba dead this morning."

Emont's expression did not immediately register the shock, but his polite smile dissolved with painful slowness. "What happened?"

Gisla expected me to deceive him, but I had not taken the time to invent a convincing lie. I feigned bewildered confusion, saying, "I . . . I don't know. Joan said that she did not wake."

"Has someone sent for the priest?"

"Not yet." Given the circumstances of Lady Alba's death, I had not considered calling the priest, though of course I should have, or people would begin to ask questions. I looked at my slippered feet to hide my burning cheeks. My great toe poked through a hole in the upper.

Emont closed his eyes and rubbed his forehead. In a strangled voice he gasped, "Oh, my God!" He calmed himself and said more firmly, "I shall have to let her sister know. Show me to Lady Alba."

I led Emont to his wife's quarters. Joan had not moved, but Ella was nowhere to be seen. We passed into the dim and airless

chamber, where the strong scent of rosewater greeted us, a loud note that failed to obscure the pungent undertone of accumulated odors. Gisla was gone. Slanting shafts of morning light filtered through the shutters. Nothing seemed out of the ordinary, except for the silence.

Gisla had arranged Lady Alba's hands so that they lay folded over her velvet-clad bosom. She looked so angelic, her pale face smooth and expressionless, her golden hair spread out like a halo, that I nearly believed my own falsehood. Emont went to the bedside and touched his wife's hand.

It was then that I saw Ella. She crouched in the shadows behind the bed, still as a statue, her eyes watchful. I did not want to disturb Emont, so I approached the child carefully, as one might approach a feral creature. Before I got within arm's reach, Gisla appeared, announcing that the priest had been summoned to anoint Lady Alba's corpse. Ella took advantage of the distraction to dart away. Her father, who was asking Gisla for details, did not notice.

Ella hid from me for several hours; I finally found her sitting behind the curtains in the solar reserved for guests. She wrapped her arms around her legs, resting her little chin on her knees. Her expression was blank and her eyes were dry. She did not look at me as I crouched beside her and stroked her back lightly.

"Ella."

She did not respond.

"Ella, your mother has gone to heaven to be with God. Jesus has welcomed her home."

Ella seemed unaware of my presence. I was used to Charlotte and Matilda's occasional stony silence, their quiet, fuming resentment, but this was not the same. Ella was simply absent. I shivered.

"We have to get ready to go to the abbey, sweetheart. There

will be a Mass for your mother. She will take her place among the saints."

I could get no response from the girl. I wondered queasily whether she knew that I was not telling the truth. That was impossible; the child had seen nothing and knew nothing of heaven's rules. I gave up trying to talk to her and picked Ella up in my arms. She stiffened, her eyes flashed with hostility, and then she became passive again. She did not fight me when I dressed her and braided her hair. I packed a trunk for both of us, and then we joined Emont in the carriage.

The trip to Ellis Abbey lasted an eternity. Emont stared fixedly out the window; the countryside that crawled past was brown and drab after a long winter, and the sky a dull gray. I worried that he would ask me questions about Lady Alba's death, but he said nothing. If he had any suspicions, he kept them buried, where they belonged.

Ella reclined on her father's lap, dozing or simply looking at the roof. At times, she hummed tunelessly. We had bread and cold chicken for supper, and I peeled an apple that was spongy from months in the cellar. I sliced off small pieces for Ella, and she took them absently from my hand. Sickness from the morning's events and my nervous excitement about seeing my daughters again made it impossible for me to eat. As the hours dribbled by, my heart pounded on my rib cage like it was trying to get free.

We arrived at the abbey as the bell rang for vespers. The sky was orange and pink in the west, and the air held the freshness of early spring. Grooms met us and helped us down from the carriage just outside the church, and Mother Elfilda herself appeared from the door to the cloister. She was attended by two nuns, one of whom I recognized as the prioress. Their veils glowed in the fad-

ing light and fluttered behind them like banners. The abbess held out a small, pale hand to Emont, saying, "I am sorry for your loss."

Emont bent to kiss her hand and replied, "It is your loss as well, Your Reverence."

Mother Elfilda bowed her head in assent. "You may use the bishop's chambers tonight, Emont. Sister Margaret will show you to them, and a manservant will meet you there." She looked to Ella, who was clinging to her father's leg, and to my astonishment, the abbess stooped to speak to the child directly. "I am your godmother, Elfilda. I shall help to care for you now that your mother is dead. We shall celebrate the ascension of her soul into heaven tomorrow."

Ella looked up at her with huge eyes, saying nothing. The abbess smiled faintly. I wondered if Ella reminded her of herself as a child. The resemblance was striking.

"Are you the nurse?" Mother Elfilda showed no sign of recognizing me.

"Yes, Mother."

"You may take Elfilda to the guest quarters. Sister Margaret will come for you when she has shown Emont to his rooms."

Servants were already unloading our trunk from the carriage.

"I know the way, my lady."

The abbess and prioress had started back toward the church without waiting for my reply, so I took Ella by the hand. She did not want to let go of her father. He kissed her head and bade her go with me, and she relented to do so as long as I carried her.

I let Ella ride on my back, holding on to her little hands so that she did not grab too tightly at my throat. She seemed to have recovered from her earlier torpor, and she chattered about the animals that she had seen during our trip to the abbey. As she seldom

went outdoors, and as there were no animals within the inner gate of the manor, even sheep were a novelty for the girl.

Although it was out of our way, I went first to the cloister in the hope of seeing Charlotte and Matilda. The sun had set, which meant that vespers was ending, and the children would soon be on their way to their dorter. I lingered in the arcade in the deepening twilight, trying to entertain Ella by watching the sky for the first stars to appear. She grew bored and cold, and guilt crept over me when I heard her kittenish yawn. Reluctantly, I left the empty cloister and brought Ella to the guesthouse. Our trunk had been delivered to the large chamber at the front of the building, where I put Ella to bed, relieved that she had returned to her normal three-year-old self. I settled beside her, knowing that sleep would be elusive. I yearned to go to my daughters; they were so close, and my mind filled in every detail of their appearances as they slept. I could see the rise and fall of their breathing, the fluttering of their eyelids, their loosely curled fists flung wide. I could feel the warmth of their brows as I kissed them good night ever so softly.

The next morning, Ella was up with the sun, and I took her to the abbey's kitchen to fetch her some milk. I planned to wait in the cloister until Charlotte and Matilda passed through, so I brought Ella's buttons on a small tray to keep her occupied. On the day that poor Ella would see her mother buried, I was as nervous as a young girl on the way to her wedding.

We did not have to wait long for the convent school girls to finish morning prayers. I watched them file out of the chapel, all garbed in the same gray frock that I had worn at Rose House so long ago. The older girls walked quietly in pairs, and the younger ones spilled out

after them, jostling one another and stifling giggles. My heart was in my throat as I searched the faces for my daughters.

When I saw Charlotte, I caught my breath. She had grown so tall! Her raven hair and dark skin stood out among the fair children like a black sheep in a flock of white. Soft contours of baby fat were gone, giving way to the hard lines of her jaw and graceful bridge of her nose. Without thinking, I stood, spilling the tray of buttons that Ella had been playing with on my lap. Ella shrieked, and I bent to comfort her, promising to gather the buttons. I did not have time to straighten before Matilda crashed into me crying, "Mama!" We fell backward onto the grass, still dead from winter, and Matilda covered my face with quick pecking kisses. When she smiled, I could see that she was missing two of her teeth. Behind her, wavering through my tears, Charlotte looked down on us, beaming.

Ella was so surprised by the commotion that she stopped crying. A nun scolded the girls sharply, and Matilda let go of me and brushed the yellow blades from her skirt. Her face was still badly scarred from the pox. Though her skin was no longer discolored, it was distorted by pits and jagged ruts. My heart ached as I remembered her smooth, perfect baby face nuzzling at my neck.

"What is the meaning of this behavior?" demanded the stout nun. Some of the younger girls lingered and stared.

"Forgive us, Sister. This is our mother," said Charlotte.

The nun raised her thin eyebrows. "Is this how a lady behaves?"

"No, Sister," the girls replied in unison.

"You must each pray a novena so that you will remember next time."

Charlotte groaned.

The nun turned to me. "I did not know that their mother had come. Are you taking them home?"

Charlotte and Matilda watched me with shining eyes, childish hopefulness written clearly on their faces.

"No, Sister. I have come for Lady Alba's funeral. This is her daughter, Elfilda. I am her nurse."

Matilda's chin quivered.

"I would like to visit with my daughters while I am here. I have not seen them in more than three years. We could spend this morning together. I must leave tomorrow to bring Elfilda home."

The holy lady looked doubtful. It was difficult to reconcile my appearance and speech—and my daughters' positions as convent students—with the fact that I was a servant. She was probably unsure of what to make of me or how to address me. Finally, she said to my daughters, "Meet us for prayer at terce. You may stay with your mother until then." The nun herded the remaining girls to the dining hall like a mother goose, leaving Charlotte and Matilda behind with me.

The girls became shy once everyone was gone, but I asked them to help me to pick up Ella's buttons, and that seemed to put them at ease. They examined Ella with fascination. With her long, graceful limbs and dainty proportions, Ella looked like a golden-haired Bathsheba shrunk down to the size of a doll. Next to her, my daughters were giants.

Charlotte, who had always been nurturing, tried to play with Ella. She made a game of counting the buttons, which made the tiny girl laugh, but when Charlotte tried to pick her up, Ella screeched and hid behind my skirts. I proposed that we go for a walk around the pond to look for frogs, and my suggestion was met with enthusiasm from the older girls, but not from Ella. She avoided water like a cat. I promised that her feet would not get wet, and she agreed to come as long as I carried her.

On the way to the pond, I peppered Charlotte and Matilda with questions about their lives at the abbey, but they were not interested in talking about it. They skipped around me, chattering about a girl who had fainted during Mass, how angry the prioress had been, what they hoped to eat for dinner, and how much they loved Ella's blue gown. I managed to gather that they were both good pupils, and that they liked some teachers and loathed others. I suppose that I got the only answer I needed, which was that they were not unhappy.

The ground around the pond was muddier than I had anticipated. I tried to herd the girls away from the edge and onto more solid ground, but they were carried away by their excitement; when the frogs tried to escape into the rushes, Charlotte and Matilda followed. I warned them that they would be punished for dirtying their shoes, but they did not care. After a while, I did not care either. I followed their movements hungrily. Their delight nourished me, and their laughter brought color back into the world.

Ella was not tempted to join the older girls, but she watched their activity with interest from her perch on my back. When Charlotte trapped a frog in her hands, Ella leaned precariously low to peer into the darkness between Charlotte's fingers. As she could see nothing, Charlotte opened her fingers wider and wider, until the frog saw its chance for freedom and sprang into the air. Ella started and I nearly lost my grasp of her, but then she giggled happily. Charlotte laughed too and promised to find her another frog.

As the time to part grew near, Matilda grew quiet and sidled closer to me. She pulled at my arm, but as I needed both hands to hold on to Ella, I could not embrace her. I tried to set Ella on some dry ground, but she squirmed and refused to get down. Matilda then whined plaintively that she did not wish me to leave, and she

tried to hook her arm around my waist, but Ella was in the way. I am not certain whether Matilda hit or pinched her, but Ella sent up a wail of fury and indignation.

"Matilda!"

She looked at me sheepishly.

"Shame on you!" I shifted Ella so that I held her against my chest, and I kissed her golden hair. "You apologize to Ella right now!"

Matilda's expression darkened as she watched me cuddle the whimpering Ella. "I'm sorry."

"She is just a wee girl. You should know better!"

"Yes, Mother."

Matilda had never called me Mother before, only Mama. Her tone was more sad than cold, and I had the urge to drop Ella and gather my own daughter in my arms. Instead, I called Charlotte over and said, "I shall help you both to get clean. The bells will ring shortly, and we should go back."

Charlotte looked stricken, and I did not know how to comfort her. I struggled to keep the tears from my own eyes. On the road, Ella consented to walk, and I gathered tufts of grass to clean the girls' shoes. They plodded silently back to the cloister with me as the bells rang for terce. When we reached the arcade, Charlotte turned to me, her eyes glistening. "When shall we see you again, Mama?" Her voice wavered.

"I don't know, my angel." Ella pulled at my skirts, and I yanked them away in annoyance.

"Shall we ever live with you again?"

"I wish it with all my heart."

"Me too."

Ella whimpered, but I ignored her. I embraced Charlotte and Matilda quickly and told them to hurry, for they were late. They

left reluctantly. As they neared the chapter house, Matilda looked back over her shoulder. I had just picked up Ella, but I managed to raise my hand to wave. Matilda turned away again without returning the gesture.

The funeral Mass was not very different from any other Mass I had witnessed at the abbey. All of the sisters were in attendance, but there were few other guests, and as far as I could tell, nobody shed a tear. The richly dressed men and women in the front pews likely came to curry favor with the abbess, whether they belonged to the Wenslock family or not. I am not even certain that Lady Alba's sister mourned her passing.

Ella and I sat in the pew behind Emont. He did not look well; his face was sallow and bloated. I had dressed Ella in her finest velvet and brushed her hair until it shone, but he did not remark on her beauty in his usual manner. He merely patted her cheek and then knelt to pray.

After Mass, the abbess led a procession to the burial ground, but Ella and I did not follow. The little girl had fallen asleep with her head on my lap, so I remained behind in the church and let her rest until we had to join the others for the abbess's reception. Though she had shown no outward signs of grief, I pitied the child for the loss of her mother. Lady Alba had been inconstant, but Ella must have loved her dearly.

Lady Alba's body was a feast for worms, but I wondered what would become of her soul. Hers was the gravest of sins, one that could not be repented. It did not seem right that murderers could go to heaven after confession, but Lady Alba would not be afforded such a chance.

I twined the ends of Ella's pale curls around my fingers as she slept. Her hair was soft and fell in perfect ringlets around her fair, heart-shaped face. I felt a shiver of wonder, just as when a huge harvest moon floats silvery bright on a purple horizon, or when the church fills with song at Christmastide.

Sadness pressed down upon me when I thought of my own daughters. Nobody would ever find them beautiful.

As the sun dropped low in the sky, the western windows glowed and cast their brilliant colors over the floor and the pews. I tried to feel grateful for my good fortune, telling myself that Charlotte and Matilda had a comfortable life. I could not help but worry that just as Ella had lost her mother, my daughters were losing theirs too.

17

BETROTHAL

After Lady Alba's death, Joan moved to Cothay Manor, and Gisla became a maid to Ella. The child did not need two servants to care for her, but I was glad for the help, and Gisla was glad for the ease of her new position. I hardly needed to justify the expense to Emont and Wills; I had by then taken over most of the household accounting, and they seldom questioned me anymore.

Black, the bailiff, was not as imposing as he first seemed. Though big and gruff, he was a reasonable man and respectful to women, most particularly to his wife, who, according to Black, was the most admirable person in all of Aviceford. Had he been a less broad-minded, thoughtful sort, it is unlikely that the bailiff would have worked with me on the idea that ultimately made the manor profitable.

The population of the village had been in decline for some years. Young men escaped to the towns, hoping to gain their freedom and learn a trade. Young women married into more prosperous manors or ran off to town with their beaux. As Aviceford was the least lucrative of the abbess's holdings, other manors poached workers.

A lord stronger than Emont or a bailiff tougher than Black might have staunched the bleeding, but as it was, the shrinking population pinched Aviceford ever tighter.

"We haven't got the men for harvest," Black complained at one of our meetings. "The grain will freeze on the stalks if it don't rot first."

It had been a wet summer and autumn, which pushed harvest back into the arms of winter. We had already had a frost and a hailstorm; yield was bound to be poor, and Black was in a rush to get whatever grains were undamaged safely into storage.

"Surely the manor can spare a few more able bodies," I said.

"I have already given as many as I can spare," Wills snapped. He disagreed with me about reorganizing labor at the manor. I was bothered by the inefficiencies, but I had no authority to tell Wills what to do with his servants.

"A few more able bodies would scarcely be enough in any case," Black said. "I asked for help from Cothay, but they claim they're just as hard up."

"A bunch of loiter-sacks is what they are," Wills said.

"The shortage gets worse every year," I observed.

"Aye."

"What if you quit planting and let grass grow for sheep?"

"We cannot feed our people with sheep alone," the bailiff said.

"You could let most of the people go. They are leaving already."

"And how can we survive without rent money and fines?"

I thought about how to respond delicately. I did not want the bailiff to think that I was accusing him of laxity, though in truth, he did a poor job of collecting payments. "Many a virgater is delinquent at one time or another," I said. "They say they will pay

with eggs, but the hens won't lay, or they will get you the money after they sell an ox. The income has never been enough to sustain the manor, and the situation is only worsening. As more villagers leave, the land becomes less productive as well. There is no way out except to change the entire arrangement."

"Your plan is to trade peasants for sheep?" Wills said. "I would sure like to see the sheep till the fields."

"Turn the fields to pasture," I said. "Sheep don't pay rent with coins or eggs. They pay with valuable wool. They never miss a payment. They rarely run away. For each virgate farmed by a peasant, we could raise whole flocks of sheep. When too many sheep are born, we need not feed them. They will feed us instead."

The bailiff was not immediately persuaded to my point of view, but over the span of three years, he turned an increasing portion of Aviceford's lands over to pasture, and the manor's fortunes improved considerably. We had no trouble paying our debts, and we were able to put villagers to work constructing new barns and helping to repoint the outer walls of the manor house. Those who lost their land and did not want to help with construction left to work at one of the abbey's other manors or to one of the nearby towns. I suppose that Lottie and Thomas were among them, as I never saw or heard from them again.

When Ella was eight years old, her godmother came to visit. This was an extraordinary event, because the abbess seldom traveled, and after the death of Lady Alba, the manor almost never received visitors. Previously, Abbess Elfilda had shown interest in her niece by sending gifts, which included a superbly rendered portrait of

the Virgin and child that we hung by Ella's bed. Ella loved the painting, perhaps in part because the beatific Madonna resembled her own dead mother.

Ella had taken over Lady Alba's chambers, and I still shared the anteroom with Gisla. As these were the largest and most richly appointed rooms in the house, we moved out in favor of Abbess Elfilda. Ella slept with me in the attic, and Gisla slept by the hearth in the kitchen to keep her old bones warm. Emont was so concerned for the abbess's comfort that he had a new feather bed and quilt brought from the city, though Ella's were still perfectly serviceable. He pestered Wills about preparations for the visit until the chamberlain was quite beside himself. Wills had grown a long ginger-and-white beard, which he yanked when he was anxious. I thought that he would pull it right off his chin in the days leading up to Abbess Elfilda's arrival.

The abbess traveled with a retinue of ten people, three of them nuns. I did not witness their approach myself, but when Gisla came to fetch Ella, she told me breathlessly that the holy lady had ridden in a gilded carriage that bore the insignia of the House of Wenslock. Upon arriving, the abbess asked to see her goddaughter. Gisla joined us, as she did not want to miss a rare bit of excitement at Aviceford Manor.

The abbess perched on one of the high-backed chairs by the blackened maw of the fireplace in the great hall, and Emont sat opposite. Two nuns flanked Mother Elfilda, surveying the room as though they expected barbarians to leap from behind the tapestries. Gisla and I nudged Ella toward her godmother. I had trained Ella to curtsy and to kiss the abbess's hand, and she carried out my instructions flawlessly. Although she was a quiet girl, Ella had not a shred of shyness, and she was good about following rules. She

was tiny, which made her look much younger than her real age, giving her the appearance of being precociously clever and poised. The abbess was charmed.

"What lovely manners!" Mother Elfilda said. Her voice was clear and lightly resonant. "How old are you now?"

"I am eight, Mother."

"And do you know your prayers?"

"Yes, Mother."

"What are the seven holy virtues?"

"Faith, Hope, Charity, Justice, Prudence . . ." Ella paused and furrowed her brow. She could become upset when she failed to remember something that she had learned. As Gisla and I watched from across the room, I held my breath.

". . . Fortitude and Temperance." Ella looked pleased with herself.

"Quite right. And can you recite the paternoster?"

Ella rattled off the Latin words to the prayer in her singsong warble.

"Such a clever girl!" The abbess looked at Emont. "Who teaches her lessons?"

"Her nurse, Agnes."

"This must be a remarkably learned nurse to teach her prayers in Latin."

"I believe that she learned her letters at your abbey, my lady."

"She was our student? Then why does she work as a nurse?"

"Not a student, my lady. Agnes worked for your mother. She married your ward." In our years together, Emont had learned nearly every detail of my past.

Mother Elfilda squinted into the shadows where I stood. "Of course. I sent you as a lady's maid to my sister. I thought that Emont would have found you a husband by now."

I moved into the light and curtsied, saying, "Your Reverence."

"Are your daughters still attending our school?"

"Yes, Mother. I am very grateful."

"I suppose it is fitting that since you have been teaching my god-daughter her prayers, I have been teaching your daughters theirs." She turned to Emont. "Elfilda will need a proper tutor soon. She is no longer a baby."

"Yes, of course, Mother."

The abbess turned back to Ella. "You have done well to remember your paternoster. Tomorrow I shall teach you the fifteen rosary promises. Your father is going to find you a real teacher from the city now that you are a big girl. Now go to bed, and I shall speak with you again tomorrow." Mother Elfilda waved her hand in my direction. "You are dismissed."

That night, Ella and I slept in the garret at the southern end of the manor house, where there were several narrow pallets raised on sagging wood-and-rope frames. The attic had housed the servants of visitors, but had fallen into disuse after the death of Lady Alba. Rodents chewed through the beds and pulled out the stuffing, leaving straw scattered over the rough floorboards, and all was blanketed by a layer of fine dust. Only one bed had not yet caved in upon itself, so I made that one up to share with Ella. When I shook the mattress, the dust rose in a great cloud, and as it settled, the last rays of sunlight captured the slowly moving motes. Ella watched with fascination, reaching into the beams of light to close her little fist around vanishing firmaments.

Despite the mischief by rodents, the garret was cozy. It smelled of pine, and there was no trace of mildew; it was warmer and drier

than many parts of Aviceford Manor. Ella did not mind ceding her chambers to the abbess or sleeping in the attic, but she grumbled about sharing a pallet with me. I tried to give her space on the bed, but we kept slipping into the valley in the center of the mattress. Fortunately, the girl's drooping eyelids were soon too heavy for her to lift, and she fell into slumber.

Ella squirmed and rolled in her sleep, wrapping herself in a cocoon of bedclothes. Each time she turned, her long braid writhed across the pillow like a golden snake. I lay awake, chilled by the cold night air, plucking at the blankets when I had the chance to steal some back. The hunchback moon crept slowly across the window, and an owl hooted in the distance. A lonely moth trying to escape whirred softly and thumped against the glazing, dashing its body repeatedly into the unyielding glass in its bid for freedom. I tried to picture Charlotte and Matilda asleep at the abbey with moonlight on their faces. Of course, at that time of year, the shutters would be closed, allowing no more than a thin blade of light to pass through.

Ella's face in the moonlight was ineffably beautiful. I turned toward the wall and closed my eyes. After what seemed an eternity, I too fell asleep.

Abbess Elfilda remained at the manor for one week, during which time Emont succeeded in maintaining the appearance of sobriety. The abbess met with Ella daily to further her religious education. On the morning of her departure, she joined Emont's meeting with the bailiff and chamberlain. When it became clear to her that I meant to join too, the faint creases on her brow deepened. She turned to Emont, saying, "Why is she here?"

Emont cleared his throat. "Agnes has been helpful with accounting, my lady."

Mother Elfilda raised her pale eyebrows. "Your child's nurse is minding the books for you?"

"Well, not exactly minding." I could tell that Emont was cursing himself for not having foreseen her reaction. Hers was no different from the bailiff's reaction years before, but we had all grown so accustomed to my role that we forgot how unconventional it was.

"What, then, if not minding?"

"She is clever with numbers, my lady. She points out mistakes."

The abbess seemed to consider this for a moment. She leaned back in her chair and waved her hand impatiently. "Get on, then. I am listening."

The meeting was routine and uneventful; Mother Elfilda asked some questions, but she did not seem to be particularly interested in the answers, and business was quickly concluded. After the bailiff knelt and bade her farewell, the abbess requested that I remain behind with her and Emont. She folded her small hands in her lap and looked at me placidly. "You have been a good nurse for Elfilda, but she has grown too old for a nurse. It is time that Emont found a husband for you. You are still young enough to have more children."

The dread that I felt was mirrored on Emont's face. He had come to rely on me not only for administration of the manor, but as his only company. The self-doubt that plagued Emont made him uncomfortable with peers and distrustful of servants; he was bewildered by manly conventions and wary of feminine artifice. As I was straightforward and uncritical, and as Ella loved him unreservedly, Ella and I were the only people he wanted to have near him.

Emont's voice was tight when he replied, "I am sure that we

can find work for Agnes here at the manor house when Ella gets a tutor. The girl is attached to her, Mother. It would be a shame to separate them."

I had not seen much evidence of Ella's attachment to me. Regardless, Emont's statement did not mollify the abbess.

"All the more reason to find a husband for her. It is not natural for children to form too strong a bond with a servant."

"Your Reverence?" I paused, waiting for an invitation to speak.

"Yes?"

"I believe, my lady, that you have been pleased with the income from Aviceford Manor these past two years?"

"That is true."

"My efforts have helped to raise that income, my lady, and I would be pleased to continue to contribute where I am needed."

The abbess shrugged irritably. "I appreciate your service, but that is the work of a lady of the manor. We shall find someone suitable soon, I am sure." Abbess Elfilda gave Emont a disapproving look and then stood, indicating that the conversation was over. "You may stay with Elfilda until her tutor arrives. I shall have one sent from the city."

After the abbess and her retinue departed for Ellis Abbey, Emont sought me out. I had settled Ella into bed in her own room and was reading my psalter by the light of a candle in the anteroom. Gisla was already asleep in her bed when Emont opened the door and beckoned to me to follow him. Someone who knew him less well might not have noticed his unsteadiness; he had evidently made up for his week of relative abstinence at dinner.

Emont led me down the corridor toward his chamber. The door

was open, and the flickering firelight guided our way. Once inside, he closed the door and sank heavily into his chair by the hearth. The room was warm, so I loosened my shawl.

"That woman should stay at the abbey and leave manorial affairs to the lords of the manors. I shall find a way for you to remain here with me."

I watched the flames dance on the hearth. The charred skeleton of a log collapsed, sending up a shower of orange sparks.

"You will stay until a tutor arrives, anyway. Then we shall find a new position here for you. Abbess Elfilda needn't know." His tongue was thick with drink.

"It would be no secret if I continued to help with the books."

"You could tell me what you think in private. Nobody else need know."

"You do not think that the servants gossip? That the abbess's steward will report the gossip back to his mistress if she asks about me? And she means to find you a new wife. What wife will tolerate my interference?"

Emont groaned and leaned his heavy head on his hands. "What would you have me do?"

I was heartsick. Everything good that I had wrought in my life was torn from my grasp. I had raised both the alehouse and the manor out of ruin, and with a heedless flick of her wrist, the abbess had taken them both from me. I blamed her for the loss of my daughters. I hated her.

"There is nothing to be done," I said hollowly. I was too dispirited and hopeless to even shed a tear.

Emont pushed the veil of hair back from his face. His gaze glittered with hectic intensity.

"You could work in the laundry."

"And what? Drink ale with you in the morning? Become your whore?" Memories of Elisabeth's degradation turned my stomach.

"I . . . I can't bear for you to leave." His expression was anguished.

A bold thought crept into my mind. Perhaps there was a way for me to stay. I needed a husband, and Emont needed a wife. My breath quickened as I imagined the impossible, and before I could snatch back the words, I heard myself say, "You could marry me."

Emont tipped his head back and laughed with a mixture of drunken amusement and bitterness. "Marry you? I could sooner marry my horse."

"Why not?"

"Why not? Are you out of your mind? You are a servant, and I am the son of Lord Henry Vis-de-Loup."

"I was married to the son of a knight. I am already functioning as the lady of the manor, and a good one at that. I am not young, but I have at least a decade of childbearing years still ahead. Besides, who will you take for a wife otherwise?" I knew that he did not want a new wife. Most women unnerved him, and he was too ashamed to let a stranger into his life. He wanted me by his side.

"The abbess would be outraged. You are not even born of gentry."

"It might ruffle her feathers, but what would she do? You are the father of her dear niece and goddaughter. She will not take the manor from you. She cannot hurt you without hurting Ella."

"You are completely mad. This idea is mad."

I knelt down before him and reached out to brush my fingertips across his lips. My shawl slipped from my shoulders, leaving my arms bare. Emont gazed down at me with an expression of con-

fused longing. Emboldened, I placed my hands on both sides of his face and pulled him toward me until his lips touched mine. His breath was hot, as though he had a fever, and stank of wine. I concentrated my senses on the prickly heat of the fire at my back. A bead of sweat slid between my breasts.

Whether in a moment of decisiveness or loss of balance, Emont lurched forward, pressing his mouth hard against mine. Our teeth clashed dully before I teetered backward, my head landing a fingersbreadth from the hearthstone. Emont slid from his chair and crawled on top of me. He straddled my waist. There was hunger in his eyes, but also pleading. His weight squeezed the breath from me, and I was relieved when he shifted forward to lay his chest against mine. As he was too short to reach my mouth, he shimmied clumsily, like a boy climbing a tree. His movement dragged my shift until it bunched around my thighs. I lay still while he planted sloppy kisses on my mouth, but when he grasped my breast, I turned my face away, saying, "No, Emont."

He grunted but sat up again, crushing my ribs beneath his hips. "Come to bed." His voice was hoarse. He staggered to his feet and held out a hand to help me up, but I didn't trust his balance. I stood on my own, brushing down my skirt.

"You will only make things worse for both of us." I stroked his arm lightly with an affection that was only partly feigned. For all of his drunken, awkward advances, he did care for me, and for all of his privilege, he was deeply unhappy.

Emont leaned forward and kissed me again. I pressed my lips briefly to his, and then I pushed him away again. "No. Please. Why don't you lie down on the bed? I shall untie your boots. It is late and time you slept."

Emont looked at me hopefully. He tried to take my hand, but

I placed my hands on his shoulders instead and guided him to the bed. When we reached the bedside, he grasped both of my wrists and searched my face intently. His eyes were lucid; perhaps he was not as drunk as I had believed. I felt a queasy flutter and could not meet his gaze.

"Agnes, you are unlike anyone I have ever met. You are so clever and kind. I . . . I wish . . ."

The naked sentiment in his voice made me uncomfortable. I did not like to hear him describe me as kind. I cut him off, saying, "Perhaps you should meet more women." I had meant to sound wry, but the words were bitter even to my own ears.

Emont held my wrists a moment longer, and then he flopped down resignedly and closed his eyes. I unlaced his boots slowly, telling him a story about Ella from earlier in the day. Before I could finish, he began to snore.

In the weeks that followed, Emont twisted and strained against the bonds of circumstance. He did not want to risk angering Abbess Elfilda, but he could not bear the thought of marrying me to another man. He made untenable proposals to hide me at the manor, but even he understood that the abbess would soon hear if he were consorting with an unwed servant.

I encouraged Emont's attachment by being warm and solicitous, hoping that he might cave in and marry me, but my attentions inflamed Emont without pushing him closer to a decision. He drank more heavily than ever, and he was intolerant of his daughter, which he had never been before.

One morning, while we sat together in the great hall, Ella squirmed on Emont's lap and knocked over his cup of ale.

"Get off me, you clumsy mimmerkin!" he bellowed and pushed Ella forcefully from his lap.

The girl landed on her knees, and she remained still for a moment, stunned. Then Ella's lovely eyes widened and she let out a shriek, an uninterrupted keening. Emont grasped her long hair, which she wore loose that day, and he hauled her to her feet with a sharp yank. He pushed his face close to his daughter's and shouted, "Take your sniveling elsewhere!"

This ended Ella's shriek, but she began to sob. Shaking, she pulled away from her father. I rose to help her, but Emont roared, "Stay!" so I sank back into my chair, and the girl ran crying to Gisla by herself.

Emont gripped the arms of his chair. I waited for his breathing to slow before daring to speak.

"You should go to her and soothe her spirits with a few kind words," I said.

Emont closed his eyes and knocked the back of his head against the carved headrest. He sighed. "I know," he said. "I will go to her."

"You are a good father."

"I am a weak father."

"Most fathers do not show so much affection to their daughters."

"She is all I have." He sounded miserable.

"She can certainly be trying at times."

Emont opened his eyes and looked at me curiously. The color of his eyes was the same arresting violet-blue as his daughter's, and it occurred to me that his gaze shared something of her innocence as well.

"You find Ella difficult?" he asked.

His words took me by surprise, for I had assumed that everyone

found Ella difficult. "She is quick to tears," I said, "and she is a fussy child."

"She is sensitive."

"Yes, I suppose that is true," I murmured. "Can I fetch you more ale? Would you care for a blanket?"

"Do you not like her?"

I had never posed such a question to myself. Ella was my labor, my duty, just as the laundry had once been. She was peculiar, certainly, a solitary woolgatherer who did not engage in play like other children. She was a stickler for quiet and rigid in her likes and dislikes. Still, she was a good girl, rarely defiant, and as fastidious about following rules as she was about routines.

"She is a dear child," I said.

"The dearest," Emont agreed. "An angel. Perfection itself."

I smiled politely.

"I do believe that she is the brightest and most beautiful girl in the kingdom."

"Undoubtedly," I said. "Certainly the most beautiful I have ever beheld. And she is clever."

After a pause, Emont said, "You would be a good mother."

"I *am* a mother."

"Of course, of course. You had daughters once too."

"I have daughters still." I had not seen my children in five years. I did not know if they remembered me. I only knew that they were alive because I begged the abbey's messenger to inquire for me.

"I hope that I did not offend you," Emont said. "I only meant that you are good with Ella."

"I shall fetch that ale for you." I left for the buttery, my eyes burning.

The days dragged on, and Emont made no decision. He was cornered, frantic for an escape but unwilling to run toward the danger he perceived on every side. He was simply unable to act.

I tried to speak about a plan for me to return to Old Hilgate. I thought that he might give me the money to make a new start; I had guided the manor out of debt, and he could afford to be generous. From Old Hilgate, I could visit Charlotte and Matilda at the abbey.

Emont refused to discuss any of this with me. He pounded his fist and told me to keep quiet and allow him to think.

Ella caught a fever, and she was sick for several days. Soon I too began to cough and ache, and then it was my turn to be confined to bed. My fever subsided, and I thought that I was improving, but the cough worsened. I had paroxysms that left me gasping, and then the fever came roaring back, worse than before. My phlegm turned putrid, then to blood, and I was frightened.

Gisla sent for the apothecary, but the medicine did not help. Troubled dreams leaked into waking hours until I could no longer distinguish sleep from wakefulness. My breathing was labored, and I had nightmares about drowning in a pond covered by gray scum and dead rushes: I sank and sank into lightless depths. The muddy bottom of the pond was as soft as eiderdown and just as yielding, and as I descended, it enfolded me until it closed over my mouth and nose. Then I would wake, heaving and struggling to catch my breath.

Often when I woke, I saw Emont's concerned face hovering over me. He rubbed my back or sat me up to ease my panic. Though I do not remember it, Gisla told me that a physician came to bleed me, and when he left, he told them not to expect me to survive.

Emont took up a vigil at my bedside. He prayed, and Gisla said that he wept when he saw how my lips turned blue as I gasped for breath. He gave up food and drink, though when Gisla saw how his hands trembled, she convinced him that he should at least take some ale.

I was ill for two weeks and wobbly as a newborn kitten when it was over. Emont insisted on feeding me broth by his own hand, and he supported my arm on his shoulders as I tried to walk again. I had never seen him so gentle, not even with Ella.

Fasting had made me gaunt; my gowns hung loose, and I was startled by the angularity of my face in the mirror. It suited me—at the end of my third decade, the soft contours of youth had given way to more sculpted features. The hollows beneath my cheekbones and sharp angle of my jaw were too austere to be beautiful, but, coupled with my large brown eyes, the effect was still pleasing.

Emont seemed to be enchanted by me. He watched me so intently that I was embarrassed and found it difficult to meet his gaze. Much to Gisla's disapproval, he gave me one of Lady Alba's necklaces, and he insisted on fastening the clasp himself. Once he had properly arranged the jewels, he held me at arm's length and told me that I was dazzling.

Though I was the servant and he the master, Emont was happy to fuss and coddle me, bringing cups of cider and tucking blankets around my knees. My infirmity seemed to give him new purpose. He was never more cheerful—or more sober—than during my convalescence.

On a sunny afternoon, Emont bundled me in one of Lady Alba's fur cloaks and took me outside for a walk. The snow had melted, leaving behind puddles and mud, but the breeze carried the loamy

promise of lilies and lilacs. My legs were still weak, but the sun-shine lifted my spirits.

"It is good to see some color in your cheeks again," Emont said.

We walked in companionable silence for some time, his arm brushing against mine, and then Emont stopped. He tapped his walking stick against the cobblestones. "You do know how much I value your company, Agnes?"

I watched him tug at his tunic where it wrinkled over his belly. When his eyes met mine, I was embarrassed by the vulnerability I perceived in them.

"I value your company also, sir," I replied.

"Sir? You haven't called me that in a while." He cleared his throat and smiled nervously. "You had suggested that we get married."

I suppose that I must have looked as uncomfortable as I felt, because he laughed and said, "Don't tell me that the formidable Agnes has become a blushing maiden!"

My heart beat almost painfully against my ribs. "It is only that I was not expecting you to speak of marriage."

"I have had time to consider."

"You are reconciled to the impediments?"

"It is not so much that . . ." He twisted his walking stick for a moment. "I have discovered that I cannot live without you. It is a ridiculous idea for me to marry you, but I don't see any other way. I . . . I know that you do not feel about me as I do about you. I do hope that you have some affection for me. I believe you do. Of course, the marriage would be a great advantage to you, as you know . . . And of course to me, because you are the best manager anyone could hope—"

When I could no longer stand for him to go on, I placed my hand on his and said, "Emont, it would be my honor to be your wife."

With a sharp intake of breath, he clasped my hand in his and bent to kiss it. He smiled at me, his eyes glistening, and said, "Thank you, Agnes. I will endeavor to be worthy of you."

The unnatural transition from servant to betrothed of a lord did not progress smoothly. There are no signposts for such an overthrow of convention. It is said that Ella rose from rags to riches by marrying a prince, but in truth, she was a high-born lady, even if her father was not wealthy by royal standards. Ella's marriage was only unusual. Mine was unthinkable.

It is fortunate that we were isolated in the countryside and that visitors had become rare, or Emont might have lost courage in the face of censure from his peers. As it was, in lonely Aviceford Manor, crouched atop a hillside and surrounded by no one but unlettered peasants, we heard objections only from Gisla and, of course, Ella.

I told Gisla the news myself, after we put Ella to bed. She looked dumbfounded. "What is this you speak of?" she asked, not trusting her own ears.

"I am to be married. To Emont."

"No! That cannot be!" She covered her mouth with a gnarled fist.

"It is. We are betrothed."

"The master must marry a lady! Marry a servant? Foul—" She searched mutely for words to express her outrage and finally spat out, "Scandalous!"

I set my candle down and lit a second one in a wall sconce. The room Gisla and I shared lacked its own hearth, though the fire in Ella's adjoining chamber kept us warm.

"I have done a great deal to right this sinking ship," I said. "The manor has never been so profitable. Emont has never been so well. You know that I do him good."

"You do, that is true, but marriage? To a nobleman?"

"Are you not happy for me?"

Gisla crossed her bony arms. "You have always acted above your station. I lay no blame on you for that. You are educated. I lay no blame on you for catching the master's eye either. 'Tisn't your fault you were born handsome. But there is right and there is wrong, and a servant marrying a master is wrong."

"Even if it will be good for the master? Good for Ella?"

"What Ella needs is a mother with proper standing. She is the granddaughter of a count and a baron. She cannot have a villein stepmother! It would ruin her reputation. How would her father find a husband for her?"

"You really doubt that Ella will find a husband?" I said teasingly.

Gisla's indignation did not prevent her lips from twitching with a smile. It was obvious that only a blind man could be unaffected by Ella's enchantment. She pressed her lips back into a thin line and said, "'Tisn't proper," but the disapproval in her voice had lightened.

"I understand your objection," I said. "This is terribly unconventional. I do not deserve Emont's love. He is likely to change his mind. If he does not, the abbess will doubtless interfere before we can be wed, and you will be gratified." I knew that Gisla disliked the abbess for her cold treatment of her sister, Lady Alba. "There is only the slimmest chance that we will arrive at the altar, but in the meantime, I beg for your compassion. You and I have always been friends and allies to each other."

Gisla waved me away irritably. She was not ready to capitulate, but she had a soft heart and did not hold out for long. A few days later, she told me how touched she had been when she saw Emont sitting vigil at my sickbed. A few days after that, she compared me with Asneth, the poor orphan who was clothed by an angel so she could wed Prince Joseph of Egypt. Perhaps unintentionally, Gisla constructed a romantic narrative around my marriage to make the unpalatable more agreeable to her strict sensibilities. The stories we tell ourselves have great power.

I was far less successful with Ella than with Gisla. The problem may partly have been my approach, for I was unaccountably nervous. I brought gingerbread to sweeten her mood, but as Ella nibbled her treat, perched on a high stool, I was at a loss for how to broach the matter. I paced awkwardly around the girl and then blurted, "Your father and I are to wed!"

Ella stopped eating and looked at me warily. "Who are you both to marry?" The detached tone of her fluting voice was disconcerting.

"Each other."

"You are to marry my father?" Ella sounded doubtful, as though I had told her that I had sprouted wings and was going to fly to the moon.

"Yes. I am to be your stepmother."

Ella's gaze was cool. She went back to nibbling her gingerbread. Perhaps I ought to have left her alone, but I wanted to be sure that she understood. She was such a quiet child; I never knew what was going on behind her pretty eyes.

"We will be a family," I said brightly, "and you may call me Mama if you wish. Gisla will still care for you as she does now."

Ella ignored me. She munched and brushed the tips of her hair against her cheek in a circular motion.

"I shan't mind if you would rather call me Mother. You are a big girl now. I suppose that 'Mama' sounds babyish to you. I forget how old you are, since you are so small." I felt foolish, running my mouth, but her silence unsettled me. I plunged on, "This is no great change, not like your father marrying a stranger. We will all continue to live together, only now as a family."

A tear trickled down Ella's alabaster cheek, followed quickly by another.

"Oh," I said, "no, dearheart, don't cry." I put my arm clumsily around her shoulders, but she shrank from me. I removed my arm and watched helplessly. Ella stared at the floor; tears made silvery paths down her face and beaded on her long eyelashes.

"Would you like your poppet?"

Ella did not acknowledge me, but I fetched the doll anyway. Guilt and annoyance followed me as I rushed through the corridor. A part of me wanted to comfort the poor child, but another part wished nothing more than to be away from her.

When I returned with the poppet, a clay doll with a fancy gown and coronet, Ella had brightened.

"Shall we find beads to sew on her train?" Ella asked. She was always improving upon the poppet's garments with bits of lace and embroidery.

"Certainly," I said. "We can snip some from your mother's old clothing."

Ella's expression wobbled, but she recovered her equanimity.

"Even though your mother lives in heaven now, she will always be queen of your heart," I said. "Death does not diminish a mother's love. Not a whit. She cherishes every hair on your head, and she sings your praise to the angels."

Ella jumped down from her stool and brushed crumbs from her lap. "Help me find some beads," she said.

Though Ella did not speak of the marriage, she clung to her father even more than usual. She sat in his lap like a tot, ate from his plate, climbed into bed with him in the morning.

Ella had always resisted lessons from me, but as her nurse I had insisted. The betrothal changed our relationship: I lost my narrow authority as governess, but I had not yet been granted the broader authority of a parent. I looked on in frustration as Ella squandered her days in idleness, and Emont colluded with her, encouraging his daughter to lounge against him hour after hour.

"She is just a small child," Emont told me.

"Eight years old," I said. "Nearly nine. I was not much older when I worked in the laundry. If a tutor is coming, she had best learn to read her prayers, not just rattle them off."

Ella yawned and pressed her face into her father's shoulder.

"She will eventually learn to read," Emont said complacently. "Let her be a child. She will have time to be a lady when she grows up. She will have little use for reading anyway."

I bristled but answered pleasantly, "Lady Wenslock is frowning from heaven."

"Abbess Elfilda does the frowning here on earth. She will ensure a tutor. That family has a fixation with educating girls."

"Idleness is to the soul as rust is to iron."

"Idleness is Ella's birthright." Emont smiled and stroked his daughter's hair as though she were a pet.

"Ella may become the lady of a great house," I said stiffly, "but no manor runs itself. She will have duties, and it is best that she does not learn to expect leisure."

"You hear that, lambie? You had best listen to Agnes. She is to be your stepmother soon."

"I don't want you to marry, Father," Ella said, her eyes wide.

"But you love your nurse!" Emont responded.

Ella wound her arms tightly around Emont's neck.

"She is worried about the change," I said.

"I shall not call you Mama!" Ella said.

"There is no need for you to call me Mama."

"I shall not call you Mother either!"

I waited for Emont to reproach her for being disrespectful, but he did not.

"Manners, Ella, mind your manners," I said mildly, knowing that my words fell on deaf ears.

Ella peered at me from over her father's arm. As was so often the case, her face was inscrutable.

It was Gisla who eventually found a way through the girl's defenses. Ella had a fascination with women's clothing that went beyond the usual childlike interest in dressing up. She sorted her mother's gowns by style and then by shade, and she made small alterations, such as pinning a skirt into the semblance of flounces, to surprisingly pleasing effect. Gisla suggested that Ella might design her own gown for the wedding. This project was a double

blessing, for it both occupied the child and distracted her from the significance of the day.

I pushed Emont to have a wedding within the month, as I did not want to give him the chance to lose courage. As we planned to wed quietly in the chapel at the manor, there was no need for a formal betrothal or the posting of banns. We informed the manorial staff of our intent, and though there was some outrage, there was also a communal sigh. Not everyone was happy to have a new lady of the manor, but at least they were familiar with me and my ways. They did not miss Lady Alba, and they had feared that her replacement might be worse.

Emont and I married in early spring with only Ella and Gisla in attendance. Ella was resplendent in a rose silk gown with her mother's emeralds around her neck. Gisla coiled her hair into cauls, provoking squirming and complaints, for Ella was not used to wearing her hair dressed. Still, she bore herself proudly and simpered happily when we told her how beautiful she looked.

Emont was pale and stiff, but he showed no signs of regret. He gave me a lovely gold ring, which I had not expected, and he smiled as he slid it onto my finger.

Although the marriage was more than I could have hoped for, my heart still ached. I longed to return to Old Hilgate, to the merry alehouse and my daughters. I even missed Fernan, who had been strong and wholesome, for all of his flaws. The same could not be said of Emont, nor of his strange daughter, who watched the world through limpid eyes but kept her thoughts secret. They lived in silent passivity and gloom, like soft-bodied creatures that dwell beneath stones in the forest floor.

On my wedding night, I ate supper in the great hall for the first time, and Ella joined us for the special occasion. Servants glided

quietly around us, carrying enough food for a party many times larger than ours. Emont said little; he looked tense and unhappy, and he gulped his wine for solace. Ella gazed absently into the distance, picking at her food.

After supper, Emont retired to his chambers, and I retired to mine. I could have taken Lady Alba's solar, but I did not wish to evict Ella from her bed. Instead, I chose the more modest guest solar as my sleeping quarters. I did not yet have a maid to undress me, so I removed my own gown and put it away. I waited until I was sure that Emont was undressed, and then I made my way down the corridor wearing only my shift. Emont was waiting for me in bed. The fire had already burned to embers; when I held my candle aloft, I could see Emont's eyes gleaming in the darkness. I fumbled with the bedclothes to get under the covers. For a long time, Emont lay with his head propped up on his hand, gazing at me and stroking my hair tenderly. He ran his fingers over my ribs and told me that I was too thin, but he said it so warmly that I knew he was not disappointed by my body. Just as I began to wonder if he was too tired to consummate our marriage, he tugged at my shift, signaling me to remove it. I obliged. His member was soft from too much wine, and it took some effort to accomplish our coupling, but when it was over, Emont sobbed with relief.

After I crept back from Emont's bed and into my own, I lay awake, staring into the dark. I would never be a servant again. I was Agnes Vis-de-Loup, the lady of the manor of Aviceford.

UGLY STEPSISTERS

My first act as lady of the manor was to gather all of the servants together in the kitchen at dawn. From that day, they were accountable to me, and I wanted to make certain of their obedience. I also wanted to establish my own discourse with the servants. Having observed firsthand the relationship of chamberlains to both underlings and master, I knew that truth frequently fell victim to expediency, self-interest, or sycophancy. I did not want to have to rely on Wills for all knowledge about what transpired in my own manor.

Scullions put out bread and ale while Wills played the reluctant shepherd, herding sleepy servants into the kitchen. Wills was unhappy about my request, which he viewed as both eccentric and a threat to his authority.

The servants gathered in silence against the back wall by the fireplace, yawning and shuffling their feet. Their eyes glinted suspiciously in the dim morning light that filtered through the grimy skylights. Those who had come in from outside were still damp from rain, and steam coiled from their cloaks along with the scent

of wet wool. The laundress tried to hide herself at the back of the group, but her effort was unavailing. It made me think of a ground-hog grown too fat to scurry into its hole in the ground.

"Welcome." My voice echoed from the high ceiling. "I know some of you better than others. I am Agnes Vis-de-Loup, your new mistress."

Several of the men glared at me with hard expressions. My resolve faltered, but I took a deep breath and continued.

"I intend to make Aviceford the most profitable of Ellis Abbey's manors. You can benefit from the manor's wealth through improved living conditions, but nothing can be accomplished unless you all do your part."

The yawning stopped, and they watched me intently.

"I shall demand that you work hard, and I shall hold each of you accountable. Today, I shall release anyone who chooses from his obligation to the manor. Leave unfettered and find your fortune elsewhere. Those who choose to stay will be given a wage, be they serf or free, and that wage shall rise or fall in proportion to our manor's fortune. Work hard and you shall be rewarded. If you will not do your part, then leave. I shall extend amnesty until the week is out."

The silence was profound. Some of the servants looked confused, and some looked angry. I resisted the temptation to wring my hands nervously. Doubt gnawed at me. I had counted on the self-interest of these men for my scheme, but I had not taken into account how hidebound they were. Why had I been so proud to think that I could change the way the manor had always functioned? If I loosened Will and Emont's grip on the servants too much, I risked rebellion. Until the day before, I had been a servant myself, and they were unconvinced of my authority.

I opened my dry mouth to break the terrible silence, and a burly man stepped forward, saying, "How much will you pay us, and what will you expect of us?"

I noted the absence of deference in his words. "Jack, isn't it? Pay will depend upon each man's position, between two and six shillings each year for most of you. An extra shilling at Christmastide in a good year. What I shall ask is that you assist with building projects, transportation of goods, harvest, shearing, or whatever other tasks need to be accomplished once you have finished with your own work. Gardeners will not be idle in winter, and scullions will not be idle when we have no guests. You will work hard, but you will be rewarded. The more profit comes to the manor, the more you will earn in your wages, the better the living quarters will become, and the more meat we can afford to feed you."

A low rumbling passed through the crowd. My breast shook with each heartbeat. Jack grimaced and wagged his head indecisively, causing the sinews of his thick, short neck to bulge. Then he nodded slowly and said, "That sounds fair. I have never been afraid of hard work." He turned to his fellow servants and said, "What she says seems fair. She is our mistress."

Another servant stepped forward, a scowling young man with a rust-colored beard. I did not recognize him. He said, "This is just a trick to get us all to work our fingers to the bone. She tricked the master into marrying her, and now she brings her sorcery to bear on us." Several others murmured in agreement.

I had to assert myself, or I would lose control. I squared my shoulders with confidence I did not feel, and I raised my voice until it rang clear in the cavernous kitchen, using a tone that I had so often heard Abbess Elfilda use from the pulpit. "You have one week to leave quietly. But make no mistake. Insubordination will not be

tolerated. Hard work will be rewarded, but if you make trouble, you will be flogged until your back runs with a river of blood. I shall have no mercy on anyone who threatens the security of my manor."

As the echoes of my voice died, the sun cast its first rays through the windows and skylight, banishing the gray pall of dawn. I held my ground, staring down anyone who met my eye. The red-bearded servant clenched his fists and snarled, but he said nothing. Most of the others looked at the floor. I decided to count it as a partial victory. If they insisted on being sheep, at least they would be my sheep. I raised my hands as though in benediction and said, "You may go."

The laundress scurried for the door, but Wills stopped her as I had instructed. He also detained the only other female servant, a wiry young woman with a ruddy complexion, ashes on her apron, and blisters on her fingers. After all of the men filed out, I approached them. Elisabeth eyed me warily from beneath the graying curls that escaped her shapeless bonnet. The laundry girl quivered like a rabbit.

"Wills tells me that you have to do more of your share of the work in the laundry now, Elisabeth. That must be hard for you."

The laundress pursed her small mouth. Fine lines now radiated from her lips, and her chin was framed by deep grooves. "I have always been a hard worker."

"I have a different memory. I see that your hands are still white and soft, not chapped and blistered like this girl here. What is your name, young woman?"

"Beatrice, my lady."

"Beatrice, do you agree that the laundress does her share?"

The woman glanced at Elisabeth's face and then mine with panic in her eyes. "Why yes, my lady." She stared fixedly at her shoes.

"Then I suppose that she can manage on her own without you for some time?"

Beatrice looked even more agonized.

"You do not need to answer. I know that she will manage fine. I do not have a chambermaid, and until I find one, I would like you to work for me."

Beatrice stared at me with dumb surprise. The laundress began to complain, but Wills cut her off sharply.

"How long will you keep her from her proper duties?" Elisabeth asked, trying to hide her frustration.

"As long as I please," I replied.

"I shall leave!"

"You haven't the courage to leave. In any event, you are not allowed."

"You just said that anyone could leave!"

"Is this how you address your mistress?"

"You said that anyone could leave, *my lady*," she said, barely moving her lips.

"That is for everyone else. You will have to earn your freedom if you wish to leave." I would gladly have been rid of the woman, but I could not ask one of the men to do laundry, and it would take some time to find a replacement.

"I cannot keep up with the laundry without help!"

I raised my eyebrows.

"My lady." She choked on the words.

"You will do your best. I believe that you remember the punishment for sloth. You set it yourself."

The laundress's face turned bright red, but she said nothing further.

"You are dismissed," I said sweetly. "Wills, show Beatrice to

my chambers and make sure that she knows her duties. She will return to the laundry when I decide. Perhaps she will get a promotion to chief laundress if she does her duty well."

In the end, only two servants left Aviceford Manor. The rust-bearded one, who worked in the kitchen, departed that same day, and the boy who kept the pigs left the next. There was resistance to change, but when the servants received pay, some for the first time, they softened. We managed the manor better with fewer staff. They became more vocal, and when we had meetings at dawn, the servants gathered gladly around the table for bread and ale. Wills grumbled that it was not properly respectful for the servants to speak with the lady of the manor, but even he had to admit that the added income was welcome.

Not long after the wedding, Abbess Elfilda sent a messenger with the news of her displeasure. Emont fretted and drank himself into a stupor, but I was too joyful to care, for the abbess also sent a gift far greater than any I could have dreamt of: Charlotte and Matilda were returned to me. Since I had vexed the abbess, she refused to continue my daughters' education. When Wills brought the news, I flew down the stairs, barely touching my feet to the ground. The girls were dark silhouettes against the bright blue sky, standing on the threshold on either side of the messenger. In the years since I had last seen them, they had grown tall; Charlotte was nearly the same height as the messenger. Matilda had not lost her old habit of standing with arms akimbo, her head tilted to the side.

When I reached the bottom steps, I burst into tears, which caused them both to hesitate in confusion, but when I called to them, they rushed into my embrace. I had never been so happy as in that mo-

ment, holding their narrow, sturdy bodies against mine, Matilda's face buried against my breast, Charlotte's strong arms around my neck. I held the girls so long that Matilda began to squirm; I let go reluctantly and looked at them. They both wore the rough woolen frocks issued by the abbey, and their hair was entirely covered by modest veils. Charlotte was more willowy than I remembered, which emphasized her doelike quality. Matilda, not yet teetering on the brink of womanhood like her sister, was sturdy, and her hazel eyes were still bright, but her pockmarked face had lost its roundness. I stood with my hands clasped, tears streaming down my face, until Charlotte wiped my cheek with the tips of her fingers and said teasingly, "Mother, we would never guess that you are happy to see us!"

After Wills put the girls' little bundles away, I gave Charlotte and Matilda a tour of the manor house. I told them that I had been a little younger than Matilda, ten years old, when I first arrived at Aviceford Manor. The girls were polite, but unimpressed by the building; compared with the abbey, Aviceford was rustic and small. They were more interested in the sleeping quarters, particularly Ella's chamber. Matilda ran to the canopied feather bed and threw herself on it with a delighted squeal, while Charlotte mused aloud about how enchanting it would be to sleep on a soft mattress next to a warm hearth.

I instructed the cooks to serve meat pies for supper, and as a special treat, I had the gardeners forage for early strawberries to serve with honey and clotted cream.

Emont was already at the table drinking wine when we arrived in the great hall for the meal; he greeted us pleasantly, but from the vagueness of his smile, I could tell that he was drunk. Ella sat shyly next to him with her head bowed.

"Ella," I said, "these are your stepsisters, Charlotte and Matilda. You met them several years ago, but you may not remember."

Charlotte stepped forward and knelt down next to where Ella sat on the bench. "Hello," she said, pitching her voice to a register friendly to young children. "I see that you have a lovely purple necklace."

Ella had tied a satin ribbon around her neck as a makeshift choker, an adornment that seemed odd then but would one day become a signature flourish. She touched the ribbon self-consciously and glanced at Charlotte with a timid smile.

Matilda joined Charlotte and put her arm over her sister's shoulders, saying, "I am Matilda. I played with the frogs with you."

At the sight of Matilda's scarred face, Ella started and squirmed backward along the bench. Matilda stood gracefully and stepped away, while Charlotte turned sharply to look at her sister. Matilda flashed her a smile that said "I am not troubled," and Charlotte's expression softened. It made me sad to realize that such reactions to Matilda's appearance were a common occurrence.

"Sit, please," I said to the girls. "I see that the food has arrived!"

We arranged ourselves on the bench opposite Ella and Emont, with Matilda farthest from her young stepsister. Servants placed a steaming meat pie in front of each of us; the aroma made my mouth water as Emont mumbled through grace.

"I recall that you both love this meal," I said.

"Oh, we do!" Matilda said. "At the abbey, we had one made all of venison, with dates and ginger spice."

"That was delicious, but remember the pork pie with almond milk?" Charlotte said. "That was my favorite."

Crestfallen, I said, "I am afraid that we haven't got venison or almond milk here at the manor."

"No matter, no matter," Charlotte said quickly. "This is lovely! Thank you, Mother."

Emont drained the carafe into his cup and signaled for more wine to be brought. "How is the battle-axe?" he asked Charlotte.

Charlotte was mystified. "I beg your pardon, sir?" she said.

"It is so wonderful to have you both home," I interjected.

"The old shrew, the old harpy," Emont said, slurring the last words together.

I knew that he meant Abbess Elfilda, but I feigned ignorance. "Ella," I said, "Charlotte and Matilda can tell you about some of the lessons they learned at the abbey."

"Oh yes," Matilda said. "We wouldn't torture you with Latin, but we know some jolly songs."

"Tilly was the best of all the girls at Latin," Charlotte said proudly. "I got the birch for botching my conjugations."

"You did fine, Lottie," Matilda said. "Edeline was the one who never knew her lessons. Sister Anne grew tired of birching her, because no matter how much she hit her, she forgot what to say. Poor Edeline."

"Remember when you wrote the answer on her hand for her? Sister Anne nearly fell over with surprise when Edeline got the right answer."

Matilda laughed.

I felt as though I were observing my daughters from a great distance. "We shall have to get you new gowns," I said. "Those gray ones are dreadful. I remember how uncomfortable they were."

Charlotte shrugged. "We are used to them."

"Oh, may I have new gowns also?" Ella asked.

"You have plenty of gowns," I said.

"I have no new ones."

"Because you have yet to outgrow the ones in your wardrobe."

"It isn't fair," Ella said.

"Let the little angel have a new gown," Emont said. He kissed the crown of his daughter's head and stroked her hair with an unsteady hand.

"I shall consider it," I said tersely.

"I shall make sure that you get the prettiest new frock," Emont whispered loudly to Ella. He smiled down at her.

"Would you like to speak with the seamstress, then?"

Emont slammed his fist on the table. "I will not be argued with! It is your fault that this has happened! That they have been sent here!"

A cold sweat prickled my brow. I knew that he was upset about the message from the abbess, but I did not want him to make Charlotte and Matilda feel unwelcome on their first day back with me. They both watched him with wide eyes, unsure of what to think.

"This will all blow over, Emont," I said. "If it does not, you may rely upon me to set it right."

"What do you know about setting things right?"

"A good deal. I do not believe that I have ever failed you."

Emont looked like he was groping for a response, but I cut him short, saying, "Ella, you should tell Charlotte and Matilda about the beautiful gown you designed. Please, Emont, do have some strawberries. They are the first of spring!"

The strawberries and cream were a distraction, and my prediction did prove true. The abbess had banished Charlotte and Matilda from the abbey as punishment for my marriage, but she took no other measures against us. Her message exhorted me to be a proper guardian for her godchild and contained a veiled threat

of reprisal in the event that we caused her further displeasure. She did not want to take Ella from us, however, nor did she wish to inflict upon herself the task of finding new management for Avice- ford Manor, particularly after I had made the manor profitable. The abbess vented her spleen, but she was a practical woman. I understood her, for I was practical too.

After supper, Matilda and Charlotte taught Ella a song with an elaborate accompaniment of hand claps and finger snaps. They giggled at the lyrics and the mistakes they kept making. Ella had trouble following along, but she joined the merriment; her shrill laugh was like the call of a shrike, humorless and louder than was warranted.

I helped Emont to bed, and when I returned, Ella asked if Char- lotte and Matilda could sleep in her chambers. I was pleased to see the three getting along so well, but also sad that my daughters were more eager to share Ella's quarters than mine.

I had Beatrice put the extra feather bed in Ella's chamber for Charlotte to use; Matilda took the trundle beside Ella's bed. While I helped Gisla with the bedclothes, Ella showed her stepsisters the pearlescent hairbrush she had inherited from her mother, and Char- lotte volunteered to brush her hair. I expected Ella to say no, be- cause she never let anyone touch her hair except Gisla, but to my surprise, she happily accepted. She sat cross-legged and serene on the bed while Charlotte gently untangled and smoothed one long golden lock at a time. Matilda lay on the trundle, out of sight of the other two, telling amusing stories about the nuns and students at the abbey. I lingered so that I could hear the stories too. The candles guttered as they melted to stubs, and though I wished to stay and listen to more of their conversation, I told them that it was time to

sleep and said good night. Charlotte and Matilda pulled me tight and embraced me fervently, but Ella ducked her chin and presented only her cool forehead to my lips. "Where is Gisla?" she asked.

"She was tired, and I sent her to bed."

Ella yawned.

"Good night, Mama!" Matilda said.

"Good night!" Charlotte chimed in.

As I closed the door, I could hear them already whispering to one another.

Even during our awkward reaquaintance, I was overjoyed to have my daughters home. Like an insecure lover, I tried to please them at every turn, serving favorite foods, purchasing new clothing, being solicitous to their needs. Despite my elation, however, worry gnawed at me. Had Charlotte and Matilda remained at the abbey, they might have become nuns, but that door had been slammed shut by Mother Elfilda. The only alternative was marriage. Emont would have trouble enough providing a substantial dowry for Ella; I was not sure that I could prevail upon him to settle dowries on my daughters. Without pedigree or beauty, I did not know what would become of them.

Matilda in particular was a concern to me. I coiled her hair in thick, lustrous braids behind her ears and gave her a gold chain to wear at her throat, but nothing could alter the fact of her disfigurement. Her intelligent eyes shone bright in her ruined face, and I tried to look only at her eyes, for without a reassuring anchor, my gaze slid and slipped from a sight that broke my heart.

Although Ella refused my lessons, preferring languid reclusiveness, Charlotte and Matilda did not resist being kept busy. Life at

the abbey had been regimented and punishments harsh, so they were used to hard work.

Charlotte remembered little of Old Hilgate and Matilda nothing, but I told them stories of the alehouse and encouraged them to learn how to brew. They seemed to understand the value of acquiring such skills.

We were by then producing our own ale at the manor and selling the excess for profit. I brought the girls to the brewery, a new outbuilding designed expressly for the purpose of making ale, and introduced them to the servants who worked there. For several hours each day, Charlotte and Matilda learned the proper way to grind the barley, wet the mash, boil and skim the wort.

"These young lasses are quick to learn," the brewer said.

"Perhaps it runs in the blood. I used to make a nice lavender ale myself," I replied.

"Ye don't say, my lady. I would not have guessed it."

He meant this respectfully; he was new to the manor and had not known me as a servant.

When Charlotte and Matilda completed their first batch, I brought some to supper for a tasting. I handed Ella a cup, saying, "Try this, sweetheart. This is your stepsisters' first effort, and I believe it is quite good. You ought to join them in the brewery someday."

Ella took a sip and made a noncommittal sound.

Charlotte smiled and said, "Yes, you should join us!"

"It would be good for Ella to get out of her chambers," I said to Emont.

Emont made a vague noise very much like Ella's.

I persisted, saying, "It cannot be healthy for her to spend so much time alone."

"Her tutor will arrive soon."

"I promised the girls a share in the profits if they continue to brew, Ella, would you not like to earn your own money?"

Ella shrugged. "I have no need for money."

"Eat your carrots," I said.

Ella had picked all of the vegetables out of her stew. She poked them with her fork and said, "I hate carrots."

"It is wrong to waste food. Look, Charlotte and Matilda have eaten theirs."

"That's because they like them."

"No it isn't," Matilda said. "We were taught to eat everything in our bowls."

"We should be grateful for the bounty God has provided," Charlotte added.

"God had an idiotic idea when He made turnips and carrots," Ella said. "They are horrible!"

"Ella! Watch your mouth! Eat up, or there will be no supper for you tomorrow."

"Why do you always carp at me? You never yell at *them*!" She pointed across the table at her stepsisters.

I looked to Emont, but he just shook his head. "It harms nobody if she leaves a few carrots," he said. "And why should she work in a brewery like a servant? Let go of your ridiculous schemes, Agnes. Ella is happy. Why must you always be plotting?"

Because misfortune does not wait idly by until we are prepared for it, I wanted to say. *Because there may not always be enough money or food. Because the world may not always be kind to your precious daughter.* I wanted to say these things, but I held my tongue.

One day, Ella asked Gisla to open the cabinet where her mother's gowns were kept. Gisla's rheumatism was bothering her, so I sent her to lie down and opened the cabinet myself. The fabric still smelled strongly of lavender, and the scent transported me back to a dark and airless chamber, where Ella crouched in shadows, gazing at the corpse that had once given her life. Ella never spoke of her mother, and I wondered how much she remembered.

Ella chose a fancy gown for Charlotte to wear, and though Charlotte was nearly fourteen and too old for dress-up, she agreed indulgently to play along. Charlotte was so tall that the hem of her gown did not even graze her ankles, though it hung loose around her shoulders and gaped at the neck. Tiny Ella disappeared into the folds of her garment; Matilda and Charlotte found ingenious ways to belt the skirt high enough that she could walk and fold the sleeves back so that her slender fingers peeked out from the ends. Even dressed absurdly, Ella was beautiful. The girls had fun until Matilda asked for a gown to wear.

"You should dress as a boy," Ella told her.

"But I don't want to be a boy! I should have a blue gown so that we may all have different colors of nature. We can pretend to be three ladies, all sisters, who are imprisoned. You can be the baby sister who is small enough to fit through the window. We can lower you to the ground."

Ella furrowed her brow. She did not like stories or imaginary games. "If you like," she said uncertainly. "But you don't look like a lady. Your face is all lumpish and ugly."

Charlotte lashed out as quick as a viper, knocking Ella to the floor. She towered over the small girl, her dark face ablaze, roaring, "Never speak to my sister that way! You are a beast! For shame!"

Ella looked horrified. Her expression crumpled into one of misery, and she began to sob.

To separate the girls, I stepped between them. I should probably have tried to comfort Ella, but her abject prostration repelled me. I helped her out of her gown and sent her, still weeping, to find Gisla in the anteroom.

I rebuked Charlotte without much force. She should not have pushed Ella, but love for her sister was a cleansing fire. Ella and her father grew like mushrooms, soft. Charlotte had unsheathed something pure, a noble loyalty that was new to Aviceford Manor, and I was glad for it.

That night, Charlotte came to me complaining that Ella would not let her and Matilda sleep in her chamber as they had been doing. I had just gotten my drunken husband into bed with the aid of two servants, and I was in no mood to arbitrate the squabbles of little girls. I strode to Ella's chamber while Charlotte trotted behind me in an effort to keep up.

"What is going on here?" I demanded as I walked through the door. Ella was sitting on her bed with her chin on her knees, and Matilda sulked nearby.

"Ella says that we can't sleep here anymore!" Matilda was indignant.

"Don't be ridiculous, Ella! Where else are they to stay?"

Ella lifted her chin. Her expression was stony. "They can sleep in the attic."

"Ella! Charlotte and Matilda are your sisters now, not servants. You will have to learn to share."

"These are *my* chambers! They belonged to *my* mother!"

"That is true, but circumstances have changed. We are your family now."

Ella leaned her forehead on her knees for a moment; when she looked up again, her eyes brimmed with tears. She said, "Fine," almost inaudibly, and then she lay down, burying her face in her pillow.

I was relieved that Ella had capitulated so easily. I told Charlotte and Matilda to go to bed and returned gratefully to my own bed.

The following morning, Ella burst into my chambers just as Beatrice finished dressing my hair. It had taken an eternity and an excessive number of pokes and tugs for Beatrice to complete the task; she was uncouth and poorly suited to the work of a chambermaid, though she was diligent and kindhearted. Ella was crying again, and I could not make out what she was trying to tell me.

"Where is Gisla?"

"Fetch—fetching bread."

I sighed. "What happened?"

"Matilda hit me!"

"Why did Matilda hit you?"

"I don't know!"

I rose and sighed again. "Come, let's go and speak with Matilda."

Charlotte and Matilda, still wearing nightcaps, were huddled together and conferring in low, angry voices.

"What is it this time?" I asked impatiently.

Matilda jabbed her finger toward Ella. "She took our stones!"

"What are you talking about?"

"The stones you gave us! She took them!"

I had not thought about my stone collection in years. I couldn't help but smile. "You still have those?"

In unison, Charlotte and Matilda answered, "Of course!" Matilda added, "They are very precious to us."

Ella, who had by then stopped crying, said, "I was only looking at them! You hit me!"

"I did not! I barely touched you! Crybaby."

As though to prove Matilda's point, Ella began to cry again.

"Where are the stones now?" I asked wearily.

Matilda pointed to the bed and said, "There's one missing. The sparkly white one."

I looked at the rows of stones on the blanket. Ella had arranged them in a perfect square with the smallest at one corner and the largest at the opposite corner. I picked up the green stone and ran my fingers fondly over its smooth surface. "Where is the white one, Ella?"

"I don't know."

"You had better think about it some more!"

"Why am I in trouble? She is the one who hit me!"

"Matilda, you will apologize for hitting her."

"Sorry," Matilda muttered. "I barely even touched her," she repeated under her breath.

"Matilda!"

"Sorry."

"Now where is that stone, Ella?"

She pulled it reluctantly from her pocket. Charlotte said, "See? She stole it!"

"I did not steal it!" Ella said, blinking back more tears. "There was no room for it in the square. Anyway, it's just a stupid stone!"

Matilda jumped to her feet and stepped toward Ella menacingly. Ella shrieked and cowered behind me.

"Stop it, all of you! I am going to separate you. Ella, you can sleep in the attic until the three of you can get along!"

Ella stamped her little foot in fury. "It's not fair! Why do I have

to sleep in the attic? This is *my* room! *They* should sleep in the attic."

"Because there are two of them and only one of you. Besides, you like the attic. We shall move up the feather bed, and I shall have Beatrice sleep there with you."

"It's not fair!"

"When you can get along, you can move back down."

"It's not fair!" Ella was by then yelling in her shrill voice. "I am going to tell Father that you are being mean to me!"

"Enough!" I thundered back. I knew that Emont would be sick in bed all morning from his excesses the night before. "Your father is still sleeping, and you will not disturb him! I shall hear no more about this!"

Ella sank to the floor, hiccupping and sobbing, as I walked out the door.

We moved Ella to the attic that day, and as it turned out, she never moved back downstairs. Like a magpie, she built a nest for herself out of colorful and shiny objects that she skimmed from her late mother's vast collection of statuary and miscellany. I was impressed by how comfortable and appealing she managed to make her garret.

Beatrice slept with Ella for the first few weeks, but as Ella preferred to have the space to herself, I returned Beatrice to sleeping in the kitchen. Once I found a more suitable chambermaid, I made Beatrice head laundress, much to Elisabeth's dismay. She was lucky that Beatrice had such a good heart, for Elisabeth deserved far worse. The young woman could not bring herself to force her former supervisor to work, and she lied to me about how the tasks were divided. Finally, I hired a new laundry girl and sent Elisabeth to look after the chickens and geese. I could count on the cook to keep her under a tight rein.

As Gisla did not like to climb the winding stairs to the attic, it became my habit to visit Ella in the garret at bedtime. I learned the location of every loose, splintering board and the warped lintel that sagged over the last turn of the staircase, so I could make my way up the narrow, dark steps without a candle. Crossing the threshold into Ella's domain was like leaving Aviceford Manor. A high, peaked roof covered the spacious southern wing of the attic, and though the windows were small, the entire space, including the rafters, had been whitewashed to a milky pallor that reflected the half-light pearlescent glow from the casements. Ella had draped her canopied bed with whimsical swaths of pastel silks, and she had strung a cascade of sparkling bits of glass and pieces of broken mirror between the posts; the effect was alluring and strange. Statues that had belonged to Lady Alba crowded the rough floorboards. Ella had chosen mostly representations of animals, and she dressed them with queer bits of clothing and jewelry.

I often found Ella singing or humming to herself, seeming to revel in her isolation. On one occasion, she was chattering merrily to the otherwise empty garret. It was midsummer, and the sun was just setting in a swamp of amber light. Ella's luminous skin was rosy in the dying rays of the sun, and her hair shone like spun gold.

"Who are you talking to, Ella?" I asked.

"Henrietta."

"And who might that be?"

Ella sighed as though she could barely abide my stupidity. "Henrietta the rat. She's right there."

I was startled to see that there was indeed a brown roof rat hunched in the corner. When I gasped, it scuttled under the armoire.

"I thought that we had closed all of the holes up here!"

Ella shrugged.

"They are disgusting." I shuddered, remembering how I hated to sleep on the floor of the kitchen. The rats would rustle in the corners at night, and in my nightmares they gnawed on my exposed flesh with their sharp yellow teeth. I loathed the furtive, hunchbacked thieves.

"Henrietta is nice. She keeps me company."

"I shall have Wills inspect for holes. It isn't healthy to have rats running around while you sleep."

Ella made a face and got under her covers. I kissed her forehead lightly and said good night. As I walked away, Ella said, "You won't hurt Henrietta, will you?"

"Don't be ridiculous, child. The world is overrun with rats."

"But you won't hurt her?"

"Even if I wanted to, I could never catch her. Rats are too fast and sneaky. Now go to sleep."

"Good night, Mother Bear." Ella had chosen this name for me from her favorite children's story. She rarely used it, but it warmed my heart when she did.

"Good night, Ella."

The next day, I told Wills to have the attic inspected for rats. They found some small cracks and sealed them, and Wills assured me that the problem was solved. I noticed rat droppings on Ella's bedclothes several weeks later, however, and when I visited her chambers in full daylight, I saw that there were crumbs and scraps of food scattered about. Ella had been feeding them. No wonder they were bold enough to climb onto her bed.

There were more droppings on the floor, some flattened to dark smears where Ella had stepped on them. I peered under the ar-

moire. Nothing seemed amiss, though the pungent, nutty smell of rodents caused me to gag.

When I opened the armoire, the stench was overwhelming. A pair of black eyes gleamed at me from a scraggly nest on the lowest shelf. Around the nest were bits of rotting apple and other decaying lumps. The rat staggered to her feet, weighed down by a half dozen pink pups that hung from her teats. Their eyes were sealed shut, and their hairless skin looked raw and angry. The dam's feet rasped against the rough wooden shelf as she tried to scramble away. She twisted violently, knocking her pups free, and then she darted past me. For a moment I stood frozen, looking at the squirming heap of naked pups. They made impossibly high-pitched, eerie squeaks.

I sent a pair of servants to clean up the mess. They did not find the mother rat, but they cleaned out the nest, spoiled food, and excrement.

Ella must have discovered that the nest was missing just before supper, for she came to the table white-faced and trembling. She fixed me with a hard gaze and said, "What did you do to Henrietta?"

Charlotte and Matilda were already seated at the table, their hands folded politely in their laps. They looked at Ella curiously. Emont tipped back his wine cup and drained it.

"Ella. That is not the proper way to address me." She sometimes still spoke to me as though I were her servant. "And you cannot feed rats in your room! I do not understand how you can live like that."

"Henrietta is my *friend*. Did you kill her?" Tears filled her amethyst eyes.

"You are not permitted to feed rats! Your chambers were a revolting mess."

"Father!" Ella appealed to Emont. "Tell her to leave Henrietta alone!"

"Tell her to leave Henrietta alone!" Matilda mimicked softly in a lisping, babyish voice.

"She killed Henrietta!" An edge of hysteria had entered Ella's voice.

"Who is Henrietta?" Emont asked wearily. He had little tolerance for arguments and wanted peace to be restored as quickly as possible.

"Henrietta is a rat. Ella has been keeping it as a pet," I told him.

"That seems harmless enough."

"It is not harmless! Rats are a pestilence."

Emont rubbed his brow and refilled his cup. "Fine. Ella, apologize to Agnes so that we may have our supper."

Ella was outraged. "She should apologize to me!" Her cheeks flushed, and her chest heaved. "Henrietta was my friend!" She ran from the room, sobbing.

Emont called after her halfheartedly. He had no appetite for disciplining his daughter, and her tears invariably melted his heart. I shook my head at him with irritation. Ella's behaviors needed to be tamed, but Emont was no help.

Charlotte and Matilda exchanged a significant glance. I sighed and patted the back of Emont's hand. "Shall I call for supper?" I asked.

CINDERELLA

E lla did not enjoy having a tutor. She found the discipline of lessons tiresome; if it were up to her, she would have spent that time sorting buttons or curled up in a corner, gazing at the ceiling. Unlike most children, Ella did not often seek out playmates or diversions, but she never complained of boredom when she had the leisure to daydream.

Despite Ella's dislike of lessons, she was an able and obedient student. She had a quick mind and a prodigious memory. She became fluent in Latin and French, and she could rattle off the names of every member of every royal family in the civilized world. Her speech had a queer cadence back then, but that has faded with age.

Ella's tutor, Frère Joachim, was handpicked by Abbess Elfilda. He had a silver beard and merry blue eyes, and he usually took dinner with us at noon. At the table, he shared lively stories about biblical and historical figures. Charlotte and Matilda grew fond of him, and for a while I had them sit in on his lessons with Ella.

"A riddle, a riddle!" the girls would say at dinner.

Frère Joachim would scratch his shorn head and pretend to be flummoxed. "I have no more riddles in this old head," he said.

"Please, Frère, one more!" Matilda pleaded. She was always the best at guessing the answer.

"One is dark, two are fair, one is small, two are tall, how many girls plague the poor old teacher for riddles?"

"Ha! You make fun of us, sir," Charlotte said. "Anyway, only two plague you, as Ella doesn't like riddles."

The monk's eyes were wreathed by wrinkles when he smiled at Ella. "Who is the fairest in the land?"

"That is hardly a riddle," I said dryly, "and perhaps it is not wise to teach children vanity."

Ella had the grace to blush. "I am no good at riddles," she said.

"You are good at many other things," Frère Joachim said kindly. "Let me see, a riddle. *I'm told a certain something grows in its pouch, swells and stands up, lifts its covering. A proud bride grasped that boneless wonder, the daughter of a king covered that swollen thing with clothing.*"

I felt the heat rise to my own cheeks and avoided meeting the tutor's eyes. I wondered if he teased me for my rebuke. Fortunately the girls were unaware of the double entendre.

"A seed sprouting?" Charlotte said.

"Bread dough!" Matilda announced triumphantly.

"Yes, dear child, bread dough. Now, one more: *On the way a miracle: water became bone.*"

"Ice," I said softly.

"Mother! You have ruined it!" Matilda said.

Frère Joachim looked at me with his piercing blue eyes. "Yes, my lady," he said. "Ice."

Deportment, music, and dance were taught by Ella's maternal second cousin, Lady Rohesia. She was a stern, matronly woman whose barrenness and widowhood were etched deeply into her sharp features. She visited the manor for one week every several months, making it amply clear that this duty was beneath her station. Lady Rohesia did not teach Ella out of charity, but because she relied on Abbess Elfilda for an income.

The deportment lessons made Ella the elegant creature she is today. Her famous gracefulness is not innate, but the result of diligent work. She had to master a tranquil air and erect carriage. No detail was too small; she even learned to lower her eyes to just the correct degree. It would surprise many people to know that dancing did not come naturally to Ella either, but she polished her steps through hours of reluctant practice.

It was Lady Rohesia who told the abbess that my daughters sat in on Ella's lessons. Frère Joachim received a letter forbidding him from taking time away from his pupil to teach her stepsisters. I tried to continue lessons for Charlotte and Matilda on my own, but their knowledge had surpassed mine. Happily, however, Frère Joachim brought several books from Lady Wenslock's collection at the abbey, and when Ella did not require them for her lessons, we read to one another. They were better readers than I, but I improved through practice. Listening to Charlotte's rich, clear voice, braiding Matilda's soft hair, watching the late-afternoon sunshine shimmer across the gilded cornice in the guest solar—those were sweet hours.

When Ella turned twelve, Lady Rohesia brought her to the city so that she might be introduced at court. They were absent for a month, which made Emont more restless than usual. He was un-

commonly attached to his daughter, who still visited him every morning in his chambers. Ella liked to jump on his bed and snuggle against his soft, round belly; sometimes she told him about her lessons, but usually they just lay together quietly. I told Emont that she was too old for such behaviors, but he merely shrugged. Ella looked and acted far younger than her twelve years, and that suited her father fine.

Upon Ella's return, Emont had the cook prepare her favorite dishes, including pigeon pie. After we had all gathered around the table, Emont welcomed Ella home with a toast. Her stepsisters were excited to ply her with questions; Charlotte wanted to know about the people she had met at court.

"Oh, I met so many people," Ella replied vaguely.

"Were there foreigners?" Charlotte wanted to know if there were women in the city with complexions as dark as her own.

"There was a man with a funny accent. He gave me a basket of sweetmeats."

"Did you see the queen? Or Princess Anne?"

Ella took another bite before she answered. "I saw the queen. I don't know which princesses. I'm no good with names."

"What about the gowns?" Matilda asked. "They must have been magnificent!"

Ella had always taken a special interest in the design of gowns, so she answered with far more enthusiasm than she had shown up to that point. "I did see the most striking gowns," Ella said. "My favorite was blue with slashes in the sleeves that showed silver underneath and a gauzy little train. Also, so much velvet! Silk velvets with floral brocades and the most astonishing finishes. Also, many of the surcoats had patterns embroidered into the back gores with gold thread . . . Who would have imagined such a thing?"

"How was the food? It must have been divine!"

"Charlotte, let Ella eat her supper," I said.

Ella dug her spoon into her pigeon pie. "I missed regular food. I don't want to go back."

"You are mad," Matilda said. She leaned forward eagerly, the long loops of her plaits nearly dragging in her bowl. "I would give anything to go to court. Did you see any of the princes? Prince Henry is said to be charming and handsome."

"He is also said to be a rake," I interjected tartly.

The girls ignored me.

"You wouldn't be invited to court," Ella said to Matilda matter-of-factly. She had no sense of diplomacy. "Anyway, you wouldn't like it. It is the most boring place imaginable. All people do is talk, talk, talk."

"I should like to talk to people," Matilda said defensively. "I like company."

"Well, you would never fit in, and people would stare at you."

"Don't mind her, Tilly," Charlotte said. "Good company is wasted on her. The way she fidgets and stares off at nothing, they probably thought she was a half-wit."

"Charlotte! Apologize to Ella!" I could see the clouds of anger gathering in Emont's face, and I wanted to head off any further bickering.

Ella dropped her spoon with a clatter. "That is not true! Lady Rohesia told me that everyone said that I was the fairest and most delightful demoiselle they had ever seen. You're just envious!"

Matilda snorted and I lifted my hand saying, "Enough! You know how your quarrels upset Sir Emont. Remember your manners!"

Ella looked sheepishly at her father, and his frown vanished.

He smiled at her adoringly. "You *are* the most beautiful girl in the kingdom," he told her, "as well as the sweetest. Now tell me what you think of the pie. I had the cook make it just the way you like!"

Ella brought back from the city several fancy gowns commissioned by Lady Rohesia and bought by Abbess Elfilda. They were intricately ruffled and pleated, and some had lace at the bodice and cuffs. Cleanliness was not among Ella's attributes, and I worried that she would ruin the expensive garments in her carelessness. I instructed her to fold them neatly and keep them in her mother's armoire.

One morning, Beatrice passed me with a bundle of laundry, and I spotted one of Ella's gowns. It was a lustrous moiré, robin's egg blue, that shimmered like rippling water. I told Beatrice to wait and sent another servant to fetch my stepdaughter.

Ella skipped down the stairs, glad to have been freed from lessons, but her pace slowed when she saw my expression.

I pointed to the dress in Beatrice's bundle. "What is that?" I asked evenly.

"A gown, my lady mother." Ella remembered to address me politely, but she did not sound contrite.

"And what is your gown doing in the laundry? You have had no occasion to wear it."

Ella shrugged. "The laundress must have picked it up by mistake."

"Do you think that Beatrice spends her time riffling through the armoire?"

Beatrice began to tell us that she had found the gown on the

floor, but Ella interrupted her. "How would I know how she spends her time? Anyway, the dress needs to be cleaned and pressed, and she can return it to the armoire."

"You see nothing wrong with leaving your dress in a heap on your dirty floor and then expecting Beatrice to clean, press, and fold it for you?"

"I should not have left the dress on the floor. I do remember now that you asked me not to. I am sorry, Mother Bear. But it is her duty. Why else do we have servants?"

"Do you not understand how hard Beatrice works?"

Ella shrugged and yawned.

"Come with me!" I grabbed Ella by her thin wrist, and her eyes widened. I dragged her down the corridor to the laundry.

"Let me go!" Ella whimpered.

The worried Beatrice trotted behind us.

The damp, acrid smell of the laundry room stung like a slap across my face. I had not been back since I was fourteen years old. The new laundry girl was up to her elbows in the basin; her bobbing white bonnet gleamed against the darkness behind her. She looked at us with curiosity.

"You may take the rest of the day to do what you like, Polly. Ella will do your work today."

The girl looked at me dumbly.

"Go on, Polly. Give Ella your apron and then off with you." I gave Ella a shove. "Put on that apron. You are going to learn how to do laundry."

Ella regarded me in disbelief. "You cannot mean to make me do the work of a servant! My father won't let you do this to me!"

I was too furious to answer her. I turned to Beatrice, who looked

miserable. "Make sure that Ella does the bucking from the beginning. You have trained Polly well. Treat Ella the same way. She is your laundry girl today."

"You cannot do this to me!" Ella looked at me with tears in her eyes.

"Yes, I can. It's nothing more than what Polly does every single day of her life. You may come to supper tonight if you have finished your duties. I suggest that you start now."

Beatrice fluttered around Ella, looking concerned.

"Do not let her get away with shirking," I snapped at her. "If you do her work, you will have to answer to me."

Beatrice did not meet my eye but hung her head and nodded.

I rode the wave of my anger out of the laundry room, but as my emotion drained away, an ache set in around my heart. I plodded through my quotidian meetings and duties, finishing in the late afternoon, and then I stood cheerlessly by a window in the great hall and watched the snow fall. The flakes were downy, and in the absence of wind, they plummeted thick and fast. Snow accumulated on the windowsill, and before long, the gargoyles wore white veils.

Charlotte and Matilda sat by the fire, embroidering. They had brief, murmured conversations, but spent most of their time in companionable silence. Servants brought cider and took a pitcher of mulled wine to Emont, who remained in his chambers. He had been fatigued, and his skin had a dull, yellow cast; he had not been down for meals in several days.

I was restless and uneasy. As the shadows grew long, I resolved to fetch Ella from the laundry room. No sooner had the thought entered my mind than the girl appeared like a dark phantom in the doorway. She was covered in ash except where her tears had carved

bright rivulets through the soot on her cheeks. To my surprise, she ran to me and buried her face against my breast. I recoiled from the filth, but when she sobbed, I twined my fingers in her silken hair and held her close.

I brought Ella near the fire and sat her in my lap as her father did. She left a smear of black on my bodice, but I did not chastise her. Charlotte and Matilda looked up from their work. I knew how it bothered them to see their stepsister behaving like a baby; they wanted me to force Ella to stop sniveling and accept her punishment bravely. In that moment, however, I felt nothing but pity. For all her beauty and cleverness, Ella had a deformed wing, which she hid by never trying to fly. Charlotte and Matilda, like common wrens, flitted competently about their business. They could not imagine that something so ordinary could be out of reach for their exotic and much admired stepsister.

"There now, Ella, it is all done now." As I stroked her hair, I could hear her muffled sniffles. I put my hand under her chin and tilted her head back gently. I could not help but smile at her black face. It reminded me of Fernan, how tenderly he had called me his cinder girl. I wondered how different my life would be if he still lived.

"You are the cinder girl now," I said aloud.

Ella snuffled and wiped her nose on her sleeve. Her chest heaved with a deep, ragged sigh.

"My little cinder Ella." I pushed the hair back from her forehead and kissed her brow. "I am sorry that the lesson was hard, but I do believe that you have learned it."

She nodded.

"Go, then. Run and tell Gisla to have a bath drawn for you. When you are clean, I want you to be sure that all of your gowns

are put away properly. Then you may come down to supper. Ronald is stuffing some hens for tonight."

"Will Father come to supper?"

"I don't think so."

"He never comes to supper anymore!"

"He is not feeling well."

Ella huffed, and with an impatient flick of her skirt, she climbed the stairs. Matilda watched her go through narrowed eyes.

The Cinderella nonsense began with a squabble about horseback riding. The Wenslocks were a horse-loving family, and they took pride in their equestrian abilities. Abbess Elfilda insisted that Ella be taught to ride, and since Emont's health was failing, it fell to me to supervise her lessons when Lady Rohesia was absent. I did not know the first thing about horses, but I was qualified to make sure that Ella got in the saddle. This was no easy matter, because unlike her mother, Ella was frightened of horses.

I brought Charlotte and Matilda with me to the stables so that they might have a chance to ride also. As a young woman, I had dreamt of galloping through the countryside on the back of a noble white palfrey, my hair streaming in the wind. Plodding in tight, dusty circles near the fly-ridden stables at Aviceford Manor was a far cry from my youthful vision, but it still pleased me that my daughters had the opportunity to do something that I never could. I might have even joined them if I hadn't been concerned about looking foolish. My authority over the servants felt tenuous, and I did not want to do anything in front of them that might be perceived as undignified.

Ella took lessons on Tuesdays and Thursdays. Our manor was

too small for a real marshal, but Peter, who took care of the live-stock, was also the head of the stables. He was a kindly giant of a man who knew the animals well and could calm the most skittish colt with the soothing rumble of his voice and a gentle hand.

One sultry August afternoon, I brought the girls to Peter for a lesson. Black clouds threatened rain, and Ella dragged her feet in hope that a thunderstorm would force us indoors. I would have been happier indoors myself, for the air was close and oppressive, like the fevered breath of a sick child upon my face. Charlotte's gown had a dark sweat stain across the back, and Matilda's ker-chief was damp from mopping her face. Though Ella complained, she looked fresh under her wide-brimmed hat, her face a mask of serenity.

Peter met us outside, holding the bridle of Ella's caramel-colored pony, Lovely. Two docile old nags for Charlotte and Matilda were tied to the fence nearby. The older girls lit up when they saw Peter and quickened their pace to meet him, while Ella lingered behind.

"There are my three favorite young ladies!" Peter said with a grin. He stroked his silver-streaked beard with his free hand. "I have got Rosie and Copper saddled and ready for you two." He beckoned to Ella. "Come and give Lovely a snack! She misses you."

Peter held a carrot out for Ella while Lovely snuffled his arm and shook her luxurious white mane, stretching her neck toward the treat. Ella cringed and put her hands behind her back.

"Come now!" Peter leaned forward, proffering the carrot. "Your pony is happy to see you!"

Ella took the carrot and held it toward Lovely at arm's length, her face turned away as though she could not bear to watch. Char-lotte and Matilda rolled their eyes when the pony nibbled the end of the carrot and Ella snatched her hand back with a shriek, drop-

ping it on the ground. Peter picked the carrot up patiently and fed the eager horse. He bowed his head to me in greeting.

"Good day, my lady. You are well, I trust."

"Yes, Peter, thank you. Good day to you."

He turned to the girls. "Are you all ready for a ride? I thought we could walk together out to the back pasture." Peter whistled, and a boy emerged from the dark entrance of the stable.

"Help the young ladies onto their horses. Come, Lady Elfilda, show me how well you can mount your brave steed." Though Ella was twelve, people often spoke to her in a singsong voice they might use for a little child.

Ella shrank from the towering man.

"Ella!" I said sharply. "It is time to get on your horse!" I wanted them to leave so that I could find a cool place to sit.

Charlotte and Matilda were impatient also, as this would be their first time in the back pasture on horseback. Charlotte frowned at the dark clouds gathering overhead while Matilda hoisted herself onto her tired-looking nag without help from the stableboy.

Ella responded to my sharp tone of voice by approaching Lovely. Peter gave her his hand, but she pretended that she could not reach the stirrup with her foot. He guided her to the proper position, but she then made a show of not being able to balance or pull herself up. Peter attempted to steady her, but Ella miscalculated and tipped farther to the side than he could have expected. The kind man assumed that she was genuinely trying to mount the pony, not wriggle free. With a thud, Ella landed on the dusty ground. She began to cry, and then she rubbed her face with her dirty hands.

"Oh look," Charlotte said under her breath, "the cinder baby is back."

Matilda was less charitable and said loud enough for Ella to

hear, "What's wong, wittle Cinderella? Did the scary pony toss you from her back?"

Ella let out an angry growl.

"Poor Cinderella. Her life is so hard."

"Stop it! Why are you always mean to me?"

"Matilda, enough." I wiped the sweat from my brow. "Ella, stop crying and get on your horse."

Peter helped her to stand. I should have said something reassuring, but I was too annoyed.

The first fat drops of rain pelted down, raising tiny puffs of dust around us. Ella pulled her hat low and made herself as small as possible by wrapping her arms around her shoulders and ducking her head. She hated to get wet, and water on her face was particularly abhorrent.

The patter quickened to a steady roar. There was no avoiding getting soaked. The rain was not cold, and once we surrendered to the drenching, it was pleasant. The clean water washed away our grime and sweat, and for the first time in days, I felt cool and refreshed.

Peter tried to shield Ella with his large hands, but it was useless.

"Turn your face to the sky and let the rain wash away the dirt," I said to Ella. "If you stop fighting it, you will find that the rain is quite nice."

Ella shook her head and hunched lower. Lovely whinnied and pulled at her reins, so the stableboy led her inside. The nags just flattened their ears and tucked in their tails.

"Very well," I said to Ella, "we can go back to the manor and get some dry clothes."

"There will be no riding lessons today!" Peter said.

Charlotte's brilliant smile was just like her father's. Water

poured off the edge of her hood and dripped from her face. "More's the pity; it would have been fun to ride in the rain."

"We should take off our shoes and run through the back meadow!" Matilda said. "Come on, Ella. Join us! We are already wet, so why not have fun?"

Ella shook her head again.

"I shall keep calling you Cinderella if you won't come," Matilda teased.

"I don't care what you call me. I want to go inside."

"Suit yourself," Charlotte said. "Come on, Matilda!"

With that, Charlotte and Matilda ran away, laughing. Ella watched them go, her face vacant.

"Come along then, let's get you to a dry place," I said.

When she reached for my hand, I pretended not to notice. I adjusted her hat to better keep the rain off of her face.

"You look like a drowned mouse!" I said with false cheer.

Ella followed me home in silence, hunching her shoulders and skirting puddles.

GODMOTHER

The girls never did ride together, but discord did not always reign in our home. The holidays were merry, particularly Saint Crispin's Day, when we went into the village for the parade, and all three girls distributed gifts to the children. For weeks before, they toiled to make a basketful of simple toys, and their faces reflected the delight of the little ones as they handed out treats.

Christmastide was also a jolly time at Aviceford Manor; the girls looked forward to the feasts all year. We provided a Christmas meal for the villagers, and Charlotte, Matilda, and Ella always volunteered to help with serving food and drink. Ella was everyone's darling. "Such a beautiful angel!" they exclaimed. "She grows more lovely every year! She is even fairer than her mother, God rest her soul!"

On Sundays, when Ella had no lessons, she spent most of the day with her stepsisters. They chattered and braided one another's hair, or sipped cider, or sang songs. Sometimes Matilda read aloud from one of Frère Joachim's books. On such occasions, they were the picture of sisterly love.

My union with Emont had happy moments as well. When the

weather was fine, he sometimes took me for strolls through the orchards. He would tuck my hand into the crook of his elbow and tell me stories from his youth, such as how he learned to joust from his older brothers, or how he stole a bucket of honey from the bee-keeper and dared his sister to eat it all. He had been fond of his siblings, and he was sorry to be estranged from them. I encouraged him to visit his family's estate, but he never did. I believe that he was too ashamed of his drunkenness and his failures, one of which was his marriage to me.

My husband visited my bed occasionally, and he was an affectionate if maladroit lover. Despite the rarity of his visits, he claimed to be attracted to me and praised my appearance; while I was never a great beauty, I looked youthful into my fourth decade, with a narrow waist, strong limbs, and a full head of thick mahogany hair. Emont was not appealing to me, but I did my wifely duty. No child resulted from our couplings.

Emont's health began to decline after the first five years of our marriage. He had always had gaps in his memory and poor balance caused by drinking, but I noticed that these problems became more of a constant for him, whether he was drunk or sober. He would give me a piece of news, and then moments later, repeat the same news to me again. After a conversation with Wills, he might say to me, "Where the devil is the chamberlain? I have not seen him all day."

When Ella was thirteen and still in the habit of visiting her father's chamber in the morning, she discovered him naked, trying to climb out of the window. She ran to fetch me, and when we returned, he was huddled against the wall, clutching a blanket to his chest.

"Emont?" I said softly.

He looked at me with frenzied eyes. "They are coming," he whispered.

"Who is coming, dearheart? We are here to help you."

Emont glanced at Ella. "Who is she?" he asked, still in a whisper.

Ella looked horrified. "Father! How can you not know me?"

"Agnes?"

"No, Emont," I said soothingly. "I am Agnes, your wife. This is Ella, your daughter."

Ella's face contorted as though she were about to cry. I touched her shoulder and said, "You should go. I will take care of him. He will be fine in a few moments."

Ella ran from us, and though her father recovered from the episode, she never visited his chamber again in the morning. She stopped seeking out his company during much of the rest of the day as well.

Despite his failing memory, Emont continued to drink heavily. Charlotte and Matilda learned how to deflect him; they understood when it was best to ignore him and when he needed to be pacified. Ella, by contrast, had little natural perceptiveness or sensitivity to moods. As she got older, she became increasingly upset by her father's behaviors, and her lack of calm made Emont worse. Ella kept Emont at arm's length, and the schism between father and daughter widened after an unfortunate conversation about Lady Alba. Charlotte had asked about the Wenslock insignia on the tapestries in the great hall.

"That is my mother's crest," Ella said. "The gold color represents virtue and generosity. The annulet is the symbol of fidelity."

Emont snorted. "Fidelity!" he said.

Charlotte paid no attention. "Do you remember your mother?" she asked.

"I remember that she was beautiful."

"Of course she was beautiful," Matilda said tartly. "We can all see that from the paintings."

"She was a lunatic," Emont said.

I placed my hand over Emont's. "I used to work for Lady Alba's mother," I said.

Charlotte smiled. "I know, in paradise. You always say that Rose House was like heaven."

"My mother was not a lunatic!" Ella said.

I squeezed Emont's hand, hoping to wake him to the trouble he was causing. "Now, Ella, your father didn't mean it," I said.

"She was stark raving mad," Emont mumbled.

"My mother was kind, generous, virtuous, and beautiful," Ella said with a quaver in her voice.

"She was a maniac," Emont said.

"It does not have to be one way or the other," I said. "People are not good or bad. God has created man in His image, but we are the inheritors of original sin. We each hold within ourselves both the dark and the light."

Matilda smiled at me sympathetically.

"You are vilifying my mother to make yourself feel better," Ella said to me.

"Why would I do such a thing?" I asked sharply.

"You want to make it seem like there was something wrong with her, because she was a noblewoman and you are a commoner. My mother was good and gentle!" She implied by her tone that I was neither good nor gentle.

"Lady Alba was a madwoman," Emont said flatly.

"Why do you always take her side?" Ella's chest heaved as she tried to keep herself from crying.

"He almost never takes Mother's side!" Charlotte said indignantly. It bothered her that Emont often interceded on Ella's behalf; she thought that her stepsister was spoiled.

"Girls, please," I said. "Let us speak of something else."

"If my mother were still alive, none of you would even be here," Ella said. "You are like great big cuckoo birds, taking over *our* home. If she had been here, none of this would have happened! All I have is my father, and he sides with the cuckoos!"

"You are agitated," I said coldly. "You do not mean to speak so disrespectfully to your father, I am certain. Perhaps you would like to take the remainder of your dinner upstairs, so that you may calm yourself."

"I shall! I shall take all of my meals in the attic. You want to lock me away up there, so you will have your wish!" Ella ran from the table, her silk skirts trailing prettily behind her as she dashed up the stairs.

Emont stirred from his lethargy; he looked confused and dismayed to see his daughter go.

"It will be fine," I said. "We will speak with her later and make peace. She misses her mother, that is all."

Ella calmed down, but I never did quite manage to make peace. She willingly abandoned her solitude for Charlotte and Matilda's company, but not for her father's or mine. Ella often ate meals in the garret, as she had threatened to do. I probably did not do as much as I ought to have done to draw her out. In the moment, it was always easier, and therefore seemed wiser, to let her alone.

After the decline in Emont's memory, he began to suffer from bouts of jaundice and lassitude; this was followed by slow but inexorable

weight loss. The change was imperceptible from day to day, but over many months, his flesh melted away, leaving him gaunt. Skin sagged from his skeleton everywhere except over his belly, which protruded, round and taut, wreathed by dark veins. By the end, his face was unrecognizable, angular and sallow with sunken eyes and hollow cheeks. He lost interest in food and then lost interest even in drink. He slept most of the day and night, and I helped the servants to nurse him. One morning, shortly after Ella's fifteenth birthday, Emont simply did not wake.

Ella was inconsolable after her father's death. Though she had seen little of Emont in his last months of life, when she heard that he was gone, she threw herself onto his lifeless body and wailed. After an hour, I tried to draw her away, but she shook me off and clung to Emont's emaciated shoulders, her head against his cold chest. It was not until the moon had risen and Charlotte had plied her with an entire bottle of honey wine that Ella consented to leave. She glared at me as she stumbled off to bed, supported between her two stepsisters. It makes little sense, but I believe that she blamed me in some way for her father's death.

Though I had no great love for my husband, Emont's departure left a hole in my life as well. It was not a hole in my daily routine, for I was used to running the manor on my own, and Emont had rarely been good company. Still, after his death, something was conspicuously missing, like food that lacked flavor or a colorless sunset. When I passed by his empty chamber each night, to my surprise, my throat tightened and tears came to my eyes.

Worse than sadness was the fear that his death brought me. I lost my home when Fernan died, and I was sick with worry that my daughters and I would lose our home a second time. The manor belonged to Ellis Abbey, and while I was an able manager, Mother

Elfilda would not pass up the opportunity to bestow lordship of the manor on the son of a wealthy nobleman willing to make a donation to her abbey. I was approaching the end of my childbearing years, and though I was still vigorous, I would not attract a husband without money of my own. Marriage had saved me once, but it would not save me again.

I woke each morning from restless sleep, my head full of wool and my heart racing, imagining the clop of hoofbeats in the courtyard, fearing that the messenger had come. My only hope was that the abbess might wait to transfer stewardship of Aviceford Manor until she found a suitable husband for Ella. Ella was of marriageable age at fifteen, and the abbess would not expend the effort to situate Ella twice if she could avoid it.

I did not share my worries with any of the girls, but Charlotte and Matilda were more than usually solicitous; they must have felt my fear. Ella was, as ever, in her own world. In her initial throes of grief, she spent several days in bed, but she gradually emerged, taking up her old routines. She even began to join us for meals more often than not.

Dressing for mourning was, oddly, Ella's greatest hardship. To my eye, she looked no less lovely in black than in any other color, but she complained bitterly about her wardrobe. Fashion was a fascination for Ella; in scholarly soliloquies, she told us about silkworms, the cleverest materials for buttons, or the most famous shoemakers in the kingdom. It should have been no surprise that she did not want to be told what to wear, but I never understood Ella's passions. While she would lecture us enthusiastically about the warp and weft of satin fabric or the art of making brilliant dyes, she was silent on almost every other subject to the point of mutism. I thought that discouraging her obsession was good for her.

In addition, though Ella had never been a vain child, I worried that she might become overly enamored of her own appearance. Ella blossomed late into womanhood; around the time of her father's death, she filled out the bodice of her gowns for the first time, and the line of her waist curved sweetly where it had so recently been straight and unyielding. Perhaps she wanted to dress in a way that flattered her new figure, but I wasn't sure that was best for her. Besides, even beyond propriety, I had good reasons to insist that Ella observe the traditional mourning period.

Ella accused me of injustice. It incensed her that Charlotte and Matilda wore fashionable clothes while she could not. In truth, I battled my own sense of injustice every day, the nagging pain, like a rotten tooth, of having to compare my daughters to the kingdom's most beautiful girl. Even if it couldn't help Charlotte or Matilda one whit, it may be that I wanted to see Ella's radiance just the tiniest bit dimmed.

Our worst argument came in early spring, toward the end of her mourning. For the hundredth time, Ella asked, "When shall I be able to wear real clothing again?" She paced irritably and did not look at me when she spoke.

A light rain pattered against the windows in the great hall. Charlotte and Matilda were bent over a game of chess. The board with figures carved from white and dark stone belonged to Frère Joachim; the girls had convinced him to teach them how to play. Ella had no patience for the game.

"You *are* wearing real clothing," I said to Ella. "As to when your mourning will end, that will be on May Day, as I have told you many times before."

She pouted prettily. Ella was more beautiful than she had ever been. Her skin was luminous and unblemished, her eyes clear

and lustrous. Although she had lost her childhood leanness, she remained delicate and slender, with dainty hands and feet. Her golden hair was her crowning glory, and even in mourning she often wore it loose, tumbling down her back in silken waves. I insisted that Gisla dress her hair when there were guests, but otherwise I let her wear it unbound and uncovered.

Matilda looked up from her game of chess to where Ella had stopped pacing before the fire. "Mourning dress suits you. You look like a sleek little raven."

"Exactly. Ravens are ugly."

"Don't be vain," Charlotte said. "Beauty is as beauty does."

"It's not vain to point out that this isn't fair! Your mother buys you new gowns but none for me! I have to wear these horrid black monstrosities. I look like a corpse!"

"Don't be ridiculous, child." I could not stand to hear someone so blessed be anything but grateful for God's gift. I would have given my right arm if that could have restored Matilda's face to even ordinary plainness.

"Why won't you buy me new gowns?"

"I have told you many times that I shall buy you new gowns when your mourning is over."

"I shall have Lady Rohesia bring new gowns for me even if you will not buy me any."

"You will do no such thing. This is not a time for frivolity, but a time to honor your father."

"If my father were still alive, he would make you act fairly! You only care about Charlotte and Matilda, and you give everything to them."

"Now you are being silly. You have everything that you could possibly need."

"You gave them my chamber and made me sleep in the attic!"

"You could have moved back downstairs anytime if you were willing to share."

With an exasperated sigh, Charlotte said, "You *like* having the garret all to yourself!"

"It's also not fair that I have to take lessons while Charlotte and Matilda sit around in fancy gowns playing stupid games, and anyway the gowns are wasted on them, for nobody ever sees them, and even if they did—well." She gestured toward her stepsisters.

Charlotte's voice hardened. "We can't all be as beautiful as Cinderella."

Ella's face flushed, and she said, "You are all mean to me! You treat me like a servant in my own home now that my parents are dead! You are glad that Father died and left you in charge!"

"How dare you say such a thing!" My voice shook with anger.

"Because it's true! You make me sleep in the attic like a servant, you make me wear these rags, you even made me do the laundry, which was the most horrible day of my life, one I can never forget, because everyone keeps calling me Cinderella!"

I took a deep breath, pushing my fury back down. To stop them from trembling, I tucked my fingers under my arms. I managed to calm myself, but an adamantine coldness filled the void where my anger had been.

"I shall forgive you, because you do not understand what you are saying. You should thank God for all that He has given to you—"

"I shan't thank *you*! You give me nothing!"

My hand shot out before I could stop it, and I cuffed the side of her head forcefully. Ella's mouth snapped shut, and her eyes widened.

"I do not want to hear another word. Get out. Now."

Ella glared at me with impotent rage, and then she fled.

Charlotte and Matilda sat frozen at the chessboard, staring at me.

"Mind yourselves!" I said.

Matilda raised her eyebrows impertinently, but they turned back to their game.

I retreated to the courtyard, where a listless drizzle pricked at dark, glassy puddles. A lone crow tore at a damp pile of kitchen refuse. The clouds relented, allowed weak rays of light to escape, and then smothered them again. I paced in circles and watched the dreary scene for as long as it took to convince myself that I had done nothing wrong.

Had it not been for these arguments with Ella, I might have been more sympathetic to her desire to attend the prince's ball at Cothay Manor. The gala was an unusual event. There had never before been a gathering of such scale and luxury within the holdings of Ellis Abbey, and the abbey had never before sponsored a social event. I am sure that Abbess Elfilda would have quibbled with the use of the word "sponsor," but everyone knew the ball would not have taken place without her initiative.

We first heard about the ball from Gisla, who was always abreast of gossip. Though she was frail and hard of hearing, she made it her business to know everything that went on at the three manors belonging to the abbey.

Gisla was still struggling out of her cloak when she found us in the great hall, where we were having dinner.

"Lady Agnes!" she called out in her reedy voice.

I was annoyed that she had let herself into the hall without

speaking with the chamberlain, but from her eager expression and breathlessness, it was apparent that she could barely contain her news. She hobbled toward us quickly.

"What is it, Gisla?" I asked.

"A ball, my lady! At Cothay Manor!" She looked around the table at our puzzled faces with a gap-toothed grin. "The abbess is organizing it in honor of Prince Henry. And she's invited everyone from hereabouts."

"Everyone including us?" Matilda asked.

"Why, yes!"

"Whatever is the occasion?" I asked. "It is very strange for the abbess to host a party for a prince."

Gisla gave a wheezy laugh. She enjoyed being the messenger. "You would not believe the rumors! The goose girl at Cothay told me the abbess is trying to find the prince a wife. I hated to be the one to tell her that goose girls were not invited to the ball. Sweet thing."

"I thought Prince Henry was already betrothed?"

"There was a foreign girl, maybe a countess? I think she died. Prince Henry has so many older brothers in line for the throne, I don't doubt that it's hard to find him a fancy wife. But a king would not be looking to marry his son off to some country girl! That is just goose girl nonsense. No, I'm sure the abbess wants a favor from the king, and Prince Henry is just the one who got sent to visit Ellis Abbey."

"Is it true that he is so handsome?" Charlotte asked.

"I sure have never laid these old eyes on him, but it's said that he claimed the maidenhood of many a lady-in-waiting!" Gisla looked suddenly guilty and clapped her gnarled hand over her mouth. "I shouldn't say such things in front of Lady Elfilda."

Ella did not seem to be paying attention. She ate placidly, a dreamy expression on her face.

"This is so exciting!" Charlotte said. "We may go to the ball, mayn't we, Mother?"

"When is the ball?" I asked.

"The Saturday after All Fools' Day."

"Oh. You and Ella will still be in mourning," Matilda said.

I sighed. "Yes, that is true."

"Please, Mother, may we all go to the ball? Ella can plan what we shall wear!"

Ella lit up and joined the conversation. "We can have ball gowns made!" she exclaimed.

"Yes! Will you help us to choose fabric and designs?" Charlotte said.

"Of course! I already have some ideas. We will need to know our budget . . ."

"Ella, our mourning doesn't end until May Day," I reminded her.

"But I want to go to the ball!"

I sighed again. "It would be unseemly for you to go while still in mourning, and you are too young to go without a proper chaperone. Do you think it appropriate for me to chaperone you in my widow's weeds when all you want is a new gown? You hate crowds and parties."

Gisla glared at me. Ella's face clouded over, and for a moment I thought she would cry, but then she surprised me.

"I shall help Lottie and Tilly with their gowns, then," she said. "It will be such fun!"

"Mother, can't Ella come too?" Matilda asked.

I wavered for a moment, but I did not give in. I wanted Ella to learn patience.

One fresh April day, the abbess's messenger came to Aviceford Manor. I was surveying the herb garden when he crested the orchard hill. The apple trees were thick with blossoms; a breeze scattered pale petals like snowflakes around him. The gardener prattled on about sage and mint, not noticing that I had turned to stone.

The messenger dismounted and handed his reins to a boy. As he walked toward the door, I wondered how he would ask for me. Lady Agnes? The lady of the manor? Or was I simply Agnes again, the penniless and homeless mother of two unfortunate young women?

I excused myself to the gardener and walked stiffly to the front entrance. When I overtook the messenger in the foyer, my panic was like a hand around my throat, strangling me, preventing me from speaking. The messenger, a slender lad of no more than sixteen, bowed respectfully. He handed me a parchment from his satchel, telling me that it was from Abbess Elfilda.

Not wanting anyone to witness me reading the letter, I instructed the boy to find some food in the kitchen, and I took the letter to my chamber. My hands trembled as I unfolded the small parchment. There were only two lines written in a cramped, neat hand. *Elfilda will be excused from mourning to attend the ball. All necessary arrangements are being made.*

I fell back on the bed, laughing with relief. A reprieve! We were safe, at least for a time.

My next thought was one of annoyance. Ella had evidently sent a complaint to her godmother through Lady Rohesia. She was

privileged by birth and would always have the upper hand. There was nothing I could do about it.

I put off telling Ella about her godmother's message for as long as I could. I suppose it was petty; I did not want to have to swallow my pride. We were expecting a visit from Lady Rohesia the week before the ball, however, and I had to tell Ella by then.

One evening at supper, I decided to get it over with. "Abbess Elfilda has requested your presence at the ball," I told her. "I imagine that Lady Rohesia will bring a gown for you to wear."

Ella gasped, and then she clapped her hands together. "How wonderful! I wish that I had some say in my gown though. This new fashion of lacing the sleeves at the shoulder is all wrong. I do hope Lady Rohesia won't bring one of those."

Charlotte rolled her eyes, but Matilda smiled, saying, "You see, I told you, dreams can come true!"

"I have learned all of the dances," Ella said. "I should teach you the steps!" She bounced in her chair.

"Nobody will dance with us," Charlotte said dryly. Ella's child-like mannerisms irked her.

Ella smiled. "Probably not, but you never know." She laughed. "Do you suppose that the prince will dance with me?"

"He will fall in love with you directly, like everyone does, I'm sure," Matilda said.

"I would not be too glad about dancing with the prince," I said. "Though he may be charming, he has no reputation for integrity."

"But he is so handsome," Charlotte said, winking at Ella.

"And rich!" Matilda added.

"Rich only matters if he marries you," I said grimly. "Handsome matters not at all."

Lady Rohesia arrived as planned, and she brought with her a gown that surpassed Ella's highest standards. The fabric was an opalescent water silk that shone like mother-of-pearl; glass beads sewn into the bodice glinted like diamonds. The shoes matched the extravagance of the gown, as they were encrusted with so many beads that they appeared to be made entirely from glass. Though the slippers were uncommonly heavy, Ella adored them. When Lady Rohesia was not watching, she danced across the great hall, fiery glitter scattering from her pretty feet.

Lady Rohesia told us dourly that the abbess would send a carriage for Ella, that she herself would accompany Ella to the ball, but that *she* would not act as chaperone. Tilting back her head, the noblewoman looked down her beakish nose at me. I gathered that I was expected to chaperone Ella, and that my daughters and I were to make our own way to Cothay Manor. This last part did not bother me, as I loathed the lady's company. I would wear my widow's weeds to the ball, and nobody would expect me to dance, or even to make conversation. Ella would soon tire of the noise and commotion, and then we would come home. Anyway, I was curious to see the prince. I had never met a member of the royal family before, and it didn't seem likely that I would have the opportunity again.

On the day of the ball, Lady Rohesia's maid dressed Ella's hair. It took two hours for her to weave pearls through a labyrinth of

delicate braids, but the effect was breathtaking. Poor Charlotte and Matilda had only Gisla and my uncouth chambermaid to help with their hair. The well-meaning servants should have kept to the common hairstyles they knew best, but in an effort to do something special for the girls, they created oddly lumpy coiffures that lacked both sophistication and simplicity.

Charlotte wore a pale blue silk gown that set off her chestnut complexion and raven hair. In typical fashion, Matilda chose fabric as yellow as summer irises. Despite her ugliness, Matilda never hunched her shoulders or shrank from anyone's gaze. Both girls had learned at the abbey to carry themselves tall, and with the flush of excitement on their faces and joy in their luminous eyes, they looked lovely to me.

Even if Charlotte and Matilda had been true beauties, however, they would have faded like ghosts next to Ella, just as the moon disappears when the sun rises in all of its glory. The older girls gasped as they beheld their resplendent stepsister at the top of the stairs. Ella stepped carefully down to where we stood and twirled self-consciously so that we could admire her from every angle. It is said that no woman since Bathsheba has been as alluring as Ella on the night of the prince's ball, and I believe that to be true. She was so exquisite, so sublimely beautiful, that it was impossible to look away.

"Cinderella, you look like an angel!" Matilda exclaimed.

Ella blushed and said, "You look nice too."

"The prince will not be able to resist you!"

"I do not want to hear such talk," I said. "Ella will behave like the proper noblewoman she has been brought up to be. I want all three of you to stay near me tonight." I lightly tapped the tip of Ella's nose. "You in particular, young lady."

Ella nodded submissively.

"I do not want any of you to gorge yourselves on sweetmeats. Take small portions of any food offered to you, and eat it daintily. Do you remember all of the proper titles of address?"

"Yes, Mother," they answered together.

"Even if you are not yet tired, I do not want anybody to beg to stay late. It isn't proper for young, unmarried women to be the last to leave. We will depart before the mid-night repast."

All three murmured their assent.

"Ella, Lady Rohesia will meet you in the foyer; wait for her there. Charlotte and Matilda, our carriage is ready. Come with me."

I turned back to Ella. "You really do look magnificent, dear-heart."

She smiled at me sweetly and said, "Thank you, Mother Bear."

THE BALL

I had visited Cothay Manor twice before, but it looked different on this occasion. Short walls of lattice had been erected on both sides of the road leading to the manor, and these were decorated with flowers and woven grass. A great rose bower covered the arch of the gate, and torches lined the walkway and staircase to the entrance. Towering over the torches were flagstaffs; a soft breeze nudged the banners open, showing rich hues in the evening light. The vivid scarlet-and-gold standard of the royal family was interspersed with banners belonging to other families, and the royal flag was also draped over the imposing iron doors of the manor.

We alighted from our carriage well before reaching the rose bower. I instructed the driver, our head stableboy, to come back after the ringing of the compline bell and wait in the same place until we returned.

As we waited for Ella and Lady Rohesia to arrive, Charlotte and Matilda looked about in wonder. Horses broke into a smart canter as they approached the arch of white roses; when the coaches came to a halt, footmen jumped down to help the ladies descend. Brightly

colored skirts peeked from carriage doors, then billowed like flowers unfurling their petals as the ladies stepped out, tugging layers of finery with them. In the light of the golden sun that hung low on the horizon, a glittering stream of guests mounted the stairs and disappeared through the dark entrance of Cothay Manor.

By the time Ella finally arrived, the stream of guests had ebbed to a trickle. Though we were not familiar with the approaching carriage, we recognized Ella's milky hand holding her favorite kerchief out the window; as it fluttered, she twisted it, flashing the green and silver sides of the fabric so that it looked like a minnow swimming through the air.

Abbess Elfilda had provided her goddaughter with a royal coach, a bulbous and heavily gilded contrivance with enormous, improbably slender wheels. Its pale sheen reflected the orange-and-pink sunset as the team of white horses pulled up to the archway. The footman helped Lady Rohesia down first. I waved, and the lady nodded slightly to acknowledge my gesture. She started up the staircase without waiting for Ella to emerge, letting me know that her duties as matron had been discharged.

Charlotte and Matilda hurried to the side of the coach; they reached out to touch its smooth surface and cooed admiringly as Ella stepped down. The three of them giggled at something Matilda said in a low voice and would have rushed up the stairs without me if I had not stopped them.

"Decorum, please, girls!"

Reluctantly, they quieted and adjusted their postures. We mounted the stairs and crossed the threshold into the torchlit screens passage. The din of voices and music greeted us, and Ella cringed at the noise. She was the first to reach the opening to the great hall, however, and she stepped boldly through. In the light

of chandeliers and torches, the glass beads on her gown came alive with fire, and her golden hair shone brightly. Women standing under the minstrels' gallery turned to stare and poked their companions to do the same. I put my hand on Ella's shoulder and guided her toward the seats at the edge of the great hall. Heads swiveled in Ella's direction, while my daughters and I passed unnoticed in her wake.

We sat in the shadows against the wall. The great hall at Cothay Manor was at least four times as large as the hall at Aviceford, and much better appointed. Ivy and flowers decorated the walls, tables, and dais. Upon the dais, the high table was draped with scarlet cloth, and silver dishes were piled with breads and sweetmeats. At the center of the table sat a handsome young man; I presumed him to be the prince. He had dark hair, as Gisla had described, and an aristocratic nose. His black eyebrows were arched in an expression of boredom. He bent his head to speak with another young man to his right; they both laughed and raised their goblets to each other. A page clad in the king's scarlet and gold hovered nearby with a flask, waiting for his opportunity to refill their cups.

I had never seen a member of the royal family before. I expected to feel a thrill, a frisson of reverence when I beheld him, but he was just a man sitting at a table, nothing more. It surprised me to find him quite ordinary.

To the prince's left sat Mother Elfilda, her back rigid, her gaze resting politely on an object proffered by a bejeweled neighbor. In her black habit, the abbess looked small and faded. I wondered whether Mother Elfilda would gain the advantage she sought from the ball.

The nobility seated at the high table ignored the crowd as though an invisible wall separated them from the rest of the gathering. In

the center of the hall, men and women bobbed and twirled in time to the music. I had never properly learned to dance, but I found it enchanting, the swirling silks, the graceful bows, the harmony of movement. I recognized few of the dancers; judging by their clothing, many guests had traveled from the city. Even the vast holdings of Ellis Abbey did not include enough wealthy families to populate a royal ball.

The girls tapped their feet and looked about eagerly. Charlotte and Matilda whispered to each other. The minstrels struck up a lively carole, and the dancers formed a ring.

"May we join, Mother?" Matilda asked, her eyes shining.

I smiled and nodded. Ella clapped her hands and jumped to her feet.

"Calmly," I said. "Remember your manners."

The three girls joined the merry circle. Ella seemed oblivious to admiring gazes; she hopped and skipped blithely with the chain of dancers, a bright smile on her face. When the song ended, several hopeful young men dogged her heels, but their schemes were interrupted by an announcement from the dais. The lord of Cothay Manor, a rotund, red-faced bull of a man, invited his guests to greet the prince.

A commotion erupted as women near the high table jostled to form a queue. The more elegant visitors watched the rush of locals with disgust. I put my arm out to signal Charlotte, Matilda, and Ella to stay seated beside me.

"But we want to meet the prince too!" Charlotte whispered.

"You may join the queue in time."

"Now?" asked Matilda a moment later.

"Wait."

Mother Elfilda had disappeared from the dais, leaving the chair

next to the prince unoccupied. The lord of Cothay Manor stood behind the empty chair, tapping his fingers on the back, looking unsure about whether to seat himself or remain standing.

Matilda pulled on my sleeve. "Now can we go?"

The line of people waiting to greet the prince had settled, and the minstrels played a quiet tune.

"Very well. Come with me."

The queue snaked beside a table laden with ale, pastries, and bowls of exotic fruit. Ella picked up one of the strange-looking orbs and explained to Charlotte and Matilda that it was an orange from Aragon; she had eaten them during her visit to the royal court. Ella peeled the fruit and handed pieces to her stepsisters, who exclaimed that the flavor was marvelous. Matilda shared hers with me; the tanginess startled me, which caused her to laugh.

It did not take long for us to reach the front of the line. As the young woman in front of us curtsied low before the dais, the prince slumped forward and leaned his jaw on his hand as though it cost him effort to stay awake. The moment he saw Ella, however, his countenance changed. Like a wolf spotting a lamb, the prince smoothly lifted his handsome head, his gaze suddenly alert and hungry.

I began to introduce our party, but the prince interrupted.

"I know for certain that we have never met before, because I have never seen anyone so ravishing," he said to Ella. "What should I call you?"

Ella finished her curtsy, and when she stood, her cheeks were flushed. Her hands twisted behind her back. The heat and intensity in the prince's dark eyes caused me to squirm also, though for a different reason.

"Cinderella," she murmured, to my great surprise.

The prince smiled. "Cinderella, will you dance with me?"

I found the lack of formality in the prince's manner peculiar, but ho ooomod to put Ella at ease. She nodded happily. The lord of the manor, still monitoring the proceedings, called to the minstrels to play dancing music. Several people still waited in line to greet the prince, but he was blind to them. The prince did not even acknowledge Charlotte or Matilda, who kept their heads bowed respectfully. He jumped lightly down from the dais and kissed Ella's hand.

A stillness descended over the guests when the prince leapt to Ella's side.

"She is so beautiful!" they whispered, and, "Who is she?"

Ella and the prince danced, oblivious to their audience. While Ella was not the most polished dancer, her partner guided her expertly. She was pure light in his arms, a glittering, dazzling sliver of sunshine, a seraph. I was as transfixed as the strangers around me.

When the dance ended, the prince kept Ella for another, and then another. Guests joined the quadrille or returned to wine and conversation. Charlotte and Matilda waited in vain for another carole so that they might join the dancing without the necessity of a partner. None of the men approached them.

The evening wore on, and I thought that the prince would never tire of dancing, but then I saw him escort Ella through an opening in the screens passage. My heart thundered as I hurried after them. Ella would be easy prey for any man, and a prince would be used to taking what he wanted.

The air was fresher in the passage, and the torches wavered in a draught from the open door. Ella's warbling laughter drifted in on the breeze. The knot in my belly loosened as I realized that they had probably gone outside for some cool air.

When I approached the threshold, I could see the prince, fac-

ing away from me, leaning casually against a stone plinth. Ella's upturned face glowed in the torchlight. Strands of hair had pulled loose from her braids, and her cheeks were pink. The dishevelment only made her more beautiful. The adoration and elation that radiated from her lovely features stirred a dark memory.

I watched them uncertainly until the prince pulled Ella close and bent to kiss her, and then I coughed loudly. I stepped out of the doorway, feigning surprise.

"Why, there you are, my dear!" I pretended to have recognized the prince just when he turned around, and I curtsied reverentially. "Your Highness."

Ella glared at me, and Prince Henry regarded me blankly.

"We were just going back inside to dance!" Ella's voice was shrill.

Before I could say anything further, she ran through the door. The prince followed without a glance in my direction. I curtsied again anyway.

True to her word, Ella danced with Prince Henry. Every time the music stopped, the prince shouted for another quadrille. The couple was lost in their own world; they had no care for anyone else. The revelers grew restless, waiting for a more lively tune, and young women grumbled that the prince should not restrict himself to only one partner.

Watching a beautiful girl dance with the prince could not hold the attention of the crowd all night. Clusters of gossiping women and drunken men grew raucous and disorderly. The high table was abandoned, and the most fashionable guests melted away. Charlotte and Matilda shifted glumly on their bench or played word games. I sent them to fetch wine just to keep them occupied.

While the servants prepared the great hall for the mid-night repast, the minstrels took a well-deserved break. I saw my chance to

extricate Ella when the prince bowed and walked briskly out the doorway behind the dais. Ella lingered in the center of the floor, no doubt waiting for her prince to return. I told Charlotte and Matilda that it was time to go home, and they looked relieved.

I knew that Ella would be unhappy to leave, but I did not anticipate the stubbornness with which she greeted me. She knew immediately why we were descending upon her, and before I said anything, she said, "I am not leaving!"

"We already talked about this, Ella. It is time to go."

"I am waiting for Prince Henry!"

"You have made a spectacle of yourself already. It is time to go home."

"I shan't leave without saying good night to Prince Henry!"

"You have had plenty of time to say good night, and you should have excused yourself long ago."

I grabbed Ella by the sleeve of her gown and pulled her toward the screens passage. Charlotte and Matilda complained that they were weary and ready for sleep. At first, Ella came docilely, but just as we left the great hall, she pulled roughly away, and her sleeve tore.

"Now see what you have done!" she said.

"Keep your voice down," I hissed. "We shall fix it later. Now come along."

"I shan't go with you!"

I wondered if she had drunk too much wine. Not knowing what else to do, I took Ella by the arm again and propelled her through the passageway and out the main entrance. Charlotte and Matilda trotted after us. I plunged gratefully into the chill night air, believing that the worst was over, but the cold reinvigorated Ella; she wrestled savagely from my loosening grasp at the top of the stairs,

ripping another seam of her gown. One of her glass-beaded shoes fell off, and she picked it up in her hand.

"You don't own me!" Her voice cracked with the threat of tears. "I don't have to do as you say. You are not my mother! My mother is dead, and you took my father from me, and now he is dead too, and you are . . ." Tears streamed down her face. "You are simply wicked! I don't care if you are my stepmother, leave me alone!" She pulled her arm back in a swift motion and threw her slipper at me with startling strength. Fortunately, her aim was poor, and the shoe merely grazed my ear. It smashed into the glazed window behind me, and one of the panes fell out with a crash.

Ella's hand flew to cover her mouth in dismay, and then she fled, abandoning her other shoe on the staircase.

"What is wrong with her?" Matilda exclaimed.

"Just one of her tantrums," Charlotte said with disgust.

Both girls descended the stairs after Ella, but I remained rooted in place, shaken. Ella's tranquil disposition had always been complicated by uncontrolled outbursts, but I had never known her to be violent. My stomach turned as I thought of her mother's rages.

Crisp footsteps warned me of approaching men, but I did not turn until one of them spoke.

"Where did she go?" The prince sounded puzzled and disappointed. He was flanked by two pages clad in royal livery; in his hand, he held the shoe that had fallen to the stones behind me.

After the required obeisance I said, "She ran away, Your Highness."

He furrowed his brow. His features were patrician, but his expression vacuous. "Why would she do such a thing?"

I had interpreted the intensity of the prince's attention to Ella as predatory, but that did not match the guilelessness of his speech.

"I do not know, Your Highness."

"I must see her again. Where can I find her?"

An absence of wit or command in his words and bearing made his handsome face less appealing.

"Why do you wish to see her, sire?"

I was rude to ask the question, and I deserved a rebuke, but instead he said, "I love her, and I wish to marry her."

The statement was so outlandish that I nearly laughed.

"Can you tell me where to find her?" he continued, ignoring the incredulity that must have been written on my features. "I saw you with her earlier tonight."

There had been a cretin in our village when I was young, a man with a perfectly sound body but the mind of a child. The look in the prince's eyes reminded me of that man. I felt queasy and tired.

"She was an acquaintance of my daughter's from the city, Your Highness," I said with a curtsy. "I am sure that you will see her at court."

As I rushed down the stairs, the sparkle of Ella's abandoned shoe caught my eye, but I did not stop. I wished only to put the evening behind us.

I found the girls waiting in our carriage. Ella sniffled; her eyes were puffy and her skin blotched. Most of her hair had come undone. Charlotte and Matilda sat on either side of their stepsister, patting her arms soothingly. They muttered consoling words, but annoyance was evident in their voices and postures.

Ella refused to look at me when I climbed into the coach. I sat opposite, saying nothing. Her little hands, like white spiders on her knees, her dirty feet, her slumped shoulders, her blank face, these held no charm for me. My mind was in tumult, my heart a stone.

We rode in silence. As we neared home, I knew that I should

speak, but my tongue was lifeless. Weariness and sadness sapped my will. It would be over soon, one way or another. Mother Elfilda would find a husband for Ella, and I would be thrown once more on God's mercy.

My face grew hot and my eyes watered. I slid to the window and pretended to peer into the darkness. Charlotte and Matilda did not need to see my distress. I would find a way to protect them as I always had. I would beg the abbess to take them as novices, and if she would not, as servants. I might find a husband for Charlotte. The right sort of man might not mind.

As I gazed beyond the feeble light of our lantern, moonlit trees emerged from the dark. After a time, I could make out some details of the underbrush, like silver ferns and coltsfoot. I caught a movement in the shadows as some animal scurried into the forest.

I did not notice that Ella had moved to sit beside me until she put her head on my shoulder. I stiffened, resisting the impulse to shrug and pull away. I knew that she meant the gesture as an apology, and that I should accept it, even if her touch was unwelcome. I stroked her cheek lightly, and Ella sighed. Charlotte and Matilda were asleep, leaning into each other, swaying with the movement of the carriage. I remained as still as I could, and Ella was soon asleep too.

GLASS SLIPPERS

Everyone knows the story about Prince Henry's hunt for the beautiful girl he met at the ball, how he searched from house to house, asking every unmarried woman in five parishes to try on the glass slippers. That is a pretty tale. As usual, the truth is more mundane.

The prince easily discovered Ella's identity. After all, her godmother had been a host of the ball, and the lord of Cothay Manor knew Ella by sight. A simple inquiry would have turned up the information necessary for Prince Henry to gallop with his retinue to Aviceford Manor on a fine Sunday morning.

The men clattered thunderously into the courtyard, shouting and waving banners as though they were headed to battle, not to woo a naive young lady with golden hair. We all rushed to the windows, startled by the commotion. The prince leapt from his white stallion and strode to the entrance, not waiting for his escort. With a squeal of delight, Ella ran to greet him. I did not admonish or call her back.

It is true that the prince brought the glass slippers, for by the

time I reached the foyer, Ella was already dancing in circles, her little feet flashing in the sunlight that poured from the open door. Her suitor watched with a besotted smile on his rosy lips.

My mouth was dry and my head ached. I curtsied low, remembering the lie I had told the night before. The prince did not acknowledge me.

Charlotte encircled my waist with her arm, and Matilda held on to my elbow. They both smiled at the scene before us. When Ella finished twirling, the prince dropped to his knees and took both of her hands in his. Members of his retinue crowded the door, casting shadows over the smiling couple.

"My lovely Cinderella," the prince said. "Come back to court with me and be my bride!"

Ella smiled happily. "Will you love me always?"

"I will love you until the stars in the sky no longer shine!"

"Will I have my own private chambers?" she asked shyly.

"You may have anything your heart desires!"

"Then my heart desires to go with you!"

The prince leapt to his feet and lifted Ella high into the air; he spun her around as though she weighed no more than a doll. While her peculiar laugh echoed through the foyer, her sparkling shoes fell off and struck the floor with two resounding bangs. After setting down the object of his admiration, the prince turned to me, beaming, no trace of recollection or resentment on his face.

"You must be Cinderella's stepmother."

Charlotte and Matilda's grips both tightened at the mention of Cinderella; I was not sure if they were cringing or amused.

I curtsied again, saying, "Indeed, Your Highness, I am Agnes Vis-de-Loup, lady of Aviceford Manor." Charlotte and Matilda curtsied with me.

The prince took a silk kerchief from his pocket and blew his nose loudly. "I assume that you do not object to my proposal to make Cinderella my wife?"

I hesitated for a moment, and Charlotte jostled me, mortified. Prince Henry did not seem to notice.

"Of course I do not object, Your Highness. We are honored. Have you spoken with her godmother, Abbess Elfilda?"

The prince shrugged. "She wants me to petition my father to give the abbey the rest of Ellismere Island. He will give it to me as a wedding gift."

Perhaps he was not so dull after all.

The prince took Ella's hand again. "We must go immediately. I shall send a messenger ahead to begin preparations for the wedding. I shall leave men here to gather your effects."

"Immediately?" Ella's smile disappeared. "Not immediately!"

"Why, yes, immediately! Why not? Do you not wish to be wed as soon as possible?"

"Of course . . ." Ella coughed, and when she began again, her voice quavered. "Can Mother and my sisters come too?" She looked at him beseechingly.

"They can come for the wedding, of course, but not now. We must be on our way."

"Will you not at least stay for dinner, Your Highness?" I asked.

"No! We have a full day of riding ahead of us and another tomorrow. We cannot waste more time!"

"Can I not stay here and follow later, with my family?" Ella pleaded.

"Do you not wish to come with me?"

Ella's violet eyes shifted uncertainly from the prince to where we stood, and then she nodded mutely.

"Then make haste! Tell your chambermaid to fetch what you require for the journey, and let us be on our way!"

Gisla had already left to make arrangements.

"Preparations will be complete soon, Your Highness. Please, enjoy a cup of wine in the hall while Ella changes her gown for riding."

"I shall wait outside." The prince kissed Ella's fingertips. "Be swift, my angel!" He strode out the door, and his escort fell in line behind him.

"Go, Ella, quickly! Do not keep the prince waiting!"

Ella threw her arms around my neck and buried her face in my shoulder. "I do not want to leave!"

Charlotte pulled her arm from my waist to make room for Ella. "I thought that you wanted to marry the prince!"

"I do!" Ella's voice was muffled against my gown.

"Well, it cannot be both. If you are to be his wife, you must do as he bids."

I felt her nod. "But I cannot bear to live so far from home!"

I sighed. "Aviceford Manor is not your home anymore, Ella. You will probably not even know the new lord and lady."

Ella looked up at me, her eyes wide. "What do you mean?"

"Abbess Elfilda will find someone new to manage the manor."

"But what will become of you, and Lottie, and Tilly?" She looked at each of us, distressed, while Charlotte and Matilda searched my face for clues about how to respond.

I had not expected Ella to be so concerned. Looking at her worried face, I felt a surge of self-pity, which I could have squelched had she not said, "I shall speak with Prince Henry. You will come to live with me at the palace!" She smiled merrily. "It will be lovely!"

I began to cry.

Ella looked even more alarmed. "Mother Bear!" she said. "What is wrong? Do you not want to live at the palace?"

I could not prevent myself from sobbing. All I could do was smile at her through my tears and pull her close. My heart swelled, straining against the bars of its cage. It was the happiest miracle of my life to hold Ella for no other reason than because I craved her nearness. She patted my back consolingly, as though she understood—I am grateful that she did not understand. She was my daughter, but that was the first time I allowed myself to be her mother.

THE ROYAL COURT

It is nearly five years since we joined Ella at court. We hoped for obscurity and prayed that the gossip would die down, but lamentably, the opposite has happened. After Prince George was killed in the jousting accident, Princes John and Hubert succumbed to bilious fever. Prince Michael, who is now heir to the throne, has always been sickly; he suffers from a sort of nervous prostration, and it is rumored that the king does not believe him to be fit to rule the nation even if he lives long enough. It is increasingly likely that Ella's husband, Prince Henry, will become the next king. Which means, of course, that my stepdaughter will be queen consort.

I do not know what to think of this situation as it pertains to Ella. She certainly has no desire to take on the responsibilities of a monarch, and she has no aptitude for politics. On the other hand, as queen consort, she could use her influence to create the sort of life she wishes, and Ella's lack of political acumen has certainly not prevented her from becoming the most celebrated member of the royal family.

While it is unclear whether or not Prince Henry's ascendency

is fortunate for Ella, it is abundantly clear that it is unfortunate for Charlotte, Matilda, and me. At first, I saw no reason why my daughters were relieved of their duties to the princess and assigned to work for a visiting countess, or why we were seated in the last pew in chapel. When we were excluded from Ella's chambers— she was expecting her third child and had entered confinement—I asked the lady-in-waiting for an explanation. "I might ask why you are even at court" was all she had to say.

It was a foreign diplomat who finally explained the circumstances to me. I was walking in the garden when a man accosted me. Though he had a pointed white beard and a head of silver hair, he looked to be about my age, two score years. He was short and slight, and he had the sort of intense, direct gaze that is unfashionable at court.

"Pardon me, my lady," he said in an accent I did not recognize, "are you the mother of Princess Elfilda?"

"I am the stepmother, Lord . . . ?"

"Niccolò Barboro. Baron of the Most Serene Republic of Venice." The man tucked the book he had been carrying under his arm and took my hand. He kissed the tips of my fingers and looked up at me with a smile. "Forgive me. I did not know this word, 'stepmother.' I know that you are also a mother, for I have met your other daughters. Dama Matelda is most brilliant. You are too young to have children of such an age!"

"You flatter me, Baron Barboro."

"Please, call me Niccolò. We are both foreigners here."

"I beg your pardon? I am not foreign."

The man scrutinized my face, and then he smiled again. His teeth were unusually white and straight. "I believe that you under-

stand me, gentle lady." He emphasized the last two words, but his tone was not nasty.

"How do you know my daughter Matilda?" I inquired.

"Ah, Dama Matelda is my tutor, and I am hers. She corrects my English, and in turn, I loan her books of Latin poetry. I believe that I have the better end of the bargain."

Though I did not get to speak with Matilda often, I was surprised not to have heard about the conversations or the poetry.

Niccolò laughed. "I see that your daughter has not mentioned me. Perhaps she thought that you would disapprove. I assure you, we have been well chaperoned."

"Oh, I . . . I did not . . ." I stopped, flustered. The need for a chaperone had not even occurred to me, as much because of the man's elfin appearance as Matilda's ruined face. To cover my embarrassment, I asked, "How are you enjoying the garden?"

"It is so cold!" He held out a delicate hand. "You see, my fingers are turning blue!"

I laughed. "But it is almost summer! How can you be cold?"

"Summer," he said grimly. "You know as much of summer as fish know of the desert. It is May, and I am still wearing my winter cloak!" He shivered dramatically.

"Then what sort of summer are you accustomed to?"

"Ah, balmy ocean breezes, the golden glitter of sun on water, the scent of oranges and jasmine mixed with warm salt air." He closed his eyes and breathed deeply, as though he could smell Venetian summer in the chilly garden air. "My home is paradise. I would never have left if I had been told that here it is always cloudy and cold."

"Why not stay inside by the fire, then? Surely the flowers do

not draw you to the garden." I waved at the topiaries that had been pruned into severe, angular shapes.

The baron's voice turned serious. "I have heard that you come here most afternoons. I wished to speak with you. May I join you on your stroll?"

My heart beat faster. "Is something wrong with Matilda?" I asked sharply.

"No, no, not exactly," Niccolò said, stroking his beard. "Please, walk with me." He touched my elbow to guide me beside him down the path. "It pains me to tell you this, but I do not think that you and your daughters should remain at court. It is not safe."

"Not safe?" I tried to keep the alarm from my voice. "Whatever do you mean?"

"You are aware that Prince Henry is likely to become king one day?"

"Yes, of course."

"There is always some, ah, *fracasso,* when power changes hands. Some fight for who will be nearest the throne."

"But we are Princess Elfilda's family."

"Yes, this is the trouble. You are not her real family. And you are not one of them, the courtiers."

"We are lowborn."

Niccolò shrugged. "Our society is not so obsessed with lineage as yours. But yes, you are foreign here at the court. Like me." He smiled wanly.

We walked in silence for a moment, and then I asked, "How can you say that we are not safe?"

"Perhaps I spoke too strongly. I hope so. I have no knowledge of plots against you. But I hear what is said, and I know that

there are some who would not mind if you disappeared into the tower."

"We have done nothing wrong!"

He sighed. "Do you know what they say about you?"

"I have heard these ridiculous tales about my daughters cutting off parts of their feet to marry Prince Henry, yes."

"It saddens me to tell you, but it is worse than that, my lady." He paused. "They call you evil. They say that you locked Princess Elfilda in the attic and spent all of her father's money on your own two daughters. They say that you forced the princess to do the work of servants. That you made her wear rags, and that you encouraged your daughters to persecute her."

My breath caught in my throat, and I blinked back tears. I had thought that I was impervious to uncharitable opinions, but his words breached my defenses. "There have always been rumors about us," I said.

"Now your king and queen are hearing the rumors," he said, "and they are persuaded that the presumptive heir to the throne should be distanced from you. I have become fond of your daughter Matelda. I would not want anything to happen to her or to those she cares about."

I tilted my face up to the bleak, gray sky to keep tears from sliding down my cheeks. A hawk soared high above us, its wings barely moving. When it crossed into the blurred edges of my vision, its flight looked erratic, as if it were underwater.

"I will find some remedy," I said into the wind. The lump in my throat was like a peach stone. For a moment, I despised the strange little man for bringing such dreadful tidings and for witnessing my humiliation.

Niccolò pressed his fingers lightly against my forearm. "I greatly apologize for interrupting your stroll. I shall leave you now."

I looked into his eyes as I said my thanks, and I saw nothing but kindness there.

The royal court is a harlot. The scarlet gown and painted face may look beautiful to a passing observer, but anyone who draws close enough can see cracks in the face powder and patched holes in the satin. She saves room in her heart only for the gold that lines men's pockets.

Once I realized how tenuous our position was at court, I saw peril at every turn. Charlotte, Matilda, and I had not done well at currying favor, and we had made powerful enemies of women like Cecily Barrett and Isabella Florivet by failing to prostrate ourselves before them. Foolishly, we had relied on our connection with Ella to protect us, but she was being swept along in the same river as the rest of us. She could ask for favors, but she had no say in matters of state, and she was unaware of the machinations of powerful cabals that determined who was invited to court and who was exiled.

Whispers and covert glances took on a sinister aspect. I was not permitted to visit Ella and her newborn son, and the chamberlain refused to seat me at supper, forcing me to ask for food from the kitchen like a servant. I did not believe that we would be thrown into the tower—we are not important enough to pose a threat—but banishment seemed increasingly likely.

Charlotte and Matilda were stationed in the palace wing closest to the river, where the less esteemed guests are housed. They attended to the foreign countess day and night, sleeping in a cham-

ber adjoining hers, so our paths seldom crossed. As I did not trust the servants to deliver a message for me, I visited the southern wing myself at daybreak. I was afraid that I would be barred from entering, so I loitered outside, hoping that one of the girls would see me through the windows. Open ditches on that side of the palace carry waste to the river; the stench was terrible, but I did not have to contend with meddlesome courtiers or guards.

The palace stretched westward from where I paced; the looming walls were at first cloaked in shadow, then warmly tinted by the rising sun. The sweep of the roof was broken by a series of crenelated towers, spectral in the pale light. Details of stonework along the parapets and balustrades emerged as the sun grew stronger; the diamond-paned windows of the living quarters glittered.

Fortunately, I did not need to wait long. Charlotte ran through an arched doorway, holding up her skirts so she wouldn't trip. My heart swelled with a pang of joy when I beheld the flushed face I so adored.

"Mother," she said breathlessly, "why have you come?"

"I wish to speak with you and your sister." I had no plan, but Charlotte and Matilda deserved to understand our predicament.

"What is it? Is there trouble?"

"Not yet, darling, but we should speak. Can you leave for a brief time?"

Charlotte's dark eyes were solemn. She nodded and said, "Meet us in the usual spot in the garden after dinner. Tilly and I should be able to get away while the countess naps." She pecked my cheek and hurried inside, casting a concerned glance over her shoulder as she disappeared beneath the sweep of the arch.

✹

I saw the girls approaching before they spotted me. They both wore dark gowns, which reminded me of the gray frocks they had worn at the abbey, and they leaned together conspiratorially, as they had when they were children. I could tell by Charlotte's tone that she was scolding her sister, though from afar, her words were mere song, like the call of a bird. Matilda laughed.

I greeted them, and Matilda said, "A secret meeting, how diverting, Mother!"

"You are in good spirits," I replied.

"Ah, but I can see that you are not. Tell me your troubles." Matilda linked her arm through mine, and we started down our usual path.

"I met your friend, Baron Barboro."

Matilda glanced at me warily. "A peculiar little man, is he not? His chambers are next to ours, so we see him often. He shares his books with us. He seems amiable enough, but there is something cloying about him."

"He certainly brought disturbing news."

Matilda squeezed my arm.

"What did he say, Mother?" Charlotte asked.

"He is concerned that we will be forced out of the court by those who believe us to be a liability to Prince Henry." I did not mention the tower. It did not seem necessary.

"Ella would never allow it!"

"When was the last time you saw the princess?" I asked.

"We have been busy."

"Have you met your new nephew?"

"No," Charlotte said uncertainly.

"It is not your duties that keep you away," I said. "You are not wanted there."

"But of course Ella wants to see us!"

I shrugged. "Perhaps. It does not bode well that she has not sent for us."

"Where would we go if we have to leave?" Charlotte asked.

"I am not sure. If we could secure a loan, we might start a brewery. You both have learned to brew."

Charlotte chewed her lip nervously. "What if the brewery failed?"

"I don't know."

"We could go to Venice," Matilda said in a small voice.

I stopped walking. "Venice?"

Matilda looked at me timidly. "Niccolò has invited me. I had said no, but I am sure that he would be happy if I changed my mind."

"But you don't want to marry him!" Charlotte said.

"Marry him?" I was incredulous.

"Why do you look so shocked, Mother? Did you think that nobody would ever wish to marry me?"

"I . . . No, of course not, it's only that . . . I was not expecting this."

"Well, it seems that Niccolò admires me despite my face." Matilda poked my side with her finger. "Who would have thought that such a thing could happen?"

"Oh, sweetheart, you are a treasure, and you know I think that you are one of the finest women ever to walk the earth. One of the finest two," I said, smiling at Charlotte. "One of the finest three," I quickly corrected myself.

"But, Tilly, you can't!" Charlotte said. She looked at me beseechingly. "She doesn't love him, and she does not want to live in Venice!"

"If Niccolò would allow you both to come with me, I could resign myself to such a fate."

"You cannot marry a man you do not love!" Charlotte said.

I was astonished at her naiveté. "Nobody marries for love," I said.

"Ella did."

"Your stepsister married a *prince*. Please do not tell me that you, of all people, are listening to these minstrel tales! These are the very reason we are being forced from the court!" I was outraged. "Prince Henry is not some heroic figure who saved Ella from a miserable fate, and Ella did not toss all reason to the wind to marry some pauper who stole her heart. She married one of the wealthiest and highest-ranking men in the land! You speak of *love*? Love is a sickness that causes men and women to do stupid things, the sorts of things that leave them sad and broken when the fever passes."

"And I suppose you think that anyone is a fool to fall in love with me?" Matilda said angrily.

"*You* are the fool if you do not realize that such fancies pass quickly when families raise the issue of inheritance!"

Matilda pulled back as though I had slapped her. The hurt in her face was wrenching. I drew a shaky breath and said, "I am sorry. I do not know how we got so cross. I love you so very dearly."

"I believe *you* are the one who got cross, Mother," Matilda said, "and isn't love a sickness?"

"Not the love I have for you!" I was perilously close to tears again. "You are my own flesh and blood and bones. You are my own heart!"

Charlotte put her arm around her sister's shoulders. "It is not right," she said, "for a woman to give her life to a man she does not esteem."

Her comment stirred my ire again. "You know little of the choices women must make," I said. "Do you suppose that most

women get to live at liberty in manor houses and castles, eating stuffed pheasant off silver plates? That most women have any control over their own fates? Every woman serves a master, be it an overlord or a husband, and she is fortunate if he does not beat her and treat her cruelly. Everything you have, I got for you either through marriage or hard work. There is no alternative. Do you suppose that freedom was *ever* a choice for me?"

"We are grateful to you, Mother," Matilda said coldly, "and we are sorry that you have suffered." She said the word as though she did not quite believe in my suffering. "If marriage is to be my only salvation, then I too will suffer. We happen to have a sister who is a princess, however, and before any of us do anything foolish, I am going to speak with her."

Charlotte, ever the peacemaker, said, "Now, Mother was not saying that you must marry."

Matilda's eyes glittered. "I know perfectly well what she said, thank you, Lottie." Matilda spun and walked away, back toward the palace. Charlotte gave me a chagrined smile and then chased after her sister, calling her name. I sank to the ground and wept, oblivious to any prying eyes that might have been watching me.

A summons from Ella came the next day. I had spent the night awake, pacing in my narrow chamber, and I was not yet clothed when a messenger knocked loudly on my door and told me to report to the princess's quarters. I was surprised that Matilda had managed to arrange an audience so soon, but I dressed as quickly as I could and hurried to the royal apartments. As hostile glances had become commonplace, I wore a long veil and kept my head bowed in the dimly lit corridors.

An uncharacteristic timidity overtook me as I approached Ella's private chamber, but before I could hesitate, a stony-faced servant opened the door and ushered me inside. Ella sat on her daybed, wrapped in a purple brocade robe and flanked on each side by Charlotte and Matilda. As I curtsied, Ella asked, "Are you ill?"

I covered my eyes for a moment with my hands, realizing that they must be red from weeping. There was no looking glass in my chamber, so I had not seen the damage wrought by my sleepless night. I touched my eyelids gingerly with the tips of my fingers; they were puffed up like bread dough. "I am fine, Your Highness," I said. "It is nothing some rest cannot cure."

Matilda jumped up and rushed to embrace me. Her expression was anguished, and I could tell from her pink-rimmed eyes that she had also shed some tears.

"I am so sorry, Mama," Matilda said. "I was an ungrateful wretch yesterday. How could I treat you so horridly when you have done so much for us? Can you forgive me?"

I did not trust my voice, so I held Matilda tightly in my arms until the storm of feelings subsided. Then I said, "I hope that you will forgive me for my harsh words, my darling. I am not myself. I have been so worried—"

Matilda took my face between both hands and kissed me. Then she smiled and said, "Our princess has found a solution to our troubles!" She put her arm around my waist and turned to the others.

Charlotte and Ella looked pleased. Ella tucked a stray lock of glossy hair behind her ear and said, "My sisters tell me that you are unhappy at court."

Out of politeness, I began to protest, but Ella cut me short, saying, "I don't always like it here either. Sometimes I wish that I could get away. I like to make pilgrimages to the abbey, because

it is always quiet and peaceful. I cannot choose to live there, but perhaps you should."

"But how can we live at the abbey?" I asked, confused. "We are not nuns, and we have no money of our own."

Ella laughed, showing her pearly little teeth. "Do you forget that the abbess is my godmother? She will deny me nothing." She cocked her head to the side and looked up through her lashes. "When my grandmother died, she left nearly all of her considerable estate to the abbey. My mother received some statuary and tapestries, a mere pittance. I was denied my rightful inheritance. Mother Elfilda settled some money on me for my dowry, but that was a tiny piece of what should be mine. If I tell her that I want the use of Rose House, she will gladly agree."

"Do not argue with her, Mother!" Charlotte said. She smiled happily. "You have longed to go back to the abbey. Think of how contented we should be there! Ella will visit often, and we can take the children to hunt for frogs around the pond without anyone telling us that it is not proper. We shall have all the books we wish to read and no awful courtiers. We shall be together!" Charlotte leapt to her feet and took my hands in hers. "Do say that we may go to Rose House, Mother!"

Ella stood also. She looked from one of us to the next with her big, luminous eyes. "If you have no objections, I shall make arrangements for the move."

I stepped forward and curtsied low. Charlotte and Matilda quickly joined me.

"I cannot properly express my gratitude, Your Highness," I said. "You are too generous."

"You are my family," Ella said simply. "We have had our differences, but I never doubted your love."

My soul shrank within me as I remembered shameful lapses in my love for Ella. My affections had never flown to her naturally; I had needed to push and shove my heart toward my stepdaughter, and I had, at times, turned a blind eye to my heart's obstinacy. I made excuses, telling myself that Ella was strange, and that anyone would find her difficult. That Charlotte and Matilda were more inherently amiable. That I was not Ella's real mother.

"Thank you," I said, bowing to Ella again. "You are far more kind than I deserve."

The perfumed air was suddenly oppressive. I could tell that Charlotte and Matilda wished me to linger, but I felt stifled and light-headed, so I excused myself. The feeling of suffocation did not improve in the corridor, however, nor could I stand to be alone in my dark chamber. I fled to the garden, seeking fresh air; when I burst from the door, bright sunshine dazzled my sore eyes, and I could draw an easier breath. Accusing glances and whispers still clung to me, however, feeding on the guilt that I had tried so long to hide, even from myself.

24

RETURN TO ROSE HOUSE

We moved to Rose House a decade ago, and I sleep in the same chamber my mistress, Lady Wenslock, slept in so long ago. Though there is plenty of room, even when Ella and her children visit, Matilda and Charlotte have chosen to continue to share a chamber. We take all of our meals together but keep busy with separate occupations for much of the day. Matilda teaches Latin to the convent students; she has become great friends with many of the nuns, and she sneaks them home for dinner whenever she gets the chance. Charlotte works in the scriptorium; she has great talent for illumination, and her volumes have gone to the best families in the kingdom. I have continued to write, mostly poetry. I don't know if anyone will read my work, but writing brings me joy. Our favorite hours are spent together in the library, where we know our favorite books by heart.

It has been a relief to escape the judgment and spitefulness we faced at court. I am certain that Ella has done nothing to promote stories about her ugly stepsisters and selfish stepmother, but she is so radiant, so simple and cheerful, and we are her shadows. In or-

der for her to embody beauty and goodness, we have to be darkness and perversity. This is the way of mankind, and it has always
been so, since God cast us out from the Garden of Eden. We can
only know virtue by understanding vice; we would be animals
otherwise, living, mating, breeding, and dying in a world without
righteousness or sin.

We did perhaps treat Ella too harshly when she was a girl, but I
know that Charlotte and Matilda truly wanted their stepsister to be
happy. So did I, though not nearly so much as she deserved. I am
still trying to make peace with my failures.

In a more complicated way, we also wanted Ella to be undaunted in the face of difficulty, thoughtful about the motives of
others, hardy in the face of God's small punishments. Charlotte
and Matilda's teasing, like my discipline, was meant to temper her
character, as fire tempers steel. It was perhaps not in Ella's nature
to learn these things, and stringency may not have been the proper
tool for teaching her, but we meant her no malice. It is only in old
age that I recognize that not all characters have a core of steel. Ella's character is made of something finer and less substantial, like
morning mist or the sparkle of sun on water.

Ella visits us every season and delights in the peacefulness of the
abbey. She usually brings some of her children. She has five little
princes and princesses now, two boys and three girls. The twins
were named Charlotte and Matilda, but little Charlotte died in the
cradle, so my daughters now share the duties of godmother to Millie. She is a sweet child, a ray of sunshine. Though she inherited
her father's brown eyes and dark hair, Millie's face is as fair as
Ella's. I am sad that Charlotte and Matilda will never know the joys

of motherhood, but they love their nieces and nephews, and they are grateful for the unusual freedom they have been granted.

Ella dutifully visits with Mother Elfilda, who is now abbess only in name. Her sight is failing, and she is frail. The prioress manages most of the daily functions of the abbey, and Ella ensures that we are well cared for.

The years pass quickly; of the half century I have been alive, the last decade has flown most swiftly. Every spring, I sit in the rose garden, where I watch the reflected light from the pond dance along the bower. When I hear the crunch of footsteps on gravel, I expect to see Fernan with his satchel slung over his shoulder, flashing his brilliant smile. Instead, it is my daughter. She takes her place beside me on the bench and strokes the back of my hand, smoothing down the blue veins that now worm beneath my spotted skin. I kiss her cheek. We may not deserve it, but we are happy.

ACKNOWLEDGMENTS

Years ago, I had a job interview with an imposing and revered chair of medicine. With passion, I described my heartfelt belief that the pursuit of science needs to be recognized as a team effort, and that the myth of the lone genius hampers progress. I thought that the gentleman would agree with what seemed a self-evident truth, but instead, he was appalled. "Why," he said, "that's like claiming that a great novel can be written by more than one author!" I didn't know how to respond at the time, but all these years later, I finally have my answer: Novels are created by teams of people too.

I am deeply indebted to all who have contributed to this book. To those who read early drafts and shared wise critiques and advice, including Jennifer Bird, Liese Schwarz, Lynn Stegner, Masie Cochran, and the astute team at InkWell Management, I am enormously grateful. Thanks also to the members of Pegasus 4, my physician writing group, for their perceptive comments and encouragement.

I am thrilled to have the opportunity to work with Jennifer Brehl and her team at William Morrow, members of the publishing pantheon that gave life to some of my most cherished stories. It is a dream come true.

Michael Carlisle, my agent, is the real Prince Charming in this

story. He was determined to lift Agnes out of obscurity, and I cannot thank him enough for his unflagging faith and enthusiasm for this work. (He also happens to be a prince of a man, and most charming.) *Un grand merci aussi à* Alexis Hurley for introducing this book to the world beyond the shores of North America.

With all my heart, I thank my family and friends for love, inspiration, and support. Special mention goes to my daughter Claire, who has been a fierce champion for my writing aspirations; to my father, whose instincts for storytelling have been my guide; and to my wonderful husband, without whom this book would not exist.

About the author

About the book

Insights,
Interviews
& More...

Meet Danielle Teller

Topher Simon

DANIELLE TELLER received her medical training at McGill University, Brown University, and Yale University. She has held faculty positions at the University of Pittsburgh and Harvard University, where she investigated the origins of chronic lung disease and taught in the medical intensive care unit. In 2013, Danielle pursued her childhood dream of being a writer. She is the author of *Sacred Cows: The Truth About Divorce and Marriage*, and has written numerous columns for *Quartz*. She lives with her husband, Astro Teller, and their four children in Palo Alto, California. ∾

Behind the Book Essay

As I age, I am increasingly fascinated with the role perception plays in human affairs. Science and mathematics have fundamental, reproducible, provable truths, but relationships do not. There are no gold standard measures when it comes to the soul. One person's "brave" is another person's "foolish," and one person's "honest" is another person's "cruel." Two individuals can witness the same human interaction and come away with vastly different stories about what they saw and heard.

When I became a stepmother, I realized that it is an intrinsically fraught relationship, where children may not want a new guardian, and stepmothers may not be prepared for parenting duties. This caused me to reconsider the portrayal of stepmothers in our culture. While mothers are placed on pedestals as paragons of virtue and sacrifice, stepmothers are painted as selfish women. I thought about the villains of fairy tales and wondered whether those stories are skewed interpretations of the complex and often difficult relationship between stepchildren and stepmothers—we only ever hear the child's perspective. ▶

Behind the Book Essay *(continued)*

I was particularly interested in Cinderella's stepmother: She is portrayed as cruel, but she is not an irredeemable murderess. She is also a mother.

I have always loved fairy tales, but these stories provide a reductive view of life, where characters are heroes or villains, good or bad. There is comfort in such portrayals because we can feel unadulterated joy when heroes succeed and villains are punished, but it worries me when we are tempted to see real life in these same terms—that we sometimes reduce ourselves and others to stereotypes of good and bad, manufacturing air cover to judge the people we don't like and excuse those we do.

I began by imagining Cinderella and her blended family as real people who are neither completely virtuous nor evil. That raised questions about their motivations to behave as they do in the fairy tale. If the stepmother and stepsisters aren't simply rotten people, why are they mean to Cinderella? Why doesn't Cinderella's father protect her? Why does Cinderella agree to help her stepsisters get ready for the ball when they are so unkind to her? From these questions, Agnes and her family were born.

Writing about the fairy tale allowed for many explorations. As a young girl, I adored Cinderella and rooted for her with every fiber of my being. At the same time, I knew that I did not fit the ideal of feminine beauty personified by Cinderella, and that it was not a reasonable aspiration to become dainty, or to grow a thick mane of golden hair. The cognitive dissonance about beauty that girls and women live with was a potent motivator for writing *All the Ever Afters*. Similarly, rescue via marriage has never struck me as a great aspiration for girls to learn from fairy tales, and it was fun to play with the theme of women rescuing themselves and each other.

If our individual perceptions and perspectives amount to millions of unique, personal realities, then the only way to bridge the gulfs between people is to try to see the world through the eyes of others. As a reader, I have always appreciated the way novels allow me to experience the world from new perspectives. It has been transformative for me as a writer to journey with Agnes through her life. I thought it would be illuminating to walk a mile in the shoes of a famous villain; I was surprised to learn that true illumination came from Agnes's failure to walk in her ▶

Behind the Book Essay *(continued)*

stepdaughter's famously tiny shoes.
Villainy does not account for much
of the heartbreak in our lives. Rather,
it is the banal barriers to understanding
and empathizing with one another
that keep us from happily ever after. ⌁

Reading Group Discussion Questions

1. Which character had the more archetypical Cinderella story, Agnes or Ella? Why? Which events in Agnes's life parallel the story of Cinderella?

2. When Ella was a girl, how did Agnes's reactions to her differ from those of Ella's tutor, maid, and father? Why did Agnes view the girl in a more negative light than other adults in Ella's life?

3. How are Agnes's feelings for her own daughters different from her feelings for Ella? How did her feelings for all three girls translate into actions? Did you feel that Ella suffered great injustice?

4. If you could talk to Princess Elfilda, how do you think she would describe her stepmother and her relationship with her stepmother? ▶

5. In *Cinderella*, the protagonist is lifted out of misery by marriage. Is that central plot point reflected in *All the Ever Afters*? How is marriage portrayed?

6. How do Agnes's evolving attitudes about men affect the way she feels about Fernan and Emont? How do you think each of those men would describe his feelings for Agnes?

7. Do you think this novel is a feminist interpretation of Cinderella? Why or why not?

8. First-person accounts are inevitably filtered through the eyes of the narrator. If you could be a fly on the wall during scenes in this book, when and how might you perceive characters and events differently from Agnes?

9. Descriptions of darkness, light, and shadows abound in the novel. How do these descriptions reflect elements of the story? Does the quality of the dark/light images change throughout the arc of the narrative?

10. When Agnes is a child, the manor is described in near fairy-tale terms, with characters presented as either good or evil. As Agnes ages, it becomes more difficult to classify characters as purely good or purely evil (except perhaps for those who affect her own children). How does this reflect the transition from childhood to adulthood?

11. Lady Alba exhibits signs of mental illness. How were her behaviors understood by her medieval society? How might her illness be seen differently if she lived in modern times?

12. Frère Joachim asks a riddle for which the answer is "ice." He pointedly emphasizes the answer to Agnes. Why does he do this?

13. In what ways does Ella resemble her godmother and namesake, Abbess Elfilda? How did their routes to power differ?

14. At the end of the book, Agnes says, "We may not deserve it, but we are happy." Why does she feel that their happiness is undeserved? Do you agree with her? ∾